A History of Canadian Architecture

Volume 2

Research was assisted by
a generous grant from

THE SOCIAL SCIENCES AND HUMANITIES
RESEARCH COUNCIL OF CANADA

Published with the assistance of

THE GETTY GRANT PROGRAM

Harold Kalman

A HISTORY OF CANADIAN ARCHITECTURE

VOLUME 2

Oxford University Press

TORONTO   NEW YORK   OXFORD

Oxford University Press
70 Wynford Drive Don Mills Ontario M3C 1J9

Oxford New York
Athens Auckland Bangkok Bombay
Calcutta Cape Town Dar es Salaam Delhi
Florence Hong Kong Istanbul Karachi
Kuala Lumpur Madras Madrid Melbourne
Mexico City Nairobi Paris Singapore
Taipei Tokyo Toronto

and associated companies in
Berlin Ibadan

Oxford is a trademark of Oxford University Press

Canadian Cataloguing in Publication Data

Kalman, Harold, 1943–
A history of Canadian architecture

Includes bibliographical references and index.
ISBN 0-19-540696-6

1. Architecture – Canada – History. I. Title.

NA740.K35 1994   720′.971   C94-931102-2

Design: Jeffrey Tabberner
Cover photograph: Ron Watts (First Light)

1 2 3 4—97 96 95 94

This book is printed on permanent (acid-free) paper. ∞

Printed in Canada

CONTENTS

Abbreviations in Captions

ANQ	Archives nationales du Québec
BCARS	British Columbia Archives and Records Service
CIHB	Canadian Inventory of Historic Building
IBC	Inventaire des biens culturelles/Ministère de la culture et des communications du Québec
MMCH	McCord Museum of Canadian History
MTRL	Metropolitan Toronto Reference Library
NAC	National Archives of Canada
NFB	National Film Board
NMC	National Map Collection, National Archives of Canada
NSM	Nova Scotia Museum
PAM	Provincial Archives of Manitoba
PANB	Provincial Archives of New Brunswick
PANL	Provincial Archives of Newfoundland and Labrador
PANS	Public Archives of Nova Scotia
PC	Parks Canada
SAB	Saskatchewan Archives Board

CHAPTER 9

THE RAILWAY AND THE OPENING OF THE WEST

THE HISTORY of Canadian architecture has so far been treated regionally because even as the second third of the nineteenth century drew to a close, present-day Canada was no more than a series of regions: self-reliant colonies and provinces, each with its own government, economy, and culture—and, in a large measure, its distinct architecture.

Two important and related events helped to change this situation. One was Confederation, which in 1867 joined the eastern and central colonies and provinces (Nova Scotia, New Brunswick, and Canada—the last comprising Quebec and Ontario) into a political union called the Dominion of Canada. It was soon increased in size by the addition of Manitoba and the Northwest Territories (1870), British Columbia (1871), and Prince Edward Island (1873). The other event was the building of the Canadian Pacific Railway (CPR), without which British Columbia would not have joined Canada. In June 1886 the first train travelled from the Atlantic port of Montreal to the Pacific port of Vancouver, inaugurating a transportation system that linked the young country from sea to sea.

These circumstances had a number of significant impacts on the built environment. For one, the CPR and the other railways were large corporations (indeed, they were the first national companies, heralding a new corporate age) that carried out immense building programs. More generally, the CPR opened up the West to development on a scale that previously would have been unthinkable. Another effect was the betterment of cultural (as well as physical) communications from one coast to the other, complementing the political union, and making it easier for architects and their ideas to move between regions, blurring regional differences. As part of the increasing control of Montreal and Toronto over the economy and culture of the West, architectural influences from those cities also took hold there.

A result of all this was a tendency towards architectural homogeneity across the country, and especially in a growing West. There the sheer numbers of towns and buildings that had to be erected in the short space of a generation necessitated much uniformity. Settlers had to provide shelter quickly and cheaply, which limited their options. The easterners who were making many of the decisions about western development saw all regions of the Prairies as being much the same. From southern Manitoba to northern Alberta the land was surveyed in a standard way, towns were laid out on standard plans, and buildings were erected to standard designs. Stations, grain elevators, stores, and houses all looked alike, though variations in building were certainly not lacking. Individuality often came about as a result of regional materials and climates, ethnic and cultural distinctions, and personal or corporate egos.

This chapter begins by looking at the many kinds of structures built by the CPR and the later transcontinental railways. It then considers the rural and urban buildings that were developed as part of the mass settlement of the West. The interplay between uniformity and individuality is an important theme that provides a thread of continuity—not only in this period and region, but in all Canadian architecture in the century to follow.

The Transcontinental Railway

By 1867 Canada had developed an efficient network of railway lines in the eastern and central provinces; but the tracks ended in the northwest at Sand Point, a short distance beyond Ottawa, and in the southwest at Windsor, Sarnia, and Goderich. The Fathers of Confederation recognized that good communication was essential to political and economic union, and so the completion of the Intercolonial Railway, linking Ontario with the Atlantic, had been made a condition of Confederation. The Prime Minister, John A. Macdonald, subsequently lured British Columbia into joining the Dominion with the promise that a transcontinental railway would be begun within two years and completed within ten—a schedule that could not be kept. Macdonald recognized that a single private corporation would have to build and control the entire line. After losing the general election of 1873 over the methods that one candidate, Sir Hugh Allan, had used to attempt to secure the contract (the Pacific Scandal), Macdonald, after his return to power in 1878, finally awarded it to the Canadian Pacific Railway in 1881—ten years after British Columbia's entry into Confederation.

The CPR was a Montreal-based syndicate initially headed by three remarkable men: Donald A. Smith (subsequently Baron Strathcona and Mount Royal), a Scot who had acquired great personal wealth while rising in the ranks of the Hudson's Bay Company; his cousin George Stephen (later Baron Mount Stephen), a canny financier with ties to the Bank of Montreal; and James Jerome Hill, a Canadian-born transportation magnate who lived in St Paul, Minnesota, and had extensive American railway and steamboat interests. The construction of the railway was an immensely difficult and expensive undertaking that required skilful management, exceptional engineering, and no small amount of financial sleight-of-hand. The first was provided by the American-born William Cornelius Van Horne, who was hired as general manager in January 1882 (he succeeded Stephen as president in 1888, and was knighted in 1894), the second by a team of talented professionals under Van Horne's strong control, and the third by Stephen.[1]

The railway had been conceived for its political mission rather than its economic viability. In order to make the latter possible, the CPR directors negotiated a generous contract with the government that provided the company with $25 million in cash, a land grant of 25 million acres (10 million hectares) along the right-of-way, the cost of surveys (worth $37 million), and a twenty-year monopoly on transportation from the Prairies into the United States. These provisions stirred up much controversy (a debate that lingers today), and gave the CPR powerful leverage that made it an important player in the development of the Canadian West.

The national railway soon became an international transportation system, with steamships crossing both the Atlantic and the Pacific—and, in time, a global airline. Before the twentieth century was a decade old, a person could travel in first-class comfort from London to Yokahama on Canadian Pacific vessels and trains, staying only in CPR hotels. The CPR consequently developed a large building program, beyond what was required to operate trains.

The dream of profits on the transcontinental line ensured that the CPR did not retain its monopoly on western rail transportation for long. Competition was felt immediately from American lines, and Canadian entrepreneurs soon began to lay new tracks across the land. The first off the mark were William Mackenzie and Donald Mann, who assembled prairie railway lines and charters, and between 1899 and 1915 built the Canadian Northern Railway (CNOR) to Vancouver via the more northerly Yellowhead Pass; they were followed by Charles Hayes, who constructed the Grand Trunk Pacific (GTP) from Winnipeg to Prince Rupert, completed in 1914. The federal government, for its part, built the National Transcontinental Railway (NTR) from the eastern terminus of the GTP at Winnipeg to Moncton.

Numerous branch-lines and smaller railways, some of them subsidiaries of the giants, were active during these years of aggressive railway construction, and the many lines that were built in central and eastern Canada continued to grow and consolidate. By the beginning of the First World War a relatively dense network of rails criss-crossed Canada from one coast to the other. The Canadian Pacific, Canadian Northern, and Grand Trunk Pacific competed vigorously in the West, often on parallel tracks that ran within sight of each other. Further competition came from the Great Northern Railroad, the American line controlled by former CPR partner, and now bitter rival, J.J. Hill.

Canada simply could not generate the traffic necessary to support all the rival lines, and hard times fell on the railways, particularly during the First World War. After the war the new railways—as well as the old Grand Trunk and Intercolonial Railways—were amalgamated and nationalized as the Canadian National Railways (CNR, incorporated in 1919). The CPR, which remained solvent, persisted as the only privately owned transcontinental railway.[2]

Standard stations

The most visible railway buildings are the stations used for passenger and light freight service. (A 'station' originally referred to a stopping place, and the building was called a 'station house'.) We saw in

Chapter 5 that Canada's early trunk lines took varying approaches to station design: the Grand Trunk Railway followed British practice in using stone to build structures that were meant to last, whereas the Intercolonial Railway heeded the pragmatic advice of Sandford Fleming, its chief engineer, spending only as much on stations as was necessary. The GTP continued to use the highest standards of engineering and design, the CNOR built for economy, and the CPR kept a foot in each camp. Together the railways built and operated several thousand stations across Canada. In order to cope with this very large number, they developed along the lines standard designs for stations and other utilitarian structures.

The CPR   The earliest stations on the CPR were those on the government-built portions of the line, including eight log buildings west of today's Thunder Bay (1877) and a series of frame stations between Yale and Kamloops in British Columbia (*c.* 1880).[3] When the CPR began to build its own stations it located them at intervals of about 8 miles (13 km), with every second station site also having a section house (for crew and staff) and a water tank. This spacing was dictated by the water capacity of the steam locomotives and the need for agent-operators to ensure control over movements along the line. Stations were therefore required

even in remote areas where communities and passengers were non-existent. When we realize that the line from Montreal to Vancouver was nearly 3,000 miles (4,800 km) long, the enormity of the task of station-building becomes evident.

The first CPR stations were adequate in size and durability to serve for a reasonable length of time without heavy maintenance costs. But within a few decades many were replaced by larger and more permanent buildings. Economies were obtained by having most of the design and construction done in-house, adopting standard plans (altered as needed for local conditions), and using wood rather than masonry for most first-generation buildings.

The first standard station design produced by the CPR's Operating Department began to appear in 1882 along the line from Ontario to the Rockies. The most familiar example of the type was the CPR **Station at Indian Head [9.1]**, Saskatchewan, photographed by Montreal's Notman Studio in 1884. The ground floor contained the passenger waiting-room, ticket wicket, and the station agent's office—indicated by the projecting bay window, which allowed him to look up and down the track. The second floor provided living quarters for the agent and his family, which

9.1 CPR Station, Indian Head, Saskatchewan, *c.* 1882. Photograph 1884. Notman Photographic Archives, MMCH/1383.

was necessary since there was no town or accommodation at most station sites. The low wing to the right was the express (freight) shed. Chimneys indicate that the passengers' and agent's sections were heated, but not the wing. The straightforward design had its decorative touches, such as the finials at the gable ends, the decoration along the strip that separates the two storeys, and the two-tone paint job. This was called a 'combination' station, since passenger, operating, and light-freight functions were combined within one structure. The division of functions is clear in the photograph: passengers, some clad in blankets, stand on the platform in front of the depot, while freight lines the platform in front of the shed.

This standard station-type, which continued to be built until about 1886, also came in a larger version, with an additional bay inserted between the office and the express shed to accommodate a separate baggage room. One example was built at Norwood, Ontario. None of these stations (of either size) remain in active use and only a few are standing, most of them now private residences—as at Poplar Point, Manitoba.[4]

The railway's publicists capitalized on the stations' sameness, as we read in a booklet on the CPR published in 1887, shortly after its opening:

We pass station after station, nearly all alike, except as to the size of the villages surrounding them. The railway buildings at these stations are uniform, and consist of an attractive station house for passengers and goods, a great round water-tank, cottages for the trackmen, and the never ending grain elevators.[5]

9.2 CPR Standard No. 10 Station, 1915. Canadian Pacific Limited.

The prairie landscape was already being perceived—and promoted—as a homogeneous entity.

The CPR continued to build stations long after the transcontinental line had been completed, replacing the first-generation buildings as they wore out or became obsolete. At the beginning of the twentieth century the company introduced a new line of standard designs, numbered from 1 to 20. Some were small, others large, but all exhibited a mature architectural design that unequivocally projected a station image. The key to this was the high hipped roof with flaring eaves, supported by triangular brackets, that provided shelter for passengers standing outside. In the CPR **Standard No. 10 Station** [9.2], designed in 1915, the two-storey portion was covered with a separate hipped roof. The ground floor contained the ticket office, with the operator's table in the bay window, a general waiting-room (finished with plaster walls and wood trim), a ladies' waiting-room, a baggage room, and an express room. The agent's four-room suite was upstairs, illuminated by windows contained within a hipped dormer. The walls were wood frame on a concrete foundation, clad in horizontal clapboard with sparse decorative trim around the doors and windows. This type was built in many western towns, including Yahk, British Columbia; Exshaw, Alberta; and Mortlach, Saskatchewan.[6]

The station often became a community's principal meeting-place, serving a host of social functions. It was centrally located near the hotel and café, and was the place to send a telegram (the fastest means of communication), to purchase a money order, or receive a parcel from the big-city mail-order house; and it had a cozy waiting-room where people could meet and relax. Politicians campaigned here from the rear platform of private cars,

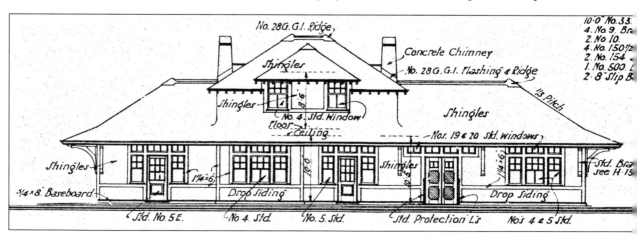

9.3 CNOR Station, Roseisle, Manitoba, 1903. Photograph by Charles W. Bohi, 1970.

and children gathered to watch the train's arrival.

The attractiveness of stations as social centres increased when their agents began to plant gardens. In the 1890s two office employees of the CPR, Manitoban David Hysop and Montrealer Stewart Dunlop, began to encourage the creation of station gardens. Dunlop, known along the line as 'the flower man', distributed seeds and instruction booklets. He reportedly told Van Horne: 'The agent with a nice garden is the agent who has a clean and tidy station; has a flower in his buttonhole; wears his coat; has a clean collar and well-brushed boots.'[7] What began as a voluntary activity became company policy. The social benefits of station gardens were promoted and design criteria were developed. Gardens were considered particularly important for prairie stations in order to help sell the West by making it look fertile. The CPR established greenhouses and a forestry department, and at the height of the garden phenomenon, in 1924, the company distributed 150,000 annuals, 60,000 pansies, and 2,000 perennials, as well as many trees and shrubs.

Other railways The rival transcontinental railways also built standard station-types in large numbers, giving them their own corporate identity. The Canadian Northern designated several 'classes' of stations. The third-class station was the most widely used; the second-class station was a larger version of it, built at divisional points (which had more staff and operational responsibilities). First-class stations were large custom-built stations in important cities; fourth-class stations were small buildings at the least-

important stops. The company also used portable stations that could be transported on a flat-car as the first depot in low-traffic areas.

The third-class station is easily recognized. The former CNOR **Station at Roseisle** (1903), Manitoba, is typical [**9.3**]. (Since the photograph was taken, the station has been moved and re-used as a private residence, and a ski lodge.) A compact two-storey house-like block is incorporated with a one-storey freight-shed; the walls of the former emerge through the roof of the latter and the platform canopy, and are capped by a distinctive high hipped roof that is pierced at the front and back by gabled dormers. The ground floor of the two-storey block contained the office (with the inevitable bay window), a small waiting-room, and the agent's living-room, and there were four bedrooms upstairs; a kitchen annex often projected at the rear. The lean-to at the left was probably a coal bin. The station's dimensions were 22 by 46 feet (6.7 by 14 m). The first 'official' version of this simple, yet elegant, third-class design (technically known as type 100-3 — a designation that brings to mind the current way of classifying commercial airplanes) was produced in 1901 by architect Ralph Benjamin Pratt (1872-1950), who came to Winnipeg from England in 1892 and worked as a draftsman with the CPR before becoming associated with the CNOR (and later the CNR) in 1901. (In 1906 he and engineer Donald Aynsley Ross [1878-1956] formed the firm of Pratt and Ross, which subsequently designed a number of large custom stations, including the CNOR terminal in Vancouver, 1917-19.) This third-class type (with several variations in roofs) was used at more than 300 stops in the West, and at many others east of the Great Lakes.[8]

The Grand Trunk Pacific believed in even stricter standardization than its rivals. More than two-thirds of its stations were built to an identical plan, Type 'E', a compact $1\frac{1}{2}$-storey structure covered by a hipped roof with bellcast eaves. The GTP **Station at Landis**, Saskatchewan (1911), represents the type [**9.4**]. Almost all were placed on the north side of the track with the waiting-room end towards the east (probably so that the uninsulated buildings could take advantage of the morning sun). Even the new towns created by the GTP were laid out to a uniform plan, imposing yet further standardization on the prairie landscape.[9]

The Canadian National Railways inherited a fully built railway system, but was required to construct new stations when earlier ones needed replacement or additional branch lines were constructed. Its own

9.4 GTP Station, Landis, Saskatchewan, 1911. Photograph by Charles W. Bohi, 1972.

third-class stations were based on the successful CNOR design. Until the Second World War both the CNR and the CPR (as well as the smaller railway companies) continued to use revised versions of old standard designs. Since the 1940s they have introduced new types whose flat roofs reflect the rectilinearity of modern architecture.

During the past half-century the removal of railway stations has been far more prevalent than construction. Many branch lines have been abandoned as part of a program of rationalization, and in response to a decline in business caused by competition from road and air transportation. Passenger service has been particularly hard hit, and as service is withdrawn stations are demolished. In 1977 VIA Rail Canada Inc. was created by the federal government to take over all the passenger operations of both the CNR and the CPR; this has led to yet further cutbacks, including the discontinuation in 1990 of public passenger service on the CPR route between Winnipeg and Vancouver. The toll this has taken on railway stations is enormous. Although many stations have been re-used as community or private facilities, the building-type remains a vanishing species. The Heritage Railway Stations Protection Act, passed by Parliament in 1988 and proclaimed into law in 1990, is intended to protect a number of surviving historic stations from demolition. But it may well be too little, too late, for this significant element of Canada's architectural heritage.

Serving the line Many kinds of structures other than stations had to be built to attend the operational needs of the line. These included water tanks, coaling stations, sand houses, and engine houses to service the locomotives; shops for

building and repairing locomotives and cars; tool sheds and stores buildings; section houses and bunk houses to accommodate the section crews; and bridges and viaducts to carry the tracks over rivers and ravines. All the competing railway lines required structures of this kind; they are introduced here by focusing on the CPR.

The CPR's engineering department drew up standard plans for the service buildings, as it did for stations. Most were economical, straightforward structures that performed their function well and were built to last. In addition, the engineers and architects who designed them kept an eye out for good and appropriate design, as in the CPR **Standard No. 4 Section House [9.5]** of 1914; its attractive asymmetry was enlivened by mock-Tudor half-timbering in its front gable.[10]

The service building most admired by railway enthusiasts is the engine house, whose best-known form is the roundhouse. The design principle is simple: a number of maintenance stalls are arranged radially to form a sector of a circle, with all the tracks converging on a central turntable located outside the building. Locomotives in need of service proceed from the yards to the turntable, which rotates to point them to a particular stall. Additional stalls could be added as needed, in some cases forming a full circle. An annex containing a machine-shop is usually attached. 'Square houses' were also used (one survivor is the CNR Prince Rupert engine house, built

9.5 CPR Standard No. 4 Section House, 1914. Canadian Pacific Limited.

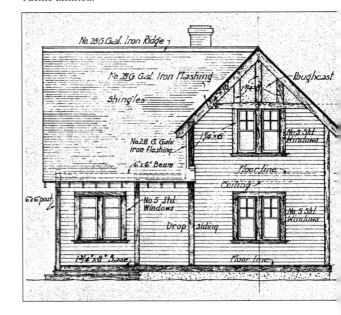

c. 1912), but the roundhouse was dominant in Canada and the US during the age of steam.[11]

Roundhouses began to be built in Canada in the 1860s. A few early ones survive; one of the oldest is the former CPR Drake Street roundhouse in Vancouver, built in the 1887-8 (and enlarged in 1911-12) as part of the line's extensive terminal service facilities. It was restored in 1985 (by Hotson Bakker Architects) for use as a pavilion at Expo 86, and will be integrated into the new Pacific Place development as a community facility.[12] Early roundhouses had a heavy timber frame and wooden roof, creating a potential fire hazard. In the first decade of the twentieth century the CPR began to build fireproof roundhouses with brick, stone, concrete, or steel walls and columns; concrete or steel roofs and 'smoke jacks' (the opening that allowed smoke to escape); and brick firewalls between the bays. As locomotives grew bigger and traffic increased, roundhouses also grew in size.

One of the largest in the country is the CPR **John Street roundhouse** [9.6] in Toronto. Replacing a 15-stall roundhouse built in 1897, the present 32-stall roundhouse was built in 1929-32. This brick structure is covered by an old-fashioned wood roof because the fires in the locomotives were extinguished before entering the facility, and the engines were powered by a central steam facility, the first in Canada. The new turntable was 120 feet (37 m) long, compared with the earlier one (1897) of 70 feet (21 m).

9.6 CPR John Street Roundhouse, Toronto, 1929-32. Photograph 1930. MTRL/T10410.

Adjacent to the roundhouse in the large yard complex were a 60,000-gallon (284,000-litre) water tank, a coaling plant, cinder plant, stores building, bunkhouse, and other service facilities. The scale of the yards is evident from the photograph, taken during construction in 1930, which shows the CPR's immense Royal York Hotel (Ross and Macdonald, 1927-9) in the background. The roundhouse remains in use, although it now services diesel and not steam engines. Its future has been challenged by the ongoing redevelopment of the railway lands along the Toronto waterfront.[13]

Railway bridges and viaducts grew ever more ambitious in the late-nineteenth and early-twentieth centuries. In the mountains of British Columbia alone, some 600 trestles and bridges were required on the CPR line, 100 of them in the 30-mile (50-km) section through the Fraser Canyon that was built for the government by American contractor Andrew Onderdonk. One was the Fraser River Bridge (1882-4) at Cisco, near Lytton, designed by noted engineer Charles Conrad Schneider (1843-1916). The steel superstructure for the daring (and early) cantilever span was fabricated in Britain and erected by the San Francisco Bridge Company. The bridge was subsequently dismantled and relocated over the Niagara Gorge on Vancouver Island, where it remains in service as a

9.7 CPR Trestle at Mountain Creek, British Columbia. Photograph by Trueman and Caple, *c.* 1892. Canadian Pacific Limited/A.11385. O. Lavallée Collection.

part of the CPR's Esquimalt and Nanaimo Railway.[14]

Towards the end of the CPR's construction period, Van Horne permitted structures to be built of wood because of the company's increasingly precarious financial position. Many were partially prefabricated: the designs were standardized and the timber stockpiled, numbered, and pre-cut for shipment and rapid assembly. The largest was the remarkable **Mountain Creek Trestle** (1885) on the eastern slope of the Selkirks, near Glacier, BC: it was 1,086 feet (331 m) long, passed 164 feet (41 m) over the Illecillewaet River, and contained more than two million board feet of lumber [9.7]. Some sense of its immense scale can be gained by comparing it with the minuscule locomotive and construction workers engaged in laying track on it.[15]

All the wood structures were subsequently rebuilt in permanent materials. The longest and heaviest trestle in the world is the CPR Lethbridge Viaduct at Lethbridge, Alberta, built in 1907-9 to designs by engineer John E. Schwitzer (designer also of the renowned Spiral Tunnels at Kicking Horse Pass, 1909),

and extending some 5,327 feet (1.6 km) across the valley of the Oldman River. The viaduct used 12,500 tons (11,250 tonnes) of structural steel.[16]

Custom buildings

While standardization may have sufficed for most structures along the line, it was inadequate for buildings of some importance. Urban terminals, special stations, and hotels all required a custom approach to design, as for any significant public or commercial building. In this section a number of these buildings are discussed (most of them erected for the CPR), along with some of the architects and styles that were brought in for these purposes.

Stations The railways adopted custom designs for their most important stations: major terminals,

9.8 CPR Station, Port Arthur, Ontario, 1883. Photograph c. 1884. Canadian Pacific Limited/A459.

and some depots at divisional points and other places where it was felt necessary to make an extraordinary impression or to accommodate a special need. Some were designed under contract by independent architects, others were produced in-house. The custom stations along the line were usually more substantial versions of the standard ones. At the terminals, however, all stops were let out. It was here, in the centres of the largest cities, that the railways could build showy edifices that

projected an image of industrial and corporate power—while also meeting some complicated functional needs. The terminal buildings were designed by leading architects who imported the latest in American corporate styles.

The CPR built more than a few custom stations during the construction era. Its reliance on talented international architects grew out of William Van Horne's personal interest in art and architecture. Three stations in Ontario were built to designs by Thomas Charles Sorby (1836-1924), an accomplished English architect who immigrated to Canada in 1883 and immediately found work in Montreal with the CPR and other corporate clients. One of these was the CPR **Station at Port Arthur [9.8]**, Ontario (1883; replaced in 1907), seen here in a photograph taken soon after its completion, before the horizontal wood siding had been painted. Until the difficult Lake Superior section of the line was built, passengers and freight travelled by CPR steamship from Owen Sound on Lake Huron, through the locks at Sault Ste Marie, and across Lake Superior to Port Arthur (now a part of Thunder Bay), giving that station particular importance. Sorby's station contained all the functional spaces of the 'Indian-Head-type' standard-plan depots, but he organized them more tightly. The

9.9 Windsor Station, Montreal, Quebec, 1888-9, and later additons. Photograph by Albertype Co. NAC/PA032307.

9.10 Principal waiting-room, Windsor Station, Montreal, Quebec, 1888-9. Notman Photographic Archives, MMCH/2510.

9.11 Main concourse, Windsor Station. Montreal, Quebec, 1910-15. Photograph by Brian Merrett.

passenger area, agent's office, and agent's suite were contained within the $2\frac{1}{2}$-storey block at the right, with the operator's bay window continued as a full-height projection terminating in a gable. It formed part of a cross-gable roof that covered the principal block, while a hipped roof above the express wing was carried as a deep eave around the entire structure to unify the two portions and shelter the platform. The eaves were supported by triangular wood brackets. The design of the building was both functional and attractive, with its composition reflecting the picturesque asymmetry that was the hallmark of the Victorian age. This station-type—which worked well, and looked good—was so successful that it became the prototype for future standard stations of both the CPR and the Canadian Northern. Sorby also designed the CPR station (1883) at Peterborough, Ontario, a brick building with a stone base whose durable materials have made it the oldest surviving station in railway use in Canada.[17]

Another talented designer Van Horne retained for custom stations was the German-born Edward Colonna (1862-1948). In the 1880s he was working in Ohio, designing railway cars for Barney and

Smith Manufacturing Co., a supplier to the CPR. Colonna lived in Montreal between 1888 and 1893, when he designed CPR stations for Banff, Calgary, Regina, Brandon, Portage la Prairie, and Fort William, and remodelled the interiors of William Van Horne's Montreal residence on Sherbrooke Street, purchased in 1890 (and demolished in 1973). He subsequently achieved an international reputation as an *art nouveau* designer in Paris.[18]

The largest and most important stations were the terminals in major cities. The CPR's principal terminal, and its administrative headquarters, was (and remains) **Windsor Station [9.9]** in Montreal. Van Horne was determined that the building should be a great landmark, and gave the commission to Bruce Price (1845-1903), a capable society architect whose practice was based in New York. (His social skills were passed on to his daughter, Emily Post, the famed instructor of etiquette.) Price's former railway experience consisted of designing parlour cars for the Pennsylvania and the Boston & Albany Railroads, which may be how Van Horne—himself a talented painter and architectural designer—first noticed him.[19]

As built in 1888-9, Windsor Station was a substantial and imposing structure, four storeys high and three bays wide at its entrance on Osborne Street (now rue de la Gauchetière), with ten bays down Windsor Street and two additional storeys at the lower end. The windows of the first three storeys are contained within tall semicircular arches in what is called an arch-and-spandrel motif (the spandrels are the rectangular panels recessed behind the arches at each floor), and the fourth floor is illuminated by three smaller arched windows per bay. The walls consist of rock-faced (rusticated) limestone. The engaged columns that support the arches, the details of the column capitals at the entrance, the corner turrets, the slender tower (intended to have had another stage at the top), and the gabled dormer windows are all medieval in their inspiration—specifically looking at buildings of the Romanesque period.

Price's design is a fine example of the Richardsonian Romanesque style, a name that acknowledges the innovative use of this manner by American architect Henry Hobson Richardson (1838-86), particularly in his Allegheny County Courthouse and Jail in Pittsburgh (1883-8) and the Marshall Field Wholesale Store in Chicago (1885-7; we have seen its influence on the Ashdown Block [7.40] in Winnipeg). Richardson's buildings adapted forms inspired by Spanish and Northern Italian architecture to suit modern requirements, and differ from earlier Romanesque revivals—such as Temple Emanuel [8.31] in Victoria, which looked more to France and less to Spain. His work made a strong impression on his American contemporaries—including Price—even before their completion. Windsor Station was one of the first buildings in Canada to adopt the style, which would become increasingly popular in the next few years for public and corporate architecture.[20]

The Romanesque character was continued in the **principal waiting-room [9.10]**, where squat polished marble columns with carved capitals, standing on high square pedestals, support arches with 'diaphragm' walls that divide the flat ceiling into square, corniced, portions. The waiting-room led to a long, low train-shed.

Van Horne was rightly proud of Windsor Station. On its completion he placed a sign on the building that bragged in six-foot-high letters: 'Beats all Creation—the New CPR Station!' Grand as the station was, however, the company quickly outgrew it. Additions made along Osborne Street in 1900-6 (by Edward Maxwell), seen at the right in the photograph, included a north-gabled *porte-cochère* (later removed). A large office addition that continued

9.12 Union Station, Winnipeg, Manitoba, 1908-11. Photograph *c.* 1920. PAM/N10937.

ion Station Winnipeg Canada

489

9.13 Union Station, Toronto, Ontario, 1914-30. Photograph *c.* 1930. MTRL/T13983.

Price's design, seven floors high with a fourteen-storey tower, was built further down Windsor Street in 1910-15 (by L. Fennings Taylor, 1862-1947, and J.W.H. Watts, 1850-1917, of Ottawa, in association with W.S. Painter); this included a new waiting-room, a wider train-shed, and a broad sky-lighted concourse (1913) between them [9.11]. Further additions were made in the 1920s and 1950s. Windsor Station was nearly demolished in the early 1970s, but public outrage led to the decision of CP Rail and Canadian Pacific Ltd. (as the railway and its parent company had become known) to preserve the building.

Just as the CPR's Windsor Station brought the Richardsonian Romanesque style to Canada, the Canadian Northern and Grand Trunk Pacific's **Union Station in Winnipeg** [9.12], built a generation later in 1908-11, introduced American Beaux-Arts Classicism, the new public/corporate style of the day. The two new transcontinental lines were determined to produce a monument that would eclipse the CPR's Winnipeg station nearby. They retained the New York firm of Warren and Wetmore, who were associate architects (with Reed and Stem) for Grand Central Station (1903-13) in New York.

The immense building, whose white limestone façade extends some 350 feet (107 m) along Main Street, is organized around a central domed rotunda, 100 feet (30 m) high, expressed externally as a grand triumphal arch on the axis of tree-lined Broadway. Union Station achieves dignity with simplicity, as the relative austerity of the flanking office wings reflects the Canadian Northern's policy of economy. In 1908 the trade periodical *Railway and Marine World* reported that 'the building will be of massive appearance, and of plain architecture, the whole being built with a view to utility rather than beauty.'[21] This perhaps underrated its monumental appearance; but the contrast between the no-holds-barred opulence of New York's Grand Central Station and the sensible, understated plainness of Winnipeg's Union Station does reflect a distinction that can often be made between buildings in the US and Canada.

The most magnificent Canadian railway terminal is **Union Station in Toronto** [9.13], erected jointly by the Grand Trunk and Canadian Pacific Railways. The opportunity to build this (Toronto's third Union Station) came about in 1904, when a devastating fire on 19 April destroyed 122 buildings along the waterfront. A year later the railways began the planning process for a replacement, and in 1913 they

9.14 Great Hall, Union Station, Toronto, Ontario.
Photograph by Bruce Litteljohn.

appointed a consortium of architects: the Montreal partnership of George A. Ross (1879-1946) and Robert H. Macdonald (1875-1942), who were the GTR's preferred consultants; Hugh G. Jones (1872-1947) of Montreal, who worked for the CPR; and John M. Lyle (1872-1945), a talented Torontonian, with grand visions for his city, who was responsible for much of the design. Designs were completed in 1914 and construction began later that year, despite the war. Although work was largely completed in 1919, the collapse of the GTR, the consequent confusion over the formation of the Canadian National Railways between 1919 and 1923—and problems in negotiating approaches—delayed the opening until 1927. The train-shed and viaducts were not finished until 1930.[22]

The scale and grandeur of Toronto's Union Station were unprecedented in this country. The immense façade extends more than 250 yards (230 m) along Front Street—its centrepiece a broad colonnade of 18 gigantic Greek Doric columns, projecting slightly at the extremities, with an undecorated cornice above. (The severe horizontality of the station might have been lessened had the statues over the cornice proposed by Lyle been executed.) The façade is divided into three parts by pavilions; on the west side of the colonnade is a three-storey office wing (the east wing was for many years the postal terminal), with the windows separated by pilaster strips. The extravagant use of giant columns is reminiscent of Pennsylvania Station in New York (McKim, Mead, and White, 1902-13). Through the portico is the entrance to the dramatic **Great Hall** [9.14], a mammoth ticket lobby, 260 feet (80 m) long and 88 feet (27 m) high, that is capped by a coved ceiling with square coffers and is illuminated by a four-storey-high arched window at either end. The walls are stone, the ceiling lightweight Guastavino tile. Around the room is a frieze on which are inscribed the names of the principal cities served by the two railways.

The plan features a complex grade-separated circulation system that permits the efficient movement of large numbers of travellers. Departing passengers use the upper level, arriving ones the lower level—a system that is now common in airports. Beyond the concourse are some 4 miles (6 km) of platform, of which more than half are covered. The pattern has since been modified to allow access as well to subway and GO Transit rail commuter services, and to the Royal York Hotel and Royal Bank Plaza to the north, across Front Street.

Toronto's and Winnipeg's Union Stations are splendid examples of Beaux-Arts Classicism—a style for important buildings that came to Canada by way of the US, as well as from architects who had studied at the École des Beaux-Arts in Paris (among them John Lyle, George A. Ross of Ross and Macdonald, and possibly Ross's former partner David MacFarlane [1875-1950], who left the firm in 1912). The teachings of the French school also stressed ways of solving complicated planning problems, and so was ideally suited for railway terminals.

A number of other large stations adopted the style, including Union Station in Ottawa (Ross and MacFarlane, 1908-12; now the Government Conference Centre), whose splendid interior also reflects that of Pennsylvania Station as well as their common source, the Baths of Caracalla in ancient Rome; and the third CPR terminal in Vancouver (1912-15; the partnership of Ernest I. Barott [1884-1966], Gordon H. Blackader [1885-1916], and Daniel T. Webster [d. 1939?]), whose broad, columned façade preceded that of Toronto's Union Station. Beaux-Arts Classicism is discussed further on pages 555, 593.

Railway hotels Once the CPR's line and stations were completed, it became necessary to generate the traffic that would make the line profitable. The CPR attracted freight and passenger business—in part, by making significant contributions to the settlement, agricultural, and industrial development of the West (discussed later in this chapter). Additional passenger traffic was induced by promoting tourism—the first initiative of this kind in Canadian history. William Van Horne was well aware that the line passed through some of the most beautiful mountain scenery on the continent, and he saw the opportunity to exploit this. 'Since we can't export the scenery,' he declared, 'we shall have to import the tourists.'[23] This was done by providing first-class travellers with excellent dining-, parlour-, and sleeping-cars; by building a series of hotels along the sublimely beautiful mountain line; and by promoting the mountains as 'the Switzerland of America'.[24]

In 1886 three hotels—or 'dining stations', as they were first called—were built in the mountains of British Columbia: the Mount Stephen House at Field in the Kicking Horse Valley; the Fraser Canyon Hotel at North Bend; and **Glacier House** [9.15], near Rogers Pass and the summit of the Selkirks. The hotels were built to attract travellers—at first, literally, as dining-stations because their restaurants were substitutes for dining-cars, which were too heavy to haul economically up the steep grades: trains arrived at mealtimes and stopped long enough for passengers to enjoy a good meal and take in the scenery and

9.15 Glacier House, Glacier, British Columbia, 1886.
Photograph *c*. 1886. Canadian Pacific Limited/A11432.

mountain air. The architect for the three hotels was Thomas Sorby, who submitted his designs in November 1885, just as Donald Smith was driving home the CPR's last spike in the mountains of British Columbia. All were similar in design (although one was reversed), having a three-storey gabled block (containing the hall, office, and kitchen), flanked by a two-storey wing on one side and a one-storey one (with the dining-room) on the other. Rooms were provided on the upper floors for travellers who wanted to stay. The wood frame was clad in horizontal siding, except within the central gable, where the wall projected slightly and was shingled—probably to suggest the appearance of a Swiss chalet. The composition was that of Sorby's Port Arthur station [9.8], rendered in a more picturesque mode appropriate to the scenic mountain location. Mrs Arthur Spragge wrote that guests appreciated the Alpine allusions: 'The Glacier House is a very artistic building of the Swiss chalet type, coloured, externally, chrome-yellow, relieved by dark brown beams and mouldings.'[25]

Glacier House was the most celebrated of the three hotels because of its magnificent location, within sight and easy walking distance of the Illecillewaet Glacier—the view of which from the trains was obscured by massive timber snowsheds that protected the tracks from avalanches. A glacial stream supplied fountains around the hotel. Demand exceeded the limited guest accommodation; initially, tents and a sleeping-car absorbed the overflow. In 1890-2 a large annex was built, with 32 bedrooms and a number of sitting-rooms (revising a plan prepared in 1889 by Bruce Price); a bowling alley and billiard room (the latter probably designed by Edward Maxwell) were also constructed. The largest addition, in 1902, was a 54-room wing by Francis Mawson Rattenbury (1867-1935). The interior was redecorated between 1906 and 1910 by Kate Reed, the wife of CPR chief hotel manager Hayter Reed, who was involved in the decoration of many of the CPR's hotels. So, by the first years of the twentieth century Glacier House had become a full-service hotel with nearly 100 guest rooms—designed by four of the country's leading architects. It declined in popularity only because the tracks were relocated in 1916 into the new Connaught Tunnel (in its day the longest tunnel in North America), and the glacier gradually retreated out of sight. The 1925 season was the hotel's last. The buildings, which were soon vandalized, were demolished in 1929.

A CPR mountain hotel that has retained its status as a world-class resort is the **Banff Springs Hotel** [9.16]. In 1883 two CPR workers discovered hot sulphur springs at Banff (Alberta) on the eastern slope of the Rockies. Van Horne strongly supported the proposal that the site should be made Canada's first national park. Sir John A. Macdonald and his wife, Agnes, passed through the mountains on the CPR

in 1886, and by the time the park legislation was introduced into Parliament in April 1887, Macdonald was an avid enthusiast. In the debate he described Banff, with great foresight, as having

> all of the qualifications necessary to make it a great place of resort . . . . There is beautiful scenery, there are the curative properties of the water, there is a genial climate, there is prairie sport and there is mountain sport; and I have no doubt that it will be a great watering place.

Van Horne had already determined to build a fine resort hotel near the springs, at the confluence of the Bow and Spray Rivers. In 1886 Bruce Price was commissioned to prepare designs for the hotel. Work began that fall and the Banff Springs Hotel opened its doors to visitors in June 1888. The 250-bed hotel was a large wood-frame structure, four and five storeys high (it was on a sloping site), with a large central hall rising the height of the building and with balconies at each level.[27]

9.16 Original Banff Springs Hotel, Banff, Alberta, 1886-8. Photograph c. 1900. Canadian Pacific Limited/B6531-1.

9.17 Banff Springs Hotel, Banff, Alberta, 1911-28. Photograph by Harold Kalman, 1990.

494

The attention Van Horne gave to its construction and to details—as well as his considerable architectural flair—are revealed by his biographer:

> The builder turned the hotel the wrong side about, giving the kitchen the finest outlook. One day Van Horne arrived and saw the blunder. His wrath amply illustrated the description of a colleague: 'Van Horne was one of the most considerate and even-tempered of men, but when an explosion came it was magnificent.' However, by the time the cyclone had spent itself a remedy was forthcoming. He sketched as rotunda pavilion on the spot, and ordered it to be erected so as to secure the coveted view for the guests.[28]

When the hotel was completed, Van Horne was satisfied that it did justice to the magnificent view, and boasted that it was the 'Finest Hotel on the North American Continent'.

The picturesque composition—created by the steep hipped roofs, pointed dormers, turrets, bay windows, and balconies—was clearly intended to be associated with the romance of historic European mountain architecture, even if nobody could pinpoint a precise source. One visitor called it 'in the Schloss style of the Rhenish provinces', and another said it was 'half way between a Tudor Hall and a Swiss Chalet . . . a Tudor Chalet in Wood.' Writing about a later addition to the hotel, CPR publicist John Murray Gibbon suggested that a Loire château was the source, 'as a gesture of recognition to the French-Canadian population and in tribute to the French explorers who had blazed the trail for the Canadian Pacific'; while a CPR promotional pamphlet drew parallels with the 'baronial style' of the Scottish highlands, noting that Banff was named by Donald Smith (who was born near Banffshire; George Stephen was from Dufftown in Banffshire) and conjuring images of 'heather-covered moors', 'highland burns', and 'Scotland's stags'.[29]

None of these comparisons were far from the mark. The same can be said of the informal composition and steep roofs of the present brick-and-stone hotel that has become a famous landmark to visitors from round the world [9.17]. One wing and an 11-storey tower (by W.S. Painter) were built in 1911-14, and the main wing (by J.W. Orrock) in 1925-8. Like Price's original hotel (the last remaining portion of which was destroyed by fire in 1926), the Banff Springs Hotel is too free an adaptation of any European prototype to reveal a precise historical source. It is best described as being in the Canadian Château Style, and not as a revival of a European source. The picturesque theme was continued in 1989-90 when a large conference centre was added to the hotel.

The Château Style had reached a climax earlier in the CPR's **Château Frontenac [9.18]** in Quebec City. Local interests had called for a luxury hotel in the Upper Town since 1880, and a dozen years later the CPR's directors accepted the challenge. They chose the most prominent point on the escarpment, next to the remains of the former Château Saint-Louis (which had burned down in 1834), and on the site of another governor's residence, the Château Haldimand. Bruce Price was the architect. Ground was broken in May 1892, and the hotel opened its doors nineteen months later, on 18 December 1893.[30]

William Van Horne again took an active interest in the design. He declared that he would not throw money away on 'marble and frills', but would 'depend on broad effects, rather than ornamentation and detail.' On at least one occasion, Van Horne went out in a boat with Price to convince himself that the hotel's appearance was sufficiently majestic when seen from the St Lawrence River.[31] The architect succeeded on all counts. The broad and effective massing of the Château Frontenac makes it the most prominent landmark seen from approaching ocean vessels. The principal elevation consists of a five-storey block flanked by two broad towers, one circular and one polygonal. The walls are faced in orange-red Glenboig brick (imported from Scotland) with ashlar trim, and stone is also used for the two upper floors to mark the best rooms and suites. The high hipped roofs, the conical roofs of the towers, the dormer windows, and the tall chimneys create a prominent and picturesque silhouette.

Inspiration for the design came from French châteaux of the fourteenth and fifteenth centuries, particularly the castles of the Loire. Although no specific building provided a source—Price heeded Van Horne's demand for 'broad effects'—it is easy to find generic prototypes, such as the fifteenth-century Château de Jaligny, whose principal block is similarly inserted between two broad circular towers.[32]

The Château Frontenac differs from the Châteauesque mansions favoured by some US millionaires (often described as being in the style of François I) that reached their zenith with G.W. Vanderbilt's Biltmore (1888-95), an immense country estate near Asheville, North Carolina. The American buildings are more assertive, angular, and loaded with historical detail; but the parallel would not have been missed. Even though the Château Frontenac was designed by an American architect (Price) for an American-born client (Van Horne), the result was plainer, less pretentious, more rounded and understated—altogether more Canadian. Nevertheless, it achieved an effect of monumental grandeur.

In an 1899 interview Price described the Château Frontenac as 'the early French chateau adapted to modern requirements.' He rightly noted that the design flowed naturally from the site, which he described as 'an inspiration':

> The result came of itself . . . . The site . . . was practically at the apex of the picturesque old City, and if ever there was the natural place and a natural reason for a picturesque building it was here.[33]

The idea of the picturesque that had developed in eighteenth-century England, and had been exploited in nineteenth-century America, had a great influence on Price—though in creating his modern architecture he used historical precedents as general inspiration, not to reiterate past styles. This spirit

9.18 Château Frontenac, Quebec, Quebec, begun 1892. Photograph *c.* 1908. Notman Photographic Archives, MMCH/4171.

of historicism informed not only Price's work, but also that of his more renowned American contemporary, Henry Hobson Richardson, in both his public buildings and in private work such as the H.L. Anderson house in Washington (1881), which uses a round and a polygonal tower to create much the same feeling for mass as the Château Frontenac.[34]

The lavish interiors of the Château Frontenac were also impressive. The original U-shaped plan arranges five wings of unequal length around a central courtyard, giving most of the exterior rooms superb views up and down the St Lawrence River. Each of the 170 bedrooms featured reproduction oak furniture in the sixteenth-century style. Three tower suites were filled with valuable antiques: the Habitant Suite was furnished in the style of early French Canada; the Chinese Suite reminded visitors that Quebec was only the first stop after Europe in the CPR's route to the Orient; and the Dutch Suite ostensibly honoured the Amsterdam shareholders who supported the company in its early stages—though here one suspects the personal touch of

9.19 Empress Hotel, Victoria, British Columbia, begun 1904. Tourism BC/03-T1971.

Van Horne, who was proud of his Dutch ancestry.

The cliff-top prominence of the Château Frontenac increased with subsequent additions. In 1897-8 Bruce Price added the Citadel Pavilion and Wing to the south, towards the Plains of Abraham, and in 1908-9 W.S. Painter designed the Mont Carmel Wing adjacent to it. In 1920-4 a massive 17-storey tower (which removed two of Price's lesser wings), the Saint-Louis Wing, and a service wing were built to designs by Edward and William S. Maxwell. The tower dwarfed Price's original elevation, which had been so prominent in its day. In June 1993 Claude Pratte wing—containing 66 rooms, a swimming pool, and health club—was inaugurated.

The building that opened in 1893 fulfilled all Van Horne's intentions. As the CPR told its shareholders in 1898:

> Your Company's Hotel at Quebec—the Chateau Frontenac—has been most successful, and a large addition was made to it last year to meet the requirements of the travel it had so largely stimulated. It has not only become profitable in itself, but has from its beginning added materially to your passenger earnings.[35]

The next of the great CPR hotels was the **Empress Hotel** (1904-8) in Victoria, BC [**9.19**]. Local entrepreneurs, who conceived the project to promote tourism, interested the CPR in it and convinced city council to grant the railway tax exemptions, and newly filled land on the inner harbour. Francis Mawson Rattenbury was selected as the architect.[36]

The steeply pitched roofs, dormer windows, tall chimneys, and turrets (domed polygonal turrets that Rattenbury borrowed from his Legislative Buildings nearby)—all features of the new Château Style—combined to create a picturesque skyline. A new emphasis on verticality was reinforced by the stacked bay windows on the projecting pavilions on either side of the entrance-loggia, whose stone facing provided a counterpoint to the red brick of the walls. The decorative detail (including Gothic quatrefoils in the cornice) was concentrated in the upper portions, leaving flat, unornamented wall surfaces that were not expressive of volume (unlike the bulges and swells of the Château Frontenac). The design of the Empress reflected a shift from Victorian to Edwardian tastes; it was also intended to evoke not only images of European castles, but also the Quebec prototype. The press quickly picked up on this, hailing it as a hotel that would 'make the Western gateway of the great transcontinental system a fitting companion to the historic pile on the heights of Quebec.'[37] The Empress was thus turned into a French château twice removed. The steep roofs and dormers—the essential characteristics of the Château Style—are the key to this associative process. The many additions to the Empress include wings by W.S. Painter (1910-13) and J.W. Orrock (1929), and a new entrance pavilion (1988-9).

Artist and connoisseur William Van Horne retained a number of talented designers—Sorby, Price, Colonna, Rattenbury, and Edward Maxwell (the only native Canadian in the group)—all of whom made significant architectural contributions. In a notable change of policy, Van Horne's successor as president, the ruthlessly efficient bureaucrat Thomas Shaughnessy (later Baron Shaughnessy), began to rely on in-house architects and engineers for almost all buildings. Shaughnessy could not tolerate independent egos and had to have total control over the people who worked for him. He complained, for example, that Rattenbury, 'like most architects, is adhering to his own ideas' in making unauthorized changes.[38]

In 1905 the CPR appointed its first chief architect, Walter S. Painter (1877-1957), who had trained in Pennsylvania and Michigan and opened a short-lived practice in Toronto in 1904 under the name of Brown and Painter. Painter returned to private practice in 1911, but not before making an impact on the CPR's buildings. His contributions to Windsor Station, the Château Frontenac, the Banff Springs Hotel, and the Empress Hotel have been noted; immediately after he left the CPR he was also involved in the Château Lake Louise (1912) and the Hotel Vancouver (with Francis S. Swales, 1912-16; demolished). Another designer hired by the CPR was John Wilson Orrock (1870-?), who rose to the position of engineer of buildings. This practice of retaining corporate designers continued after Painter's and Orrock's departure, and as as result later CPR buildings were less remarkable.[39]

The Château Style appeared in many more railway hotels across the country in the first third of the twentieth century. The story of how it was heralded as a national style will be told in Chapter 14. We shall return now to the late nineteenth century, and the continuing account of architectural development in the West.

The Opening of the West

In 1870 Canada acquired Manitoba and the Northwest Territories with the purchase of Rupert's Land from the Hudson's Bay Company. Despite the

incentives offered by the Dominion Lands Policy, which were intended to attract settlers, growth was slow. When the CPR was completed in 1885, only 150,000 people lived on the Prairies. The federal government and the CPR knew that the West would have to be settled far more densely—to justify the government's annexation, and so that the CPR could develop a solid base of freight and passenger traffic, and generate enough activity to sell or develop some of its 25 million acres of land. The federal and Manitoba governments, and the CPR, therefore undertook aggressive programs of attracting new settlers, particularly after the economy took an upturn in 1896. In that year the energetic Clifford Sifton, who had been named Minister of the Interior in the new Laurier government, began a determined campaign of urging Americans and Europeans to settle in 'The Last Best West'. The federal government continued to distribute free land on certain conditions that included its cultivation. Sifton's ministry commissioned propaganda literature, such as Edward Robert Peacock's *Canada: A Descriptive Text-book* (1900), which made utopian promises to prospective British immigrants to the Prairies, noting that

> every settler is given, practically free, a large farm in a country which produces the best wheat in the world . . . . The feeling of equality with one's neighbours, and particularly the knowledge that the land is one's own is worth a good deal.[40]

The department paid European agents five dollars for each farmer and two dollars for each family member they recruited. The CPR also maintained a network of land agents and issued its own advertising. Many English Canadians attacked Sifton for his efforts to lure Eastern European peasants, whom they alleged lacked 'quality'; these prejudiced objections led Sifton to retort:

> I think a stalwart peasant in a sheepskin coat, born on the soil, whose forefathers have been farmers for generations, with a stout wife and a half-dozen children, is quality.[41]

For his part, Van Horne recognized the Prairie West as 'our great gold mine', and he and his successor, Shaughnessy, set out to achieve agricultural, mineral, and urban development.[42] The CPR's initial policy was to help the government attract settlers, since an established population would ensure long-term profitability better than a one-time land sale. 'It is *settling*, not *selling* that we must aim at,' George Stephen wrote in 1881. 'If our lands won't sell we

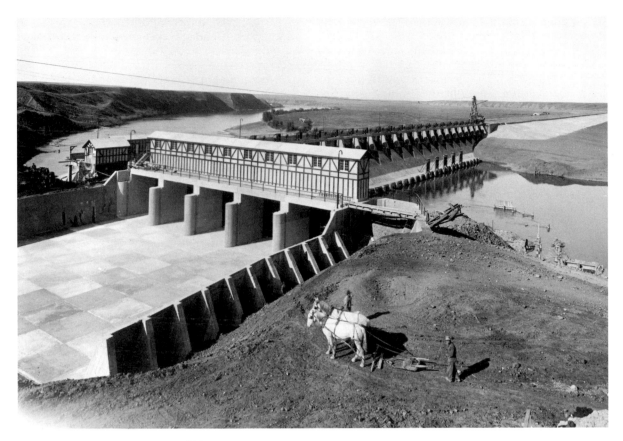

9.20 Irrigation dam near Bassano, Alberta, 1912-14.
Photograph *c.* 1914. Glenbow Archives/NA3641-1.

will give them away to settlers.'[43] The advice was not followed, however: the company was never willing to give away land. In that same year it appointed a land agent in London and began to advertise the sale of its lands in Britain. Initial sales were slow. Between 1881 and 1896 only 1.7 million acres (680,000 hectares) had been sold; but in the next eighteen years—between 1896 and 1914—12.6 million acres (5 million hectares) on the Prairies were sold, reflecting a number of innovative and agressive ways of promoting settlement.[44]

One was irrigation. Captain John Palliser (page 337) had recognized that southern Alberta was dry, yet the region was too important to the CPR to allow this verdict to impede its development. In 1904 the CPR began to build a system of dams and canals to divert water from the Bow River. The irrigated land could be sold to new settlers at a far higher price than unimproved, arid property. The **Irrigation dam** (1912-14) near Bassano, Alberta, designed by CPR engineer Hugh B. Muckleston and constructed of reinforced concrete, brought water to 245,000 acres (100,000 hectares) of land [9.20]. The mock half-timbering provided an appealing

touch of gentility to the otherwise utilitarian structure. The dam generated hydroelectric power as well, some of which was used by the CPR's Ogden Shops in Calgary.[45]

The CPR devised several schemes for 'assisted settlement' within this irrigation block. Its Development Branch provided new arrivals with contractors to build fences and prepare and seed the land at a cost well below the going rate. It introduced a 'crop payment plan', whereby new settlers could pay for their land mostly in crops rather than cash, allowing them to invest their limited capital into developing the land. Another program was the 'loan farm', in which the CPR provided cash advances to experienced farmers to help them set up the farm and build a house and a barn. The CPR also built demonstration farms to show the viability of planting in the irrigation area, carried out (with the federal government) a program of tree-planting, and even provided some settlers with 'ready-made farms' [9.26].

These government and CPR initiatives were largely successful in attracting people to the Canadian West, although they were certainly assisted by global circumstances beyond Canadian control, such as poor crop yields in the American dry belt and the Russian government's intolerance of cultural minorities. Whatever the causes, by the beginning of the First World War—twenty years after the introduction of rail service—the Canadian prairie population had increased tenfold to 1.5 million people.[46] The West attracted Canadians and Americans seeking more or better land (or simply a new life), Europeans who were looking for new opportunities, and members of cultural minorities who were suffering persecution in their own countries.

Rural settlement

The settlers' first task was to build a shelter against the elements. As at the Red River Settlement nearly a century earlier, the frontier's powerful environmental forces led different cultural groups to arrive at similar temporary building solutions. But before long—usually in the first permanent house that was erected, and particularly among those settlers who could not afford (or chose not) to use industrialized building products—individual architectural traditions emerged, and produced clearly differentiated ethnic building-types. In time, however, industrialization became dominant, and the availability (and intensive advertising) of cheap milled lumber and standardized building systems led to a blurring of cultural identities as the Bodnarchuks, Tarasoffs, and Silbersteins all strove to keep up with the Joneses. Within a few generations, a sameness prevailed in prairie housing, and the differences among groups was seen only in details and ancillary features, such as colours, fences, and gardens.

This section discusses the buildings that accompanied rural agricultural development, including the temporary shelter and the first substantial house—both of which were built quickly and cheaply out of necessity—and finally the second house, in which cultural and social aspirations could be expressed more directly. Schools and churches are also introduced.

Homesteading: the first house Most prairie settlers rode a CPR colonist car to the nearest station (after an arduous crossing, for many, of the Atlantic), then found transportation by wagon to their quarter-sections of empty land. Suddenly they were faced with the reality of having to build a farm out of nothing. One new arrival described that feeling:

> We reached our homestead at last. I'll never forget the desolate feeling that came over me, when, with the contents of the waggon out on the ground, we sat on a box and looked around, not a sign of any other human habitation or a road leading to one to be seen, nothing but bluff and water and grass. Then I realized that we were at the end of our journey, that this was to be our home, that if we wanted a house to cover us, a stable for our horses, a well for drinking water, it would all have to be the work of our own hands.[47]

9.21 Roy Benson homestead near Munson, Alberta, *c.* 1910. Glenbow Archives/NA2543-1.

9.22 Pail house near Viking, Alberta, *c.* 1900-10. Glenbow Archives/NA1758-13.

Many came with a canvas tent, which served as home until they built their first dwelling. Other temporary shelters included a lean-to made of saplings lashed together and placed over a dug-out hole in the ground; or a 'Prairie Schooner', an arch of saplings constructed over a wagon (if the settler had one) and protected with the canvas wagon-cover.[48] This sufficed until the first house, usually only a semi-permanent dwelling, could be built.

Those settlers who could afford to buy lumber at the nearest sawmill or lumber-yard would build a shack, or shanty. It was usually a rectangular one-room structure, often as small as 10 by 12 feet (3 by 3.7 m)— sometimes a more generous, but still small, 14 by 16 feet (4.3 by 4.9 m)—in which a family would eat, sleep, and socialize. Shacks were typically framed with 2-by-4 studs, sheathed with horizontal shiplap, and covered with a gently sloping shed roof. Many were clad only in scrap lumber, tarpaper, or anything else that was available cheaply or free. A door and a window or two provided access and light, and a small wood-burning stove was used for cooking and heat. The first **Roy Benson homestead** (*c.* 1910), near Munson, Alberta, was built in this way [**9.21**]. (Benson and his wife pose in front with their ox-cart and two ploughs.) Shacks of this kind were frame versions of the log shanties of Upper Canada [**4.25**], and may well have been introduced to the Prairies by people from that

region. As most offered poor (if any) insulation, this kind of shelter was popular among people who lived on their land only during the summer and had jobs elsewhere during the winter.

Most new arrivals did not have the money to buy lumber and used whatever materials were available at no cost. The most prevalent substance on the grassland was the turf that was upturned by ploughing; consequently sod houses were an expedient and common solution. Unlike the *semlin* built by Manitoba Mennonites in the 1870s (pages 349-50), which was partly dug out and partly above ground, the post-railway prairie sod house (or 'soddie') was usually a reasonably substantial dwelling built entirely above grade. A well-built sod house had walls two sods thick. The **Pail house** [**9.22**] near Viking, Alberta, built in the early 1900s, is one such dwelling. Frank Pail and his wife stand proudly in front of their home. Behind them is a person in a wagon, and a log barn and a lower sod structure.

James Rugg has described the sod house his family built in 1905:

The walls were built like laying bricks. The sods were cut about two feet long, were thirteen inches wide and four inches thick laid with grass side down. We had one rough-made door about six feet high and 2-foot-6-inches wide which was difficult to fit into the sod walls. The roof was lean-to type, there were three windows 2 feet by 2 feet with four lights in each. Being set in two foot wide walls not much light could come in, of course no storm windows. Many cold days in winter an inch or more frost would gather on the inside of the windows.

Inside, it was 12 feet wide and 22 feet long. Ten feet was curtained off for a bedroom, and the other 12 by 12 feet was used as a kitchen and living room. Later a porch was added which came in very handy. Poles with hay and sods on top were used for the roof over the bedroom; we used boards with tarpaper on top over the kitchen. The lumber for roof, door and windows cost about 20 dollars. One good fortune by having boards over the living room was the reasonable freedom from insects and dirt falling from the ceiling . . . .[49]

Mrs Ed Watson of Keeler, Saskatchewan, recalled how she and her children built a sod barn with few tools, making a harness for the cow and recruiting it (with only limited success) to help haul the sod.[50] Sods were sometimes banked up against wood shacks to provide them with insulation. Some settlers endeavoured to finish the interior well. The **Moorhouse house [9.23]** at Lashburn, Saskatchewan, built in 1906, had sod walls that were lined with white building paper and hung with pictures, with wood flooring, knick-knacks, and a large iron stove for warmth.

In the parkland and forest-margin regions, where there were trees, the initial house was often built of horizontal logs, with dovetail or saddle-notched joints—again, in much the same manner as the log houses of early Ontario, although the first prairie house was usually roofed with sod or thatch rather than shingles. The **Summers house [9.24]** near Erskine, Alberta, was built in 1902 of large logs with crude saddle-notched joints. It was called 'Our First Homestead Mansion' when it was built by Asa Darrah, who accompanied the Summers family from Nebraska, and it was occupied for three years.

In areas where the trees were not big enough to provide logs that were long or straight enough to be laid horizontally, the logs were placed vertically into a trench—like the *pieux en terre* seen among early French settlers, or the palisades of the NWMP. Upright logs were used in the **Roland house [9.25]** near Alix, Alberta, built around 1903 and seen with Gus Roland and his family in the doorway. (A rare example of a church built of vertical logs is Christ Church at Millarville, Alberta, built in 1895, a year after the area was settled; it still stands.[51]) Other materials were also used. Some prairie settlers built their initial houses of sun-dried adobe bricks made out of mud and straw, and other early settlers built crude houses of stone.[52]

The reminiscences of Sarah Ellen Roberts—who

9.23 Interior of the Moorhouse house, Lashburn, Saskatchewan, 1906. Photograph *c.* 1908. SAB/R-A3483.

came with her husband, father, and two sons from Illinois to homestead near Talbot, Alberta, in 1906—provide wonderful insights into the types of shelters, and the agonizing choices, that were available to new settlers. The Roberts family began by living in a tent, which was soon destroyed by a storm. Until they built their own house, they lived in the one-room shack of their friend and neighbour, Jack Gatliff, which 'had been very cheaply built' and was 'very cramped and crowded'.

> The walls were of the thickness of just one board, nailed to the studding over building paper. The ventilation was more than adequate even when the window and the door were both closed, and it was not a building in which one could spend the winter.[53]

Sarah Roberts explained that the decision about what kind of house to build was made rationally:

> We had at first intended to build a sod house, but the more I knew about sod houses the more I was

convinced that I could not be satisfied with one. They are warm and cheap, but are very hard to keep clean . . . . Most of the homesteaders who have money enough to do so build frame houses . . . . We had no money with which to buy lumber, so a frame house was out of the question for us. We therefore decided to build a log house . . . . As there were no logs large enough or straight enough to build a house of the usual style, with the logs laid horizontally, it was decided to dig a trench, put two rows of smaller logs in it vertically, and fill the spaces between them with mud . . . .

'I do not know of another house of this vertical-pole-and-mud construction,' Roberts noted, as the house was being built. It was 28 by 18 feet (8.5 by 5.5 m), with one half taken up by the living-room, and the other half by two bedrooms.

The walls are of upright poles, most of them six or eight inches in diameter. These poles are set in a double row in a trench two feet deep, and the space between the poles is filled with clay, which the boys dug near the shore of the lake and which they thought would dry to give a firm impervious wall. They conservatively estimated that they dug and hauled forty tons of this material and tamped it into the walls . . . . The ceiling was made by laying small poles together on stringers made of larger poles. Tarpaper was laid on these poles, and this was covered with a layer of sod, grass side

down. So, in spite of my aversion to a sod house, I am living in one that is made partially of sod.

The sod provided insulation; above this, the roof was gabled with poplar rafters, tarpaper, and shingles. After the roof was finished, a floor was made of boards hewed from poplar logs; before that the family had walked on 'ground-up hay or that clammy, cold dirt floor.' Despite these efforts, the Roberts' house was very cold in winter: 'The intense cold has opened up many small cracks in the walls and they let in much cold air.'

The family finally decided to abandon their log house and build a sod house. Roberts described the difficult task of building the soddie—which she had tried so hard to avoid. It was 22 by 24 feet (6.7 by 7.3 m), with the sod walls 28 inches (70 cm) thick—

9.24 Summers house near Erskine, Alberta, 1902. Glenbow Archives/ NA1592-2.

9.25 Roland house near Alix, Alberta, c. 1903. Glenbow Archives/ na648-2.

two rows of parallel sods, 'laid alternately crosswise and lengthwise, with the grass side down.' A hipped roof was constructed with long logs, on top of which were laid small poles, tarpaper, and a double layer of sod. The family plastered the interior walls with clay dug from the cellar, and built a proper wood floor and partitions. Much to their surprise, they found the house 'to be very warm and comfortable'. Nevertheless, in 1912—six years after they arrived in Alberta—the Roberts family returned to Illinois.

The second house   An estimated four in ten applicants for prairie homesteads failed to 'prove up', and never obtained a patent to their quarter-section.[54] For those homesteaders who did remain, the time eventually came to build a larger, more comfortable, and more permanent house. Second houses on prairie farms were typically $1\frac{1}{2}$- and 2-storey wood-frame buildings in a wide range of plans and styles that correspond to the types of houses that will be discussed in Chapter 11. Milled lumber and manufactured building supplies were readily available through a large network of retail outlets; the railway system allowed easy transportation of products; and the lumber industry controlled distribution and prices. Mail-order lumber sales were introduced to the Prairies in 1909, accompanied by more aggressive and competitive marketing that somewhat reduced the cost of building supplies.

Even with these benefits, many settlers still did not have the money, or the carpentry skills, to design and build their own wood-frame houses from scratch. For them, a compromise between comfort and cost lay in mass production and standardization. Pre-built farmhouses, prefabricated buildings, mail-order houses, and published plans all offered urban and rural residents snug and affordable frame dwellings that either replaced, or were more comfortable alternatives to, the crude initial dwellings.[55]

The pre-built homestead provided a no-hands approach to settlement. Homesteads were produced by a number of commercial colonization companies, which offered prospective settlers everything they needed as an incentive to buy their land. As early as 1882, the Qu'Appelle Valley Farming Company marketed 300 tenant farms near Indian Head, 'each with dwelling house, stabling and shedding', although it and several similar schemes failed.[56] One of the few successful ventures of this kind was the CPR's 'ready-made farms' in the Alberta irrigation district as a part of its assisted-settlement program. This involved the company's building a house, barn, implement shed, and fencing, and also hav-

ing 50 acres ploughed and sowed before the settlers arrived. The first tract developed in this way, called the Nightingale colony, was readied for British settlers in 1910. A **ready-made farm**[9.26] near Brooks, Alberta—seen in a photograph of 1920—shows the farmer, his wife and their three children, and their dog and team of horses and equipment in front of a standard $1\frac{1}{2}$-storey gable-roofed house, and a small barn with a granary loft and a shed. Many ready-made farms had these same tiny structures, although standard plans were available for at least six house models of varying sizes. By 1919 some 419 settlers had purchased ready-made farms in central and southern Alberta.[57]

Prefabricated buildings (also called 'ready-mades') form an interesting and innovative chapter in architectural history. Sectional prefabs, which provided the owner with standard wall panels that he could assemble without special skills (similar, in principle, to the knock-down furniture that is so popular today), had been produced in the UK and Canada for several decades (see pages 346, 393), but not until after the turn of the century were improved products marketed actively on the Prairies. The railway made it possible to ship these and other industrialized construction products quickly and efficiently from the East, and from the West Coast. First off the mark was the British Columbia Mills, Timber and Trading Company of Vancouver, which manufactured a large line of well-constructed prefabs between 1904 and 1910. The wall panels' many layers of wood and tarpaper (separated by internal air spaces), and the effective joints, provided rigid and draft-free walls. All sections were numbered for easy assembly. **Design B [9.27]**—a 12- by 16-foot (3.7- by 4.9-m) one-room cabin, pre-painted and with a galvanized iron chimney—could be purchased for little more than $100, providing an alternative to a hand-built initial house; a four-bedroom, two-storey house was available for under $800. The company was more successful, however, in selling to farmers its larger buildings—commercial as well as residential (see page 523-4)—in towns, and smaller structures, such as cabins, chicken coops, and sheds.[58]

An alternative mass-produced system, one that required greater assembly skills than a sectional house, was the mail-order building. Shopping from a catalogue or an advertisement in a farm journal, a property-owner could send away for a package that consisted of all the lumber (sometimes pre-cut), doors, windows, roofing, hardware, other components, and plans that were required to build a house. (The furnace and plumbing were extra.) Nothing

9.26 Ready-made farm near Brooks, Alberta. Photograph by Harry Pollard, 1920. PAA/H.Pollard Collection/P591.

9.27 Design B for a one-room cabin. From the British Columbia Mills, Timber and Trading Company, *Catalogue of Patented Ready-Made Houses,* 1905.

For price, etc., see page following Design " D."

was preassembled, and economies of scale lowered the cost below that of purchasing parts at the local lumber yard. The T. Eaton Company of Toronto first included houses and building materials in its 1910 catalogue [9.28]. The next year's catalogue offered five houses and a barn, ranging from a 'shack' ($165), and a 'cottage' for the homesteader, to a nine-room house ($1,025); three years later the line was expanded to require a separate 80-page catalogue of houses and barns. The **W.A. Van Lohuizen house [9.29]** near Monarch, Alberta, a $2\frac{1}{2}$-storey building with a hipped roof, was an Eaton's house; built in 1918, it is still in use. (A similar Eaton's offering was the 'Eastbourne' [11.32].) Eaton's faced competition from a number of other suppliers of prefabricated houses, mostly American—including Sears Roebuck of Chicago and the Aladdin House, manufactured by the North American Construction Company of Bay City, Michigan (which opened a branch in Toronto).[59]

Would-be house-builders could simply opt for buying an advertised plan. While this was not a labour-saving move, it ensured a tried-and-true design and building system (while imposing a further element of standardization on the landscape). Eaton's charged $2.50 for the plans of its houses. Several lines of American plans were advertised in Canadian periodicals, such as *The Nor'West Farmer* and *The Farmer's Advocate*.[60]

Standardization was also the order of the day

among the rural schoolhouses of the Prairies, as it had been in the eastern provinces following the introduction of public education. The first schools were usually built by individual communities, following provincial or territorial guidelines. Most were one-room buildings in a variety of materials, covered with a gable roof and poorly illuminated by domestic-type windows. Provincial and territorial governments gradually asserted central control over school-building and issued standard plans. Winnipeg architect Samuel Hooper (1851-1911) was commissioned to produce standard plans and specifications (published in 1903) for three sizes of schools for Manitoba. The **school at Ridgeville [9.30]**, Manitoba, follows Hooper's plan no. 1, the smallest of the three. The neat frame building, planted forlornly on the open prairie, had large windows, a ventilating cupola, a draft vestibule, and a lean-to shed.[61]

In the Northwest Territories in 1885, the Board of Education issued standards for school construction, following Ontario and Manitoba guidelines; responsibilities for schools passed to Saskatchewan and Alberta when they achieved provincehood in 1905.

As the Saskatchewan authorities were unable to agree, they relied on standard plans offered by a private corporation, the Waterman-Waterbury Company of Minneapolis, which opened a Regina branch in 1912. The firm promised to 'provide everything but teacher and pupils', offering free school-plans and installing its own patented stove; by 1918 it claimed to have supplied plans for more than 1500 rural schools in the province. Most followed the **Waterman-Waterbury design no. 1 [9.31]**, a small one-room cottage-type, with a hipped roof and small windows, probably intended to conserve the stove's heat. Other private firms also jumped into the fray: the BC Mills, Timber and Trading Company, for one, offered a sectional one-room schoolhouse in its 1905 catalogue.[62]

Despite the promises of equality for all, stated in immigration propaganda and reflected in mass-produced housing systems, social and economic distinctions were inevitable. People who came with

9.28 From the Fall and Winter Catalogue, 1911-12, of the T. Eaton Company. Archives of Ontario/F229-2-0-14.

Lumber Direct from the Mills at Lowest Prices

NINE-ROOMED HOUSE

ize 28x40.   Compact and easy to heat.

..K200. **EATON** price for the material, including Rough Lumber, Siding, Flooring, Finishing, Mouldings, Windows, Doors, Window and Door Frames, Lath and Shingles, including Plans and full Specifications complete, eight paid to most stations.... **1.025.00**

4K201. Plans and Specifications...... **2.50**

.f Lumber is ordered, we refund the price of ans.

IVE ROOMS—WARM AND HOMELIKE

ve-Roomed House, size 22x28

.... EATON price, complete for all necessary Lumber, Windows and Doors, Window and Door Frames, Mouldings, Building Paper, Lath and Shingles, and also Plans and Specifications, freight paid to most stations. Price.. **645.00**

.K203. Plans and Specifications, if ordered separately.......... **2.50**

.f Lumber is ordered, the price of Plans will be refunded.

We supply both fir and cedar lumber cut on the British Columbia Coast, and properly seasoned before shipment. We guarantee all our lumber to be fully up to standard.

To secure the advantage of our low prices, we require an order for at least 16,000 feet of lumber, which makes a carload. If necessary get your neighbor to join with you in ordering.

If you can place an order for at least a carload of lumber it will pay you to write us for our price on the necessary material for any buildings you may contemplate erecting. When writing, send us your bill of material. If you have no bill of material, send us a plan or rough sketch, showing the dimensions or layout of proposed buildings. We will reply by early mail giving you our price, including freight charges to your nearest station.

For the convenience of our customers, we have prepared some ready-made plans for several standard houses and barns. Particulars of these are shown on this page, also the cost of all lumber entering into their construction. You may order the plans first at the small cost of $2.50, and then if you send us your order for the lumber called for in the plans, we will refund price of the plans. We do not draw plans of special order. The only plans we have for sale are described below.

The prices named below for houses and barns include freight to stations between the Rockies and Winnipeg, with the exception of Northern Saskatchewan and Manitoba. To such points, we shall be pleased to quote special prices on application.

We reserve the right to lower or raise our prices of lumber, in accordance with market fluctuations. We cannot guarantee the prices quoted below, as we can only give a price based on present market figures. Before ordering, write us, and we will give you the lowest possible prices applying at that time.

All our houses are of frame construction, with one-ply of No. 1 Shiplap, paper, and No. 1 clear Bevel Siding on the outside ; on the inside one-ply of No 1 Shiplap, paper, strapping, and lath and plaster, giving two air spaces. For lining floor, No. 1 Shiplap is used, and No. 1 Fir Flooring for finishing floors.   No. 1 Shiplap, paper and No. 1 XXX Red Cedar Shingles for roof.

HOMESTEAD COTTAGE

Four-Roomed Cottage, size 22 ft. 4 ins. x 26 ft. 4 ins.

44K204. Our price includes all the necessary Lumber, both common and finishing ; Windows and Doors, Window and Door Frames, Casing, Mouldings, Lath and Building Paper, also complete Plans and Specifications. The price of material for Cottage, freight paid to most stations.... **404.00**

44K205. Plans, Specifications and Bill of Material for above Cottage.... **2.50**

If Lumber is ordered, we refund price of Plans.

The material for a Homestead Cottage or Homestead Barn makes only about a half carload. As our price is conditional on a carload order, it is necessary to order the material for two cottages or two barns, or for one cottage and one barn.

HOMESTEAD BARN

Square Pitched Roof Barn, 36 ft. 6 ins. x 40 ft., with 12-ft. posts. Barn is sheeted with Shiplap, Tar Paper and Drop Siding to height of stable. Above stable line Drop Siding only.

44K206. Our price for No. 1 quality Lumber, Shingles, Barn Sash, Doors and Tar Paper, with Plans, Specifications and Bill of Material, freight paid to most stations, is........ **337.00**

44K207. Plans, Specifications and Bill of Material for this Barn........ **2.50**

Price of Plans refunded on receipt of Lumber orders.

SENSIBLE EIGHT-ROOMED HOUSE

Eight-Roomed Ho..... .... A warm and well-lighted house, attractive in appearance, and a most desirable country home.

44K208. EATON price for all necessary, rough Lumber, Siding, Floorings, Mouldings, Windows and Doors, Window and Door Frames Shingles and Lath and Building Paper, including Plans, Specifications and Bill of Material, freight paid to most stations...... **895.00**

44K269. Plans, Specifications and Bill of Material...................... **2.50**

If Lumber is ordered, price of Plans will refunded.

HOMESTEADER'S SHACK

This Shack is specially designed for the homesteader, is built in sections, and can be put up in a day. It measures 12 x 18 feet, with 8-foot ceiling. Has double floors, with building paper between. The top floor is of matched lumber The wall construction is as follows : Matched siding outside, then building paper, shiplap, building paper on studs, 4-in. air space, then sheeting and building paper inside. Roof is shiplap covered with building paper and prepared 7-year roofing. Weight of material 4500 pounds, at third-class freight rate, if shipped singly. If four are shipped at once, the low carload rate of freight is obtained.

44K210. EATON price for Shack complete, including Windows, Doors, Hardware, Nails and Paint. f.o.b. Winnipeg........ **165.00**

(F. O. B. Winnipeg means that the purchaser pays freight from Winnipeg.)

9.29 Van Lohuizen house near Monarch, Alberta, 1918. Photograph by Thelma B. Dennis, 1982.

money and invested it wisely, or who worked very hard to accumulate capital, gained the advantage; and those with certain backgrounds, particularly English-speaking settlers from Eastern Canada, began in a privileged position. For them, class and cultural distinctions were clearly expressed in the second house.

One of the best-known success stories on the Prairies is that of William Richard Motherwell. The son of a farmer from Lanark County, near Perth, Ontario, and a graduate of the Ontario Agricultural College, the 22-year-old Motherwell homesteaded near Abernethy, in the Pheasant Hills district north of Qu'Appelle, Saskatchewan, in 1882, the year the CPR tracks reached Qu'Appelle. He spent one season in a tent, then built a small three-room log house (which he subsequently clapboarded)—a kind that was (and still is) abundant in eastern Ontario. Motherwell worked hard, made good use of his scientific knowledge of agriculture, and prospered; he and his wife accumulated wealth, and became leaders in their community. In 1897, after a bumper wheat crop and the end of the recession, they built their permanent residence: a large stone house that clearly displayed their wealth and position in society. The **Motherwell homestead** [9.32, 33] is on the farm they named Lanark Place, after their home county.

The house consists of a 2½-storey principal block with a hipped roof, central door, and formal centre-hall plan. At the rear, a 1½-storey kitchen-wing projects, with a separate entrance, an Ontario-type central gable, and a long side veranda; it originally contained the summer kitchen and servants' quar-

ters. This arrangement of a main block and wing ('ell') was common in eastern Ontario, and the design represents a simplified version of the Italianate style that was popular there when Motherwell left Perth. The principal façade has a two-tiered central gabled porch and a pair of projecting pedimented windows, both of which have handsome fretsawn details (no doubt based on pattern-book designs). The windows have Italianate segmented heads, and the round-arched dormers fan-like mullions (there are no dormers on the side, which suggests that the attic storey was used only for storage). Cast-iron cresting outlines a rectangular space at the peak. The attractive ornamentation clearly made this house stand apart from most prairie houses of the day.

The walls are constructed of large grey, black, and brown fieldstones that Motherwell had been collecting over a period of years from his and neighbours' properties and from the Pheasant Creek

9.30 School, Ridgeville, Manitoba, c. 1903-10. Photograph c. 1911. PAM/School District Albums/N13578.

9.31 Waterman-Waterbury design no. 1 for a one-room school. Courtesy June Rowand.

coulee, indicating that he had set his heart on a stone house for quite some time. (Stone, the most popular building material for substantial houses in Perth, is also common in this part of Saskatchewan.) Motherwell later remarked that he knew the history of each stone that went into the walls. Care was taken in placing each one, calculating the effect of its colours and size. Adam Cantelon of Lorlie was the mason, P. Kerr of Indian Head was the contractor, and Motherwell himself participated in the construction. He did not retain an architect and likely drew up the plans himself, although it is possible that he was assisted in this by the Indian Head

9.32 Lanark Place, the Motherwell homestead near Abernethy, Saskatchewan, 1897. Motherwell is driving the carriage. SAB/Motherwell Collection/R87-219.

builders Fraser and Cameron. The source of the superb fretsawn elements and the decorative detail, in a land where such things were still little used, remains unknown.[63]

At Lanark Place, Motherwell recreated an entire Ontario farmstead, using trees to divide the area occupied by the house and farm buildings into four portions: domestic, garden, water supply, and barnyard. The large barn, built between 1896 and 1907, has a gambrel-roofed wood superstructure on a stone foundation. A diamond-shaped window with small panes—familiar to us from Ontario sawmills—is placed within the gable. The plantings of ornamentals, fruits, and wind-sheltering trees—so familiar to Ontarians—included roses, Niagara plums, apples, and maples. The trees and fences provided protection from winds and animals, while also offering a sense of security in the empty and lonely prairie landscape.[64]

Motherwell continued to prosper as both a farmer and a politician. He helped form the Territorial Grain Growers' Association in 1901, was appointed Saskatchewan's first minister of agriculture in 1905, and served in that portfolio in the federal government twice in the 1920s. The Motherwell Homestead was donated to the people of Saskatchewan in 1965 and purchased by the federal government a year later. The house and gardens were restored by Parks Canada and are open to the public.

9.33 Lanark Place, side view. SAB/Motherwell Collection/R82-219.

Motherwell's life and estate show many parallels with those of Charles R. Prescott and his Acacia Grove [3.41], in the Annapolis Valley of Nova Scotia a century earlier. Both were industrious farmers and politicians who expressed their aspirations and achievements in a large and formal country house that had explicit associations with the architecture of a more established society: Motherwell's with Ontario and Prescott's with England and New England.

Ethnic distinctions in architecture

Interesting variations in design are also seen in the dwellings of the various ethnic communities, particularly those built by people who could not afford to buy manufactured building products. Immigrants from Britain, France, Belgium, Iceland, Sweden, Germany, Hungary, Ukraine, and many other places converged on the Prairies both in organized colonies and as individuals. Some lived together because of a common nationality; others—such as Jews, Doukhobors, Mennonites, Hutterites, and Mormons—because of shared beliefs. (The Mennonites and Icelanders, who arrived before the railway, were discussed in Chapter 7.) Like every other group of new Canadians in the previous three centuries, each replicated the architecture of their homeland as they remembered it—inasmuch as this was feasible, given the Canadian environment, the limited available materials, and the emerging local building practices. The diffusion of their traditions in the Canadian Prairies provides a fascinating picture of cultural and architectural assimilation. The discussion that follows looks at the buildings of selected ethnic and cultural groups that settled in the rural West.

Ukrainian architecture The Ukrainians have been described as the most visible of the southeastern European peasant cultural groups that came to the Canadian Prairies—because of their numbers and their tenacious determination to retain their culture. They came principally from Galicia (Halychyna) and Bukovyna, a part of Ukraine that then comprised two provinces in the Austro-Hungarian empire and is now divided among Poland, Romania, and the present Ukraine. All were known at the time as Ruthenians. (Not all immigrants from these provinces were ethnic Ukrainians; they also included Germans, Jews, Poles, and Romanians.) Immigration began slowly in 1891 under the leadership of Ivan Pylypiw and Wasyl Eleniak. In 1895 the Department of the Interior received an eloquent letter explaining that many Ukrainian

farmers 'desire to quit their native country, due to overpopulation, subdivision of land holdings, heavy taxation, and unfavourable political conditions.' The writer, Dr Josef Oleskow, a professor of agriculture and an influential leader of the Ukrainian peasantry, successfully negotiated with the Canadian government for land, financial aid, and travel assistance. In the years that followed, large Ukrainian settlements were established in many parts of Manitoba, Saskatchewan, and Alberta. By the beginning of the First World War there were between 120,000 and 170,000 Ukrainians living in the Prairies, most of whom maintained their traditional language, clothing, and housing.[65]

The Ukrainians, skilled farmers with little capital, were generally unable and unwilling to avail themselves of milled lumber and other mass-produced building components. Most settled on homesteads along the northern fringe of the parkland, on land that was reminiscent of western Ukraine and forested with tamarack, white pine, spruce, aspen, and poplar (rather than the oak of their homeland). Wood was therefore readily available for construction.

Community life in Ukraine focused on the village, but the provisions of the Dominion Lands Act forced the settlers to live on their own quarter-sections. (Unlike the Mennonites, they were unable to benefit from the 'hamlet clause'; page 347.) Four settlers would sometimes claim contiguous properties and build their houses at the 'four corners', where they converged, but this method created difficult access to the road system.

The new settlers' first concern, like that of all other groups, was quick shelter. Using some of the temporary shelter-types discussed above, they resorted to a small dug-out, called a *zemlyanka* or *borday*, cut into the side of a slope, facing south, and roofed with branches and sod—a traditional folk-form that is said to have been based on the mountain hut of the Hutsul shepherds of the Carpathian Mountains. Some built lean-tos and tipis from small trees and poles.[66]

Their first and second houses, built of materials that could be taken from the land, bore a strong resemblance to the dwellings the people had known and built in Ukraine. Houses were typically rectangular two- or three-room structures built of horizontal logs with saddle-notched or dovetailed joints, with pegs inserted through the joints for stability. The partitions were also built of horizontal logs, and so joints were clearly visible where they met the external walls. Roofs were frequently constructed from poplar poles and thatched with prairie grass, steeply sloped to shed the rain, and hipped or having a truncated (hipped) gable form. Other roofs were shingled or covered with sod, and the slopes were correspondingly lower to accommodate these materials. The log walls were covered inside and out with mud plaster—usually a mixture of mud, straw, animal dung, and lime that was applied by the women. If the logs were squared, willow laths were usually affixed to them on the diagonal to provide a secure key for the plaster. A coat of white lime was

The difference between the first and second houses was seen in the quality of the materials, the care taken in construction, and the size. For the former there was little time and almost no money available, and it was often made of thin round logs with rough notches. A **Ukrainian house near Gimli [9.35]**, Manitoba, photographed about 1905, is clearly a first house because of the evident haste with which it was built. The unpeeled logs are joined with saddle notches, the roof is crudely thatched, the gable ends are

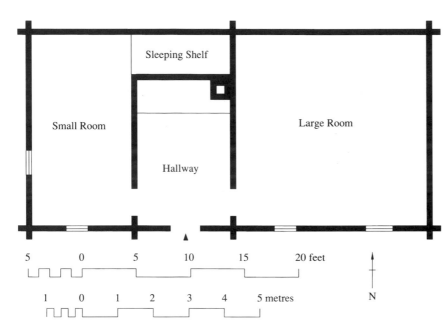

9.34 Floor plan of a Ukrainian house. Drawing by David Byrnes after John C. Lehr.

9.35 Ukrainian house near Gimli, Manitoba. Photograph *c.* 1905. PAM/W.J. Sisler Collection/N12856.

placed over the mud plaster and provided a base for decoration. The floor might be earth covered with plaster or, less often, wood planking.[67]

The house was always oriented east-west [9.34], with two principal interior spaces: the large room (*velyka khata*), at the east end, and the small room (*mala khata*), containing a large mud stove (*pich*) vented by a clay chimney (later replaced by an iron stove). It was in the small room that the family ate, slept, and carried out its daily activities; a sleeping shelf on the stove provided a warm bed for the elderly and the children. The large room was usually reserved for holiday or ceremonial use and for guests, although large families would use it as the bedroom of the head of the family. Icons, embroidered linens, and other decoration and memorabilia hung on its eastern, or holy, wall. The houses built by Bukovynians usually had a third space, an entrance hall (*siny*) located either between the two rooms or at the west end. The entrance faced south.

covered with coarsely cut planks, and the plaster is thinly applied. The upper floor was for storage.[68]

Vertical logs and the Red River frame were also used on occasion, in areas where good timber was not available. In the Stuartburn district of south-eastern Manitoba (just south of the Mennonite East Reserve), of forty-three houses whose structural technique has been identified by John Lehr, twenty were built of horizontal logs, fifteen of Red River frame, and eight of vertical logs. On the other hand, of

9.36 Bukovynian house in Alberta. PAA/Ernest Brown Collection/B683.

more than 100 early Ukrainian houses he examined in Alberta, only one example of vertical logs was found (as an addition to a horizontal-log structure); all others were built of horizontal logs.[69]

When the settlers became established, often within about eight to ten years, they would replace the initial house with a second, more carefully constructed residence. The logs were larger, peeled, and often squared and joined with dovetails. The external finish was smoother and harder, and often decorated. Roofs were properly thatched, floors boarded, and doors and windows milled.

Subtle variations are found between the houses of the Bukovynians and Galicians. The former were usually larger—the sample in Alberta averaged 35 by 18 feet (10.7 by 5.5 m)—and had a separate entrance hall; they were also more flamboyant in their details and more closely resembled the prototypes in Ukraine. They had deeply projecting eaves: typically $2\frac{1}{2}$ feet (75 m), but sometimes as deep as 5 feet (1.5 m) along the south front, and slightly less at the sides and the rear. A soffit beneath the eave concealed the rafters, and the eaves were often supported on flared brackets formed by allowing the ends of the top logs on the walls to project further through the joint. A **Bukovynian house [9.36]** in

Alberta, photographed by Ernest Brown of Edmonton early in the century (he called it a 'Russian thatched house'), shows all these features. Others had small eyebrow dormers in the slope of the roof that may have been inserted to help ventilate the smoke. Galician houses were somewhat smaller and more sober, with shallower eaves. Many had gabled, rather than hipped, roofs with a distinctive shallow eave below the gable. Decorative trim was more likely to be green on Bukovynian houses and blue on Galician houses, although other colours were used as well. (Brightly coloured trim is also characteristic of Ukrainian houses in urban areas, such as Winnipeg.)

This vernacular house-form, which continued centuries-old folk traditions from the homeland, became well established in Ukrainian communities across the Prairies. Sketches of **houses in western Ukraine [9.37]** at the end of the nineteenth century clearly show their similarity to the Canadian houses. However, as the process of acculturation occurred, characteristic Ukrainian features began to disappear; houses built after 1920 were likely to acquire some 'Canadian' features while retaining many of their

9.37 Drawings of houses in western Ukraine. From V.P. Samojlovych, *Ukrains'ke Narodne*, Kiev, 1972.

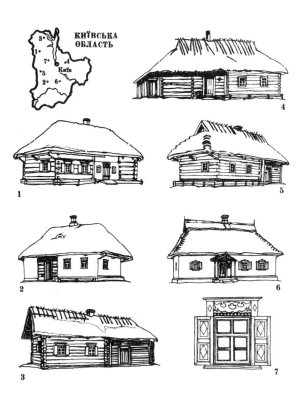

traditional components. The Canadianization of the **Wenger homestead [9.38]** near Radway, Alberta, is seen in a picture taken in the early 1950s. At the left is the second house, built around 1909, its original sod roof since replaced with a shingled one but the flared eaves and plastered log walls revealing its Ukrainian heritage. At the right is the third house, built in 1937, a $1\frac{1}{2}$-storey frame house with no identifiable ethnic character. The new car is proudly displayed between them.

Although few of the older houses are still being used, the folk traditions are being preserved in the Ukrainian Cultural Heritage Village, east of Edmonton, where a collection of early houses, churches, commercial and public buildings from various Ukrainian communities in Alberta have been restored and interpreted by the provincial government.

Ukrainian Canadians developed a distinctive and attractive religious architecture. Most Galicians adhered to the Catholic faith and Bukovynians to the Orthodox faith. (Until its organization in Canada in 1918, the Ukrainian Greek Orthodox Church was known as the Eastern Rite Byzantine faith.) Differences between the churches of the two denominations, however, are inconsequential. The immediate source of their design is the nineteenth-century church architecture of Ukraine; the origins of the style are found in domed Byzantine churches, the earliest of which were built in the sixth century.[70]

9.38 The Wenger homestead near Radway, Alberta. Photograph *c.* 1953. PAA/Wenger Collection/85.228, UV709.

St Michael's Ukrainian Orthodox Church [9.39] in Gardenton, Manitoba, the first Ukrainian church in Canada, was built in 1898-9 by settlers from Bukovyna. It is seen here in a photograph taken around 1915, just after carpenter Menholy Chalaturnyk had elaborated the original design to reflect the congregation's more settled state, and its improved ability to express its cultural identity. As altered, the church has a large, domed central nave—called a *bani*—covered by an octagonal drum and an onion-shaped cupola, a narrower narthex in front of it with a smaller onion dome, and a sanctuary beyond the nave (not visible in the photograph) that also has a small dome. Each of the three main parts of the plan—the barrel-vaulted narthex, the domed nave, and the low sanctuary—is an independent structural component (a *zrub*). This three-chambered church was common in both Galicia and Bukovyna. St Michael's, like most other early Ukrainian-Canadian churches, is built of horizontal logs and its construction is similar to that of the two- and three-room Ukrainian houses. The logs were protected with horizontal siding in 1901, at which time the roof—not yet domed—was shingled. The enclosed entrance porch is a later addition intended to help keep out the winter cold.[71]

The **interior [9.40]** is richly decorated. The view shows the scripture stand and a pair of hand-carved candelabra, which stand before the decorated east wall (the *ikonostas*), covered with icons (designed *c.* 1902 by Wasyl Chornopysky) that represent the Holy Family and religious scenes. This icon wall separates the nave from the sanctuary, which only the

9.39 St Michael's Ukrainian Orthodox Church, Gardenton, Manitoba, 1898-9. Photograph 1956. Courtesy *The Carillon* (Derksen Printers).

priest and certain privileged persons in the parish hierarchy are permitted to enter, and screens the congregation's view of the altar inside. Blue paint on the walls (covered with gold stars within the dome), artificial flowers around the icons and the doors, and the patterned floor (a later alteration) all reveal the penchant for decoration that is also seen in Ukrainian houses, dress, and Easter eggs.

Like most prairie Ukrainian churches, St Michael's is located in relative isolation, with a free-standing belltower—a two-tiered structure capped by a hipped roof—a short distance away. The open space has a liturgical purpose, since some ceremonies call for a procession around the church. A larger church was subsequently erected at Gardenton. Both stand today, the newer one in regular use and the older one preserved as a historic site.

In a more elaborate variant of the three-part plan, the nave was expanded laterally to produce a transept at each side. The transepts were often narrow—perhaps 4 to 5 feet (up to 1.5 m), but sufficient for a small side altar to be placed in each, one dedicated to Christ and the other to the Virgin. In some cases—as at the Church of the Assumption of the Holy Virgin Mary near Meacham, Saskatchewan, built in 1911 with commercial lumber—the plan is fully cruciform.[72]

A superb cruciform structure is the **Ukrainian**

9.40 Interior, St Michael's Ukrainian Orthodox Church, Gardenton, Alberta. Photograph 1984. Manitoba Culture, Heritage and Citizenship, Historic Resources.

Greek Catholic Church of the Nativity of the Blessed Virgin Mary [9.41] at Dobrowody (near Buchanan), Saskatchewan. St Mary's, as it is known, was built by a community of Galicians—some of whom had come from the village of Dobrowody in western Ukraine—who settled in Saskatchewan in 1904. Responsibility for the construction of the church was shared by the forty families in the parish: they raised $2500 (the Roman Catholic diocese provided another $200) and volunteered their labour. Work began in August 1911, with F. Nowakowski of Rama serving as foreman and the Reverend A.

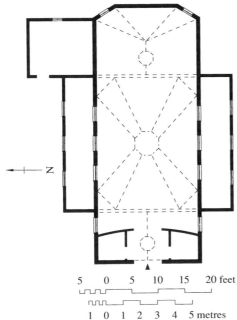

9.41 Ukrainian Greek Catholic Church of the Nativity of the Blessed Virgin Mary, Dobrowody, Saskatchewan, 1911-12. Photograph 1972. Church Historical Information Research Project, Canadian Centre for Folk Culture Studies, Canadian Museum of Civilization/74-16585.

9.43 Interior of the Ukrainian Greek Catholic Church, Dobrowody, Saskatchewan. Photograph by John de Visser, 1975.

9.42 Plan of the Ukrainian Greek Catholic Church, Dobrowody, Saskatchewan. Drawing by David Byrnes.

Delaere providing direction; the first service was celebrated on 1 July 1912.[73]

The dominant architectural feature is the magnificent tin-clad onion dome, topped by a small cupola, which covers the entire nave; cupolas are also placed over the narthex and sanctuary. The complicated structural transition from the rectangular nave to the eight-sided dome was made by inserting a curved triangular support, known as a squinch (or pendentive), at each corner. The plan [9.42] has the shape of an elongated cross. The overall length—including the narthex, nave, and sanctuary—is 50 feet (15 m), and the combined width of the nave and transepts is nearly 33 feet (10 m).

The *bani* is impressive; its generous proportions (despite the modest dimensions) can be appreciated in a photograph [9.43] taken from the small balcony over the narthex. The interior of the dome is painted blue, with gilded stars, and the walls are yellow, with decorative trim at the base of the dome, over the arch, and above the transepts. The *ikonostas* (uncommon in Latin-rite churches) is a pierced screen rather than a solid wall, and partially obscures the view of the altar in the sanctuary. Paul Zabolotny, an artist who decorated a number of churches in the area, painted the interior decoration and the icons of the *ikonostas* in 1936; other icons were brought from Ukraine. The side altars are located on the east wall of the transepts, with paintings above and beside them. The church is well maintained; it was placed on a concrete block foundation in 1960 (replacing the original stone foundation). St Mary's also has a separate belltower nearby—a tapered wood structure that is 10 feet square at the base and rises 24 feet to its tiny hipped roof, with an open frame supporting the bell.

Ukrainian churches, like houses, gradually adopted elements from Canadian architecture. One of the first signs of assimilation was the introduction of the twin-towered façade. Although many Baroque churches in Ukraine did have two towers, the source for the prairie churches is found closer to home, in the French-Canadian churches of Alberta. His Beatitude Msgr Andrey Sheptytsky, the Metropolitan in L'vov, western Ukraine, advised worshippers to accept the aid of the Canadian Roman Catholic Church until their own church was organized and incorporated. The towers flanking the entrance of many Ukrainian Catholic churches are therefore an adaptation of the French-Canadian form, with its *clochers* transformed into onion domes. An early example is seen at **St Mary's Ukrainian Catholic Church [9.44]** in Chipman, Alberta, built in 1916 by Jarema Janishewski. At each side of the entrance stands a slender tower topped by an octagonal drum and a dome, and there is a larger dome over the nave. The appearance of the exterior has been altered by stucco, but the interior retains the splendid decorative scheme painted in 1928 by the most renowned of Ukrainian-Canadian church artists, Peter Lipinski. The parish was organized in 1900; a founding member was Vasyl Eleniak, one of the first two Ukrainians to settle in Canada. This is the congregation's second church.[74]

Although the traditional building techniques have disappeared, recent Ukrainian churches have maintained their distinctive appearance: the large central space covered by a broad onion dome and surrounded by smaller domes. A number of remarkable Ukrainian churches, designed from the 1920s to the 1940s by the Reverend Philip Ruh, are discussed in Chapter 14.

Other ethnic settlements Many other national and ethnic groups that settled in the Canadian West also transplanted something of their folk architecture

9.44 St Mary's Ukrainian Catholic Church, Chipman, Alberta, 1920. Iwan Boberskyj Collection/Ukrainian Cultural and Educational Centre.

on the prairie soil, each in its own way. It was important for them to be surrounded by familiar things in a strange land, and at a practical level their own building and planning traditions were the only ones they knew when they first arrived. A look at several groups reveals the diversity of the new Canadian architecture.

The Doukhobors, a sect of Russian peasants from the Caucasus and north of the Black Sea, were a much-persecuted group that had broken away from the Orthodox church (probably in the seventeenth century) and rejected church liturgy, secular governments, and all externalities—espousing pacifism and a belief in the equality of all. In 1898-9 the first group of 7,400 Doukhobors arrived in Saskatchewan, where they formed a number of separate communities. Like the Mennonites a quarter-century earlier, they were able to use the 'hamlet clause' in the amended Dominion Lands Act to establish street-villages, typically accommodating twelve to fifteen families. Various groups adopted differing social and economic practices: the 'Community' Doukhobors were organized communistically, the 'Independents' individualistically. In the Community villages, such as **Khristianovka [9.45]**, Saskatchewan, as many as forty houses were built on both sides of a wide street; a short cross-street was terminated at either end by the community buildings—one or two barns, ware-

houses, and bathhouses—and by a park. The view of Khristianovka, perhaps taken as early as 1903, shows the village already well built up, with the trees and gardens planted. In the Independent villages, residents held private property and often built connected house-barns, similar to those of the Mennonites.[75]

As with other prairie settlers, houses were constructed with the materials that were available, including log, sod, and wattle-and-daub. The fronts of many houses featured an extended eave supported on posts to form a veranda.

Verandas are seen on a larger scale in an Independent village, in the so-called **Doukhobor Prayerhouse** (1917) at Veregin, Saskatchewan, a two-storey building with double verandas on all four sides **[9.46]**. (The shed in front is the entrance to the basement.) The Doukhobors did not require a building in which to pray; this 'prayerhouse', whose name in Russian means 'Orphans' Home', was used as the administrative centre, the leader's residence, for guest accommodation, and for public meetings that did not distinguish between religious and secular matters. (This last function was similar to that of the Congregationalist meeting-houses of the eighteenth century.) The building measures 50 by 52 feet (15.3 by 15.9 m) and was designed by Alex Horkoff. The squarish hipped-roof form (with dormers), also characteristic of later Doukhobor building, may have been adapted from English-Canadian neighbours. The attractive decorative work on the verandas—the upper tracery was cut from tin—was executed by John J. Mahonin, and

9.45 View of main street, Khristianovka, Saskatchewan, *c*. 1903. BCARS/Tarasoff Collection/47194.

9.46 Doukhobor Prayerhouse, Veregin, Saskatchewan, 1917. Photograph by Wayne Zelmer, 1986. Heritage Branch, Government of Saskatchewan.

reveals the relative materialism of the Independent Doukhobors.[76] The building is still in use.

Peter P. Verigin (Peter the Lordly), the Doukhobors' leader, was released from exile in Siberia and arrived in present-day Saskatchewan in 1902. He immediately set about organizing the communities more tightly. Architecture, as well as life, became more uniform under his control. In 1905, however, things went badly for the Doukhobors, since the new Minister of the Interior, Frank Oliver, who replaced Clifford Sifton, interpreted the Dominion Lands Act more literally than his predecessor and ordered that the Doukhobors take an oath of allegiance and farm every quarter-section in order to obtain title to land. Many refused to take the oath and lost their land.

Verigin reacted by purchasing private land in southeastern British Columbia, near Grand Forks and Castlegar, and led about 6,000 Community Doukhobors there in 1908. In the absence of land restrictions or other settlers, Verigin devised a distinctive architectural form that responded to his beliefs, and his desire for communal living: the **Doukhobor double house [9.47]**. It consisted of two 2-storey buildings with hipped roofs built about 50 feet (15 m) apart and joined by a U-shaped 1-storey structure that formed a partly enclosed courtyard between the two houses; a pair of archways provided access. The 2-storey buildings each had two rooms on the ground floor, a living-/meeting-room and a kitchen-/dining-room, and upstairs a central corridor led to eight bedrooms. A cellar provided storage for food. The 1-storey structure was used for services—including a laundry, a steam bath, and storage. Many double houses were built of brick and finished very plainly, without ornament. Verigin organized a number of collective industries, including fruit-preserving and sawmilling. Several large community buildings were erected as well.[77]

9.47 Doukhobor double house near Brilliant, British Columbia. BCARS/47364.

9.48 Hutterite colony near Cayley, Alberta. Photograph by Jim Merrithew.

Verigin died violently in 1924 and was succeeded by his son, Peter V. Verigin (the Purger), who was unable to maintain cohesion among the Community Doukhobors. They were wracked by dissent, incendiarism—and ultimately foreclosure of their land. Although many individual Doukhobors bought back land in the 1960s and maintained their customs, the communal villages have been abandoned; most of their buildings were demolished, burned, or have reached a state of advanced deterioration.

Another immigrant group whose way of building accommodated communal living was the Hutterite Brethren. Anabaptists, like the Mennonites, the Hutterites migrated from Czechoslovakia to Hungary, Romania, and then Russia; they left Russia and came to the Dakotas in the 1870s with the Mennonites. One group from South Dakota settled near Dominion City, Manitoba, in 1893; but the principal relocation from the US to the Canadian Prairies occurred in 1918 because of persecution associated with the Hutterites' refusal to participate in US military service.

The Hutterite agricultural colonies are village-like settlements in which the siting of the buildings reflects the highly structured life of the brethren. The distinctive planning system has changed little since the nineteenth-century settlements in South Dakota. The nucleus of the **Hutterite colony [9.48]** near Cayley, Alberta, is the residential court: four long, narrow buildings that are row houses containing a private apartment for each family, with the kitchen-/dining-building and the kindergarten located between them. A few single-family houses behind the row houses are intended for community leaders such as the minister, the German teacher, the kitchen manager, and the farm manager. The English school is located apart from this group, indicating its connection with the outside world; German classes are held either there or in another school building. The farm buildings—barns, granaries, and storage sheds—are placed in an outer ring around the residential core, and extensive fields occupy the periphery. The design of the buildings is not distinctive, but reflects prevailing popular architectural forms. When the population of a village reaches about 125 to 150 it sub-divides and forms a new colony; in 1987 there were 243 colonies in the three Prairie Provinces.[78]

Jews made up another group that came from Russia to escape persecution. Beginning in 1881, organized physical attacks (pogroms) and anti-Jewish laws in Russia left 100,000 Jews homeless, forcing mass immigration to other countries. Sir Alexander Galt, Canada's High Commissioner in London, became a trustee of the Russo-Jewish Committee formed in that city and persuaded Sir John A. Macdonald to accept a number of Russian-Jewish refugees. In May and June 1882, 340 Jewish immigrants arrived in Winnipeg with the intention of homesteading, but because of concerns about the their 'suitability' for farming—few had an agricultural background, because Russian law prohibited Jews from owning land—it was two years before land was made available to them.[79]

The first Jewish agricultural settlement was established in 1884 on 51 quarter-sections near Moosomin,

Saskatchewan. Known as New Jerusalem, it suffered a series of setbacks and was declared a failure within half a decade; many of the residents moved to Winnipeg. But a dozen successful farm settlements followed. The earliest was the Wapella farm settlement, located on the CPR line near Moosomin, begun in 1886. The colony was formed through the assistance of Hermann Landau, a prominent Anglo-Jewish financier who was also an agent for the CPR in London. He sponsored an initial group of eleven people—five members of the John Heppner family and six young men who had been trained as farm hands at Aylesbury, Buckinghamshire—and sent them to Canada in 1886. The CPR Land Commissioner, J.H. McTavish, advanced them money, and a special concession—arranged jointly by the CPR and the federal government—provided the group with eight adjacent quarter-sections. About thirty other Jewish families, some from countries other than Russia, had joined them by 1892. All Orthodox Jews, they formed the Wapella Hebrew Congregation and found spiritual leadership from Edel Brotman, a homesteader from Galicia who had qualified as a rabbi.

The land was covered with poplars and so the settlers built log houses with sod roofs. Fanny Pelenovsky Brotman recalled in old age:

> Sam and I built the house. And his brothers and sisters used to come and help us. We cut down poplar trees for logs and chinked the cracks with mud. We'd make a plaster out of a mixture of the clay, straw and manure from the cattle. And we mixed it with our feet . . . . And you'd put the log down, then you'd put the plaster, then you'd put the log—until the walls were built.[80]

The **Kalman Isman house [9.49]** at Wapella, built in 1889, is typical of the first homesteads. To the small log house on the left in the photograph was later added the larger portion on the right. The original sod roof of the log house was replaced with shingles before the photograph was taken.

In 1906 the last of the major Jewish colonies was founded 225 miles (360 km) to the northwest, near Melfort, Saskatchewan, by a group from the Baltic states and other eastern European countries who had settled in South Africa but chose to relocate in Canada. The wooded community along the Carrot River remained nameless until it was granted a post office and a name had to be chosen. The residents resorted to the Canadian Postal Guide and settled on Edenbridge, an Anglicized combination of *Yidden* (Yiddish for 'Jews') and bridge. In 1908 the settlers built a house of worship, the **House of Israel Synagogue [9.50]**. It is a simple frame building that avoided all the features that might associate it with a church: it has no tower or pointed windows, and the pitch of the roof is softened by a second slope at the top. The round-headed windows at the east end, behind the cantor's desk and the ark, may have been intended to evoke associations with architecture that was vaguely Romanesque (as at Victoria's Temple Emanuel [8.31]). The synagogue closed its doors in 1968 when the declining Jewish population could no longer provide a *minyan* (the ten men required for a formal service), but the building has been restored and dedicated as a provincial historic site by the government of Saskatchewan.[81]

In the late nineteenth century an intensive recruitment campaign was directed at the British Isles.

9.49 Kalman Isman house, Wapella, Saskatchewan, 1889. Courtesy Cyril E. Leonoff.

9.50 House of Israel Synagogue, Edenbridge, Saskatchewan, 1908. Photograph by John de Visser, 1975.

An interesting English colony was Cannington Manor, Saskatchewan, established in 1882 some 40 miles (65 km) south of what was then the end of rail. Captain Edward Michell Pierce, a gentleman of some refinement who had come to Canada after suffering a bank failure, acquired the land and named it after his hometown in Somerset. He advertised in English newspapers for settlers of means and good breeding, and also for farm apprentices—preferably public-school lads—who would pay £100 in return for room, board, and an education. Pierce established an agricultural college for the 'pups', as the students were called. The colonists seem to have preferred breeding racehorses (in mahogany-lined stables), playing tennis and cricket, and staging gala balls to the rigours of agricultural life. They spent a week during the harvest hunting and playing polo. Sixteen homes boasted pianos, and one 26-room house contained a ballroom, billiard room, and servants' quarters. As Pierce's daughter later recalled, 'it was all such a change from our luxurious life in England, but . . . everything seemed a joke and we were very happy.'[82]

Cannington Manor failed within a generation, but not before it had provided a legacy of English-inspired buildings. The community's church [9.51], **All Saints, Cannington Manor** (1884), has a cruciform plan with a large square entrance tower, much like a simplified Early Gothic Revival Anglican church that might be found anywhere in English Canada. The entire community participated in its construction. Its genteel appearance conceals the effort that went

into building it; the walls were constructed of logs (covered with commercial siding) and the rafters were hand-sawn. Every effort went into denying the environmental forces of the frontier. Care went into making pointed-arched windows and the band of decorative trim around the tower suggesting quatrefoils—both Gothic features. Cannington Manor is now a provincial historic park, and some of the original buildings, including the church, have been preserved, and others have been reconstructed.

The Englishness of the houses of many English settlers on the Prairies is embodied in **The Grotto** [9.52] in Davisburg, Alberta, built around 1887 by Dr Albert E. Banister, a veterinarian from Bridport in Dorset. The 1½-storey house had the character of a cozy Victorian English cottage, with its simplified Georgian façade and dormer windows poking above the eaves, which were decorated with fretwork trim. The neatly trimmed lawn and the garden plantings were equally English in character.

9.51 All Saints Anglican Church, Cannington Manor, Saskatchewan, 1884. Photograph by John de Visser, 1975.

9.52 Banister house (The Grotto), Davisburg, Alberta, *c.* 1887. Photograph *c.* 1900. Glenbow Archives/NA1808-1.

Towns

The railways were the most significant factor in the location and development of prairie communities. The CPR chose the site for each of its stations, and actively developed some townsites, mostly at divisional points (rail-service centres at intervals of about 125 miles, or 200 km, the distance a locomotive of the day could travel without refueling). The Grand Trunk Pacific took a highly interventionist approach. It was interested not in bringing in agricultural settlers (as were the CPR and CNOR), but rather in establishing towns along the line that would grow with the settlement of the countryside. The GTP, which was built with no government land grant, bought land for 86 townsites and laid them out according to a standard plan. The towns were named according to the sequence of the alphabet, going back to A when Z was reached: they went from Atwater to Zelma, Allan to Zumbro, Bloom to Zenata. By imposing a form of land-use planning, the GTP went beyond the efforts of the other railways—providing, in effect, the first zoning in Canada. A newspaper article of the day described the planned beginnings of GTP townsites:

'We will put down a town here,' said the engineer in charge . . . . These towns-to-be would grow up straight and orderly according to explicit instructions, just as babies are raised nowadays according to formula instead of by the old pot-luck methods of other days. Before the first settler arrived the streets were marked out and the parks were labeled, the stables put in a certain section, the market place determined upon . . . . The main street always runs down to the railway station. It is 80 feet wide and no building costing less than a $1000 can be erected on certain parts of it.[83]

The GTP also built a city—Prince Rupert, BC [**12.10, 11**]—at its western terminus.

Historian Gerald Friesen has identified a hierarchy of five scales of towns that developed on the Prairies between 1870 and 1930. The smallest were the hamlets, perhaps numbering about 1,300 or 1,400 in the late 1920s, which had fewer than 50 residents and six businesses; many consisted of little more than a grain elevator along the track, or a general store and garage at a crossroads. The next level comprised villages—about 1,000, each having between 50 and 500 people, and between eight and thirty businesses. They provided the residents of the surrounding rural districts with groceries, mail, hardware, lumber, and farm implements, as well as social amenities such as a hotel, café, community hall, and hockey rink. These first two levels were extensions of a rural society whose inhabitants related closely to the farm families. At the third tier were some sixty towns that had populations of between 1,000 and 5,000—such as Dauphin (Manitoba), Melville (Saskatchewan), and Red Deer (Alberta), whose residents were more likely to take on airs of self-importance. These towns might boast between forty and seventy businesses, a wide range of retail and professional services, a movie theatre, and a high school. The fourth level comprised the small cities, and the fifth level the major urban centres.[84]

Main Street Most of Friesen's second- and third-level towns developed along the same plan. A road along the tracks was called Railway Avenue, and one perpendicular to it, on or near the axis of the station, was Main Street. This T-intersection formed the town's centre, and before long a hotel and a bank were built there. Along Main Street were the stores of the local merchants, the town hall, the post office, the Chinese café, the barber shop, the office of the weekly newspaper, and a host of other businesses and services. The rest of the streets formed a grid pattern, with those on the far side of the tracks accessed by one or two crossings. Main

9.53 Vermilion, Alberta. Photograph by A.B. Wright, *c.* 1905. Glenbow Archives/NA1259-1.

9.54 Dominion Day parade at Vulcan, Alberta, 1914. Glenbow Archives/NA748-57.

9.55 Hudson's Bay Company store, Fort Qu'Appelle, Saskatchewan, 1897. Photograph by Edgar C. Rossie, *c.* 1910. SAB/R-B921.

overnight: a picture of the young town of **Vermilion [9.53]**, Alberta (*c.* 1905), shows a number of completed buildings along one side of Main Street—the largest building, left of centre, is the pretentiously named King Edward Restaurant, already open for business—while a tent and piles of lumber indicate anticipated construction on the other side. Main Street became the social, as well as the commercial, heart of the community, and was always used for politicking (called 'mainstreeting') and parades. The **1914 Dominion Day parade at Vulcan [9.54]**, Alberta—named after the Roman god of fire because of a large prairie fire that had occurred nearby—attracted as many participants as observers; behind them is a row of plain, false-fronted frame buildings, a few ornamented with a hint of a cornice or a flagpole.

Backed by substantial capital, builders might use brick or stone for their Main Street buildings, as in the **Hudson's Bay Company store at Fort Qu'Appelle [9.55]**, Saskatchewan. The Company's long-established trading post had served the Indians and Métis well, but it did not attract the patronage of the new agricultural settlers. In 1897 the directors in London reluctantly agreed to build a store on Main Street at Fort Qu'Appelle—one of the earliest 'Bay' retail outlets in Canada, and probably the oldest to survive. The two-storey building has a brick façade and side and rear walls of stone (plentiful in the Qu'Appelle Valley, as was seen at the Motherwell house), 2 feet (60 cm) thick. Four vertical pilaster-like strips are carried up above the roofline; they and the triangular parapet, with the Company's name inscribed, give the building a picturesque silhouette. High display windows framed in wood open up the ground floor in the front. The store has a 30-foot (9.2-m) frontage and is 60 feet (18.3 m) deep; attached to it at the left was a one-storey warehouse 20 feet (6.1 m) wide with a castellated roofline, perhaps an attempt to associate the building with the Company's forts. The building was probably designed by Chief Factor Archibald McDonald, continuing the company tradition of posts being designed by senior administrators.[86]

For banks, competing aggressively to be the first to locate in a town (and gain initial control of the area's trade)—and being able to build quickly, yet imposingly—posed a challenge. The best solution came from the Canadian Bank of Commerce. Between 1906 and 1910 the BC Mills Timber and Trading Company supplied the bank with some seventy prefabricated 'Prairie Type' buildings in three sizes. The designs were by the eminent Toronto archi-

Street usually had a generous allowance of 66 or even 99 feet (20 and 30 m; 66 feet was the length of a surveyor's chain). This width served horses and wagons, and showed the town's ambition (today it accommodates diagonal parking on both sides). Roadways were all numbered: 'streets' in one direction and 'avenues' in the other. To avoid negative numbers, First Street had to be at the edge of town and Main Street (which also received a number) at the centre. The range of numbers reflected a community's ambitions, and streets often had to be renumbered if a town grew beyond expectations. High River, Alberta, has its principal intersection at a modestly selected Fourth Street (now Fourth Avenue); in the more ambitious towns of Lacombe and Red Deer, also in Alberta, the ante was raised and Main Street is 50 Street. Edmonton just kept growing, and its central artery had to be renamed 100 Street.[85]

The architecture of Main Street typically consisted of 1- and 2-storey commercial buildings with false 'boom-town' fronts whose horizontal parapets concealed the gabled roofs behind them and presented a false impression of the building's solidity. Most were wood, built with milled lumber. It seemed that a town and its Main Street were constructed

9.56 Canadian Bank of Commerce, Crossfield, Alberta, 1906. Photograph 1914. Glenbow Archives/NC29-3.

tectural firm of Darling and Pearson. 'Knocked-down' banks, made from 3- and 4-foot-wide (0.9-to-1.2 m) wooden wall sections, were sent over the mountains by train; once at their destination, the buildings could be assembled in a day. The **Canadian Bank of Commerce at Crossfield** [9.56], Alberta, was built on 17 April 1906—a year in which the Bank opened a new prefabricated branch every fortnight. The building achieved dignity and an impression of

9.57 St Andrew's Anglican Church, Humboldt, Saskatchewan. Photograph 1916. Courtesy the Diocese of Saskatoon.

strength with its gracious proportions and classical temple-front; yet it was also well scaled, and did not overwhelm its assertively plain boom-town neighbours—a ubiquitous real-estate office on the right, and the hotel (typically three storeys high) on the left. The second storey of the bank was used as dormitory space by junior clerks (or in some instances as a suite for the manager)—just as the upper floors of stations in new towns provided accommodation for employees.[87]

Standard, or prefabricated, designs were used for other types of buildings as well, even for churches. The Reverend George Exton Lloyd, who in 1903 assisted in establishing the Barr colonists at Lloydminster, on the Saskatchewan-Alberta border, subsequently rose in the church hierarchy to become Bishop of Saskatchewan. As archdeacon, he helped persuade the Anglican leadership to establish a church in every centre of population in the province. The new churches were built cheaply and quickly to a standard design—like railway stations, schools, and banks. Plans and specifications were carefully worked out so that any local carpenter could assemble the buildings easily from fixed quantities of standard materials. **St Andrew's Church at Humboldt** [9.57], Saskatchewan, is typical of the group. The designer may have been the Reverend D.T. Davies of Saskatoon, who was a skilled carpenter. The churches, pretentiously called 'Canterbury Cathedrals' (but generally known as 'Bishop Lloyd churches'), squeezed sixty worshippers into a nave

16 by 20 feet (4.9 by 6.1 m). A contemporary description recorded that they

> are to be thoroughly ecclesiastical in design, with tower, Gothic windows, and high-pitched roof . . . . The tower, which costs about $15, serves as the hallmark of the Church of England throughout the Diocese of Saskatchewan.

A complementary design for a neighbouring small shed-roofed dwelling for a missionary or priest, called a 'Lambeth Palace', was also available. (The small house beside St Andrew's is not one of these.)[88]

Grain elevators   The most prominent buildings in every town were the 'prairie sentinels'—those quintessentially Canadian structures, the country grain elevators. Farmers hauled their wheat and other cereal products to the station stop, where they would be stored in an elevator until loaded on a train, to be sent either to the big-city mills or to a terminal grain elevator in a port city for transfer to ships for export. One or more grain elevators—towns were ranked by their number, as in a 'four-elevator town'—stood along the railway line, a short distance (usually across the tracks) from the station. Elevators were originally constructed by elevator and milling companies with close ties to the railways, and their practices led farmers to complain of being overcharged and underpaid. The

farmers retaliated by organizing their own co-operative grain growers' and elevator companies, culminating in the formation of the Alberta, Saskatchewan, and Manitoba Wheat Pools in 1923 and 1924.

The earliest grain-storage facilities were 'flat' warehouses—low wood buildings erected along the track, in and out of which grain had to be shovelled by hand. The first tall elevator in Canada is believed to have been a circular stone structure built at Niverville, Manitoba, in 1879, a year after the first shipment of western Canadian grain for overseas markets reached Glasgow. Easier-to-build square and rectangular designs soon replaced circular ones; the first in the West was built in 1881 at Gretna, Manitoba, by the Ogilvie Milling Company. In all vertical elevators, the farmer's wagon or truck entered a lean-to drive-shed at the base, where the grain was unloaded into a pit or other holding area; a bucket conveyor then lifted the grain to the top, where it fell through a distributor spout into one of several storage bins (as in a grist mill). The grain was subsequently unloaded by gravity feed through chutes into train cars.[89]

In the late nineteenth century two alternative designs, distinguishable by the shape of their roof,

9.58 Grain elevators and CPR station at Wolseley, Saskatchewan. Photograph 1902. SAB/R-B2969.

became popular. In the cupola design, the four exterior walls terminated at eaves about two-thirds of the way up, at which point a hipped roof supported a square cupola. In the monitor-roof design, two sides of the elevator had 'sloping shoulders' (so described by novelist W.O. Mitchell), which led to a narrower portion at the top that was capped by a gable roof; the other two sides were flush from bottom to top. Both kinds were commonly built until the early twentieth century, when the monitor-roof design became dominant.

One of each kind can be seen in the view of **two grain elevators [9.58]** at Wolseley, Saskatchewan, taken in February 1902: a monitor-roof elevator stands near the centre, and beyond it to the right is a cupola elevator. At the left is a first-generation standard CPR station, and a water tank is just visible over the drive-shed of the closer elevator. As Wolseley had an active wheat market, a large number of wagons and sleds (it is early winter) were filled with bags of grain.

Grain elevators were traditionally constructed of 'crib' walls made of stacked lumber, usually 2-by-6s and 2-by-4s, one on top of another, to the height of the lower eaves. The cupola and the drive-shed were frame construction—as was the power-house, a separate building located about 20 feet (6 m) or more away from the elevator, to reduce the hazard of fire. The earliest elevators had horse-powered conveyors; these were later replaced by gasoline engines. A photograph of a **grain elevator under construction** (*c.* 1910) at Estevan, Saskatchewan, shows the structure clearly **[9.59]**; the framed skeleton on the left is the power-house. (The contractor is identified as Ed Johnson of Macoun.) The walls would have been covered with either horizontal wood or pressed-metal siding, and painted a bright colour, with the name of the elevator company (and usually the town) in large letters. A small country elevator was about 30 feet (9.2 m) square, 55 feet (16.8 m) high, and had a capacity of 30,000 bushels (912,000 litres); a more typical one might be about 33 by 36 feet (10.1 by 11 m) and 65 feet (19.8 m) high, holding 40,000 bushels (1.2 million litres); some large elevators rose 100 feet (30 m) or more. An annex was sometimes built adjacent to the elevator to increase the capacity. Each of the elevator companies used standard designs; one set of extant drawings of a standard elevator—built by the Grain Growers Grain Co. of Winnipeg, probably *c.* 1916—identifies the designer as Theodore Kipp Company Limited.[90]

Nearly 6,000 country grain elevators were standing in the 1920s and 1930s; since then their num-

9.59 Grain elevator under construction at Estevan, Saskatchewan, *c.* 1910. NAC/PA38590.

9.60 Medalta Stoneware (Medalta Potteries), Medicine Hat, Alberta, begun 1912. Photograph by Harold Kalman, 1978.

bers have steadily decreased. One reason for this is the sharp decline in the rural prairie population, accompanied by the gradual shift in agriculture from subsistence farming to farming as a major industry, with fewer and larger producers—a situation requiring fewer grain-storage locations. Another cause has been the improvement in roads and truck transportation, and the related abandonment of branch railway lines. Elevator companies—even the farmer-owned pools— have been rationalizing their activities by operating larger and more cost-effective elevators in medium-sized and large communities. Many village elevators have been abandoned or demolished, and the attrition continues at an alarming rate—a highly visible symbol of the transformation, and loss, of many prairie villages and towns.

Economically and politically, as well as architecturally, the West related to central Canada in a colonial way, much as Canada had related to Britain a century earlier. Industry was based on the extraction and processing of primary resources—agriculture, cattle, metals, lumber, and (later) petroleum—most of which were exported from the region by the eastern-owned railways. Some investment capital, however, was local, particularly after Alberta and Saskatchewan achieved provincehood in 1905—and this increased after the First World War. Only in 1921 was the first western manufactured non-cereal product sent to eastern Canada; this consisted of ceramics from **Medalta Stoneware** (later Medalta Potteries) in Medicine Hat, Alberta [9.60]. The firm's slogan was 'Canadian-made Stoneware from Canadian Clay, made by Canadian Workmen and financed by Canadian Capital'. The Medalta plant was located in Medicine Hat because of the local abundance of natural gas (Rudyard Kipling, on his visit to Canada in 1907, declared that the town 'had all Hell for a basement'). The original factory, built in 1912, still stands, although it has not produced pottery since 1966. Four linked buildings have wood structural frames supporting wood monitor roofs, and the dividing walls are made of brick and clay tile. The utilitarian principal elevation, facing a CPR spur line, is basic brick. The expansion of the plant over the years included the addition of four large beehive kilns in the 1920s.[91]

Cities

In the 1920s small prairie cities, with between 5,000 and 20,000 people, were becoming important supply centres for a large region. Many—such as Brandon (Manitoba), Moose Jaw (Saskatchewan), and Medicine

Hat (Alberta)—were divisional points along the CPR. Five major cities developed a full range of services and industries, and institutions that included post-secondary education, major hospitals, and a concentration of government departments. Winnipeg continued to be the dominant urban centre, but its control of commerce was challenged by Calgary, Regina, Saskatoon, and Edmonton. Of these, Calgary emerged in the 1890s as the largest and most important city between Winnipeg and the west coast.[92]

Calgary In 1875 the North-West Mounted Police's Fort Calgary was built at the confluence of the Bow and Elbow Rivers, and a small community grew up next to it to supply the young cattle industry, trade with the natives, and provide freighting services. It was anchored by a branch store of the I.G. Baker Company of Fort Benton, Montana, whose billiard-room was used for dances on Saturday and church services on Sunday. The main supply route was north-south and came from the US; even mail was channelled through Fort Benton, and required American postage.[93]

Calgary would likely have remained a small settlement with close ties to the western US had it not been for the CPR, which arrived in August 1883 and made the town a divisional point. The CPR owned Section 15, across the Elbow River from the original settlement, and succeeded in attracting the town-centre to its own land by building the station there (an 'Indian Head type'), and offering to donate land for a town hall and fire station. People rushed to buy lots from the CPR when they were put on sale that winter; somebody even tied a rope around the post office and hauled it across the frozen Elbow to the new townsite.

The focus of the bustling young town was the intersection of McTavish (now Centre) Street and Stephen Avenue (now 8th Avenue S). These and many other streets were named after CPR officials; in 1904 the city replaced the names with numbers, as in most Prairie communities. A view of **Stephen Avenue [9.61]**, photographed in 1884, shows predominantly 1½-storey frame structures with gabled roofs; elsewhere on the street, false fronts prevailed. Some lumber was milled locally and some was brought in from the East by the railway. (Colonel James Walker, a former NWMP officer turned businessman, opened Calgary's first sawmill in 1882, and the Eau Claire Lumber Co. of Eau Claire, Wisconsin, opened a large mill in 1886.) The simple residence in the right foreground was built of squared logs and covered with a corrugated metal

9.61 Stephen Avenue (8 Avenue), Calgary, Alberta (looking east). Photograph *c.* 1884. Glenbow Archives/NA1075-14.

9.62 Stephen Avenue (8 Avenue), Calgary, Alberta. Photograph by Boorne and May, *c.* 1892. PAA/E. Brown Collection/B.3154.

roof; logs were also used for many other buildings in the town.

As happened in so many hastily built communities, a major fire (in November 1886) destroyed a large number of wood buildings, which were quickly replaced with bigger and better ones, using fire-resistant materials. Calgary had an excellent local source of sandstone. Joseph Butlin and Wesley Orr opened the first two of many quarries in 1886, both of them just outside town; and a number of brick-yards also opened, the first in 1885. The results were soon evident. Fine sandstone buildings began to rise along Stephen Avenue, and elsewhere in the city. (The first was Knox Presbyterian Church, built in 1887 and replaced in 1912-13.) They proved to be as permanent as their builders hoped, and a remarkable legacy of stone structures still stands.[94]

A view looking east on **Stephen Avenue** [9.62], taken around 1892, shows the amazing transformation that had occurred in only a few years. Large rough-faced sandstone buildings dominate the street. In the left (north) foreground is Alexander Corner (1889, demolished), a $3\frac{1}{2}$-storey gabled block with a round tower (barely visible at the far corner). It dwarfs the Sing Lee laundry, on the extreme left, one of several such establishments operated by members of the large Chinese minority. Across Scarth Street (now 1st Street SW) is the Bank of Montreal (1889;

9.63 Beaulieu, the house of James Lougheed, Calgary, Alberta, 1891. Photograph c. 1914. Glenbow Archives/NA2623-7.

replaced by the present Bank of Montreal, 1930), whose corner tower, gable, and street-level round arches mirror those of Alexander Corner—both of which have a Romanesque Revival character. Beyond the bank is the Norman Block (1890), built by Senator James Lougheed and named after one of his sons; it was designed by William Dodd (1870-1948). Farther down the street, beyond a low wood survivor of pre-fire days, loom two more sandstone buildings developed by Lougheed: the Clarence Block, named after another son (1891; both the Norman and the Clarence Blocks were subsequently rebuilt) and the Lougheed Block. Beyond them, flying a flag, is the Hudson's Bay Company store. Canvas awnings project from many of the buildings, and electric wires distribute power.

On the opposite (south) side of Stephen Avenue, past three low buildings and across from the bank, rises the three-storey Alberta Hotel, built of sandstone in 1888-9 and designed by James Llewellyn Wilson (1855-1931). This popular hotel boasted the longest bar (125 feet, 38 m) between Winnipeg and Vancouver. Future Prime Minister R.B. Bennett, Lougheed's law partner, lived here for several years and had his own table in the bar. Of these buildings, the only survivors are the Alberta Hotel (though it was converted to offices and stores in 1916 when prohibition reached Alberta) and the Hudson's Bay Company store; but many sandstone blocks erected in the 1890s still stand on what is now the 8th Avenue Mall.[95]

Sandstone was also the predominant material for a number of Calgary's early private houses. One was **Beaulieu** [9.63], the residence of James Lougheed, who came to Calgary from Ontario in 1884 and was the town's first lawyer. Successful at law (his clients included the CPR), real estate, and politics, he amassed considerable wealth and power, was appointed to the Senate in 1889, and was subsequently knighted. (Former premier Peter Lougheed is his grandson.) In 1891 he built a fine house ten blocks southwest of the city centre, on what was then still open prairie. An octagonal tower and a gable face the street, and a steeply pitched hipped roof with flamboyant cresting rises above the rear (south) elevation, which once faced an extensive terraced garden. The design is based on the neo-medieval Romanesque Revival and Château styles, although its historical references are imprecise. The interior contained (and retains) many superb finishes, including wall panelling of Spanish mahogany, marble fireplaces from Italy, and many stained-glass windows. Beaulieu (which awaits a new use) was a social focus for Calgary's business and political élite, and royalty were included among the Lougheeds' many guests.[96]

Sandstone remained a popular building material in Calgary through the first decade of the twentieth century, and at one point City Council considered requiring that all buildings on main business streets adopt this warm brown sedimentary stone. Lending itself to a rough 'rock-faced' texture that was appropriate to the picturesque tastes of the 1890s, sandstone must have appeared too rustic to the changing tastes of the Edwardian age. It began to be superseded by imported limestones, which could be cut to produce sharp edges and smooth surfaces, and allowed the addition of relief sculpture. As a result, the last of the dozen-or-so sandstone quarries that served Calgary were closed (or were ready to be closed) by 1915.[97]

Two fine municipal buildings that were among the last to use sandstone illustrate this change in taste, while also showing the continued association of sandstone with the city's public image. The first is **Calgary City Hall** (Dodd and Hopkins, 1907-11) [9.64], a scaled-down version of the Toronto City Hall [10.31] in the Richardsonian Romanesque style,

with rusticated walls and a tall central clock tower. It has been preserved, and acts as the frontispiece to the large new stepped-profile addition finished in mirrored glass (Christopher Ballyn and Webb Zerafa Menkès Housden, 1983-5).[98]

The other is the **Carnegie Library** [9.65]. Now the Memorial Park Library, it was built in 1909-12 in Central (now Memorial) Park, in the as-yet undeveloped parkland bordering on the Victoria Park residential area, and a short distance east of the Lougheed house. This was one of 125 Canadian libraries that were supported by the foundation established by American steel magnate Andrew Carnegie. (Even with the subsidy, there was no universal acceptance among Calgarians that such a cultural service was needed; one newspaper suggested that 'people were too busy to read'.)[99] The design—prepared by an American firm, McLean and Wright of Boston—is a fine, if small, expression of the Beaux-Arts Classicism that was then finding favour in Canada, particularly in the West, where it was adopted for the new Legislative Buildings of all three Prairie Provinces (pages 555-9). Nearly square—and covered by a low, flat-topped hipped roof—the library presents a classical exterior to the park. The high principal storey, containing the main reading-room, is illuminated by large windows that have balustrades at their sills and ornate heads. A projecting portico contains two Ionic columns *in antis* (inserted between projecting ends of the wall), and a pediment with relief carving. Neo-Greek acroteria (projecting ornaments) rise from the pediment and around the cornice. The basement is clad in channelled stone, and the second floor is treated like a shallow attic. Tightly composed and crisply executed, the building is a true jewel of classical design. The walls are of the same yellow-brown Paskapoo sandstone, quarried at Calgary's Oliver quarries, as those of the City Hall; but the sandstone has been worked to produce a smooth finish that is more easily achieved with harder stone. By now the rustic appearance of the first generation of sandstone buildings was looking old-fashioned.

With the phasing-out of sandstone, Calgary's architecture became indistinguishable from that of other western Canadian cities. Office buildings with steel frames and terracotta façades—such as the Burns Building (Hodgson, Bates, and Beattie, 1911-13) and the Canada Life Building (by Brown and Vallance of Montreal, 1911-13), both six storeys high and recently rehabilitated—resembled the Edwardian Commercial buildings in other urban centres (see pages 575-8). The frame dwellings that

9.64 City Hall, Calgary, Alberta, 1907-11. Photograph by Harold Kalman.

9.65 Carnegie Library (now Memorial Park Library), Calgary, Alberta, 1909-12. Photograph by Harold Kalman.

were the predominant housing for the middle and working classes also followed the same patterns as in other cities.[100]

A significant number of Chinese settled in Calgary, many of whom had come to Canada to work as labourers on the CPR. At first the community lived in two separate areas on either side of the tracks, but around 1910 it coalesced into a single Chinatown near Centre Street and 2nd Avenue South. As in other Canadian cities, Chinatown was formed partly as a defence against racism—which was always present, and occasionally erupted into violence—and partly to assist the formation of institutions that would help provide jobs and services and enable the people to maintain their language and culture. Immigration from China was discouraged by a head tax, which rose in 1903 to a prohibitive $500 (two years' income for many people).

Calgary's Chinatown did not develop a particularly distinctive architecture, as Chinatowns in other cities did—particularly in British Columbia. The principal architectural feature was a proliferation of balconies, usually external, as in the former frame buildings of Victoria's Chinatown [8.33]. In masonry buildings, balconies were often recessed behind the line of the façade—a feature of buildings in Canton—as at the **Chinese Benevolent Association Building** (1909) on East Pender Street, Vancouver

9.66 Chinese Benevolent Association Building, Vancouver, British Columbia, 1909. Photograph by John Roaf, 1973.

[**9.66**]. Many Chinatown buildings had 'cheater stories' (low-ceiling mezzanines that were not taxed) and Chinese motifs such as dragons, lions, and tiled roofs. One of the few Chinese-Canadian architects was W.H. Chow, who practised in Vancouver in the early twentieth century.[101]

Calgary's overall population passed 3,000 in 1894, the year in which it was incorporated as a city. Although growth was slow during the recession of the 1890s, the city experienced rapid expansion between 1905 and the First World War, reaching 43,700 in 1911 and 56,500 in 1916. The economy was based primarily on resource industries: cattle-ranching and meat-packing, and farming and milling. (Much the same remains true today, although the main current resource is oil.)

The CPR contributed to the city's prosperity and also determined the principal patterns of development. Its large shops at Ogden, southeast of the city centre (by engineers Westinghouse, Church, Kerr and Company, 1912-13), employed as many as 2,000 people.[102] The decision to locate the railway's freight sheds downtown, just east of the station, caused the area south of the tracks to become a wholesale warehouse district, which it remains. In 1907 the CPR built a large new station (by Edward Colonna)—its third in 24 years—and in 1912-14 it erected the nine-storey Palliser Hotel (by Edward and W.S. Maxwell) adjacent to the station, in the downtown core that it had created.[103] In these same years the company developed two exclusive suburbs in the southwestern part of the city, Mount Royal and Sunalta, and also opened up the working-class suburb of Bridgeland on the north side of the Bow River.[104] The city's growth continued throughout the century—although it has been very cyclical, responsive to booms and busts in the resource-based economy.

The Prairie West experienced rapid development in the thirty years between the completion of the CPR and the First World War, beginning as a formidable territorial frontier and culminating with a well-established network of multicultural cities and towns that served the region's economic and social needs. The built environment progressed from one of expediency, often displaying strong rustic and ethnic character, to a sophisticated urban architecture that would not have been out of place in the older parts of Canada.

CHAPTER 10

BUILDING THE YOUNG DOMINION

IT WAS fortunate that the 1860s, the decade when the Dominion of Canada was born, marked the peak of the High Victorian period, a time when architects excelled at designing grand building complexes. (They became even more adept during the next two generations.) As a happy consequence, the young Dominion amassed a remarkable collection of public and institutional buildings during its first fifty years. Although a world-wide depression clouded much of the period between 1873 and 1896, Canada experienced steady industrial expansion; and when international commerce began to bustle again in 1896, the ensuing active growth of business was marked by a potent optimism in commercial architecture. This chapter looks at the principal government, commercial, and institutional buildings erected across the country during the period 1860-1914. It focuses on 'high' architecture—cosmopolitan work by trained architects that was based on study and on elaborate historical precedents, and was produced to express authority. The buildings reveal a succession of clearly identifiable styles. (Chapter 9 offered samples of some of these styles in the custom buildings for the railways.) Ambitious building programs stimulated the development of new materials and techniques, and by the end of the period many Canadians were working in steel and reinforced-concrete 'skyscrapers' rising more than ten storeys.

All in all it was an exciting time for architecture. New specialized building-types emerged, encouraging public and domestic architecture to diverge in their ways. Whereas in Upper Canada in the 1820s a house, a bank, and a Parliament Building may all have looked similar and followed the same Palladian-Georgian models, half a century later a city hall, a bank, and an office building each revealed its particular function. So too did houses (discussed in Chapter 11).

By the beginning of the twentieth century, archi-

tects and engineers attained new levels of professionalism and organized themselves into formal associations. They also began to provide formal training and produced specialized periodicals, helping the flow of information about recent buildings and blurring regional distinctions. Their social position improved as well.

The 1860s and 1870s saw the emergence of three related High Victorian styles, all of which fall under the broad rubric of Picturesque Eclecticism. Two of them, High Victorian Gothic and the Second Empire style, were particularly well suited for public buildings; and Victorian Italianate was at its best in commercial architecture. The reliance on models from the past and a fondness for picturesque effects, which were the essential characteristics of Early Victorian architecture (see Chapter 6), continued and intensified. Rather than emphasize a single historical source for a building, as the Ecclesiologists had done with churches, the architects of the High Victorian age combined forms and details that were inspired by a variety of earlier styles in a dynamically 'synthetic' or 'creative' eclecticism. Although usually constrained within a single broad historical era or locale—High Victorian Gothic combined various medieval sources, and Victorian Italianate synthesized forms whose origins were found in Italian classicism—the buildings that resulted did not at all resemble the models. And the picturesque taste that revealed itself in a love for asymmetrical compositions and jagged silhouettes was carried much further than previously, producing playful variations in colour and texture.

The second half of the period under consideration, the Late Victorian and Edwardian eras, saw a gradual reaction to what were seen as the excesses of High Victorian architecture. The eclectic use of past styles showed a greater consistency within a single building (although, again, new creations looked nothing like those of the past), and compositions became quieter and more self-contained. As the First World War approached, an architectural manner deriving from the teachings of the École des Beaux-Arts in Paris began to dominate the public architecture of Canada.

Government Architecture

The buildings of the federal government

The first architectural priority of the new Dominion government was to provide accommodation for parliamentarians and civil servants. This was resolved without issue, since the federal government simply moved into the Parliament Buildings that were just then being completed for the former Province of Canada (Canada East and Canada West, now the separate provinces of Quebec and Ontario), which was dissolved upon Confederation. Although they were built for a province, the Parliament Buildings quickly became identified with the federal government, and the most visible symbol of the young Dominion.

The Parliament Buildings   Formed as a result of the Durham Report of 1841, the Province of Canada had gone for years without a proper capital. Kingston, Toronto, Montreal, and Quebec all assumed this role in turn. The competing claims were squelched when Queen Victoria selected Ottawa as the capital in a proclamation delivered on 31 December 1857. The choice was a compromise: Ottawa—until two years earlier known as Bytown—was a rough-and-tumble community dominated by the lumber industry. Its most attractive quality was its location at the Ontario-Quebec border—and its not being one of the competing cities. The capable Governor General, Sir Edmund Walker Head, put it succinctly in a private memorandum to Her Majesty: 'Ottawa is the only place which will be accepted by the majority of Upper and Lower Canada as a fair compromise.'[1] The choice was unpopular and the question was debated for another year; but, as Head had predicted, the legislature finally accepted Ottawa, in February 1859.

The Department of Public Works moved quickly. It was decided (probably by Head) that the Parliament Buildings should be built on Barrack Hill, the strategically located site above the west bank of the entrance locks of the Rideau Canal, which Colonel John By had set aside as a government reserve. In May 1859 the Department advertised an open archi-

tectural competition for four public buildings: a parliamentary building, two departmental buildings flanking it, and a residence for the Governor General. Competitors were given less than three months to submit designs for any or all of the buildings, with the requirement that they be built of coursed hammer-dressed local stone and in a 'plain substantial style'. Using pseudonyms, seventeen architects submitted 33 schemes (several prepared more than one) in a variety of styles, described as Civil Gothic, Classic, Norman, Elizabethan or Tudor, Lombard Venetian, Italian, and Plain Modern. The submissions were judged by two civil servants: engineer Samuel Keefer, now the Deputy Commissioner of Public Works, and F.P. Rubidge (1806-97), the engineer and architect in Keefer's department. They used a numerical evaluation system proposed by John Morris, a little-known Toronto architect who ended up being Clerk of the Works for the project. Keefer presented the recommendations to Head (a scholar, art historian, and known connoisseur of Gothic architecture). After an exchange of memos with Head, the Executive Council on 29 August announced the winners: Thomas Fuller and Chilion Jones would be architects of the main Parliament Building, and Thomas Stent and Augustus Laver of the Departmental Blocks; each also came second to the other. (F.W. Cumberland and W.G. Storm were awarded the premium for the Governor's residence, but it was never built. Rideau Hall, begun in 1838, eventually became Government House.)[2]

The winning designs were in the 'Civil Gothic Style'. Keefer felt that Fuller and Jones's centre-piece showed 'great unity of design', and was confident that Stent and Laver's Departmental Blocks would harmonize with it, being 'in the same style . . . though of somewhat different expression.' The competition had announced no preference for any particular style, but the assessors' comments showed that they were swayed by associations. Keefer thought that the 'conventual and collegiate appearance' of Stent and Laver's entry for the Parliament Building 'seems to associate it with . . . devotion and learning rather than with purposes of Legislation'; and that Cumberland and Storm's Norman design was in a 'heavy castellated style' that 'renders it prison-like and defiant in aspect, and therefore unsuited to become the seat from whence should emanate the laws of a free country.' The Classic designs generally received low marks or were considered to be too costly—one suspects they were non-starters. Keefer and Head must surely have had in mind, as they considered the entries, two highly prominent and

10.1 Centre Block, Parliament Buildings, Ottawa, Ontario, 1859-66. Photograph by W.J. Topley, 1880s. NAC/PA8338.

symbolic buildings just then nearing completion—the Gothic Revival Houses of Parliament (1837-67) in Westminster and the domed classical Capitol (1792-1864) in Washington—and settled on the former as being a more appropriate model. To the architects and clients of the High Victorian era, associationism was an important determinant of historical sources, just as it had been for their Early Victorian predecessors: these comparisons with Britain and the US could not have been disregarded.

Who were the winners? Thomas Fuller (1823-98), a native of Bath, began his architectural career in England and moved to Toronto in 1857. He designed the Gothic Revival church of St Stephen-in-the-Fields [6.38] in that city before teaming up with the younger Chilion Jones (1835-1912), a well-connected Brockville-born engineer. Fuller went on to a controversial practice in the US—he and Jones entered the competition for the Capitol buildings in Albany, NY, in 1863 and Fuller eventually won (with Arthur

Gilman), but the work went badly and he left in disgrace. He returned to Canada in 1881 as the nation's Chief Architect. Jones subsequently became a contractor for railway, canal, and harbour work. Thomas Stent (1822-1912) and Augustus Laver (1834-98) had shorter Canadian careers. Laver temporarily teamed up with Fuller in Albany and New York, worked on commissions in Montreal and Quebec, and arrived in San Francisco in 1870 to meet his second Waterloo (after Albany) as the architect, with Fuller, of that city's third City Hall, whose construction was thick with scandal. Stent also found his way to San Francisco.[3]

Construction of the Parliament Buildings in Ottawa began in glory, with ground being broken for the three buildings in December 1859 and the Prince of Wales laying the cornerstone on 1 September 1860, during his celebrated Canadian tour. Work did not proceed, however, without its own share of controversy. As the competition had been rushed, and the architects were given only one month in which to make changes to their designs, too many issues were left unresolved when the project went out to tender. Costs quickly got out of hand, and in 1862 work was suspended; a Royal Commission was appointed to inquire into the severe disagreements between the government and the contractor for the central building, Thomas McGreevy of Quebec City. Work resumed in April 1863, with Charles Baillairgé (1826-1906) of Quebec (who had submitted an unsuccessful classical design in the competition, and was appointed to the thankless position of associate architect) thrust into the centre of disputes among government, contractor, architects, and politicians. Things have a way of resolving themselves, however, and the first (and last) session of the Parliament of the Province of Canada opened in Ottawa on 6 June 1866. A year later the Dominion of Canada was born, on 1 July 1867, and the buildings became available to its House of Commons and Senate, and the newly formed departments. Construction continued for some time however: the Library, tower, and landscape were not finally completed until the late 1870s.[4]

The three buildings—the **Parliament Building** (its replacement now called the Centre Block), and on either side the Departmental Blocks (now called the East and West Blocks)—were arranged around three sides of an open forecourt some 650 feet (200 m) square [**14.7**]. In the centre, set well back from Wellington Street, was Fuller and Jones's Parliament Building [**10.1**]. The composition was bold and effective. The architects intended that it should present 'a dignified, elegant and also cheerful appearance, and that its character should tend more to the Palatial than the Castellated.'[5] A broad elevation faced the south and Wellington Street, having two principal storeys over a raised basement, and a full attic floor contained within the mansard roofs. The entrance was in the centre through the 252-foot-high (77 m) Victoria Tower, whose gabled sides and bulbous conical roof were capped by an open iron crown. The façade projected forward at either end, with each of the salient wings enclosed, as by bookends, by a pair of three-storey pavilions with tall hipped mansards. The two legislative chambers, equal in size, were situated at either side of a central courtyard [**10.2**]. The tower, pavilions (which were repeated at the rear), and turret-like ventilating shafts gave the building a truly picturesque silhouette.

At the centre of the rear elevation, the magnifi-

cent sixteen-sided **Library of Parliament** [**10.3**] related to the main building in the same way as did a medieval chapter-house to its cathedral (or a monastic kitchen to its monastery). It projects towards the Ottawa River, a setting that the architects appreciated as being scenery 'of the boldest and grandest character', distinct from the 'park like' setting of the front.[6] The Library consists of a tall reading-room, illuminated by a ring of large pointed-arched windows and covered by a vaulted ceiling and a lantern (a Gothic version of a cupola), and is finished in exquisite panelling of white pine. The lowest level contains a number of alcoves with stacks for the collection. Elegant flying buttresses make the transition between tiers; and the composition terminates in spiky window-gables and the tall conical roof of the lantern. Alpheus Todd, the Parliamentary Librarian, specified the circular form of the library, showing his respect for the Round Reading Room at the British Museum (Sidney Smirke, 1855-7).[7] A Gothic source that had a similar function was the chapter house at Westminster Abbey, which was then being used as the Records Office for Westminster Palace. (The Library of Parliament fortunately survived the tragic fire of 1916, which destroyed the Parliament Building, and another fire in 1952.)

The buildings combined three kinds of stone: local Nepean sandstone, whose rich and varied colours, encompassing a range of deep browns, predominated; buff Ohio limestone was used for the window surrounds and other trim; and red Potsdam sandstone for decorative panels. This polychromatic effect—so important to Victorian sensibilities—was continued on the roofs, which were covered with slates arranged in decorative patterns of yellow and green—striped on the Parliament Building, and with alternating bands of rectangular and hexagonal slates, in floral designs, on the Departmental Buildings.[8]

The statement submitted by Fuller and Jones for the competition said that they were 'fully convinced that a Gothic building only could be adapted to a site, at once so picturesque and so grand.' Their decorative vocabulary, and that of the two Departmental Buildings, was indeed 'Civil Gothic', in that the pointed arches of the windows and doors, the gables, the towers, and the corner turrets found their inspiration in Gothic architecture—particularly in 'civil' (i.e. non-ecclesiastical) buildings. But in the composition and details, the past provided only a series of isolated ideas that were carefully synthesized. One source was evidently the medieval public buildings of Belgium, such as the famous fourteenth-century Cloth Hall at Ypres (destroyed in the First World

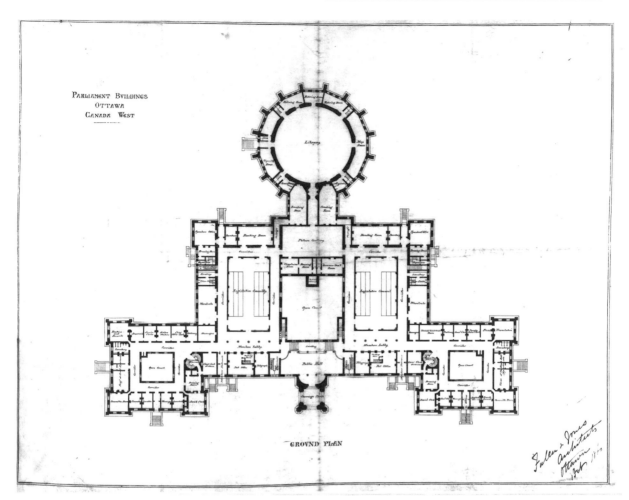

10.2 Ground-floor plan of the Centre Block, Parliament Buildings, Ottawa, Ontario, 1859. NAC/23174.

10.3 Library of Parliament, Ottawa, Ontario, 1859-77. Photograph by S. McLaughlin, *c.* 1880. NAC/C18371.

War), and the City Hall at Brussels (1402-54)—both of which featured a tall tower in the middle of a broad windowed façade. Another source may well have been the fourteenth- and fifteenth-century Doges' Palace in Venice, with its two-over-one bay pattern, having a pair of narrow pointed-arched apertures on the second floor placed above each broader opening on the ground floor. The architects (and here we surely recognize the role of the more worldly Fuller, rather than the Ontario-bound Jones) must have been referring to models such as these when they said:

> The designers have endeavoured not slavishly to copy the Gothic of any particular period or country[,] but the noble civic buildings of the Low Countries and Italy have afforded them suggestions.[9]

This statement—which architectural historian Carolyn Young has shown was borrowed from a contemporary British source—expressed the very spirit that lay behind Picturesque Eclecticism and High Victorian Gothic. The architecture of the past, along with compositions of the present, were culled for ideas that would produce a 'modern' building.

Fuller was evidently up-to-date in his knowledge of contemporary English practice, since the Parliament Building reflected several new and highly acclaimed designs in addition to the British Museum Reading Room. One was the **University Museum [10.4]** in Oxford (1855-60), designed by the Irish firm of Thomas Deane (1792-1872) and Benjamin Woodward (1815-61), under the watchful eye of the influential critic, aesthete, and designer, John Ruskin (1819-1900), whose famous work *The Stones of Venice* (1851-3) had awakened British sensibilities to the beauties of medieval Italian architecture. The Oxford Museum established important precedents—with its use of Italian Gothic sources, polychromatic masonry (also Italian-inspired), multicoloured slate roofs, a central tower with a hipped roof and iron finials, and an attached 'chapter house' (the laboratories pavilion, modelled on the Abbot's Kitchen at Glastonbury)—all features that appear in the Ottawa building. Another English model was the competition design (unexecuted) submitted by Sir George Gilbert Scott (1811-78) for the **Foreign Office [10.5]** in Westminster (1857), which was also indebted to the Oxford Museum for its composition and detail, although its façade and plan were more formal and symmetrical. Fuller and Jones alluded to Scott's project in their notes, in reference to its being cheaper than a classical design. British architectur-

10.4 University Museum, Oxford, England, 1855-60. Photograph *c*. 1860. Centre for Oxfordshire Studies, Oxford County Library/1992/1/1.

al historians Roger Dixon and Stefan Muthesius have called the Ottawa building 'perhaps the most important derivative' of Scott's design. (The Foreign Office was eventually built in 1862-73 to an Italianate scheme by Scott, after a prolonged and highly political debate.) The Ottawa Parliament Building looked at non-Gothic sources as well. For example, the mansard roofs, with their iron cresting, reflect the early French Renaissance, as interpreted by the architects of contemporary France; the formal plan also seems to acknowledge the emerging Second Empire style [10.7, 8].[10]

A direct connection between the design for University College, Toronto (1856-9; **6.63**), and the Parliament Building—a possible go-between was

10.5 Design for the Foreign Office, Westminster, England, 1857. From *Building News*, 14 August 1857. MTRL.

John Morris, who served as Clerk of the Works for both buildings—has long been speculated, but never verified. Designed by Cumberland and Storm, University College also exhibits parallels to the University Museum at Oxford; and architect F.W. Cumberland was acquainted with it, and with Ruskin. The College anticipates many features of the Parliament Building—including a central tower, mansarded end pavilions, and a circular 'chapter house'—although the Toronto building's historical detail is Norman rather than Gothic. Another link was the direct involvement of Governor General Head in choosing the style to be used as a source. The similarities were not lost on contemporaries. Politician and journalist George Brown called the Ottawa buildings 'really magnificent', and noted: 'The architecture is something like the Toronto University but infinitely finer. The work is beautiful and of the most substantial character.'[11]

Whatever the sources of the Parliament Building, it was very much a product of its time, in keeping with the newest and best architecture in Britain, France, and Canada. Unlike Canadian work of a half-century earlier, which was very *retardataire* in comparison with British and American prototypes, the architecture of leading Canadian buildings had caught up with the rest of the world by the High Victorian period.

Stent and Laver's Departmental Buildings, which were intended to accommodate the offices of all government departments, provided a perfect complement to the Parliament Building. Located at the sides of the huge expanse of the courtyard and closer to Wellington Street, they were composed far more casually, with asymmetrical elevations, unmatched corner towers, and witty details. Samuel Keefer instructed Stent and Laver to introduce this picturesque irregularity when modifying their competition designs:

> It is desirable, for appearances sake, to vary the designs of the two blocks on the East and West side of the Square . . . and so to do away with the formality of two similar buildings.[12]

The principal entrances of both buildings are in the centre of the façades that look onto the courtyard; the one in the East Block, protected by a porch, was reserved for the exclusive use of the Governor General, whose office, until 1942, was directly above it.

The **East Block [10.6]** is a controlled Gothic fantasy of arched windows, towers, pinnacles, and chimneys, whose fanciful profile is softened by colour—the stone (the same kinds as on the original Centre Block) ranges from cream through ochre and red to grey, and the roof was originally patterned with muted green and yellow slates—and by the delicate wrought-iron roof cresting. The bizarre public entrance in the southwest tower (which Sir John A. Macdonald likened to a cowbell, and in whose elevation many people see a face) places the door and its tympanum (carved with the arms of the Province of Canada) within a large tear-shaped relieving arch that contains a five-sided panel of random Potsdam stone topped by a crescent-shaped frame of Ohio stone, which is perforated by a circular opening (containing an intricate carved tendril roundel) and two elongated trefoils. Gargoyles, grotesque faces, and other carvings occur all over the building. Wood dormer windows—a later addition—add to the building's liveliness. The Department of Public Works recently cleaned the stone and reinstated the original exterior colour-scheme, which includes maroon window frames, so that the contrasts in colour and texture that were so important to the Victorian aesthetic can be fully appreciated. A portion of the interior—including the Privy Council Chamber and the offices of the Governor General, Sir John A. Macdonald, and Sir George-Étienne Cartier—has been restored to its appearance in 1872.[13]

The success of the three buildings depends to a large extent on their siting around the large central court, and on the effective landscaping of the courtyard. The original call for competitive designs treated the site as if it were level, even though there is a considerable rise from Wellington Street to the north. The Parliament Building was therefore about 20 feet (6 m) higher than the East and West Blocks. The courtyard and its treatment were ignored during construction, but required a creative resolution after the buildings were completed. An Ottawa newspaper, for example, commented in 1872 on the 'expediency of cutting down the unsightly high ground which interrupts the view of the Parliament Buildings.'[14]

Thomas Seaton Scott (1826-95), the Chief Architect of the Department of Public Works, was sent to New York to commission designs for the 'public grounds' from Calvert Vaux (1824-95). This highly talented London-born architect and landscape designer—whose career has been somewhat overshadowed by those of his celebrated associates, Andrew Jackson Downing and Frederick Law Olmsted—submitted his design in June 1873. Vaux proposed the construction of a two-tiered terrace across the front of the Centre Block to make the transition in grades. (Work was completed in 1879.) The terraces, and their balustraded retaining walls (faced in Nepean

sandstone), survive with only minor alterations as
the principal landscape feature of Parliament Hill.
The lower terrace carries curving roadways from the
lower to the upper level; a broad staircase in the centre connects the lawn with the central tower. The
level upper terrace has stairs and a flagpole at either
end. Vaux explained to Scott how he cleverly exploited what had been perceived as a deficiency:

> As The Parliament House stands at a conspicuous-
> ly higher level than the Department Buildings, it
> seems very desirable to make the whole arrange-
> ment of the ground seem to grow out of this con-
> trolling and somewhat peculiar circumstance of the
> site. I propose therefore to carry the front of the
> upper terrace on a level—and to terminate it with
> a flag staff at each end, also to introduce projecting
> bays and steps at the angles, so that the appear-
> ance of steepness may be still further increased.[15]

Some years later Vaux recalled that the terrace

10.6 East Block, Parliament Buildings, Ottawa, Ontario,
1859-65. Photographed during the funeral of Sir John A.
Macdonald, 10 June 1891. NAC/C7126.

served to bring the base line of the upper building
to the same level as the lower buildings, and this
did away with the apparent incongruity to the eye.[16]

Sculptor Marshall Wood claimed credit for the work,
but Scott made it clear that it was executed by Vaux
and himself. The other important landscape feature
from this period is the fence (1873-5) along
Wellington Street, which combines a stone wall with
an iron fence and features a magnificent central gate.
The design was by Frederick J. Alexander (1849-1930),
an architect with the Department of Public Works,
who also completed the Library of Parliament.[17]

The Parliamentary complex received international praise even before its completion. One of the best
tributes was also among the first. In 1862, while the
buildings were still under construction, English nov-

elist Anthony Trollope visited the site, inspected the model, and expressed his rapture:

> The glory of Ottawa will be—and, indeed, already is,—a set of public buildings which is now being erected. . . .I take it upon myself to say that as regards purity of art and manliness of conception the work is entitled to the highest praise. . . . I know of no modern gothic purer of its kind, or less sullied with fictitious ornamentation. . . . I know no site for such a set of buildings, so happy as regards to both beauty and grandeur.[18]

Trollope, like many of his contemporaries, used the term 'Modern Gothic' as a stylistic description; today we prefer the historical perspective provided by the term 'High Victorian Gothic'. The significance of the Parliament Buildings has been widely recognized in our own times as well. Architectural historian Henry-Russell Hitchcock, for example, has stated that 'the variety of form, the gusto of the detail, and the urbanistic scale of this project made [it] a major monumental group unrivalled for extent and complexity of organization in England.'[19]

Over the generations many observers have considered High Victorian eclecticism to be a Canadian national style, a manner of building that was particularly appropriate to the Canadian psyche. We may recall that Vice-Chancellor John Langton described the architecture of his University College as being in 'the Canadian style' (page 312). Members of the Canada First movement, the nationalist and imperialist group organized in 1868, drew upon Ruskin's Victorian Gothic aesthetics when they exalted the superiority of our 'northern' race.[20] In 1907 poet and historian Wilfred Campbell applied these sensibilities to architecture in his romantic description of the Parliament Buildings:

> For while we speak of [our majestic buildings] as Canadian, every tower and arch, every buttress and carving, every groin and bastion, every window and doorway is an evidence of the spirit and ideal of our Celtic, Saxon, and Norman forefathers. In these buildings we have as a people, both French and British. . . . epics in stone, revealing to us not only universal beauty and inspiration, but emblematic of our common ideal, our common artistic sense, our common ancestry, and our common Christianity.[21]

More recently Alan Gowans proposed that the High Victorian architecture of University College, the Parliament Buildings, and many other public buildings of the era—inspired by Gothic and diverse historical styles—with their mixed forms and broadly general associations, represent a Canadian National Style, and that 'the feeling for it remains deep and instinctive'.[22] This is a valid observation, and although other forms of expression for public building were used as well—several are described later in this chapter—Canadians have shown an inherent attraction to a historically allusive 'northern' architecture of steep roofs and vertical proportions. This was particularly evident in the first half of the twentieth century, when federal authorities proposed the Parliament Buildings, and the castle-like Château Laurier [14.15], as models for the nation's public architecture.

The Department of Public Works The government of the young Dominion soon addressed the need to construct buildings across the country to provide expanding federal services, while at the same time creating a much-needed national identity. More than 300 public buildings were built by the federal government between Confederation and the First World War. All were erected under the direction of (even if not all were designed by) the Department of Public Works, which became an increasingly well-organized and powerful ministry. Canals, railways, and national trunk roads also fell under its jurisdiction. (The coastal waterways and their associated buildings were the responsibility of the new Department of Marine and Fisheries.)[23]

The first significant building project undertaken after Confederation was a new **General Post Office** [10.7] on Adelaide Street East, Toronto. Officials of the Post Office Department searched for an appropriate architectural expression; and rather than choosing the High Victorian Gothic of the Parliament Buildings, or looking to England for the latest developments there, they selected the Second Empire style, which was then (in 1870) in vogue for important public buildings in the United States. The style was based on the recent public buildings of the French Second Empire of Napoleon III, particularly the bombastic new additions to the Louvre in Paris, built in 1852-7 to designs by L.-T.-J. Visconti (1791-1853) and H.-M. Lefuel (1810-80)—which in turn were derived from the sixteenth- and seventeenth-century architecture of France. It began to be used in the US after the Civil War for federal buildings in Washington and across the country. The Courthouse and Post Office in New York (1869-75) was representative of the group; the largest and perhaps the best was about to be begun: the State, War, and Navy Building in Washington (1871-89). All were designed

10.7 General Post Office, Toronto, Ontario, 1871-4. Photograph by Frank W. Micklethwaite. NAC/RD336.

under the direction of (and likely by) the Supervising Architect to the Treasury Department, Alfred B. Mullett (1834-90).[24]

In March 1870 John Dewe, the Postal Inspector for Toronto, submitted a set of plans for the new Post Office to the Department of Public Works, describing the design as

> chaste, elegant and in perfect taste, and highly creditable to Mr Mullett, the architect by whom they have been drawn. The interior arrangements have been planned out with great care and after consultation with some of the best practical Post Office officials in Canada and the United States.[25]

The Post Office intended that these plans by Mullett—which we presume were commissioned formally—should become a model for future buildings. The same drawings were re-submitted a few weeks later for a proposed post office in Quebec City, and were described as 'a general plan applicable to all city Post Offices to be hereafter built.'[26]

The plans for the Toronto Post Office, as built in 1871-4, were prepared not by Mullett but by architect Henry Langley (1836-1907) of that city. Since

Mullett's drawings have been lost, we do not know to what extent Langley followed the American model. Whatever the relationship between the two may have been, the executed building displayed all the features of the new style—and exhibited an urbane elegance that was unprecedented in Toronto. A rooftop architectural forest sprouted above the cornice, its complexity catering to picturesque tastes. Characteristic of the style were the steep mansard roofs (a corruption of the name of French architect François Mansart) with their ornate dormer windows and iron cresting; variations of the mansards were seen over the corner pavilions and on the bulbous 'square dome' above the entrance. The wall ornament was classical in its derivation, its complexity and deep relief creating lively patterns of light and shade. It featured columns in the projecting pedimented central portion (a separate order for each storey, one piled on top of another); deep window surrounds made up of pilasters, round-headed arches, and keystones carved in the form of heads; and heavily channelled masonry at the corner pavilions. The entrance was framed by paired columns and a semicircular pediment, over which was placed the Royal Coat of Arms. As lively as the composition may appear, it did not rival those of American buildings in the style. Indeed, the control exerted by the pedimented frontispiece seems to be a holdover from Toronto's dominant Palladian-Georgian public buildings of a half-century earlier. The Post Office was sited directly on the axis of Toronto Street, grandly terminating the vista from King Street; unfortunately it was demolished in 1960 and its banal replacement does not respect this alignment.[27]

Langley had already shown his facility for the Second Empire style (as a partner in the firm of Gundry and Langley) at Toronto's Government House, and this achievement may well have been the reason for his selection as the architect for the Post Office. Langley presumably followed the Mullett model to a considerable extent, since his client remained the Department of Public Works and Thomas Seaton Scott, who was appointed architect to the Department in May 1871 (replacing the retired F.P. Rubidge). Scott, who was introduced above for his involvement in the landscape of the Parliament Buildings and in earlier chapters for his work for the Grand Trunk Railway and Christ Church Cathedral in Montreal, had been in private practice in that city.

Soon after his appointment, Scott was sent to inspect the public buildings of Portland (Maine), Boston, and New York. We may guess that this orientation tour focused on Second Empire monuments, particularly the Custom House in Portland (by Mullett, 1868-72), Boston's City Hall (Bryant and Gilman, 1862-5) and Sub-Treasury Building (Mullett, 1869-74), and Mullett's federal building in New York. Less than a year later, in February 1872, the post of Chief Architect (sometimes called Dominion Architect) was created for Scott. He and his staff, the Chief Architect's Branch, were responsible for the acquisition, construction, and maintenance of all buildings controlled by the federal government—a mandate similar to Mullett's. Some buildings were designed by private architects and others were designed in-house and only supervised by private firms; but the distinction was not always clear, since Scott kept a tight rein on all buildings erected during his ten-year tenure and ensured consistency in federal architecture. The Branch operated on the model of a private architectural office, with Scott as principal, providing overall design guidance and being responsible for all decisions. The day-to-day design work was in the hands of staff architects and draftsmen.

One of the largest public buildings in the Second Empire style was the **Custom House in Saint John** [10.8], New Brunswick, built in 1877-81 to replace the austerely Neoclassical Custom House (by John

Walker, 1840-2) that was destroyed in the city's Great Fire of 1877. The earlier Custom House had been dressed up in 1870 with a mansard roof, to identify it as a federal building, when it was purchased by the Dominion government (which had previously leased the space). Scott now took advantage of the opportunity to build a proper symbol of the Dominion. There was considerable interplay between his Branch and the local architects J.T.C. McKean (1840-1911) and G. Ernest Fairweather (1850-1920). Scott insisted on towers and additional ornament, while McKean and Fairweather successfully argued for using stone (rather than brick) for the entire building, and not just the principal façade on Prince William Street. The result, seen in a photograph taken soon after completion (while the devastation from the fire was still visible), was imposing. Some 200 feet (61 m) wide and three storeys high, the rigidly symmetrical building was composed with projecting pavilions in the centre, capped by a stepped gable and a large square dome, wedding-cake ends made up of gables, pavilion roofs, and the two-stage square towers demanded by Scott. Broad

10.8 Custom House, Saint John, New Brunswick, 1877-81. Photograph by A. Stoerger, 1889. NAC/C30871.

arched windows with exquisite surrounds set a *grandioso* rhythm on the first two floors, and smaller paired windows illuminated the third storey. Pilasters enlivened the pavilions. The capitals of the central ones had carved heads representing Europe, Africa, Asia, and America, and the keystone over the central door bore a bust of Britannia. Tall chimneys enhanced the picturesque qualities of the silhouette; this and the overall composition reveal the parallels between the Second Empire and the High Victorian Gothic styles and remind us that both are products of Picturesque Eclecticism. The Custom House was praised as 'a monument of elegance' and the press also noted its 'free rendering of the classic style. . .[and] the striking harmony of its proportions and the suggestion of the French Renaissance style, conveyed by its central dome.' The building was demolished in 1961, in the same wave of destruction that took the Toronto Post Office.[28]

Smaller and simpler buildings served as custom houses, post offices, and offices for other government services across the country. Many designs were prepared by Branch staff, particularly after 1873, when the Liberals came to power and promoted departmental self-sufficiency for reasons of economy. (Prime Minister Alexander Mackenzie, a former contractor, served as his own Minister of Public Works, and he surely felt that he could run a building business without outside help.) The **Custom House in Victoria** [10.9], British Columbia, known locally as the Malahat Building (1873-5), is one of the plainest, presenting a square brick front enlivened by segmental window heads and quoins to Wharf Street. The mansard roof, with its pedimented dormers and tall chimneys, is sufficient to convey the federal image. Other buildings of this scale and character adopted a central tower-like pavilion; two that were designed in-house were the Post Office at Saint-Jean, Quebec (1877-80, demolished) and the Post Office and Custom House at Fredericton, New Brunswick (1878, now the National Exhibition Centre).[29]

Scott and his Branch were capable of working in other styles when appropriate. They designed a handsome large addition (1875-8) to the West Block on Parliament Hill, adopting the High Victorian Gothic style to fit in with the existing Parliament Buildings. The extension presented a new façade to the west, facing away from the central court and culminating in the tall Mackenzie Tower, in which the Prime Minister had his large office.

By the end of the decade, when the Second Empire style began to fall out of fashion, the Branch responded by modifying its pattern. The **Post Office in**

10.9 Custom House, Victoria, British Columbia, 1873-5. Photograph by Harold Kalman, 1992.

10.10 Post Office, Stratford, Ontario, 1883-4. Photograph *c*. 1893. Stratford-Perth Archives.

Stratford (1883-4, demolished), Ontario, designed under Scott's direction in 1881, reveals a significant deviation in composition and plan [**10.10**]. The dominant exterior feature was a clock tower located at a corner— rather than in the centre—and containing a door and a staircase leading to the second- and third-storey offices (the ground floor was the post-office hall). Besides providing for separate entrances, the new layout revealed that close attention was paid to the siting, since the corner tower was visible as a landmark feature from two approach routes. The tower was actually the left-hand pavilion of the familiar Second-Empire formula, but its prominence skewed the design, giving it an asymmetrical and picturesque aspect. This post office was structurally more adventurous than many earlier buildings, consisting of load-bearing masonry walls and iron girders and columns (as well as timber joists). It is particularly interesting that its plans were signed by Scott on 8 September 1881, his last day as Chief Architect; on 9 September he took a leave of absence and never returned to his desk. Yet the Stratford Post Office was a prototype for the many post offices and federal buildings designed by Scott's successor, Thomas Fuller.[30]

Yes, Thomas Fuller! Hearing that Scott was about to retire, Fuller wrote to his old client, Samuel Keefer, stating: 'I should like the appointment.' Keefer quickly passed on a glowing recommendation to Prime Minister Macdonald (who had returned to power):

> . . . if it is the intention to fill Mr Scott's place, you have here a rare opportunity of securing on your own terms, the services of the best architect I know of in North America.[31]

Sir Hector-Louis Langevin, Minister of Public Works, appointed Thomas Fuller as Chief Architect of the Department of Public Works on 31 October 1881. The 58-year-old Fuller was to remain in the position for sixteen years, during which time the Branch erected some 140 public buildings across the country. (Under ten years of Scott's direction, it was responsible for about one-quarter that number.)[32] Langevin expanded the program of public building, insisting on high standards of design. He was determined to create an imposing government presence across the country, and felt that the Department of Public Works should set a good example that would encourage local developers to erect substantial buildings.[33]

Fuller's post offices and federal buildings in large towns and small cities—about eighty—were all individually designed. They display considerable variety in their materials and details, but all have a decid-ed family resemblance. (Although properly designated 'federal buildings', most were usually known as 'post offices' because that was the most widely used service.) The buildings typically have two storeys beneath a steep roof (variously mansarded, gabled, or hipped), with a central gable, and an end or corner tower and a lower one-storey annex; all are carefully sited. Some have a central tower, as in the Post Office at Lachine, Quebec (1889-90), and others have no tower at all, as in the **Post Office in Baddeck** [**10.11**], Nova Scotia (1885-7; now known as Gilbert H. Grosvenor Hall). Both buildings have exterior walls of rough-faced sandstone and feature broad round-headed arches with large voussoirs, showing an affinity to the Romanesque Revival style then in vogue. Others were built of red brick with light horizontal banding—as in the post offices at Port Hope, Ontario (1882-3, demolished 1971) and Strathroy, Ontario (1889); although they also have prominent round arches at street level, they reflect features of the Queen Anne style as well. Indeed, none follow a single historical style; they reveal an eclectic approach towards the past, in keeping with the spirit of the time and the genius of Fuller.[34]

The professional periodical *Canadian Architect and Builder* praised Fuller's federal buildings for helping

10.11 Post Office, Baddeck, Nova Scotia, 1885-7 (Gilbert H. Grosvenor Hall). Photograph by Robert Bailey, 1979.

to 'form the public taste' and for having 'a merit that will make them an influence for good.'[35] The continuity between Scott's and Fuller's buildings (their post offices were similar in design) indicates that much of the design initiative came from the staff within the Branch. Some of its architects were given specialized tasks with considerable autonomy: John Bowes (1820-94), for example, was allowed a large measure of freedom as superintendent of penitentiaries. Private architects rarely participated in government projects, and those who did were carefully controlled.

The most important structure erected under Fuller's direction was the **Langevin Block [10.12]** in Ottawa, which contained government offices (now principally the Prime Minister's Office). Built in 1883-9, directly across Wellington Street from the Parliament Buildings, it was originally known as the Southern Department Building. The scale and massing relate positively to its neighbours across the street, by then twenty-five years old, but the design makes no reference to their High Victorian Gothic. The composition is more sober, the lively polychromy gone. The mansard roofs, the emphasis on the centre and the ends, and the use of channelled and smooth masonry (olive sandstone from New Brunswick) are clearly reminiscent of Scott's large productions of a decade earlier and show a continuation of the federal imagery. The omission of columns or pilasters distances it somewhat from the Second Empire style, which by now was becoming quite *passé*; the relentlessly repeated heavy arches—Fuller claimed that round-arched windows would provide more light in the offices— with voussoirs supported on engaged colonettes, are features of the Richardsonian Romanesque [**10.19, 10.31**], which was just then becoming known outside the northeastern US (where Fuller had been practising before his return to Ottawa).[36]

The largest of Fuller's buildings was the Toronto Armouries (1891-3, demolished 1963) on University Avenue, a huge castellated red-brick structure with grey limestone trim, whose towers and turrets associated it with armies and war (even if medieval ones). The drill hall alone was as large as a football field, and the building accommodated other needs of the local militia. Larger than required by modern military activities, it was one of many armoury buildings erected across the country. The survivors present a mammoth preservation problem.[37]

Fuller retired in 1897, a year before his death. His successor as Chief Architect was David Ewart (1843-1921), the son of an Edinburgh builder, who would serve in that position until 1914. Ewart had been employed by the Department of Public Works since May 1871, the month of Scott's arrival and the time of the formation of the Chief Architect's Branch, so his appointment ensured a strong measure of continuity. Like his predecessors, Ewart was responsible both for federal buildings across the Dominion and for new government buildings in Ottawa.[38]

One of the first tasks that the Branch faced under Ewart's direction was the provision of federal buildings in Dawson during the Klondike Gold Rush. Their design and construction were ably handled by T.W. Fuller, the son of Thomas Fuller and himself a future Chief Architect (1927-36), who was assisted by Ewart's own son, Henry Ewart (see Chapter 13).

The old-fashioned Palladian-Georgian style revived at Dawson found no place in the new mainstream federal buildings of southern Canada. The new image for the Dominion forged by Ewart and his staff was based on yet one more up-to-date style: the Edwardian Baroque, which came to Canada from Britain in the early years of the century. The **Post Office in Vancouver [10.13]**, British Columbia— built in 1905-10 on Hastings Street—is representative of those in larger cities. A stately row of giant columns spans the second and third storeys, standing on a rusticated ground floor, and the colonnade supports a deep entablature, above which rise a mansard roof and a corner clock-tower with a square dome and little cupola. Many of these features are holdovers from the Second Empire public buildings of Scott, and therefore continue an established image; but their arrangement is more controlled and ordered—and less picturesque—while still making no less grand an impression than their forebears. Behind the granite façade lurks a steel frame fireproofed in concrete, the first in Vancouver. The building has been rehabilitated and now forms part of the much-acclaimed Sinclair Centre [**15.98**].[39]

The immediate sources of the design are the bombastic public buildings of the Britain of Edward VII— monuments such as the War Office (1898-1906) on Whitehall, Westminster, designed by Ewart's co-patriot and contemporary, the Scotsman William Young (1843-1900). Described by contemporaries as being in the English Renaissance style, and now called the Edwardian Baroque, the composition finds its inspiration in the architecture of late-seventeenth- and early-eighteenth-century Baroque England, with the work of architects such as Sir Christopher Wren, Nicholas Hawksmoor, Sir John Vanbrugh, and— once again!—James Gibbs. (This was the very style from whose excesses the Palladians had sought to escape.) The alleged Englishness of the style (although

10.12 Langevin Block, Ottawa, Ontario, 1883-9. Photograph by John Roaf, 1982.

10.13 Post Office, Vancouver, British Columbia, 1905-10. Photograph by John Roaf, 1973.

it certainly acknowledged continental architecture) appealed to the patriotism of Britain, which was inflamed first by Queen Victoria's Diamond Jubilee (1897) and then by the Boer War.[40]

Small cities received a simplified, but nevertheless imposing, version of this design. The **Post Office in Lethbridge [10.14]**, Alberta, built in 1912-13, is almost identical in composition to the Vancouver building, including the corner tower and the emphasis on the ends; but the engaged columns have been reduced to thin pilasters and the classical detail is more restrained.[41]

Federal buildings in smaller centres were much simpler in design, reflecting the quieter side of Edwardian Classicism. To cope with the growing need for federal buildings, and taking a cue from the standard designs that were proliferating on the Prairies (pages 504-7), Ewart's office produced plans around 1907 for two 'Standard Public Buildings'. Both were compact two-storey brick buildings with classical door and window surrounds and a heavy cornice at the top. Design 'A', the smaller of the two, was four bays wide with a door at either side; one example is the Post Office (1908) at Lachute, Quebec. Design 'B' was five bays wide and decorated with channelled pilasters (also in brick) that spanned the two storeys; executed examples are the **Post Office at Westville [10.15]**, Nova Scotia, and the one at Maple Creek, Saskatchewan (1908; both with entrances in the centre and at one end), and at Ladysmith, British Columbia (with a door at either side of the façade). Standard designs were also used at this time by the Department of Militia and Defence—independently of the Department of Public Works—for small drill halls. This practice was continued into recent times by the Post Office, which used a series of standard plans (called the 'SP' series) in the 1960s.[42]

David Ewart was more directly involved in the large custom-designed buildings erected in Ottawa by the Department of Public Works. These include the Dominion Observatory (1899-1900); the Victoria Museum (1905-12), which served as the temporary Parliament Building after fire destroyed the Centre Block in 1916; the Dominion Archives (1904-7, now the Canadian War Museum); the Royal Canadian Mint (1905-8); and Ewart's personal favourite, the Connaught Building (1913-14). The Observatory has Romanesque detail; the others are all buttressed and battlemented buildings that follow Elizabethan and other English late-Gothic sources.

Named after the Governor General, the Duke of Connaught, the **Connaught Building [10.16]**—a large office block on the east side of Mackenzie

10.14 Post Office, Lethbridge, Alberta, 1912-13. Photograph by Hellmut W. Schade.

10.15 Post Office, Westville, Nova Scotia, 1908. Photograph by G.A. Waldren, 1908. NAC/PA46728.

548

Avenue, across from Major's Hill Park, not far from the Château Laurier and across the locks of the Rideau Canal from Parliament Hill—is an imposing pile, with tiers of low-arched Tudor windows, replete with tracery, and castellated turrets defining pavilions at the centre and the ends. The design was originally opened to public competition in 1906-7. The Montreal firm of Edward and W.S. Maxwell placed first, with a chaste Gothic Revival scheme, but much to the chagrin of the Maxwells and other competitors, their work was passed over, and Ewart (who had sat on the jury) provided the final design for a smaller and less expensive building—and revealed that he had learned not a little from the submissions. This was one of many abuses of competitions that drove architects to organize their profession.[43]

Despite the classical image purveyed by federal buildings across the country, Ottawa was to remain decidedly medieval, following the High Victorian Gothic example set by the Parliament Buildings. Ewart had been sent to England in 1901 to study Windsor Castle, Hampton Court, and other royal buildings, and he followed his lessons well, leaning towards Tudor models from the period of Queen Elizabeth I. An anonymous peer of Ewart characterized his style as

> severe, plain but not bold. . . a charm which combined pure artistic taste with Puritan severity, even choosing severe late Gothic types. . . which he fashioned with marvellous simplicity and delicacy of taste.[44]

More than thirty years of building by the Department of Public Works produced a wide range of architectural types that ran the gamut of styles popular during the High and Late Victorian and Edwardian eras. Beginning with the High Victorian Gothic of the Parliament Buildings, the image of the young Dominion was promulgated successively by the Second Empire, Richardsonian Romanesque, Queen Anne, Edwardian Baroque, and Elizabethan Revival styles. The Chief Architects and their staffs kept abreast of the latest design work in Europe and the US, and in many cases set examples for the rest of the country.

10.16 Connaught Building, Ottawa, Ontario, 1913-14. Photograph by Hellmut W. Schade, 1980.

In the remainder of this chapter, we shall see how these examples and others were followed in the buildings of provincial and municipal governments, and in those erected by private business.

The provincial legislative buildings

The first colonial and legislative buildings, erected in the early nineteenth century, all adopted versions of the Georgian and Palladian styles to express their roles as the focus of political authority. New Brunswick, Nova Scotia, Prince Edward Island, Newfoundland, Lower Canada (Quebec), and Upper Canada (Ontario) all relied on this architectural image, despite its being long out of fashion in Britain and the US. The first departure was in the Parliament Building, Ottawa—though built by the Province of Canada, it was emphatically identified with the idea of a new federal government. In response to the growth of the young Dominion, eight new provincial legislative buildings would be built between 1880 and the First World War. All abandoned the Georgian models and, following the example of federal architecture, chose the fashionable styles of the day in an attempt to express a budding nationalism.

The first three, begun between 1877 and 1881, adopted the Second Empire style. The first and the largest was the **Hôtel du Parlement [10.17]** in Quebec City, built on the former garrison cricket field in the Upper Town. The design was by architect Eugène-Étienne Taché (1836-1912)—the son of former Premier Sir Étienne-Paschal Taché, and a devoted Quebec nationalist who coined the provincial motto 'Je me souviens' (and had it inscribed over the entrance). Execution was supervised by Pierre Gauvreau (who had been involved in the previous Parliament Building, 4.62) and Jean-Baptiste Derome (1837-1910). Plans were drawn up in 1876, construction began the following spring, and work was completed in 1887.[45]

The building forms a quadrangle with a large interior courtyard. The centre of the principal elevation (the Palais législatif) is marked by a tall tower, and each of the three other wings (containing the departmental offices) by a high square-domed pavilion (only one is seen in the photograph, facing chemin Saint-Louis). Smaller tower-like pavilions project near the corners. The plan is clearly derived from the new wing of the Louvre (page 541). After the practice of naming a pavilion for a famous historical figure, at Quebec they commemorated Jacques Cartier (the centre tower), Champlain (on the left), and Maisonneuve (on the right). The Louvre provided

the precedent for the Second Empire style, with its mansard roofs, classical vocabulary, and rich Renaissance-inspired ornament concentrated around the windows and doors. Taché selected the public buildings of France as appropriate models to express Quebec's national identity. It would be an oversimplification, however, to identify them as the sole prototypes, since Taché evidently followed Fuller and Jones's Parliament Building in the composition of the façade and the design of the tower, and was also aware of the use of the Second Empire manner for federal architecture in both Canada and the US. Taché's intention to combine British as well as French sources is revealed by his complex iconographic program, which transformed the façade into a pantheon of Quebec's founders. Bronze statues (several by the celebrated sculptor Louis-Philippe Hébert) and stone reliefs provide likenesses of clerics, explorers, soldiers, and politicians (as well as allegories), representing both founding cultures—from Mère Marie de l'Incarnation and Bishop Laval to James Wolfe and Robert Baldwin. The wife of the Governor General, Princess Louise, recognized the building's Frenchness, and also sensed its expression of Canadian nationalism, when she wrote:

> All this architecture is truly French, with, in addition, a particular character of its own in which the learned, original, distinguished and very Canadian personality of the architect, Mr Eugene Taché, manifests itself.[46]

The building was dramatically sited at the rear of a large landscaped forecourt—which, in the second quarter of the twentieth century, was largely filled with additional government office buildings.

The Second Empire style was also followed in the **New Brunswick Legislative Building [10.18]**, on Queen Street in Fredericton, reflecting the popularity of the style in the Maritimes after the rebuilding of Saint John. The original home of the Assembly, Province House, had come to be seen as 'disgraceful looking and shabby', and brought about calls for a building 'that will be a credit in point of design, elegance and architecture to the province . . . commensurate with the progressing spirit of the age in which we are living.'[47] New Brunswick was the only Atlantic province to become dissatisfied with—and replace—its Georgian legislative building (until Newfoundland did this with the Confederation Building, by A.J.C. Paine and Lawson, Bettes and Cash, 1958-60). The ensuing competition to find an architect selected James Charles Dumaresq (1840-1906), a Nova Scotian practising in Saint John.

10.17 Hôtel du Parlement, Quebec, Quebec, 1877-87. Photograph by Neuville Bazin, 1965. ANQ/E6-7/1207-65.

10.18 New Brunswick Legislative Building, Fredericton, New Brunswick, 1880-2. Photograph by Harold Kalman.

(McKean and Fairweather, the supervising architects for the Saint John Custom House, placed second.) While the designs were out for tender, in February 1880, fire severely damaged Province Hall; this merely reinforced the need for a replacement. Dumaresq's building (1880-2) is similar to (but smaller than) its Quebec counterpart, although its calmer design and less-ornamented surfaces show characteristic British restraint, as do the pedimented frontispiece and the octagonal cupola. The interiors contain some particularly attractive features, including an elegant wooden spiral staircase beyond the octagonal entrance hall, and the Legislative Assembly Chamber, with its overhanging balconies.

The first Manitoba Legislative Building in Winnipeg (1881-3; demolished) also adopted the Second Empire style—not surprisingly, since it was designed by the federal Department of Public Works. J.-P.-M. Lecourt (1824-1913), an architect with the Branch, supervised construction.[48]

Ontario was the next province to build a new legislative building, replacing the Palladian-Georgian structure of 1832 [4.37], which Provincial Architect and Engineer Kivas Tully reported was in 'a dilapidated and dangerous condition'.[49] Tully was instructed to prepare designs for a new building, which he

551

submitted in preliminary form in February 1880, for a magnificent site on Queen's Park, at the head of what is now University Avenue. He proposed a brick building in the Gothic Revival style; his own description revealed that he was still thinking in terms of the Early Gothic Revival and its literal reliance on associationism:

> The buildings have been designed in the Early English or Pointed architecture of the 13th Century when Parliament was first instituted in England. . . . The Grecian or Roman, commonly called the Classic style, is also well adapted for buildings of this description, and is in much favour with the architects of the United States, but it would be found to be much more expensive in construction.[50]

Tully's design met with indifferent response (probably because it was old-fashioned) and the Commissioner of Public Works, C.F. Fraser, called an international competition in April of that year. The High Victorian Gothic design of Toronto architects Darling and Curry was judged the best artistically, although they were not awarded the commission. Tenders for both designs exceeded the budget, so Fraser consulted with Richard A. Waite (1848-1911),

an English-born architect working in Buffalo, New York, who had received commissions in Toronto and Hamilton and had been one of three members of the jury. After Waite pronounced that 'none of the plans was suitable', Fraser appointed him (in January 1886) to prepare drawings for the building. This was a highly unpopular decision that the Toronto architectural profession denounced in unison (to no avail), and was another important factor that spurred them to create a formal professional organization: the Ontario Association of Architects, established in 1889.[51]

The **Ontario Legislative Building [10.19]** was finally built to Waite's design between 1886 and 1892. It is composed of a large central block, containing the Legislative Chamber on an upper floor (Ontario had abolished its upper house) and connected by short arms to a pair of deep wings, which define a courtyard at the rear (north). The south façade, including the *porte-cochères* that project off each side-wing, is a majestic 490 feet (150 m) wide. Each of the individual components is marked by its own steep hipped roof covered in blue slate (since

10.19 Ontario Legislative Building, Toronto, Ontario, 1886-92. Photograph by Bruce Litteljohn.

10.20 Legislative Buildings, Victoria, British Columbia, 1893-7. Photograph by Philip E. Graham, 1982.

replaced); the tall central roof is accompanied by four low-domed cupolas covered with copper, and the roofs over the end pavilions are preceded by gabled wall dormers. All combine to produce a highly picturesque profile, while leading to a measure of fragmentation. The rock-faced red-brown Credit Valley sandstone, quarried a short distance west of Toronto, confers warmth to the building. The inner walls and load-bearing partitions were made of more than 10 million bricks manufactured at the prison on Strachan Avenue.

The principal doors and windows are all contained within the heavy round arches that are the hallmark of the Richardsonian Romanesque style. Begun in the year of H.H. Richardson's premature death—two years before the CPR's Windsor Station [9.9], and three years before Toronto's third City Hall [10.31]—this was the first significant Canadian appearance of the style, which was just then beginning to gain popularity in the US. Waite gave Toronto, and the Ontario government, a showpiece in the latest American architectural fashion, one that in retrospect certainly makes Darling and Curry's High Victorian Gothic design seem outdated. The arches in the central pavilion are supported by clustered colonettes with intricately carved foliated capitals, while those at the ends contain two storeys sepa-

rated by spandrels—the two manners in which Richardson excelled at using arches. The surfaces abound in superb stonecarving. The largest relief composition is the 70-foot-wide (21-m) frieze over the main entrance, and the windows of the Legislative Chamber, depicting allegorical figures of music, agriculture, commerce, and other endeavours, and containing the Great Seal of Ontario in the centre. The spandrels beneath the side-windows of the chambers contain heads of great Ontarians, from Governor Simcoe to Robert Baldwin. Playful grotesques, beasts, and lacy stylized foliage appear everywhere—on columns, arch surrounds, bosses, and gables. The high level of craftsmanship is continued inside in the sumptuous public spaces, from the iron handrail of the great staircase to the beamed ceiling of the Legislative Chamber.[52]

Fire gutted the west wing in 1909, and it was rebuilt under the guidance of architect E.J. Lennox (1855-1933). At the same time a library, designed by George W. Gouinlock (1861-1932), was built within the north courtyard; its fine Romanesque doorway continued the original spirit. The frontispiece, which lies directly on the axis of University Avenue, remains essentially as it was designed by Waite.

The same scale and grandeur appeared in the **British Columbia Legislative Buildings** [10.20], which were being planned just as Ontario's were being completed—to replace the 'Birdcages' [8.27], which the *Colonist* deplored:

Mean and insignificant public buildings are out-ward and visible signs of a sordid, narrow-minded and uncultivated State or Province. Visitors are sure to judge the whole people by the buildings they erect for public uses. Those buildings ought to be handsome as well as commodious.[53]

This comment reflected the general sentiment and provided motivation for a spate of public buildings during the period.

A competition, open to Canadian and American architects, was announced in July 1892 and attract-ed 65 sets of drawings, from which five were short-listed for a second competition. In March 1893 the winner was declared to be Francis Mawson Rattenbury (1867-1935), a young man of 26 who had come to Vancouver from England less than a month before the competition was announced. (Never prone to understatement, Rattenbury presumptuously iden-tified his drawings with the motto 'A B.C. Architect'—which carried little weight with the eastern-Canadian judges, who rendered it as 'A.B.C. Architect'.) Rattenbury had trained in architecture with his uncles, William Mawson (d. 1889) and Richard Mawson (1834-1904), partners in a successful Yorkshire prac-tice that was best known under the name Lockwood and Mawson.

Rattenbury's winning design was for a large build-ing in the shape of a T (or an irregular H), with the 'top' of the T providing the façade (facing north to Belleville Street and the inner harbour) and the stem extending towards the rear and containing the Legislative Chamber. To either side is a freestand-ing block, connected by an open arcade and intend-ed for the Printing Office on the right and the Land Registry Office, although the latter was used instead as the Provincial Museum (which, since 1968, has occupied its own building nearby). The magnifi-cent round-arched entrance, which might be found on a Romanesque cathedral, features a series of archi-volts (receding concentric mouldings) supported on colonettes, all richly carved. In the spandrels to either side of the arch are niches containing stat-ues of Governor Sir James Douglas and Chief Justice Sir Matthew Baillie Begbie—the two men who were credited with bringing British rule and order to the West Coast. To either side of the entrance rises a tower capped by a small dome (features that are repeated as corner turrets elsewhere across the façade), and above the entrance is a row of arched windows and a row of roundels, all features that were seen on the frontispiece of the Ontario Legislative Building. The Victoria building has many

other Romanesque features as well, but the source and the effect are not Richardsonian or American, so much as Late Victorian British. The central cli-max is most un-Richardsonian: a tall dome set on an octagonal drum some 42 feet (12.8 m) across, on top of which is a cupola and a gilded statue of Captain George Vancouver (by Viennese sculptor and tinsmith Albert Franz Cizek). The dome was a feature of American capitols, seen in many states, as well as in Washington, DC.[54]

The tightly organized and symmetrical horizontal composition—which emphasizes its breadth (the buildings have a combined frontage of about 500 feet, or 150 m), and is given a majestic presence by the central dome and the end pavilions—recalls Late Victorian public buildings in London. Rattenbury's scheme is particularly close to the Imperial Institute in South Kensington (1887-93, all but the tower demolished in 1957)—an appropriate source for a monument to the imperial tradition—which was designed by Thomas E. Collcutt (1840-1924). It had similar round arches, small cupolas, and gabled end pavilions, except that Collcutt's monument termi-nated in a tall tower rather than a central dome. Parallels in composition and detail may be seen as well in the Imperial Institute's neighbour to the south, the Natural History Museum (1873-81) by Sir Alfred Waterhouse (1830-1905), which has similar corner turrets—and (not to be overlooked) in Fuller and Jones's Parliament Building in Ottawa. The Imperial Institute and the Natural History Museum are fine proponents of what is called the Late Victorian Free Style (known in its day as Free Renaissance or Free Classic, and today sometimes confused with the style known as Queen Anne)—a mixture of early English and continental historical sources, combined with sophisticated planning and lively detail. In 1898 the Colonist gamely tried to explain the ingredients of the free-style design of the new Legislative Buildings, describing it as

a combination, or blending into one design of the Romanesque, Classic and Gothic, not a jumble by any means, but an adaptation and modulation to the general effect in a masterly and artistic whole, pleasing to the eye and yet not sacrificing the util-itarian purposes which public departments of busi-ness demand. Seen from a distance the main out-line of the building is classic. . . .[55]

Construction of the British Columbia Legislative Buildings began in 1893 and was completed in 1897—not without some tension between the gov-ernment and its architect over matters of finishes and costs. Rattenbury insisted on—and mostly obtained—a high quality of craftsmanship; he was assisted in this by painter and decorator Victor Moretti. Local materials were used throughout, both as a form of provincial patriotism and to aid the ailing economy, then suffering from a recession. The walls were built of light grey andesite from Haddington Island and the foundations of Nelson Island granite. The bricks and slates were also produced in the province, as were the woods used for both structural members and interior finishing.

The entrance leads to a handsome octagonal rotunda, finished in Tennessee marble, that serves as a circulation hub and provides an exciting view up into the dome, 90 feet (27 m) above. The pendentives feature allegorical representations of the province's four major industries, painted in the 1930s by George Southwell. The Legislative Chamber is finished in green Italian marble and oak. On 21 June 1897, to celebrate Queen Victoria's Diamond Jubilee, the profile was illuminated with a string of 2,500 incandescent lights, and this form of exterior lighting remains in use.

In 1912-15 Rattenbury was commissioned to provide additions that doubled the size of the buildings. The work consisted of a large Legislative Library beyond the Legislative Chamber and a pair of wings, containing departmental offices, extending towards the rear (north) from the end pavilions. The woodcarving in the Library (by Edinburgh-born George Gibson and H.H. Martyn and Company of Cheltenham), and the stained and art glass, are superb.[56] The buildings have undergone no significant changes—other than major restoration and rehabilitation work carried out, in the 1970s, by architect Alan Hodgson.

10.21 Minnesota State Capitol, St Paul, Minnesota, 1895-1904. Library of Congress/usz62-13315.

Rattenbury went on to a distinguished architectural career. Some of his work for the Canadian Pacific Railway has already been noted. Always the eager and confident entrepreneur, his colourful life included ventures into politics and development. It ended tragically with his murder in Bournemouth, England, in 1935—which formed the subject of Terrence Rattigan's play, *Cause Célèbre* (1977), and a television adaptation.

The central dome of the British Columbia Legislature proved to be a potent image, one that reappeared on the legislative buildings that were built in the three prairie provinces in the first two decades of the twentieth century. Alberta and Saskatchewan became provinces on 1 September 1905, and within three years both were constructing new seats of government. Not to be outdone, Manitoba soon replaced its Second Empire building with a newer, larger, and more up-to-date one. The three have much in common: all are grand, domed classical buildings that resemble the American state capitols of the day, and whose planning owes much to the teachings of the École des Beaux-Arts. The architects represented three different nationalities—the US, Canada, and Britain respectively—showing that the style and vocabulary of their buildings went beyond national boundaries.[57]

Alberta was first off the mark. Rattenbury was invited to Edmonton in January 1906 and apparently was offered the job of architect of the Alberta Legislative Building, but he agreed only to provide a design, not to supervise the work, and consequently went home empty-handed.[58] Edward C. Hopkins (1857-1941) was appointed architect of the Department of Public Works in March, and two months later he submitted a proposal that was reported to be 'similar to the British Columbia Parliament Building'.[59] Minister of Public Works W.H. Cushing rejected this, and a subsequent scheme by Hopkins, and looked instead for an appropriate architectural source in the United States. In January 1907 he

> made a trip to Minnesota and Wisconsin where he visited the state capitol buildings at St Paul and Madison to get new ideas regarding the proposed buildings for Alberta.[60]

These were the nearly completed **Minnesota State Capitol [10.21]** built in 1895-1904 by Cass Gilbert (1859-1934) in St Paul, a city that had played an important supply role in the development of the Canadian Prairies; and the new Capitol that was just then under construction in Madison, Wisconsin (by George P. Post and Son, 1906-17). Both were landmarks of the new Beaux-Arts Classicism. So impressed was Cushing with the Minnesota Capitol that he convinced Premier A.C. Rutherford to visit it later that year. The relentless classical vocabulary and monumental domes of the two buildings owed their concept to the US Capitol in Washington and its many derivatives in the states, but they also introduced a more modern and sophisticated rigour of planning and composition associated with the teachings of the École des Beaux-Arts in Paris.

That famous school taught a method (not a style) of design. It offered the student instruction in the academic principles of design, as well as supervised work in the *atelier* of a teacher-architect. Emphasis was placed on bringing together the plan, the interior spaces, and the exterior volumes into a unified and clearly expressed whole. The architecture of the past was used to provide instruction and inspiration for the buildings of the present. While the products of the school—seen particularly in the competitions for the coveted Grand Prix de Rome—were most often treated in a classical vocabulary, the historical sources varied considerably, as did the degree of ornamentation, depending on the intended purpose of the new design.[61]

A third, and equally important, American source for the Alberta Legislative Building was introduced by another means. A new design was submitted in the summer of 1907 by a recently arrived member of the Public Works staff, Allan Merrick Jeffers (1875-1926), a native of Rhode Island who had received his training in Providence. Jeffers' preliminary drawings showed that he was familiar with the new Rhode Island State Capitol in Providence (1895-1905), another building of the same type, which was designed by McKim, Mead and White, the New York firm that was arguably most responsible for introducing Beaux-Arts values to North America. Henry-Russell Hitchcock and William Seale, the historians of the American state capitols, have declared:

> The Capitols of Minnesota and Rhode Island . . . became important models which were never really copied, but which loomed behind every other project of that kind for a whole generation. If any American capitols ever represented the high style of their period, it is these two.[62]

History has shown that Cushing and Jeffers chose their models well.

The Alberta government consulted a number of outside professionals, the most important of whom was Percy Erskine Nobbs, professor of architecture at McGill University, who noted that Jeffers' design 'is an excellently worked out example of the "Academic Style" [the Beaux-Arts style] of work so popular just now in the United States', and that it has been 'carried to its perfection in France', though

> it has two drawbacks to lay against its stately grandeur. (1) It is thoroughly non-British in feeling, the English tradition of classical architecture being far more sincere, freer and bolder and consequently more elastic in treatment. The design prepared is precisely the class or work to be found in every state in the Union and every Republic in South America . . . . (2) The French Academic style is essentially an expensive one in which to design, the relation between actual utility space as against passages, halls, stairs, walls etc. being rarely better than two to one.
>
> The modern Free Classic evolved for English Public Buildings and sometimes called the Anglo-Classic or Imperial Style has this to recommend it: that it has distinctive national character while the planning can be far freer and closer than in Academic work, the proportion of used to non-used space being rarely less than three to one, a very decided advantage where economy is to be considered. I would suggest that your architects devote some attention to English models of public buildings with which they are I believe quite unfamiliar.[63]

Nobbs therefore criticized Jeffers' design on grounds of nationalism and economy. In citing the 'modern Free Classic' style, he was recommending the very manner that had been used by Rattenbury in Victoria. The distinction between English and French Renaissance sources provided a very real issue at the time, though it may seem moot to our own distant eyes.

Jeffers responded to these comments with a number of changes. Among them were the removal of the colonnade around the drum of the dome (seen at the Rhode Island and Wisconsin Capitols, as well as in Washington), and its replacement with an octagonal drum pierced with windows that are capped by broken pediments and separated by brackets that rest on a balustrade. Another amendment was the removal of low dome-like lanterns from the roofs of the east and west (side) wings, similar to those on the Minnesota and Rhode Island Capitols (where each covers one of the legislative chambers), and the use of a lantern instead over Alberta's single chamber in the rear (south) wing. These changes notwithstanding, the building still looks very much like an American state capitol.

10.22 Alberta Leglislative Building, Edmonton, Alberta, 1908-13. PAA/Alfred Blyth Collection/BL.1196.

In the final design for the **Alberta Legislative Building** [10.22], the plan is T-shaped, with the entrance—marked by a free-standing six-column composite portico—facing north. The three-storey elevations are treated as a rusticated and arcaded basement with the two floors above united by giant columns, some paired and some single, at the end pavilions. A continuous parapet runs around the roof. The steel structure is clad in warm buff sandstone, some quarried near Calgary and the rest from Ohio, with the lower storey of colder white granite. The rear wing looks out towards the high banks of the North Saskatchewan River. The Legislative Building occupies a superb property along the river that had been the site of the Hudson's Bay Company's Fort Edmonton—which the government purchased in 1906 for both its prominence and its history. (The buildings of Fort Edmonton have been reconstructed on parkland west of the city.) Construction began in 1908. The Legislative Assembly first sat there in November 1911, and work was completed two years later.

By that time construction was finished as well on the **Saskatchewan Legislative Building** [10.23] in Regina, which is similar in many respects to the Edmonton building. The government purchased a 168-acre (67-hectare) site on the south side of Wascana

Creek, just south of the city, and invited landscape architect Frederick G. Todd to lay out the grounds. Premier Walter Scott, who was also the Minister of Public Works, offered the commission to Toronto architect John M. Lyle, recently returned from the École des Beaux-Arts; but Lyle refused. Scott also met with Rattenbury; then decided to hold a limited competition, and asked Percy Nobbs to serve as adviser. Seven architects were invited: one each from the US and Britain, one from Saskatchewan, and the other four from elsewhere in Canada. The American architect was Cass Gilbert, designer of the Minnesota State Capitol, which Scott described as 'one of the really successful buildings on this continent.'[64] Despite the presence of two Americans on the jury (the third was Nobbs), the winner, selected in December 1907, was the Montreal firm of Edward and W.S. Maxwell. Edward Maxwell (1867-1923) had trained in Boston with Shepley, Rutan and Coolidge, the successors to H.H. Richardson; his brother William Sutherland Maxwell (1875-1952) had spent two years at the École des Beaux-Arts, working in the *atelier* Pascal. Together they offered a wealth of experience and talent, and they quickly rose to the top of their profession.[65]

Almost predictably, the winning scheme offered a monumental and symmetrical classical building dominated by a central dome. All but one of the submissions were in a classical mode, drawing in varying degrees on the English Baroque and/or American-French Beaux-Arts Classicism; remarkably, the only exception was provided by Cass Gilbert, who submitted a Gothic-inspired design (probably to distance the building from the American capitols the Canadians sought to emulate!). The Maxwells described their design as 'a free adaptation of English Renaissance work . . . that marks it unmistakably as representative of the British sovereignty under which the Province is governed.'[66] They took the American type and gave it a measure of British character with the details of its dome, pavilions, and other features. The plan is cruciform; the longer arm, which extends 542 feet (165 m), contains departmental offices, and the shorter arm projects forward with the entrance, has the Legislative Chamber and library at the rear, and an elegant rotunda at the crossing, capped by the 183-foot (56-m) dome. The hybrid structural system adopted steel for the Legislative Chamber, reinforced concrete for the office wings, and load-bearing exterior masonry walls. Above the granite basement the walls are faced with cream-coloured fossil-rich Tyndall limestone from Manitoba. (Nobbs had recommended brick with stone trim, but Scott retorted: 'Our buildings would be cheapened in appearance by the use of red brick; they are to be entirely of stone.')[67] Construction began in 1908 and was completed in 1912, but not before it was damaged by a tornado in June of that year. The building is set in lovely Wascana Park (see **12.8**).

The third (and last) of the Prairie landmarks, also dominated by a tall dome and classical columns, was the **Manitoba Legislative Building [10.24]** in Winnipeg, erected in 1913-20. Not to be outdone by its neighbouring provinces, Manitoba held a competition that was open to British subjects (including Canadians) and selected Francis L. Worthington Simon (1862-1933) of England, another former student at the École des Beaux-Arts. (The Maxwells competed without success.) Planned in the form of an H, the building is richly decorated with allegorical sculpture and the dome is topped with the famous 'Golden Boy', a statue that represents eternal youth and the spirit of enterprise.[68]

Thus was Canada left with a truly impressive series of provincial legislative buildings that expressed

10.23 Saskatchewan Legislative Building, Regina, Saskatchewan, 1908-12. Watercolour by Edward Maxwell, 1911. National Gallery of Canada/306.

10.24 Manitoba Legislative Building, Winnipeg, Manitoba, 1913-20. Travel Manitoba.

both patriotic sentiments and provincial pride. The surface ornament drew upon a range of fashionable styles, yet the underlying compositions and plans remained remarkably consistent. All seem to pay homage to the first and grandest legislative building of the Victorian era, the Parliament Building in Ottawa, while the immediate inspiration for their Romanesque and classical vocabularies came from the US. Ultimately, however, they reflected political ties to Britain, just as had the Georgian legislatures of the pre-Victorian age; and a somewhat unexpected homogeneity was thereby established among all the provinces.

Municipal buildings

Municipalities across the country have left an impressive architectural legacy, accommodating their administrative activities as well as the various services and utilities they manage. The basic building is the town (or city) hall; the basic space a room in which the citizens or their representatives can hold regular meetings. In early years the meeting-houses of the dissenting religions often fulfilled this function: the Barrington Meeting House (1765, **3.30, 31**)

was used for town meetings, although before the day of the elected council, as well as religious worship. In Quebec, parish halls sometimes doubled as a *salle des habitants*; an example is the former Parish Hall at Mont-Saint-Hilaire, Quebec (1889). Elsewhere a union hall might be used for town meetings, like the Society of United Fishermen's Union Hall in Newborn, Newfoundland.[69]

During the nineteenth century civic duties passed from appointed magistrates to ratepayers and their chosen officials—in Ontario, for example, this occurred with the Municipal Act of 1849 (known as the Baldwin Act)—leading to a spate of new town and township halls. When communities became incorporated as villages, towns, or cities their responsibilities increased. Since government was only a part-time avocation for the mayor and councillors (and it remains so in the smaller centres), office space might be required for only a part- or full-time administrator or clerk. The architectural response to so simple a program could be very modest: a structure with a single large room, similar in design to a school or a small church. Countless town halls of this kind were built in Ontario and across the country. The **Kenyon Township Hall [10.25]** in Greenfield, Ontario—a rural township that at the time it was built had a population of 4,800, many of them Scottish—is representative. Local resident Lachlin McGillis drew the plans and contractor Roderick McMillan built it in 1862. It is a simple stone building, 30 feet (9.2 m) by 45 feet (13.7 m), with the entrance in the gable end. The interior was treated as a single hall, with its ceiling 15 feet (4.6 m) high. (The dimensions in the ratio of 1:2:3 may follow a Georgian tradition of using simple mathematical proportions in building design.) A raised platform (for the council) was located at the east end and a bench was placed around the other three walls. After a fire in 1895 a small room was enclosed at one side of the platform; in 1966 further spaces were partitioned off.[70]

Similar in approach, although one-third smaller (20 by 30 feet, 6.1 by 9.2 m) and built of wood, was the **Municipal Hall in Surrey Centre [10.26]**, British Columbia, built in 1881, two years after the incorporation of this settlement across the Fraser River from New Westminster. Local carpenters W.J. Brewer and H.G. Ballson built the hall, giving it a wood frame with board-and-batten cladding. Sited near the church and school, it was used by a number of community groups, including the Orange Order (which built its own hall nearby in 1891) and the Agricultural Society. The expanding District of Surrey soon outgrew the single-room building and replaced it in 1912 with a two-storey municipal hall with separate offices for each of the various municipal services. The old town hall was subsequently used as an exhibition building, then was moved to become a component of the Surrey Centennial Museum and Archives.[71]

Community social activities and growing municipal services were two factors that brought an end to the one-room town hall; a third was civic pride. In addition to accommodating administrative needs, many town halls provided space for other functions, often including an auditorium, the fire department, the police department, and jail cells. Following British precedent, markets were often combined with town halls in Ontario—we saw this, for example, at the Kingston City Hall [4.41]. The auditorium (or, as it was often called, the opera house) was used for community meetings and cultural performances and was placed on the second storey, separate from the council chamber. Town functions were sometimes combined with those of the county, as in the restrained

Second Empire County Court House and Town Hall at Lunenburg, Nova Scotia (by Henry F. Busch, 1826-1902, built in 1891-2).[72]

Pride drove many councils to plan prominent landmarks that would give physical expression to their ambitions. Numerous municipalities of only moderate size built town halls that were large in comparison to their population. The most absurdly overscaled was **Victoria Hall [10.27]** in Cobourg, Ontario, designed by Kivas Tully and built in 1856-60. Fanned by ambition, inspired by competition with St Lawrence Hall [12.17] in Toronto and Kingston City Hall—Cobourg lies midway between the two cities—and permitted easy credit by the province's Municipal Loan Fund, the town fathers included in the building program the county courts and offices, a concert hall, a Masonic hall, a bank, and considerable commercial rental space (although they omitted the market). They produced a splendid classical monument, with nearly an acre (0.4 hectare) of floor space, but it far exceeded the town's finances: the building quickly became—and remains—a heavy financial burden. Like the Kingston City Hall, it represents the transition from Georgian Classicism to Neoclassicism, retaining the compositional elements of the former but augmenting them with more classical detail, a picturesque roofline, and a plastic treatment of the façade that achieves a lively play of light and shade.[73]

Multi-purpose town halls began to proliferate, particularly in Ontario. One of the earliest was the Town Hall at Perth, designed by John Power (1816-82) and built in 1863-4, which included a market, a public hall, a fire station, a lock-up, and a band room, in addition to the town offices and the council chamber. Most town halls used the styles current in the region, and at the time. High Victorian Gothic was adopted at the beginning of our period in the Town Hall (1872-4) at Belleville, Ontario, by John Forin (1826-1901). Towards the end of the period the Tudor Revival—which was very popular in British Columbia, particularly for houses—is seen in the second municipal hall at Surrey, BC, built in 1912 to designs by C.H. Clow (1860-1929).[74]

Many towns erected large buildings that may not have been as large as Cobourg's but nevertheless would seem to have stretched their resources. St Marys, Ontario, a community with a remarkable collection of stone architecture, was one of many that sought to impress with size, even though it had only 3,500 residents. In 1889 fire destroyed the two-storey frame town hall and market building (built in 1865)— an event described by a historian of the time as 'a

10.25 *(top)* Kenyon Township Hall, Greenfield, Ontario, 1862. Photograph by Dana Johnson, 1978. PC.

10.26 *(above)* Municipal Hall, Surrey Centre, British Columbia, 1881. Photograph 1918. Surrey Museum and Archives/ 91.2.01.

10.27 Victoria Hall, Cobourg, Ontario, 1856-50. Photograph 1990. PC Heritage Recording Services.

merciful interposition of Providence'—providing an opportunity for a fitting monument. Dr Mathieson, chairman of the building committee, was speaking for the councillors of many communities when he described what he wanted for the new **St Marys Town Hall**:

> We should not adopt a florid style of ornamentation, but yet we should not erect a perfectly plain building simply because it is cheaper. The ornamentation should be of a lasting and permanent character. We are not building a hall or market for now, but for years or generations to come.[75]

The committee retained Toronto architect G.W. Gouinlock, who used Romanesque forms and rusticated limestone to give 'lasting and permanent character' to the building, which was erected on Queen Street East in 1890-1. The robust extravaganza is seen in a photograph of 1899 [10.28] behind the spray produced by the town's firemen, who are demonstrating the new high-pressure municipal water system. A lofty central gable with a stepped profile is flanked on one side by a tall square corner tower, with a lantern and a flagpole perched atop its root, and on the other by a lower round turret. A multi-arched portico provides one entrance, and there is a secondary entry along the side at the left. Decorative stonework above the windows adds to the texture and the overall picturesqueness. In addition to the council chamber and offices for the mayor and four salaried staff, the building contained the

fire and police departments, a police court, and on the second floor a large auditorium, with a stage and balcony. The performance hall was built even though St Marys already boasted a fine turreted High Victorian Gothic Opera House (by Weekes and Smyth of London, 1879-80), because by now an auditorium was expected to be part of the town hall of every aspiring community. The town was certainly over-supplied with cultural facilities, and as a result the Opera House spent most of the twentieth century as a flour mill. (It was recently adapted as residential suites.)

The auditorium idea spread across the country, although nowhere was it as widely used as in Ontario. Prince Albert, Saskatchewan, built a combination town hall and 'opera house' as early as 1891.[76] The *Western Municipal News* published an article in 1908 recommending a standard **'design for a small town hall'** [10.29]. The central feature of the interior is an auditorium with a stage and two small dressing-rooms on the ground floor; the office of the mayor or reeve is also situated on that level. The second floor contains the council chamber and the office of the clerk-treasurer, and the municipal telephone exchange is accommodated in the basement. Brick walls and stone trim are recommended as the materials for the gable-roofed building, which is dressed up with corner pilasters and a classical porch. Several municipal halls in Saskatchewan, including those in Strathclair and Perdue, adopted this general arrangement.[77]

Most large cities erected monumental municipal halls, following the example of Europe.[78] The administrative and community needs of cities were obviously far greater than those of towns, as was the determination to make a good show. City halls, like legislative buildings, understandably followed the latest architectural fashions. In the 1870s the Second Empire style was popular, as it had been for federal and provincial buildings. Saint John (McKean and Fairweather, 1877-9), Ottawa (Horsey and Sheard, 1874-7; demolished), and Victoria (John Teague, 1878-91) all adopted the style in that decade.[79] The **Hôtel de Ville** [10.30] in Montreal was the finest of the group, built in 1872-8 to designs by Henri-Maurice Perrault (1828-1903) and Alexander C. Hutchison (1838-1922). The architects allegedly modelled their design on the Hôtel de Ville in Paris, a sixteenth-century building that was extensively restored and enlarged in 1837-49 (and then rebuilt after being burned during a political insurrection in 1871). The Montreal building may be the most perfect Canadian expression of the Second Empire style, reflecting the best of contemporaneous buildings in both France and the US. The central pavil-

10.28 St Marys Town Hall, St Marys, Ontario, 1890-1. Photograph 1899. St Marys District Museum.

10.29 Design for a small town hall. Manitoba Legislative Library/*Western Municipal News*, March 1908.

10.30 Hôtel de Ville, Montreal, Quebec, 1872-8.
NAC/C16468.

ion contains a masterly build-up of forms, progressing from a staircase to a two-storey pedimented portico, and a multi-tiered square stage above that culminates in a tall square dome with complex dormers (containing clocks) and capped by a square tier with open arches and iron cresting. The wedding-cake effect recurs in reduced form in the end pavilions. The connecting wings have two arcaded storeys over a rusticated basement and the *de rigueur* mansard roof and iron cresting. Much of the interior was devoted to ceremonial uses: halls, reception rooms, staircases, and other spaces commonly thought of as being non-productive but were essential to a building that was in the French tradition of grand public architecture. In the photograph the building is seen in its urban context, facing Place Jacques-Cartier, the old city's most important public square, and its market—continuing the association of city halls and markets. At the left is the Nelson Column (page 304).[80]

The Hôtel de Ville suffered a major fire in 1922 that left only its exterior walls standing. It was rebuilt in 1922-6 to designs by Louis Parant (1890-1958) and J.-L.-D. Lafrenière (1874-1929) of the city's staff, augmented by a half-dozen prominent consulting architects. The image of the existing building was so powerful that the walls up to the cornice were retained and restored. Above the cornice everything is new. An independent steel frame within the walls supports an additional storey and a high mansard roof (containing two more floors) that dwarfs the restored roofs of the pavilions; a slender cupola with open arches rises above the entrance.

The Richardsonian Romanesque entered city-hall design in the late 1880s as it had with other building-types. We have already seen in Calgary City Hall [9.64] a relatively late example of the manner. The prototype, and for many years the largest municipal building in Canada, was **Toronto City Hall** (1889-99), the city's third [10.31]. The immense scale of the building—it consists of a four-storey-high quadrangle around an open central courtyard—reflects the combination of municipal and county offices, the growing complexity of civic administration, and

10.31 Old City Hall, Toronto, Ontario, 1889-99. City of Toronto Archives/sc587-19.

the desire of Toronto's politicians to express the strength of their growing metropolis (then a city of 150,000 people, second in population only to Montreal). A competition for the design of a courthouse was announced late in 1884, and it was several years before the building program had expanded to include a city hall and before the winner emerged: Toronto-born and Toronto-trained Edward James Lennox (1855-1933). Costs expanded along with the functions, from $200,000 (for the courthouse) to an eventual $2.5 million. But Mayor John Shaw justified the expense at the official opening, delivering what may be taken as a hyperbolic apology suited to all splendid public edifices:

Why people will spend large sums of money on great buildings opens up a wide field of thought. It may, however, be roughly answered that great buildings symbolize a people's deeds and aspirations. It has been said that, wherever a nation had a conscience and a mind, it recorded the evidence of its being in the highest products of this greatest of all arts. Where no such monuments are to be found, the mental and moral natures of the people have not been above the faculties of the beasts.[81]

Dominated by a tall, off-centre clock-tower that rises beside the triple-arched entrance, and stands directly on the axis of Bay Street, the heart of the city's financial power, Toronto's Old City Hall (as it is now called) is certainly a landmark. (The quadrangular plan and tower of the City Hall are indebted to a parallel monument designed by Richardson: the much-imitated Allegheny County Courthouse and Jail

(1884-8) in Pittsburgh.) Pink rock-faced blocks of Credit Valley stone and New Brunswick stone (both sandstones) in shades of russet and beige, enlivened by many carved surfaces, combine to soften and enrich the building's monumental appearance. The repeated arches, the use of the arch-and-spandrel motif, the towers, and the intricately carved ornament all follow the Richardsonian Romanesque, whose Toronto début had occurred a few years earlier with the Ontario Legislative Building. The richness is continued inside, where there is an enormous stained-glass window by Robert McCausland, along with murals painted by George A. Reid and fine detailing in wood, iron, bronze, and marble. The building was threatened with demolition in the 1960s in the first plans for the Eaton Centre [**15.72, 73**], but public protest led to its preservation.

The Late Victorian free style also had its municipal champions: for example, the City Hall in Charlottetown, PEI (by L.J. Phillips, 1839-1904, and C.B. Chappell, 1857-1931, built in 1887-8), which has been allowed to deteriorate and is only a shadow of its former self.[82] The most celebrated example of the style, however, was the former Winnipeg City Hall (1884-6; **7.37**).

A separate building-type that many towns and cities (and their agencies) erected during this era was the exhibition building on municipal fair grounds, used for annual agricultural displays and other shows. The ultimate source for late-nineteenth century North American buildings of this kind was the Crystal Palace, built by Joseph Paxton (1803-65) in London's Hyde Park for the Great Exhibition of 1851. A hybrid between a greenhouse (Paxton was trained as a landscape designer) and a train shed, it encouraged the building of

10.32 Aberdeen Pavilion, Ottawa, Ontario, 1898. Photograph by Harold Kalman, *c.* 1982.

countless large glass-and-metal or glass-and-wood structures around the country. Many—such as the iron-framed one in Montreal (J.W. Hopkins, 1866), the wood-framed ones in Hamilton's Victoria Park (Albert H. Hills, 1860) and Picton's Prince Edward County Fairgrounds (1887), and the replacement in 1878 by Strickland and Symons of Toronto's Palace of Industry in the new Exhibition Grounds—were called Crystal Palaces; others bore a variety of names.

One of the most impressive of the exhibition buildings, and a rare survivor of its era, is the **Aberdeen Pavilion [10.32]** in Ottawa, commonly known as the Cattle Castle because of the livestock that have been exhibited in it during the annual Central Canada Exhibition. Designed by architect Moses C. Edey (1845-1919) and built in 1898, its steel trusses achieve a remarkable clear span of 133 feet (40.5 m), and reach a height of 74 feet (22.4 m) through the use of a three-hinged arch, in which pins allow the arches to pivot at the apex and the bases. This innovative structural system had been adopted for the Galérie des Machines at the Paris Exposition of 1889 (where the span was an incredible 377 feet, or 115 m). In the Aberdeen Pavilion, thirteen of these arches, placed side by side, create an overall length of 309 feet (94.7 m). The exterior is enclosed with pressed-metal panels and glass panes to create a light and elegant space. The no-nonsense functionality of the structure is somewhat disguised—one might say compromised—by the persistently classical exterior decoration. The ends exhibit turrets and Palladian windows, the side-entrances are marked with frontispieces reminiscent of Renaissance church façades, and the centre is crowned by a large dome. The inspiration for this vocabulary was certainly the classical buildings of the World's Columbian Exposition in Chicago (1893), the single architectural event on the American continent most responsible for promoting classical and Beaux-Arts values (see page 651).[83] The Aberdeen Pavilion was restored by the City of Ottawa in 1993-4; the architect was Julian S. Smith.

The Architecture of Business and Commerce

Commercial architecture came into its own in the second half of the nineteenth century with the rapid growth of the mercantile sector. Retail stores, warehouses, banks, and office buildings emerged as discrete building-types. Many followed the prevailing architectural styles, yet developed in a way that was unique to their respective functions. Commercial buildings grew increasingly large and more elaborate as the business community became more affluent and downtown land values rose. Some served as a laboratory for the development of new structural materials and techniques.

Stores and warehouses

Although the regulated separation of land use, known as zoning, is a child of the twentieth century, retail stores became increasingly concentrated and segregated in business districts in the nineteenth century. In the larger cities, the principal commercial thoroughfare (often known as King or Queen Street) would be lined with buildings three or four storeys high—about as high as a person could comfortably climb in the pre-elevator era—with shops on the ground floor and storage, offices, or residential suites above. In smaller centres buildings might have only two floors, with the proprietor often living over the shop.

Until about 1860 the predominant type featured rows of square-headed windows on the upper floor, larger display windows on the ground floor, and a gently sloped gabled roof with a straight eave along the façade. A photograph of **Princess Street [10.33]** in Kingston, Ontario, taken around 1863, shows a harmonious row of commercial buildings (most constructed between the 1830s and 1850s), all with wood-and-canvas awnings protecting the sidewalk from the weather. The exterior walls were built of stone, the predominant building material in Kingston, but in other cities they might be brick or wood, depending on local custom. The effect was ordered and somewhat dour, a variant of the Georgian domestic and public architecture of the day.

The advent of Victorian eclecticism animated commercial building in the years just before Confederation. The predominant style was the Victorian Italianate, which we have seen in the Rithet Building **[8.24]** in Victoria, begun in 1861. The style is a free adaptation of Italian Renaissance and post-Renaissance forms characterized by windows with round- and segmental-arched heads and decorated surrounds, often with a horizontal course between storeys and an elaborate cornice at the top. A particularly impressive group in the style was built on **Granville Street [10.34]** in Halifax immediately after a disastrous fire in September 1859 that destroyed more than two city blocks in the heart of the city's wholesale and retail district. Many property owners

10.33 Princess Street, Kingston, Ontario. Photograph *c.* 1863. NAC/PA62177.

took advantage of the opportunity for co-ordinated redevelopment. Six dry-goods merchants combined their outlets under one roof and commissioned the firm of William Thomas and Sons to design the 12-bay-wide Palace Buildings (1859-60) on the west side of Granville Street, north of Duke Street; the same architects subsequently designed no fewer than six other smaller buildings on both sides of the block, ensuring a uniformity of scale and design. The English-born William Thomas (1799-1860) had established a successful practice in Toronto in the 1840s. His became probably the first architectural firm in Canada to have a branch in a second city when his son and partner Cyrus Pole Thomas (1833-1911) opened the Halifax office in 1858; four years later (after the post-fire rebuilding had slowed down) C.P. Thomas moved to Montreal, where he was soon joined by his brother, William Tutin Thomas (1829-92; see page 598).[84]

The 1870 photograph of part of the east side of Granville Street shows the variety of arched Italianate window treatments on seven buildings, all of them four storeys high and most built in 1860. All contained retail shops on the ground floor, and the upper floors were primarily used for wholesale storage. The

building at the extreme left, a warehouse built for Duffus and Company, has narrow round-arched openings at street level, and upper-level windows with stilted segmental-headed arches and heavily moulded heads. On its right, also built for Duffus, the building containing two retail stores has pairs of arched windows separated by slim colonettes, a Venetian feature. The Thomas firm designed it and the three-bay building beyond, erected for dry-goods merchant J.B. Bennett. The latter has round-headed arches separated by attached columns, derived from the Renaissance buildings of Rome. The voussoirs over the windows bear wonderful carved heads. Thomas also designed the six-bay-wide structure with a similar elevation near the right of the photograph, built for William J. Coleman.

Just beyond the Bennett block is a particularly interesting building, distinguished by the semicircular arch that fills the second storey, whose glass originally bore the name English Shoe Store. Built for W.G. Coombs by P.J. Boris of Halifax, it has a façade that is made entirely of cast-iron components—simulating stone and some of it with fine classical detail—that were fabricated by the Architectural Iron Works in New York. The foundry was established by Daniel Badger (1806-84), a leader in the promotion and manufacture of architectural cast iron, who had been developing the technique

Building the Young Dominion

since the 1840s. C.P. Thomas was aware of Badger's products and visited the New York plant in February 1860. Most Thomas-designed buildings used cast-iron store fronts in the form of decorative columns and ornate entablatures that permitted the walls to be opened up on the ground floor to provide large display windows. All these buildings were otherwise conventional, with brick bearing-walls at the sides and rear, stone façades (above the ground floor), and timber beams, joists, and floors.[85]

In an imaginative and successful adaptive re-use, the upper floors of most of the buildings on the east side of Granville Street (as well as several buildings nearby on the waterfront) have become classrooms and studios of the Nova Scotia College of Art and Design. Those on the west side of Granville, including the Palace Buildings, were dismantled in 1977

10.34 Granville Street, Halifax, Nova Scotia. Photograph *c.* 1870. PANS/N-450.

and their façades rebuilt as a part of the Barrington Inn.[86]

In the 1860s, and the two subsequent decades, commercial buildings of a similar character were built across the country. Entire city blocks were often filled with rows of them—all built individually, but achieving an admirable sense of harmony because of the consistency of their height, scale, and window rhythms. **Victoria Row [10.35]** in Charlottetown, Prince Edward Island, is a superb example. This group of brick shops and offices on Richmond Street, most of them constructed immediately after a fire in 1884, contains a number of separate but perfectly compatible buildings. The building on the left, identified by the triangular and semi-circular bumps on its parapet, was built in 1884-5 by furniture manufacturer and importer John Newson to designs by the talented Charlottetown architect William Critchlow Harris (1854-1913; see page 583). With the stilted segmental arches on the second storey

10.35 Victoria Row, Charlottetown, Prince Edward Island. Photograph 1894. Prince Edward Island Public Archives and Records Office/PARO3218/28.

and the flat-headed windows above, it offers a tranquil version of the Victorian Italianate style. Beyond it is the Morris Block, built a few years later, in 1890, and therefore showing the influence of the Richardsonian Romanesque with its broad top-storey arches. The architects were Phillips and Chappell, designers of the Charlottetown City Hall. Harris designed the broad Cameron Block (1884-5) in the centre, with its three small triangular gables; and Phillips and Chappell the Brown Block (1884-5) beyond, which consists of three separate small buildings. The Stamper Block (1892) at the far corner is also by Phillips and Chappell. The buildings were owned and occupied by merchants, and it is said that three-quarters of the doctors and lawyers in town had their offices here as well.

The row forms an assertive wall that is offset by the attractively landscaped Queen Square Gardens, at the other side of which stands Province House [3.54]. Developed after the 1884 fire and designed partly by Assistant Provincial Secretary Arthur Newbery and partly by William C. Harris and his mentor and partner, David Stirling (1822-87), the gardens had many ornamental features, including the fountain seen in the photograph, which reproduces the one that stood at the time in front of the Parliament Buildings in Ottawa. The landscaping has largely been removed to accommodate the Confederation Centre of the Arts [15.62], but the buildings remain intact.[87]

Other outstanding buildings in the Victorian Italianate style include Winnipeg's Empire Hotel (L-A. Desy, 1882) and the row of commercial buildings

on Princess Street, introduced on pages 360-1. Buildings such as the Benson and Bawlf Blocks in Winnipeg (Barber and Barber, 1882) and those on Granville Street in Halifax were used for storage as well as sales. Most cities developed wholesale districts with warehouses that were well serviced by transportation facilities and set apart from the retail and office districts.

The steady growth and prosperity of Toronto made it inevitable that its commercial activities would require many warehouses. The **John Macdonald Dry-goods Warehouse [10.36]** on Wellington Street East was begun in 1863, at the peak of the High Victorian Gothic, and so it adopted that style with its pointed windows of Venetian descent. As originally built to the designs of Gundry and Langley, the warehouse was five bays wide (at the right in the photograph), and went as high as the corbels above the fourth-floor windows. The addition on the left was erected in 1878 (by Langley, Langley and Burke) and the top storey was added in the twentieth century. The building was demolished in 1965.[88]

One block south, on Front Street, the real centre of warehousing developed because it was closer to the railway and waterfront. A row of Victorian Italianate and Second Empire warehouses, with shopfronts at street level and storage space above, has survived on the south side. The photograph shows the former warehouse of wholesale grocers **Perkins,**

Ince and Company [**10.37**], a double warehouse designed by Frank Darling (1850-1923) and built in 1873. It is notable for its groupings on each floor of very different window treatments and for its crowning glory, a cornice with two semi-circular pediments in pressed metal. Next to it on the right is part of the former Griffiths Building (now the Beardmore Building), designed by David Roberts, Jr, and built in 1871-2. Its three units (partly visible in the photograph) are tied together by rows of arched windows and a high-dormered Second Empire mansard roof. On the ground floor, piers that once divided arched doors and display windows are faced with cast-iron Corinthian pilasters. On the left of the photograph can be seen part of a warehouse—built in 1872-3 for Homer Dixon—whose entire façade is composed of cast-iron components, fabricated by the St Lawrence Foundry in Toronto and believed to have been designed by Strickland and Symons.[89]

Frank Darling enjoyed a long and prolific practice in Toronto. A graduate of Trinity College, University of Toronto, he learned his profession in London in 1870-3 in the offices of G.E. Street and Sir Arthur Blomfield, architect to the Bank of England. When he returned to Toronto, the Perkins, Ince and Co. warehouse was one of his first commissions. Darling had a succession of partners, the most important of whom were S. George Curry (1854-1942), with whom he won the premium (but not the commission) for the Ontario Legislative Building, and the English-born John Pearson (1867-1940). The Royal Institute of British Architects recognized Darling's achievements by awarding him its Gold Medal in 1916. Darling was notable for buildings of great sophistication, including a number of office buildings and banks, building-types that will be examined next.[90]

Office buildings, department stores, and banks

New technologies and old forms Many of the buildings cited in the previous section were non-specialized commercial structures that included some combination of retail, wholesale, and office uses. Victoria Row in Charlottetown and the Empire Hotel (Cauchon Block, **7.38**) in Winnipeg both contained office space; the latter was an important early purpose-built rental office building (although it failed within the year—maybe an indication that it was slightly ahead of its time). By the end of the 1880s the office building had become more common as a

10.36 John Macdonald Dry-goods Warehouse, Toronto, Ontario, begun 1863. Panda Photography Limited.

10.37 Perkins, Ince and Company Warehouse, Toronto, Ontario, 1873. Photograph by William Dendy.

distinct building-type. Some were erected by large business enterprises (many of them insurance companies, which enjoyed prosperity in this era) for their own offices, with or without some additional rental space, whereas others were entirely speculative. In those days before the telephone, office tenants demanded downtown locations near one another on expensive real estate, and so land economics required that property be developed as densely as possible—in other words, that the building be tall. Another incentive necessitating height was egotism: pride (and competition) led corporate builders into a never-ending spiral of trying to be the highest and the biggest, a form of competition that continues a century later.

Two technological developments permitted buildings to grow upwards: the metal structural frame and the elevator. Cast-iron columns had been used in factories in Britain ever since the eighteenth century, and we have seen iron adopted in Canada, as in the Iron Church [8.30] in Victoria and in commercial buildings in Victoria, Halifax, and Toronto. It was not until the end of the nineteenth century, however, that the metal frame became a self-supporting system that could be carried upwards to great heights independently of load-bearing external masonry walls. The breakthrough occurred in Chicago in the mid-1880s, when architects reduced the exterior wall to an envelope (or 'curtain') that was supported by the interior metal frame, and whose function was simply to protect the interior from weather and the frame from fire. The nine-storey Home Insurance Building in Chicago (1884-5), by William Le Baron Jenney (1832-1907)—utilizing cast-iron columns and both wrought-iron and steel beams—is often credited with being the first such 'skyscraper'. It was raised to eleven floors in 1890. In the next few years other architects developed designs that better expressed the skeletal nature of the structure, and rolled steel soon replaced the more brittle iron.[91]

The elevator, for its part, was a slightly earlier invention. Steam-powered hoists had been known for some time, but they were too dangerous to permit use by passengers. Elisha Graves Otis demonstrated the first safe elevator in New York in 1853, and installations of the device began later in that decade. A number of buildings in New York rose to heights of more than 200 feet (60 m) in the 1870s—containing around ten storeys and towers—using elevators and conventional masonry structures, often with internal iron columns and beams. (The limitation of masonry bearing-walls was that they had to be made thick-

10.38 New York Life Insurance Company Building, Montreal, Quebec, 1888. Photograph by Albertype Co., c. 1900. NAC/PA45937.

er and thicker at ground level to support the mass of the building above.)

Until the late 1880s, office buildings in Canada were restricted to five storeys (sometimes with an additional attic), although few rose higher than four. The first 'tall' building in the country was the **New York Life Insurance Company Building** [10.38] in Montreal, built in 1888 to designs by the New York firm of Babb, Cook, and Willard. Senior partners George Fletcher Babb (1836-1915) and Walter Cook (1846-1916) had developed a strong commercial practice, and this was one of several buildings they erected in different cities for the same corporate client. The Montreal building is eight storeys high, with another floor and a clock inserted in a corner tower (which may respond to the towers of the Church of Notre Dame, a few dozen yards away on an adjacent side of Place d'Armes). The floors and roof are supported by steel beams, but they bear on exterior walls of red Scottish sandstone, which are as thick as 40 inches (1 metre) at the base, and so the New York Life Building does not display true skyscraper construction. The principal elevation is organized

10.40 *(below)* Central Chambers, Ottawa, Ontario, 1890-1. Photograph by John Roaf, 1982.

horizontally through the use of entablatures and mouldings at four levels, and vertically by arches that enclose the top three floors and their windows. The arch-and-spandrel motif, which we have seen in the work of H.H. Richardson and his followers, was characteristic not only of Chicago architecture, but also of New York office buildings built earlier in the 1880s by Babb, Cook, and Willard, and others. The stone walls are enlivened by quoins at the corners and beneath the tower, and by arabesque carvings by sculptor Henry Beaumont around the arched doorway, imposts, and spandrels. Although the arches acknowledge the Romanesque manner, and the balustrades and quoins recall classical sources, the New York Life Insurance Building presents a rational and relatively non-historicist design. Fortunately it remains in use.[92]

Not so Canada's other tall office buildings of the late 1880s and early 1890s (many of them also by American architects), which continued the eclecticism that dominated the public buildings of the day, and also continued to use traditional load-bearing masonry walls. The Standard Life Assurance Association Building on rue Saint-Jacques (then known as St James Street) in Montreal (by Richard

Waite, 1886-7; demolished) displayed a series of somewhat clumsy superimposed stages that reached five storeys and was ornamented with richly sculpted classical forms, including two statues over the entrance of Atlas bearing a heavy globe. The Toronto Board of Trade Building (1889-90; demolished), designed after a competition by James and James, English-born architects with offices in Kansas City and New York (and completed under the supervision of J. Francis Brown, 1866-1942), had Gothic-inspired gables over the arched entrances and at the top (sixth) floor high gabled and arched windows that rounded the corner facing the intersection of Front Street East and Yonge Street.[93]

One of the largest commercial buildings of the day, the **Confederation Life Building** [10.39] in Toronto, was originally a romantic Romanesque-Gothic castellated fantasy. Built in 1890-1 at Richmond Street East and Yonge, it had grand arcades on the ground floor, and ogee arches at the fifth and sixth floors, some of them providing caps to tiers of windows. At the centre and corners rose towers with pyramidal roofs and corner turrets, the central tower perforated by traceried windows and enlivened by balconies. Iron was used internally for columns and beams, their loads borne by the walls of red Credit Valley sandstone, some of it beautifully carved, and matching brick. The architects, also selected by competition, were the Chicago firm of Wilm Knox (1858-1915), John Harlock Elliot (c. 1862-1925?), and Edgar Beaumont Jarvis (1864-1948). Their design shows that even architects who practised in architecturally progressive Chicago relied on eclecticism, while at the same time attempting to accommodate new uses and programs. The Confederation Life Building initially contained the company's offices on one side and a department store on the other, but the latter failed as a business and the upper floors were converted entirely to offices around 1899-1900, at which time some of the ground-storey stonework was opened up and replaced with plate-glass display windows for retail shops. The building has been rehabilitated and remains in office use, but the extravagant towers, which were removed earlier, have not been replaced.[94]

Central Chambers (1890-1) in Ottawa, by John James Browne (1837-93, the son of George Browne),

also has a row of gables across the top windows, but these medieval references are entirely subordinated to the expanse of glass [**10.40**]. Bay windows with large plate-glass central panes (which open on a central vertical pivot), flanked by smaller casements, dominate the façades on the oblique corner of Elgin and Queen Streets. Once again, steel beams are supported by masonry walls. (Its five storeys and partial mezzanine were serviced by one of the first electric elevators in Ottawa.) The building was rehabilitated and integrated into a large new development in 1993; the architects were Brisbin, Brook, Benyon. Similar features appeared earlier on Browne's Nordheimer Building, on rue Saint-Jacques in Montreal (1888; rehabilitated in 1989 to become part of the Centre de Commerce Mondiale), but its awkward piers, spandrels, and central gable lacked the finesse of the Ottawa block.[95]

It was a department store and not an office build-

10.41 Robert Simpson store, Toronto, Ontario, 1895. Photograph by Hellmut W. Schade, 1980.

ing that would become the first tall building in Canada to be constructed with a true self-supporting metal frame—what is called skyscraper construction. **The Robert Simpson store [10.41]** in Toronto, taking up a city block at Yonge and Queen Street West, was given credit for this innovation in the year of its construction, 1895, by a local newspaper and the honour has been sustained.[96] A previous Simpson's store had been designed by Toronto-born architect Edmund Burke (1850-1919) and built in 1894 as a structure combining steel, wood, and masonry. Steel was used because it is capable of achieving long spans that could provide the unobstructed space required for effective merchandising. That building was destroyed by fire in March 1895, shortly after its completion. (The columns and beams of the two steel-framed lower storeys had been encased in stone, brick, and terracotta and survived the fire intact, demonstrating that steel and iron were fireproof if protected by masonry in this way.) Robert Simpson immediately commissioned Burke and his new young partner, J.C.B. Horwood (1864-1938), to produce a replacement that was built entirely of a fireproofed steel frame. The steel columns and beams along the outside were covered with brick and stone, and those inside were enclosed in concrete; the floors were concrete slabs. The result was a progressive and austerely handsome non-historical six-storey building whose structural cage-like frame was clearly and rationally articulated on the exterior. The columns are indicated by vertical piers, the beams and slabs by spandrels. The elevation is organized in three portions: a two-storey base, whose entrance arches and other surfaces are richly adorned in ornamented terracotta (like a picture frame around the display windows), a three-storey intermediate portion that is essentially undecorated, and the top storey, whose smaller windows form a stage that leads to the strong cornice. The large expanses of window provided displays on the ground floor and allowed ample light to reach the interior. In 1928-9 a nine-storey wing was added at Bay and Richmond Streets, and in the late 1960s a 32-storey tower was added by John B. Parkin Associates, containing a further addition to the store (now the Hudson's Bay Company) and rental office space.

The reduction of historicist detail to a bare minimum—only the capitals of the lower piers and the cornice allude to the past—puts the Simpson store at the vanguard of North American proto-modernist design. It was built only a few years after the first such Chicago structures, like Jenney and Mundie's Ludington Building (1891), and it precedes by several years so obvious a comparison as Chicago's Carson Pirie Scott Department Store (originally the Schlesinger and Mayer Company, begun 1899), designed by the American architect Louis H. Sullivan (1856-1924).[97] The Toronto architects remained abreast of the most recent developments in New York building as well. Horwood, who had apprenticed with Burke (and Burke's former partner, Henry Langley), had worked in New York in 1892-3, when he wrote detailed letters to his mentor about new structural techniques. He explained, for example, that a steel frame could either be supported by the exterior masonry walls, be self-supporting but independent of those walls, or be self-supporting and also carry the exterior walls. The last is true skyscraper construction, and is the method that Burke and Horwood used in the second Simpson store. Burke himself was aware of the advantages of using thin curtain walls. In a newspaper article written two months before the Simpson's fire, he noted:

> The increased thickness of walls which would be necessitated by [conventional] methods in the erection of a high building would occupy so much valuable floor space and reduce the light to such an extent that the commercial success of the building would be interfered with.

He suggested that only when rising land costs, concerns about fire safety, and the need for long spans and wind bracing became issues would the steel cage come into common use. The opportunity for Burke to use the system arrived sooner than he expected, and the technique became increasingly common.[98]

Department stores and warehouses were the two building-types in which historical ornamental forms were allowed to be reduced or abandoned. The **Daly Building [10.42]** on Rideau Street in Ottawa (by Moses Edey, 1904-5; demolished 1992), initially a department store, used a reductionist design entirely expressive of its steel frame (with concrete-slab floors). Rusticated limestone piers (with vestigial capitals) and thin stone covering on the floor-beams protected the structural members; but they were so thin that it was clear that the stone did not support the building. The space between the structural members was entirely glazed—using the tripartite 'Chicago windows', with wide central lights, that could be seen in the Carson Pirie Scott store, and elsewhere in Chicago. The Daly Building went beyond the Simpson's store in omitting the relatively fancy treatment of the ground floor. The photograph was taken after an addition in 1913 raised the three storeys (four on the east elevation) two more floors and

eight-storey building whose piers and recessed spandrels describe an assertive grid and do not attempt to revive any historical style. Each structural bay is filled with three windows of equal size. The building is framed entirely in heavy timber (except for steel beams in the areaway beneath the sidewalk). Hefty 18-by-18-inch (46-cm) posts support the building in the basement. Each succeeding floor has narrower columns, tapering to 8-by-8 inches (20 cm) at the top. This stalwart building was rehabilitated in 1988 (by Soren Rasmussen) to accommodate retail, office, and hotel uses.[100]

'Progressive' non-historical elevations and the new structural systems evidently did not necessarily go hand in hand, since new forms were used at The Landing (and other warehouses) with traditional wood constructional methods. Old wine was put into new bottles, showing that appearance and structure were based on their own criteria and conditions. The reverse was often true with office buildings, which retained their dependence on the past—particularly after the wave of classicism inspired by the Chicago World's Columbian Exposition of 1893— while embracing the introduction of the new (and more expensive) structural techniques. Ironically, as the 1890s progressed, office design became increasingly historicist.

The transition is seen well in a series of office buildings in Montreal that were designed by Edward Maxwell. This native of Montreal returned home in 1892—after a stint with Shepley, Rutan and Coolidge of Boston (successors to H.H. Richardson)—to supervise construction of that firm's building for the Montreal Board of Trade (1892-3, destroyed by fire), a relatively plain structure dominated by Richardsonian arches and spandrels. Maxwell followed this precedent in his first independent commercial building, a large store and office for jeweller Henry Birks (1893-4), and in the **Bell Telephone Company Building** [10.44] of 1895-7 (demolished). The latter was treated in three stages (as was the Board of Trade), with the arches encompassing the three floors of the middle tier and smaller windows in the rounded corner. The ubiquitous cornice crowned the composition. It is a somewhat more ornate rendition of the Richardsonian warehouse formula—appropriate, since it contained the offices of a prestigious corporation—that was seen in the Ashdown Block [7.40] in Winnipeg, built in the same period.[101]

Maxwell's **London and Lancashire Life Assurance Building** [10.45] on rue Saint-Jacques is far more revivalist in its design, revealing the veil of classi-

10.42 Daly Building, Ottawa, Ontario, 1904-13. Photograph *c.* 1927. NAC/PA155404.

extended the building to the north; this later work used a timber frame.[99]

Warehouse design also discarded arches in favour of a straight trabeated (beamed) design. **The Landing** [10.43], on Water Street in Vancouver, built for wholesale grocers Robert Kelly and Frank Burnett (later Kelly, Douglas and Company), is one of countless such structures across the country. Erected in stages between 1905 and 1910 to designs by Newfoundland-born William Tuff Whiteway (1856-1940), it is an

10.43 The Landing, Vancouver, British Columbia, 1905-10. Photograph by John Roaf, 1973.

cism that had fallen over Canadian and American architects. Built in 1898-9, this seven-storey office building, faced in buff sandstone, is in some respects a throwback to the Second Empire manner. Lavish French Renaissance ornament appears in the heavy pediments and cartouches over the street-level openings, and in the channelled masonry of the ground floor and the higher corner bays, in the bracketed wrought-iron gallery outside the sixth storey, and particularly in the mansard roof (containing the boardroom), with its encrustation of floral and figurative detail. The life-insurance company and a bank occupied the two lower storeys, and the third to sixth floors were rental offices. Edward Maxwell was assisted in the design by his younger brother William (W.S.), who had been working as a draftsman in Boston (where he studied design at the Boston Architectural Club under Professor Constant Désiré Despradelle [1862-1912], a graduate of the École des Beaux-Arts), and was about to leave for architectural studies in Paris.[102]

Classicism remained the guiding principle throughout the building boom that preceded the First World War. The **Dominion Express Building** [10.46] in Montreal—designed by the fertile partnership of Edward and W.S. Maxwell for a company that was associated closely with the Canadian Pacific Railway—is characteristic of tall office buildings across the country. Like the London and Lancashire Life Building, it was situated on prestigious rue Saint-Jacques in the heart of the city's business and financial district. Built in 1910-12 and ten storeys high, it has a steel frame that supports exterior walls of white glazed terracotta—a lightweight, fireproof, and easily moulded clay product. (The ground floor is faced in light-coloured granite.) The elevation is again divided into three units, conceived as a base, a shaft, and a crown. The base, consisting of the ground and first floors, is marked by giant pilasters supporting a cornice, on top of which are perched four larger-than-life-size figures and, at the ends, bronze shields bearing the emblems of the provinces and supported by female figures. The seven intermediate floors are more simply treated, but the ends are emphasized by solid channelled piers, which rise to the top, and by decorative spandrels. Windows are grouped in pairs, except at the ends, where they are in threes. The top floor, originally occupied by the exclusive Montreal Club, is marked by a broad balcony and large segmental-headed windows embellished with decorative foliage, and terminates in a balustrade.[103]

This composition was widely advocated, most

10.44 Bell Telephone Company Building, Montreal, Quebec, 1895-7. From *Canadian Architect and Builder*, September 1897. MTRL.

10.45 London and Lancashire Life Assurance Building, Montreal, Quebec, 1898-9. Photograph by Hellmut W. Schade, 1992.

notably by Louis H. Sullivan, who wrote that 'a three-part division' arose from the very functions of the tall office building.[104] The reliance, in designing office buildings, on classical forms, and the frequent (but by no means universal) use of terracotta, became standard across Canada and characterized what has come to be called the Edwardian Commercial Style—parallel to the Edwardian Classicism that was seen in public buildings of the day. Examples are found in all cities, including those in the West, where many were designed by American architects. The eight-storey Canada Building in Saskatoon (1912-13), and the nine-storey McLeod Building in Edmonton (1913-15), were steel-frame skyscrapers clad in terracotta and brick, and were the tallest in

their cities. Each was built by a local developer (who was also a municipal councillor), who went outside the city to find an architect. The Canada Building was designed by James Chisholm and Son of Winnipeg, the McLeod Building by John K. Dow (1860-1961) of Spokane, Washington.[105]

Similar in composition, but more elegant in treatment, was the attractive **Birks Building** [10.47] in Vancouver, designed for Montreal jewellers Henry Birks and Sons by the Seattle partnership of W. Marbury Somervell (1872-1939) and J.L. Putnam, who established a prosperous Vancouver practice. The Birks store occupied the ground floor and mezzanine; rental offices—once the most desired in town—filled the remainder. Built in 1912-13 (demol-

10.46 Dominion Express Building, Montreal, Quebec, 1910-12. From *Montreal Old and New*, 1915..

10.47 Birks Building, Vancouver, British Columbia, 1912-13. Photograph by John Roaf, 1972.

ished 1974), the structural frame was made of reinforced concrete rather than steel and was covered
with glazed white terracotta on its two façades, with
decorated spandrels and elegant arches gracing the
top-floor windows.[106]

Reinforced concrete—which consists of concrete
(a mixture of cement, sand, and an aggregate, such
as gravel) that is given tensile strength by the insertion of metal bars, wires, or mesh—was just beginning to be used on a non-experimental basis. Non-
reinforced concrete (invented by the ancient Romans,
and very strong in compression) had been used for
some time for foundations (including those at the
Parliament Buildings in Ottawa), for fireproofing
metal, and for some grain elevators; but it had little strength under tension without metal reinforcement. The first building in Vancouver with a
reinforced-concrete frame was the Europe Hotel at
Powell and Carrall Streets. Designed by the partnership of J.E. Parr (1856-1923) and Thomas A. Fee (1859-
1929), it was built by the Ferro-Concrete Construction

Company of Cincinnati, Ohio, which only six years
earlier had built the first tall concrete building in the
world: the 16-storey Ingall's Building.[107]

The earliest reinforced-concrete structure in Canada
was likely the Bell Building (1904) on Granville Street
in Halifax, built to designs by R.A. Johnson (1871-
1949). Located just east (to the right) of the buildings in **10.34**, it is a four-storey building erected for
hardware merchants A.M. Bell and Company and is
now used by the Nova Scotia College of Art and
Design. Concrete was used in the Bell Building for
the exterior walls (left exposed), as well as for the
structure. Subsequent builders discovered that it was
more efficient to limit the reinforced concrete to
columns, beams, and (usually) floor slabs, and to use
lighter, non-bearing materials for the exterior walls.[108]

Department stores—which had led the way in non-
historical design—went classical during this Edwardian

10.48 Hudson's Bay Company store, Vancouver, British
Columbia, begun 1913. Photograph by John Roaf, 1973.

period. The Hudson's Bay Company commissioned nearly identical stores in Vancouver, Victoria, and Calgary from Burke, Horwood and White (the architects of the Simpson's store in Toronto had been joined in practice by Murray A. White [1870-1935]). The **Hudson's Bay Company store in Vancouver [10.48]** was begun in 1913 as an appendage to the company's earlier store, located directly across the street from the Birks Building; subsequent additions in 1925-6 and 1948 brought it to its present size. Above a high pilastered base rise four storeys that are held together by a stately row of giant engaged Corinthian columns; an attic and a balustrade complete the elevation—covered, like the Birks store, with white glazed terracotta. An important precedent for this composition was Selfridges Department Store in London (begun 1907), which was designed by a team of architects that included Daniel H. Burnham of Chicago, the supervising architect of that city's World's Columbian Exposition, and the young American Francis S. Swales (1878-1962), who later worked in Canada for the CPR. Classicism remained the hallmark of Hudson's Bay Company stores for some time, notably in their Winnipeg store (E.I. Barott, 1925-7).[109]

Banks Although many banks simply occupied ground-floor space in an office building—in Montreal, for example, the Bank of Nova Scotia had a branch office in the London and Lancashire Life Assurance Company Building—purpose-built banks differed in design from office buildings until the 1920s, when they too began to contain floor upon floor of rental offices. Previously most bank buildings were intended to accommodate the financial institution alone and to promote the bank by means of a design that conveyed permanence and stability, qualities individuals and corporations look for when deciding where to entrust their money. Indicating the growing social and economic status of banking and bankers, bank buildings became increasingly large and ornate—culminating, of course, in the high-rise towers of our own time.

In his introductory essay to an exhibition of American and Canadian bank architecture, sociologist Robert Nisbet reflected on the physical presence of banks in alluding to the Bank of Montreal's headquarters in Montreal:

. . . one sees at the Place d'Armes in Montreal a telling juxtaposition: on one side the Church of Notre Dame, across from it the Bank of Montreal. Each building conveys a message about the social forces that underlie it. The church institutional-

izes a religion; the bank institutionalizes the concept of the banker as a high priest of finance.[110]

From its founding in 1817 the **Bank of Montreal** was notable for conveying through its architecture images of trustworthiness, permanence, wealth, and eventually power. Its original building, erected in 1818-19 as the first purpose-built bank in Canada, used the restrained vocabulary of Georgian Classicism. This was replaced in 1845-8—when the Bank had attained a position of power and prestige in the country—by a larger and more explicitly classical building [5.52], designed by John Wells. The principal feature of the new building [10.49], which was adjacent to the old one, was a six-column Corinthian portico whose temple-like pediment contains reliefs of allegorical figures and the coat of arms of the bank (executed in Scotland by sculptor John Steele). Among the assembled company are a sailor, a colonist, the muses of music and literature, and two natives—one depicted as the 'noble savage' and the other as rejecting the products of European civilization. Behind the columns is a two-storey façade (a low dome that once rose above it was removed in 1859 when its wooden structure became rotten). The unequivocal classical design has its origins in both Britain and the US, but its source has generally been cited as the Commercial Bank of Scotland in Edinburgh (1844-6) by David Rhind (1808-83): the two buildings are indeed quite similar, especially their porticoes. American banks, however, had also fixed on classical imagery. A general source for the six-column portico and a domed block was the Bank of Pennsylvania in Philadelphia (1798-1800) by Benjamin Henry Latrobe (1764-1820). (Latrobe adopted a similar design for the Roman Catholic Cathedral in Baltimore, 1804-18; both were loosely modelled on the Pantheon in Rome.) The association of classical architecture with banks was indelibly established by the Parthenon-inspired Greek-Revival façade of the Second Bank of the United States, also in Philadelphia (1819-24), by William Strickland (1788-1854).[111]

At the beginning of the twentieth century growth and changing banking needs led to a new building campaign at the Bank of Montreal's head office. Ambitious renovations and additions (1901-5) were designed by McKim, Mead and White of New York, with Andrew T. Taylor (1850-1937) of Montreal serving as the local supervising architect. Taylor, who was the nephew of the vice-president of the bank (and whose firm, Taylor and Gordon, had designed a fine Richardsonian Romanesque branch for the bank at Mansfield and Ste Catherine Streets in 1889),[112] brought the New York architects to the directors' attention. Charles Follen McKim (1847-1909), William Rutherford Mead (1846-1928), and Stanford White (1853-1906), America's leading proponents of Beaux-Arts Classicism, were introduced earlier in this chapter as the architects of the Rhode Island State Capitol. In Montreal they placed a new dome, constructed of light-weight Gustavino tile (a new and popular material in New York), atop Wells's 1840s building, and it was transformed internally into a vestibule and ceremonial entrance leading to a magnificent new banking hall—said to be the largest in the world—which was placed within a new addition to the rear. The

basilica-like hall has walls of pink Tennessee marble between which are two rows of 31-foot-high (9.5-m) columns of green Vermont marble, with bases of black

10.49 *(below)* Head office of the Bank of Montreal, Montreal, Quebec, 1845-8 and 1901-5. Photograph by Brian Merrett, 1989.

10.50 *(right)* Canadian Bank of Commerce, Winnipeg, Manitoba, 1910-12. Photograph by Henry Kalen, 1970. Henry Kalen Limited.

10.51 *(below, right)* Main banking hall, Canadian Bank of Commerce, Winnipeg, Manitoba, 1910-12. Photograph by Henry Kalen, 1970. Henry Kalen Limited.

Belgian marble and solid bronze capitals plated with gold. The exquisitely detailed coffered ceiling is also trimmed with gold. The opulence and scale left no doubt in anybody's mind that the Bank of Montreal was Canada's foremost financial institution.

This was not the Bank of Montreal's first impressive hall. In Toronto, in 1885-6, the Bank replaced its seemingly old-fashioned Main Branch at Yonge and Front Street West, built in 1845 to designs by Kivas Tully—a handsome three-storey building that looked like a London mansion or club, as had the first bank in Montreal—with an even more splendid building. For it, Darling and Curry created a large square hall, with a coffered ceiling rising two storeys to a domed skylight of stained glass. The classical exterior echoes the portico of the Montreal bank, with pilasters and pediments on the two façades and a chamfered entrance bay between them. No longer in use as a bank, the building has been incorporated into a new development by Bell Canada Enterprises. The façade now marks the Hockey Hall of Fame, which is mainly underground, in BCE Place.[113]

The head office of the Bank of Montreal attracted a great deal of attention, some of it favourable, some critical. Percy Nobbs, who was not an admirer of the American Beaux-Arts manner (as we have seen), poked fun at it during the renovations by describing the astonishment of the ghost of a gargoyle, who left his perch on the Church of Notre-Dame to investigate the bank, then under construction, and assumed ' . . . that it was here the men of Montreal did their real worship and he concluded that the God must be very great to be worthy of so fine a temple.'[114] Years later, a mellower Nobbs said that McKim, Mead and White ' . . . showed Canadians for the first time, on their own soil, what modern classic [architecture] and planning in the grand manner really meant.'[115]

Not only the Bank of Montreal, but Canada's other chartered banks responded by erecting grand limestone-and-marble piles in cities across the country. Winnipeg was particularly blessed with a group of grand classical temples along its 'Bankers' Row' on Main Street, as the eastern banks rushed to the city to attract a share of the booming prairie business. The Bank of Montreal once again retained McKim, Mead and White as its architects, and the Winnipeg bank (1910-13) presents a row of tall Corinthian supports along each of its façades (columns on Portage Avenue and pilasters on Main Street): in Beaux-Arts splendour it was second only to its Montreal head office. The Royal Bank of Canada also retained a New York firm, Carrère and Hastings (architects of the

10.52 Merchants Bank of Canada (now Brandon Public Library), Brandon, Manitoba, 1907. Manitoba Culture, Heritage and Citizenship, Historic Resources.

New York Public Library); its narrow bank (1909-12) has a relatively restrained façade on Main Street inspired by an Italian Renaissance *palazzo*.[116]

The firm of Darling and Pearson, the designers of many banks—it was they who added classical dignity to the prefabricated prairie branches of the Canadian Bank of Commerce [9.56]—was commissioned to design four large banks in downtown Winnipeg. These were the Union Bank of Canada (1903-4, now known as the Royal Tower), the Bank of Nova Scotia (1907-10), and the Canadian Bank of Commerce (1910-12), all on Main Street; and the Imperial Bank of Canada (1906-7) on Portage Avenue.[117]

The Winnipeg regional office of the **Canadian Bank of Commerce [10.50]** is arguably Darling and Pearson's most splendid bank, as well as one of the country's finest examples of Beaux-Arts Classicism. It replaced an earlier and smaller classical building by the same architects, built in 1900, which was dismantled stone by stone in 1910 and reassembled in Regina (where it still stands). The sublimely simple façade on Winnipeg's Main Street is a monumental Roman temple front: a row of eight Doric columns (paired at either side) rests on a rusticated basement and supports a heavy entablature and balustrade. A closer look reveals that the temple front masks a six-storey (and two-basement) building. Behind the wall of Stanstead granite (from Quebec) are a steel frame and concrete-slab floors, indicating the continued compatibility of traditional design and contemporary materials. Most of the rear por-

tion of the lower floors is occupied by the **main banking hall [10.51]**—100 feet (30.5 m) long, 72 feet (22 m) wide, and 50 feet (15.3 m) high—a marble-panelled room that rises nearly the full height of the building. It is illuminated by a circular glass dome that is almost as wide as the room. The east (rear) wall features a row of Doric columns, smaller versions of those outside, between which are five tall stained-glass windows that flood the room with warm light. The rest of the building consists of offices, arranged in the form of a U around the other three sides of the banking hall. The most impressive is the handsome 40-foot-long (12.2-m) oak-panelled office of the western regional superintendent on the third floor.[118]

The Canadian banking system encouraged the large, centrally controlled chartered banks to build branches in virtually every city and smaller centre. The prairie prefabs demonstrate this initiative. More typical in design, however, were two-storey masonry buildings with strong classical allusions. Brandon, Manitoba, for example, had several banks of this type on Rosser Avenue—including the Bank of Montreal (1903), by local architect William Alexander Elliott (1866-1957); the Canadian Bank of Commerce (Darling and Pearson, 1905); and the **Merchants Bank of Canada [10.52]**, by Montreal architects Taylor, Hogle and Davis. Now the Brandon Public Library, the Merchants Bank (1907) is a graceful, modestly scaled example of Beaux-Arts Classicism, with its central feature a pediment and Ionic portico *in antis* (i.e. a portico that is inserted between two pilasters at the ends of the wall—in contrast to *antae*, a projecting or *prostyle* portico).[119]

Religious and Institutional Architecture

Churches

In the late nineteenth century religious architecture was characterized primarily by a continuation of the stylistic revivals—particularly the Gothic Revival—that had emerged in the early Victorian period and were introduced in Chapter 6. The principal deviations from the revivals were seen in the West, in the mission churches that served the natives and in the houses of worship of the new European immigrants on the Prairies. This section focuses on the sophisticated revivalist churches of three architects

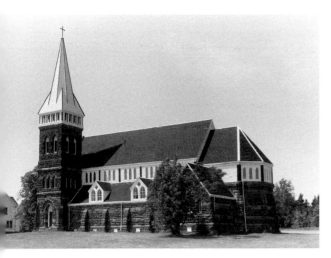

10.53 St Paul's Church, Sturgeon, Prince Edward Island, 1887-92. Lionel F. Stevenson, from *Historic Churches of PEI*, by H.M. Scott Smith.

or firms and concludes by showing how the teachings of the École des Beaux-Arts made their influence felt at the beginning of the twentieth century.

The first of the church architects is William Critchlow Harris, whom we met as the designer of several commercial buildings in Charlottetown [10.35]. The younger brother of painter Robert Harris, he was born near Liverpool and immigrated to Prince Edward Island with his family when he was two. In

10.54 Design for the proposed Methodist Church, Windsor, Nova Scotia, 1898. Private collection of Keith Pickard.

1870, at the age of sixteen, he went to Halifax to serve as an indentured apprentice in the office of architect David Stirling and his younger partner Andrew Dewar (1844-?). Harris remained, and in 1877 he and his teacher formed the partnership of Stirling and Harris, which lasted until Stirling's death ten years later. Harris spent the rest of his life in Prince Edward Island and Nova Scotia, except for two years looking for work in Winnipeg, where he placed second to Barber and Barber in the City Hall competition [7.37]. His firm maintained a general practice, which included many houses, as well as public buildings for the federal Department of Public Works. In 1899 Harris formed a second partnership, with Halifax architect William T. Horton (1840-1926). The buildings erected during the partnerships are properly those of the two firms, but Harris is generally credited with the lion's share of the design work. He is best known for his ecclesiastical buildings, which included twenty churches in Prince Edward Island, and others in Nova Scotia. 'What a number of churches he designed,' Robert Harris wrote to his sister after William's death in 1913, 'and how fine many of them are! That was work he really liked, that's one comfort.'[120]

Harris's earlier churches—including the Methodist Church at Tryon, PEI (1881), and St Thomas Anglican Church at Long Creek, PEI (1887-8)—were straightforward Gothic Revival designs built in wood (several have board-and-batten siding), with a rectangular nave, square altar wall, and corner entrance tower. They followed the English tradition that we have seen was introduced into the Maritimes by Frank Wills and translated brilliantly into wood a generation earlier by Edward Medley [6.40].

Harris's manner matured with his first work for the Roman Catholic church, **St Paul's Church** [10.53], Sturgeon, PEI. Commissioned in 1887 and completed five years later, St Paul's is more monumental than the earlier churches, having a tall nave with lower side-aisles and a high polygonal choir—a feature of French Gothic, and probably intended to distance the Catholics from Anglican Ecclesiology (as at St Patrick's Church [6.41] and Église Saint-Pierre-Apôtre [6.42] in Montreal). The church is built primarily of rock-faced Island sandstone, quarried nearby, with trim of Nova Scotia freestone, producing a warm brown colour and rugged texture such as we have seen in Richardsonian Romanesque buildings of this time. The entrance passes through a square three-tiered and spired tower at the southwest corner. The detail is all Gothic-inspired, with narrow lancet windows on the façade and the tower, as well as in the wood-faced clerestory. The nave was originally illuminated from the clerestory, as the aisle walls—articulated externally only by buttresses—are windowless; but the effect must have been too dark, since awkward dormer windows were subsequently installed over the aisles to admit more light. The free mixture of historical sources from France (the plan) and England (the lancet windows), with the very up-to-date masonry treatment, reveals a free eclecticism characteristic of this Late Victorian period. In 1973 the interior was drastically modernized (by architect Peter McNeill), a result in part of the impetus for change brought about by Vatican Council II; but the exterior fortunately retains its original warmth and dignity.[121]

The freedom of expression that Harris was capable of is evident in a rendering for the **Methodist Church, Windsor [10.54]**, NS, drawn in 1898 but not built. The elegant and upward-reaching nave projects from—and contrasts markedly with—a burly ground-hugging block that was probably intended to contain the church hall and school. The nave is clearly ecclesiastical, illuminated by a large Tudor

window and accentuated by a tall tower and spire; the hall is domestic, almost castellated, with an arcaded entrance, rooted to the ground by a pair of squat round towers—Romanesque in character, yet Gothic in window treatment—and covered by a high, heavy hipped roof with a central chimney.

The finest church designed by Harris is also his smallest: **All Souls' Chapel in St Peter's Cathedral [10.55]**, Charlottetown. Originally called Hodgson Memorial Chapel, in memory of the Reverend George Hodgson, the chapel is a small, self-contained sandstone building attached to the cathedral and has one of the most exquisite Late Victorian interiors in Canada. Built in 1888-9, it is entered either from a door at one end or through the cathedral at one side. Its dark and dramatic interior, which took many years to complete, contains eighteen paintings by Robert Harris, including a roundel depicting *The Ascension of Christ* directly opposite the entrance, in the chancel—which is set off from the nave by handsomely proportioned nestled arches. Paintings along the walls on both sides are fitted within an architectural framework. The mural to the right of the altar is the Sarah Harris Memorial Painting, honouring Robert's and William's mother, and show-

10.55 Interior of All Souls' Chapel, St Peter's Cathedral, Charlottetown, Prince Edward Island, 1888-9. Barrett and MacKay Photographers.

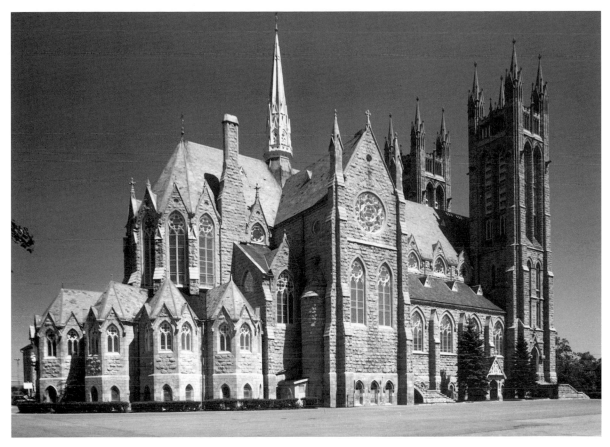

10.56 Our Lady of the Immaculate Conception, Guelph, Ontario, 1876-1926. Photograph by Hellmut W. Schade.

ing members of the Harris family (including the architect) being blessed by Christ. The exquisite finishes include walnut and oak panelling, and roof beams by local woodcarvers Whitlock and Doull; stained-glass windows by Kemp and Sons of London, England; and encaustic tile over the paintings and the windows.[122]

The quality of the work of William Critchlow Harris was matched by that of Joseph Connolly (1840-1904). Born in Limerick and trained in Dublin with architect J.J. McCarthy (1817-82), who was sometimes called 'the Irish Pugin', Connolly moved to Toronto about 1873, at a time when the urbanization of Ontario and the growing numbers (and increasing acceptance) of Catholics led to the construction of many substantial new churches. Connolly was responsible, in whole or in part, for 34 Roman Catholic churches and chapels in Ontario, as well as for the cathedral in Sault Ste Marie, Michigan.[123]

Some of his early work, like that of Harris, looks back to the Early Gothic Revival of A.W.N. Pugin and his contemporaries. For example, the Church of St Mary's (1875), Grafton, Ontario, has a simple nave (without aisles or a clerestory), a separate square-ended chancel, corner tower, and Early English detail, rendered in brick. A rather different approach is revealed in the magnificent Church of St Bartholomew [10.56], later **Our Lady of the Immaculate Conception** (1876-1926) at Guelph, Ontario. Like Harris, Connolly turned to French and other continental European sources as an appropriate vehicle for Roman Catholic expression, just as Gothic Revival Catholic churches in Quebec had looked at French models. According to local tradition, the parish priest, Father Hamel, had been impressed by Cologne Cathedral on his European travels and asked Connolly to use it as a model. Although the Guelph cathedral does not attempt the literal reproduction of features seen at Cologne, the result is a fusion of German, French, English, and Irish sources, rendered with a freedom characteristic of the High Victorian period.[124]

The Church of Our Lady is magnificently sited on the crest of a hill, and is certainly cathedral-like in

its scale and complexity. The plan, clearly articulated on the exterior, consists of a tall nave, side-aisles, transepts, and a polygonal apse (rising as high as the nave), with an ambulatory and radiating chapels—features that are associated with the great French cathedrals of the Gothic age. A spire rises over the crossing, twin towers frame the entrance façade, and buttresses, along the aisles and at the corners of the towers and transept, continue the Gothic language. Only the absence of flying buttresses, and the chimney alongside the apse—necessary in a country where winter heating is essential—are major deviations from the medieval sources. And the relatively broad expanses of plain wall (rather than profuse *rayonné* open-work of the Gothic style in France) tell us that this is a 'modern' nineteenth-century Canadian church.

The inspiration of Cologne Cathedral, a fourteenth-century church that was finally being completed in the 1870s, is more evident in a **preliminary study** [10.57] by Connolly that shows tall spires atop the two entrance towers and a profusion of gables, windows, niches, buttresses, and finials across the façade (all, of course, far more restrained than in the German church). At Guelph, the executed façade and towers—which were not built until 1925-6 and are more English in appearance, with their perforated parapets and corner pinnacles—deviate considerably from Connolly's design. The true sources for the Church of Our Lady are European and American Gothic Revival churches of the previous decades, including several Irish churches by Connolly's mentor, J.J. McCarthy (particularly St Macartan's Cathedral at Monaghan, 1861-83); and the twin-towered St Patrick's Cathedral in New York (1859-88) by James Renwick (1818-95), which in turn finds parallels in European churches of the time, such as Sainte-Clothilde in Paris (by F.G. Gau—a native of Cologne—and Théodore Ballu, 1846-57) and the Votivkirche in Vienna (by Heinrich von Ferstel, 1856-79).[125]

The interior of the Guelph cathedral fulfils the expectations created by its exterior. The nave features a tall pointed arcade with richly carved capitals, a triforium—rare in Canadian churches—and a clerestory with cusped circular windows. The apse is brilliantly illuminated by its tall, narrow windows, and succeeds in approaching the medieval architects' objective of using light to create a feeling of insubstantiality. In 1907 the walls were adorned with magnificent murals (by church artist Peter Charles Browne). Msgr Sbaretti, the Apostolic Delegate to Canada, praised the murals as the 'finest example of gothic decoration in the country'; but they were tragically overpainted in the 1960s.[126]

Connolly also designed a few churches that clearly recalled prototypes in Italy. **St Paul's Church** [10.58], at Queen Street East and Power Street, Toronto, was built in 1887-9, and was one of several churches he designed for the Roman Catholic Archdiocese of that city. With its pink-and-grey stone façade making a radical departure from the Gothic Revival norm, it has a two-storeyed central frontispiece capped by a pediment, and single-storey wings in front of the side-aisles, whose sloping roofs imply the form of a split pediment. The detail is all classical: Ionic and Corinthian pilasters frame the various components; arcades supported by engaged columns enframe doors, windows, and niches; and discs of coloured marble are inserted in the spandrels. The tightly organized composition, an amalgam of Italian precedents, is closest to San Miniato al Monte, near Florence, built around 1100, but long believed to have been a work of antiquity—and therefore associated with Early Christian basilicas, such as the fourth-century S. Paolo fuori le Mura (St Paul's Outside the Walls) in Rome (restored in 1854 after its destruction by fire). The Toronto church also recalls the progeny of San Miniato, namely the façade of Santa Maria Novella in Florence (1460-7), by Leon Battista Alberti (1404-72), and its many imitations—such as Il Gesù in Rome (*c.* 1575-84), which became the standard church-type in the Baroque era—and its earlier revival at Notre-Dame-de-Grâce [6.64] in Montreal. The large *campanile* (belltower) at one side—designed by Connolly, but built in 1905, after his death, by his colleague and successor Arthur W. Holmes—reinforces the Italian imagery. The use of these models echoes the Baroque Revival in Quebec. The Right Reverend Timothy O'Mahony, Bishop of Toronto and Connolly's client at St Paul's, had spent extended periods in Rome and was fond of the Eternal City. He encouraged use of the Italian prototypes to establish close associations with the Vatican, just as Bishop Ignace Bourget had turned to St Peter's as a model for his Montreal cathedral [6.65, 66].[127]

The remarkable **interior** of St Paul's [10.59], praised by Eric Arthur as 'quite the most beautiful church interior in Toronto',[128] continues the Italian theme. The nave arcade consists of unfluted columns, bearing the same Ionic capitals as the façade, that support a stately row of round arches. A continuous

10.57 *(left)* Preliminary study for the Church of Saint Bartholomew, Guelph, Ontario. From the *Historical Atlas of Waterloo and Wellington Counties*, 1881.

entablature runs around the entire church, and above it are arched clerestory windows and a barrel-vaulted ceiling painted with scenes of the missionary activities of St Paul. The aisles are covered by shallow domes with pendentives that are supported by the nave columns and by pilasters engaged to the exterior wall.

St Paul's not only shows a change from Gothic to classical inspiration, but indicates a shift from the picturesque and energetic design of the High Victorian era to the more sedate and sober compositions of the Late Victorian period. As the nineteenth century approached its end, architecture became more tightly organized and self-contained, eschewing the animation, vigour, and frequent humorous touches achieved by the best High Victorian work—such as the Parliament Buildings in Ottawa and the Toronto City Hall.

Connolly died in 1904, and his place as the favoured architect of the Toronto archdiocese was taken by Arthur Holmes (1863-1944), who had been Connolly's draftsman in the late 1880s and emerged as a church architect in his own right around 1891. Holmes was brought up in London as an Anglican, but subsequently converted to Catholicism. Like Connolly, he demonstrated his facility in the Gothic, Romanesque, and classical modes.

One of Holmes' most interesting, if atypical, ecclesiastical commissions was **St Ann's Church [10.60]**, built in 1912-14 on Gerrard Street East, Toronto. Standing in front of the undecorated basilican sanctuary, very much like a false front, is the simple façade of the higher narthex, which consists of a four-column Corinthian portico set off against a disarmingly plain wall. The rough cobble-like texture of the stone contrasts with the smooth, channelled masonry of

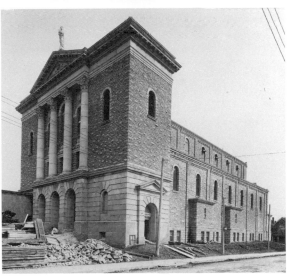

the lower storey. A professional magazine noted that St Ann's was inspired by 'a Roman church of the six-teenth century', and it does indeed bear comparison with the churches of such architects as Giacomo da Vignola and Giacomo della Porta (the designers of Il Gesù). Architectural historian Christopher Thomas has suggested that these churches of the Counter-Reformation provided suitable sources for Catholic churches built during the rule of Pope Pius X (1903-14), who was a very conservative pontiff. The focus on the entrance, and the bold use of classical forms, go far beyond these centuries-old models, however, and reflect values seen in the architecture associat-ed with the École des Beaux-Arts.[129]

Some of the best work in the Beaux-Arts manner was, understandably, produced by French-Canadian architects who had studied in Paris. The first was J.-Omer Marchand (1872-1936), who spent ten years in Paris, beginning in 1893, and worked in the promi-nent *atelier* of Victor Laloux (1850-1937). On his return to Montreal, Marchand quickly established a reputation as an architect of religious buildings. Among his best churches were Sainte-Cunégonde (1906) on rue Saint-Jacques in Montreal and the **Cathedral in St Boniface [10.61]**, Manitoba. (Built in 1907, it was destroyed by fire in 1969; the ruins were stabilized, and a new cathedral, by Étienne Gaboury, was built in 1970-2.) Marchand's cathe-dral, as well as the Montreal church, had imposing twin-towered elevations of cut stone, with the recessed entrance and rose window contained with-in an assertive, although graceful, semi-circular arch; the towers have classical, somewhat Renaissance, detail, and the entrance is Romanesque.[130]

Marchand's most extensive and impressive reli-gious building—constructed in 1905-8—was the **Maison Mère des Soeurs de la Congrégation de Notre-Dame [10.62]** in Montreal, which he designed in association with Stevens Haskell (1871-1913). The Mother House is a large complex on Sherbrooke Street West, near Atwater, that is now used as a col-lege campus by CÉGEP Dawson. It is H-shaped in plan: the principal entrance is in the centre of one long arm and leads to the large chapel, which forms the cross-bar of the 'H' and is appropriately the central feature of the convent. The church-like frontispiece (similar in composition to the façades of Ste-Cunégonde and St Boniface Cathedral), the dome behind the twin entrance cupolas, and the mass-ing of the central block all indicate the presence of the chapel (now the library). The grand scale, sym-metrical layout, rational planning, exterior expres-sion of interior use, and adoption of an appropri-

10.61 St Boniface Cathedral, St Boniface, Manitoba, 1907. Photograph 1956. PAM/St Boniface Cathedral (1908) 16.

10.62 Maison Mère des Soeurs de la Congrégation de Notre-Dame, Montreal, Quebec, 1905-8. Photograph 1976. Communauté urbain de Montréal.

10.63 Bibliothèque de Saint-Sulpice (now Bibliothèque nationale du Québec), Montreal, Quebec, 1912-15. Bibliothèque nationale du Québec.

Institutional buildings

ate historical style are all principles that Marchand would have learned in Paris. He used a Romanesque Revival vocabulary, which had been accepted as a proper mode for monastic buildings ever since Julien Guadet (1834-1908) won the Grand Prix at the École des Beaux-Arts in 1864 with a Romanesque design for a Hospice in the Alps. Guadet subsequently became a noted theorist who taught at the École during the years Marchand was in Paris.[131]

Institutional buildings

The early part of the twentieth century saw the maturing of public institutions that served educational, health, and other social needs. Some were supported by municipalities or provinces, others by churches or private organizations. Many of these institutions erected new buildings, particularly during the period of economic growth that preceded the First World War; and most turned to Beaux-Arts Classicism, a manner perfectly suited for public architecture. A small sampling reveals the quality of the work that was produced.

The educational buildings include schools and colleges (several of which are discussed in other chapters) as well as libraries. A small but precious library that follows Beaux-Arts principles is the **Bibliothèque de Saint-Sulpice [10.63]** on rue Saint-Denis in Montreal. Built in 1912-15 as the Sulpicians' library, it is now the Bibliothèque Nationale du Québec. The architect was Eugène Payette (1874-1959), who subsequently designed the much more monumental

591

Bibliothèque municipale (Montreal Public Library, 1914-17) on Sherbrooke Street East. Exquisitely proportioned and detailed, the Bibliothèque de Saint-Sulpice is perfectly scaled, fitting well into a secondary street, yet stately enought to be noticed. The model is the private *hôtel* of a Parisian aristocrat, appropriate for a private library, and the vocabulary is that of the seventeenth and eighteenth centuries. The central portion and the entrance are recessed between projecting pedimented end-wings, and relief carving on the parapet gives the impression of a balustrade. Restrained engaged Doric columns define a *première étage* (the central portion contains the two-storey-high principal reading room, whereas there are two separate floors in the wings) that is elevated above the ground-level base.[132] The composition is an inversion of Arthur Holmes's St Ann's Church in Toronto, which was built at the same time—the one projects where the other recedes. Each uses a classical vocabulary to establish a clear link with the past, while imitating no specific source and aspiring to be a wholly 'modern' building.

Many libraries were built during this period, most of them with financial assistance from the Carnegie Foundation. We have seen the Carnegie Library (now Memorial Park Library) in Calgary [9.65]. Another that received Carnegie funding was the Toronto Public Reference Library at College and St George Streets (1905-9), designed by A.H. Chapman (1879-1949) in association with Wickson and Gregg. This dignified brick building served as both a reference library and a branch library: a hierarchy of entrances and public spaces, expressed in part through the ornament, made this distinction clear. After undergoing a series of alterations and additions in 1984-5, the building is now the University of Toronto Bookroom and Koffler Student Centre.[133]

Courthouses, land-titles offices, prisons, museums, hospitals, concert halls, railway stations, and other public buildings across the country adopted a similar architectural vocabulary. Even a raw young city like Saskatoon—founded as a temperance colony in 1881, still a village of 100 persons in 1901, and achieving city status only in 1906—built a Courthouse (1907, demolished) and in 1909 a **Land Titles Building** [10.64] in sophisticated versions of the manner. Both were designed by the Regina firm of Edgar M. Storey (1863-1913 and William G. Van Egmond (1883-1949). The Land Titles Building, on 21st Street East, is particularly accomplished. It might have been mistaken for being in a more established city, were it not for the frame houses that surrounded it. One storey high, it was built of variegated brown

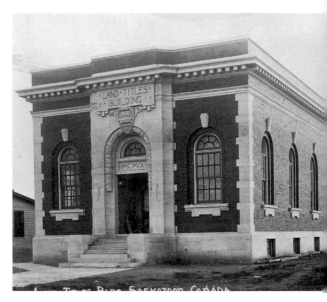

10.64 Land Titles Building, Saskatoon, Saskatchewan, 1909. SAB/R-A5772.

brick, with cream-coloured Tyndall limestone and terracotta used for the entrance, base, quoins, and cornice. Gracious arched windows, recessed behind the plane of the wall, are accented with stone keystones and sills. It was evidently modelled on the similar Land Titles Offices in Yorkton (1907) and Battleford (1908), both designed by Darling and Pearson, showing how quickly Toronto classicism became entrenched on the Prairies. The Saskatoon building soon became too small for the volume of land transactions resulting from that city's real-estate boom, and Storey and Van Egmond designed an addition only a year later, in 1910.[134]

Even industrial and utility buildings with little public access adopted a similar architecture. A particularly remarkable monument of this kind is the **Toronto Power Generating Station** [10.65] at Niagara Falls, Ontario, built in 1903-13 by the Electrical Development Company of Ontario, which was owned by railway-builder William Mackenzie, financier and soldier Sir Henry Pellatt, and electrical manufacturer Frederic Nicholls. Water was diverted from behind the Horseshoe Falls into a tunnel carved through bedrock and passed through turbines built by Canadian General Electric with a capacity of 15,000 horsepower; the electricity was transmitted at 60,000 volts to Toronto, 80 miles (130 km) away. Both the power and the voltage were the largest in the world at the time.[135]

The power-generation occurred underground, but the building over it—on a prominent site, seen by all visitors to the Falls—was required to be well designed, subject to approval by the Niagara Parks Commission. The Electrical Development Company retained as its architect E.J. Lennox, who subsequently created the mammoth Casa Loma in Toronto as a residence for Pellatt. The power-house is a large classical building dominated by a central cubic block, a pedimented portico, and broad wings that feature an Ionic colonnade—similar in concept and scale to the slightly later Union Station in Toronto [**9.13**]. Lennox described the building as being in the 'Italian Renaissance' style, which he called 'a characteristic appearance to answer the purpose for which it is intended.' Although the association remains obscure, he may have been referring to either the permanence of Renaissance buildings or the capitalism of the Renaissance age. The grandiose power house reveals that Lennox's architectural versatility went far beyond the Romanesque Revival of his Toronto City Hall, and certainly shows that he had absorbed the principles of Beaux-Arts Classicism.

The Electrical Development Company was absorbed by the provincially owned Ontario Hydro in 1922. As the Toronto Power Generating Station's 25-cycle generators were never upgraded to 60 cycles,

it was closed in 1974; but the station is a familiar landmark near the Canadian falls, awaiting a new lease on life.

Beaux-Arts Classicism nearly became a universal style, blurring regional differences, although it was never thought of as being particularly Canadian; it was certainly not embraced as a national style, like the High Victorian Gothic and the Château styles. We have seen Percy Nobbs' dismissal of what he called the 'French Academic style' of the Alberta Legislative Building as being 'thoroughly non-British', and Edward and William Maxwell's somewhat contradictory attempt to justify the style in the Saskatchewan Legislative Building as being 'representative of . . . British sovereignty' (pages 577-8). Despite these often defensive attitudes, classicism became established as the lingua franca of public building in Canada (and abroad) during the first third of the twentieth century.

The teachings of the École des Beaux-Arts entered the Canadian educational system as well. Teachers in Montreal, as well as elsewhere in Canada, recognized the value of the Parisian system. A chair in architecture was established at McGill College in 1896, providing the country's first university-based classes in architecture. The head of the new department, S. Henbest Capper (1859-1925), was educated first in Edinburgh and then at the *atelier* Pascal

10.65 Toronto Power Generating Station, Niagara Falls, Ontario, 1903-13. Photograph 1914. NAC/PA61167.

at the École des Beaux-Arts. The courses at McGill were based on those at Columbia University, the Massachusetts Institute of Technology, and other American schools that followed the Beaux-Arts method—although they deviated from them in 1903 when Capper was replaced by Percy Nobbs, who leaned more towards Arts and Crafts principles (page 619). French-speaking students in Montreal were introduced to Beaux-Arts instruction through the École Polytechnique, particularly after the arrival of Max Doumic in 1907. Montreal acquired an École des Beaux-Arts of its own in 1922. Many of its teachers of architecture were brought over from France and the Paris curriculum was followed closely. The school retained its name until 1959, and its programs were subsequently amalgamated with those of the Université de Montréal.[136]

Beaux-Arts Classicism provided a vital link between the revivalist architecture of the nineteenth century and the modernism of the twentieth. The inculcation of the principles of clear, rational, ordered planning, and of the need for appropriate expression and scale, were all indispensable lessons for the architects who would lead Canada and the western world into a new era of architectural design. The reliance on the formal and decorative vocabularies of the past, also basic to the curriculum, has led to its teachings' being erroneously branded as conservative, whereas in many respects they paved the way to the future. The persistence of these lessons, in the period between the First and Second World Wars, will be seen in Chapter 14. Only with the suppression of historicism during the modern era did the trappings of Beaux-Arts Classicism fade. But even then, its principles of planning continued as a basis for public architecture.

CHAPTER 11

DOMESTIC ARCHITECTURE

THE HOUSE is society's elemental building-type. At its most basic level it is intended for survival—to provide its inhabitants with shelter—but it is also designed to accommodate a particular way of life and indicate its occupants' place in their society. Residential forms are therefore determined partly by the environment and available materials, and partly by accumulated social and cultural traditions.

We have already seen many different forms of basic shelter in which environmental factors play a larger role than cultural ones; these include the wigwams of the Algonquian tribes, the tilts of Newfoundland, the log houses of the Métis, and the sod dwellings of the pioneer prairie farmers. We have also examined many kinds of residential building in which the socio-cultural determinants were heeded more strongly than the environmental ones; among these are the Georgian houses of the Maritimes and Upper Canada, the dwellings of the coastal tribes of British Columbia, and the mansions of the newly established power élite on the Prairies. Houses in the first group represent the vernacular traditions; those in the second aspire more to high-style architecture. When Sarah Roberts reluctantly toiled with her family to erect a dreaded sod house because it was the only way that she could keep warm in winter (page 503), she was responding to the environment. On the other hand, when Dr John Helmcken went to the trouble to procure finished cedar boards for his house [8.18] from a far-away trading-post, he was putting his desire to impress people with his taste and his money far above a pragmatic response to local skills and materials.

The same situation existed when a number of families or groups chose to build their houses close to each other. They might have sited their dwellings with particular regard for factors such as protection from the wind or from enemies, whether the plot was level or sloped, and ease of access, but without caring about formal land division. These were the prin-

cipal determinants of an Iroquoian village and a Newfoundland outport. In contrast, many towns were planned according to ideal principles that responded to the need for order, for social hierarchies, and to make a political statement: such was the case with the royal towns of New France, the British Imperial gridiron town plan, and the Hutterite villages on the Prairies. Little regard is shown for topography, if being straight is more important than providing an easy-to-negotiate grade, when a street marches up and down a steep hill—like the imperial roads of the Romans and the streets in the British-inspired gridiron plans that were imposed on steep terrain, as in parts of Montreal, Toronto, and Vancouver.

Most often, however, a residence or a town took a middle path, heeding both natural and cultural factors. The houses of New France respected the conditions of the region and also provided an ideal ambience for *habitant* life. The Mennonite villages in Manitoba were laid out with a rigid and rectilinear plan having clearly stated hierarchies, yet their grids were aligned to follow streams so that everyone had access to water.

This chapter looks at domestic architecture, focusing particularly on the second half of the nineteenth century and the first part of the twentieth. Houses are discussed from the point of view of style, type, and function, beginning with single-family dwellings and concluding with multiple housing.

The Single-Family House

House is a word that denotes a particular building-type and is synonymous with 'dwelling' or 'residence', whether one is referring to a mansion or a humble homestead. The term *housing* usually alludes to the houses of the working class, particularly those built for it by government authorities or private developers. (Canada Mortgage and *Housing* Corporation is the federal agency responsible for this activity.) Most houses are considered also to be a *home*, a more emotive word that eludes definition; it represents ideas of comfort, intimacy, and domesticity.[1] (The closest word in French is *foyer*, which also describes the hearth and implies its warmth.) Ask any child to draw a picture of a house, and he or she will likely sketch a building with a few windows, a door, a peaked roof, and a chimney emitting an evocative curl of smoke. No matter that the majority of Canadian children do not live in dwellings of this type; this representation of the house as a cozy, freestanding, middle-class, single-family dwelling pervades our culture.

The image—perhaps one should say the myth—has not come about by accident. Although variations in size, structure, plan, materials, and form are considerable, this was the standard form of housing for most Canadians of European and mixed background, regardless of their economic status, until the second half of the nineteenth century. No matter that Charles Ramage Prescott's Acacia Grove [3.41] in the Annapolis Valley was a large brick building in the Georgian style, and Jean-Baptiste Charette's house in St Norbert, south of Winnipeg (page 331), built at the same time, was a simple log structure a fraction of its size. The two share a generic family resemblance.

The principal exceptions were in crowded urban centres, such as Quebec and Montreal, where land values were too high to permit freestanding houses. Here party walls and row houses became the norm (pages 55 and 251). As the nineteenth century brought increasing urbanization, more and more Canadians began to live in multiple dwellings within densely populated cities. For them, the self-contained, self-owned house became the dreamt-of objective. The goal of living in a true 'home', rather than in mere 'housing', was one that residential builders would promote and exploit in the suburban housing developments of the twentieth century. Writing in an American context, Canadian architectural historian Alan Gowans attributes the popularity of the individual suburban house, on its own lot, to 'images of sturdy independence in [the occupants'] apartness from their neighbours'. And, as is revealed by the illustrations in Gowans' book, *The Comfortable House*, the houses that were being promoted often had much in common with the child's image of a dwelling.[2]

The text that follows looks at a number of house-types that were popular in Canada between the middle of the nineteenth century and the early years of the twentieth. It begins with a brief overview of those styles that were considered in the last chapter in the discussion of public and commercial buildings; it then looks in greater depth at types and styles that were used primarily for houses. A number of the houses discussed were introduced in earlier chapters.

The 'high' styles in domestic architecture

Most of the styles that were illustrated in the two previous chapters, with respect to public and commercial buildings, were also used for houses. They appear in their 'purer' form in large architect-designed houses for wealthy Canadians, yet their distinguishing features are recognizable as well in developer-built residences for the middle and working classes. The choice of which particular style to use depended mostly on what was fashionable at a given time—architectural styles, like furnishings and clothing, quickly go in and out of vogue—and also to some extent on what was most appropriate to a particular client's position or needs.

The Gothic Revival is a case in point. We saw in Chapter 6 that it was introduced primarily for churches because of its association with an earlier—and supposedly better—period of Christianity. The style was used for domestic design as well. The motivation was sometimes its religious associations—as in the Bishop's Palace [6.26] on Church Street in Toronto (William Thomas, 1845), the residence of the Roman Catholic archbishop, adjacent to St Michael's Roman Catholic Cathedral.[3] But more often it was used simply because a person *liked* it, and wanted his house to be built that way—this was surely the incentive for Elizabeth Cottage [6.25] in Kingston and Manoir Campbell [6.47] at Mont-Saint-Hilaire. The Gothic Revival was also chosen for its picturesque qualities, and for the easy way a house in this manner seemed to fit into the landscape. Henry John Boulton certainly chose the style for these reasons when he built Holland House [6.24] on park-like grounds in Toronto.

As will be discussed later in this chapter, the Gothic Revival had a significant impact on domestic building, both through its reliance on the picturesque and through its emphasis on craftsmanship and the 'honest' use of materials. The cottage, the villa, the Queen Anne Revival, and the Arts and Crafts Movement all trace their roots to the principles, if not the forms, of the Gothic Revival. This pervasive influence was also reflected in vernacular building: we shall see its

11.1 *(above)* George
Stephen house, Montreal,
Quebec, 1882-4.
Photograph 1903. Notman
Photographic Archives,
MMCH/147,451—Misc. II.

11.2 Entrance hall of the
Stephen house, Montreal,
Quebec. Photograph by
Brian Merrett, 1993.

impact in the rural Ontario Cottage, and in common urban houses in cities across the country.

The classical revivals were likewise transferred from public to domestic architecture. In the first half of the nineteenth century, Temple Grove [6.53] in Montreal and Martock [6.57], near Windsor, NS, were domestic examples of the two strains of Neoclassicism. In the second half of the century, Greek and Roman Revivals gave way to a reinterpretation of Italian (as well as northern-European) classicism of the Renaissance period—allowing the introduction of more intricate forms and compositions that responded to the love for complexity and eclecticism that was so characteristic of the High and Late Victorian periods. The Italianate manner was thus a Victorian counterpart to the earlier Georgian classicism.

The **George Stephen house [11.1]** in Montreal is one of the most sumptuous mansions to have been built in what is variously called the Italianate or the Renaissance Revival style—a domestic equivalent of the Victorian Italianate commercial buildings of the time. The house was built in 1882-4—for George Stephen (later the first Baron Mount Stephen), president of the Bank of Montreal and a principal in the building of the Canadian Pacific Railway—on Drummond Street, in the lower portion of Montreal's '(Golden) Square Mile', where the city's English-speaking power élite built their residences. Stephen's architect was William Tutin Thomas (1828-92), a son of the Toronto architect William Thomas and a member of the family partnership that designed fine Italianate commercial buildings in Halifax and Toronto as well as Montreal (page 567). W.T. Thomas had become the most fashionable Montreal architect of the day, and it was fitting that he should be selected by Stephen, who was intent on expressing his elevated position in the financial community, and desirous of (but unsuccessful in) creating a niche for himself in Canadian society. Stephen lived in the house for only four years before returning to Britain in 1888. It was purchased by his brother-in-law, Robert Meighen, and since 1926 has served as the exclusive Mount Stephen Club.[4]

The house retains its imposing aspect and tastefully opulent interiors; the only significant alteration has been the replacement of the glass walls of the conservatory wing, on the left, with stone in 1927 (by Grattan D. Thompson, 1895-1971). The two-storey principal block looks like (and was inspired by) an Italian urban palace, suggesting those of the bankers of a previous age. The stone façade is treated symmetrically, with a projecting bay and porti-

co supporting a balustraded balcony, and with paired windows (arched on the ground floor) on either side— reinterpreting the Georgian elevation of sixty years earlier. A rounded three-sided bay projects from the side overlooking the conservatory; the decorated middle marks an interior fireplace. The roofline right round the building is ornamented with a bracketed cornice and sculpted parapet. The exterior decorative vocabulary is derived primarily from Italian sixteenth-century sources, although it is indebted as well to the later Italian and English Baroque. The highly ornamented wall surfaces, and the layering of the ornament—with the columns, arches, and entablatures applied on top of, and projecting from, the wall plane—recall the sixteenth-century Northern Italian buildings of Jacopo Sansovino (in Venice) and Michele Sanmicheli (in Verona), rather than the more austere palaces of Rome and Florence—but the historical quotations are too indirect to pinpoint precise sources.

The Renaissance Revival began in Britain with a series of men's clubs (ironically foreshadowing the subsequent use of the Stephen house) on Pall Mall in London, especially the Reform Club (1837-41) by Sir Charles Barry (1795-1860), which looked at Roman sources; and the Carlton Club (1845-56), by Sydney Smirke (1798-1877), which adopted Northern Italian sources. The elder William Thomas (a contemporary of Barry and Smirke), who came to Canada in his forties, frequently used Renaissance features in his public buildings, such as St Lawrence Hall (1849-50; **12.17**) and the Don Jail (1858) in Toronto and the City Hall in Guelph (1856); it was his son, W.T. Thomas, who brought the style to its maturity in residential buildings.[5]

The interior of the Stephen house—the work of 'a small army of carvers and craftsmen in wood and marble [who] were brought from Europe'[6]—is particularly impressive. On passing through the portico and front doors, the visitor comes to the sumptuous **entrance hall [11.2]**. Its magnificent staircase, arches, balustrade, wall-panelling, and beam-and-pendant ceiling were made from Cuban mahogany. A skylight and a large stained-glass Palladian window, depicting scenes from Shakespeare, flood the stairs with light, and tapestries depicting Greek goddesses line the walls above the wood panels. This high level of design and craftsmanship (and expense) is maintained throughout, with walls and ceilings of carved oak, bird's-eye maple, English walnut, Ceylonese satinwood, and southern pine; fireplaces of marble, onyx, and hand-painted tiles; and doorknobs and hinges plated with 22-carat gold.

11.3 Lowden house, Charlottetown, Prince Edward Island, 1868-9. Prince Edward Island Public Archives and Records Office/PARO 2806/6.

11.4 W.H. Lyon house, Winnipeg, Manitoba, 1881. Photograph 1905. NAC/PA38465.

The Italianate manner had entered into builders' vernacular by way of the United States some two decades before the construction of the Stephen house. It is seen in two wooden houses at opposite ends of the country: the Richard Carr house [**8.34**] in Victoria of 1863, which was modelled on American pattern-book designs; and the **Lowden house** [**11.3**] on Haviland Street in Charlottetown. The latter was built in 1868-9 by Esther Lowden, the widow of a prosperous merchant, to replace a house burned in the city's fire of 1866. Undocumented—it is believed to have been designed by David Stirling—the Lowden house is two-storeys high and features a projecting central bay with a small pediment, and a hipped roof that culminates in a balustrade and a square cupola. The windows in the outside bays are paired on the upper floor (as in both the Carr and Stephen houses), and are contained within projecting bays on the ground floor. After Lowden's death, the house was leased by the American consul, Delmer J. Vail, who noted that it would 'show respect to the United States'—suggesting that he recognized its American character. It is now the United Services Officers' Club.[7]

The Second Empire style became very popular for

houses, even more so than the Italianate style—from which it is largely indistinguishable below the mansard roof. It was adopted for both great residences and ordinary houses. Government House in Toronto (Gundry and Langley, 1868-70; demolished 1912) established the style for fine residences. Fronting on Simcoe Street at King Street West, it was relatively restrained—but only because it was one of the earliest examples of the style in Canada. Built in red brick with limestone dressings, it had a picturesque central tower over a *porte-cochère*, a mansard roof with prominent bonnet-topped dormer windows, and on the south side—facing the gardens and looking towards Lake Ontario—a large balustraded porch, echoing the one at the entrance.[8]

At their most ornate, Second Empire houses could present a wonderful brocade of decorative gewgaw. The **W.H. Lyon house** (1881, demolished) in Winnipeg was one such gem [11.4]. Designed by Edward McCoskrie (*c*. 1821-93) and Joseph Greenfield (1845-1910), it was composed like a wedding cake, rising relentlessly from the ground floor, with its broad veranda; through the brick walls of the second floor, with a balcony in the central bay; past the mansard roof, with its pedimented dormers, chimneys, iron cresting, and finials; to the cupola, with its own mansard roof and crested cap. The turned spindles of the porches were triumphs of the lather's craft. The cupola and

veranda were slightly later additions, designed about 1890 by George C. Browne (1852-1919).[9]

The Second Empire style adapted easily to existing regional vernaculars. The **Morency house [11.5]** at Sainte-Marie-de-Beauce, Quebec, has many of the same elements, but all are rendered quite differently. Built in 1885 for merchant Gédéon Beaucher *dit* Morency, it retains many of the features of the traditional Quebec house. The veranda is raised high above the ground, and is covered by the flare of the mansard, rather than by a separate roof—just as the flaring eaves had traditionally provided shelter for the verandas in the farmhouses of the *habitants*. The tower over the entrance has an orthodox square dome that is truer to architectural sources in Second Empire France than the cupola of the Lyon house.[10]

Smaller in scale, and reduced in its complexity—yet in many ways just as sophisticated—is a small **farmhouse at Maitland [11.6]**, Nova Scotia, probably built in the 1870s or 1880s. It has the mansard roof, eaves brackets, projecting central bay, classical ornament (seen in the window and door surrounds, and the pilaster strips) that are indicators of the Second Empire style. The delicate wood detail, with its painted highlights, continue a long Maritime tradition of fine woodwork.[11]

The Richardsonian Romanesque style was also used for domestic architecture. The most ostenta-

11.5 Morency house, Sainte-Marie-de-Beauce, Quebec, 1885. Photograph 1970. CIHB/05207000700052.

11.6 *(below)* Farmhouse at Maitland, Nova Scotia, 1870s-1880s. Photograph 1973. CIHB/02004800000030.

11.7 Craigdarroch Castle, Victoria, British Columbia, 1887-90. BCARS/5445.

11.8 The stairhall of Craigdarroch Castle, Victoria, British Columbia. Photograph by Nigel Drevor. Courtesy Craigdarroch Historical Museum Society.

tious example in the country is **Craigdarroch Castle** [**11.7**] in Victoria, built in 1887-90 by coal baron Robert Dunsmuir. The Scottish-born Dunsmuir first worked in the Hudson's Bay Company's coal mines on Vancouver Island. In 1869 he discovered the rich Wellington coal seam north of Nanaimo and set up his own company, ruthlessly exploiting cheap Chinese labour in order to maximize profits. In 1884, bolstered by California capital, Dunsmuir and his son James began construction of the Esquimalt and Nanaimo Railway (now a part of the CPR) to transport coal from his mines to the port at Esquimalt for the San Francisco market. As an incentive they received a land grant that comprised nearly one-quarter of the area of Vancouver Island, including much of its prime timber. Dunsmuir's other business endeavours included an iron foundry, a fleet of steamships, and a newspaper: he and his family dominated the economy and the politics of British Columbia until just after the turn of the century. Robert Dunsmuir became president of the Executive Council (the cabinet) in 1888, and James Dunsmuir subsequently served as provincial premier and lieutenant governor.

On a 28-acre (11-hectare) site, on the highest point of land in Victoria, Robert Dunsmuir built the opulent castle of which he and his wife Joan had long dreamed. He looked south for his architect, and in 1885 retained Warren H. Williams (1844-88), the leading designer in Portland, Oregon, who worked in association with the little-known Arthur Smith. Craigdarroch Castle began to rise in 1887—but Dunsmuir died in 1889, a year before its completion, and so never had the opportunity to enjoy it; it became the residence of his widow and their three remaining unmarried daughters. After Joan Dunsmuir's death in 1908 the house was occupied by a number of institutions, including Victoria College and the Victoria Conservatory of Music. It is now a historic-house museum owned by the City of Victoria.[12]

The total effect of Craigdarroch is certainly castle-like, with its formidable stone walls and its picturesque silhouette punctuated by a tower, turrets, gables, and balconies. It was intended to evoke the image of a Scottish baronial castle, but like the contemporaneous wood-frame Banff Springs Hotel [**9.16**]— built by another American architect (Bruce Price) for a different railway magnate (William Van Horne)—it was a free adaptation of 'generic' European castles. The rusticated stone (likely from Dunsmuir's own quarry at Koksilah, near Duncan, on Vancouver Island), the repeated round arches,

the turrets, and the foliated capitals of the ground-floor veranda are all features of the Richardsonian Romanesque, which was just then being introduced into Canada at the Ontario Legislative Building [**10.19**] and the CPR's Windsor Station [**9.9-11**], both also designed by American architects. Craigdarroch displays the superficial features of the new style, and its spindly proportions stand in contrast to the compact massing that was characteristic of Richardson's own work.

The interior of Craigdarroch is opulent almost beyond belief. On the ground floor the oak panelling and ceiling of the **stairhall** [**11.8**], the mahogany and stained glass in the library, the plasterwork in the drawing-room, and the Minton tiles in the carriage entrance set a grand theme. The ballroom—never used by the Dunsmuirs—was on the fourth floor; from it one could see the lights of the city far below. Higher still is the tower, which the Prince of Wales visited in 1919 to enjoy the magnificent view.

A purer example of the Richardsonian Romanesque residence— this one built in a very urban setting with a restricted garden— is the **Gooderham house** [**11.9**] in Toronto, built in 1889-92 for George Gooderham, president of Gooderham and Worts distillery [**12.18**] and then of the Bank of Toronto. He commissioned a design from David Roberts, Jr (c. 1830-1907), whose father had designed the distillery's most important building in 1859. Though the house is massive, it is relatively simple in form. Above the double-arched main entrance is a high, wide gable that displays an arrangement of deep windows, pilasters, arches, and a balcony under the peak. To the left of the entrance is a *porte-cochère*, and a pinnacled tower faces the corner of St George and Bloor Street West. It is harmonious in colour and materials—red rock-faced sandstone, brick, and terracotta—and has smoothly integrated and richly carved picturesque elements. Still an impressive presence in Toronto, the mansion is now the York Club. (Roberts also designed for Gooderham, immediately afterwards, the triangular office block in Toronto known as the Flatiron Building.)[13]

Architects possessed a wide vocabulary of historical styles for residences, as for other building-types. This versatility is seen, for example, in the work of Edward and W.S. Maxwell, who designed a number of houses for well-to-do businessmen in Montreal's Square Mile. Edward Maxwell adopted the Richardsonian Romanesque style for his earlier houses, such as the James Crathern house (1892) on avenue Docteur-Penfield (formerly MacGregor

11.9 Gooderham house, Toronto, Ontario, 1889-92. Photograph by William Dendy.

11.10 J.K.L. Ross house, Montreal, Quebec, 1908-9. Photograph by Hellmut W. Schade, 1992.

Avenue), which was built shortly after Maxwell's return to Montreal from the Boston office of Richardson's successors, Shepley Rutan and Coolidge.

A decade-and-a-half later, and a few blocks away on Peel Street, Edward and his brother W.S. Maxwell designed a **house for J.K.L. Ross [11.10]**, the sportsman son-and-heir of CPR contractor James Ross, that revealed the vast distance that had been traversed by the firm—and by architectural tastes. Built in 1908-9 (after the Maxwells had produced several similar schemes over a five-year period), the Ross house is coolly and elegantly classical. Its façade was composed like a Palladian villa, although with exquisite detailing derived from the buildings of Baroque and eighteenth-century France. The arrangement of elements resembles those on the end pavilions of the Maxwells' contemporaneous Saskatchewan Legislative Building [10.23]. The historical sources, and the rigid symmetry, reveal William Maxwell's Beaux-arts training and his love for classical forms. His touch is evident in the central bay—in the curved reveal of the arched doorway, the delicate brackets and cartouche above it, the charming wrought-iron balcony, and the layering of the window frames and pilasters that lead up to the thin pediment and parapet. The arch of the doorway is echoed in the windows cut out of the channelled ground-floor masonry that stands in striking contrast to the darker smooth-faced stonework above. The classical character is continued in the interiors, which feature delicate plaster ceilings, and cornices above handsomely panelled walls.[14] The building was used by Marianopolis College from 1946 to 1976, when it was purchased by McGill University; it is now used by the Law Faculty.

The cottage and the villa

The detached house of modest proportions became a desired alternative to crowded city dwellings in the last years of the eighteenth century in Europe, and in the mid-nineteenth century in the United States—where urban density was becoming a problem—and spread from the US into Canada. Over sixty illustrated books offering designs for small and mid-sized houses were published in Britain between 1790 and 1835, and many more appeared subsequently. All were intended to provide architects, builders, and property-owners with models. Their authors devoted considerable attention to developing the ideas of the 'cottage' and the 'villa'. Although the two terms were often used interchangeably, the cottage was generally accepted as being a small, rustic dwelling based on the vernacular residences of the working poor and transformed into a modest house-type for both the middle and working classes, combining utility and economy with good taste and a picturesque aesthetic. The design might be plain, or treated in any of a number of historical styles. The romantic cult of the picturesque was a dominant force: these buildings were often seen as being ornamental and rustic features set within a landscape. The villa, on the other hand, was often defined as a larger and more elegant version of the cottage—even associated, sometimes, with the country villas built by Pliny the Younger outside Rome in the first century AD.[15] Three of the most widely read volumes in this genre were *Rural Residences* (1818), by John B. Papworth (1775-1847), an architect who had apprenticed with John Plaw (page 112); *Villa Rustica* (1832), by Charles Parker (1799-1881), a former student of Jeffry Wyatville (page 257); and the *Encyclopaedia of Cottage, Farm, and Villa Architecture* (1833) by John Claudius Loudon (1783-1843).[16]

Americans read these and other books avidly. Some even produced popular books themselves that were also intended to provide models for suburban and rural dwellings for the expanding middle class. By far the most widely read were by gardener-turned-author A.J. Downing (1815-52). His publications included *Cottage Residences* (1842) and *The Architecture of Country Houses* (1850), both of which describe and illustrate buildings designed by others as well as himself. Downing has been credited with having engendered an 'architectural revolution' that 'changed the face of rural America'. Two other influential American books were *The Model Architect* (1852) by architect Samuel Sloan (1815-84) and *Villas and Cottages* (1857; 2nd edition, 1864), by Downing's sometime collaborator Calvert Vaux (page 539).[17]

These books were also purchased and read by Canadian architects and builders. The few architectural libraries whose contents are known to us all possessed some books of this type. William Storm, for example, owned the Loudon and Parker books, as well as other titles by Papworth and Downing; and Charles Baillairgé had copies of Parker and Sloan.[18] Bookstores in Kingston offered six different titles by Downing between 1849 and 1853; one, the City Book Store, published notices on three occasions that it was re-ordering *The Architecture of Country Houses*, and it advertised in 1854 that 'a fresh supply of Downing's works' had just arrived, implying an eager market.[19] Nothing comparable was published in Canada until the first appearance in 1864

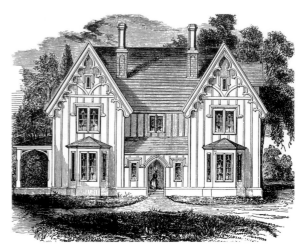

11.11 'Plain Timber Cottage-Villa', Brunswick, Maine. From A.J. Downing, *The Architecture of Country Houses*, 1850.

of *The Canada Farmer*, a periodical that published model buildings irregularly under the headings 'rural architecture' and 'farm architecture'.[20]

Pattern books must have had an immense impact on the designs of Canadian architects and builders, but few specific instances have been identified. One case of a possible model-copy relationship is the evident similarity between **'a plain timber cottage-**

11.12 The Cone, Port Hope, Ontario, begun 1858. Photograph by Ralph Greenhill.

11.13 Claverleigh, Creemore, Ontario, c. 1870. Photograph 1978. PC/Heritage Recording Services.

A SMALL GOTHIC COTTAGE.

11.14 'A Small Gothic Cottage'. From *Canada Farmer*, February 1864. Archival Collections, University of Guelph Library.

11.15 Plan of 'A Small Gothic Cottage'. Drawing by David Byrnes after *Canada Farmer*, February 1864.

villa' [11.11] in Brunswick, Maine, designed by Gervase Wheeler (c. 1815-70; he too was an author of pattern books), and illustrated by Downing in *The Architecture of Country Houses*; and two Ontario houses: **The Cone [11.12]** at Port Hope, the home of renowned railway engineer Thomas Curtis Clarke (1827-1901), that was begun in 1858 and described as 'a Villa erected upon the model of the Swiss Cottage' by the local press, which presumed that Clarke was the designer; and **Claverleigh [11.13]** at Creemore, a house built around 1870 about which little is known. Claremont in Gagetown, NB—built c. 1850 for Nathaniel De Veber— is another house of this type.[21] The similarities may be more generic than specific, particularly with The Cone, since its right-hand portion was built twenty years before the matching one on the left. All three houses follow the lines of Gervase Wheeler's 'cottage-villa': in the twin projections covered by steep gabled roofs and connected by a low entrance; in the pointed Gothic arch (around the doors in Maine and Creemore, and above the door in Port Hope); and particularly in the board-and-batten siding. The use of vertical boards, whose joints are covered by narrow strips (called 'battens'), was advocated by Downing in *The Architecture of Country Houses*:

> . . . not only because it is more durable, but because it has an expression of strength and truthfulness which [horizontal siding] has not. The main timbers, which enter into the frame of a wooden house and support the structure, are vertical, and hence the vertical boarding properly signifies to the eye a wooden house.[22]

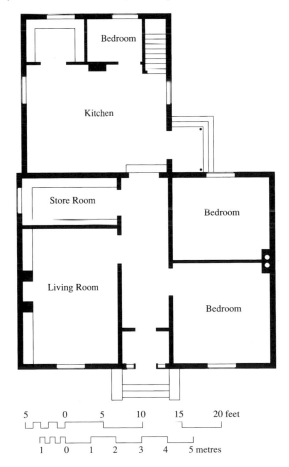

The desire for 'truthfulness' in construction and materials—a value held by residential designers with inclinations towards the picturesque—would have a lasting legacy in the domestic architecture of subsequent generations. This led, particularly in the US, to the use of 'stickwork'—vertical, horizontal, and diagonal boards on the exterior wall that suggest the structural frame—and to what has been called the Stick style.[23]

The most common form of suburban dwelling in Ontario, in the third quarter of the nineteenth century, was a small building, three bays wide, with a straight eave on the façade interrupted by a gable above the central entrance. This house-type is known as a 'Gothic cottage' because of the frequent presence of pointed windows, hood mouldings, pointed finials, and decorative bargeboard (also called vergeboard or 'gingerbread') in the gable or under the eaves—all features that are associated with the Gothic Revival style. It is sometimes known as an 'Ontario cottage', particularly in that province, although the term is often used in a broader context. Examples occur in wood (both board-and-batten and horizontal siding) and in brick and stone.

The *Canada Farmer* promoted this kind of cottage in its second issue in February 1864, illustrating and describing the basic version, designed by Toronto architect James A. Smith (1832-1918): one storey high, it had a decorative trefoil in the gable and a hipped roof behind. The house was referred to as '**a small Gothic cottage**' [11.14], and as 'a dwelling suitable for a small family.' The accompanying **plan** [11.15] shows the front door leading into a central hall, off which are a living-room and closet on the left, and two bedrooms on the right—a main block, 36 by 28 feet (11 by 8.5 m), covered by a hipped roof. A smaller kitchen wing, with a pantry and servant's bedroom, extends behind. (The kitchen extension was typical of Ontario houses: the back door was the entrance in general use, and the front door was said to have been reserved for weddings and funerals.) A year later the *Canada Farmer* presented a slightly larger version, $1\frac{1}{2}$ storeys high, with the upper floor created by a cross-gable roof. Also designed by Smith, it was described as 'a cheap country dwelling house'.[24]

These house-types abound throughout Ontario, and are also found in the Maritimes and the western provinces. One example is the **Coulchard house** [11.16] in Perth County, Ontario (seen in the photograph with the Coulchard family), which was built of buff brick, likely in the 1860s, and has a pointed gable window and bargeboard. Another is Inge-Va

11.16 Coulchard house, Perth County, Ontario, *c*. 1860s. From *Weekend Magazine*, October 1969.

[4.22] in Perth, Ontario (begun 1824), although the central gable was a later addition. The insertion of a gable over what had once been a straight eave is particularly evident at **Stonestable** [11.17] at Richardson, a short distance east of Perth. A modestly scaled one-storey stone house, begun around 1825, it was modified by adding a gable and one bay at the left. The new work was finished in wood, creating a remarkable contrast between the two portions.

Another instance in which a likely pattern-book

11.17 Stonestable, Richardson, Ontario, begun *c*. 1825. Photograph by Harold Kalman, 1991.

11.18 Burpee house, Saint John, New Brunswick, c. 1865. Photograph 1971. CIHB/04101008100101.

Frank [**4.27**] in Toronto (1795-6), are paradigms of the temple-house— suggesting attempts at literal interpretations of Pliny's villa, set in a picturesque rural/suburban landscape.[26]

The romantic cult of the picturesque may have provided the incentive for building these pseudo-rural retreats, but early cottages and villas generally retained the symmetry and formality (and usually the centre-hall plans) of Georgian classicism. The asymmetry associated with picturesque aesthetics gained a foothold in house-planning only after the mid-century—primarily with the Italian Villa, another type that was promoted by authors of pattern books.

Bellevue [11.19], on Centre Street in Kingston, Ontario, is an early Italian Villa—believed to have been the first example of the style in Canada—and has a particularly interesting history. It was built by well-to-do grocery merchant Charles Hales in, or shortly after, 1841; he also erected a row of five cottages along the King Street frontage of the property. (George Browne was the architect of the cottages; it is not certain if he also designed the principal house.) Bellevue attracted attention from the start, and Hales' line of work gave rise to several nicknames for it: 'Teacaddy Castle', 'Muscavado Mansion', and 'Pekoe Pagoda'. Hales lived in the house for only a few years, and subsequently rented it out. The most illustrious tenant was the 33-year-old John A. Macdonald, then a Kingston lawyer and a member of the Legislative Assembly of the Province of Canada. He lived in Bellevue for a year, beginning in September 1848— referring (in a letter to his sister-in-law) to his new 'Eyetalian Willar' as 'the most fantastic concern imaginable'.[27]

Bellevue raised the eyebrows of the time for its extreme picturesque asymmetry, provided by its three-storey tower, covered by a low hipped roof and a finial, and two Italianate balconies outside the top windows (hence the name 'Bellevue'). Three wings seem to pivot around this tower. One projects forward on the right, another on the left, from which a hooded balcony over an elaborate wooden bracket hangs; and a lower kitchen wing (not visible in the photograph) extends at the rear. Each wing is covered by its own gabled roof. The tower rises above the entrance hall on the ground floor and is surrounded on two sides by a veranda (whose roof and decorative railing form a deck supported by posts), which is reached by steps at one side rather than from the front. Gone are the quiet profile of a unified roof and the formal symmetry of the central-hall plan. The ground floor contains reception

source has been identified is the Richard Carr house in Victoria (1863; **8.34**), which appears to have synthesized two designs that appeared on the same page of Samuel Sloan's *The Model Architect*. With its full two storeys, and the slight projection of the central gabled bay, the Carr house is a larger version of the Ontario cottage and displays Italianate detail. Similar designs are found across the country. One particularly impressive rendition is the **Burpee house [11.18]** on Burpee Street in Saint John, New Brunswick, built around 1865 on what was then a suburban site. It features a three-storey frontispiece with Gothic Revival pointed-arched openings on all levels and a projecting bay, and ground-floor bays on either side. Pendants hang from the eaves, a balcony projects from the gable on the side, and there is fine detail in wood on the door, window surrounds, and eaves brackets. The composition is a Gothicized—one might say romanticized—version of the classic Georgian façade, with the central pediment transformed into a projecting gabled bay.[25]

These houses represent the simpler 'cottage' strain of the cottage-villa phenomenon. But another, larger, and often more formal and classical type leans towards the 'villa' aspect. Temple Grove [**6.53**]—the McCord residence (1836) on Mount Royal in Montreal—and Governor Simcoe's more rustic Castle

it is reversed in plan from Bellevue, has board-and-batten siding, and differs in its details. The essential features of the Italian villa are the presence of one or more towers (also called a *campanile* or *belvedere*), and the asymmetrical composition. Prototype Italian villas were built earlier in Britain by that early master of picturesque design, architect John Nash, at Cronkhill (1802), Shropshire; and Sandridge Park (1805), Devon. The first Italian villa in the US is usually cited as Riverside (1839) in Burlington, New Jersey, by John Notman (1810-65). Bellevue therefore stands close to the top of the list of those built in North America; and if it was indeed designed before 1842 it preceded Downing's popularization of the mode. The historical and architectural importance of Bellevue is reflected in its being open to the public as a national historic site; its restored gardens emphasize the relationship of the villa to its landscape.[28]

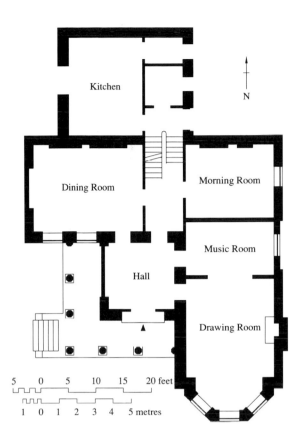

11.20 Ground-floor plan, Bellevue, Kingston, Ontario. Drawing by David Byrnes.

11.19 *(left)* Bellevue, Kingston, Ontario, *c.* 1841. Photograph by Ralph Greenhill.

11.21 'Italian Villa'. From A.J. Downing, *Cottage Residences*, 1842.

rooms [11.20] and the second floor bedrooms. The new freedom achieved in the plan permitted variation in the rooms and a thoughtful approach to planning that attempted to address the needs of domestic living. On the ground floor the morning-room is intimate and is oriented towards the eastern sun; the drawing-room is larger and faces south; the dining-room, generally used in the evening, has little natural illumination. The house is finished in stucco (as were the adjacent cottages) and decorated with scalloped bargeboard.

Houses of this kind were published in England by Loudon and in the US by Downing, as well as by many contemporaries. An **Italian Villa** [11.21], illustrated in Downing's *Cottage Residences* (1842), displays the same principal components, although

Italian-inspired towers began to appear in Canadian architecture in the 1830s. Sir Allan Napier MacNab's Dundurn in Hamilton, Ontario (by Robert Charles Wetherell, 1834-5), a substantial house overlooking Burlington Bay, has two such towers on the garden elevation. The formal symmetry of the design, organized around a central hall and dining-room, precludes its being described as a true Italian villa.[29]

The most sumptuous and extravagant Italian villa in Canada is **Ravenscrag** [11.22], above Pine Avenue in Montreal, the house of Scottish-born Sir Hugh Allan. He made his fortune principally in shipping (he owned the Allan Line), and also had business interests in fields as widespread as coal-mining, paper-manufacturing, textiles, telephones, and banking. His attempt to obtain the contract to build the CPR

11.22 Ravenscrag, Montreal, Quebec, 1861-3 and following. Centre Canadien d'Architecture/ Canadian Centre for Architecture, Montreal/ copyright Phyllis Lambert and Richard Pare.

11.23 Ballroom, Ravenscrag, Montreal, Quebec, 1872. Photograph by Brian Merrett.

created the Pacific Scandal that brought down the Macdonald government in 1873. He chose to exhibit his wealth by building Ravenscrag on a large estate high on the slope of Mount Royal. Its picturesque profile could be seen from much of Montreal, and from its *campanile* Allan could observe his ships in the city's harbour. The design was conceived by architect Victor Roy (1837-1902), and construction was supervised by William Spier (1801-78) and Son. Initial work was undertaken in 1861-3, but by 1872 the house had been enlarged with a ballroom and conservatory (by Alexander G. Fowler [1824-99], and Victor Roy) and a billiard room and antechamber to the ballroom (by John William Hopkins [1825-1905]—to whom the design of the entire house has traditionally been credited—and his partner, Daniel Wily). In 1889-98, when the house was occupied by Sir Hugh's son, Sir Hugh Montagu Allan, the east wing and stables were enlarged (by Taylor and Gordon). An advantage of asymmetry was the ease with which additions could be made.[30]

Although Allan is said to have modelled his residence on Ravenscraig, the ancestral home of the Marquis of Lorne (Governor General, 1878-83) in Ayrshire, near Allan's own birthplace, one looks in vain for any meaningful architectural links with Scottish tradition. The plan and elevation of the Montreal mansion are based directly on the Italian villa. The dominant feature is the tall square tower,

11.24 The Octagon house, Dartmouth, Nova Scotia, 1871. NSM/68.178.56.

around which the wings of differing heights and massing appear to be casually organized. The exterior walls are built of rough-faced Montreal greystone, with smooth quoins and window surrounds, and the windows display a variety of Italianate profiles and details. The main entrance is through a columned portico at the base of the tower. Over the door is carved the Allan motto: *Spero* (I hope).

The magnificent interior displayed Allan's wealth and taste. A variety of decorating styles was used, all classically derived: Italian Renaissance for the hall and dining-room, Georgian for the drawing-room, French Baroque for the **ballroom [11.23]**—a very grand room whose coved ceilings and colonnaded entrances evoked images of Versailles. Royalty, nobility, and political and business leaders from Canada, Britain, and around the world frequented the house, which was sometimes described as a second government house. In 1940 Sir Hugh Montagu Allan and Lady Allan donated Ravenscrag and its grounds to the Royal Victoria Hospital, and the building now serves as the hospital's Allan Memorial Institute. The original interiors have been lost in the massive transformation that followed (by Lawson and Little, 1941-5; annex by Barott, Marshall, Montgomery and Merrett, 1952-3; new west pavilion, 1962).

A peculiar variant of the villa was the Octagon Mode, a short-lived but surprisingly popular fashion that lasted from the 1850s until the 1870s. The source was *A Home for All* (1848), written by phrenologist Orson Fowler, who promoted octagonal buildings for reasons that were both utilitarian (an octagon encloses 20 per cent more floor area than a square with the same total length of wall) and aesthetic (it is allegedly more beautiful because it approaches the sphere, 'the predominant or governing form of Nature'). The book went through six editions in eight years. Octagonal houses quickly appeared throughout the US and Canada, many of them in New York State and Ontario.[31]

The **Octagon House [11.24]** on Dahlia Street, Dartmouth, Nova Scotia, is one of many Canadian survivors. It was designed by architect Henry S. Elliott (1824-90) for Gavin Holliday, the manager of a local factory, and built in 1871. Three storeys high, with an octagonal cupola and fronted by a two-storey veranda, it was built of wood, the predominant local material. The ground floor contains a central staircase hall and four nearly rectangular rooms with left-over triangular spaces between them—hardly an efficient use of the extra space provided by the octagon![32]

The Queen Anne Revival and the vernacular house

So strong was the legacy of the picturesque that in the last decades of the nineteenth century, asymmetry became common in urban houses (those that relate principally to the street and not to a private landscape) as well as in suburban and rural ones. The dominant type of town-house before that time was a regularly planned building whose principal façade and eaves were parallel to the street; any wings, or other deviations from the containment of a basic rectangular plan, were inconspicuous or invisible from the street. Derived from the vernacular houses of the Maritimes and Quebec, and influenced by the formality of Georgian classicism, the elements of this house-type were fairly consistent throughout Atlantic and Central Canada—whether they

11.25 Elevations, Haddon Hall, Toronto, Ontario, 1883. Archives of Ontario/C11-637-0-0-1.

were detached, or shared a common party wall—and varied principally with respect to size, materials, and details. (See, for example, the Short view of Halifax [3.20]; the Jacquet house [2.29] in Quebec City; and the shops with upstairs residences along Princess Street in Kingston [10.33].)

The stylistic vehicle for the change to picturesque composition was the Queen Anne Revival, a manner that developed in England in the early 1870s and first appeared in both Canada and the US towards the end of the decade. This speedy migration can be attributed to the rise of illustrated architectural periodicals—not only those published in England (especially *The Builder*, which began publication in 1842) and the US (particularly *American Architect and Building News*, from 1876), but also the first Canadian periodical in the field, *Canadian Architect and Builder*, which was first published in Toronto in 1888.[33]

A house in Toronto that exhibited the principal features of the Queen Anne Revival was **Haddon Hall** [11.25], the residence of Robert Simpson (the

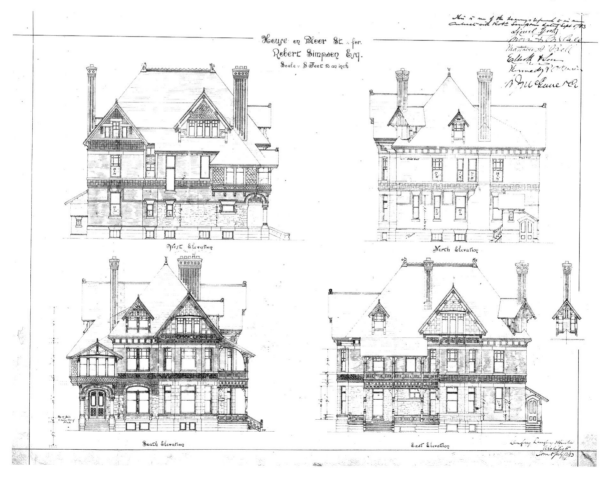

House on Bloor St. for Robert Simpson Esq.
Scale 8 feet to an inch

West Elevation

North Elevation

South Elevation

East Elevation

owner of the famous Toronto department store, **10.41**), built in 1883 to designs by Langley and Burke and demolished in the 1930s. It was characterized by a picturesque, irregular massing of forms and a rich variety in materials and details. The principal (south) elevation—which faced the north side of Bloor Street, east of Church—had the entrance at the extreme left, recessed beneath an overhanging gabled window supported on columns. The principal mass, which projected forward to the right of the entrance, was covered by a high hipped roof and terminated, to the right, in a bay window capped by its own gable. A two-storey veranda at the southeast corner provided access to the garden and further fragmented the composition. The gable roofs that covered wings on the east and west sides were clearly visible from the front, and the irregular roofline was further punctuated by tall chimneys, with decorative stacks and caps, and by dormer windows: the dormer at the northeast corner was oriented at a 45-degree angle and supported a chimney. The external materials and textures were as varied as the composition. Rough-faced stone was used for the ground floor of the façade, brick on the second floor, half-timbering (a decorative treatment on a masonry backing) in the gables, turned wood for the veranda, and iron cresting along the ridge of the roof. Most of the windows were rectangular, with double-hung sash—although the entrance arch, and the window beside it, had broad segmental heads. The complex massing of the house afforded considerable variation in the size and shapes of the rooms, allowing the plan to respond to the particular requirements of domestic living, and providing splendid opportunities to let light flood the house.[34]

All of these seemingly disparate elements were effectively balanced by a masterly composition that was utterly alien to the rational and ordered taste that, only a half-century earlier, had produced Georgian buildings such as The Grange [4.17] and Osgoode Hall [4.38]. The factor that brought about this change was the whole-hearted acceptance of the picturesque aesthetic, which had been introduced to ecclesiastical architecture by the Gothic Revival and to domestic architecture by the Italian villa. The Queen Anne Revival firmly established picturesque design principles.

The British origins of the Queen Anne Revival are evident in the buildings of Richard Norman Shaw (1831-1912), and his partner W. Eden Nesfield (1835-88), and in the designs and writings of John James Stevenson (1831-1908). The style was used mostly for residences. It began with a number of private designs in the 1860s, and went public with several highly visible buildings erected shortly after 1870, including Shaw's Lowther Lodge on Kensington Gore (1872-5) and Stevenson's Red House on Bayswater Road (1871-3, demolished)—both on thoroughfares along the edge of Hyde Park in the west end of London. Their picturesque compositions, roof-lines, and varied materials (particularly red brick and tile) offered a vaguely historical revival of features taken from English domestic architecture of the late medieval and early Renaissance periods. Although Queen Anne reigned from 1702 to 1714, the style has little to do with the buildings of that era, apart from the propensity for red brick. The compositions and ideals of the founders of the style were broadcast to a wide audience in Stevenson's book, *House Architecture* (1880).[35]

North American architects adapted the Queen Anne Revival to regional economic and environmental conditions as well as to architectural traditons. H.H. Richardson drew on the Shavian sources (as well as the American colonial vernacular) in his innovative W.W. Sherman house (1874-6) in Newport, Rhode Island, which is generally accepted as the first Queen Anne Revival house in the US.[36] In Canada the style was initially used for detached houses of moderate size, usually much smaller than the English prototypes and therefore more in conformity with Canadian budgets, as well as being easier to heat in winter. Such decorative materials as tiles and carved stone were used less because they were vulnerable to the climate, so contrasting textures were often achieved with wood shingles and stone. Brick remained the primary material in Toronto, Montreal, and other places where it was common; but wood was prevalent in the Maritimes and the West. The style's links with the British architectural past must have appealed to devoted Anglophiles (numbering most English-speaking Canadians) at the time, in the very same way that the Georgian architecture of the previous era had been found attractive.

The Laurels [**11.26**], on Rockland Avenue in Victoria—built around 1890—is a particularly fine 'Canadianized' Queen Anne house by Thomas C. Sorby, an architect who was practising in England at the time of the style's inception, and who was a contemporary of Shaw and his colleagues. Sorby came to Canada in 1883, and finally settled in Victoria after a transcontinental migration working as an architect for the CPR. He designed The Laurels—one of many fine houses then being built in the prosperous coastal city—for Robert Ward, a wealthy Victoria businessman and politician. (Ward's good architectural taste was later revealed in his selecting Samuel Maclure [page 621] as the architect for his office block, the Temple Building, in 1893.) The entrance tower of the eight-bedroom wood house was flanked by shingled gabled projections of different sizes, and punctuated by balconies at various levels. A local journalist displayed his confusion over its style:

> The principal feature of the front is the large Moorish window, above which are graceful balconies. The general style is Ionic . . . a grand stair window just above the entrance gives a fine view over the lawn . . . . A mantle piece in what may be called the Renaissance style almost fills the eastern side of the room [the stairhall]. It is highly ornamental and has an alcove at either end in which Bijou lamps will be placed . . . . The Belvedere or observatory-smoking room above all is sixteen feet square. It is sixty feet above the lawn and has a northern balcony; the vane rises to ninety feet above the lawn.[37]

Shorn of its tower, its wood walls stuccoed, and the interior subdivided into suites, the building retains little of its original character inside or out.

The attention paid to the stairhall of The Laurels, with its fireplace and flanking alcoves, is characteristic of Queen Anne Revival houses. What began as a revival of the old English hall became a central feature of new houses. The Victoria journalist's interest in The Laurels' relationship with the exterior landscape (expressed architecturally in its large windows and verandas) reveals the persistence of the villa idea.

Bartra [11.27], at 28 Circular Road in St John's, Newfoundland, also renders the Queen Anne revival style in wood. Designed and built in 1906 for Irish-born merchant W.S. Munroe, by contractors Thomas and Chalker, the house presents a dynamic grouping of polygonal and semi-circular bay windows, and a medley of gables and dormers in clapboard, with decorative shingles and eaves brackets. In the stairhall the grandeur and elegant decorative woodwork of the staircase, the panelled walls, and the fireplace are all illuminated by a hidden window on the landing. Torch-bearing nymphs on the newel posts provide additional illumination.[38]

A number of American pattern books made the style accessible to builders, as well as architects, by providing models for houses. A documented example of the use of a published source is a **drawing of an elevation of a house** [11.28] by Kingston architect William Newlands (1853-1926) that directly

11.26 Robert Ward house (The Laurels), Victoria, British Columbia, *c.* 1890. Photograph by Richard James Maynard. BCARS/57022.

copies a plate from *Picturesque California Homes* (1884), by Ontario-born virtuoso California architects Samuel Newsom (1854-1908) and Joseph Cather Newsom (1858-1930). Newlands subsequently used the bay window on the right corner, and the oriel

11.27 W.A. Munroe house (Bartra), St John's, Newfoundland, 1906. Photograph 1983. PC/Heritage Recording Service.

11.28 Drawing by William Newlands of the elevation of a house. Queen's University Archives, William Newlands Architectural Collection/208 (detail).

11.29 Parkins house, Montreal, Quebec, 1885. Photograph 1983. PC/Heritage Recording Service.

above it, in a richly decorative unexecuted scheme for the John Hazlett house on Frontenac Street in Kingston—although the executed house (1893) was much simplified.[39]

The Queen Anne Revival quickly found its way into the Canadian vernacular. A good example of its adaptation to middle-class speculative housing is seen in the **Parkins house [11.29]** at 3492 rue Durocher, Montreal. Merchant James Duncan Adams built the house in 1885 and immediately sold it to insurance agent Frank Fairleigh Parkins, the first occupant. The architect (if one was involved) has not been identified. The $2\frac{1}{2}$-storey red-brick building has a heavily pronounced gabled projecting bay that is tied to the relatively plain entrance by a terracotta band near the top of the ground-floor openings. A semi-circular second-storey oriel window, with a conical roof, projects along the side as a modest substitute for a corner tower. Wood shingles in the gable provide a contrasting texture. (The stone house next door, partially visible on the left, boasts a full tower.) The Parkins house was restored in 1980-3 by architect Mario Biocca and now contains condominium units.[40]

The new taste for gables and the penchant for asymmetry— both products of the Queen Anne Revival that were derived from the Gothic Revival— allowed houses to be shifted so that their principal axes were perpendicular to the street, rather than parallel to it. This, in turn, permitted the subdivision of land into narrow lots of 25 or 33 feet (7.6 or 10.1 m)—the latter half the length of a surveyor's chain. The resulting higher densities led to increased profits for developers.

These factors produced a new generation of ordinary builders' housing. The group of **three houses at 449-59 East Pender Street [11.30]** in Vancouver, built in 1903, are based on design principles that are similar to those of Queen Anne houses, with irregular massing and varied colours and textures; and all have asymmetrical gabled ends facing the street. Bargeboard, decorative shingles, eaves brackets, and bay windows enliven the façades, while porches with turned columns protect the off-centre entrances. The house on the left (no. 449) has a hipped roof behind the gable, whereas the other two have multiple gables.[41] Houses such as these were usually painted in combinations of earthy tones. (Colour schemes were more assertive in the US than in Canada. It is in California, for example, that the recent interest in rehabilitating houses of this kind has produced the much-admired 'painted ladies', with their remarkable combinations of colours.)

11.30 449-59 East Pender Street Vancouver, British Columbia, *c.* 1903. Photograph by John Roaf, 1973.

Even simpler in design was the most prevalent vernacular house-type that appeared across Canada in the years leading up to the First World War: a 1½- or 2-storey house with its gable facing the street, a ground-floor porch or veranda, and an off-centre entrance. Sometimes a cross-gable produces a shallow wing at one side. The front door opens into a narrow hall and, usually, a staircase. The living-room is at the side, with the dining-room beyond it; the kitchen is at the far end. In the east and west of the country this house-type is typically clad in wood (as in the illustrated **house on 13 Avenue SW [11.31]** in Calgary, built around 1912), but in the central provinces it is usually faced in brick. Ironically it is so common, and so taken for granted, that it does not have a name in general usage (although 'Queen Anne' is sometimes used); it may be described as a 'gable-front' house.[42] Houses of this kind were made available to the masses through pattern-books, and in the catalogues of builders, who would sell the plans for between ten and one hundred dollars. Others were available pre-cut or prefabricated ('ready-made' housing of this kind was introduced on page 504).[43] But often no specific prototype or source existed; like the vernacular houses of any other era, this was just the accepted way of building.

Equally common in both urban and rural Canada was the 'foursquare' house, which first appeared around 1910. Typically square in plan, it was two storeys high, had a front veranda, and was covered by a pyramidal hipped roof with a front dormer. The illustrated example, the **Eastbourne [11.32]**, was one of a dozen foursquares included in the Eaton's catalogue for 1919, which offered the purchaser pre-cut components requiring assembly on site. (Not all foursquares originated in this way.) Many foursquares, like the Eastbourne, were entered through a side-hall (as in the gable-front house), although some larger ones (the type could be quite expansive) had a central doorway and staircase hall, with a living-room

11.31 13 Avenue sw, Calgary, *c.* 1912. Photograph by Harold Kalman.

IDEAL HOMES

EASTBOURNE
EATON PLAN BOOK
E15

An exceptionally well planned home of the modern type of square house, which is the one type where you obtain the maximum of space at the minimum of cost of both material and labor. The treatment of the lower walls with siding and the upper walls with shingles produces a pleasing and well balanced effect.

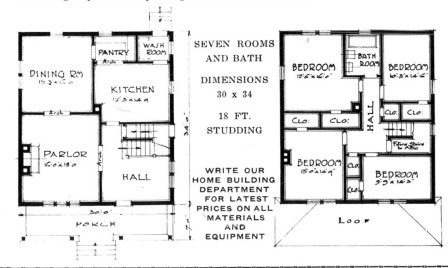

SEVEN ROOMS AND BATH

DIMENSIONS 30 x 34

18 FT. STUDDING

WRITE OUR HOME BUILDING DEPARTMENT FOR LATEST PRICES ON ALL MATERIALS AND EQUIPMENT

11.32 Eastbourne. From the T. Eaton and Co. catalogue, 1919, reproduced in *Plan Book of Ideal Homes: Homes Designed for the West*. Eaton Collection, Western Development Museum, Saskatoon.

11.33 'Wedding-cake' houses, Moose Jaw, Saskatchewan, *c.* 1913. SAB/Rice Studio Album 53.

or parlour at either side. Bedrooms and bathrooms were upstairs. The foursquare—as solid and dignified in appearance as its name implies—was usually embellished with classical columns, and might have decorative brackets and a cornice below the emphatically straight eaves. It offered the same image of stability as the Georgian house did a century earlier, and provided an alternative—perhaps a reaction—to the picturesque designs of only a few years before. A smaller, one-storey, version was often called a 'cottage'. Brick (in central Canada) and wood (in the East and the West) were the prevalent materials, but houses of this kind were also built of stone and 'artistic' concrete block (imitation stone).[44]

Sometimes the porches and verandas went wild and dominated the rest of the house. The so-called **'wedding-cake' houses** [11.33] in Moose Jaw, Saskatchewan—built around 1913—feature bulbous three-tiered circular porches facing Oxford Street that all but hide the main blocks of the buildings behind them. Eccentric as they may be, the massing of these dressed-up foursquares fits in well with the more conventional gable-front houses beyond them.[45]

Builders of the period showed a particular interest in making houses work better. Concerns included the design of efficient layouts tailored specifically to the clients' needs, the provision of sunlight and fresh air, and the introduction of effective heating, ventilating, plumbing, and illumination systems—

in short, the creation of a *comfortable* and sanitary home. Among the many technical developments in the last quarter of the nineteenth century were the introduction of hot-water and warm-air heating systems, the invention of the enamelled bathtub and siphonic-action wash-down water closet, and the replacement of gas-lighting with electricity. The new disciplines of 'domestic engineering' and home economics began to make themselves known at this time in American universities and periodicals, following the initiatives of the American Christine Frederick and numerous other women.[46]

Canadian architects were well aware of these developments. Edmund Burke, for one, used the new jargon in a lengthy article on house-planning published in *Canadian Architect and Builder* in 1890:

A poor plan, a crude plan or a complex one may be, and often is, a continual source of discomfort to the occupants of a house, especially to the wife, as housekeeper, and to the servants, while one which is carefully considered and thoughtfully put together, is of the most material assistance in the smooth-working of the domestic machinery.

Burke noted that the abundant British labour market contributed to 'careless and diffuse planning', whereas in the US and Canada the comparative short-age of domestic labour and 'the lack of means, have conduced to more careful and scientific planning . . . and to the invention of many labor saving appli-ances, which have been born of necessity.'[47]

The Arts and Crafts Movement
and the bungalow

Closely related in its origins to the Queen Anne Revival was the Arts and Crafts Movement, a paral-lel product of Late Victorian Britain. More an ide-ology than a style, it emerged in England among a circle of artists and architects that centred on William Morris (1834-96) and Phillip Webb (1831-1915). Both had trained in the office of George Edmund Street (1824-81), as had Richard Norman Shaw; so all began with a firm grounding in the architecture of the High Victorian Gothic Revival, and all espoused its governing principle that a design must be appropriate to the purpose for which the build-ing is intended. Morris and Webb admired John Ruskin, and in particular the latter's disdain for machine production as a substitute for art. In *The Seven Lamps of Architecture* (1849), Ruskin had declared that 'the use of cast or machine-made orna-ments of any kind' was an 'Architectural Deceit'; in his next book, *The Stones of Venice* (1851), he argued that buildings, decoration, and decorative objects must show that they are man-made.[48]

Inspired by Ruskin's polemical advocacy of 'truth' in design and materials, Morris determined to uphold good craft traditions, in part as a bulwark against the poor taste and machine-made products that had been popularized by the Great Exhibition of 1851. He organized a commercial firm—Morris, Marshall, Falkner & Co. (later Morris & Co.)—to commission and sell decorative arts by good designers and crafts-men who sought to maintain the practices of the pre-mechanical age. Morris's interest in the work-ingman led to his espousal of a utopian socialism. He also demonstrated a very real concern for his-toric buildings, and was instrumental in organiz-ing the Society for the Protection of Ancient Buildings (1877), through which he attacked the insensitive cathedral restorations by G.G. Scott and others. Morris's early interest in preservation was impor-tant for recognizing the value of all styles of historic building, and not only certain phases of the Gothic.

The architect who first put Morris's architectural ideals into practice was his friend Philip Webb. His Red House (1859-60) at Bexleyheath, Kent—built as a residence for Morris—is an unpretentious brick house whose picturesque irregularity comes out of the Gothic Revival tradition, as does the use of indige-nous English vernacular building forms, to create a building of its own time. The approach to design and the use of materials are straightforward and util-itarian. Webb's admirer, William Richard Lethaby (1857-1931)—a former principal assistant to Shaw—praised Webb for attempting 'to revitalize [building] by returning to contact with reality.'[49]

In 1884 Lethaby, and four former pupils of Shaw, formed the Art Workers' Guild, whose primary objec-tive was to promote 'the Unity of all the Aesthetic Arts', especially in building. The Guild included painters, sculptors, and designers as well as archi-tects. William Morris joined the Guild in 1888, in the same year that some of its members formed the Arts and Crafts Exhibition Society. A parallel ven-ture was the Guild of Handicraft, an experimental workshop (subsequently located in the Cotswold Hills) that was founded in the same year by metal-work designer (and architect) C.R. Ashbee (1863-1942).[50]

This 'new-old' approach to architecture and the arts—which combined a deep respect for tradition-al domestic building forms and craft practices with a commitment to design in a modern manner, and is known as the English Domestic Revival—came to Canada at the turn of the century. One architect in Toronto (Eden Smith) and one in Montreal (Percy Nobbs) stand out as the most prominent Canadian advocates of the new movement, and an architect in Victoria (Samuel Maclure) was its most accom-plished practitioner. The Arts and Crafts Movement was particularly important to domestic architecture, although its influence was felt as well in churches and other building-types.

The key event in Toronto was the organization of the Toronto Architectural Eighteen Club in 1899 by a group of young architects of that city whose principal motive was to protest what they perceived to be the self-serving activities of the Ontario Association of Architects (established by an act of legislature in 1889). The Eighteen Club espoused the belief that architecture is an art rather than a pro-fession and therefore should not be regulated by leg-islation. Many of the Club's members shared an artis-tic vision similar to that of the founders of the Arts and Crafts movement, and spread that vision through a series of annual exhibitions, beginning in 1901.[51]

The first president of the Eighteen Club, and an especially talented member, was Eden Smith (1859-1949), who used only his double last name. Born near Birmingham and trained as a watercolourist and draftsman, he and his family immigrated to Canada in 1885. After a year or two of homesteading in southwest Manitoba, they moved to Toronto. Eden Smith first took a job with the firm of Strickland and Symons, then passed the new examinations administered by the Ontario Association of Architects and opened his own practice. He is best known for his domestic architecture (though the claim, in his obituary, that he had designed more than 2,500 houses seems incredible), but he also produced a number of fine religious and public buildings. He used British models in an effort to develop and market a new Canadian architecture, concealing his English background in the interest of promoting Canadian nationalism.[52]

His Arts and Crafts leanings are evident in the **Eden Smith house [11.34]** on Indian Road, near High Park in Toronto, which he designed for himself and his family in 1896. The compact dwelling uses a variety of local materials to provide attractively rich textures. The general form is that of an Ontario cottage, with a steep gabled roof and plain brick walls. Stone lintels and sills above and below the small casement windows contrast with the brick. A half-timbered cross-gable (a feature of English medieval vernacular building) projects over the entrance (behind the bushes to the right) and dominates this south façade, while the west elevation (at the left) is more American in character, having a shingled gable and broad veranda. The bare shaft of the chimney and the projecting bay on the west side, with its pyramidal roof, add elements of geometric intricacy to the otherwise simple form. The overall appearance is much quieter than that of a Queen Anne Revival house. The principal interior feature is a two-storey hall with a staircase, surrounded by rooms on three sides. Simple squared-oak panelling, and a hand-beaten copper hood over the fireplace, are typical Arts-and-Crafts decorative touches. The house therefore pays its respects to the vernacular traditions of Canada, the US, and Britain, while exhibiting fine craftsmanship, and combines these sources in a unified composition that is essentially forward-looking and non-revivalist.[53] Eden Smith subsequently had the opportunity to design a number of fine houses in a superb landscaped setting, working with and for—and living next to—several talented painters, sculptors, and craftsmen in Wychwood Park, Toronto [12.21].

Eden Smith actively promoted the alliance of architecture and crafts. In an address to the Architectural League of America, with which the Eighteen Club was affiliated, he declared that architecture was 'the

11.34 Eden Smith house, Toronto, Ontario, 1896. From *Canadian Architect and Builder*, November 1902.

harmonious association of all the crafts', and that the role of architects was to form 'societies with the intention of mutually advancing their own interest and that of architecture for the good of the community.' Quoting Lethaby, he advanced the cause of guilds 'to improve the quality or raise the standard' of architecture.[54]

Four years after the formation of the Eighteen Club, in 1903, a 28-year-old Scotsman named Percy E. Nobbs (1875-1964) arrived in Montreal to take up the position of Macdonald Professor of Architecture at McGill University. (McGill's department of architecture—the first in a Canadian university—had been formed in 1896.) After receiving an academic education, he trained in Edinburgh with Robert Lorimer (1864-1929), a member of the Art Workers' Guild and a contributor of furniture to the Arts and Crafts exhibitions in London. Nobbs remained committed to the importance of skilled craftsmanship in his forty-year career as an influential teacher and a practising architect in Montreal.[55]

Nobbs valued the expression of nationalism in architecture, as was evident in his comments on the Alberta Legislative Building [10.22]. Believing that nationalism could be achieved through the study and emulation of indigenous vernacular building, he noted that Lorimer had succeeded in this and lauded him as 'the last of the great romantics, with a name to put beside that of Philip Webb and Norman Shaw . . . . It was given him to materialize in building the very essence of the Scottish spirit.'[56] Hermann Muthesius, the chronicler of the English house at the turn of the century, wrote that Lorimer 'was the first to recognize the charm of unpretentious old Scottish buildings, with their honest plainness and simple, almost rugged massiveness.'[57]

In the **Percy Nobbs house** [11.35] on Sunnyside Avenue in Westmount, which Nobbs designed for himself and had built in 1913-15 in that well-to-do suburb of Montreal, he blended English and Scottish influences with elements of the local domestic tradition in an attempt to develop a local vernacular. Prominent gables and steeply sloping roofs were popular among architects of the Arts and Crafts Movement, and Lorimer had used the motif frequently during Nobbs' period of apprenticeship. The exterior walls consist of unadorned plain stock red brick with small windows, characteristic of Montreal housing, and there are no overtly historicist features. The design takes advantage of the steeply sloping site by placing the main rooms in the principal block, with a view, and the service spaces in a lower wing. The artisans of the Arts and Crafts Movement were represented by Morris wallpaper and a fireplace with hearth tiles by William de Morgan. Charles Reilly, director of the School of Architecture at Liverpool University, left his impressions of the house, describing it as:

11.35 Percy Nobbs house, Westmount, Quebec, 1913-15. Photograph by Hellmut W. Schade, 1992.

. . . a tall, austere pile, standing prominently on the mountainside, and commanding a vast view of the town, the St Lawrence, and the distant mountains. The big, bare rooms, with their polished hardwood floors and an occasional choice rug, contained a few very good pictures. His rooms were inhabited by his wife and children rather than by bronzes and statuettes. It was a house full of modern conveniences, efficient in service, yet fine in its shape, a notable if somewhat rare combination. Historically its ancestry could be traced back to the Scotch castle and the Teutonic schloss, and, of course, ultimately to Italy.[58]

On the West Coast, Arts and Crafts principles were interpreted somewhat differently in the striking and sensitive houses of Samuel Maclure (1860-1929). Like both Eden Smith and Nobbs, Maclure was an accomplished watercolourist, and so the 'the Unity of all the Aesthetic Arts' was a concept that came easily to him. Maclure was born at Sapperton, British Columbia— the first white child whose birth was registered in New Westminster—the son of a Scottish surveyor who served in the Royal Engineers. When he was a boy the family moved to the Matsqui Prairie in the Fraser River valley. At the age of 24 Maclure went to the Spring Garden Institute in Philadelphia to study art; he also visited New York and Boston. Essentially self-taught in architecture, he went into practice in New Westminster in 1887, first in partnership with Charles Henry Clow (1860-1929) and subsequently with Richard P. Sharp. During five years in that city Maclure participated in the design of a number of houses and public buildings, mostly wood-frame structures in the Queen Anne Revival (notably the Royal Columbian Hospital, New Westminster, by Clow and Maclure, 1889).[39]

Maclure and his family moved to Victoria in 1892 on the basis of a commission to design the Temple Building (1893), a small, precious brick-and-terracotta office building, for Robert Ward—his brother Charles's employer and the future occupant of The Laurels [11.26]. The architect then launched a long and successful practice in Victoria, devoted almost entirely to houses. A sensitive family man, he was a foil, colleague, and sometime associate to the more flamboyant and arrogant Francis Mawson Rattenbury. Maclure's clients included a number of wealthy members of Victoria's social and business élite, some of whom were drawn from Ward's circle of friends and associates.

The **Biggerstaff Wilson house** [11.36] on Rockland Avenue, Victoria—built in 1905-6—is characteristic

11.36 Biggerstaff Wilson house, Victoria, British Columbia, 1905-6. Photograph by Dane Campbell, *c.* 1973. Courtesy Martin Segger.

11.37 Stairhall of the Biggerstaff Wilson house, Victoria, British Columbia. Photograph by Dane Campbell, *c.* 1973. Courtesy Martin Segger.

of Maclure's best work. The second son of pioneer Victoria entrepreneur William Wilson, W. Biggerstaff Wilson continued his father's food-warehousing business and inherited the fortune of the London bachelor after whom he was named. Above the rustic stone walls of the ground floor, the house is finished in the (false) half-timbered patterning that is usually described as Tudor Revival. The black-on-white bands—mostly perpendicular, but radiating in the gable peaks and in a quatrefoil shape beneath the windows— create a striking decorative effect. The massive hipped roof, cross gables, and tall brick chimneys create a truly picturesque effect, as does the setting: a large, attractively landscaped suburban property. The half-timbering occurs only on the front and sides; wood shingles—an indigenous North American material— are used on the rear.[60]

The principal interior feature (here and in many other Maclure houses) is the magnificent **hall** [11.37], a two-storey space that contains the principal staircase at one end and a gallery around the other three sides. A variety of handsome materials is introduced to good effect. The door from the entrance vestibule (not seen in the photograph) is inserted between a pair of windows with small leaded panes; the staircase rises on the opposite side and is illuminated by a bank of four leaded-glass windows, with some decorated panes interspersed among the clear ones. Fir is used for the wall panelling, the beamed ceiling, and the balustrade of the staircase and the gallery, which consists of vertical rails—enlivened by a delicately carved curved motif beneath the handrail— and heavier posts that extend below the floor line as pendants. The fireplace is tiled, and the natural illumination is supplemented by brass sconces and suspended light fixtures. An elegant hall of this quality provided a perfect setting for the sophisticated entertainment that was so important a part of Victoria society.

The Wilson house may seem to be somewhat more 'revivalist' than the houses by Eden Smith and Nobbs, but it is so only insofar as Maclure looked for sources in the half-timbered walls and living-halls of medieval and Tudor England—a historical point of departure that was appropriate for the strong British element in the young west-coast city. In the absence of a centuries-old heritage of domestic building, Arts and Crafts architects on this continent were forced to select an external tradition that had appropriate meaning in the new setting.

The house has links to current, as well as historical, building practices in both Britain and the US. The focus on the living-hall was a priority among Shaw, Webb, and the other British architects in both the Queen Anne Revival and the Arts and Crafts manners. This feature of planning was picked up by American architects who designed in the Shingle Style, an Americanized version of the Queen Anne that had strong affinities with the Arts and Crafts Movement. Originating in New England around 1880, the Shingle Style quickly spread throughout the US. Bruce Price, the New York architect whose work for the CPR has been discussed, was an accomplished practitioner, as was H.H. Richardson. In Philadelphia there was Wilson Eyre (1858-1944), whose work Maclure may have seen when he was a student in that city. Eyre's Charles A. Newhall house (c. 1881) in Chestnut Hill, Pennsylvania (a suburb of Philadelphia), combines external half-timbering with shingles and has an impressive entrance hall with a staircase and a gallery on three sides—elements that appear in the Wilson house. Maclure's future partner, Ross Lort, noted: 'The impact of the eastern cities on him was so great that it was to this [architecture] that he turned and found in it what he wanted to do with his life.'[61]

Maclure may be best known for his half-timbered houses, but he applied his Arts and Crafts approach to a number of other modes as well. The **John James Shallcross house (Tor Lodge)** [11.38] on Foul Bay Road, Victoria, was built in 1907 for an English-born friend with a passion for art and a deep interest in the Arts and Crafts Movement. (The Shallcrosses and the Maclures participated in establishing the Vancouver Island Arts and Crafts Society—which, in turn, founded the Victoria Art Gallery, now the Art Gallery of Greater Victoria—and the Arts and Crafts Institute, which provided formal education in art.) The house is sited on a high, rocky prominence with a spectacular view of the Olympic Mountains in Washington State. Ever the landscape painter, Maclure sited his buildings and framed his views with great care. (A workman once found him high in a tree, determining whether the master bedroom would have a good mountain view.) A broad gable dominates the façade. Split granite boulders were used for the ground-floor of the front elevation, while siding of rough sawn pine stained with creosote filled the gable and the other three elevations.[62]

In a development of the hall seen at the Wilson house, a two-storey living-room, entered at one corner from a vestibule, occupies the centre of the nearly square plan. The hall sets up a cross-axial flow that parallels the spatial manipulations of Frank Lloyd Wright—whom Maclure admired and with whom he corresponded—as in the latter's Isabel

Roberts house (1908) in River Forest, Illinois.[63] Maclure and Mrs Shallcross worked together on the Victoria house to ensure that even small details of interior design were carefully attended to. The crafts were well represented, including the use of brass latches by Morris and Co. to secure the leaded casement windows.

Maclure's practice spread to Vancouver, where he opened an office in 1903. Placed in charge of the Vancouver office was Cecil Croker Fox (1879-1916), a young English architect who had worked in the office of C.F.A. Voysey (1857-1941), an important member of the Arts and Crafts community. The Vancouver office, known as Maclure and Fox, fared well during the building boom that preceded the First World War, but its success was short-lived because Fox was killed in action during the war.

The **W.F. Huntting house [11.39]** in Vancouver was built in 1911, to designs by Maclure and Fox, for sawmill-owner Foster Huntting, on Angus Drive in the CPR's affluent residential subdivision of Shaughnessy Heights. The entrance is twice protected from the Vancouver rain: by its own pyramidal roof and by the deep eave of the main roof above it. The austere roughcast (stucco) surface of the façade, broken only by a pair of gables, had become a Voysey trademark, and is seen in houses such as his own residence, The Orchard, at Chorley Wood, Hertfordshire (1898-1900). The inspiration for Voysey was the vernacular cottage of the West Country of England, and this became a new 'cottage' prototype for the years around 1900.[64]

Maclure and Fox designed a number of other fine houses in Shaughnessy Heights, most of them displaying Tudor Revival half-timbering on the exterior walls. The largest was Rosemary (1913-15), the residence of lawyer and liquor magnate A.E. Tulk; the most effectively composed was Miraloma, the home of publisher (and later Lieutenant Governor) Walter C. Nichol, which is contained within a massive hipped roof and whose property was developed with superb gardens.[65]

The Tudor Revival was a popular mode for houses across Canada during the first third of the twentieth century, and the half-timbered gable became its most recognizable feature. The style gained a notably persistent grasp in Victoria and Vancouver, because of those cities' powerful associations with Britain—Victorians were said to have been 'more English than the English'[66]—and it remains in use in both cities to express their roots. Home-builders liked the Tudor Revival for many of the same reasons they liked Georgian Classicism a century ear-

11.38 John James Shallcross house (Tor Lodge), Victoria, British Columbia, 1907. Photograph by Dane Campbell, *c.* 1973. Courtesy Martin Segger.

lier: it displayed the features of a tried-and-true architectural style as an emblem of colonial values and imperial loyalty.

Maclure was very conscious of his blending of traditions. In his description of the Alexis Martin house (1904) on Rockland Avenue in Victoria, which he

11.39 W.F. Huntting house, Vancouver, British Columbia, 1911. Photograph by John Roaf, 1973.

published in both *Canadian Architect and Builder* (1907) and *The Craftsman* (1908), he wrote that it was an

> unusually interesting example of a house that is built of local materials and is absolutely suited to its environment, but which yet shows decided evidences of the tastes and traditions of another country . . . .

He noted that in the large central hall, 'part of the furniture is Craftsman and the rest was designed by Mr M.H. Baillie Scott'—indicating a tangible link between himself and leading proponents of both the British and the American Arts and Crafts Movements.[67]

Baillie Scott (1865-1945) was a leading Arts and Crafts designer, while *The Craftsman* was a monthly magazine published in the US between 1901 and 1916 by furniture-manufacturer Gustav Stickley (1848-1942), who used the journal mainly to publicize and sell his own line of 'Craftsman' products and designs. Stickley succeeded in attracting a large and loyal readership among followers of the Arts and Crafts Movement because he invoked the spirit of Morris and Ruskin (to whom the first two issues were dedicated), and showed how their and his ideals could combine to improve the lives of ordinary Americans. Stickley's 'Mission' furniture was starkly plain, with straight oak rails and little upholstery; his furnishings used handcrafted materials such as copper, glass, and earthenware. His importance to architecture lies in his having published houses as well as their furnishings. His favourite image of the American 'home' was the 'bungalow', a new house-type that developed out of the Arts and Crafts Movement and would soon dominate mass housing in the western US and Canada.[68]

The bungalow—also known as the 'California bungalow', but more appropriately called the 'Craftsman bungalow'—is a 1- or $1\frac{1}{2}$-storey suburban house of modest size that is entirely contained within a low- or medium-pitched gabled roof (separate roofs may cover the entrance porch and/or the kitchen), and exploits wood as a structural, cladding, and decorative material. Triangular brackets or false beam-ends support broad eaves, and the rafter ends are often exposed. The roof over the porch rests on tapered square posts and stone pedestals; and random stone or brick—usually soft bricks, including a number of 'clinkers', or overburnt discards—is used for the chimney. The first bungalows of this type were built in the Bay Area around San Francisco in the first decade of the century. Some of the most

elaborate were the seminal bungalows designed by brothers Charles Sumner Greene (1868-1957) and Henry Mather Greene (1870-1954) of Pasadena. Greene and Greene (as their firm was called) learned much from *The Craftsman*, and their own custom-designed residences for individual clients were, in turn, published by Stickley. Their exploitation of the structural and decorative properties of wood was wholly within the Arts and Crafts spirit.[69]

The source of the 'bungalow' idea was the colonial bungalow, a low-slung hipped-roof building with flaring eaves that sheltered verandas around the perimeter. The form emerged in British India (the name is derived from Bengal) and appeared throughout the warmer parts of the Empire. This kind of bungalow provided a model for the Colonial Administration Buildings [8.25] in Victoria. Maclure, and his British Columbia contemporaries, occasionally alluded to the type in their houses. Maclure's own residence on Victoria's Superior Street (1899) is one such example; from there it was but a short jump to the Craftsman bungalow.[70]

Designers and builders in the US and Canada quickly distilled and popularized the essence of the Craftsman bungalow, and made the type accessible to first-time home-owners of the rapidly growing urban middle and working classes. Many periodicals—popular ones such as the *Ladies Home Journal*, as well as professional ones like *The Craftsman*—published a variety of bungalow designs intended for a broad market. In the 1910s and 1920s bungalows were spread effectively through the catalogues of American builders. Two of the many houses illustrated in the 1920 edition of *Craftsman Bungalows*—the catalogue of Yoho and Merritt of Seattle, Washington—represent typical **large and small bungalows** [11.40]. The former is $1\frac{1}{2}$ storeys high, with the gables on the sides and a large forward-facing dormer containing an upstairs bedroom. The plans show a new openness because rooms are interconnected, with space flowing from one room to another: no longer is each room entered from a common hall. In the small bungalow one enters the front door and passes through the living-room, dining-room, and kitchen to reach the rear door, without ever setting foot in a hall. The eaves are supported by brackets, the rafters are exposed, and the walls are clad in cedar siding. The smaller house is only a single storey high, with a cross-gable covering the broad porch. The shingle cladding is varied by half-timbered stripes in the porch gable. (The upper windows illuminate only attic space.) Both houses have an open sleeping porch at the rear, a feature

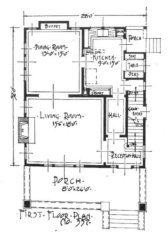

11.40 Large and small bungalows. From Yoho and Merritt, *Craftsman Bungalows*, 1920. Courtesy Michael Kluckner.

11.41 Bungalows, 2950-3040 West 5th Avenue, Vancouver, British Columbia, 1919-21. Photograph by John Roaf, 1973.

derived from the casual lifestyles of California. The lack of a parlour reflects this same informal way of life. Other firms that produced catalogues of this kind included E.J. Stillwell and Company of Los Angeles, William A. Radford's Radford Architectural Company and Fred Hodgson of Chicago, and Henry Saylor of New York—whose book, *Bungalows* (1911), was published in a second edition in Toronto (1913).[71] Producers of ready-mades—such as Sears Roebuck and Company—quickly added bungalows to their catalogues.

Houses like these are found in abundance in Vancouver, Victoria, and throughout the Canadian West; and many were also built in central and eastern Canada. Some were erected singly by individual property owners, others in groups by developers. A row of **eleven bungalows [11.41]** on West 5th Avenue, Vancouver, shows the simplest form: a one-storey building with a single gabled roof whose end faces the street. All are similar in plan and appearance, although on closer inspection minor variations in the decorative touches are revealed. The houses were erected between 1919 and 1921 by two separate contractors: Fred Melton built five, and the partnership of W.J. Hawkins and C. Cook six. The row is located in the Kitsilano district, which was developing rapidly at this time—mostly with bungalows—in response to the extension of the B.C. Electric Railway Company's streetcar line. Shingled walls, wood verandas, brick chimneys, stained glass, and simply detailed and darkly stained woodwork all provide rich textures and interesting forms at an affordable cost.[72]

The Arts and Crafts Movement had a lasting impact on architecture and design in Canada, as it did in Britain and the US, fostering a continuing respect for fine craftsmanship, the 'truthful' nature of materials, and the integration of architecture and the arts—while also making good design available for a middle-class market. A number of Canadian organizations were formed to develop handicrafts and train workers, among them the Canadian Handicraft Guild of Montreal and the Women's Art Association of Toronto.[73]

The most interesting and persistent of these groups was the Guild of All Arts, founded by Spencer and Rosa Clark in 1932 at Scarborough, just east of Toronto. The Guild was a residential community, set up somewhat like Ashbee's Guild of Handicraft, which provided 'pleasurable conditions' for the pursuit of arts and crafts. Among the early artists associated with the Guild were sculptors Emanuel Hahn and Frances Loring, silversmith Harold Stacey, and

musician Sir Ernest MacMillan. The Guild continued with diminishing vigour for more than half a century, its site becoming better known today for its hotel—the Guild Inn (1914, many subsequent additions)—and the Spencer Clark Collection of Historic Architecture, a grouping of some 100 fragments from demolished Toronto-area buildings, displayed outdoors in an attractively landscaped lakeside setting.[74]

Country houses and vacation retreats

Large country houses for wealthy members of the establishment—so important a part of European landscape and society—appeared early in Canada's history. The manor houses of New France were the country estates of a new aristocracy, although they were occupied more often by agents or tenant farmers than by the seigneurs themselves. Towards the end of the eighteenth century a number of British notables acquired country retreats in the image of those they had known in their homeland. In 1781 Governor Frederick Haldimand built Montmorency House (or Kent House), a residence overlooking Montmorency Falls, near Quebec; and Prince Edward, the Duke of Kent (who lived in Montmorency House a decade later), made many improvements to the Prince's Lodge [3.50] near Halifax, which Governor John Wentworth had lent him, after 1794. Another early country seat was Charles Ramage Prescott's Acacia Grove [3.41].

Around 1780 General Henry Watson Powell built **Powell Place [11.42]** at Sillery, just west of Quebec, as a two-storey Palladian villa, with a central gable, that was given a pair of wings in the 1830s by new owner Henry Atkinson (it was then known as Spencer Wood; the detail from the lithograph by Lemercier shows it at this time). It was enlarged again in 1852 by George Browne to be used as the governor's residence, but it burned down in 1860.[75] Typical of the first generation of Canadian country houses—of which there were many in the suburbs of Quebec—its classical design resembled that of the urban house. Classicism served as an effective foil to the wilderness: in the spirit of the Enlightenment, art was made to triumph over nature. By the middle of the nineteenth century, select areas of the United Canadas had concentrations of country estates of this kind.

Improved travel facilities, and growing affluence among the middle class in the last quarter of the century, led increasing numbers of Canadians to build rural retreats intended for week-end, vacation, and summer use, often as bases for hunting and fish-

ing. People of high position or wealth erected manors on large country estates; those of more modest means either built cottages on smaller properties or patronized the many resort hotels that began to spring up along the beaches and in the mountains. This period marked the beginnings of tourism, encouraged in a large measure by the efforts of the CPR and others to sell Canadian scenery.[76] Since most of the new country residences were built between 1880 and the First World War, the popular Romanesque and Queen Anne revivals, and the Arts-and-Crafts-influenced styles, were favoured. Whether through their choice of model or materials, many were designed to reflect, rather than reject, the natural landscape. The remainder of this section looks at a selection of houses and hotels of this kind.

Country houses often consciously sought to achieve a rustic character by the use of an appropriate prototype or style. **Stanley House [11.43]**—built around 1888 on Chaleur Bay, near New Richmond, Quebec; originally the Gaspé fishing retreat of the Governor General, Lord Stanley of Preston—was an attempt to acknowledge the rural environment, for its design was based on that of a scaled-down château (a country house of the French aristocracy). It consists of a two-storey rectangular

11.42 Powell Place (Spencer Wood), Sillery, Quebec, *c.* 1780 and following. Lithograph by Lemercier, 1849. ANQ/P600-5/GH-470-64.

11.43 Stanley House, near New Richmond, Quebec, *c.* 1888. Photograph by Harold Kalman, 1973.

block with a polygonal projection (containing the living-room) at the left, and a square one at the right—both of which seem as if they should have risen higher to become towers (as they do at the Château Frontenac, 9.18). A veranda extends across most of the front, and there is a lower kitchen wing at the rear. The exterior walls are board-and-batten, the interiors are finished with vertical pine boards. The rustic character may be as much a product of necessity as of choice, given the relative isolation of the site, although the proximity of the Intercolonial Railway made it quite accessible. Lady Aberdeen, the wife of Lord Stanley's successor as Governor General, described the house in her *Journal*.

Lord Stanley, who was devoted to carpentering as a hobby, took a great deal of interest in the designing, building & fitting up of the house & Reid the old Aberdeenshire house carpenter (of Government House Ottawa) or under-clerk of works, carried it all out capitally & economically . . . . It is built of common pine wood & the furniture is of the simplest—plain deal boards for tables with legs of small trunks of unbarked trees—shelves of wood with curtains hanging from them . . . . There are eighteen bed-rooms, a nice big octagonal drawing-room with a big open fireplace & a brick hearth . . . . The menservant's bedrooms & carpenter's shop etc. are all outside. Of course it is all arranged for summer living only . . . .

The house, still owned by the federal government, was used for many years by the Canada Council as a venue for small conferences.[77]

A popular summer vacation area frequented by both Canadians and Americans was the southern coast of New Brunswick, in the area around St Andrews (known at the time as St Andrews-by-the-Sea) and the nearby islands. Sir William Van Horne had his summer house in the area—Covenhoven, on Ministers Island—which he built to his own design shortly after 1891. Problems with construction, and the need for more space, led him to ask Edward Maxwell to alter and extend it in 1898-9.[78]

Many of the summer residents in the St Andrews area were Americans, and their presence made the region a Canadian outpost of the American Shingle style, a version of the Queen Anne Revival that is dominated by gabled rooflines, shingled walls, and simpler compositions. The best-known building in this manner is the Algonquin Hotel in St Andrews, built in 1889—to designs of Rand and Taylor of Boston—by the St Andrew's Hotel Company of Boston. It was subsequently acquired by the CPR and

rebuilt after a fire in April 1914.[79] The most impressive of the early hotels in the region was the **Tyn-y-Coed Hotel** [11.44] on Campobello Island, NB, built in 1882 for New England clientele by a consortium of New York and Boston businessmen, and designed by the distinguished Boston architectural partnership of Charles A. Cummings (1833-1905) and Willard T. Sears (1837-1920). (The most famous summer resident of Campobello Island would be President Franklin Delano Roosevelt.) Four storeys high, including the portion within the slope of the roof, the Tyn-y-Coed Hotel featured a broad veranda, shingled walls, shuttered double-hung windows, and a picturesque roofline punctuated by numerous gables and a polygonal corner tower. The hotel (which has been demolished) would have fit in well at Newport, Rhode Island, or in resort areas along the Maine coast.[80]

A fascinating country house was **Château Menier** [11.45] at Port-Menier (Baie Ellis) on Anticosti Island, Quebec. The 140-mile-long (225-km) island, at the entrance to the St Lawrence River, was purchased in 1895 by Henri Menier, a wealthy chocolate manufacturer from France, who played out his pastoral fantasies by attempting to maintain it as a private sports preserve and to colonize a portion with a model town based on a medieval fiefdom. Menier's château, built in 1903 to designs by the French architect Stéphane Sauvestre, is based on European models, yet it also fitted comfortably within the North American Queen Anne Revival. It was dominated by a tall central gable that enclosed several floors within the slope of its roof, much like a Swiss chalet—which was apparently regarded as an appropriately picturesque prototype for the Canadian wilderness. The exterior walls were framed in a grid of vertical and horizontal wood beams with wood-panel infills. (This method had Swiss antecedents, yet one finds a parallel in the Stick style prevalent in the US in the last decades of the nineteenth century.) The irregular massing, with wings and gables of varying heights, and the use of turrets and verandas, all suggested the Queen Anne Revival. The sumptuous interiors featured heavy carvings, grand fireplaces, hunting trophies, and tapestries. Menier visited the island for only a half-dozen summers; the town (Baie-Sainte-Claire) failed; and the manor burned down in 1953. The legacy of the eccentric 'chocolate king' is now most evident in the herd of more than 100,000 white-tailed deer that are descended from the 220 he brought out in 1896.[81]

Percy Nobbs predictably adapted regional traditions in his country-house designs. At the **John L.**

Domestic Architecture

Todd house (1911-13) in Senneville, Quebec, he and his partner George Hyde (1877-1944) took the steep hipped roof, tall chimneys, lateral veranda, and shuttered casement windows from the farm houses of New France and adapted them in a manner that made them non-revivalist, modern, and timeless [11.46]. Located on a bluff by the shore of the of Lac des Deux-Montagnes, west of Montreal, this attractive house was built in a warm, locally quarried limestone with a roughly textured finish—another Quebec tradition—and the same stone was used for the terrace and garden pergolas, further linking the building with the site. The use of vernacular forms and materials was, of course, the Arts and Crafts approach; here Nobbs found satisfactory indigenous Canadian sources, casting only a few glances at Britain (with polygonal Scottish dormers), in keeping with his ongoing search for an appropriate national expression.[82]

The Victoria-born Dr John Todd was Professor of Parasitology at McGill (he had been instrumental in discovering the parasites that cause sleeping sickness), and his wife was the daughter of wealthy Montreal banker Sir Edward Clouston, whose large summer house, called Boisbriant (built for J.J.C. Abbott, who succeeded John A. Macdonald as Prime Minister, and enlarged by Edward Maxwell, beginning in 1899), was on the adjacent property.[83] The

11.44 Tyn-y-Coed Hotel, Campobello Island, New Brunswick, 1882. New Brunswick Museum/Ganong 115A.

11.45 Château Menier, Port-Menier, Anticosti Island, Quebec, 1903. NAC/C76312.

630

11.46 John L. Todd house, Senneville, Quebec, 1911-13. McGill University/Canadian Architecture Collection. Copyright Francis J. Nobbs.

Todds wanted a house that was smaller and more casual than that of the Cloustons, and so the living-room and the oval dining-room are relatively modest in scale, and the bedrooms include a sleeping porch, a feature that was common in the houses of British Columbia and California.

Another way in which a country house might

11.47 Perspective view of the Hodgson cottage (Château-du-Lac), Sainte-Agathe, Quebec, *c.* 1896. McGill University/Canadian Architecture Collection.

achieve a rustic character was by using materials that look unfinished—which the rubble stonework adopted by Nobbs in the Todd house, and by Maxwell in Boisbriant, succeeded in doing. Even more effective was the use of round logs rather than finished lumber, as in Edward Maxwell's **Château-du-Lac [11.47]** at Sainte-Agathe, Quebec, built in 1896 for Thomas Hodgson, one of a series of houses that Maxwell designed in the Laurentians, north of Montreal, for businessmen from that city who wanted to fish in the mountain lakes and rivers. The house is not unlike an Ontario cottage in its form, with a projecting central bay (enclosing the living-room) illuminated by a pointed-arched Palladian window that breaks through the eaves as a dormer, and a lower wing to the right (barely visible in the watercolour) containing a woodshed and an ice-house. What is unusual is that the walls were built of horizontal logs joined with saddle-notches, exposing the butt ends, and the house was encircled by a broad veranda whose supports were unpeeled logs with branches at the top in the place of capitals.[84]

Unsawn logs had occasionally been used as a rustic conceit in 'polite' architecture—as in Governor Simcoe's Castle Frank [4.27] and John Galt's Priory [12.2] at Guelph, and in a cottage proposed for R.H. Place in West Oxford, Ontario (John G. Howard, 1835), whose veranda was supported by tree-trunks with branches spreading at the top, as at Château-du-Lac.[85] However, a more immediate source for the

Hodgson house is found in the cottages and summer 'camps' that were being built by wealthy Americans in the Adirondack Mountains of New York State, and that have been described as forming an 'Adirondack style'.[86]

As log construction became rarer in principal dwellings, it was used with increasing frequency for country houses in the twentieth century. **Pethern Point** [11.48], near Perth, Ontario, was built in 1919 on Big Rideau Lake by the Hicks family of Perth. Engineer Thomas Norman Hicks, the son of carriage-maker Thomas Hicks, had the cottage built as a hunting and fishing lodge—though before long his family was living in it the year round. Built by local carpenters Wesley James and Milford Rabb, it is constructed of western red cedar logs that are insulated and chinked with oakum (tarred rope or hemp) and connected with saddle-notched joints. The projecting central gable features a curved peak, a detail shared by all the outbuildings—cabin, workshop, garage, boat-house, and ice house—although they have frame, and not log, construction. A Hicks family tradition recalls that Thomas, who had visited New York, wanted the house to be constructed in a Finnish technique and to resemble Adirondack lodges. This is supported by a 1908 manual on log construction, found in the house, that refers to Scandinavian and Swiss techniques and illustrated cottages in the Adirondacks.[87]

The building that claims to be the largest log structure in Canada is the **Château Montebello** [11.49]

11.48 Pethern Point, near Perth, Ontario, 1919. Photograph by Larry Turner, 1988.

at Montebello, Quebec, where the Laurentian Mountains meet the Ottawa River. Now a Canadian Pacific hotel, it was built in 1930 as the Seigniory Club, an 186-bedroom private fishing lodge. The large X-shaped main building (whose wings are joined at a tall six-sided central lounge), and its outbuildings, were constructed from 10,000 western red cedar logs in only four months by Finnish-Canadian master-builder Victor Nymark and a crew of about 800

11.49 Château Montebello (Seigniory Club), Montebello, Quebec, 1930. Photograph 1930. Canadian Pacific Limited/ASN-8209-4.

men—most of them Europeans who were familiar with Scandinavian techniques. While the basement walls are uncoursed stone on concrete foundations, all the exterior walls above were made of logs. Montreal architects Harold Lawson (1885-1969) and Harold Little (1887-1948) provided the design. (Edwin S. Kent and George W. White were associates for the project.) The club was the brainchild of Swiss-American millionaire H.M. Saddlemire. It was built by the Lucerne-in-Quebec Community Association, which was sponsored by the Canadian Pacific Railway, and its initial directors represented the power élite of both the French- and English-speaking communities. They included L.A. Taschereau, Premier of Quebec, and E.W. Beatty, Chairman of the CPR, as well as the presidents of three Montreal-based banks. Membership in the Seigniory Club came with 10,000 square feet (930 sq m) of land in the adjacent hills, on which many members built their own log houses. The land was the former *seigneurie de la Petite-Nation*, whose most illustrious seigneur had been Louis-Joseph Papineau, the leader of the Rebellion of 1837-8 in Lower Canada. Papineau's manor house—a stone building with a hipped roof, widow's walk, and twin towers, designed by Louis Aubertin and built in 1847-50—stands a short distance away from the Château Montebello.[88]

Most Canadians could not afford to buy a country property, stay at a grand hotel, or join an exclusive club—yet many wanted to enjoy the lakes, rivers, and mountains. A popular solution was the rental cottage or cabin, available on a daily, weekly, or monthly basis. A **row of cottages [11.50]** at Notre-Dame-du-Portage, Quebec, on the St Lawrence River near Rivière-du-Loup, built in the shadow of the parish church, offered vacationers water and clean air, but very little privacy.[89]

Multiple Housing

The provision of adequate housing for people of modest and low incomes has always posed social and architectural challenges. Working people must live within reasonable access of their place of employment; so when transportation was limited, urban industries required housing nearby. But the high cost of city property made it difficult for wage-earners to procure private houses. By increasing the density of land use (i.e. by increasing the number of dwelling units on a parcel of land), the cost of land (per unit) became lower and the housing correspondingly cheaper. The preferred solution, therefore, was the introduction of multiple housing—buildings with two or more self-contained suites. The mid-nineteenth-century houses on rue Wolfe [5.54] in Montreal provided an effective solution, with four units contained in a two-storey building. The construction of a separate residential building at the rear of the property, common in Montreal, provided still denser land use, but it was accompa-

11.50 Cottages, Notre Dame-du-Portage, Quebec. Photograph by Dudley Witney.

nied by a corresponding degradation in the residents' quality of life. For many years Montreal had a larger proportion of its population living in rental suites than other Canadian cities because of the strong industrial basis of its economy (requiring a large working-class population) and its high land prices. Consequently the city's developers—many of them small contractors who erected one building at a time—produced a wide variety of multiple-dwelling-types.

Another answer, more common in other cities, was to produce a cheaper single-family house. Nothing could be smaller or cheaper than the one-room ready-made house (Design B) produced by the British Columbia Mills, Timber and Trading Company [9.27]. But the overriding determinant remained the high cost of urban land, and so houses of this tiny scale achieved very limited sales in cities. Once a person bought a city property, he or she was much more likely to acquire it with a house of a more reasonable size. The mass production of plans and building materials made houses such as those illustrated in **11.31** and **11.40** fall within the reach of people of modest incomes.

Housing in self-sufficient industrial communities—such as Marysville, NB [**5.40**], and those that are discussed in the next chapter—was even less problematic. The proprietor of the industry usually also owned the land surrounding the mill or factory, and was able to build housing and rent it to the workers at below market price.

After the introduction of streetcars in the second half of the nineteenth century, people working in large cities could live on less costly suburban land served by public transportation. And in the early twentieth century the popularization of the automobile allowed commuting from even greater distances, permitting proportionately more people to own single-family houses in the suburbs. In large cities, however, multiple residences were a common solution for housing people of both low and middle incomes. This section provides an overview of the different kinds of buildings that contained multiple-dwelling units.

Row houses and duplexes

Side-by-side row houses provide a simple and effective means of reducing the land area occupied by each living unit. The common 'party walls' ensure that no space is left between suites as undeveloped land—although this results in reduced light, air, and privacy. Row houses had long been common in

11.51 Row of houses, Spruce Street, Toronto, Ontario, 1887. Photograph 1970. CIHB/06101002400119.

England (where they are called terraces) and France, and were therefore familiar in colonial Canada. They were built in the eighteenth century in the centres of Halifax, Quebec, and Montreal.

11.52 Row houses, Maynard-Creighton district, Halifax, Nova Scotia, *c*. 1870s. Photograph by Kathleen Flanagan.

Row houses remained popular through the nineteenth century for people in all income groups. The **row at 119-33 Spruce Street [11.51]**, Toronto, was built in 1887 for working people. Each unit is only two bays wide. The few rooms were illuminated on the front and back by a door and a window on the ground floor and by two windows upstairs—contained as dormers within the mansard roof, the hallmark of the Second Empire style. The elegant arched heads over the doors and windows, and the iron cresting along the top of the roof, provide some relief to what would otherwise be a rather dreary brick ensemble. Similar in scale, but very different in detail and materials, is a **row in the Maynard-Creighton area of Halifax [11.52]**, Nova Scotia, built in the 1870s, and recently rehabilitated. The clapboard and shingle walls, gently sloped roof, polygonal dormers, and classically inspired doorways are all familiar features of Nova Scotia building.[90]

Hollywood Parade [11.53], on James Street in Ottawa's Centretown, was built for people with somewhat higher incomes and had a more grandiose design. This flamboyant brick row, erected in 1892 by prolific builder James A. Corry, contains six narrow five-bedroom suites, 16 feet (4.9m) wide at the front, and narrower at the rear to allow light courts. The façade is a Victorian eclectic delight. The Romanesque-inspired entrance arches and corbels are complemented by Moorish 'keyhole' arches around the living-room windows beside them and by the Italianate segmental-headed arches in the bedrooms above. Terracotta reliefs, marble colon-

nettes, and art glass produced an extraordinarily rich design.[91]

For people at the high end of the income scale, the elegant Prince of Wales Terrace [5.57] in Montreal provided a series of eight three-storey (plus basement) townhouses in the heart of that city's gracious Square Mile.

A building that contains only two living units is called a duplex. In North American cities like Montreal—that for long had high urban densities and land values, and consequently developed a tradition of multiple dwellings rather than single-family houses—generations of people (even including moneyed and professional families) grew accustomed to living in relatively confined spaces. In these cities, duplexes usually contained one unit per floor, one over the other: the 'downstairs' unit (which often included the basement) and the 'upstairs' unit. One duplex of this kind is **4910-12 Victoria Avenue [11.54]**, Montreal, built in 1939 and designed by Maxwell M. Kalman (b. 1906), whose family occupied the downstairs suite. The pair of entrance doors, encased in a somewhat *retardataire* Georgian Revival surround within the central projecting bay, immediately reveals that the house is a duplex. The door on the left (no. 4910) leads into a vestibule and central hall, with a living-room at one side and a dining-room on the other; while the right-hand door (no. 4912) opens onto a staircase that leads to the second floor (an internal version of Montreal's traditional exterior staircase). The Georgian theme, declared in the door surround and central hall, is maintained in the red brick walls, white wood trim, and small-paned windows. A steep driveway provides access to a basement garage.

11.53 Hollywood Parade, Ottawa, Ontario, 1892. Photograph by John Roaf, 1982.

Duplexes were sometimes built with one entrance on the front elevation and the other along one side (unseen from the street), so that the building might pose as a large single-family house. In Westmount, the well-to-do residential suburb of Montreal— which did not want to be perceived as a municipality that had multiple dwellings—this arrangement was actually enforced by law for a period.

Buildings with more than two living units having exterior entrances can be called triplexes, fourplexes, and so on. The houses on rue Wolfe [5.54] and rue Jeanne-Mance [5.55] in Montreal, both of which have suites beside and above/below each other, fall into this category. Those that are inhabited by low-income people are often described as 'tenements'. The word denotes a rental dwelling of any kind, expensive or cheap, and may include single-family dwellings in the heart of a major city rented out for multiple-family occupancy—a use that caused them to be considered slums.

For other cities, like Toronto, that had developed a tradition of single-family dwellings, up-and-down duplexes were seen as being too confining, and lacking in privacy, to be widely accepted by the housing market (though they were certainly built in some numbers). Consequently a double dwelling was designed with the units side-by-side—forming, in effect, a two-unit row house, or two semi-detached houses. The pair of residences at **64-6 Madison Avenue** [11.55], Toronto, built in 1891 for a middle-class market, are typical of countless others there, and in other Ontario cities. The plans of the two Toronto houses are similar, with the doorway (located to the left of centre) leading to the staircase (and the upper-floor bedrooms) and ahead to the kitchen, and the living-room is on the right with the dining-room behind it. The elevations, on the other hand, have been treated differently to provide variety—in contrast to the look-alike treatment of the lower-cost row on Spruce Street. The dwelling unit on the left presents a somewhat conventional Queen Anne Revival exterior: the dormer window (with its decorative scalloped shingles) provides a gable-like peak, the living-room and principal bedroom windows share a bowed projection, and a porch protects the entrance. The right-hand unit terminates in a stepped gable (resembling a Dutch or Flemish townhouse), and the bay window occurs as an oriel on the second and third floors. Both units are faced in the same brick, but on the left side it has been painted a light colour. As so often occurs in Toronto, the separate owners decorated their respective dwellings differently.

11.54 4910-12 Victoria Avenue, Montreal, Quebec, 1939. Photograph by Brian Merrett, 1994.

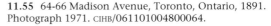

11.55 64-66 Madison Avenue, Toronto, Ontario, 1891. Photograph 1971. CIHB/061101004800064.

Apartment houses

A building in which numerous self-contained units are entered internally from a common corridor or courtyard, rather than directly from the street, is usually called an apartment house. (This is distinct from a rooming house or hotel, in which the rooms or suites are not self-contained, and may share some living and cooking facilities.) Such structures—common on the European continent and in Scotland in the eighteenth century, mostly providing accommodation for working-class people—gained acceptance in England (where they were called 'flats') in the second half of the nineteenth century. English developers often named blocks of flats with the euphemism 'Mansions' (as in R.N. Shaw's Albert Hall Mansions, London, 1879-86) in order to attract the middle classes.[92]

Canadians observed this trend with mixed feelings: some saw it as a solution to the growing housing problem, others as an assault on the quality of residential life. Both sides were correct! In 1890 an anonymous contributor to *Canadian Architect and Builder* asked:

Why should not cities such as Toronto, London, Ottawa, Hamilton or Kingston, have apartment houses? The old time citizen accustomed to his 'bit of garden' is apt to hold up his hands in holy horror at the suggestion, forgetting that times have changed, and that these places have got beyond the village conditions.

It is contended that there is no privacy in these great piles, that there is no place for children, and that many other things are lacking to the man who considers his home his castle. But what are the conditions and surroundings of the average citizen in Toronto . . . ? He is squeezed into a narrow slice of building say 12 to 16 feet wide—one of perhaps a dozen domiciles in one long uninteresting block. . . .

With a well laid out apartment house, a greater proportion of sunlit living rooms may be obtained, while a well-lit court beautified with flowers and a fountain would replace the narrow and ill-kept backyards[93]

The advocates were heard. During the building boom at the end of the nineteenth century, apartment houses catering for tenants of various incomes began to be built in Canada in response to the wave of urbanization and the consequent increase in city land values. By the beginning of the First World War the building-type was well established in cities across the country. Several means of laying out

the plan competed for favour; we shall look at an example of each type.

One popular layout, among relatively small buildings with low rents, had a single entrance off the street leading to a central stairwell that was open the full height of the building (usually three or four storeys). Access to the individual apartments was from the landings, or from an open hallway that surrounded the stairwell. Many structures of this kind were built by (now-anonymous) small-scale developers. **The Warrington [11.56]**, on Elgin Street in Ottawa, is a brick apartment house that was built in 1910 with this plan, containing ten suites on its four floors. A superb four-tiered balcony on the façade provides the tenants with a way of getting fresh air and compensating, to some extent, for their having no direct access to the ground. (For this reason balconies have always been an important feature of apartment-building design.) The provision of access off an interior stairwell (called an atrium today) was adapted from office buildings: the Central Chambers [10.40], a dozen blocks to the north, has such an arrangement.[94]

Narrow light courts commonly penetrated the building block in order to provide more opportunity for windows, and to allow increased light and air to reach the suites (they also permitted a larger number of suites). The entrance to the building was often located at the end of a narrow forecourt; such was the case at the **Manhattan Apartments [11.57]**, at Thurlow and Robson Streets in Vancouver, a large (32-suite) building erected in 1907 by Scottish-born lumberman and developer William Lamont Tait. The architects were John E. Parr (1856-1923) and Thomas A. Fee (1859-1929), a highly successful partnership that specialized in functional commercial buildings. Parr and Fee advertised that 'their chief endeavour [was] the production of buildings that will pay . . . . *Utilitas* is their motto, and revenue their aim.'[95]

The opening to the deep forecourt is seen near the left in the photograph, beyond the two cars parked on Thurlow Street. The entrance opens onto a small lobby and a staircase, and corridors lead from there to the apartments. Buff brick walls, with red brick quoins, are enlivened by three-storey-high bay windows (a popular feature in Vancouver's commercial buildings) and a heavy cornice. Retail shops occupy most of the ground floor. Praising the building shortly after its completion, a newspaper reported that

the flats are arranged so that all the principal rooms overlook the main streets. There is not a suite in the building overlooking out upon backyards, or that has not a good view.

It concluded that the Manhattan was 'in advance of anything else of the kind yet erected in the city.'[96] Despite the amenities, however, most Vancouverites were slow to accept apartment living, and for many years clung to the ideal of owning a house. They saw apartments as an American and European scourge (an impression reinforced by the name 'Manhattan'), as an item in the *Province* suggests: 'In the big, bad cities, such as New York and London, the acute issue is the rent question—the tenement house evil.'[97] The Manhattan was a success, however, attracting residents with middle incomes, and in 1912 a narrow five-storey addition was constructed (seen at the right of the photograph). Recently rehabilitated, the building is now operated as co-operative apartments.

Many apartment residents preferred a more direct means of access from the outside. An alternative plan, therefore, provided a series of separate entries off the courtyard, each with its own lobby and stairs, that led to a limited number of suites. This layout, common in Britain, was less space-efficient than the plan of the Warrington or the Manhattan, since multiple staircases were required, and it was a more expensive solution adopted in buildings for people of higher incomes. A handsome example of this type, built in 1904, is the **Bishop's Court Apartment Building** [11.58] on Bishop Street in Montreal (located within the Square Mile), designed by Saxe and Archibald. (Charles J. Saxe [1870-1943] and John S. Archibald [1872-1934] had both worked in the office

11.56 The Warrington, Ottawa, Ontario, 1910. Photograph by John Roaf, 1982.

11.57 Manhattan Apartments, Vancouver, British Columbia, 1907. Photograph by John Roaf, 1973.

11.58 *(right)* Bishop's Court Apartments, Montreal, Quebec, 1904. From *Canadian Architect and Builder*, June 1905. MTRL.

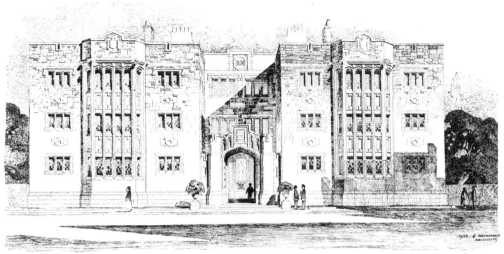

PERSPECTIVE OF FRONT

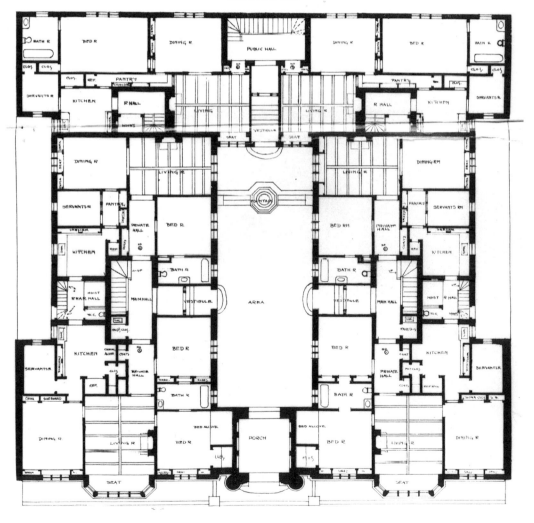

639

of Edward Maxwell before striking out on their own in 1897.) The deep and narrow forecourt, anticipating that of the Manhattan, is separated from the street by an arched porch. Three doors open off the court, each of them serving a wing containing two apartments on each of three floors, for a total of eighteen one- and two-bedroom suites. The social status of the tenants for whom the apartments were built is shown by each unit's having a servant's room, and access (from the kitchen) to a back staircase and a service elevator, so that trades people and servants could come and go through a door to the basement on the rear lane. The interior finishes are marble in the public spaces and chestnut in the apartments. The exterior, which is faced with random-coursed brown sandstone and artificial stone trim, is treated in the Gothic Revival—not the ecclesiastically inspired Gothic of the early and High Victorian eras, but a version of Gothic that was derived from secular architecture and would soon become a popular style (see page 228).[98]

The 'court', in the name Bishop's Court Apartments referred to the forecourt. (A progenitor in Montreal is the nearby Stanley Court Apartments, designed by D.R. Brown [1869-1946] and D.N. MacVicar [1869-1929] and built in 1897.) The courtyard originally contained garden sculpture and a fountain, transposing the landscape features of great homes to an apartment house.[99] Courtyards became broader with time, creating the 'courtyard apartments' or 'garden apartments' that were popular in later years (see **11.60**, **14.86**).

An alternative apartment-house plan, and the one that ultimately dominated mid-twentieth-century high-rise buildings, was the rectangular block with a long corridor running along its spine and providing access on either side to the suites, all with an exterior aspect. This is the plan of the **Arlington Apartments** [**11.59**] in Edmonton, built in 1909 to designs by R. Percy Barnes (1857-1926). The Arlington was that city's first—and for many years its largest—apartment building, offering its tenants an attractive residence near the city centre. The five storeys contain 49 suites of three to six rooms. A fire-escape provides emergency egress at either end of the corridor, and a tearoom 'for all the elegant clientele and their friends' (as former owner Phyllis Barham recalled) was once located on the top floor. The many modern conveniences included china cabinets that

11.59 Arlington Apartments, Edmonton, Alberta, 1909. PAA/Ernest Brown Collection/B4220.

rotated out of sight to reveal retractable 'murphy beds' (allowing a living-room to serve also as a bedroom), refrigerators, internal telephone communication, and an elevator. Barham, who purchased the Arlington in 1972, noted that 'It was the most elegant building,

> and housed all important lawyers, doctors, judges, and some titled British aristocracy. It was more or less like a Club. Whenever, for some reason, they sold their big old homes, they moved to the Arlington, to 'join the crowd.'[100]

The apartment building may have been perceived initially as providing housing for the masses, but those like the Arlington and Bishop's Court Apartments served a far more affluent market. Private-sector developers recognized (as they do today) that there is little money to be made in constructing low-rental units. Consequently workers continued to live in old, poorly serviced, and poorly maintained tenements that provided considerable profits for the landlords.

Efforts were made to improve the situation, but changes came slowly. In Toronto a survey made in 1887 of 654 working-class people and their families revealed that 278 were tenants, 341 boarders, and only 35 owned their residences.[101] Reformers such as William Holmes Howland, Toronto's mayor from 1886 to 1888, fought for better housing. He noted that in St John's Ward

> you will find houses built in front and then others built in at the back end, the result being that there's no space or air room and that they are very unwholesome.[102]

Howland also campaigned against crime and alcoholism, earning for the city the epithet 'Toronto the good'.

Pressure from reformers such as Howland led Prime Minister Macdonald to strike a Royal Commission in 1889 to investigate the effects of industrialism and 'the conflict of labor and capital'. The report of the Commissioners noted:

> In many places no effectual means are taken to secure proper sanitary conditions in workingmen's dwellings. Testimony supports a belief that these houses yield to the owners a much larger revenue than houses of a better class, and certainly landlords can afford to make them safely habitable.

It recommended inspections and regulations to help provide safer housing, as well as some form of rent controls based on 'fair and legitimate interest on the amount invested.' The report also stated:

> If the hours of labor be shortened workingmen will be able to seek homes in the suburbs of towns, where they will have the benefit of lower rents and will secure better sanitary conditions.[103]

The Commission did little more than expose the problems. The only recommendation that was heeded was the declaration of Labour Day as a statutory holiday.

Progress was finally made more than two decades later, in 1912, when the Toronto Housing Company was organized on a British model as a limited-dividend corporation with a mandate to provide affordable housing for the working people of the city. The City of Toronto was a participant, and retired businessman (and reformer) G. Frank Beer directed the company. Combining business with philanthropy—investors were permitted a five-per-cent return—the Company built two developments that together provided homes for 256 families. They succeeded in attracting tenants with moderately low incomes, although the rents were beyond the reach of the working poor. Twenty-one Canadian cities and a number of American municipalities expressed interest in the experiment, but its success was limited as a result of the recession of 1913 and the subsequent war.[104]

One of the two projects, and architecturally the more interesting, was **Riverdale Courts [11.60]** in Toronto, on Bain Avenue in North Riverdale, east of the Don River. Designed by Eden Smith and Sons, the development was built in 1914-16. The units were called 'cottage flats', described by the Company as 'modern apartment[s] with [their] own front door to the street.' The 204 units were arranged in $2\frac{1}{2}$-storey blocks around three 80-foot-wide (24.4-m) landscaped 'courts' spanning Bain Avenue. The steep shingled roofs are interrupted at intervals by gabled projections, some of which enclose two-storey porches. (Many of the porches have been filled in with windows.) Hipped dormer windows provide illumination within the roofs. The north-facing gables (normally in shadow) are finished in half-timbering to provide a contrast with the light stucco walls. With the roofs, gables, and detailing giving the exterior a domestic character— which is further expressed by the angled arrangement of the ground-floor and second-floor entrances, and by the comfortable interiors the project provided both privacy and a sense of community, and avoided the sterile public-housing aspect of so many later developments. Riverdale

11.60 Riverdale Courts, Toronto, Ontario, 1914-16. City of Toronto Archives/sc18-1.

Courts is today very much alive—a handsome co-operative that is an architectural ornament of its district.[105]

The Toronto Housing Company undertook no construction after 1923, although it continued to maintain its properties until the early 1960s, when it disbanded. It formed an important precedent by involving the public sector in the provision of housing and by demonstrating that affordable housing was as much a social, economic, and planning issue as an architectural one.

In subsequent decades a number of other Canadian cities—notably Montreal—followed the Toronto example and provided non-profit public housing. The federal government became involved in housing during the Second World War, when it created Wartime Housing Limited, a crown corporation that built and managed thousands of rental units (both multiple and detached housing) for war workers and, subsequently, returning veterans.[106] The National Housing Act of 1946 created Central Mortgage and Housing Corporation—now Canada Mortgage and Housing Corporation (CMHC)— which absorbed Wartime Housing Limited a year later. The federal agency remains active in providing assistance to the private sector in building affordable housing.

CHAPTER **12**

TOWN PLANNING

TOWN PLANNING is often thought of as a creation of the twentieth century, but this is not so. It is true that town-planners became recognized professionals only in our own time, but towns and cities have always been planned. Most Canadian communities, even in colonial times, were the result of conscious planning decisions. Quebec was first laid out by governors Samuel de Champlain and Charles Huault de Montmagny, and engineer Jean Bourdon; Halifax by Governor Edward Cornwallis, engineer John Brewse, and surveyor Charles Morris; New Westminster by the Royal Engineers; and the farms and towns of the Prairies by the Dominion Land Survey and the railways' surveyors. The plans and land policies that were chosen shaped the communities' social structure, ownership patterns, physical well-being, and future development patterns. Most of the time these choices favoured the interests of the established economic and political order.[1]

In the early days of settlement, direct government or corporate intervention was usually restricted to the initial survey and sale of lots. Thereafter, market forces played an increasingly dominant role. An exception is seen in the regulations, usually in the form of building codes, that were introduced from time to time (beginning in New France) to reduce the risk of fire, or building collapse, or to otherwise ensure public safety.

This chapter looks at a selection of town-planning activities. It begins with private-development ventures in the nineteenth century, then turns to the early-twentieth-century movements that led to urban planning as we know it today. After Toronto is singled out to demonstrate the effect of these tendencies, a number of resource communities conclude the chapter. We shall see how, in every period, it was firmly believed that proper planning of the built environment would provide a high quality of life, and that good design was essential to overall well-being.

The Settlement of the Interior

Land development companies and colonization schemes

In the middle years of the nineteenth century, land speculators played an important role in opening up the interior of eastern and central Canada and in promoting settlement. A number of privately owned land companies, most of them organized in England, grasped this opportunity with varying degrees of success and profit. Of course the principle of private initiative was not new. In New France, the Compagnie des Cents-Associés had been organized in 1627 to encourage settlement, although it did not succeed in attaining its objectives (page 27).

One of the most important of these new organizations was the Canada Land Company (commonly known as the Canada Company), formed in 1824 under the leadership of the Scottish-born novelist and promoter John Galt (1779-1839). The gap between Galt's ideals, and what he was actually able to accomplish, reveals much about the realities of developing the new land.

The Canada Company acquired nearly 2.5 million acres (1 million hectares) of Crown land in western Upper Canada between Lake Ontario and Lake Huron, establishing agents in Canadian, American, and European—including German—cities, and advertising widely to help sell its land. It became a powerful commercial and political organization, with close ties to the Tory government. Galt was the Company's superintendent between 1826 and 1829, when his frequent quarrels with the directors led to his dismissal.[2]

Architecture and planning interested Galt immensely. As he wrote in his autobiography:

Having myself a kind of amateur taste in architectural drawing, and being, in consequence, from

643

the period of my travels, led to adopt as a rule in art, that the style of a building should always indicate and be appropriate to its purpose, I thought that the constructing of a city afforded an opportunity to edify posterity in this matter.

In 1826, on his way to Upper Canada from England, Galt visited and studied a number of land developments in New York State. He was particularly impressed by the radial plan of Buffalo, which he called a 'very prosperous and handsome town.' Buffalo had been developed by the Holland Land Company, and planned in 1797 by Joseph Ellicott,

who had assisted his brother in surveying the radial avenues of Washington designed by French architect Pierre L'Enfant (1754-1825). Galt put these lessons to work in his plan for the Canada Company's first two towns: Guelph and Goderich.[3]

Galt launched **Guelph [12.1]** with due ceremony on 23 April 1827. A large maple tree was felled, and the stump became the focus of the town plan, which featured a series of streets radiating from it in a fan-like arrangement. Important sites were reserved for

12.1 Plan of Guelph, Ontario, 1827. From Joseph Bouchette, *The British Dominions in North America*, 1832.

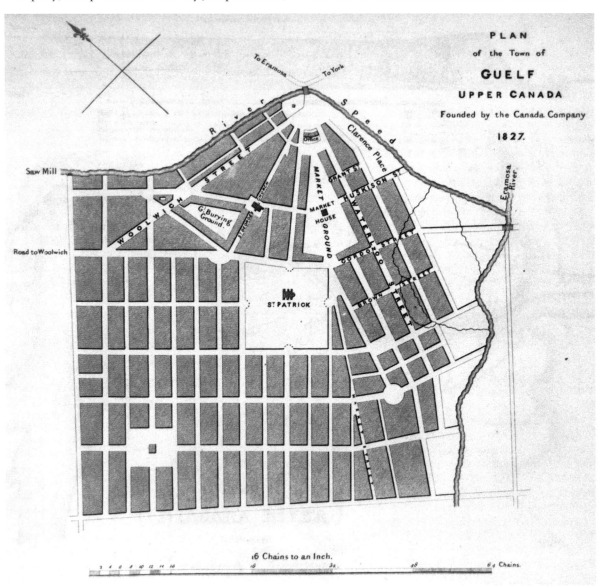

644

12.2 View of Guelph, Ontario, 1830. From *Fraser's Magazine*, November 1830 (detail).

a large triangular market-place and several churches. Based on the principles of Baroque planning, Guelph made a significant break with the Georgian gridiron that could be seen at Halifax, and in other early townsites planned by the British government.

The Canada Company cleared the land, built roads, and erected the first public buildings. Galt was true to his word, making each structure's style 'indicate and be appropriate to its purpose.' The principal building in which new arrivals were received and temporarily accommodated was a house called **the Priory** [12.2]—the large building in the centre foreground of the illustration, the name a punning allusion both to a medieval monastery and to Charles Prior, the Company's superintendent of operations. It was built of 'round logs, the bark untouched'; the principal block was 54 by 42 feet (16.5 by 12.8 m), with a kitchen wing projecting at each end. Galt explained that it

is but a log one, the first that was erected in the Town: but it is not without some pretensions to elegance. It has a rustic portico formed with the trunk of trees in which parts of the Ionic order are really somewhat intelligently displayed.[4]

Classically symmetrical, yet deliberately coarse in its appearance, the Priory was one of Canada's first self-consciously rustic buildings (compare Castle Frank, **4.27**). The classical portico not only added dignity, but surely also produced associations (at least in Galt's well-educated mind) with the mythical 'primitive hut' that late-eighteenth-century architectural theorists believed had been created by linking four trees with horizontal poles.[3]

The **Market House** at Guelph (behind, and to the left of, the Priory in the illustration) was described by a contemporary English magazine as being 'a rude

copy of a Greek temple. The ingenious may see that, in a certain sense, it resembles the Bourse of Paris'— a reference to the large temple-like commercial exchange built in 1808-26.[6] A third building, the Canada Company's office, was a stone structure also in the classical manner.

Construction of the first buildings began in 1827, and some eighty properties were sold in less than a month. Scottish traveller Alexander Dunlop visited Guelph in May 1827 and wrote a lengthy description:

We entered the site of the intended city. Five weeks before it was a portion of the wilderness. Now the giant elms, the maples, the cedars and the oaks, fallen from their high state, were crumbling into ashes or blazing into flames. We stalked through the avenue of burning trees, and descending towards a beautiful little stream were received by his Guelphic Majesty at the entrance of his Rustic Palace. This regal mansion was neither more nor less than a square apartment formed by trunks of the largest trees piled on each other, covered over with planks and floored with the same. An elegant log house was in the course of completion, intended as a caravanserie for the reception of travellers . . . .

The streets form a semi-circle. Eighty lots were taken while we were there. Many houses have already commenced.

The site of the town was chosen because it is equidistant from Lakes Erie, Ontario, Simcoe and Huron. The soil is the finest I have seen in this part of Canada . . . . Ruder shanties with open fronts were ranged around our own.[7]

By 1831 a gristmill, a sawmill, a tannery, two distilleries, a brewery, five inns, five retail shops, four blacksmiths' workshops, and three churches were either built or under construction. Guelph's role as the administrative centre and staging point for the settlement of the Canada Company lands had been secured. The illustration, published in 1830, shows the young town and its principal structures, with the Priory in the foreground, the Market House in the middle distance in a large clearing, and the Catholic church on the street that climbs the hill in the background. The stump of the maple tree from which the streets radiate is just to the left of the Priory. A measure of order had been imposed on the raw Canadian landscape, although in the artist's romantic rendition nature still prevails.

A year later, in 1828, the Canada Company founded the town of **Goderich** [12.3] on Lake Huron and built a road to connect it with Guelph. Goderich was intended as a port that would receive and sup-

ply settlers, although it never achieved this level of importance. The layout was more sophisticated than that at Guelph, reconciling the radial and grid plans in a more symmetrical and satisfying manner. Eight streets radiate from a central market place (today called 'the Square') to describe both a grid aligned with the principal compass points and a series of diagonals that run parallel and perpendicular to the harbour shore. Beyond the inner blocks of the plan the grid predominates. The town was surveyed under Galt's supervision, although the plan may have been sent out from London.[8]

Like Jean Talon before him and many who followed, John Galt believed in the importance of the town-plan to the future success of a community. He wrote that 'the first effectual step in colonization is

12.3 Aerial view of the Square, Goderich, Ontario. Photograph by Gordon Henderson, 1950. Huron County Museum.

to plant a village . . . for we see it is from towns in all countries that cultivation proceeds.'⁹ He was a thoughtful and cultured man who tried to base town planning on humanistic, rather than military, values.

Galt's examples were not followed elsewhere. Other developers tended to be more conservative and to avoid innovations in planning and building design. The Georgian gridiron plan, sometimes adorned with a central square (as at Fergus, founded by Adam Fergusson in 1834, and Galt—now a part of Cambridge—which was named after John Galt), prevailed for the remainder of the century. Rather than providing a humanistic amenity, the gridiron moulded civilization by imposing imperial order. Only with the introduction of the more expansive ideals of Beaux-Arts and City Beautiful planning in the early twentieth century would elements of the radial plan reappear in Canada.

Hundreds of miles to the east, the New Brunswick and Nova Scotia Land Company acquired a half-million acres (200,000 hectares) of land in New Brunswick between the St John and Miramichi Rivers. The company was formed in London in 1831 with the objective of buying large tracts of land and making them available to emigrants from Britain and Ireland in a spirit of 'mutual co-operation and assistance'. It offered very favourable terms, promising to open roads, clear lands, build houses before the settlers' arrival, and provide transportation to the lands. It would rent 100-acre (40-hectare) lots with 5 acres (2 hectares) cleared and a log house on a 50-year lease for 1 shilling

12.4 View of Stanley, New Brunswick. From *Sketches of New Brunswick*, 1836. New Brunswick Museum/Webster Canadiana collection/w1669.

per acre—with an initial period of free rent and food—and provide the settlers with constant employment in preparing the land for future arrivals.¹⁰

Stanley [12.4], New Brunswick, was founded some 24 miles (39 km) north of Fredericton, on the Nashwaak River, in 1834. E.N. Kendall, the company's talented commissioner, put his energies into clearing and building the town. In the summer of 1835 Bishop John Inglis visited the site and wrote favourably of it:

> The house in which we lodged has been built for an inn; and, like all the other houses and cottages, displays excellent architectural taste combined with economy . . . . I . . . was particularly struck by the commanding situation of Church Hill, the spot already allotted as the site for a church, for which a design has already been prepared, in the same excellent taste in which everything here is done. There is also a very superior saw mill, which is essential to a new settlement.¹¹

By the time the first emigrants arrived two years later, Kendall could boast that the town had a 14-room inn (later known as the tavern), a storehouse, a bunkhouse for 100 labourers, six frame houses, a log house for the miller, two sawmills, a flour mill, shops for the blacksmith and carpenter, barns, and stables.

The planned church was never built; instead, a tower and chancel were added to the schoolhouse in 1842.

The designs for the buildings were either prepared by Kendall, who was a capable surveyor and draftsman, or were sent over from England. The principal structure was the tavern (in the centre of the illustration), a two-storey, nearly cross-shaped frame building with a hipped roof over the central core and gables on the arms. The clapboard walls were enhanced with eaves brackets, and the gable ends were decorated with a half-timber motif in the manner of the picturesque cottage advocated in English pattern-books of the day. One of the original frame houses was a low verandahed Regency cottage with a two-storey rounded projecting bay in the centre of its long façade. Both are early examples of the picturesque, which would dominate Canadian architecture for the next generation. (In the mind of a British designer, surely nothing could have been more picturesque than this settlement in the New Brunswick wilderness.) The original town plan was irregular, although a more conventional grid developed behind it.

A series of lithographs of the Stanley settlement was published in England in 1836 and helped to advertise the company. Forty-five families from the Isle of Skye were among the first arrivals, reaching Stanley late in the season, in November. These crofters were totally unprepared for the demands of their new life, and forty-one people died during the first winter. This was a bad beginning for the company and discouraged prospective settlers. The town never prospered, although it maintained a population of between 500 and 900 through the subsequent decades.

Other land-development companies were also active during this period, but few (if any) reached their objectives with regard to numbers of settlers or profits. The British-American Land Company, formed in 1831 and chartered three years later, acquired nearly 850,000 acres of land in the Eastern Townships of Lower Canada, intending to settle them with British emigrants and thereby overcome the 'prejudicial influence' of Americans and the 'extravagant pretensions' of the French Canadians. After promising beginnings in the settlement of Scottish Highlanders, the company ran into financial difficulties and defaulted on its payments for the land.

The government also contributed to the effort to settle the hinterlands of Canada, both by encouraging immigration and by making new land available for habitation. At the conclusion of the War of 1812—apprehensive about Upper Canada's being 'a Country already too much inhabited by Aliens from the United States, very many of whom are avowedly disaffected to the British Government'—the authorities opened up a range of townships west of the Rideau River as a barrier to American invasion or encroachment, and settled them with demobilized soldiers and Scottish Highlanders intent on emigration; they also attempted (with little success) to discourage additional American immigration.[12] Participants were offered free passage, 100 acres (40 hectares) of land, free rations for a limited period, and implements at a reduced price. The town of Perth (pages 156-60), founded in 1816, was at the centre of this new territory.

The benefits of putting the control of land development into the hands of government authorities rather than private speculators was advocated for the first time by John Arthur Roebuck (1802-79), an English MP and political reformer who spent his youth in Upper Canada and continued to consider himself a Canadian even though he moved to England in 1824. A disciple of Jeremy Bentham and a friend of John Stuart Mill—and for many years a leading spokesman on Canadian affairs—Roebuck was the first to apply Bentham's utilitarian principles (a good action is one that provides 'the greatest happiness to the greatest number') to urban planning. In a pamphlet he wrote in 1836 (that sounds like a plea of the 1990s for responsible resource management) Roebuck advocated central planning of Canadian land:

> Wild land is the great means of the improvement of Canada . . . and could, by careful management, be made the means of supplying all the expenses of government . . . . The most appropriate solutions for new settlements can only be determined by persons conversant with the country and its wants. The management of these lands . . . influence[s] the well-being of the entire colony.[13]

Although Roebuck's wisdom had no immediate impact, he set the stage for twentieth-century planning in both Britain and Canada.

In the middle of the nineteenth century, however, limited government initiatives did follow. In Canada West (as Upper Canada was called after 1841), the Public Lands Act of 1853 enabled the government to give to newcomers as many as 100 acres (40 hectares) of land free 'in the vicinity of any Public Roads in any new settlements which shall or may be opened.' (Although land had originally been granted at no cost, after 1827 Crown lands were generally available only by purchase.) The legislature set aside money for the construction of a series of 'colonization roads' between the Ottawa River and

Georgian Bay, known as the Ottawa-Huron Tract. Most of this area was at best marginal agricultural land within the Canadian Shield, although the optimistic promotion of free land by Crown agents, and the extensive advertising in foreign newspapers, did not always make this clear.

Thirteen colonization roads were built in all. The Opeongo Road was cut through the forest from the Ottawa River, near Renfrew, in a northwesterly direction. By 1857, 40 miles (64 km) were passable for wagons the year round and the first settlers, mostly Irish-born, were taking possession of their land. The Hastings, Addington, and Bobcaygeon Roads were the first of several north-south routes that opened up the marginal farmland in the Shield, mostly north of today's Highway 7. The response was disappointing. By 1860, only 1,139 settlers had taken up free land on these first four roads. Nevertheless, a steady stream of Canadians and new immigrants migrated to this area and made a genuine attempt to establish farmsteads.

Each settler was obliged to build a log house at least 20 by 18 feet (6.1 by 5.5 m) and put a minimum of 12 acres (4.8 hectares) into cultivation within four years. The regulations noted:

> The LOG-HOUSE required by the Government to be built is of such a description as can be put up in four days by five men. The neighbours generally help to build the Log-cabin for newly arrived Settlers, without charge . . . the roof can be covered with bark, and the spaces between the logs plastered with clay, and whitewashed. It then becomes a neat dwelling, and warm as a stone house.[14]

On the other side of the Ottawa River, the Roman Catholic Church encouraged the agricultural development of the hinterland on the Shield fringe. Curé Antoine Labelle, the parish priest of St-Jérôme de Terrebonne, north of Montreal, worked energetically to settle the Shield fringe with French-speaking settlers. He established some twenty new parishes and sixty villages between 1869 and his death in 1891. Recognizing the potential value of railways in providing access to the interior, Labelle was a principal advocate of the Northern Colonization Railway, which opened between Montreal and St-Jérôme in 1876. This was augmented, shortly after Labelle's death, by the Montfort Colonization Railway, a narrow-gauge line begun in 1893 that reached a number of remote communities in the Laurentian Highlands.[15]

Another church-sponsored settlement was in the Lake Témiscamingue region, near the headwaters of the Ottawa River, encouraged in the 1880s by Fathers Paradis and P.-E. Gendreau of the Oblate Order. This, too, was made accessible by a narrow-gauge line, the 6-mile long (10-km) Lake Témiscamingue Colonization Railway, as well as by light tramways around three rapids above Mattawa.[16] The colony formed the basis for the later pulp-and-paper town of Témiscaming [12.23].

Colonization schemes played an important role as well in the subsequent settlement of Western Canada. Several of these initiatives were discussed in Chapters 7 and 9.

The City Beautiful and the Garden City

The City Beautiful Movement

The previous chapter described efforts, around 1900, to introduce an urban-reform movement that would make cities more healthy, moral, and equitable. Mayor Howland of Toronto (page 641) was one pacesetter; another was J.S. Woodsworth, the first leader of the CCF (now the New Democratic Party), who used his base at the All People's Mission in Winnipeg to work for democratic social action. The activities of these and other reformers were reflected in planning initiatives aimed at providing a better quality of life for urban residents through improved sanitation, parks, housing, and other much-needed amenities.[17]

Architects and landscape architects listened to these urban reformers. They became convinced that the ills and ugliness of the city could be overcome with a program of civic beautification achieved through good design and effective regulation. The impetus for the City Beautiful Movement, as it came to be called, came from the United States and began with the park movement associated with the work of the distinguished landscape architect Frederick Law Olmsted (1822-1903). The creation of Central Park, New York (Olmsted and Calvert Vaux, begun 1858), set a widely admired precedent that other cities were quick to follow. Vaux's work on Parliament Hill in Ottawa (1873-9; pages 539-40) shows an interest by Canadians in planned urban landscaping. Olmsted's ambitious design for **Mount Royal Park** [12.5] in Montreal, which covers a marvellous 550-acre (220-hectare) site atop the city's mountain, was an impressive achievement in picturesque design. Olmsted produced his plans in 1874-7 and the park was developed in the years following.[18]

The most visible event that furthered the City

12.5 Mount Royal Park, Montreal, Quebec, begun 1878.
Notman Photographic Archives, MMCH/944.

Beautiful Movement was the World's Columbian Exposition held in Chicago in 1893, popularly known as the Chicago World's Fair. The design was co-ordinated by architect Daniel H. Burnham (1846-1912), the site plan was produced by Olmsted—it was his last important project before passing his practice on to his sons—and the buildings were designed by McKim, Mead, and White and other leading architects of the day. The 'White City'— with its Neoclassical buildings, formal avenues, water and landscape features, and advanced transportation and sewage systems— impressed everyone who visited it. (The Canadian Building, designed by federal architect David Ewart, was an unassertive classical structure with a circular entrance tower and perimeter veranda applied to a plain two-storey block.)[19] The aesthetic and pragmatic lessons promoted by the fair were to have an enormous impact on American and Canadian urban planning for the next generation.[20]

The City Beautiful Movement had no clear philosophy or dogma, although it was guided by the aesthetic principles of coherence, visual variety, and civic grandeur. Its adherents believed that the City Beautiful would come not simply from filling the city with beautiful creations, but rather through a concerted planning effort that would address the city's every aspect.[21]

Percy Nobbs expressed his faith in this process in an article published in 1904:

. . . it is not merely by erecting a fine structure here and there that you will make any great improvement, or even laying out a little bit of park, although that may be an item; the construction of the city throughout should be made as beautiful as it can be.[22]

Other Canadian architects took a similar position. They advocated that the city should not only be a thing of beauty but that its circulation and hygiene systems must be improved through proper planning. Architect William A. Langton (1854-1933) of Toronto, who served a term as president of the Ontario Association of Architects, made these points on several occasions in *Canadian Architect and Builder*, the influential periodical he edited. In his article 'City Planning' (1902) he said that beautification would come through planning, particularly by means of land-use segregation and by reworking the grid pattern. Three years later the journal told its readers: 'Beauty must be massed to tell, in a city as in any other work of art.'[23] And as early as 1895, Langton had urged the establishment of municipal associa-

tions on the models of those in New York, Boston, and Chicago.[24]

The advocates of civic beautification also promoted the new profession of town-planning. An early venture was the formation in 1903 of the Canadian League for Civic Improvement, followed by the founding in 1919 of the Town Planning Institute of Canada.[25] The amateur, 'grass-roots', side of the City Beautiful Movement was seen in the formation of horticultural societies, and in the pressure placed on municipal councils to create parks, landscape public buildings, plant street trees, and place flower boxes on Main Street. The railways, led by the CPR, planted gardens beside their stations (page 483). Citizens participated in clean-up campaigns and urged their neighbours to improve the landscape in front of their own residences. All these beautification efforts expressed values that remain precious today.[26]

The earliest initiative to beautify an existing Canadian city through an intensive exercise in planning was seen in the formation by the federal government in 1899 of the Ottawa Improvement Commission. Prime Minister Wilfrid Laurier was acting on a promise he had made to the Ottawa Reform Association in 1893—the year of the Chicago World's Fair—as Leader of the Opposition:

. . . when the day comes [to form a government] . . ., it shall be my pleasure and that of my colleagues, I am sure, to make the city of Ottawa the centre of the intellectual development of this country, and the Washington of the North.[27]

The Ottawa Improvement Commission was a volunteer organization with limited jurisdiction and a small budget, but through it the federal government participated in the beautification of the heavily industrialized lumber town. Among its early achievements were the cleaning up of the banks of the Rideau Canal (which had become littered with lumber yards, sheds, and industrial detritus) and the creation of a landscaped 'driveway' (now known as Queen Elizabeth Driveway) on its west bank, the first of several scenic roadways in the national capital [12.6].

In 1902 the Commission retained the services of Frederick G. Todd (1876-1948), who had trained with Olmsted and Sons in Brookline, Massachusetts, and moved to Montreal in 1900 to become Canada's first resident professional landscape architect and town-planning consultant. The Todd Report (1903) on Ottawa's parkway system was the first of innumerable planning studies to be prepared for the Ottawa Improvement Commission and its succes-

12.6 Queen Elizabeth Driveway and Pagoda, Ottawa, Ontario. Photograph 1904. From Ottawa Improvement Commision, *Annual Report*, 1904. City of Ottawa Archives/CA15983.

sors, the Federal District Commission (organized in 1927) and the National Capital Commission (1959), and set an important precedent in being the first co-ordinated plan for an established Canadian city.[28]

A Federal Plan Commission, chaired by businessman and banker Sir Herbert S. Holt, was formed in 1913 to develop a master plan for the cities of Ottawa and Hull, and to make suggestions for the design of new government buildings. The commissioners retained the services of planner Edward H. Bennett (1874-1954), an Englishman who had been trained at the École des Beaux-Arts and had years of experience in the United States, including working with Daniel H. Burnham on plans for San Francisco and Chicago. In the Holt Commission's report, completed in 1915, Bennett and his associates revealed their strong admiration for the Parliament Buildings, 'because of the general harmony of the group and the happy expression which has been given to them, seemingly in character with a northern country.' The report recommended that the style of the proposed new buildings should display

> an architectural character with vigorous silhouettes, steep roofs, pavilions and towers, never competing with, but always recalling the present group . . . . In the design of these, inspiration may be derived from the close and sympathetic study of the beautiful buildings of Northern France of the 17th century.
>
> Generally speaking, the external architecture of the Château Laurier, though it may require refining in detail, may be regarded in general outline and character as a worthy suggestion for an archi-

tecture of vertical composition, such as is suggested for the new group.[29]

A drawing published with the report shows the streets along the Ottawa River lined with scores of new châteauesque government buildings, all with steep roofs and dormer windows. This was the first of several documents advocating the Château Style for government buildings; the others—and the buildings that resulted—will be discussed in Chapter 14.

Ideas of civic beautification, often coupled with park development, were promoted across the country. The grandest was the **plan for Calgary** [12.7] prepared by the celebrated English landscape architect Thomas H. Mawson (1861-1933), a devoted follower of the City Beautiful Movement and a persuasive speaker and writer who ably promoted town-planning schemes for a number of Canadian cities. He made four North American tours and opened an office in Vancouver.[30]

In his elaborate proposal for Calgary, published in 1914, Mawson criticized 'the American "chess-board" system of planning' and 'the absence of those diagonal routes which are essential to a well-planned city.' He recommended that Calgary abandon the gridiron plan, and suggested instead that 'we ought to arrange our plan so that certain streets naturally become traffic routes and others remain mere means of access to the buildings which line them on either side.'[31] This anticipated the now universally accepted planning principle of a hierarchy of roadways. His plan would have replaced one British imperial town-planning model, the gridiron, with another—the neo-Baroque plan in which neighbourhoods of varying forms are organized within a structure of oblique avenues and boulevards that create long vistas terminating in architectural and sculptural landmarks.

Mawson's design proposals were exciting, far-reaching, ambitious, grandly scaled—and utterly impracticable. He proposed a network of avenues, squares, and circles lined by large, uniform towered and domed classical buildings interspersed with parks, obelisks, fountains, and other urban embellishments. The proposals varied in character from area to area, from the dignified symmetry of the magnificent Civic Centre—a necessary feature, it seems, of every City Beautiful plan—to the gently ordered informality of the Connaught residential area. Mawson tried in vain to persuade his audience that he was describing the possible by making the project sound smaller than it really was:

> City planning is not the attempt to pull down your city and rebuild it at ruinous expense. It is merely deciding what you would like to have done when you get the chance, so that when the chance does come, little by little you may make the city plan conform to your ideals.[32]

Although a few of his individual proposals—such as the construction of the Centre Street Bridge in 1916—did come to pass, his document remains an eloquent and seductive, but unexecuted, testament to the City Beautiful.

One of Mawson's few Canadian designs to be implemented were the gardens in front of the Saskatchewan Legislative Building in Regina [10.23]. These are set in Wascana Park, one of many large urban parks created in the early years of the century as a result of the City Beautiful Movement. The park was planned in 1906 by Frederick Todd as an oasis within the flat and dry prairie landscape around man-made Wascana Lake. Todd proposed a naturalistic scheme with meandering roadways and the irregular planting of more than 100,000 trees and shrubs, many of which were grown in the government nursery in Regina from seeds and plants acquired from as far away as Siberia and Korea. They contrasted with formal rows of trees along the city streets at the edge of the park. When provincial officials became disillusioned with Todd's design, and the high death-rate among the newly planted trees, they called in Thomas Mawson.[33]

Mawson arrived in 1912, amid much ballyhoo, as a guest of the Lieutenant Governor. He succeeded in walking away with the commission not only to redesign the legislative gardens and Wascana Park,

12.7 'The Civic Centre of Calgary as It May Appear Many Years Hence'. From Thomas Mawson, *Calgary: A Preliminary Scheme for Controlling the Growth of the City*, 1914. City of Calgary Archives, Town Planning Commission/File 6.

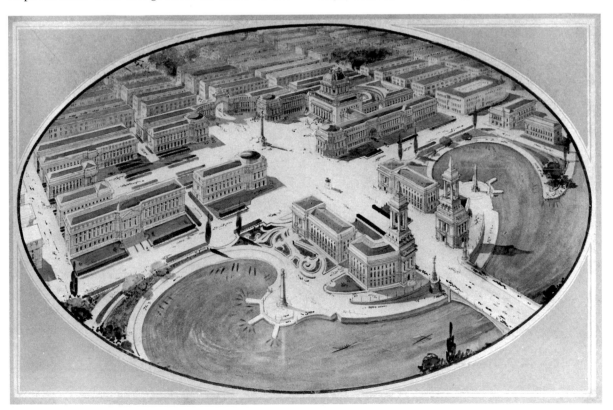

but also to find a site for Government House and to recommend civic improvements for the entire city of Regina. Fervently believing that parks should be integrated with their surroundings, Mawson proposed an 'architectural' **layout of the gardens [12.8]** of the classical and symmetrical Legislative Buildings. A series of formal and linear flowerbeds and walkways were to lead from the entrance of the buildings to Wascana Lake— similar in effect to the *parterres* of Baroque France and England (a style known best in the gardens of Versailles). The grounds around the Legislative Buildings were executed according to his design, and the gardens are still much admired.

Mawson's other—unexecuted—proposals for Wascana Park included the pretentious idea of building a new Government House across the lake so that the Lieutenant Governor could sail across it on a royal barge to open the legislature. His suggestions, however, did form the basis for improvements to Wascana Centre (as the park was later renamed), designed in 1962 by American architect Minoru Yamasaki (b. 1912) and landscape architect Richard Church. Mawson's proposed improvements to downtown Regina—similar to those for Calgary—were also unbuilt.

Civic-beautification designs on a smaller scale than those proposed for Calgary or Regina were executed at **Maisonneuve**, a municipality at the eastern boundary of Montreal that was founded in 1883 and annexed by the larger city in 1918. A group of promoters, led by industrialist and politician Alphonse Desjardins and biscuit king Charles-Théodore Viau, lured a number of industries to

12.8 Thomas Mawson's plan for the gardens of the Legislative Building, Regina, Saskatchewan, 1912. SAB/B620.10.

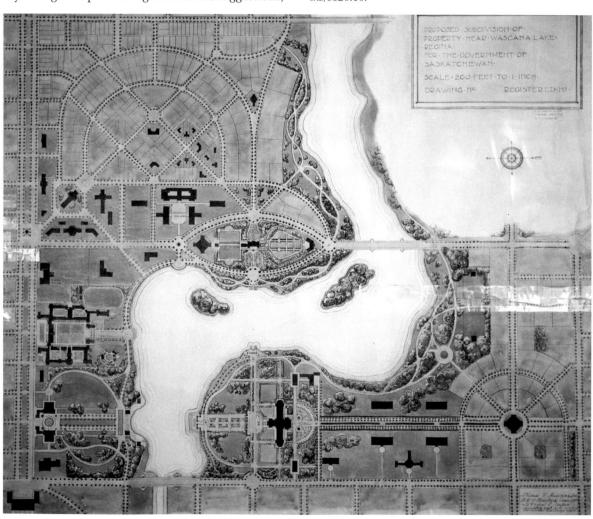

12.9 Morgan Boulevard, Maisonneuve, Quebec. Photograph *c.* 1915. Notman Photographic Archives, MMCH/16185.

Maisonneuve in the years preceding the First World War. Municipal officials boasted in 1912 that Maisonneuve—promoted with images of smoke-belching chimneys—was fifth in Canada in industrial production and called their city the 'Pittsburg of Canada.'

A new crop of politicians, more attuned to improving the quality of life, resolved to transform Maisonneuve into the 'Garden of Montreal'. The leaders were mayor Alexandre Michaud and shoe manufacturer Oscar Dufresne. The artistic vision apparently belonged to Oscar's brother Marius Dufresne (1883-1945), the city engineer. Many public improvements followed. The municipality built a new City Hall (Cajetan Dufort, 1910-11), Public Market (Marius Dufresne, 1912-14), Public Baths (Dufresne, 1914-16), and Fire Station (Dufresne, 1914-15; **14.58**), and created a new broad, treed street called **Morgan Boulevard [12.9]**. The baths are seen at the right in the photograph, with the cupola of the classical market building at the end of the axis. Pie IX Boulevard (named after the incumbent pontiff) was built along the western boundary, and Sherbrooke Street East was widened along the northern edge. Brothers Oscar and Marius built their large classical double mansion—the Château Dufresne (1915-18), re-used as the Musée des Arts Décoratifs de Montréal—at the intersection. The city also created the immense Maisonneuve Park, which now accommodates the attractive Botanical Gardens (begun in 1931) and the large athletic complex built for the 1976 Olympic Games **[15.65]**.[34]

Rarely did the opportunity arise to design a new city from scratch. This happened, however, at **Prince Rupert**, the northern British Columbia coastal locale that was chosen as the western terminus of the Grand Trunk Pacific Railway by Charles M. Hays,

the line's visionary president. The first surveyors and engineers reached the hilly and heavily forested site in May 1906. Hays selected Boston landscape architects Franklin Brett and George D. Hall, both former students of John C. Olmsted, to design a grand plan for what he intended as no less than Canada's Pacific metropolis. Brett and Hall visited Prince Rupert in 1908. They marvelled at 2,300-foot-high Mount Hays ('a natural park of great possibilities'), the superb natural harbour, and 'the views over the harbour . . . [that will] remain, for all time, the revelation of a grand harmony of Nature.'[35]

Brett and Hall responded with an ambitious **plan [12.10]** that combined the formality of the City Beautiful and the École des Beaux-Arts with the picturesque controlled naturalism of the English landscape tradition. (They later produced a plan for Westmount, Quebec [1910], and designed the grounds of Hatley Park on the estate of James Dunsmuir at Sooke, near Victoria [1908-16; for many years Royal Roads Military College], with its manor by Samuel Maclure.)[36] Broad processional avenues terminating in circles and crescents—and accented by set-pieces of classical public architecture—were contrasted with informal meandering residential streets determined by the topography and the scenic prospects. The attempt at formality is seen in the **vista along 2nd Avenue [12.11]**, past a totem pole (carved by the legendary Charles Edenshaw) that was erected as an intermediate focal-point, to the classical Provincial Courthouse (1923) and the circular drive in front of it that was set aside as a market place. The intended effect was diminished, however, by the many lots

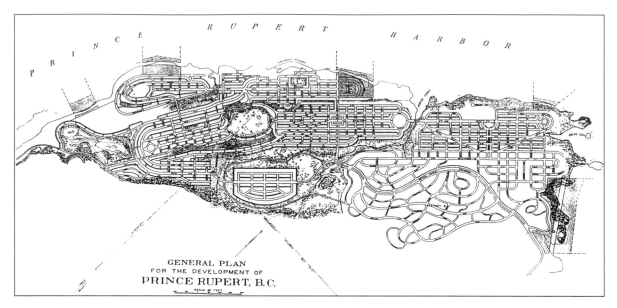

GENERAL PLAN
FOR THE DEVELOPMENT OF
PRINCE RUPERT, B.C.

12.10 Plan of Prince Rupert, British Columbia, 1908. From *Architectural Record*, August 1909.

that were never built upon, and by the insubstantiality of many of the buildings that were erected.

The planners divided Prince Rupert into nine 'sections'— divisions that are still used today for planning purposes—each of which was intended to serve a particular function and was laid out according to

12.11 View east along 2nd Avenue, Prince Rupert, British Columbia. Photograph *c.* 1925. Prince Rupert City and Regional Archives/Wrathall Collection.

its distinctive plan. The commercial sections were laid out in rectangular gridirons on two plateaus, the industrial section was separate, and the residential sections each had a distinct character. The most affluent section was supposed to have been Section 9 (at the lower right on the plan), which featured curved streets that would offer 'a certain charm and variety in sharp contrast to the greater dignity of the broad straight avenue.' The skeleton of the plan, intended to 'tie the whole development together', was a system of arterial streets (called 'fundamental roads') that would maximize the efficiency of transportation links through and between the sections.[37]

The plan was unique, innovative, and bold. It adapted classical formality to the limitations of the difficult and highly scenic topography, maximizing the effect of breathtaking views, while using the practical aspects of gridiron planning. (It was published in 1909 by the renowned English planner Sir Raymond Unwin [1863-1940].)[38] Prince Rupert was developed according to the essentials of the Brett and Hall plan and, despite some deviations, the designers' intentions remain clearly legible and the original section numbers are still used.

The Grand Trunk Pacific intended major improvements of its own—including an extravagant steamship terminal, railway station, and château hotel complex designed by Francis Rattenbury—that were never built.[39] Prince Rupert never achieved its intended glory, chiefly because Charles Hays went down with the *Titanic* in 1912, and his successor, Edson J. Chamberlin, lacked the former's dynamism and vision.

Mawson, the Dufresne brothers, Brett and Hall, and other proponents of the City Beautiful believed that good physical planning and design would somehow make the city's problems disappear. But congestion, poor health, and poverty did not vanish upon the creation of a monumental avenue or a civic centre. Growing opposition to the belief that a grandiose design would solve the city's ills was summed up in *The Canadian Municipal Journal* for 1911, which contended that the provision of sanitary housing for the poor was 'the real meaning of city planning':

> Magnificent avenues, leading to grand buildings, are desirable. Lovely and artistic parks should be in every city. But the dwellings in which those live who cannot get away from their homes the whole year long, really decide whether any city is to be healthy, moral and progressive. The common people are in the great majority: their proper accommodation is the greatest problem.[40]

The Garden City Movement and the development of suburbs

One of the most exciting planning concepts to come out of Europe, and arguably the most powerful and pervasive planning idea of the twentieth century, was the Garden City. Ebenezer Howard (1850-1928), an English reformer who was appalled by the living conditions in the slums of industrial London, made seminal proposals in his book *To-morrow: A Peaceful Path to Real Reform* (1898). (Reprinted in

1946 as *Garden Cities of Tomorrow*, it is better known by that name.) He stated that the growth of cities should be limited, and that people leaving rural areas should be redirected towards new satellite communities set in agricultural surroundings. Land use within each of these new towns was to be strictly segregated: residential and industrial uses would be kept apart to promote healthy conditions. The first Garden City was Letchworth, Hertfordshire (1903, planned by Raymond Unwin and Barry Parker), 30 miles (50 km) from London; the most influential was Welwyn Garden City (1919, with many buildings designed by Montreal-born Louis de Soissons) in the same county.

The Garden City idea caught on quickly. It spawned the development of countless suburban communities, particularly in North America. Dormitory suburbs, green belts, and separated land uses—leading planning theories of the mid-twentieth century—all owe a great deal to the theories of Howard.

The immediate effect of Howard's ideas on Canadian planning is seen in the particularly innovative **Town of Mount Royal [12.12]**. The Canadian Northern Railway gained access to a terminal in downtown Montreal by a bold and expensive means: a 16,315-foot-long (5-km), double-tracked tunnel through Mount Royal. To help offset the cost of the tunnel, which exceeded $12 million, the railway purchased 4,800 acres (1,950 hectares) of cheap land near its north end and planned a modern community—the Town of Mount Royal—that would be only a ten-minute ride by electric train from the heart of the city. The tunnel was begun, and lots went on sale, in 1911; on the first morning more than a million dollars' worth of lots was sold, and land sales in the new 'Garden Suburb' eventually surpassed the cost of the tunnel.[41]

Frederick Todd designed the town. Its plan is formed by two diagonal boulevards that intersect in the centre—with the railway station, the town hall, and a park located at that point, and other institutional buildings and some shopping facilities near their intersection. The rest of the town is residential. The plan is based on a grid, but monotony is avoided by the boulevards, and by the 'green necklace of parks' that Todd wove through the underlying rectilinear geometry.[42]

The principle of the Garden City—or, as it came to be called in Canada, the Garden Suburb—directed suburban planning for the next half-century. In the early years of the century suburban development occurred rapidly, spurred on both by the rapid pop-

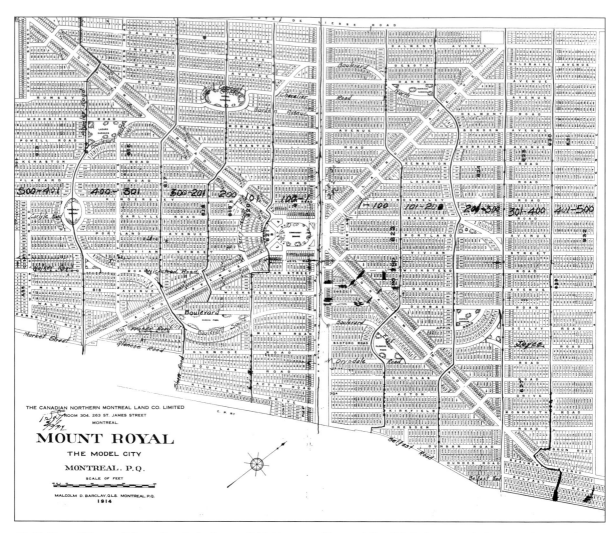

12.12 Plan of Town of Mount Royal, Quebec, *c.* 1910-11. Town of Mount Royal Library Archives.

ulation increase and by the desire of the middle class (rather than the working class cited in the 1889 Royal Commission) to leave congested and unhealthy city centres. The new forms of inexpensive multiple-housing described in Chapter 11, the effective sales techniques of land promoters, and the development of urban mass transit encouraged a new generation of home-owners to make the move. Suburbs rose across the country—in the early years from Tuxedo Park, the 'suburb beautiful' near Winnipeg (planned by Rickson Outhet, 1906, and revised by Frederick Todd),[43] and Uplands, near Victoria (John C. Olmsted, 1908-9, with F.M. Rattenbury as architectural adviser),[44] to developments after the Second World War that included Don Mills, outside Toronto (Macklin

Hancock [b. 1925], director of planning, begun 1952),[45] and Lorraine, north of Montreal (J. André Laferrière, surveyor, and Maxwell M. Kalman, consulting architect, begun 1960).[46] In enlightened designs such as these, developers and their planners conceived landscaped, self-contained communities—with curved streets, cul-de-sacs, T-intersections, generous lot sizes, and parks that eventually became clichés of suburban planning—whose quality of life was intended to be superior to that of inner-city living.

But suburban growth has had its dark side. Canadian (and American) suburbs were not planned to be economically self-sufficient, as were Howard's Garden Cities. Most were residential 'dormitory' communities that forced people to commute to work in the city centre. (An exception was Don Mills, which includes a large commercial district with many good early International Style buildings [e.g. Oxford

University Press, by Fairfield and DuBois, 1963], but observers quickly noted that the workers tended to live elsewhere.)[47] Electric streetcars, and their interurban extensions, made commuting feasible. Rather than alleviating problems of growth and congestion, however, streetcars and buses aggravated them, because the improved transit links brought about the creation of yet more and larger suburbs, as well as denser city centres.[48] This situation worsened with the increase in private automobiles and the development of freeways. Since few cities put limits on growth, as Howard had urged, cities and suburbs merged into a single sprawling agglomeration. Worse still, the move of affluent residents out of the cities to the suburbs often created urban conditions that were even poorer than before.

These ills began to be recognized and understood in the 1950s. In her classic study *The Death and Life of Great American Cities* (1961), Jane Jacobs, a resident of Toronto since 1967, argued persuasively against the theories of Howard and the 'Decentrists', and demonstrated both the need and the methods to revitalize city centres with residential life. But this takes us far beyond our period, and we must wait until Chapter 15 to see how this has been addressed.

The Commission of Conservation The social and health concerns expressed by the urban-reform movement, and the design initiatives promoted by the City Beautiful Movement, came together to some extent in the Garden Suburb. Further key developments occurred in the years immediately preceding the First World War, a period of enormous urban expansion created by massive European immigration and an unprecedented economic boom. Between 1881 and 1921 Montreal's population expanded nearly four times from 177,000 to 618,000, and Toronto's six times to 522,000—while Vancouver grew from an unincorporated hamlet of a few hundred souls to a worldly city whose metropolitan area had 125,000 people in 1911 and 260,000 in 1927.[49] Many Canadians expressed concerns about unchecked growth and the depletion of natural resources, anticipating the conservation movement of the 1980s and 1990s.

In 1909 the Laurier government responded by establishing an advisory board called the Commission of Conservation, acting under some pressure from the Roosevelt administration in the US to work towards a continental conservation policy. The Commission was charged with providing information and recommendations on the conservation of

human and natural resources. Its first chairman, Clifford Sifton, had recently resigned as Laurier's Minister of the Interior.[50]

Charles Hodgetts, an Ontario medical health officer who served as chairman of the Commission's Standing Committee on Public Health, recognized the need to improve the urban environment, and saw improved town-planning as a necessary dimension of sanitation and health:

I would say no government can justify its existence unless it carefully considers this important question [of town planning] and places upon the statute book a law with ample and adequate regulation for dealing with unsanitary houses of all classes in the community and for conferring power on the city, town, or village municipality whereby they may not only control, but in a measure direct, town and suburban planning.[51]

The eminent British planner Thomas Adams (1871-1940) was retained by the Commission in 1914 as its Adviser on Town Planning—a brilliant appointment that left a lasting impact on Canadian planning. Adams was familiar with Raymond Unwin, Ebenezer Howard, and the Garden City movement; he had been secretary of the Garden City Association that had brought about the development of Letchworth, and was also a founder, and the first president, of the British Town Planning Institute. He recognized that land can be efficiently managed for the public good through the effective application of scientific knowledge, a central tenet of Canadian planning that owes its origins to J.A. Roebuck. In the decade Adams was a consultant to the Canadian government, he urged the provinces to adopt legislation regulating planning and development, was responsible for the planning of Kipawa (Témiscaming), Quebec [12.23], founded the Civic Improvement League (1916) and the Town Planning Institute of Canada (1919), and lectured and published widely. He also pressed, with only limited success, for government intervention in the provision of affordable housing. The provinces balked, although in 1918 the federal government initiated a program of lending money to the provinces to encourage new housing—which led to the establishment of the Central Mortgage and Housing Corporation in 1946.[52]

Adams' approach to planning has been described as representing the 'city-efficient' or 'city-functional' school, which holds that each portion of the city should be designed and serviced for its particular functions, with land developed to its 'highest and

12.13 View of The Hydrostone, Halifax, Nova Scotia, *c.* 1918-20. Photograph by Harold Kalman, 1978.

12.14 *(below)* Houses in Lindenlea, Ottawa, Ontario, *c.* 1918-24. Photograph by Edward H. Dahl, 1991.

best' use, and all of the parts connected by good communications systems. As he wrote:

> We should plan to have artificial beauty, but not at the expense of business efficiency, or health, or cleanliness . . . . A city that is healthy and clean may be beautiful even if it is without excessive ornament.[53]

These principles, which were seen at work in Brett and Hall's plan for Prince Rupert, may be taken for granted today but were considered new in Adams' time.

Two districts designed by Adams stand in their maturity today. **The Hydrostone [12.13]** is a 23-acre (9-hectare) redevelopment in Halifax's north end that replaced a working-class area devastated by the Halifax Explosion of 6 December 1917. The collision between a Belgian relief vessel and a French munitions ship in Halifax harbour levelled the north end of the city, destroyed or damaged more than 13,000 buildings, and left more than 10,000 people dead or injured. The Halifax Relief Commission retained Adams, and the Montreal architectural firm of Ross and Macdonald, and together they designed Canada's first public-housing project in seventy-five days. Construction took place from 1918 to 1920. Adams' rectangular blocks, with service alleys, are oriented both east-west and north-south. The eastern portion is overlaid by two diagonal avenues intersecting in a square, and curved roadways add variety near the centre. Architect George Ross determined that the 326 houses should be built of hydro-stone, a concrete block that gave the neighbourhood its name. He produced seven house types—including both row houses and duplexes—with half-timbering and stucco on some of the upper floors and a

variety of roofs. All were provided with indoor plumbing and central heating, which many houses in the working-class district had lacked. The result was an attractive, yet unpretentious, neighbourhood—a combination of good planning and good architecture—with a decidedly Old English flavour.[54]

In the 1920s poor management set the rents too high and led to 40-per-cent vacancy rates. The houses began to be sold in the 1940s, and today The Hydrostone is a fully occupied neighbourhood protected by heritage legislation.

The second residential neighbourhood planned by Adams was **Lindenlea [12.14]**, a 22-acre (9-hectare) garden suburb at the northeastern edge of Ottawa. Developed under the authority of the Ottawa Housing Commission and built in 1918-24, it was based in part on designs by town planner J.-E. Noulan Cauchon (1872-1935). Lindenlea has much of the character of an English hamlet, with a grassy commons, street trees, and winding streets and culs-de-sac that discourage through traffic. A broad, 66-foot-wide (20 m) boulevard called Rockcliffe Way was intended to be part of the city's 'driveway' system, but the other streets were only 20 feet (6 m) wide. Most of the original houses are modestly scaled and undistinguished two-storey brick single-family residences with mansard roofs whose gables face the street. Those in the photograph are at the corner of Rockcliffe Way and Elmdale Avenue. Adams emphasized the importance of landscaping, writing that 'the ultimate success of the scheme will depend on the enterprise shown in improving the surroundings of the buildings.'[55]

Zoning

A fundamental principle of the City Efficient (as contrasted with the City Beautiful), promoted by Adams and others, was the separation of land uses. This was seen as a means of achieving a healthier city—residential districts could be located at a distance from dirty industrial emissions—and also as a way of enhancing property values. Segregation was best achieved through the principle of municipal 'zoning': the creation of distinct zones, each with a stipulated use (or uses) for land, and with regulations controlling the size, height, location, and appearance of buildings. These restrictions met with initial resistance, but in time they came to be widely accepted as necessary and beneficial controls.

Land-use regulation began to appear in the early years of the century. At Maisonneuve, for example, a statute of 1912 forbade industrial development along Pie IX Boulevard. It also stipulated set-backs, minimum heights, and masonry construction (and prohibited outside staircases) along the street.[56]

A 'Town Planning By-law' was enacted in 1922 by the municipality of Point Grey, a middle- and upper-income suburb of Vancouver that had seceded from working-class South Vancouver in 1905. The new by-law made Point Grey 'the first of the municipalities and towns throughout Canada to adopt a zoning ordinance as part of a definite town planning policy.'[57] The by-law differentiated between residential and commercial areas, set high levels of public amenities, and provided for the hiring of professional planning staff. In the same year the British Columbia government passed the Shaughnessy Heights Building Restriction Act to limit construction in Shaughnessy Heights (the well-to-do residential enclave of Point Grey, laid out in 1907 on CPR land by Frederick Todd and Danish engineer L.E.

Davick) to single-family houses, and prohibited the subdivision of properties beyond the original plan.[58]

Things moved quickly after that. British Columbia passed the Town Planning Act in December 1925, calling for municipalities to prepare Official Plans, and within the next three years zoning by-laws were passed by both Point Grey (replacing the 1922 regulations) and Vancouver. The City of Vancouver (which in 1929 absorbed both Point Grey and South Vancouver) continued to promote enlightened planning by commissioning a major study from the St Louis-based firm of Harland Bartholomew and Associates. Many of Bartholomew's recommendations—which followed City Beautiful principles—were included in a far-reaching new zoning by-law of 1931 that established a central business district surrounded by roughly concentric zones permitting—at increasing distances from the core—industry, multiple housing, duplexes and conversions, and finally single-family houses.[59] The initial Point Grey and Shaughnessy regulations had both clearly been intended to maintain the property values of the privileged classes, but the later by-law was more broadly based and democratic.

Another early zoning by-law was introduced in Kitchener, Ontario, in 1924. Originally known as Berlin, but renamed in 1916 because of wartime anti-German feelings, Kitchener had been on the leading edge of the planning movement for some time. In 1904 it adopted a 'Building Line Act' that allowed the creation of residential streets, with lines beyond which houses could not be built. New York planner Charles W. Leavitt, Jr (1871-1928) prepared a plan on City Beautiful principles for Berlin and neighbouring Waterloo in 1913-14, including diagonal arteries and circular boulevards; like so many other plans of this kind, however, little was done about it.[60]

Thomas Adams and his associate, Horace L. Seymour (1882-1940), were subsequently commissioned to prepare a plan for Kitchener and Waterloo. Completed in 1924, the pragmatic design did not propose a radical intervention to the existing urban landscape, but rather provided a framework for rational future development. Land-use zones were delineated, but were not retroactive. The plan 'placed emphasis on preventive rather than corrective measures in the interest of obtaining both economy and the most permanent results.'[61] The council of Kitchener—but not Waterloo—passed the plan as a zoning by-law in December 1924.

The principles of municipal planning were established and appreciated. Most other cities soon followed with comprehensive plans and zoning by-laws. The challenge of devising town-plans that may provide healthy communities with satisfied residents continues; subsequent schemes will be examined at the end of this chapter.

Toronto

Changing approaches to town-planning are evident in the successive layers of development activity in Toronto, the largest city in Canada. The site of present-day Toronto, situated between the Humber and Don Rivers on the north shore of Lake Ontario, was originally inhabited by Huron and Petun Indians, but by 1600 they had withdrawn to the north. In the late seventeenth century the French claimed the area for the fur trade, using Toronto as the head of an important portage route to Lake Huron and the interior, and developing a number of posts, the largest of which was Fort Rouillé (1750-1)—also known as Fort Toronto—which fell to the British in 1759. Although the natives and the French left few signs of their occupation, their use of the land anticipated the city's role as a significant lake port and transportation centre.

Continuous European settlement in Toronto began in July 1793, when John Graves Simcoe, the Lieutenant Governor of the newly formed province of Upper Canada, arrived with his family and officials at its well-protected harbour, with the intention of creating a naval arsenal. Not long after, an unimaginative rectilinear gridiron plan for the town of York was drawn up under Simcoe's direction by surveyor Alexander Aitkin. This was the familiar British imperial layout, which asserted imperial control and order, ignoring the area's natural topography. The townsite consisted of ten blocks just west of the Don River, bounded by George (in the west), Duke (on the north), Berkeley (in the east), and by Front Street facing the lake, where lots were reserved for top officials. We have seen the houses of D'Arcy Boulton Jr [4.17] and Sir William Campbell [4.20], both of which were in this area. Properties were speedily acquired and the town limit moved north to Lot (Queen) Street, north of which 100-acre (40-hectare) lots were reserved for Simcoe's officials—such as the Receiver-General, Peter Russell, and John Elmsley, Sr, who became Chief Justice—as a reward for having settled there. Simcoe built his own suburban house, Castle Frank [4.27], north of the town

near the bank of the Don River, although he and his wife Elizabeth lived with the garrison.[62]

Simcoe chose York as the capital of Upper Canada, rather than the established towns of Niagara or Kingston, because it was less vulnerable to American attack. York became the capital in 1796, when Simcoe left for England. By then most of the 100-acre lots had been granted and were cleared for farming, but only a small number of houses had been built—most of them log, and located near the Don. Russell, who had become Simcoe's successor as administrator, extended the town limit westward to Peter Street. Two main roads were begun: Dundas Street, running east-west across the province, and Yonge Street, running north towards Lake Simcoe. In 1799 a contract was let to an American, Asa Danforth, for a road from York eastward to the Bay of Quinte. These formed the basis of the present interurban highway system, now overlaid with expressways.

The commercial vitality of York began with the arrival of numerous tradesmen—blacksmiths, carpenters, and masons were the first; by sawmills, tanneries, breweries, distilleries, a pottery, and potasheries; by shopkeepers; and by the agricultural development of the area surrounding York—farms on Yonge Street were producing a surplus of flour by 1801. Between 1797 and 1814 the population increased from 437 to 1427. In 1809 there were just over 100 dwellings: 14 round-log houses, 11 one-storey and 27 two-storey squared-timber houses, and 55 one-storey frame houses.[63] The first church of St James—called the 'English Church'—was erected in 1807. The clapboarded building was designed by William Berczy (1744-1813)—colonist, land developer, contractor, architect, and, above all, artist—whose first design in stone was rejected for reasons of cost. Berczy also designed Russell's house on Front Street, a frame building with a central portion having a gabled portico and two projecting wings. The effect of its elegance on the simple architecture of York led to its being called Russell Abbey.

Although wood predominated as a building material, brick was used for the first Parliament Buildings, near the lakefront (1797; page 172), and for the **house and shop of Laurent Quetton St George** (1807; demolished 1904), a Royalist officer and prosperous trader [12.15]. At King Street East and Frederick, it had a two-storey, five-bay elevation, embellished by a small Ionic porch with a three-part Palladian window above it and covered by a low hipped roof. It set an important precedent, and established Georgian Classicism—and brick construction—as the style of the establishment.[64] The house

12.15 Laurent Quetton St George house, Toronto, Ontario, 1810. MTRL/T10080.

of St George (who left York in 1815 and returned to France) was followed by such landmarks as The Grange [4.17] of 1817-18, John Strachan's house [4.19] of 1818, and Chief Justice William Campbell's house [4.20] of 1822, as well as by commercial and public buildings such as the Bank of Upper Canada of 1825-7 and the Second and Third [4.37] Parliament Buildings (1820 and 1832 respectively).

On King Street, north of Front, Simcoe had reserved 6 acres (2.4 hectares) for public buildings that would define the civic core. Several appear in a **view of King Street [12.16]** looking east from Toronto Street, executed in 1835 by architect and artist Thomas Young (c. 1805-60). It shows, on the left (north) side of the street, the jail, the courthouse (both by W.W. Baldwin and John Ewart, 1824), and the second St James Church (by Thomas Rogers, 1831-3; the steeple, included in the illustration, was never built). The south side of the street is lined with two-storey residences, many with shops and large display windows on the ground floor, indicating the arrival of merchants. (All these buildings have been demolished.) The pervasive Georgian (and English) character of this, the main street of the capital, is evi-

dent. In 1840 a three-storey commercial row—known as the Wellington Buildings (demolished)—would be inserted on the north side of King, directly in front of the jail and courthouse, marking, in the words of geographers Gunter Gad and Deryck Holdsworth, 'the ascendancy of the merchants' world over that of the government'.[65]

By 1834, the year York was incorporated as the City of Toronto, the population exceeded 9,000; and the New Town, west to Peter Street and south of Lot (Queen) Street, was becoming well developed. The economic depression that helped bring about the armed uprisings of 1837-8, and continued for some years afterwards, was followed by a development boom that lasted from the 1850s to the 1870s. The surge of building activity was brought about not only by the stabilization of the political situation, but also by the opening of grain, timber, and trapping resources in the North, and of breweries and distilleries in Toronto; by English investment and the development of the banking system; and above

all by the onset of the railway age. Toronto matured quickly from being a colonial capital to becoming a major centre for regional trade, transportation, and finance, with its own industrial base.

This period produced many important architectural monuments whose designs exhibited the Victorian revivals. A number have been discussed: they include landmarks such as St James Cathedral [6.37] and University College [6.63]. Another was **St Lawrence Hall [12.17]** at King Street East and Jarvis, which was built in 1849-50 as a grand centre for the city's expanding cultural and social activities (replacing the Market Building that had been destroyed by fire in 1849). William Thomas designed a richly ornamented three-storey building, fifteen bays wide—with shops on the ground floor, an assembly room above, and a market behind—that represents the transition from the Palladian Georgian manner to the Neoclassical style. (Its treatment was similar to that of Kingston City Hall [4.41] and Montreal's Bonsecours Market [6.56].) The design of St Lawrence Hall incorporates a triple-arched entrance (leading originally to the market arcade) with a frontispiece of four engaged Corinthian columns above, and a pediment containing the city's arms, supporting an attic storey (over the assembly room). Above this a temple-like cupola, with twelve white-painted wooden columns, rises to a domed roof with clock faces. Built in white brick and honey-coloured stone, and embellished with classical detail and ornamental sculpture, St Lawrence Hall had a

12.16 View of King Street, Toronto, Ontario. Lithograph by Nathaniel Currier of a drawing by Thomas Young, 1835. Royal Ontario Museum.

12.17 St Lawrence Hall, Toronto, Ontario, 1849-50. Photograph by William Dendy.

commanding presence that made it Toronto's most impressive building in the middle of the nineteenth century. After the turn of the century it was often unused, but in 1966-7 it was beautifully restored. It stands today as a fine Toronto monument that has historical, cultural, and (particularly with the Saturday market stretching behind) commercial significance.[66]

Along King Street, St Lawrence Hall marked the beginning of the replacement of the restrained Georgian façades with larger and more highly embellished Victorian ones. In the following decades the street became the retail showpiece of Canada. An observer characterized it in the 1880s:

> On the south side, the 'dollar' or fashionable side, of King Street, continuously from York Street to the Market, are the spacious plate-glass windows, glittering with jewelry, with gold and silverplate, with elaborate china and brick-a-brac, with sheen of satin-shining tissues for Toronto's brides . . . . There are restaurants, where men and ladies can dine in comfort, and as luxuriously as in any in New York or London, photographers, art warerooms.[67]

12.18 Gooderham and Worts Distillery, Toronto, Ontario, 1859-60. Photograph by Hugh Robertson.

In 1849 King Street East acquired a horse-drawn omnibus that ran up Yonge Street, linking the St Lawrence Market with the village of Yorkville, which had been laid out in the previous decade. This was followed by a horse-drawn streetcar in 1861—the first public transit in Canada—and an electric streetcar in 1892, when the trackage of the horse-car system was over 68 miles (110 km).[68]

Toronto's economy was fuelled by commerce and industry, which brought about the prosperity of a new class of merchants and manufacturers, most of them newcomers and not the old-moneyed lawyers and politicians descended from the Family Compact. Among them were Scottish-born dry-goods merchant, Methodist lay preacher, and senator John Macdonald, whose warehouse [10.36] on Wellington Street East was seen earlier; Irish-born department-store magnate Timothy Eaton [14.10]; his rival Robert Simpson, whose store [10.41] and house [11.25] have been described; and Hart Massey [14.1], who relocated his father's farm-implement manufacturing business to Toronto in 1879.

Two Yorkshiremen who rose to prominence were William Gooderham and his brother-in-law James Worts, who set up business in Toronto in the 1830s as millers and soon branched into distilling. They developed a large complex at Trinity and Mill Streets, in the industrial area east of downtown along the Don River. Several of their buildings still stand, the oldest being the **Gooderham and Worts Distillery Building** [12.18], built in 1859-60 to designs by civil engineer David Roberts, Sr (d. 1881), and rebuilt after a fire in 1869 by his son, architect David Roberts, Jr. Originally used for grain storage, milling, and distilling, it replaced a windmill. Four and one-half storeys high, the structure comprises load-bearing walls of Kingston limestone, some $3\frac{1}{2}$ feet (1 m) thick at the base, with internal supports of wood. The austere 300-foot-long (92 m) façade, in front of which was a Grand Trunk Railway siding, was articulated with segmental-arched windows resting on stone sill courses at every floor. The central bay (rendered off-centre by a later addition) projects slightly and terminates in a gable, reminiscent of the familiar Georgian design formula. The building is no longer in use and its future is uncertain.[69]

In 1889-92 George Gooderham, who succeeded his father as president of the distillery, built a magnificent house [11.9], in the Richardsonian Romanesque style, on St George Street at Bloor Street West, in the developing uptown area near the University of Toronto (to which he made a generous endowment). David Roberts, Jr, was the architect, as he was of the Gooderham Building (1891-2, also known as the Flatiron Building), a 4½-storey office building on the narrow triangular site where Wellington and Front Street East meet. From here, Gooderham managed his many business interests; one of them was the Bank of Toronto, of which he was president. Both his house and his offices were built of red brick, with Credit Valley sandstone trim.[70]

Most members of the new commercial establishment, like Gooderham, built their houses on or near Bloor Street, as the original élite residential area centred on Front Street gave way to warehouses, offices, and rooming houses—a result of the railway tracks along the waterfront. The Grand Trunk and Great Western Railways built their stations west of Yonge Street, where the third (and present) Union Station stands today. Housing for working people developed in a number of areas, most notably Cabbagetown, east of Parliament Street.

King Street remained the principal business thoroughfare. An upsurge of business activity led to an increase in property values, which brought about higher buildings and greater density. A photograph of the **north side of King Street East [12.19]**, taken around 1910, shows a new generation of five- and six-storey buildings. (The picture looks east from Yonge Street, a block west of Thomas Young's watercolour view of 1835.) The Janes Building (1892) in the foreground, with the rounded corner bay, shows some influences from the Romanesque Revival, with its brick corbels and round arches at the fourth storey; whereas the Royal Bank of Canada (1906), two buildings beyond, exhibits the classicism of the Edwardian age. Toronto office buildings reached ten storeys in 1895 (the Temple Building at Richmond and Bay Streets, designed by G.W. Gouinlock) and twenty in 1915 (the new Royal Bank at 2 King Street East, by Ross and Macdonald, replacing the 23-year-old Janes Building).[71]

As Toronto entered the twentieth century, the city centre had moved only slightly west of the orig-

12.19 North side of King Street East, Toronto, Ontario. Photograph *c*. 1910. City of Toronto Archives/James 7227.

inal ten-block plot, although the gridiron had been extended far beyond its original limits. As we have seen, land uses changed—the most dramatic being the waterfront's shifting from residential to transportation and industrial use. The rectilinear plan, with its narrow streets and repetitive blocks, must have seemed tedious and inadequate to a new generation of Torontonians imbued with Beaux-Arts and City Beautiful principles. A major downtown fire in 1904 provided an opportunity for grandiose redevelopment. The Toronto Guild of Civic Art (founded in 1897) and the Ontario Association of Architects combined in 1906 to propose a plan that showed park development along the waterfront, a system of parks and driveways around the city, and a series of diagonal avenues intended to connect downtown with the suburbs, the driveways, and inter-city routes. The proposed diagonal thoroughfares with long vistas revived the town-planning improvements implemented in Europe from the sixteenth-century Rome of Pope Sixtus V to the nineteenth-century Paris of Georges-Eugène Haussmann. The plan was well received, but not acted upon.[72]

A **second plan for Toronto** [12.20], prepared for a new Civic Improvement Committee by architect John Lyle (page 276), and submitted in 1911, repeated the idea of radiating avenues (which, it was hoped, would solve problems of congestion) and also proposed a grand Federal Avenue linking the proposed new Union Station on Front Street with a large civic plaza north of Queen, featuring a complex of new municipal and federal buildings inserted between Osgoode Hall [4.38] and the City Hall [10.31], with public gardens and a parade ground behind. Federal Avenue was intended as a dignified processional route for the downtown core that would provide opportunities for new commercial development and would replace city blocks of 'the poorest possible character.' Lyle's training in Paris, and the report's frequent references to Daniel Burnham's unexecuted Chicago Plan of 1909, left no doubt about the joint influences of the École des Beaux-Arts and the American City Beautiful Movement.[73]

Neither Federal Avenue nor the diagonal street plan was ever built, and Toronto continued to expand on the grid. The Federal Avenue proposal was halted because of the war, although it was revived (without issue) in 1929 as Cambrai Avenue— aligned somewhat differently and conceived as a memorial to Canadian war veterans. A number of important structures, including the Toronto Star

Building and the Royal York Hotel, were planned with the proposed thoroughfare in mind. A half-century later a new City Hall and a public square (Nathan Phillips Square; **15.32**) were built on the site of Lyle's intended municipal complex.

As downtown development intensified in the 1880s, new residential areas were developed above Bloor Street. The Annex— extending from Avenue Road west to Bathurst and north to Davenport— was so named because it was annexed to the city in 1887. (It is just west of Yorkville, which had itself been annexed in 1883.) Rosedale, to the northeast—planned with large properties and much greenery—was partly carved out of the estate of Colonel W.B. Jarvis and was intended for the wealthy. The streets of Rosedale deviated, to a great extent, from the gridiron plan, acknowledging some of the ravines that punctuate Toronto outside the old central core. But the natural landscape predominated in the west—in High Park, the public recreational area that was deeded to the city in 1873 by architect John G. Howard in return for an annual pension of $1,200.[74]

The most attractive residential enclave was—and remains—Wychwood Park, on the escarpment to the northwest. A privately developed 22-acre (9-hectare) colony for well-to-do artists and professionals, it was developed on picturesque principles. Landscape painter Marmaduke Matthews, who built his house there in 1874 and named it Wychwood (after a forest in his native Oxfordshire), drew a subdivision plan in 1888 in partnership with his neighbour, businessman Alexander Jardine. They showed a number of 'villa lots' that retained the earlier, suburban idea of the villa (page 603)—surrounded by a circular Park Drive, with a large private park where Taddle Creek passed through the property. The plan was revised three years later; it restricted land uses and controlled design, anticipating zoning by-laws of a generation or two later. The first lot was not sold until 1905— to the well-known painter George A. Reid (who called his house Upland Cottage)—and many of the others were not claimed until the next decade. Architect Eden Smith (page 619), who built his own house there, helped to reorganize the Wychwood Corporation with even tighter restrictions, and designed a number of other houses in the park.[75]

Nineteen houses were built between 1905 and 1917—eight or nine of them by Eden Smith—and their character probably represented the combined vision of Matthews, Reid, and Eden Smith. Typical is the **Agnes and Mary Wrinch house [12.21]**,

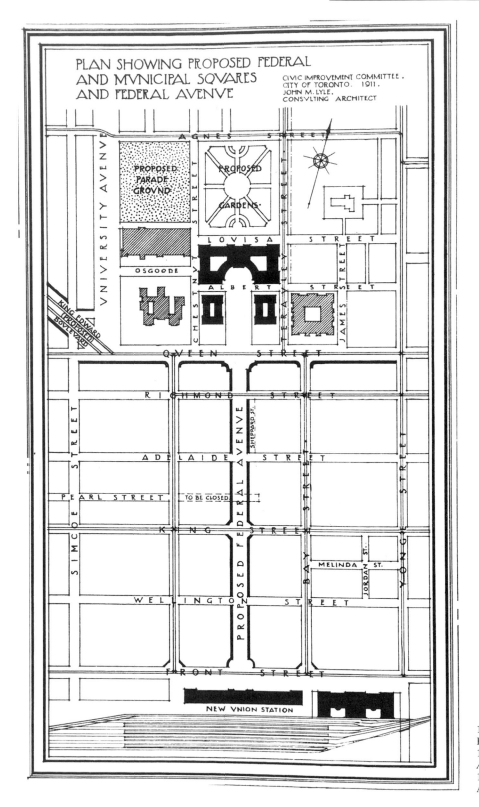

12.20 Plan of proposed Federal Avenue, Toronto, 1911. From *Report of the Advisory Planning Commission*, 1929. City of Toronto Archives.

designed by Eden Smith and Son and built in 1911 in the free English Domestic Revival style that came out of the Arts and Crafts Movement (page 619). Mary Wrinch was a painter who had studied with Reid and would marry him in 1922. Everything about the house is suggestive of early English building, yet nothing copies specific sources. Beige walls of shingles and stucco are contained beneath a broad hipped roof, with a gable at the rear (seen in the photograph), facing the park. The Wrinch house, and the others built at this time, nestle comfortably in the landscape and are glimpsed through the trees, much like a series of three-dimensional paintings. The trees and shrubs are predominantly native species planted in a casual manner, reflecting the teachings of English landscape architect Gertrude Jekyll, a respected colleague of the Arts and Crafts practitioners.

At the outbreak of the First World War, Toronto's population reached nearly 400,000, and only Montreal challenged its bid for economic supremacy. In the years that followed, the city continued to grow rapidly. The principal buildings erected between the wars will be discussed in Chapter 14, and a selection of more recent architecture in Chapter 15.

12.21 Agnes and Mary Wrinch house, Wychwood Park, Toronto, Ontario, 1911. Photograph by Harold Kalman, 1981.

Resource Communities

A kind of town that has been particularly important to the Canadian economy is the resource town, a community built near the place where a natural resource—usually minerals or timber—is extracted or processed, and whose economy is based on that activity. Many are 'single-enterprise or company towns', built and managed by the corporation that operates the industrial enterprise, while others are 'service and supply towns' with a broader base of control, yet still dependent on a resource industry. Resource towns often were born—and died—very quickly. They have always been vulnerable to fluctuations in market prices for their commodities, and to decisions made by far-away corporations or governments.[76]

A number of communities sprang up as a result of the nineteenth-century gold rushes in the West. Two such towns— Barkerville in British Columbia (1862; **8.44**) and Dawson in the Yukon (1896; **13.19**)—were settled by independent fortune-seekers who worked their own claims, though the government controlled their development. At their peak, Barkerville had an estimated 10,000 people and Dawson 16,000. Both became service and supply towns that met the needs of a region and not just a single company, and Dawson served for many years as the administrative capital of the Yukon Territory. Today both are interpreted historic sites with dozens of restored buildings.

12.22 Miners' houses, Cumberland, British Columbia. BCARS/11672.

Nelson and Kaslo in British Columbia, and Cobalt and Sudbury in Ontario, are other examples of resource-based service and supply towns. Sudbury was laid out in 1883 by the CPR, which found nickel and copper deposits during railway construction. The Canadian Copper Company built a smelter five years later; in 1902 it became a part of International Nickel (INCO Ltd). As the nickel industry developed, mainly in the second quarter of this century, Sudbury's residents were divided between miners who commuted to nearby mining camps, and people employed in town at the smelter and in service industries.[77]

Cumberland [12.22], British Columbia, was a resource community of a different kind—a single-enterprise town whose growth and progress were directed by one man, Robert Dunsmuir (**11.7**). After discovering coal at the Wellington Mine and establishing a town there, he found rich seams of anthracite coal further north on Vancouver Island, and in 1888 he acquired the Cumberland mine, near Courtenay. Dunsmuir planned a townsite in 1891 and six years later incorporated the City of Cumberland, named after the coal-mining centre in northern England. The familiar gridiron pattern formed the basis for the town; there was little planning intervention beyond the initial survey. The population reached 13,000 at its peak, shortly before the First World War. Dunsmuir Avenue, the main street, was lined with two-storey frame com-

mercial buildings, while the residential area was crammed with row upon row of one-storey four-room cottages, many of which had no street frontage. The city had an estimated 3,000 Chinese inhabitants, who lived on the edge of a swamp west of town and formed the largest Chinatown north of San Francisco; its main streets, Shanghai and Chang, lacked the order of those in the principal town. Cumberland also had a black district. As the twentieth century progressed, oil replaced coal as the fuel of preference, and Cumberland's prosperity, which had been based on a single resource, waned. The population has since dwindled to below 2,000: and the people who are left are sustained by logging and tourism. Clearly visible today are the original grid, several mine-heads, some of the old public buildings, and blocks of old cottages (most of them modified).[78]

Glace Bay, Nova Scotia, is another coal town that originated in this period. Coal had been extracted in the area on a small scale since 1720, when it was used to supply Louisbourg. In 1893 the Dominion Coal Company established itself there and turned Glace Bay into a booming company town. The firm operated eleven collieries, including some of the largest on the continent. Living conditions were poor, with little separation between industrial and residential uses and no waste-management program. Testimony given in 1925 before a Royal Commission studying labour unrest in the coal fields revealed that

> the mortality rate among infants is very high. Glace Bay had the highest death rate last year, perhaps of any place in Canada . . . . the infant death rate was, I think, 110 per thousand.[79]

Little was done to improve life. In 1967 Dominion Coal abandoned Glace Bay, and a government agency operated the last colliery until 1984. The town now supports itself largely on tourism, taking pride in the Miners' Memorial Museum that commemorates the coal miners of the past.

Before the First World War, Canadian corporations involved in the resource industries built townsites in the interest of increasing production and profits but with little regard for the comfort or well-being of their employees. This approach contrasts with the benevolent attitude represented by many company towns in England, such as Titus Salt's Saltaire, near Bradford in Yorkshire (by Lockwood and Mawson, 1851-76), and George and Richard Cadbury's Bourneville, near Birmingham (begun 1879), where industrial barons (the former producing textiles, the latter chocolate) laid out communities with an eye to health and amenities, despite an absence of government regulation.

The Canadian situation began to change in the post-war period, partly because provincial governments decided to become involved in planning. The first totally planned resource town was **Témiscaming** [**12.23**], Quebec, a pulp-and-paper community developed by the Kipawa Fibre Company, a subsidiary of the Riordan Pulp and Paper Company. Everybody in town—except the postal workers—was an employee of the company. The firm 'decided that the completed town should be a model industrial community which would attract and hold the best class of men.'[80] In 1917 it invited Thomas Adams and the Commission of Conservation to prepare a plan that, in Adams' words, was 'designed to secure convenience of access between its different parts [in order to achieve] economical and healthy development.'[81] Streets were curved and followed the topography, parks and playgrounds were reserved as open space, and different house types were provided for the various social classes. Managers lived separately from production workers, and English- and French-speak-

12.23 Plan of Témiscaming, Quebec, 1917. From Thomas Adams, *Rural Planning and Development*, 1917.

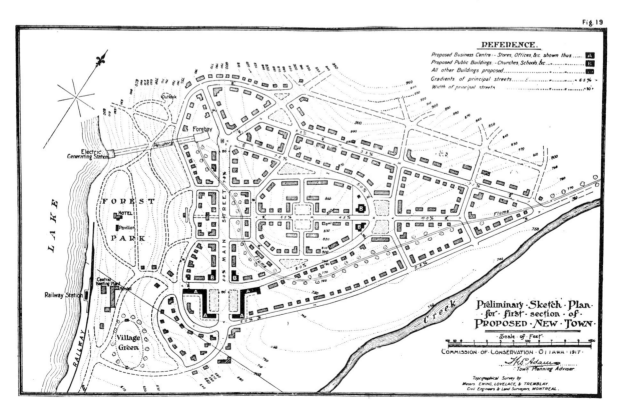

12.24 Houses, East Fullerton Avenue, Hamilton, Ontario, *c.* 1903-5. From *Canadian Architect and Builder*, May 1907.

ing families tended to live in separate parts of town.

Kapuskasing, Ontario, a pulp-and-paper town planned in 1921 by the Ontario government for the Kimberly-Clark Corporation, and Arvida, Quebec, an aluminum-smelting town planned in 1926, went even further by providing zoning controls, greenbelts, and reserving land for future growth.[82]

Major industries in established urban areas often built residential subdivisions adjacent to their plants. While not complete communities, they comprised neighbourhoods whose inhabitants all worked for 'the company'. When the International Harvester Company located an agricultural-machinery plant in Hamilton, Ontario, around 1903, it formed a subsidiary, the Eastern Building Society, to construct workers' housing. Some 150 two-storey brick dwelling units—some of them single-family houses, others rows and duplexes—were built on **East Fullerton Avenue [12.24]**, Hamilton, to be rented to employees. Many workers objected to paying the rent, preferring to buy a house of their own. The company then gave them the opportunity to purchase the dwellings, with 10 per cent down and $16 per month (for employees who were earning $2.50 per day or more).[83]

In a similar gesture, during the Second World War, the federal government's Wartime Housing Limited (see page 642) built **Burkeville [12.25]** on Sea Island, in the municipality of Richmond adjacent to the Vancouver airport, with 328 houses for workers who were employed at the plant of Boeing Aircraft of Canada Ltd. (The streets were named after airplane manufacturers.) The plain, no-frills dwellings, designed by Vancouver architects McCarter and Nairne, came in three sizes: a 'Small Four' (a tiny four-room cottage), a 'Big Four', and a 'Big Six' (which had six rooms, including two bedrooms in a second storey). When Boeing left British Columbia after the war, the company sold the houses of Burkeville to returning veterans. The area—on the noisy main approach to Vancouver International Airport—remains largely intact, although virtually all the houses have been enlarged and modified. But Burkeville retains a strong sense of community.[84]

The most successful example of a comprehensively planned resource town is **Kitimat [12.26]**, British Columbia, planned in 1952 and developed by the Aluminum Company of Canada (Alcan) to serve its mammoth smelter. Like Prince Rupert, only 70 miles (110 km) to the west, Kitimat was an entirely new community planned thoroughly and conscientiously, using the state-of-the-art techniques of its day. And as at Prince Rupert, the Canadian corporate developer turned to American planners.[85]

The large design and consulting team for Kitimat was directed by Clarence S. Stein (1883-1975) and the principal planners were Mayer and Whittlesey—all of New York. Stein was an accomplished architect-turned-planner whose lasting fame was ensured by his design for Radburn, New Jersey (with Henry Wright, 1926), as a 'town for the motor age'. It introduced a circulation plan that separated pedestrian and vehicular traffic, directed through traffic away from local activities, and created residential superblocks around interior parks. Stein's colleague Albert Mayer (1897-1981), for his part, had already

demonstrated a commitment to addressing social needs through large-scale housing projects.

The design of Kitimat combined Stein's Radburn idea, the Garden City, the Greenbelt City (in which a city is preplanned to maximum growth and surrounded by a greenbelt), and the concept of organizing superblocks into discrete neighbourhood units. The objectives were intended to ensure the industrial success of the plant by creating a place in which workers would enjoy themselves, despite the remoteness and difficult climate of the region. Another goal was to plan for the diversification of industry, which has since occurred. The team's holistic approach looked at virtually everything—from retaining a sociologist (to help solve the problems of family life in an isolated area) to addressing the conservation of natural resources.

The smelter and deep-sea port of Kitimat are located in an industrial area at the head of Douglas Channel. Bauxite ore from Jamaica is made into aluminum, using hydroelectric power from a massive generating plant 50 miles (80 km) away, and the metal is sent to world markets. The Kitimat townsite is 4 miles (6 km) from the industrial area, from which it is separated by a flood plain and an agricultural reserve. Service industries are grouped in a separate service centre. The city itself has been planned to have, eventually, ten residential neighbourhoods of 5,000 persons each—its focus being a community centre with a school, shops, offices, and recreational facilities. The city centre was placed at the point where the roads from the neighbourhoods converge to lead to the highway.

The prototype buildings (begun in 1953) were

12.25 Aerial view of Burkeville, Richmond, British Columbia. Photograph by Charles Wishart, 1944. City of Richmond Archives/1984 17 84.

designed by Vancouver architects with a reputation for progressive modern design. The **commercial buildings and shopping centre [12.27]** were by Semmens and Simpson, the school and recreational buildings by Sharp and Thompson, Berwick, Pratt (see Chapter 15). J. Russell Baxter, the only architect resident in Kitimat in its early years, designed an elementary school, a cinema, the public-safety building, and a church.

Alcan built no rental housing, but it provided financial bonuses and second mortgages to make houses affordable, with an agreement that enabled workers to sell back homes if they moved within ten years. By the end of 1954, builder Norman Hullah of Vancouver had constructed more than 80 one- and two-storey post-and-beam houses with wood-panel construction, and builders Johnson and Crooks built 250 two-storey houses, including singles, twins, and rowhouses. All houses face traffic-free green areas, and children can walk to school, and adults to stores, without crossing streets.

The architecture of Kitimat's first decade has left the imprint of a 1950s modern period-piece, but its planners created a community with a high quality of life. The population reached 14,000 by 1957, but soon dropped to 9,000 because of the soft aluminum market; in the 1980s it stabilized at around 13,000. Kitimat achieved its goal of being a comfortable place for family living. The population now includes grandparents and the trees have matured.

12.26 Aerial view of Kitimat, British Columbia. Courtesy Alcan Smelters and Chemicals Ltd.

12.27 Shopping centre (City Centre), Kitimat, British Columbia, *c.* 1953. Courtesy Alcan Smelters and Chemicals Ltd.

12.28 View of Africville, Halifax, Nova Scotia. Photograph by Bob Brooks, c. 1960. PANS/N7832.

Most of the walkways are still used as planned, but some new neighbourhoods have been built with houses facing the streets and no walkways. Residents complain about the lack of life in the town centre and the inadequate retail stores.

Kitimat was planned to achieve economic diversity. A pulp-and-paper mill and a sawmill opened in the 1970s, and a petrochemical plant opened in 1982. Kitimat will likely survive, even if world markets for aluminum should fail.

Few other resource communities have been so enterprising. They tend to be built in times of economic growth and often suffer—and sometimes die—in periods of recession. Schefferville, Quebec, was one such community. It was founded by the Iron Ore Company of Canada in the early 1950s, during the post-war industrial boom, in the heart of the rugged Labrador-Ungava peninsula. Iron ore was extracted and shipped south to Sept-Îles on the company's own Quebec North Shore and Labrador Railway. Although lacking the imagination of Kitimat, its plan, drawn up jointly in 1953 by the company and the government of Quebec, attempted to create a comfortable environment in a hostile land. The mines were soon producing two-thirds of Canada's iron ore and the town's popu-

lation reached 2,000. But when, in the recession of 1983, Iron Ore Company of Canada president (and future prime minister) Brian Mulroney announced the closure of all operations, Schefferville was dead.[86]

Sometimes communities are not planned at all, yet achieve a high degree of cohesion—and even thrive—in spite of contrary efforts by planners. Such was the case of **Africville [12.28]**, a black community at the north end of Halifax, on the shore of Bedford Basin. Eight families, led by W.M. Brown, purchased property and settled here in the 1840s, on what was then called Campbell Road (later renamed as an extension of Barrington Street). Others joined them in the years that followed. In 1849 they formed a Baptist congregation; in 1883 they were provided with a one-room public school—a small frame building heated only by a stove and with no running water; and in 1916 the residents built the Seaview African United Baptist Church. The community coalesced: its institutions worked, and its people felt at home, even in their poverty and with virtually no municipal services. A view of the street shows the school, the church, and a handful of houses—mostly two-storey shingled buildings with low gabled roofs, following the Nova Scotia vernacular tradition.[87]

The authorities seem to have done everything they could to harass the residents. The railway went through Africville in 1855 and before long a large network of tracks bisected the neighbourhood. The city's disposal pit for 'night soil' was located on the edge of the community in 1858; also in the vicinity the Infectious Diseases Hospital was built in 1870, a stone-crushing plant and an abbatoir developed in the early twentieth century, and in the 1950s a large open city dump was located 350 feet (100 m) from the end of the settlement. Despite these incursions, the community flourished, attaining a population of about 400. The planners, however, were determined that Africville should not exist, and so in 1962 the City of Halifax's Development Department recommended its relocation. Between 1964 and 1970 the city bought all the properties, dispersed the residents, and demolished most of the buildings (including the church). But even the bulldozer could not destroy the community's spirit. In 1982 the former residents founded the Africville Genealogical Society, and they hold annual reunions on the site.

CHAPTER **13**

THE TRUE NORTH

THE CLIMATE and terrain of the Canadian Arctic may seem remarkably hostile to southerners, but that vast region has supported habitation for millennia. The glaciers from the last Ice Age retreated to the mountain peaks of the eastern Arctic about 7,000 years ago. During the next 3,500 years the Arctic climate was warmer than it is today, and vegetation on the tundra became sufficiently established to support large herds of caribou, muskoxen, and bison, as well as human inhabitants who hunted those animals.[1]

The Arctic has two seasons: a short summer and a long winter. The summer is a period of constant light and warmth, the winter one of darkness and cold. The range of available building materials is severely restricted, since there is little tree growth across much of the Far North. The region is subject to permafrost—ground that remains at, or below, freezing throughout the year. The presence of ice in the ground makes it heave during seasonal freezing and thawing, causing severe problems with conventional methods of construction. Heaving occurs when the ground is warmed unnaturally: for example, buildings—or even a slight disturbance of the vegetation cover—can transfer heat and cause movement.

The history of building in the North is in part the story of how the aboriginal peoples understood and worked in harmony with these unique conditions; how Europeans and southern Canadians at first ignored these circumstances, but gradually came to respect them, and adapt to them by means of new construction techniques; and how some builders learned from the natives' centuries-old experience. The outcome was a distinctively new architecture—a process that continues.

Buildings of the Far North remain relatively unstudied. What is known about native building there (as elsewhere) is the result of research by archaeologists and anthropologists, not architectural historians. This chapter offers a brief summary of native and non-native building based on our current knowledge.

Early Inuit Building

While archaeologists have found the remains of sites in the northwestern Arctic that were occupied as long ago as the eighth millennium BC, the history of Arctic building may go back as many as 25,000 years. Our knowledge of the earliest cultures, and their dwellings, remains scanty. Somewhat more is known about the Dorset culture (or paleoeskimos), which originated around 800 BC, occupied an area from western Victoria Island to northeastern Greenland and southern Newfoundland, and may have lasted until about AD 1300. The dwellings of the Dorset culture consisted of a round skin tent for summer use, and a rectangular semi-subterranean house, presumed to have been covered by a tent-like superstructure, for winter use. Archaeologists have found snow knives and inferred from them that the Dorset also built snowhouses.[2]

The realities of the North led its inhabitants—the Inuit of today and their ancestors, who are known to anthropologists as Eskimos—to build separate dwellings for each of two seasons, winter and summer. The winter was a time devoted to indoor life, the summer to intense outdoor life with constant hunting and fishing. Inuit houses were built to respond to the resulting environmental and behavioural needs.

The Thule winter house

Similar habitation patterns are found among the people of the Thule culture, who, about AD 1000, began to displace those of the Dorset culture across the Arctic, from Alaska to Greenland. The Thule people (named for the district in Greenland, halfway between the Arctic Circle and the North Pole, where their remains were first found) were the ancestors of today's Inuit. They too adopted separate house-types for summer and winter. The Thule winter houses were complex and permanent, providing comfort and warmth for prolonged periods of indoor living. Archaeologist Robert McGhee has written that they are 'the most impressive archaeological remains found in arctic Canada, and attest to an economy considerably richer and more secure than that of most Inuit of the historic period.'[3]

The typical Thule winter house formed an oval whose external diameters were between about 10 and 30 feet (3 and 9 m), and it was dug as much as $3\frac{1}{2}$ feet (1 m) into the ground. The floor and walls were lined with solid materials, and a frame superstructure supported a roof. The actual materials varied from region to region, depending on what was available to the builders. In the central and eastern Canadian Arctic, the Thule used whalebone and stone, while in Alaska the abundant driftwood prevailed. Common to all regions, in the form of the house, was a narrow underground entrance passageway a few metres long that angled up into the floor to provide an effective cold-trap. (Since warm air rises, cold air was displaced to the lower end of the passage, away from the living space.) The passage could be sealed during storms. Sleeping platforms around the perimeter were raised off the ground to take advantage of heat given off by bodies and blubber lamps. A hole in the roof (called a 'nose') and a window covered with gut or skin provided some ventilation and light. Houses were usually oriented to face the shoreline.[4]

A group of Thule winter houses at Brooman Point, NWT, in the Bathurst-Cornwallis Islands region of the High Arctic, was excavated in the late 1970s by a team led by Robert McGhee. The exterior of the largest (House 3) was 30 feet (9 m) across and 23 feet (7 m) from back to front (exclusive of the entrance passageway), and it contained two rooms, while others were somewhat smaller and generally contained only a single room. The builders set the houses less than 3 feet (1 m) into the ground, and paved the floors with large slabs of stone. They lined the inner walls with boulders and slabs set on a layer of moss and backed with fill consisting of earth, gravel, and stones. The walls originally rose 3 feet (1 m) or more above the floor—$1\frac{1}{2}$ feet (50 cm) or more above grade—and were as thick as $6\frac{1}{2}$ feet (2 m). Roof frames made of whalebones rose from the top of the walls.[5]

House 4 [13.1]—seen in the photograph with its roof reconstructed—provided the best evidence of the whalebone roof structure. The roof was originally supported by seven mandibles (jawbones). The largest—nearly 10 feet (3 m) long, and spanning the width of the house—rested on piles of flat boulders and functioned as a ridge-pole. The other six

mandibles served as rafters: one end was supported on the front or rear wall and the other end on the larger bone. Interlaced among the rafters were whale ribs (less strong than the mandibles), and the roof was filled with moss, earth, and gravel.

The Thule winter community at Brooman Point, which was smaller than many other Arctic settlements, had an average population of about 15 to 30 people—probably consisting of an extended family unit. Some five or six houses were in use at any given time, and each house seems to have been occupied for only a few years.

There are numerous variations among Thule houses. At Cumberland Sound on Baffin Island, Peter Schledermann found single-family dwellings, two-family living quarters, and a communal house with a cloverleaf floor plan. Roofs were variously covered with sod, stone, and baleen.[6] (A flexible substance that grows from the roof of the whale's mouth, baleen became a precious commodity to Europeans, who used it for corset stays and other products for which we now use plastics.) In Labrador, sod was commonly used for walls and roofs, with some reliance on whalebone and wood.[7]

A large, undisturbed whalebone house at Izembek Lagoon on the Alaskan Peninsula—similar in construction to Thule houses in the Canadian Arctic—had about 31 mandible rafters. Assuming that the average winter house used at least 20 of these bones, each house would have required the jawbones from between ten and fifteen whales—more for a single household than would be acquired during a season's hunting by an entire settlement.[8] Whalebones must therefore have been an important commodity. Abandoned houses were re-used, or their bones scavenged for other houses—which explains why so many of the surviving winter houses have been disturbed, as at the **Learmouth site [13.2]** at Creswell Bay on Somerset Island.

The Inuit continued the habitation patterns of their Thule ancestors until the beginning of the historic period. In 1577, when the English mariner Sir Martin Frobisher returned to what is now called Frobisher Bay on southern Baffin Island, he noted Eskimos living in 'tents made of Seale skinns' (the summer dwelling), and also saw winter buildings 'raised of stones and Whale bones'.[9] The whalebone winter houses were abandoned shortly afterwards—perhaps because of their decreasing effectiveness with the cooling of the climate during the 'Little Ice Age' that occurred in the Far North between 1600 and 1850; the decline of whaling; or because new house forms had been learned through contact with

13.1 Thule house 4, Brooman Point, Northwest Territories. Photograph by Robert McGhee. Archaeological Survey of Canada, Canadian Museum of Civilization.

13.2 Thule house ruins, Learmouth site, Somerset Island, Northwest Territories. Allen P. McCartney, University of Arkansas.

Europeans. For example, in Saglek Bay in Labrador some Inuit houses, built about 1850, had planked floors, peaked roof-frames on sod walls, and wood-burning stoves—surely the influence of the Moravian missionaries who were based at Hebron, 25 miles (40 km) to the south (see page 689).[10]

The Inuit snowhouse

The most familiar image of an Inuit dwelling is certainly the domed snowhouse, usually known as the igloo (or *iglu*)—a word that properly refers to a permanent house of any form.[11] Most authorities believe that the snowhouse was used since the Dorset culture, if not earlier, and some suggest that it was inspired by the domed skin-tent. Other (more Euro-centred) people have claimed that the snowhouse came into use as the common winter dwelling only in the historic period, when the Eskimos learned techniques of vaulting from Europeans—but this seems highly unlikely.

Whatever its origin, the snowhouse was not only the primary Arctic winter dwelling from the early nineteenth century until the middle of the present century, but its construction techniques have continued to amaze observers from the South. The way of building allows the construction of a vault without a scaffold or external support, uses the catenary curve intuitively to avoid bulging or collapse,

and attains excellent heat conservation through the natural insulation of snow and the use of cold-traps.

When the renowned anthropologist Franz Boas first visited the Arctic in 1883-4, he was very impressed by the snowhouse and described its construction in detail:

> Two men unite in building a house, the one cutting the blocks, the other building. At first a row of blocks is put up in a circle, the single pieces being slanted so as to fit closely together. Then the first block is cut down to the ground and the top of the row is slanted so as to form one thread of a spiral line. The builder places the first block of the second row with its narrow side upon the first block and pushes it with his left hand to the right so that it touches the last block of the first row. Thus the snow block, which is inclined a little inward, has a support on two sides. The vertical joint is slanted with the snow knife and tightly pressed together, the new block resting on the oblique side of the former. In building on in this way the blocks receive the shape of almost regular trapezoids. Every block is inclined a little more inward than the previous one, and as the angle to the vertical becomes greater the blocks are only kept in their places by the neighboring ones. In order to give them a good support the edges are the more slanted as their angle is greater.[12]

Boas drew the **plan and section of a typical snowhouse in the Davis Strait region [13.3].** A curved wall at the entrance acted as a windbreak. Typically a $2\frac{1}{2}$-foot-high (75-cm) door led to a small dome about 6 feet (1.8 m) high, which in turn opened onto a passage of the same height formed by an elliptical vault. From there, a door 3 feet (90 cm) high opened into the main room, whose floor was 9 in-

13.3 Sections through a snowhouse, Davis Strait region, Northwest Territories. Drawing by Franz Boas. From Boas, *The Central Eskimo*, 1888.

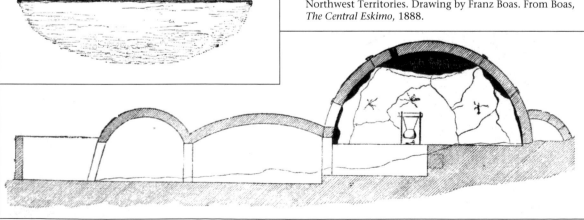

13.4 Iglulik snowhouse, Cape Fullerton, Northwest Territories. Photograph by Albert Low, 1903. NAC/C24522.

13.5 Two snowhouses at Little Whale River, Quebec. Photograph by James L. Cotter, 1874. Notman Photographic Archives, MMCH/MP3914.

ches (23 cm) higher than the entrance passage. Benches at the left and right sides and a bed across the rear half rose two and one-half feet (75 cm) above the floor. Small domed rooms at the side and rear provided storage space.

Inside, the vault was lined with skins (sometimes the same skins that covered the summer tent) that prevented the interior heat from melting the roof. A window was cut over the door and covered with seal gut, and a small hole was cut through the wall near the top to provide ventilation. The bed was covered with wood, shrubs, and skins. On the side-benches were soapstone lamps and a framework that supported cooking utensils.

Snowhouses were built for two distinct purposes. Large ones—perhaps 10 to 12 feet (3 to 3.5 m) high and 12 to 15 feet (3.5 to 4.5 m) in diameter—were built to house a family through an entire winter, particularly among the Central Eskimo. The **Iglulik snowhouse at Cape Fullerton [13.4]**—on the west shore of Hudson Bay, photographed in 1903 by Albert Low—comfortably accommodates a family and its needs. Smaller snowhouses, used as temporary dwellings during winter hunts or journeys, were about 5 feet (1.5 m) high and 7 feet (2 m) in diameter. The two **snowhouses at Little Whale River**

[**13.5**], Quebec, in a photograph taken by James L. Cotter in 1874, were being built for this purpose. The man at the left is cutting blocks of snow for the entrance passage, while the man on the right is tending to the sled. A skin on a semi-circular stretcher frame leans against the snowhouse at the right.[13]

Details differed from one region to the next. Some groups did not use the skin lining, with the result that there was dripping and noticeably cooler interior temperatures. The Copper Eskimo—the westernmost of the Central groups—made entranceways that were straight-sided and flat-topped rather than vaulted or domed. In 1822-3 Sir William Parry documented a house among the Iglulik Eskimo of northern Baffin Island that consisted of three domed sleeping rooms connected to a common feast-house and entrance; and in the 1860s Charles Hall recorded a cluster of four igloos entered from a common domed hall. Twentieth-century anthropologists have noted many variations of cluster plans—with some spaces being shared by several families and others private.[14]

Other dwellings

As temperatures rose above freezing, in late April or May, the winter house would begin to melt. The Inuit would remove the dome and place a superstructure of skins on the base of the snowhouse. This interseasonal dwelling was known as the *qarmaq*—a name that also described a hut of stone, turf, or whalebone that was roofed with skins and might be used in autumn as well as spring.[15]

In summer, when the weather became warm and the community was more mobile, engaging in hunting and fishing, the Inuit lived in tents. Cooking was now done out of doors. The tent, or *tupiq*, was sewn from skins (usually seal or caribou, but sometimes walrus or even salmon) and supported on poles, with the edges of the fabric weighted down

13.6 Summer tent, Hopedale, Labrador. Photograph by William N. Pierce Sr, 1864. Copyright President and Fellows of Harvard College. Peabody Museum, Harvard University/N26858/H3150.

with rocks. The skins were dehaired, and scraped thin at the entrance to admit light.

The form of the tent varied among the different Inuit groups. On the Labrador coast, and among some Central Eskimos, the tent often had a triangular entrance area formed with a horizontal ridge-pole and a conical-shaped rear portion made by joining a series of vertical poles at the apex. The **summer tent at Hopedale [13.6]**, Labrador, has this form: the entrance is in the foreground and the ridge-pole extends back towards the crossed poles. With its longitudinal entrance and domestic living space, this compound shape resembled the snowhouse.[16] The Iglulik Eskimo favoured a simpler ridge-type tent, similar in shape to the pup tent used by hikers of today.[17] The Inuit of the Belcher Islands (in Hudson Bay), NWT, used a conical tent with a framework of poles and a central smoke hole, similar to that of an Indian tipi.[18]

The Mackenzie Eskimo, who lived in the northern part of the Mackenzie River Delta, were unique among the Inuit of Canada in that they—like the North Alaskan Eskimo—had access to timber. Their winter house was a semi-subterranean building framed and planked in wood, covered with sod, and glazed with ice. It was entered by a tunnel and contained raised sleeping platforms.[19]

Inuit communities had a special building for social and religious functions called the *kashim* or *qaggiq*. Authorities have described them as 'singing houses', 'dance houses', 'feast houses', or 'men's clubhouses'. A central role was taken by the shaman, or *angakok*. The *kashim* had the same form as the characteristic dwellings of the region, but was usually larger— and so the Central Eskimo used snowhouses, the Mackenzie Eskimo built rectangular frame structures, and in the summer most groups used large tents. Boas described a *kashim* about 20 feet (6 m) in diameter and 15 feet (4.5 m) high, and Vilhjalmur Stefansson described one 30 feet (9 m) in diameter (both could accommodate more than 100 people); missionaries in Labrador recorded a *kashim* 70 feet (21 m) across.[20]

Not many years ago visitors to the Arctic could describe the traditional buildings of the Inuit in the present tense. But the massive changes that have affected Inuit society in the last half-century brought an end to most of these building-forms as viable dwellings and social facilities. DEW-line construction, the introduction of wage labour, a decline in the caribou herds, snowmobiles, television, and countless other southern influences have caused the centralization of Inuit in relatively large communities, rendering the snowhouse and other winter

dwellings largely obsolete. In their place the Canadian government has provided the Inuit with oil-heated plywood and frame houses (see **13.22**)—imposing on a centuries-old way of life a degree of change that has had an immense impact.

Explorers, Fur-Traders, and Missionaries

In 1576, on the first European voyage through the Arctic in search of a northwest passage, Sir Martin Frobisher found ore that he believed to contain gold, and he returned twice more to the Arctic to try to recover it. The Company of Cathay was formed to participate in this, the first gold rush in Canada's history— and even Queen Elizabeth invested £1000 in the venture.

In 1578, on his third expedition to 'Meta Incognita' (the unknown shore), as the land was named, Frobisher—with fifteen vessels and more than 400 men—landed at Quallunaaq (or Kodlunarn) Island, which they knew as Countess of Warwick's Island, in today's Frobisher Bay, off the shore of eastern Baffin Island. They intended to erect a large prefabricated wooden 'house', but the ship that carried two sides of the building had been sunk by ice. This event, and the realization that provisions were short, led Frobisher to abandon the attempt to leave a colony of men in the Arctic over the winter.[21]

Before leaving, they built a small mortared stone house, about 10 by 13 feet (3 by 4 m), in order to test English construction against Arctic conditions, and to set the Inuit an example. Diarist George Best described it:

This day the masons finished a house which Captain Fenton caused to be made of lime and stone upon the Countess of Warwick's Island, to the end we might prove against the next year, whether the snow could overwhelm it, the frosts break up, or the people dismember the same. And the better to allure those brutish and uncivil people to courtesy, against other times of our coming, we left therin divers of our country toys, as bells, and knives, wherein they specially delight . . . . Also in the house was made an oven, and bread left baked therein, for them to see and taste . . . . Also here we sowed peas, corn, and other grain, to prove the fruitfulness of the soil against the next year.[22]

The first of many such attempts by Europeans to

construct familiar building-types in the Arctic environment, this ended in failure—as did Frobisher's search for gold. He never returned to the house, and the 'gold' proved to be worthless pyrites.

The site was visited in the summer of 1990 by a party from the Archaeological Survey of Canada, led by Robert McGhee, and the next summer McGhee directed a larger group that undertook archaeological investigations and various other studies. They found the stone foundations of a number of small, crude structures, probably Frobisher's workshops. They also uncovered the remains of barrels of dried peas (accounts of the expedition note that these and other supplies were buried) and 400-year-old ship biscuits!

Most important from the architectural perspective, McGhee and his associates studied the **remains of the stone house [13.7]**—'a jumble of boulders lying amid a pile of mortar or plaster fragments.'[23] Despite having been disturbed, the foundation is largely intact. The walls were built of large stones that had been roughly hammered into shape and held together with lime mortar containing English flint—indicating that the mortar had been brought from England. The single room is 8 by 10 feet (2.4 by 3 m) on the inside, with walls 2 feet (0.6 m) thick. About 400 stones were counted and measured, revealing that the stone walls were originally about 3 feet (1 m) high; wood was probably used for the upper part of the walls. In shape and construction, the house finds parallels in vernacular English cottages and farm outbuildings of the Elizabethan age. Modest though these ruins may be, they represent the first permanent buildings erected by the English in the western hemisphere.

Forts and posts

The Hudson's Bay Company If Frobisher's stone cottage was a folly, **Prince of Wales's Fort [13.8]**, built a century and a half later, was an absurdity. The immense fort was located at the mouth of the Churchill River on Hudson Bay, across the river from today's town of Churchill, Manitoba. The strategic importance of the remote northern site had been appreciated ever since it was discovered in 1619 by the Danish explorer Jens Munk. John Abraham, of the fledgling Hudson's Bay Company, sailed into the river in 1686 and named it after John Churchill, the newly appointed governor of the Company (and a forebear of Sir Winston Churchill). Governor James Knight built a permanent post in the area in 1717 as a fur-trade and whaling station.

In 1731 construction was begun on a larger and stronger fortification against possible attack by the French. Twenty-four men were sent from England to begin the work, and Chief Factor Richard Norton optimistically estimated that it would take six or seven years to complete. The mammoth task took some forty years—work went on until 1771— although enough progress had been made by 1740 for Norton to inhabit the post.[24]

Prince of Wales's Fort (it was later renamed Fort Prince of Wales) is a structure of remarkable scale. Some 300 feet (91.4 m) square, with large angular corner bastions for defence, the outer walls were built of 'Extraordinary good Durable stone' (found nearby), and more than 15 feet (4.6 m) high and between 30 and 40 feet (9.2 to 12.2 m) thick. The inner walls are 10 feet (3.1 m) high and separated from the outer ones by an earthworks rampart. The fort was defended by nearly four dozen cannon,

13.7 Remains of Frobisher's stone house, Kodlunarn Island, Northwest Territories, 1578. Photograph 1990. Archaeological Survey of Canada, Canadian Museum of Civilization.

some of them in separate gun emplacements located outside the stone walls. A number of buildings stood within the courtyard, including the residence of the governor—a two-storey-high stone building covered by a flat lead roof.

Life at the fort must have been cold, lonely, and desolate. Perhaps for that reason, far fewer men were posted there than the intended three or four hundred. Such was the situation in August 1782, when three French ships with 300 men under the command of the Comte de Lapérouse sailed into the mouth of the Churchill River. Governor Samuel Hearne had only 39 men, with none trained to operate the 42 large guns. He recognized the futility of

13.8 Aerial view of Fort Prince of Wales (Prince of Wales's Fort), near Churchill, Manitoba, 1731-71. Photograph 1966. PAM/Prince of Wales 2.

trying to fight and immediately surrendered. The astonished Lapérouse took the English defenders as prisoners and did his best to destroy the massive fortress. His men burned the wood buildings and immobilized the cannon, but they failed in their

attempt to blow up the stone walls. The Hudson's Bay Company returned to the Churchill River a year later, but never again occupied the large fort. A portion has been restored, and it is now operated as a national historic site by Parks Canada.

More sensibly built and scaled—and far more useful as a trading post—was **York Factory** [13.9], about 140 miles (225 km) southeast of Prince of Wales's Fort, near the point where the Nelson and Hayes Rivers (the main canoe routes into the northern interior) come together and empty into Hudson Bay, in the present Manitoba. Rival fur traders from

13.9 Aerial view of York Factory, Manitoba, c. 1830s. Photograph c. 1926. PAM/York Factory/N3950.

Britain, France, and New England landed there independently in 1682, so that proprietorship of the site was disputed for some years. The post was attacked and rebuilt several times—the Comte de Lapérouse, for one, burned it during his escapade of 1782—but York Factory nevertheless became established as a British possession. It emerged as the undisputed administrative centre of the fur trade when the Hudson's Bay Company and North West Company merged in 1821.[25]

During the next two decades a number of new buildings were erected, including residences, warehouses, a church, a library, and a school. The most impressive was the large depot (the principal warehouse), which still stands as one of only two surviving structures of an immense building complex. Construction was begun shortly after Chief Factor A.H. Christie was appointed in 1830. Its completion was delayed until 1838 owing to the scarcity of timber and outbreaks of influenza. As clerk (and later Chief Factor), James Hargrave reported that the new depot was built because of

> the crowded state of our Stores. Every garret . . . is groaning under its own burden & the Old Factory has at length become Crazy & leaky & unfit to be filled with property.[26]

The depot is about 100 feet (30 m) square, three storeys high on the side facing the Hayes River and two floors high elsewhere. The exterior walls and those facing the large inner courtyard were generously filled with windows to provide light, since lamps were banned because of the threat of fire. Although no architect has been identified, the plan follows ideas that had been sketched by William Kempt, the Company's surveyor, and Simon McGillivray, a former partner in the North West Company who became a chief trader of the Hudson's Bay Company in 1821, the year the two companies merged.

The depot was built of timber that had been felled far up the Hayes River, floated down to the site, and hauled up the 30-foot-high (9-m) river bank. Other supplies—such as nails, wrought-iron hardware, and lead for the roofs—had to be brought over from England. Attempts to produce bricks failed, and even stones were hard to find. The building has survived for a century and a half because of a number of important engineering innovations that acknowledged the northern conditions. The wood columns and beams were connected in a manner that allowed for movement that was generated by the heaving and settling caused by the permafrost. Another threat to the stability of the

depot and the other buildings, surface water, ran off through a drainage system that included open ditches, wooden troughs, and metal pipes. (Despite the thoughtful construction, the extreme climate and the encroaching river are relentlessly destroying the building and the site.) The building was filled with furs, which the company obtained by trading items such as tobacco, knives, blankets, sugar, and axes. The largest of the storage halls (on the second floor, along the rear) extends the length of the building.

The winters at York Factory were intensely cold, and the short summers were plagued by flies and mosquitoes. The only contact with the outside world was the annual supply ship, due every August. The community grew what little food it could, but the short growing season made it dependent on what could be sent from Britain. And game was hunted: in one year, in the early eighteenth century, the eighty men ate 90,000 partridges and 25,000 hares. A still produced 'high spirits' for the consumption of the European visitors—and for trade with the natives.

The development of the Canadian West—when riverboats and railways provided a more viable form of transportation than the long voyage to Hudson Bay—spelled the decline of York Factory. Fort Garry (page 323), at today's Winnipeg, eventually succeeded York Factory as the Hudson's Bay Company headquarters—though the venerable northern trading post went on for another century, finally closing its doors in 1957, after 275 years of service. York Factory has been designated both a provincial and a federal historic site, and ownership has passed to the Government of Canada.

Fort Conger A remarkable combination of EuroAmerican construction techniques and native building practice occurred at **Fort Conger [13.10]**, a base camp for polar exploration in northern Ellesmere Island, NWT—located above 81° latitude, and in its day the most northerly base camp in the world. In the late summer of 1900 the American explorer Robert Peary (1856-1920) was forced to improvise a group of small structures when his supply ship failed to appear. He built a shelter for himself and for each of the two other Americans in his party, one for his Inuit employees, and a kitchen a short distance away, safely separated in the event of fire. Three dwelling huts (two for Americans and one for the Inuit) and the kitchen were built of frame, in part using wood salvaged from a house that had been left by the earlier expedition of US Army Lieutenant Adolphus

13.10 Fort Conger, Ellesmere Island, Northwest Territories, 1900. Photograph by Admiral Robert Peary, 1900. National Geographic Society/Robert Peary Collection/31547.

Greely. For his own shelter, Peary modified an army wall-tent that he had used as a summer dwelling—in his words, 'partly to economize the lumber, partly as a practical experiment, and partly to furnish occupation and amusement' for himself. He chose a well-drained sloping site that provided some protection and facilitated excavation for the partly dug-out structures. His efforts were successful, allowing his party to endure the winter in relative comfort—the first time this standard had been achieved by people other than Inuit.[27]

Peary made a number of well-considered design decisions about how best to use the limited materials available to him. He made each of the shelters small—roughly igloo-sized, or about 10 feet (3 m) long and 8 feet (2.4 m) wide (the size, also, of Frobisher's stone house)—in order to reduce the need for fuel. The walls and roofs of the wood shelters consisted of many separate layers for good insulation. The inner and outer walls were made of boards (those on the inside were tongue-and-groove lumber) and the space between them was filled with silt and gravel. Tarpaper was tacked to the outside of both walls, and the inside face of the inner wall was lined with charts and asbestos paper. Earth, snow, and snow blocks were banked against the outside walls nearly to the height of the eaves; and sand, gravel, and dirt were heaped on the roof. The tent was stiffened with wood, the walls lined with old blankets, the wood floor carpeted with old tarpaulins, and the ensemble covered with a large tarpaulin and banked with gravel, turf, and old mattresses (from Greely's house). In addition, a snow-block wall was built around the tent and the space

between it and the mattresses was filled with loose snow and water, creating a solid envelope of ice that was impervious to the wind.

All shelters except the kitchen were connected by low passageways that were partially tunnelled and covered with canvas, and a domed vestibule of snow blocks provided added protection. The passages and the low entrances served as heat traps, as in Inuit houses. The layout reflected the military hierarchy of the little group: Peary's tent was accessible only from the hut of his second-in-command, surgeon T.S. Dedrick, whereas Dedrick's quarters communicated with the other two huts.

His shelter was so successful that on his return from a hunting trip, Peary was able to 'warm the interior of [his] tent to a comfortable temperature by the judicious burning of a yard of tar roofing paper in [his] sheet iron stove.' He also noted that 'very little coal keeps [Dedrick's] house so warm now that he goes naked to the waist practically all the time, and some of the time entirely nude.'[28]

Peary acknowledged his indebtedness to Inuit building practices. As he wrote:

> The matter of winter quarters is one of pronounced importance to polar travellers, ranking second only to the question of an abundant supply of food . . . . A knowledge of Eskimo methods of house-building, combined with a little ingenuity, enables these needs to be secured with few and simple materials.[29]

By combining Euro-American frame construction with native techniques of siting, scale, and heat retention (using low passageways between dwellings, snow blocks, and banking for this purpose) Peary found a highly creative solution to the urgent problem of survival. His method of anticipating and solving problems suggested the process that is adopted in the development of all vernacular building-forms.

Police posts The North-West Mounted Police (after 1919 the Royal Canadian Mounted Police) built a number of posts in the Arctic as part of the mission to assert Canada's northern sovereignty. In a remarkable combination of naïveté and bureaucratic bungling, the police were quite unsuccessful at adapting to the environment of the northern frontier. The first posts above the tree-line were established in 1903 at Herschel Island in the western Arctic, and at Cape Fullerton off the northwestern coast of Hudson Bay. At Herschel Island, two officers arrived without having made arrangements for food or shelter. The resident Anglican missionary rented them a rudimentary sod house of the kind used by local natives—the walls made of boards, driftwood, or staves, roofed with sod (with a hole in the roof for ventilation), and lined inside with canvas. Though dark and damp, it remained in use until 1906, when the men acquired a frame building from the American whaling company that was the ostensible object of their police work. At Fullerton the

commanding officer, Superintendent Moodie—who had no training in architecture—designed small frame buildings to be constructed from lumber that the men had brought with them, but they ran out of wood and could not finish their quarters. Fortunately, the next spring they were able to buy a shelter from the American whalers at that site. Then in 1914, at Port Nelson (at the mouth of the Nelson River), the comptroller in Ottawa sent prefabricated structures that were warped in transit, arrived without a carpenter to assemble them, were constructed with only a single layer of boards, and had no provision for insulation. The superintendent likened them to 'the usual sort of houses erected at summer resorts'.[30]

In the 1920s the situation improved somewhat as the RCMP set up additional detachments in the High Arctic, after it began to rely on the Department of Public Works to provide standard plans for living quarters and storehouses, and to arrange for their manufacture and delivery. A standard detachment

13.11 Bache Peninsula Detachment, Ellesmere Island, Northwest Territories, under construction 1926. NAC/PA176641.

13.12 Moravian mission at Hopedale, Labrador. PAN/A1-20.

building in the eastern Arctic was about 20 by 40 feet (6 by 12 m), accommodated three men, and contained three rooms: a kitchen and general living area, the commanding officer's room, and a bedroom for the two constables. Enclosed porches, at the front and rear doors, helped reduce heat loss. The photograph shows the **Bache Peninsula Detachment [13.11]** under construction in 1926. The components were all pre-cut and marked to help with assembly. The buildings were constructed of a double layer of boards (separated by tarpaper) on the inner and outer walls, with insulation limited to the air-space between the studs—although additional insulation was provided by banking snow against the walls. Since the plain appearance of the buildings did not convey the authority and prominence that were appropriate to police stations in the region, they were transformed into symbols of authority by means of accessories: recognizable paint colours (grey with a bright red roof), carefully manicured grounds (pathways marked with white-painted stones), and flagpoles.

Only slowly did the RCMP adopt new building technologies and insulating materials—far behind builders in southern Canada. Rock-wool insulation was first used by the RCMP in 1937, at Eskimo Point on Hudson Bay, and only in the late 1940s and early 1950s—following the example of the Hudson's Bay Company—did they begin to use stressed-skin construction (in which plywood outer and inner walls assumed most of the building load, and allowed the use of lighter framing members) and double- and triple-glazed windows. As historian James de Jonge has concluded: '. . . the Mounted Police can perhaps best be described as followers, rather than leaders.'[31]

Missions

Several religious orders were active in the Far North, in spite of the rigours of the climate and the sparse population. They typically erected buildings that were designed and constructed in traditional Euro-Canadian ways, in part to impress the natives— as Frobisher, the fur-traders, and the police had all done—but mostly because they ignored the environmental conditions and used methods of buildings that were familiar to them.

The Moravian mission in Labrador An early attempt to proselytize aboriginal people in the North was the eighteenth-century Moravian mission to the Inuit of Labrador. The Moravian Church— known also as the Unitas Fratrum (United Brethren), who claim to have been the first Protestant community to break away from the Roman Church (in Bohemia in 1467)—sent missionaries to the West Indies and Greenland in 1732-3, and subsequently went from Greenland to Labrador. The first missionaries arrived in Labrador in 1752 with a prefabricated dwelling and some garden seeds. Their attempt to set up a mission station ended when seven members of the crew of the mission ship were killed, apparently by natives. A decade later the Moravians made further exploratory voyages and successfully negotiated with the British government for a land grant of 100,000 acres (40,000 hectares). A mission was established in 1771 at Nain (Nunaingok), about 220 miles (360 km) north of the present Happy Valley, Goose Bay; and another one at Hopedale, to the south, in 1780. Additional stations were installed later along the coast to the north.[32]

At **Hopedale [13.12]**—where trees grew in abundance—the missionaries built a water-powered sawmill. This produced lumber that was used to build a combined church and residence in 1872. (It has been restored by Parks Canada.)[33]

Missionary activity at Hopedale was combined with a trading operation in an attempt to keep the Inuit from travelling south and making contact with more Europeans who might expose them to alcohol and other undesirable influences. Trading also provided the Moravians with money to support their work. While wanting to protect the Inuit from what they saw as inappropriate change, the missionaries had a profound impact on their lives by converting them to Christianity, teaching them to read and write their own language, and urging them to live in European-style communities and buildings. They established the first schools for the Inuit in 1792, and remained responsible for their education until 1946, when schools and health care came under the control of the Newfoundland Department of Education. The Moravians operated their trading post at Nain until 1926, when its operation was taken over by the Hudson's Bay Company; it is now run by the provincial government.

Missions to the Northwest We have seen that the Oblates of Mary Immaculate were active in British Columbia and Alberta. This Roman Catholic order maintained an effective policy of reaching the native people by planting missions in close proximity to Hudson's Bay Company posts.[34]

The most northerly of the Oblate missions was **Our Lady of Good Hope [13.13]** at Fort Good Hope in the Northwest Territories—a fur-trading post founded by the North West Company in 1805—20 miles (32 km) below the Arctic Circle, and one of several missions in the Mackenzie River basin. This mission was established in 1859, and its remarkable church was begun in 1865 under the direction of—and to designs by—Father Émile Petitot (1838-1917), a celebrated ethnologist, linguist, and geographer, who lived at the mission from 1864 to 1878. Father Jean Séguin was responsible for most of the skilled carpentry, assisted by Brother Joseph Patrick Kearney. As the short summer season, and the priests' missionary tasks, made for slow progress, the basic structure was not completed until 1876 (and the building was still not quite finished in 1885).[35]

As originally built, the church was a rectangle 45 feet (13.7 m) long and 20 feet (6.1 m) wide, but in

13.13 Our Lady of Good Hope, Fort Good Hope, Northwest Territories, 1865-76. Photograph 1980. PC/Heritage Recording Services.

13.14 *(right)* Interior of Our Lady of Good Hope, Fort Good Hope, Northwest Territories, begun 1865. Photograph 1980. PC/Heritage Recording Services.

1877 an addition 20 feet (6.1 m) deep was placed at the rear. The structural system was the familiar grooved post, the Red River frame associated with the fur trade; since it provides flexibility in the wall joints (the horizontal logs can slide within the grooves), the technique was reasonably well suited for the North. The main façade was sheathed in wood siding from the start, but early in the twentieth century the entire building was covered with horizontal clapboard. The medium-pitched roof is gabled at the front and hipped at the rear. (The hip cannot be seen easily in the photograph.)

Father Petitot made a conscious effort to give the church a Gothic Revival appearance. The entry, the two flanking windows, and the six windows along each side all have pointed Gothic arches, and a rose window is set over the doorway. All have intricate tracery carved by Séguin after patterns drawn by Petitot, who said that his designs were inspired by Chartres Cathedral—endearing hyperbole, perhaps,

painted pale blue speckled with gold stars. Along the side walls are paintings of religious scenes with elaborate ornamental borders. (Petitot initially planned ten, but a total of fourteen were executed once the nave was extended.) The paintings, begun by Petitot, were continued after his departure (for reasons of health) by Father Xavier Ducot and Brother Julien Ancel, and completed only in the late 1950s or early 1960s by subsequent Oblate artists. Petitot also designed the altar, and Brother Ancel created the retable, which features kneeling angels adoring Our Lady, and the magnificent sacristy doors, whose carved panels are flanked by marblized green pilasters set off against red trim. Petitot said that he wanted to astound the natives, and give them an exalted idea of his religion. He certainly did that; but his work has also surprised generations of southerners who have been fortunate enough to visit Our Lady of Good Hope.

Missionaries of the Anglican Church competed with the Catholic orders for souls. The Reverend William W. Kirkby was the first to enter the upper basin of the Yukon River, travelling from Fort Simpson to Fort Yukon in 1861 to work among the Kutchin Indians. He and other Anglican missionaries returned to the area in the years that followed. In 1865 William Carpenter Bompas came from England to become 'priest-at-large' under Kirkby, and in 1873 he was made Bishop of Athabaska, a new western diocese, and subsequently Bishop of the Selkirk (later Yukon) diocese.[36] Catholics and Anglicans were therefore well positioned when gold was discovered in the Yukon. Missionaries, along with the North-West Mounted Police, quickly came to Dawson and the sites of other major strikes, to preach the gospel and help to ensure the maintenance of order.

but a clear indication of his source of inspiration in the cathedrals and churches of medieval Europe. The original steeple had the same general profile as the present one of the 1920s; but it was much more ornamented, with pairs of arched windows in its base and pointed gables at the base of the spire, and rows of 'crockets' (knob-like projections) running along the eaves of the façade and the gables on the spire.

The exterior is spartan when contrasted with the lavish decoration of the **interior [13.14]**, which would be considered remarkable in any setting, but is astonishing in this remote northern outpost. Carved woodwork, painted ornament, and figurative paintings cover almost every surface—all of it vividly Gothic in inspiration. Immediately upon entering, the visitor encounters the tribune arch, an elaborately carved wooden screen composed of three arches—a taller pointed central arch flanked by two ogee (S-like double-curved) arches—with delicate white tracery supported on two multi-coloured posts. The ceiling is

Resource Development and Settlement

Dawson

Skookum Jim, Klondike Kate, Sam Steele, Sam McGee, Dan McGrew. Some of these people were very real, others were romantic creations of poet Robert W. Service, but all are indelibly linked to the Klondike Gold Rush, the opening of the Yukon, and the boom and bustle of Dawson, Canada's most westerly city and one of its more northerly. In 1898 Dawson boasted a population of between thirty and forty thousand, making it the largest city in Canada west of Winnipeg.

Prospectors had looked for gold along the upper valley of the Yukon River since the 1870s, searching for the 'mother lode' that had left a trail of gold from California to British Columbia. Some finds occurred in the 1880s, but the big strike was made on 17 August 1896 by George Washington Carmack—a Californian who had prospected in Alaska for a dozen years—and his two partners, Skookum Jim and Dawson Charlie, Tagish brothers (and Carmack's brothers-in-law). In the rocky bed of Rabbit Creek, near where the Klondike River flowed into the Yukon River, they found gold between the stones, 'thick between the flaky slabs, like cheese sandwiches.' Carmack renamed it Bonanza Creek, he and his friends staked their claims, and before long word was out. In the following year prospectors from near and far flocked to Dawson—which became an instant city at the junction of the Klondike and Yukon Rivers—in what has been called the world's greatest gold rush.[37]

The federal government was well prepared for these events. Anticipating the gold rush, and determined to establish and maintain law and order—as well as Canadian sovereignty—Ottawa created in 1895 the District of Yukon, separate from the North-West Territories, and dispatched a detachment of twenty North-West Mounted Police. (Yukon became a territory three years later, with Dawson as its capital.) Boats took would-be miners to the notorious port of Skagway, Alaska—where, according to veteran policeman Sam (later Sir Samuel) Steele:

Neither law nor order prevailed [and] honest persons had no protection from the gang of rascals who plied their nefarious trade.[38]

The Canadian police discouraged the entry of transients and scoundrels by insisting that every prospector have money and supplies to last not less than six months—which meant hauling a ton of goods by foot over the tortuous Chilkoot Pass.

In Dawson order was maintained and an ordered city laid out in the familiar gridiron pattern by the NWMP and the Department of Public Works, who jointly assumed the role of city-building taken by the Royal Engineers in the Fraser River gold rush. An important government initiative, aimed at asserting control over the territory, was the construction of an imposing group of public buildings in Dawson to accommodate federal services. Commissioner William Ogilvie had only modest architectural ambitions—unlike the Department of Public Works' resident architect in Dawson, Thomas W. Fuller (1865-1951), the son and namesake of the chief federal architect (a position the son would later hold), who had retired in 1897. The

younger Fuller, who arrived in Dawson in July 1899, provided the community with an administration building, post office, courthouse, Commissioner's residence, telegraph office, and public school. All were wood-frame buildings in a *retardataire* Palladian-Georgian style, looking much like the government buildings that had appeared in eastern and central Canada nearly a century earlier. Their form had a similar purpose: to be a central government's symbol of its political authority in a distant possession. Just as Britain used Georgian Classicism to express sovereignty over its North American colonies, so too did the Dominion government adopt the ordered image in the Yukon—which in many respects was a colony of Canada.

Most of the public buildings were built on the government reserve in the south end of town, an enclave located several blocks from the commercial core and the waterfront. The largest of the group was the two-storey wood-frame **Territorial Administration Building** [13.15]. Built in 1901 in a city of small buildings, it was immense: 160 feet (48.8 m) wide and 43 feet (13.1 m) deep—far larger than was required by the Commissioner's building program. The plan was organized to achieve a broad, imposing façade on Fifth Avenue that would express government control. The central portion and the ends project as pavilions— each capped by a pediment, and the central one by a tall flagpole—while the main structure is covered by a low hipped roof. Pedimented ground-floor window-heads, and giant pilasters between the windows of the main block (emphasized by being painted in a contrasting colour), provide traditional classical detail. The largest room (40 feet, or 12.2 m, square) was the recording office, where all mining claims in the Yukon were documented; and a second large space, 40 feet by 24 feet (12.2 m by 7.3 m), served as the council chamber; the remainder provided offices for employees of the Department of the Interior, as well as for some local and territorial officials. The Administration Building was enhanced by the extensive landscaping of the grounds, and the adjacent development of Minto Park—which included tennis courts, a ball-park, and a grandstand, and became a social and recreational focus for the community. The building was surrounded by a low, white fence that increased its aloofness, and provided a garrison-like definition of its territory. It was restored in the 1980s (by The Iredale Partnership) for use as government offices, courts, and the Dawson City Museum.[39]

Fuller's **Courthouse** [13.16], built in 1900-1, continued the classical theme. Like the Administration Building, it is a wood-frame building constructed on the government reserve. It is wider than deep, with

13.15 Territorial Administration Building, Dawson, Yukon Territory, 1901. Photograph by Harold Kalman, 1984.

13.16 Courthouses, Dawson, Yukon Territory: log courthouse, 1898; Fuller's courthouse, 1900-1. NAC/PA 16308.

pedimented end pavilions, each containing a court-room on the upper floor, connected by a block that featured a two-tiered veranda and a square cupola. It replaced a temporary two-storey log courthouse (seen in the foreground of the photograph)—made from local unseasoned wood and covered by a galvanized sheet-iron roof—that had been built in November 1898. The striking contrast between the two build-ings, erected only three years apart, shows how quick-ly Dawson matured. The initial vernacular structure, built hastily in frontier conditions, was soon con-sidered inappropriate, and had to be replaced by a properly designed Classical building that projected an image of authority. To ensure quality, many mate-rials were brought in from the south along the steep narrow-gauge White Pass and Yukon Railway (com-pleted in 1900) from Skagway, Alaska, to Whitehorse, Yukon Territory, where freight was transferred to sternwheelers or barges that descended the Yukon River. This supply route replaced the Chilkoot Pass.[40]

The new government buildings were mostly erect-ed in 1901 or later (the post office had been com-pleted in December 1900), after the first, hectic, gold rush had passed. The initial boom ended in April 1899, when a fire destroyed much of downtown Dawson. Many of the more transient goldseekers moved on to Nome, Alaska, but those who stayed made a long-term commitment to their enterprises and to the city. In the years that followed, Dawson entered a period of relative equilibrium. Mineral extraction became more capital-intensive, requiring large mechanized dredges, and this encouraged an atmosphere of social stability. As a result, the city experienced a building boom as the log cabins and shanties that had been thrown together by the first wave of residents were replaced by substantial build-ings made of proper materials. What emerged was an Edwardian frontier city just below the Arctic Circle.

Southern techniques of frame construction had to be modified for the Yukon climate and conditions. Thomas Fuller quickly recognized this and wrote to his supervisor, chief federal architect David Ewart:

> I tell you, it is a hard job to know what is best to do in the way of building here, no one has the very faintest idea of what is best. I will tell you what I have to contend with. The ground here is frozen solid all the year, at a depth of 18" . . . . You will see by this what great difficulties I have to con-tend with. I can only act as I think best and hope and trust it may prove satisfactory.[41]

Because of the permafrost and poor drainage, the foundations of the government and other well-con-structed buildings in Dawson consisted of mud sills—horizontal timbers placed directly on trenches in the ground—that projected a short distance beyond the walls, on top of which were placed round posts secured by spikes. The main sills that supported the building frame, in turn, rested on the posts. The restricted movement that resulted during the spring thaw worked reasonably well as long as the struc-ture was maintained, but once abandoned it was quickly deformed by frost heaves. In 1902—by which time the post office was sagging seriously and other new buildings showed signs of deterioration—Fuller placed concrete foundations beneath the furnaces of all government buildings.[42]

Heating and insulation systems proved to be inad-equate for the cold winters, when the temperature might dip below -60° F (-50° C). Frame buildings were erected with double and even triple walls, with heavy building paper inserted between each wall and a 4- to 6-inch (10- to 15-cm) air space between the walls. Floors were also doubled, with the space between them filled with sawdust. There was no shortage of materials because by 1901 Dawson had six sawmills producing good seasoned lumber; bricks and hardware were also being produced locally. Municipal services, including drainage and sanita-tion, were introduced, and the use of non-com-bustible materials was encouraged.[43]

Of the original dwellings of 1897-8, none survive. But one that evokes their qualities—and can still be seen—is the **Robert Service cabin [13.17]**, the log house where the celebrated poet lived between 1909 and 1912. (It is seen in the photograph with Service, and his bicycle, in front.) It was built around 1901 by sometime miner and broker Whitney Clarke, who rented it to Service. The two-room house, on the hill behind town with a view of the river, is 18 feet by 14 feet (5.5 by 4.3 m), augmented by a front porch. It was built of round logs laid horizontally with the bark still on them, and the roof was cov-ered by sod; the natural insulation provided by the materials, and the wood stove, kept it cozy in win-ter. Service adored his house, and eulogized it in 'Good-Bye, Little Cabin':

> *Your roof is bewhiskered, your floor is aslant,*
> *Your walls seem to sag and to swing;*
> *I'm trying to find just your faults, but I can't—*
> *You poor, tired, heart-broken old thing!*

It was here that Service wrote his first novel, *The Trail of Ninety-Eight: A Northland Romance* (1910). His famous ballads of the Klondike, 'The Shooting of Dan McGrew' and 'The Cremation of Sam McGee',

13.17 Robert Service's cabin, Dawson, Yukon Territory. *c.* 1901. Service is seen with his bicycle. Yukon Archives/ Martha Black Collection/3288.

13.18 Canadian Bank of Commerce, Dawson, Yukon Territory, 1901. Photograph by Harold Kalman, 1984.

were published in 1907 when he was a clerk at the Canadian Bank of Commerce in Whitehorse.[44]

The **Dawson branch of the Canadian Bank of Commerce [13.18]**, where Service worked for a year until his income from royalties allowed him to quit his job, was another building that projected an image of stability and security (a necessary condition for a bank that competed to assay prospectors' gold and attract people's money). The two-storey building (seen here with the historic steamship *Keno* beyond it) adopted the Italian Renaissance Revival style, posing as a Medici palace on the banks of the Yukon River. It was built in 1901, probably to designs by Warren Porter Skillings (d. 1939), a native of Portland, Maine, who went to Seattle after that city's fire of 1889, practised in Dawson between 1900 and 1902, then ended his career in California. The building is remarkable for its liberal use of pressed-metal for two exterior walls, where it imitates sandstone, and for the walls and ceiling of the banking hall. (Metal panels—providing dura-bility, fire-resistance, and status— had been readily available in Canada since the early 1890s.) The Bank of Commerce had come to Dawson in 1898—at the invitation of Clifford Sifton, the Minister of the Interior—and opened in June in a 'shack' with a windowless garret, in which the staff slept. This was replaced in August or September by a two-storey log building. The logs were sawn on three sides, but the bark was left intact on the exterior (suggesting that its rustic appearance was intended) and the roof was covered by boards, moss, and mud. The 1901 bank was therefore a 'third-generation' structure, though it was erected only three years after the first bank.[45]

A photograph of **Queen Street**, **Dawson [13.19]**, taken at midnight on 4 July 1904 (when many Americans were celebrating), shows the common commercial building-types in Dawson—most of them more ornate than the buildings we saw on the main streets of prairie towns. The Bank of British North America (subsequently the Bank of Montreal) stands in the left foreground. Replacing a substantial log structure, which burned down in the fire of 1899, it was a frame building whose design looked back to earlier, Georgian, sources. The gable end of the two-storey building was finished as a pediment. The exterior wall was clad in corrugated iron, placed over asbestos building paper and wood sheathing; metal shutters also helped to keep out the winter cold. A balcony outside the second floor, at the corner of Queen and Second Streets, was used by the staff.[46]

Immediately beyond the bank, the clapboard façade of the dentist's office is a false front that masks a building whose side and rear walls were exposed logs; the peak on the parapet responds to the ridge of its gabled roof. The building across the street from the bank, in the right foreground, has large windows on the ground floor, which was in retail use, and smaller windows upstairs that probably lighted residential rooms or suites. An entablature separates the two floors, and a straight parapet marks the top. The building next to it has prominent bay windows on the second floor—a common feature of vernacular commercial buildings on the west coast, from San Francisco to Vancouver. Just past it is a lower 1½-storey gable-roofed building (without a false front), containing a barber shop. All of these types were repeated throughout the downtown. Plank sidewalks line the unpaved streets.

Despite the confidence shown in building (and rebuilding) Dawson, the city suffered a long and gradual decline. Many buildings were abandoned, and eventually collapsed. The construction of the Alaska Highway during the Second World War allowed Whitehorse to surpass Dawson as the commercial hub of the Yukon, and in 1951-3 the capital was

transferred to that city to the south. In 1960, in an attempt to bolster tourism in Dawson, the federal government reconstructed the Palace Grand Theatre (where Klondike Kate Rockwell performed), and subsequently committed itself to a long-term program of land acquisition, restoration, and interpretation. Park Canada's Klondike National Historic Sites now includes numerous buildings and other structures, and every year Dawson attracts thousands of visitors who come to relive the romance of the Klondike.[47]

While Dawson became a built-up city soon after the beginning of the Gold Rush, other communities were slower to develop. For example, a view of a **street in Whitehorse [13.20]**, Yukon Territory, taken in 1901, shows a row of commercial premises housed in tents, whose trade was identified by prominent signs— including the familiar stripes of a barber shop.

Contemporary housing and communities

For the aboriginal peoples of the North, the twentieth century has been a time of massive transition. Traditional ways of living and building began to be transformed as soon as the native inhabitants were exposed to southern practices—first by the example of explorers and missionaries, with the consequent introduction of new tools and implements, and more recently by the opportunities offered by modern communications and travel. In recent years change has accelerated, as new cities have been established and many natives have been relocated to new government-built housing and communities.

The centuries-old types of shelter discussed at the beginning of this chapter—which were perfectly suited to the harsh environment and the few natural materials available—were building-types that in modern times could no longer be regarded as adequate. Together with a rise in expectations came a change in economic practices (chiefly the introduction of wage labour) that led to a decline of nomadic lifestyles, and consequently a reduced need for portability.

One of countless northern native communities in transition is the **Willow Lake camp [13.21]** in the Mackenzie Basin, northeast of Fort Norman, NWT. Archaeologist and anthropologist Robert Janes undertook a detailed study of the settlement in 1975, at which time the old ways were in the process of being replaced by the new. The 'Willow Lakers', as they call themselves, are Slavey Dene, who live for four to six months a year in this residential camp, where they engage in traditional activities such as hunt-

13.19 Queen Street (looking west), Dawson, Yukon Territory. Photograph 1904. NAC/C14546.

13.20 Street in Whitehorse, Yukon Territory. Photograph 1901. Notman Photographic Archives, MMCH/MP2024 (22).

13.21 Willow Lake camp, near Fort Norman, Northwest Territories. Photograph by Robert R. Janes, 1975.

ing, fishing, and gathering—with the help of such modern implements as high-powered rifles, snow-mobiles, and nylon gill-nets. The transition from the old to the new ways is poignantly illustrated by their buildings. Each of the seven families at Willow Lake inhabited, or used, several structures. Most had both a log house and a tipi—in the traditional spirit of having separate winter and summer dwellings. (Log construction was introduced to the Mackenzie Basin by fur-traders in the eighteenth and nineteenth centuries. In the case of the Willow Lakers, however, their oral history indicates that the first log cabin was built there between 1906 and 1915.) A former log house was used for storage; for outdoor storage a stage (raised platform) was erected away from the reach of predators and dogs. Some families had canvas tents.[48]

The primary living space was provided by log houses. No partitions divided the single room; beds, mattresses, shelves, and cupboards lay against the walls, an oilcloth on the floor near the centre provided an eating area, and a drum stove (made from a 45-gallon oil drum) provided heat in winter (to be replaced in the spring by a less intensely hot commercially made airtight stove). All the houses were constructed with logs extracted from the nearby bush and floated downriver, although some commercial building materials were used, such as nails, plywood, roofing paper, and milled lumber (made available through

a government-assistance program). Large flat stones were placed under the corners of the houses to reduce settlement of the sills.

The houses exhibited three different techniques for making the corner joints. In decreasing order of the time and skill involved in the carpentry, they were dovetail notches, saddle notches, and what the residents called an 'HBC corner'—so named because it was derived from the log construction used by the Hudson's Bay Company, and was a modern and simplified version of the Red River frame. Two 2" x 8" milled boards fastened at right angles were set upright at the corners; the logs on the long side were inserted into the angle so formed, while those on the short side butted against one of the boards; and the logs were spiked into place. The HBC corner was considered to be inferior to the other two techniques; in 1975 two households who used it did so, they said, only because it was easy, fast, and required no special axe-work. The choice of which method to use appeared to be pragmatic, and not cultural.

Tipis were used for drying meat or fish, and for other processing activities—and also, according to one resident, because tipis were valued for being 'part of the old days'. Although they were smaller in diameter, and proportionally taller than those built in ear-

13.22 Houses, Grise Fiord, Ellesmere Island, Northwest Territories. Photograph by Fred Bruemmer, 1967.

lier generations, they were constructed of poles in the traditional manner (**7.1, 2**). Rather than caribou skins, however, their coverings included combinations of canvas, polyethylene, cardboard, burlap, spruce bough, and birch branches—the latter two were also used as windbreaks at the bases of the tipis. These coverings were reduced, or removed, in warm weather.

While the Willow Lake people, and others like them, are able to live and hunt on their traditional lands, many other Dene and Inuit have been relocated to new settlements. A particularly extreme instance of relocation occurred at **Grise Fiord [13.22]** on the southern coast of Ellesmere Island, NWT, in the High Arctic— Canada's most northerly Inuit community. Beginning in 1953, some families were relocated to this very remote area, allegedly to provide them with better game, but actually (it has recently been revealed) to assert Canadian sovereignty in the High Arctic. Most came from the east coast of Hudson Bay; a few were from northern Baffin Island. The first arrivals built frame dwellings from scrap lumber and canvas and insulated them with local plant material (between the double walls), and with imported buffalo and reindeer hides. As seal-oil lamps could not warm the houses sufficiently in winter, they continued to build snowhouses for several winters until fuel-oil-burning stoves were introduced.[49]

As the community grew, the hand-built houses were replaced by prefabricated rigid-frame (stressed-skin) plywood houses provided by the federal government as a part of its Eskimo Housing Loan Program. These buildings were poorly designed and constructed; with an area of only 288 sq. ft. (26.8 m²), they were quickly dubbed 'matchboxes'.[50] A typical one is seen in the photograph. Grise Fiord has continued to grow—its population in the 1980s was slightly over 100—but it is a small and artificial community whose long-term viability remains in doubt.

The provision of public housing has been a major initiative of the Government of the Northwest Territories. After the failure of the 'matchboxes' and other early programs, the Northwest Territories Housing Corporation was formed in 1974 with a mandate to provide functional, cost-effective, and energy-efficient housing—all part of a concerted effort to define a true northern, and Canadian, architecture. Building design began to originate in the new territorial capital of Yellowknife, rather than in Ottawa, and the architects were therefore more in touch with regional needs and conditions. Nevertheless, for the first five years most of the houses continued to display southern-type construction, with vented trussed roofs (which did not work because of snow infiltration) and poor insulation.

5   0   5   10   15   20 feet

1   0   1   2   3   4   5 metres

Since around 1979, houses designed specifically for northern conditions have at last been built. Beginning in that year Number Ten Architectural Group of Winnipeg, and Woolfenden Group Architects Limited of Edmonton were commissioned by the Territorial government to produce designs for single- and multiple-family residences that deviated from standard houses in the South. Taking their work a step further, in 1985 the Northwest Territories Housing Corporation's own architects took over the design of most new housing. A standard plan for a **two-bedroom duplex** [13.23], produced by the Corporation in 1987, displays many of the lessons that had been learned. The building is elevated off the ground, with a false floor suspended below the structural floor to keep internal heat from thawing the permafrost. The roofs have no overhangs, to prevent the 'ice dams' that tend to build up at the eaves. Semi-rigid insulation some $1\frac{1}{2}$ inches (38 mm) thick is inserted into the wood walls and the metal-clad roof. Heat is provided by boilers in a furnace room sandwiched between the two units, and sewage holding tanks are located beneath the stair-landings. Each unit has a draft vestibule, large living-room, kitchen, and bathroom on the ground floor, and two bedrooms and a utility room upstairs. The few windows are small, leaving broad expanses of wall to retain the heat.[51]

13.23 Ground-floor plan of a two-bedroom duplex, 1987. Drawing by David Byrnes after Northwest Territories Housing Corporation, *Northern Housing Identification Guide*.

Entire communities—not just individual buildings—have been constructed with the intention of coming to terms with the environment. The most ambitious experiment in northern design has been the new town of Inuvik, NWT, on the Mackenzie River Delta. Now the administrative centre of the western Arctic, Inuvik ('place of man' in Inuktitut, the Inuit language) was created as a result of a federal-government decision in 1953 to relocate the established community of Aklavik because recurrent flooding, and the construction of buildings directly on the permafrost and silt, were causing severe land erosion and building deterioration. (The Inuvialuit and Loucheux Dene refused to move, and so Aklavik has remained alive.) Located 125 miles (150 km) north of the Arctic Circle, and 60 miles (100 km) south of the Beaufort Sea, Inuvik was planned and constructed by the federal Department of Public Works between 1954 and 1961. The principal public buildings were designed by private architectural firms— principally Rule, Wynn and Rule, and Rensaa and Minsos, both of Edmonton. Inspired in part by Prime Minister John Diefenbaker's 'northern vision', Inuvik demonstrated intense optimism about the capability of science and technology to solve environmental challenges. This evangelical spirit is evident in the dedication plaque on the monument to the town's official opening:

> This was the first community north of the Arctic Circle built to provide the normal facilities of a Canadian town. It was designed not only as a base for development and administration but as a centre to bring education, medical care, and new opportunity to the people of the Western Arctic.[52]

Once they saw the buildings at Aklavik being deformed by frost-heaving, the planners determined that the moss that covers (and insulates) the permafrost should not be disturbed. As a result, the surface was covered with gravel, and all permanent buildings were set on piles and raised clear of the ground, allowing air to circulate beneath them so that heat from the buildings would not thaw the permafrost. The piles were inserted into holes blasted with jets of steam, and allowed to freeze in place throughout a winter before buildings were placed on top of them. This technique refined the method adopted at Dawson, a half-century earlier, that used piles and mud sills, but disturbed the soil.

The **aerial view of Inuvik [13.24]**, taken in 1967, shows the principal residential area and a number of multiple-housing units that were built with the assistance of the Central Mortgage and Housing Corporation. Shadows beneath the buildings show them to be raised above the ground. Some single-family houses stand on Bompas Street at the left (named after the first Anglican Bishop in the North), and others were later built on the piles and sills near the lower-right corner. Mackenzie Road, the main street, runs across the centre of the photograph; to the left, just out of sight, is the town square. At the upper left, beyond Bompas Street, is the large Anglican hostel (*c*. 1957-9).

Fresh water (drawn from a lake above town), sewage, and heat from a central heating plant are supplied through 'utilidors'—conveyors that are seen snaking their way through town. The original utilidors were heavily insulated boxes, about 3 feet (1 m) high and wide, containing four pipes and set on piles. (The pipes of incomplete utilidors can be seen in front of the house piles at the bottom right.) Although their design was later modified to reduce construction costs, the principle remains effective. The first experiment of this type was made in 1933 in Flin Flon, Manitoba; by the 1960s, utilidors were standard in many northern communities.[53]

Although the buildings in the photograph are all conventional in appearance, with rectangular plans and low-gabled roofs, distinctive symbolic forms were occasionally adopted for public buildings in the North. Some had either domed or conical shapes, imitating the forms of the snowhouse and the tent respectively. The **Roman Catholic church of Our**

13.24 Aerial view of Inuvik, Northwest Territories. Photograph 1967. Institute for Research in Construction, National Research Council of Canada.

Lady of Victory [13.25] in Inuvik, completed in 1960, is a circular building constructed of blocks of white wood and covered with a bronze dome. While the form is supposed to indicate the northern location, the pointed arches over the narrow windows use Gothic Revival associations to identify the building's ecclesiastical function.[54]

The largest community in the Northwest Territories is Yellowknife, a city of about 12,000 on the north arm of Great Slave Lake—more than 600 miles (1,000 km) southeast of Inuvik, and situated within the Canadian Shield. Since 1967 it has been the territorial capital (though, ironically, it is one of the

13.25 Our Lady of Victory, Inuvik, Northwest Territories, 1960. Photograph by John de Visser.

least-northern of towns in the Territories, and boasts that it is 45 miles [70 km] closer to San Francisco than it is to the North Pole!). Named after the Yellowknife Dene, the city began as a boom town in the gold rush of 1934 that followed the accidental discovery of gold-bearing quartz by prospectors Hugh Muir and C.J. Baker. Commercial gold production began in 1938, and in the half-century since, Yellowknife has grown into an important mining, administrative, and transportation centre.

13.26 Weaver and Devore Trading Ltd, Yellowknife, Northwest Territories, 1936-8. Photograph 1988. City of Yellowknife Heritage Committee.

13.27 Legislative Assembly of the Northwest Territories, Yellowknife, Northwest Territories, 1992-3. Photograph by Tessa Macintosh, 1993. Government of the Northwest Territories.

The first settlement occurred in the area known as Old Town, in the centre of which is 'the Rock'—a hilly outcrop surrounded on three sides by water and accessible by boat, barge, and float or ski plane—where small log buildings, frame shacks, and tents were crowded together. A number of 1930s structures remain on the Rock—buildings such as the **store and warehouse of Weaver and Devore Trading Ltd** (1936-8); and next to it the Wildcat Café (1937), and the 'House of Horrors', a former rooming house built in 1938 [**13.26**]. Typical of vernacular frontier architecture, they are simple and unpretentious log and frame structures erected expediently with the limited materials available. The Old Town of Yellowknife was the Barkerville or Dawson of its day; its development was dictated by similar motivations and values.[55]

In the 1940s and 1950s, on a gravel ridge (not subject to permafrost heaving) less than a mile away, the New Town of Yellowknife began to be developed. Many residents who resented Ottawa's decision to relocate the town nicknamed it 'Blunderville'. Mundane office towers—the first was the Bellanea Building (1972)—three-storey walk-ups, shopping malls, banks, stores, apartment houses, and trailer subdivisions make the new town an undistinguished kin of many small cities in the South.

A few notable public buildings have been erected, however. One is the Prince of Wales Northern Heritage Centre (John Keith-King and the Number Ten Architectural Group, 1977-9), a light grey con-crete building on the shore of Frame Lake—but it too was designed by southern architects (from Vancouver and Winnipeg) and uses essentially southern forms, with the addition of extra insulation and other technical modifications.[56] Another is the **Legislative Assembly of the Northwest Territories** [**13.27**], the newest of Canada's provincial and territorial legislative buildings. The design is a joint venture between Pin/Matthews and Ferguson Simek Clark of Yellowknife, in association with Matsuzaki Wright of Vancouver. Built in 1992-3 and located in downtown Yellowknife, on Frame Lake, the building offers a variety of symbolic forms and materials. Shallow domes cover (and illuminate) the circular Legislative Chamber and the caucus meeting area. The circular vocabulary is intended to represent the Northwest Territories' approach to government, in which there are no official political parties and the elected Members, who together choose a house leader, sit around a ring as equals. The Great Hall, between the entrance and the Chamber, is a large, open, public meeting-space flooded with light through large areas of window. The open and expansive building is closely integrated with its site, nestled between three large rock outcrops and bordered by stunted trees, and the landscape design (by Cornelia Hahn Oberlander)

features indigenous plants, such as sedges and grasses. The exterior walls are clad in glass and zinc panels (over a structural steel frame), because zinc is durable, it develops a patina that will blend with the grey of the rock outcrops, and is a reminder of a large zinc mine in the area that provides employment for the community. In a time of governmental economic constraints, the building was funded through a public bond issue and a conventional mortgage.[57]

Many Northern designers have adopted an approach to design that is more pragmatic, and consequently less appealing, than that of the Inuvik church or the Heritage Centre and Legislative Assembly in Yellowknife—producing, in the words of Yellowknife architect Stephen Barr, 'tight and well constructed buildings [that] strive to work in harmony with the local climate and circumstances.'[58]

His firm's **Tuktoyaktuk Community Centre [13.28]** in Tuktoyaktuk, NWT (Barr Ryder, 1983), is an example of this movement towards 'a leanness of form'. It maximizes the ratio of interior volume to exterior skin, minimizing heat loss—a compact plan is therefore created that has relatively little exterior articulation—and steamlines the design to reduce the impact of snow accumulation. (These criteria, of course, also describe the snowhouse!) Clad in corrugated metal siding, the building is raised on piles to conserve the permafrost. Entrances are high enough to remain above the surface of the snow, and the windows are

13.28 Tuktoyaktuk Community Centre, Tuktoyaktuk, Northwest Territories, 1983. Barr Ryder Architects.

few and small. The wing to the left, behind the wheelchair-ramped emergency exit, contains the large community hall, while the wider portion to the right contains offices and services. (The entrance is on the far side.) The Community Centre may seem plain and undistinguished by conventional standards, but its very qualities of conservatism and simplicity make it work well in its difficult environment.

As the development, in the Far North, of a true northern architecture represents a rare attempt to define specifically Canadian forms for Canadian conditions, it is very significant. Once architects discovered that European and American prototypes (which have played so important a role in the history of Canadian building) did not work well in the northern environment, they went back to basics, and strove to develop a pragmatic response to the unique conditions of the North. In so doing they looked at traditional native building-types, such as the snowhouse, and learned from the principles that lay behind those timeless and effective solutions. Rather than importing sources, Canadians have exported technological and design achievements, sharing their work with Russian and Scandinavian architects. That effort continues, and the next generation or two should produce some very interesting new architecture.

CHAPTER **14**

ARCHITECTURE
BETWEEN THE WARS

FROM THE 1910s to the 1940s Canadian architects strove to develop a 'modern' and 'Canadian' architecture, within an established tradition that was highly dependent on past and imported styles. However, rather than choosing a revolutionary denial of the past, as their contemporaries had done in Europe and the United States, Canadian architects adopted a conservative and evolutionary route to modernism, based on the gentle modification of existing practices. In Canada there was no inexorable march to modernism, nor an inevitable 'triumph' of the moderns over the revivalists—an interpretation that has often been applied to descriptions of Canadian buildings of the time. Canadian architects hardly seemed to notice what was happening at the Bauhaus, and in other hotbeds of international modernism. While searching for new directions, most continued to work with traditional forms as they focused on trying to develop a distinctively Canadian architecture.

In the mid-1930s, however, there were several notable attempts to deviate from historical precedent, as the spirit of modernism inspired by the age of automobiles and jazz finally began to touch the architectural profession. But not until the social and cultural upheaval that followed the Second World War did the new ideas find broad acceptance, and lead a significant number of Canadian architects to make a real break with the past.

It is therefore in historicism that we find the most characteristic Canadian architecture of the period. Revivals of past architectural styles continued the momentum generated during the second half of the nineteenth century. Not only were historical forms maintained, but so too were the symbolic associations and the social patterns that governed their choice. Many architects committed to the renewed historicism felt keenly that they were designing in a 'modern' manner. In the face of rapid social and industrial change, architects and clients alike revealed a desperate need to cling to the past, much as our own period has 'discovered' conservation in an era of fast change. But there was also a genuinely modern trend in the treatment of the less-conscious aspects of design: forms became far simpler than in the pre-war period, with flatter wall surfaces, fewer advances and recessions, less ornament, and quieter silhouettes. These were all passive responses to new architectural currents abroad.

This chapter examines not only the buildings but also the theory of the period, beginning with the continuation of the nineteenth-century stylistic revivals. The principal styles—first those based on medieval precedent, such as the Château Style and the Tudor and Romanesque Revivals, then those inspired by classicism, including the Neoclassical Revival—are considered separately, followed by a look at domestic architecture, which turned to both sources. A discussion of the initial Canadian responses to European and American ideas of modernism—the Prairie Style, Modern Classicism, Art Deco, and Moderne—concludes the chapter.

The Late Revivals

The revival styles that proliferated during the Victorian age continued into the twentieth century, although with some notable changes. Designs tended to be less boisterous and less colourful, as the new age tamed the High Victorian picturesque aesthetic and showed a preference for simplicity and order. Buildings often exhibited a greater academic correctness. When new structural materials (steel and reinforced concrete) were introduced, they were usually disguised by traditional finishes. The names of several styles of the period adopt the prefix 'late' or 'second' to distinguish them from their Victorian predecessors. For example, St Ann's Church in Toronto [10.57] represents the Second Renaissance Revival.

The Late Gothic Revival

Previous chapters have shown the close association between the nineteenth-century Gothic Revival and ideas about Christianity, education, government, and imperial solidarity. This retained its vigour in the 'late' version of the style that flourished during the first half of the twentieth century. Although the Late Gothic Revival began before the Great War, it continued vigorously throughout the inter-war period and is therefore considered here.

Collegiate Gothic   A most enthusiastic champion of the Gothic Revival was architect Henry Sproatt (1866-1934). A third-generation Torontonian, he spent time in New York and Europe before returning home in 1890 to enter practice. After a period as a partner in the firm of Darling, Sproatt, and Pearson, he formed a lasting partnership in 1899 with another Toronto architect (and a former Darling employee), Ernest R. Rolph (1871-1958), whose previous practice had included work as an architect and engineer with the Canadian Pacific Railway.[1]

Sproatt and Rolph's opportunity came with a series of commissions at the University of Toronto for the prominent Massey family. Beginning in 1910, the firm designed several Gothic Revival buildings for Victoria College, all of them the gift of the Hart A. Massey estate. They included Burwash Hall (residence, common rooms, and dining-hall and kitchens) and a library (now the United Church Archives).[2] These were followed in 1911 by the commission for **Hart House**, arguably the finest Canadian exercise in the Late Gothic Revival—or, as it was called in its day, 'modern Gothic'. Sproatt's client was Vincent Massey (1887-1967), the grandson of farm-equipment manufacturer Hart Massey. Vincent—who graduated from University College, Toronto, in 1910 and earned a second degree from Balliol College, Oxford, in 1913—had a lifelong interest in architecture and was inspired by the hallowed traditions of Oxford and Cambridge and, inevitably, by their architecture. He was a lecturer at Victoria College in 1913-

14.1 *(below)* Hart House, University of Toronto, Toronto, Ontario, 1911-24. University of Toronto Archives/93-45 31/A65-004/0055 [2.49].

14.2 *(right)* Great Hall, Hart House, University of Toronto, Toronto, Ontario, 1911-19. Photograph by Bruce Litteljohn.

15 and later became a diplomat and Canada's first native-born governor general.

Hart House was built as a men's union for the University of Toronto; in today's university jargon it would be called a student union or student centre (women are now members). Its components include library, reading-room, common rooms, chapel, dining-hall, and athletic facilities, all organized within four wings that are distributed around a quadrangle, under which is a theatre. Construction continued from 1911 to 1919. The **south front [14.1]** is framed on the west by the pinnacled Soldiers' Tower—a memorial to the university's war dead added in 1924—and on the east by the high arched window and turrets of the Great Hall. Between are a long three-storey block and a cloister of Gothic arches, with mullioned and transomed casement windows, some in bays, and at each end an enclosed porch (the western porch housing the main entrance). The tall stone chimneys, rising from the green slate roof, enliven the roofline. At the west end, adjacent to the Soldiers' Tower, is a lower block containing the main entrance, a reading-room, and the second-floor library. Sproatt worked in stone, brick, and wood to suggest the Gothic character associated with the great English universities, and employed decorative carving that is complementary without being overwhelming.[3]

The most impressive space in Hart House is the **Great Hall [14.2]**—used daily, when the university is in session, as a dining-hall and occasionally for concerts and other functions. It has a hammerbeam roof of oak braced with steel, and high windows—notably the great south window, fitted with armorial glass honouring ten of the benefactors of the university and founders of its colleges. The lower walls are panelled oak. At the south end the panels are painted with the Royal Arms and the crests of universities of the Commonwealth; at the north end a fireplace is surrounded by crests of universities in countries allied in the First World War. Around the cornice of the panelling is inscribed a passage from Milton's *Areopagitica*, chosen by Massey. A corkscrew staircase at the south end, set in a windowed tower, leads to the Senior Common Room above.

Grand and beautifully detailed though it is, the overall design of Hart House bespeaks restraint and good taste. The Gothic elements unite in a harmonious whole to create an atmosphere of comfort warmed by tradition, and an environment that sustains a centre of lively activity.

Hart House represents a particular a variant of the Late Gothic Revival known as 'Collegiate Gothic'—

a manner that had become widely accepted in the US as the most appropriate mode for university buildings. The Philadelphia firm of Cope and Stewardson popularized the style, with significant additions to the campuses at Bryn Mawr College (1886-1904), the University of Pennsylvania (1895-1901), and Princeton University (1895-1903).[4] All adapted Gothic and Jacobean sources, and composed them in cloister-like arrangements punctuated by towers. Hart House followed this lead admirably. Jacobean (or 'Jacobethan'—referring to the reigns of King James and Queen Elizabeth) features are seen in the rectangular windows with stone mullions, bay windows, and stacked chimneys. The principal components, such as the Great Hall and Soldiers' Tower, are more strictly Gothic in inspiration.

Hart House compares favourably with the much-admired Graduate College at Princeton University that was being designed and built at the same time (1911-13). Sproatt's Toronto landmark is equally well composed and detailed, although it is more restrained—more Canadian, perhaps—with its use of fewer bay windows and its calm, relatively unbroken skyline. The Princeton Graduate College was designed by the firm of Cram, Goodhue, and Ferguson, specifically by senior partner Ralph Adams Cram (1863-1942), the leading American champion of the Late Gothic Revival. Writer, author, critic, scholar, and teacher as well as architect, Cram was a distinguished medievalist and ecclesiologist, a founder of the Medieval Academy of America, and, above all, a passionate believer in the potential of Gothic architecture to flourish as a living, modern style. He believed that architects should

> take up English Gothic at the point where it was cut off during the reign of Henry VIII and go on from that point, developing the style England had made her own, and along what might be assumed to be logical lines, with due regard to the changing conditions of contemporary culture.[5]

Henry Sproatt shared Cram's enthusiasm for the Gothic style—though he did not show it the same rigorous commitment as Cram. In his obituary of Sproatt, the archaeologist and renowned museum director Charles T. Currelly wrote:

> He loved Gothic architecture because he saw in it a type of work easily adapted to growth . . . . The classical style produced a building of completion, balance, finality. He also loved the intimate warmth of Gothic as opposed to the formal. In his talks he always said, 'Each style has a place, but Gothic

collegiate architecture is the one architecture developed for scholastic work. It has proved a success and a joy. Why throw it away?'[6]

Hart House was widely praised, and among the honours it received was the American Association of Architects' gold medal for scholastic work. Compliments came from other quarters as well. Eric Arthur, then (in 1932) a 34-year-old architect—at the beginning of an influential career as a teacher, critic, and historian—declared that 'Hart House is, I think, superior to any modern "medieval" building, not excluding work in the American Universities.'[7]

Sproatt and Rolph used the Gothic Revival for other educational and ecclesiastical buildings, including Bishop Strachan School in Toronto (1913-14) and the Chapel at Ridley College in St Catharines, Ontario (1925).[8] As Currelly noted, Sproatt felt free to use other historical styles when their associations were more appropriate. Sproatt and Rolph's National Research Council building in Ottawa (1930-2; **14.39**), one of the last projects to be built before Sproatt's death, adopts an entirely classical vocabulary. The firm showed the same kind of eclecticism that was seen a generation earlier in E.J. Lennox's adopting the Richardsonian Romanesque for Toronto City Hall [**10.31**] and Beaux-Arts Classicism for the Toronto Power Generating Station [**10.65**].

Collegiate Gothic found a warm reception across Canada. In 1906—when the government of Saskatchewan, shortly after achieving provincehood, decided to form a university in Saskatoon—University of Saskatchewan president Walter Murray and two members of his board toured nine North American campuses. They especially admired the US college buildings. Murray reported:

14.3 College of Agriculture, University of Saskatchewan, Saskatoon, Saskatchewan, 1910-12. Saskatoon Public Library/Local History Room.

The style of architecture adopted is Collegiate Gothic, a style introduced into America by Cope and Stewardson. Some of the best examples of this style are to be seen at Bryn Mawr, Princeton, and Washington University, St Louis. The buildings of the University of Chicago in the same style are close copies of the more notable buildings of Oxford.[9]

With these American sources in mind, the university hired the Montreal architects David Brown (1869-1946) and Hugh Vallance (1866-1947), who had used the style for the Strathcona Medical Building at McGill University (1907-11). Brown and Vallance drew up a plan for the Saskatchewan campus in 1909 and designed five buildings. Construction soon began on the most imposing of the group, the **College of Agriculture** [**14.3**], Saskatoon. Built in 1910-12 (and now the Administration Building), the two-storey building, with projecting ends, has three oriel windows in the centre (illuminating the library)—the middle one, over an arched doorway, combining with a stepped gable to form a central frontispiece. The textured walls of local greystone, windows with 'crossed' stone mullions, gargoyles (included here with some restraint), shields (that include prairie gophers!), and the notched parapet are all features of the popular Collegiate Gothic style. Fully contemporary materials, however, were used in the structure: a reinforced concrete frame with steel roof trusses.

At the same time, British Columbia decided to build a provincial university. A magnificent 260-acre (105-hectare) site was selected near Vancouver

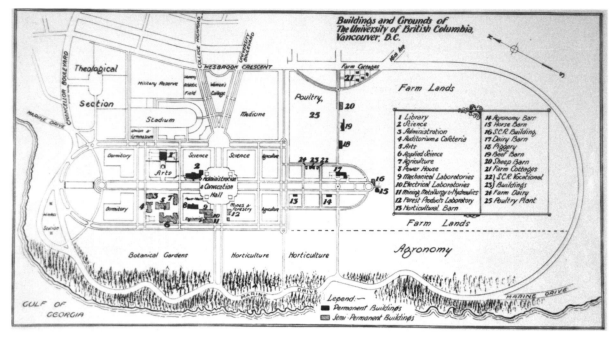

14.4 Site plan, University of British Columbia, Vancouver, British Columbia, 1925. UBC Special Collections. Library Special Collections and Archives Division/University Campus and Endowment Lands/Maps and Plans/B1925.

on the cliff-tops of Point Grey, overlooking the Strait of Georgia. The mountains of Burrard Inlet's north shore, and the peaks and snowfields of the Coastal Range beyond the city, form a natural backdrop of sometimes breathtaking beauty. In 1912 a competition was called for the design of the new campus; the assessors (who included Samuel Maclure) were known for their fondness for traditional British architecture. While claiming to give the competitors 'the freedom to choose among styles', they offered 'a definite suggestion . . . as to the appropriateness of three distinctive styles, namely: a free rendering of late Tudor or Elizabethan or Scotch Baronial.'[10] One competitor, Victoria's Thomas Hooper (1859-1935), offered buildings based on Renaissance and Baroque precedents; the judges dismissed his presentation as 'a classical scheme of grandiose and palatial character', and concluded:

> It is quite clear that the Instructions had in view the dignified but simpler and often domestic types of the older English Universities, rather than the more grandiose modern American examples.[11]

The unanimous winners of the UBC competition were George L. Thornton Sharp (1880-1974) and Charles J. Thompson (1878-1961), two young English-trained architects recently arrived in Canada. Sharp had worked in London with T.E. Colcutt, and in Montreal with Saxe and Archibald, before coming to Vancouver. Thompson had been employed by the CPR before entering private practice. Their partner-

ship, which began in 1908—and its successors—remained one of the most important architectural firms in Vancouver. The practice—later known as Thompson, Berwick, and Pratt (see page 785)—removed the last founder's name only in 1990, when it became Hemingway Nelson.[12]

Sharp and Thompson's **plan for the University of British Columbia [14.4]** applied Beaux-Arts planning principles to the scenic site, and proposed Collegiate Gothic for the design of the buildings. The administration was intended to occupy the highest part of the site, at the intersection of University Boulevard and Main Mall, and each faculty was assigned one or two blocks near the crossing. A hierarchy of educational values was clearly embedded in the plan. Science received the choicest sites; the southern part of the campus was reserved for agriculture ('agronomy'); and the periphery was left for theology, athletics, the military, and the botanical gardens.

Construction began in 1914, but the First World War and the death of President Frank Wesbrook brought work to a halt, until a massive student demonstration in 1922 reminded the government of its commitment. Contracts for the completion of the first three buildings were let in 1923, and the Point Grey campus was open for classes in the fall of 1925.

14.5 Science Building, University of British Columbia, Vancouver, British Columbia, 1914-25. Photograph by Robin Ward, 1992.

The **Science Building** (**14.5**, Sharp and Thompson, 1914-25, with later additions; now the Chemistry Building), and the central portion of the Library (1923-5, later additions), were the only structures completed to the high standards of design and fin-

14.6 Point Grey Secondary School, Vancouver, British Columbia, 1928-9. Photograph by Robin Ward, 1992.

ishes initially specified by Sharp and Thompson. With its mullioned windows and buttresses, the Science Building is a good example of Collegiate Gothic, though the architects described the design as 'a free rendering of Modern Tudor, depending chiefly on outline and a careful disposition of voids and solids, detail only being lavished on central features.'[13] The first two floors, containing laboratories, are articulated by alternating projecting and recessed window bays; the third storey, with lecture rooms, is treated as an attic with smaller arched windows. A reinforced concrete structure supports exterior walls of random ashlar, using multi-coloured BC granite. Windows are steel casements with leaded glass throughout. The interior corridors feature Welsh quarry tile floors and brown brick walls. When the British-inspired Science Building is compared to the American-inspired College of Agriculture at the University of Saskatchewan, the similarities are far more apparent than the differences. Perhaps the latter's greater emphasis on the centre and corners, contrasted with Sharp and Thompson's subtler modelling, is the best indication of a different touch.

Subsequent buildings at UBC had cheaper frame construction and a stucco finish. Only in 1951, when a new building program was instituted, was modern design introduced to the campus; the first of the new breed were the War Memorial Gymnasium (1951) and the Buchanan Building (1956-8, with later additions), both by Sharp and Thompson, Berwick, Pratt.[14]

The Collegiate Gothic Style was used in several other campuses, notably at McMaster University in Hamilton, where the first buildings were designed by W.L. Somerville (1886-1965)—with J. Francis Brown (1866-1942) and F. Bruce Brown (1899-1983)—and built in 1929-30.[15] In 1920, for the Provincial Normal School in Saskatoon, provincial architect Maurice W. Sharon (1878-1940) created a fine Collegiate Gothic design in brick with stone trim (the central portion of which shows the influence of the College of Agriculture at the University of Saskatchewan).[16]

As the Gothic Revival mode became associated with education in general, variations on the Jacobean, Tudor, and Gothic Revivals came to be used as well for high schools. Daniel McIntyre Collegiate Institute in Winnipeg, built in 1923 to designs by J.N. Semmens (1882-1960), is a large brick complex designed as a quadrangle with an entrance tower and hints of medieval sources throughout.[17] **Point Grey Secondary School** [**14.6**] in Vancouver (1928-9), by the partnership of Fred L. Townley (1887-1966) and R.M.

Matheson (1887-1935)—while structurally explicit in its use of concrete—is more overtly Gothic, with its end pavilions having pointed-arched blind arcades that repeat the rhythm of the windows, and side entrances marked by octagonal turrets that extend above the roofline. The walls of 'monolithic concrete' (i.e. poured continuously to provide a single structural unit) are articulated by tall window strips, those in the centre with pointed arches. The concrete surface is covered with cement paint.[18]

These Collegiate Gothic schools, and many others like them, stand in contrast to the high schools of the previous two decades that were built according to classical principles.

Public buildings The most familiar landmark of the Late Gothic Revival is the **Centre Block of the Parliament Buildings [14.7]**, built between 1916 and 1927 in Ottawa. The previous High Victorian Gothic Centre Block of Fuller and Jones [10.1] was destroyed by fire on 3 February 1916; the Library of Parliament [10.3] was saved from the flames because the alert parliamentary librarian shut the iron fire-door separating the two buildings. Within two weeks architects John A. Pearson (of Darling and Pearson) and J. Omer Marchand were called in.

It went without saying that Gothic would be followed, because of the style of the surviving East and West Blocks, and for continued associations with Canada's British heritage and the Gothic of the Parliament Buildings at Westminster. The detail that was designed by Pearson and Marchand is consistently Gothic, particularly in the magnificent public interior spaces, such as the fan-vaulted Confederation Hall (the Rotunda), the House of Commons, and the Senate. Even today a team of sculptors continues to chip away at completing the interior ornament.[19] Pearson and Marchand originally intended to keep the old walls and rebuild with some changes; but owing to the high cost of this plan (some six million dollars), they ordered in the end a 'hurried and secret demolition', as one newspaper branded it, and created a new steel-framed building half again as large as its predecessor (the increased size was achieved with additional storeys).[20]

The façade follows the lines of the original Centre Block, and the walls were faced in the same Nepean sandstone. The effect, however, was comparatively tame. Gone were the rugged textures, the deeply shadowed window reveals, the colourful Potsdam sandstone accents, the polychromatic slate roof, and the iron cresting. While the new building was given a somewhat sleek appearance, it was unquestion-

ably dignified by Pearson's soaring, majestic Peace Tower (1919-27), which has become a powerful national symbol. Rising 300 feet (90 metres), it contains a Memorial Chamber honouring Canada's war dead and a 53-bell carillon.

The Late Gothic Revival was adopted for numerous public buildings across the country. One example is **Westmount City Hall [14.8]** on Sherbrooke Street West. Built in 1922 for an affluent English-speaking suburb of Montreal, it was designed by Robert Findlay (1859-1951) and Francis R. Findlay (1888-1977), who used the style to assert a British presence in their ivy-covered building, facing a small park. It features a stalwart castellated entrance tower flanked by gabled and buttressed wings.[21]

Churches The Late Gothic Revival produced some fine ecclesiastical architecture. The association between Christianity and Gothic that inspired the original revival of the medieval style continued to affect church design. Unlike the nineteenth-century work, however, the later version displayed an impressive knowledge of historical precedent and an academic interest in using 'correct' detail, while tending to be composed with broader and quieter strokes. The principal dispute was a subtle one that would have been lost on everybody except the architects: whether to pursue a modern Gothic based on the Perpendicular style of the fourteenth and fifteenth centuries, as recommended by Cram and followed by many American designers; or whether to remain with the Early English and Decorated styles of the twelfth to early-fourteenth centuries, which had found favour with the followers of Pugin three-quarters of a century earlier.

The American firm of Ralph Adams Cram—known in the 1910s as Cram, Goodhue, and Ferguson—left its mark in Canada in stone as well as in print. Two of its designs were executed. One was a small church (1903-4) commissioned by the wealthy distillers, the Walker family, at St Mary's, Windsor, Ontario.[22] The other was a much larger and more important building, **All Saints' Cathedral [14.9]**, on College Street in Halifax, Nova Scotia. The Halifax Cathedral (1907-10) was designed in the New York office of Cram,

14.7 *(top, right)* Aerial view of the Centre Block of the Parliament Buildings, Ottawa, Ontario (1916-27), with the Library of Parliament behind and the East and West Blocks on either side. Photograph 1930. City of Ottawa Archives/CA1039.

14.8 *(bottom, right)* City Hall, Westmount, Quebec, 1922. Photograph 1976. Communauté urbaine de Montréal.

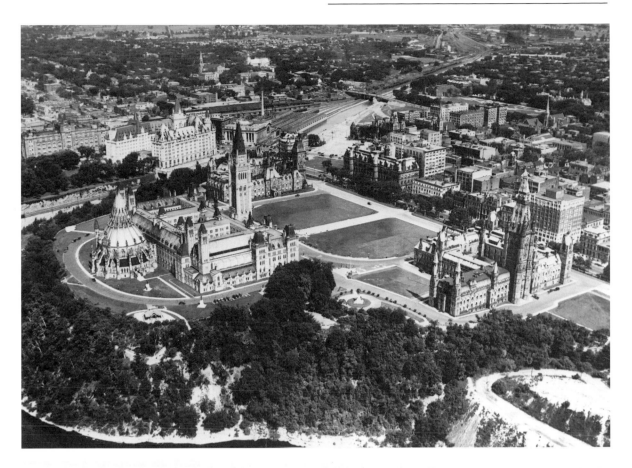

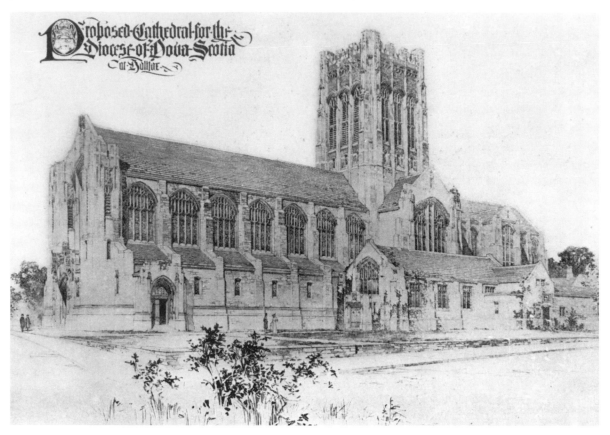

14.9 Perspective of All Saints' Cathedral, Halifax, Nova Scotia, 1907-10 (drawn 1906). From *Architectural Record*, January 1911/MTRL.

Goodhue, and Ferguson, and was therefore the responsibility of the gifted New York principal, Bertram Grosvenor Goodhue (1869-1924). (Cram was in charge of the Boston office.) Goodhue's Perpendicular Gothic design won the commission over the Maritime firm of Harris and Horton. William C. Harris, fifteen years Goodhue's senior, had proposed to use the Decorated Gothic. Percy Nobbs arbitrated between the two designs and gave Goodhue's the nod: a decision that marks the acceptance of the American idea of Gothic as a 'modern' style. In its obituary of Goodhue, the *Journal* of the Royal Architectural Institute of Canada noted: 'His churches, although based on the principles of Gothic, are in every way modern in their expression.'[23]

The design for All Saints' Cathedral was both grand and simple, with a tall nave and transepts and, rising high above the crossing, a square tower heavily encrusted with Late Perpendicular carved stone detail. The procession of tall buttresses along the

sides sets a majestic tempo. The spaces between them are nearly filled by the large nave windows (their scale and tracery pattern inspired by Perpendicular sources), whose openness contrasts with the expanse of stone on the walls of the low side-aisles. The lightness and delicacy—indeed, the modernity—was achieved without being overly fussy, and may be contrasted with the relatively stodgy (although more picturesque) other great Atlantic cathedrals: Frank Wills's Christ Church Cathedral in Fredericton [6.32], and George Gilbert Scott's Cathedral of St John the Baptist in St John's, Newfoundland [6.36], both designed some sixty years earlier.

At All Saints' Cathedral in Halifax only the chancel, transepts, and six of the seven nave bays were built (not the west façade or the crossing tower). Inside, the ceiling is dark-stained wood, designed so that masonry vaulting could later be replaced; but this substitution never occurred. Severe structural problems emerged before the building could be finished, and for most of this century the energies and moneys of the diocese have been spent on repairing and maintaining the original defective building rather than on completing it.

714

Until mid-century the Gothic Revival remained by far the most popular style for Anglo-Canadian churches. With their strong ties to Britain, however, Canadian architects—still heeding the advice of the Ecclesiologists of a half-century earlier—tended to look at the Decorated period of Gothic rather than follow the American idea of using the Perpendicular style as the source for modern Gothic. Other Protestant denominations also participated in the Gothic Revival. Roman Catholics used the style liberally as well, although we have seen attempts in Montreal and Toronto to look towards Italian sources that might be more readily associated with Rome (see **6.65**, **10.58**).

A large complex built for a Methodist congregation—and now administered by the United Church of Canada—is **Timothy Eaton Memorial Church** [**14.10**] in Toronto (1909-14), a rambling cluster of Gothic-inspired buildings on a large site on St Clair Avenue West, and commissioned by the widow, Flora McCrae Eaton, of Sir John Craig Eaton, son of the department-store magnate. (The architects—A. Frank Wickson [1861-1936] and Alfred H. Gregg [1868-1945]—also designed Ardwold in 1909, the Georgian Revival mansion of John Craig Eaton, off Spadina Road on the crest of Toronto's escarpment, demonstrating their stylistic versatility.) The monumental character of the obviously richly endowed church is immediately revealed by a square tower—100 feet (30 m) in height—containing a carillon with 21 bells. The tower rises next to three massive but-

14.10 Timothy Eaton Memorial Church, Toronto, Ontario, 1909-14. Photograph by William Dendy.

tresses supporting two arches, behind which two deep recesses frame traceried windows that light the south end of the nave. On the west (left) is a low *porte cochère* with two openings, one for pedestrians and one for cars. The two-storey Sunday School, which was built first, stands at the far east (right) end; its hipped roof and the blind arcade on the ground floor provide a sense of classical order. Between the school and the church (and obscured in the photograph) is a block with a two-storey bay window and tall chimney, containing reception rooms and offices. The buildings are faced in warm Credit Valley stone that is randomly coursed and rock-faced, except at the base and the top of the nave and the bell-stage of the tower, where it is smoothly finished. The elegant, but restrained, ornament includes the fine stone tracery of the nave windows (along the sides as well as the ends), a solitary pinnacle in the centre of the south end of the nave, and reveals around the doorways.[24]

Irregular not only in its composition, but also in the treatment of individual components, the ensemble is grandly but calmly picturesque. The interior of the church was originally T-shaped in plan, following the Methodist preference for arranging the congregation close to the pulpit, with the choir-loft behind. Above this rose a tall stained-glass copy of Richard Holman Hunt's painting, *Light of the World* (1854). However, in 1938—largely as a result of Lady Eaton's infatuation with English ways, including Anglicanism—a chancel was added to the auditorium (designed by W.L. Somerville of Toronto and Hardie Philip of New York); and this was only one of several other alterations.

In 1925 Canadian Methodists, Congregationalists, and two-thirds of the Presbyterians joined together to form the United Church of Canada (hence the changed allegiance of Timothy Eaton Memorial Church), and architectural design was an early consideration of the new union. The Montreal Presbytery of the United Church formed a Committee on Architecture that produced memoranda on church design and decoration written by two ministers and Percy Nobbs. While concerned primarily with seeking solutions to liturgical needs, the second memorandum did address architectural style. It differentiated between an English Classic church style (deriving from the buildings of the Church of Rome and Sir Christopher Wren) and an English Gothic church style; and while acknowledging that 'throughout the English-speaking world, pointed windows have come to connote an ecclesiastical purpose in a structure', it showed a preference for the former.

14.11 St Andrew's-Wesley United Church, Vancouver, British Columbia, 1931-3. BCARS/86202.

Nobbs and his colleagues noted that because the members of the United Church 'share a certain inheritance of Early Christian tradition', 'Basilican church forms are in this sense more appropriate to its uses than the mediaeval models with their stressed sacerdotal and conventual planning.'[25] This recommendation evidently fell on deaf ears, because Gothic remained by far the more popular source.

For example, the principal source of the decoration of **St Andrew's-Wesley United Church [14.11]** in Vancouver (1931-3), designed by British-born brothers Robert Percival Twizell (1879-1964) and George Sterling Twizell (1885-1957), is Gothic. Hindsight reveals a contradiction between the structural and finishing materials, although this would not have been sensed by the architects. St Andrew's-Wesley is one of many churches of the time constructed of reinforced concrete, yet covered with more traditional materials—in this case exterior granite and a stone-like coating inside—that offer no hint of the structural system. The church features a superb, rich stained-glass window by Gabriele Loire of Chartres, France (installed in 1969), and a tall corner tower, producing a façade that is more elegant in its composition—because it is more contained—than that of Eaton Memorial Church.[26] In the background of the photograph is the earlier—and clumsier—First Baptist Church (Burke, Horwood, and White, 1910-11).

A few churches dared to leave the concrete exposed.

An extraordinary venture into exposed concrete—combining traditional and modern impulses—is **St James's Anglican Church [14.12]** in Vancouver (1935-7). Sharp and Thompson served as associate architects to Adrian Gilbert Scott (1882-1963) of

London. The grandson of Sir George Gilbert Scott, who had designed the cathedral at St John's nearly a century earlier, and the brother of Sir Giles Gilbert Scott (1880-1960), the architect of Liverpool Cathedral and of Toronto's Trinity College Chapel (1952), Adrian Scott had just completed a cathedral in Cairo; a decade later he would achieve fame for his post-war rebuilding of the British House of Commons at Westminster. St James's was a conservative parish, in the sense that it proudly retained the Anglo-Catholic liturgy, but it was also a liberal one in its role of delivering social services to an area inhabited by the needy. This dichotomy was reflected in the design.[27]

Scott produced an ingenious solution to the constricted corner site, which was squeezed in between

the Clergy House and St Luke's Home (Sharp and Thompson, 1924) on East Cordova Street and the Parish Hall (Sharp and Thompson, 1925) on Gore Street. As seen in the **plan [14.13]** the angled entrance leads into a central space **[14.14]** whose nave extends to the west, the sanctuary to the east, with transepts of unequal depth. An octagonal Lady Chapel opens behind the sanctuary. The crossing is almost Byzantine in feeling, with its deep arches supporting a flat coffered wood ceiling, above which rises an octagonal tower that is

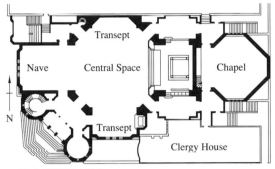

14.12 *(lower left)* St James's Anglican Church, Vancouver, British Columbia, 1935-7. Photograph by John Roaf, 1973.

14.13 *(right)* Plan of St James's Anglican Church, Vancouver, British Columbia, 1935-7. Drawing by David Byrnes.

14.14 Interior, St James's Anglican Church, Vancouver, British Columbia, 1935-7. Photograph by Leonard Frank, 1937. Vancouver Public Library/4671.

also a belfry. The 8-inch (20-cm) outer wall and 5-inch (13-cm) inner wall are built of poured reinforced concrete and separated by a 2-foot (60-cm) space. (The building was as ambitious a monolithic pour as Canada had seen.) The tower is braced by four internal concrete trusses and covered with a steep slate roof, pierced by copper louvres and topped by a silver cross.

St James's—at once both a traditional and a radical building, representing the conflicts and contradictions of Canadian reactions to history and modernity—is a revivalist church, in the sense that its forms and decoration were derived from the past. While the massing may be associated with the Romanesque or Byzantine styles, Gothic provided the source for the narrow pointed lancet windows, the reticulated parapet walls suggesting crenellations, the projecting gargoyles, and the tracery of the chapel ceiling—decorative features that are integral with the structure. The union of structure and decoration, as well as the austere rectilinear geometry—seen in such features as the reveals of the main entrance and the parapets—owe much to the aesthetic of the new Art Deco manner (discussed later in this chapter). The frank exposure of the structural material inside and out makes it also somewhat of a pioneer of the modern movement.

The Late Gothic Revival gained relatively little following in French Canada because of its associations with Britain. Quebec church architects favoured the late Romanesque and classical revivals (also discussed later in this chapter).

The Château Style and other medieval revivals

The Late Gothic Revival and its variant, Collegiate Gothic, were only two of several medieval revivals that continued to be built well into the twentieth century. Medieval forms of European building styles continued to be considered especially appropriate for Canada.

The Château Style The origins of the Château Style in the hotels and terminals built by the Canadian Pacific Railway during the 1880s and 1890s were discussed in Chapter 9. Continuing well into the twentieth century, the style was expressed in the luxurious, castle-like hotels that were built by the competing transcontinental railways, and was adopted as an official national style for government buildings.

The success of the CPR's early hotels, such as the Château Frontenac in Quebec and the Empress Hotel in Victoria, inspired rival railways to build their own

castles. In 1907 the Grand Trunk Railway commissioned Bradford Lee Gilbert (1853-1911) of New York—who had worked for a number of railways in the United States and Mexico—to design a railway terminal and luxury hotel in Ottawa. His proposal for the hotel was vertical in composition, with steep roofs, and bore a family resemblance to the Empress, although it exhibited more explicitly Gothic detail; the station across the street was entirely Neoclassical in design. Hotels were evidently firmly associated with châteaux, and stations with the public buildings of Rome.

A year later Gilbert was dismissed and replaced by Ross and MacFarlane of Montreal. Ottawa's **Château Laurier** [14.15]—built in 1908-12, with later additions and alterations—and Union Station (1908-12), for which the Montreal firm took full credit, were similar to the designs by Gilbert. When the hotel opened its doors in 1912, the first person to sign the guest register was Prime Minister Sir Wilfrid Laurier, after whom it was named (and whose government was encouraging the construction of the Grand Trunk's Pacific line). The Château Laurier marks the full flowering of the Château Style. Steep copper roofs are broken by towers, turrets, dormer windows, and carved gables to convey a lavishly romantic impression. The amply decorated and picturesque roofline contrasts with the austere ashlar walls—characteristic of the new tendency to simplify forms—that are interrupted only by timid advances and recessions.[28]

The two decades that followed saw the construction of fanciful châteauesque railway hotels across the country. The Grand Trunk Pacific engaged Ross and MacFarlane to design the Fort Garry Hotel in Winnipeg (1911-13) and the Macdonald Hotel in Edmonton (1913-15), and the line's successor, the Canadian National Railways, retained Archibald and Schofield to design the Bessborough Hotel in Saskatoon (1930-2) and the Hotel Vancouver (1928-39). All have benefited from recent renovations and remain fine luxury hotels, although the Fort Garry and Bessborough are no longer under railway ownership, and the Macdonald and the Hotel Vancouver are operated by Canadian Pacific Hotels, which purchased the CNR's hotels in 1985.

For a time the CPR used the Château Style only for its Rocky Mountain resorts: the present Banff Springs Hotel (**9.17**, by company architects W.S. Painter, 1912-14, and J.W. Orrock, 1926-8) and the new wing of the Château Lake Louise (Barott and Blackader, 1924-5). The CPR was busy building foursquare urban hotels that were classical in inspiration and had no

14.15 Château Laurier, Ottawa, Ontario, 1908-12. Photograph by John Roaf, 1982.

explicit references to the Château style, among them the Royal Alexandra Hotel in Winnipeg (Edward and W.S. Maxwell, 1904-6), the Palliser Hotel in Calgary (E. and W.S. Maxwell, 1911-14), and the Hotel Saskatchewan in Regina (Ross and Macdonald—successors to Ross and MacFarlane—1926-7). Probably as a gesture to keep up with its own imitators, the CPR placed a château roof on Toronto's large Royal York Hotel (Ross and Macdonald, with Sproatt and Rolph, associate architects, 1927-9, seen in the background in 9.6), whose ornament was otherwise inspired by the Romanesque. The Château Style sig-nified more than just hotels. It represented deluxe accommodation, and hence was adopted for a num-ber of luxury apartment buildings, such as the Château Apartments (now Le Château; Ross and Macdonald, with H.L. Featherstonhaugh, 1925) on Sherbrooke Street West in Montreal, within the city's upper-crust Square Mile.[29]

The Château Style—which came to be considered distinctively Canadian not only because of its shared British and French roots, but also because Canada was so closely identified with its railways—began to be advocated as a national style appropriate for gov-ernment buildings. We have seen that the Holt Commission of 1913-15 recommended that new public buildings in Ottawa be influenced by the design of the Parliament Buildings or the Château Laurier (page 652). This was the first of several fed-eral documents advocating the Château Style for government architecture. In 1920 a committee of three designers—David Ewart (1841-1921), Dominion Consulting Architect and the former Chief Architect of the Department of Public Works; R.C. Wright (1860-1927), the current Chief Architect; and Thomas Adams, town planner—was asked to make further recommendations. Its members submitted two dif-ferent schemes, but were unanimous in 'agreeing on the style of architecture to be adopted, viz: Northern French Gothic (French Château).'[30]

In 1927 the scheme for government buildings that had been submitted by Wright and Adams was approved by the Department of Public Works. The official report summarized the opinion:

> That as the Federal Plan Commission [of 1915] and Messrs. Wright, Adams and Ewart all agree that the [new government] building should be Gothic in character and suggest Norman French Gothic Type; furthermore as it is the general consensus of opinion that Gothic should be adopted to har-monize with the Parliament Buildings, being the type of architecture most suitable to our Northern climate, the Deputy Minister [J.B. Hunter] further recommends the adoption of the French Chateau style of architecture, of which the Chateau Laurier is a modernized type.[31]

The writers were rather loose in their stylistic terminology, combining the Gothic Revival and Château styles; but nomenclature aside, they agreed that the Château Laurier stood as an appropriate model for the new buildings.

The first tangible result was the **Confederation Building [14.16]**, which was built in 1928-31 at the

14.16 Confederation Building, Ottawa, Ontario, 1928-31. Photograph by John Roaf, 1982.

corner of Wellington and Bank Streets, just west of the Parliament Buildings (and their newly completed Centre Block). The design was prepared by the Chief Architect's Branch of the Department of Public Works under the supervision of Thomas Dunlop Rankin (1886-1965), who had formerly worked for Ross and MacFarlane. The eight-storey government office building—which was intended to be part of a larg-er group—is L-shaped in plan and dominated by a picturesque asymmetrical entrance in an angle between the two principal wings (as in the Macdonald Hotel). The central high-pinnacled tower rises above a circular stair-turret on the right; on the left a mansarded-roof projection begins the west wing. (A third wing extends obliquely into the court-yard behind.) The walls are faced in the warm-coloured Nepean sandstone that was used on the Parliament Buildings. The ornamentation is restrained and not immediately evident, but the arches over the fifth-floor windows on Wellington Street (seen at the left in the photograph) bear carved heads representing different occupations; the dormers have representations of Canadian wildlife; and other carved areas show the maple leaf, fleur-de-lis, rose, thistle, and shamrock—symbols of the nation and its founding peoples. The steep copper roofs provide a picturesque silhouette that certainly complements that of the Parliament Buildings and the Château Laurier.[32]

The completion of the Confederation Building marked the first time that a so-called *Canadian* style was identified and promoted (even if its roots were all European), although we may recall John Langton's private description of University College in Toronto as being in 'the Canadian style' (page 312). This was a period of new nationalistic feelings and a growing emancipation from British political control. Prime Minister W.L. Mackenzie King was in the process of developing a foreign service, and between 1925 and 1929 the first legations (now embassies) were opened in Washington, Paris, and Tokyo.

Government construction slowed down with the onset of the Depression, but received a boost in 1934 with the passing of the Public Works Construction Act. This provided $40 million in supplementary funds for the construction and improvement of a variety of public works across the country—a much-needed shot in the arm to the economy.[33] Three additional public buildings were erected in downtown Ottawa as a consequence of the Act: the Justice Building, the Central Post Office, and the Supreme

14.17 Supreme Court of Canada, Ottawa, Ontario, 1938-9. Photograph by John Roaf, 1982.

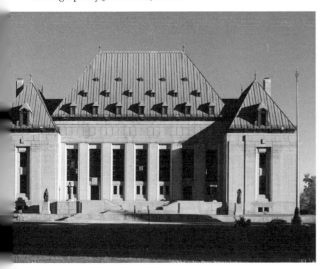

Court. All adopted the Château Style, although in varying degrees. The Justice Building (1934-6), designed by the Department of Public Works, is located just west of the Confederation Building and looks very much like its neighbour. In the Central Post Office (1938-9), by W.E. Noffke (1878-1964), a steep copper roof and corner tower are placed over classical lower storeys.[34]

The commission for the **Supreme Court of Canada** [**14.17**], the next building west on Wellington Street beyond the Justice Building, was awarded to Ernest Cormier (1885-1980), a superbly talented Montreal architect whose other principal buildings will be introduced at the end of this chapter. From the cornice down, Cormier's building—which was constructed in 1938-9—is a pristine and dignified example of Modern Classicism (a style that will also be discussed below). Cormier's original design called for a flat roof, which was the customary and appropriate cap for such a design. The Department of Public Works, however, dictated that the architect should provide steep roofs with dormers—the hallmarks of the Château Style—and Cormier believed that the directive had come all the way from the prime minister, Mackenzie King. The designs were changed and the roof built, initially without any use being allocated to the immense interior space that was inevitably created: only during construction was it decided to place the library there.[35]

King showed a passionate interest in improving the appearance of Ottawa and giving it the grandeur due to a capital city. It was he who demanded a co-ordinated plan for the national capital and brought in planner Jacques Gréber from Paris to provide it. King evidently believed that one aspect of achieving consistency was by imposing the Château Style—or at least its most salient feature, the steep, dormered roof—upon all new public buildings in the national capital.[36] It is perhaps significant that tall hipped roofs were being placed on official buildings in Ottawa in the very year that the federal government was erecting them atop the reconstruction of Champlain's *Habitation* at Port Royal, which was praised as being the first Euro-Canadian building.

The Château Style was adopted for government buildings outside Ottawa as well. The Chief Architects of the time were Thomas W. Fuller, whom we first met as an architect in Dawson, and who held the post from 1927 to 1936; and Charles D. Sutherland (1879-1957), a career bureaucrat who served from 1936 to 1947. Fuller and Sutherland used the style for numerous 'federal' or 'dominion' buildings (combinations of post offices and other federal departments) in small communities around the country. One stands at **Pointe-au-Pic [14.18]**, Quebec: a one-storey brick building of 1938-9, trimmed with stone, with a corner entrance and a steep, dormer-pierced roof that rises as high as the walls.[37] The style is also seen in a much larger building at the **Bureau de poste [14.19]** in Lower Town, Quebec City, by Raoul Chènevert (1889-1951). Built in 1939-40, it is a thoroughly châteauesque design from top to bottom.[38] The elaborate entrance elevation is dominated by a five-storey gabled frontispiece with large clustered windows and a turret to one side. Steep roofs, gabled and shed dormers, chimneys, and finials abound, and the picturesqueness is increased by the asymmetrical plan and composition. The walls are faced in brick with stone trim. The Quebec postal terminal surely reflects the domination of the Château Frontenac, looming high above in Upper Town, and responds as well to its châteauesque neighbour, the Gare du Palais (Union Station), built by the CPR in 1915 to designs by architect Harry Edward Prindle (1873-?).[39]

The final flowering of both the Château Style and Beaux-Arts planning in government architecture is seen in the **Memorial Buildings [14.20]** in Ottawa, a pair of large office buildings across Wellington Street from the Supreme Court, and erected after the Second World War for the Department of Veterans' Affairs (1949-56) and the Department of Trade and Commerce (1954-8). The Toronto architectural firm of H.L. Allward (1899-1971) and G.R. Gouinlock (1896-1979) was commissioned shortly before the end of Mackenzie King's term of office (he retired in 1948 and died two years later), and once again the prime minister's fondness for the style is revealed. The bland six-storey stone elevations have pitched copper roofs with dormers, and a pair of towers rise where the two buildings meet at the ceremonial Memorial Arch—a gateway that was intended to frame an avenue that never developed.

The Château Style was an important force in Canadian architecture for two-thirds of a century. Introduced as a picturesque solution for a series of railway hotels, it became the principal mode for federal building, and for a time was advocated as a uniquely Canadian architectural style.

The Tudor Revival and Rustic Tudor styles Features of the buildings of Tudor England—principally the half-timbered gable—became popular in Canada around the turn of the century. We have seen how the Tudor Revival became important in domestic architecture (page 623), in part as an expression of

14.18 Federal Building, Pointe-au-Pic, Quebec, 1938-9. NAC/PA124534.

14.19 Bureau de poste, Quebec City, Quebec, 1939-40. Photograph by M. Trépanier, 1989. PC.

allegiance to the values of the Empire. The federal government adopted the Tudor Revival to provide an image of imperial solidarity, particularly in a series of customs and immigration buildings erected at Canada/US border crossings, beginning in 1932. With the growth of automobile traffic, these became the new 'gateways to the nation'—the offspring of railway stations. Here the Department of Public Works selected the Tudor Revival (rather than the more bombastic Château Style) to express a distinctly Canadian identity.

The first crossings of this kind were erected in 1932 at **Beebe Plain [14.21]** and Trout River, Quebec, at the Vermont border. Both are small, one-storey buildings, with a flat canopy extending at one side to provide a shelter for customs officers and cars. A decorative pattern of darkly stained vertical boards set off against white stucco, augmented by scalloped circular roundels over the windows, provide the Tudor Revival imagery. The building at Beebe Plain contrasts nicely with the American customs building across the road in Vermont, whose brick walls, pedimented canopy, chimneys, and small-paned sash windows clearly allude to the American Colonial Revival. Each structure draws on an architectural style associated with its country's past to make a succinct nationalistic statement.[40]

Similar couplets were replayed across the long border. On the west coast, on the Pacific Highway that

14.20 Memorial Buildings, Ottawa, Ontario, 1949-58. Photograph by John Roaf, 1982.

14.21 Customs and Immigration Building, Beebe Plain, Quebec, 1932. Photograph by Harold Kalman.

14.22 Museum Building, Riding Mountain National Park, Manitoba, 1933. PC/Photo Services.

linked Vancouver with Seattle (it is not the only highway link today), the higher volume of traffic led to the construction of larger buildings, but the images were the same. The Canada Customs Post at Douglas (Surrey), BC (1935-6; demolished), used the Tudor Revival, while the American station at Blaine, Washington, adopted the Colonial Revival—here with a high gambrel roof.[41] Standing in austere contrast to them both is the International Peace Arch, erected in the park that straddles the border. Built in 1921 as a joint project between the two governments, the Neoclassical monument was an American initiative, and therefore adopted the classical vocabulary commonly used for US government architecture.[42]

For buildings throughout the growing system of national parks, the federal government developed a rustic variant of the Tudor Revival. The familiar half-timbered gable was combined with log construction, rusticated stone, and wood trim to convey the joint messages of 'Canada' and 'park'. Unfortunately, they also helped to reinforce the visitor's image of Canada as an unrefined northern wilderness populated by bears and Mounties—one that was nurtured by Hollywood in such films as *Rose-Marie* (1936), starring Jeanette MacDonald and Nelson Eddy.

The Rustic Tudor Style is seen best in the structures erected at Riding Mountain National Park in southeastern Manitoba, which was elevated from being a forest reserve to a national park in 1930. Some 86 government buildings were constructed in the park during the 1930s by a skilled work-force—including many Scandinavian-Canadians familiar

with log construction—provided by federal unemployment relief programs. They were designed by the Architectural Division of the National Parks Branch, and credit for the concept may be shared by an architect—English-born William David Cromarty—the head of the division—and J.B. Harkin, the Commissioner of National Parks.

The **Museum Building** [14.22], now called the Interpretive Centre, at Riding Mountain National Park—built in 1933—presents the fullest expression of the Rustic Tudor Style. The $1\frac{1}{2}$-storey building presents an amalgam of several construction techniques. The central portion, containing a large community room, is faced in native fieldstone and features a massive stone chimney—a symbol of 'home' and comfort—with a double brick stack, which responds to a large stone fireplace on the inside. The wing on the left, which accommodates a large museum room for natural-history exhibits, is built of round bearing logs with saddle-notched joints. The complementary wing on the right has a projecting gabled bay finished in half-timbering with rough-cast infill, quatrefoil and circular insets, and leaded windows—all features derived from English Tudor cottages. (Behind this wing is a 250-seat lecture hall, for meetings and religious services, that is also constructed of logs.) An assertive hipped roof, with exposed log rafters, unites the ensemble. The logs are exposed inside as well, and the roofs of the museum and lecture hall are both supported by open log trusses. The museum, and the nearby log Administration Building, were set in a planned landscape that complemented their appearance, including 'broad lawns, picturesque walks, . . . and pergolas constructed of native oak'. A small garden behind the museum was 'landscaped in the English style, containing a fountain and a rustic summer house with thatched roof'.[43]

The same Rustic Tudor image was continued throughout the western national parks, including Prince Albert, Waterton Lakes, and Banff. Some were designed by the National Parks Branch and others by private architects. The most familiar portal of this kind is surely the **East Gate at Banff National Park** [**14.23**], designed by Harold C. Beckett (1890-1970) and built in 1934; it is passed by every motorist who crosses the Rockies along the Trans-Canada Highway. Uncoursed fieldstone forms the primary material, but the most noticeable features of the pair of cross-gabled buildings are the peaked gable-ends, one with vertical half-timbering and the other with 'Banff National Park' inscribed in wood relief-lettering.[44]

The government's Rustic Tudor style complemented the private-sector penchant for log-building that was seen in small vacation cottages and the large Seigniory Club (Château Montebello, **11.49**). In the 1920s and 1930s the federal government developed a resort of its own at Jasper National Park.

14.23 East Gate, Banff National Park, Alberta, 1934. White Museum of the Canadian Rockies/George Noble Collection/v469,2423.

The large complex of Jasper Park Lodge included the main lodge (burned in 1952 and later replaced), bungalows, cabins, and service buildings—many using a system of construction, with vertical posts and horizontal log infill, that was butt-jointed, toe-nailed, and left rounded on the outside—forming a modernized version of the Red River frame. This nostalgic exercise in Canadiana was designed by Godfrey Milne, an architect in the office of John Schofield.[45]

The Late Romanesque and Byzantine Revivals In the years between the wars other architectural styles of the Middle Ages—particularly Romanesque and Byzantine—enjoyed late revivals in Canada. Many of the results are impressive, although they had a lesser impact than the Gothic Revival, the Château Style, and the Tudor Revival. Their existence, in the middle years of the twentieth century, underlines the persistence of traditional values in Canadian design.

During the 1930s the Toronto firm of Chapman and Oxley produced some fine designs in the Late Romanesque Revival. The firm's senior partner, Alfred Chapman (1879-1949), was born in Toronto and trained with E. Beaumont Jarvis (1864-1948) and with Burke and Horwood. He then attended the École des Beaux-Arts in Montreal for two years and worked for another two years in New York City, before return-

ing to Toronto in 1907. Chapman immediately won the competition for the Toronto Public Reference Library (1907-9, now the Koffler Student Services Centre in the University of Toronto) on College Street (executed with Wickson and Gregg). He headed two successful practices—first with R.B. McGiffen (1875-1945) until 1919, and subsequently with J. Morrow Oxley (1883-1957); a 1928-9 addition to the Library was designed by Chapman and Oxley, with Wickson and Gregg. Chapman—who is generally accepted as the designing partner—produced a number of fine buildings in a wide range of historical styles over more than three decades of practice.[46]

Chapman and Oxley's east wing (1931-2) of the **Royal Ontario Museum [14.24]** in Toronto presents a broad three-storey elevation to Queen's Park Avenue (then called Queen's Park Drive). The monumental entrance bay features a large round-headed arch rising three storeys, with three tall stained-glass windows in the centre and a carved frieze and tympanum at its apex. Within the archivolts of the arch, ornamental columns with griffons on the capitals form part of the elaborate carving scheme by William F.K. Oosterhoff. Beyond a trio of doors at the lowest level is a magnificent octagonal rotunda, whose vaulted ceiling sparkles with a golden mosaic (conceived by museum director Charles T. Currelly), whose symbols and patterns represent the world's cultures and reflect the breadth of the museum's collection. The exterior wall is faced in random-coursed Credit Valley sandstone and trimmed with Queenston limestone. The complexity of the decorative program stands in marked contrast to the large scale and simple masses of the overall composition, characteristic of the period's growing preference for relatively plain, if textured, surfaces. The ensemble makes a nice contrast with the more plastic Richardson-inspired Romanesque of the original west wing, built in 1912-14 to designs by Darling and Pearson—the two wings formed an 'H'-shaped plan. The spaces between them were filled in with a major expansion in 1978-83 (by Moffatt Moffatt and Kinoshita, with Mathers and Haldenby).[47]

In his critique of the east wing of the ROM (which received an honourable mention at the 1932 exhibition of the RAIC), architect A.S. Mathers admired the composition of the façade and the impression left by the rotunda; but he recognized the Museum's *retardataire* character and—with only an implicit glance at the advancing modernist tide—suggested that it

is perhaps a little too strongly styled. The Romanesque manner sets a great many limitations for the designer

14.24 East wing, Royal Ontario Museum, Toronto, Ontario, 1931-2. Industry Science and Technology Canada.

. . . . It is as I hope, for this country, a brilliant climax and finale to that great school of North American architecture founded by the late H.H. Richardson.[48]

Actually, there are few parallels in the ROM with the earlier Richardsonian version of the Romanesque. The ambitious scale, calm horizontality, relatively unbroken surfaces, and attention to historical detail of the Chapman and Oxley east wing are very different from the picturesqueness and bulk of the true Richardsonian Romanesque, as seen in E.J. Lennox's Toronto City Hall **[10.31]**, built some 40 years earlier.

Chapman and Oxley—with Maurice D. Klein (b. 1896) as associate—used the Late Romanesque Revival with particular success for **Holy Blossom Temple [14.25]** on Bathurst Street in Toronto, built in 1936-7 for a Reformed Jewish congregation on a large property in an area (below Eglinton Avenue) that was largely rural and in the process of development. The entrance, and the main block behind it, were placed at a 45° angle to Bathurst Street, facing southeast, so that the commanding and beautiful frontispiece is sunlit for much of the day. It has three

14.25 Contractors' display sign for the construction of Holy Blossom Temple, Toronto, Ontario, 1936-7. City of Toronto Archives/sc648026.

14.26 Interior, Holy Blossom Temple, Toronto, Ontario, 1936-7. From *IRAIC*, October 1938.

entrance doors—with a pierced lattice on either side to light an interior staircase—below a tall round-headed arch set deep in a smooth wall of poured concrete. Under the arch a rose window, with the Star of David in the centre, is surrounded by tracery filled with stained glass, and below this are nine tall, narrow, round-headed windows with rampant lions—the piers of the entrance doors—on either side of the middle three. The façade is topped by a simple cornice outlining a low gable. The high round arch over the entrance, the tall round arches along the sides of the wood-roofed sanctuary, and the *campanile*-like tower at the junction with the school-and-auditorium wing are all reminiscent of Romanesque churches. Concrete is exploited at Holy Blossom; even the elaborate archivolts and tracery on the front are formed in that material. Elsewhere the ornament is understated, allowing the concrete to assert itself as a monolithic and plastic material. This is particularly evident in the remarkable **interior [14.26]**, which features a stately line of five unadorned arches separating the nave from the galleries and leading to a tall arch at the Ark end, which has been described by architectural historian William Dendy:

A flight of steps leading between the pulpits to the Ark, and a lattice screen of fine concrete framing the pierced oak doors of the Ark, give it the architectural importance its religious significance demands. The pulpits and steps, finished in a polished pink-beige marble, complement the lighter colours of the auditorium. Behind, on the screen, are relief panels of religious symbols with backgrounds of an intense sky blue—the colour of the vault of the apse, which is a metaphor for the Dome of Heaven.[49]

The space has the dignity and simplicity of a Late Classical basilica (the parallel extends to the exposed truss that supports the heavily beamed wood roof), as well as the reduction to essentials of contemporaneous modernist design. Holy Blossom was begun only a year after St James's Church in Vancouver, which also uses exposed concrete in a progressive manner, and whose interior round arches are also suggestive of Late Classical and Romanesque (as well as Gothic) sources.

The Romanesque Revival was popular for synagogues, whose architects had sought for years to achieve an appropriate and identifiable Jewish image. The Moorish and Byzantine modes that appeared in the nineteenth century—characterized by bulbous domes, and chosen because of the Eastern origins of Judaism—gave way in the twentieth century to Romanesque-inspired forms with round arches and corbels. Implicit in the choice was the fact that the Romanesque style preceded the Gothic, just as Judaism preceded Christianity. (Painters of the early Renaissance often used Romanesque forms to symbolize the Old Testament.) Early uses of this style for synagogues were seen at Temple Emanuel [**8.31**] in Victoria, the oldest standing synagogue in Canada, and at the Shearith Israel Synagogue [**6.62**] in Montreal. A mature version with Romanesque features (although still retaining small Moorish cupolas) was the impressive Congregation Shaar Hashomayim in Westmount, Quebec, designed by John Melville Miller (1875-1948) and completed in 1922 to become the largest synagogue in Canada; it is still in use, although the façade has been hidden behind an insensitive later addition (Eliasoph and Berkowitz, 1965). The Romanesque design of Holy Blossom Temple is said to have been inspired by the large Temple Emanu-El on Fifth Avenue in New York (Robert D. Kohn, Charles Butler, and Clarence Stein, 1929); but whereas the American precedent was constructed of stone (with a steel truss roof), the Toronto temple was poured and finished in reinforced concrete. A Romanesque model closer to home was the previous Holy Blossom Synagogue on Bond Street, Toronto, which has both Moorish domes and Richardsonian arches (John Wilson Siddall, 1895-7; now the Greek Orthodox Church of Hagios Giorgios).[50]

Romanesque and Byzantine forms were also used

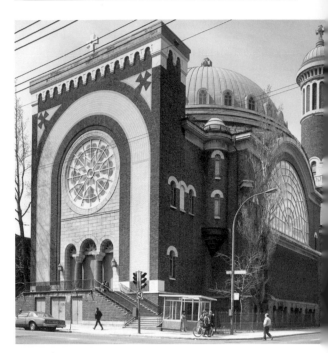

14.27 Église Saint-Michel-Archange, Montreal, Quebec, 1914-15. Photograph by Brian Merrett.

for churches during the period, particularly for Roman Catholic churches in Quebec. The reason would seem to have been a continued effort to disassociate the churches of French-speaking Catholic congregations from those of the anglophone communities, despite the popularity of Gothic in some francophone circles. The **Église Saint-Michel-Archange** [**14.27**], on rue Saint-Urbain in Montreal, is wholly Romano-Byzantine in inspiration, its domed central space following the examples of the Byzantine churches of Istanbul and the Romanesque churches of Aquitaine. Built in 1914-15, the building might be dismissed as an awkward curiosity, were it not the first church in Quebec—and likely in Canada—whose structure was built of reinforced concrete. The architect was Aristide Beaugrand-Champagne (1876-1950), then professor of architecture at Montreal's École Polytechnique, and subsequently at the École des Beaux-Arts. The engineers were C.M. Morssen, with E. Brown and W.D. Lawrence.[51]

Dom Bellot and Quebec rationalism The enthusiastic use of concrete makes Saint-Michel-Archange a precursor of the rationalist movement that was to dominate ecclesiastical architecture in Quebec between the wars. A number of architects and clerics, among them Gérard Morisset and Mgr

Olivier Maurault, criticized the use of imitation materials—'the architecture of tin and false marble' in the French classicism associated with Abbé Jérôme Demers (page 194).[52] They admired Byzantine, Romanesque, and Gothic architecture primarily for their structural logic and the frank use of materials, less for their historical associations. This preference parallels the Arts and Crafts Movement associated with William Morris, in contrast to the more romantic approach that we recognize in the English-Canadian and American late revivals.

The rationalists found their hero in the Parisian-born monk-architect Dom Paul Bellot (1876-1944), who trained at the École des Beaux-Arts and was a member of the Benedictine order. Before Dom Bellot visited Montreal in 1934 to deliver a series of nineteen lectures on architecture—in that city, and also in Quebec and Sherbrooke—he was esteemed for designing a number of impressive churches and abbeys across Europe whose roofs were supported by repeated arches. (First built of brick and then of concrete, these churches included decorative and colouristic effects that were produced by the structural materials themselves.) Bellot's invitation to Canada, proffered by the Institut scientifique franco-canadien, had been instigated by two of his Quebec disciples: architects Adrien Dufresne (1904-82) and Edgar Courchesne (1903-79). Courchesne explained his admiration for Bellot in an article written to drum up interest in the lectures:

And so in the shadow of the cloister is born a new style. Created from tradition, this architecture is classical in its spirit, but practical and modern in its execution.[53]

In his lectures, which were widely attended by students and the general public, Bellot expressed his admiration for French architect and theorist Eugène-Emmanuel Viollet-le-Duc (1814-79), particularly his belief that a modern architecture should emulate, rather than imitate, the lessons of the Middle Ages. Texts of the lectures were circulated among Bellot's admirers and published in 1948.[54]

Dom Bellot's Canadian visit had immediate consequences. One was the appearance in 1935 of the periodical *L'Art sacré*, devoted to promoting a new 'modern' expression for religious art and architecture. Another was the construction of several churches in what has been called the 'Dom Bellot Style', featuring parabolic arches, brickwork in fiercely contrasting colours, and the radical geometric modernism of the post-First World War period. In Dufresne's **Église Sainte-Thérèse-de-Lisieux [14.28]** at Beauport (1936), near Quebec City, a row of powerful parabolic arches dominates the nave and gives the church a grandeur that belies its relatively small scale. The arches and walls are constructed of red brick, the former vividly garnished with zig-zag brick patterns in black, ochre, and grey. The structural elements serve as decoration, true to the rationalist spirit of Viollet-le-Duc. Dufresne was paying homage not

14.28 Interior, Église Sainte-Thérèse-de-Lisieux, Beauport, Quebec, 1936. Photograph by Nicole Tardif.

14.29 Abbaye de Saint-Benoît-du-Lac, near Mansonville, Quebec, begun 1939. Courtesy of Abbaye de Saint-Benoît-du-Lac.

to the polychromy of High Victorian Gothic, but to the similar treatment seen inside Dom Bellot's church at Noordhoek, Holland (1921). The simple and stocky exterior of Sainte-Thérèse is articulated along the sides by transept-like gabled projections at every second bay, which act similarly to buttresses by resisting the lateral thrust of the arches. Dufresne subsequently designed a number of other churches and chapels in the Dom Bellot style, using several forms of nave arches, including polygonal arches of reinforced concrete at Saint-Pascal-de-Maizerets, Quebec (1946).[55]

Dom Bellot returned to Canada to serve as a member of the architectural teams for two important building projects: the Benedictine Abbey of Saint-Benoît-du-Lac, near Mansonville, Quebec; and the completion of the Oratoire Saint-Joseph-du-Mont-Royal in Montreal. He died in Quebec City in 1944.

In 1935 the Father Superior of the **Abbaye de Saint-Benoît-du-Lac** [**14.29**]—where Dom Bellot would be buried—invited the French monk to design a large new addition on a scenic hilltop site overlooking Lake Memphramagog in the Eastern Townships. Dom Bellot accepted, and associated himself with two architects registered in Quebec: Félix Racicot (1903-73) and Dom Claude-Marie Côté. The plan arranged the monks' wings and the church around a pentagonal courtyard, with the hostel wing and its tall *clocher* attached but separate. Construction began in 1939; but after three building campaigns, portions of the complex remain incomplete. Nevertheless, the architects' intentions are clear. The picturesquely massed

abbey is built of reinforced concrete and faced in local granite. The exterior treatment offers a simplified rendition of Romanesque and Gothic sources, with stylized pointed-arched windows, buttress strips, and corbels, and such traditional forms as an octagonal monastic kitchen. The ornament is again integral, and can be rationalized as serving both a structural and an articulative function. Dom Bellot's touch is evident most notably in the **cloister** [**14.30**]. Exquisite parabolic arches of red brick, supporting a wood roof, define a space that is illuminated by repeated small stained-glass windows. Polychromy is introduced on the tile floors and in the perimeter walls.[56]

The **Oratoire Saint-Joseph** [**14.31**], Montreal's most familiar architectural landmark—whose dome is one of the largest in the world—is perched on the northern slope of Westmount Mountain (adjacent to Mont Royal). In 1904 Frère André, a simple man renowned for his healing powers, received permission to build a small shrine to Saint-Joseph, his patron saint. Twenty years later, in 1924, an imposing basilica (the principal building) was begun on its site to designs by J. Dalbé Viau (1881-1938) and L. Alphonse Venne (1875-1934) in a late revival of the Italian Renaissance style—continuing the affinity for this style that was seen at the Cathedral of Saint-Jacques-le-Majeur [**6.65**].

Work on the Oratoire, which had progressed only to the base of the vaulting, resumed in 1937—the year Frère André died, by which time the shrine had been visited by millions of people, many of whom had claimed to be cured—under the direction of Dom

14.30 Cloister, Abbaye de Saint-Benoît-du-Lac, near Mansonville, Quebec, begun 1939. Courtesy of Abbaye de Saint-Benoît-du-Lac.

14.31 Oratoire Saint-Joseph, Montreal, Quebec, begun 1924. Collection of Harold Kalman.

14.32 Interior, Oratoire Saint-Joseph, Montreal, Quebec, begun 1924. Communauté urbaine de Montréal.

Bellot and Lucien Parent (1893-1956). Bellot, the principal designer, continued in the revivalist spirit, although he avoided any direct imitation of historical sources. His principal contribution was the dome, a magnificent technical achievement that he designed as two thin concrete shells—covered in copper and topped by a cupola—in a shape reminiscent of that of the Duomo in Florence. Inside, Dom Bellot's influence is seen in the polygonal concrete arches of the nave, crossing, and choir, which give a distinctly modernist and stylized appearance to this otherwise traditional building. The vivid colour scheme he proposed for the **interior** [**14.32**]—green, violet, ochre, pink, brown, black, and turquoise—was not followed by the architects who subsequently

completed the building. Exterior work on the Oratory was completed in 1955, and on the interior in 1967.[57]

The architectural vocabulary of the churches designed and influenced by Dom Bellot was based in the religious buildings of centuries earlier, but the new spirit of rationalism and structural decoration took those forms and made them into something quite contemporary. The modernism of Bellot's buildings had its personal touches, but his reconciliation of new materials with a stylized version of historical styles shows a clear parallel with St James's Church in Vancouver and Holy Blossom Temple in Toronto, also designs of the mid-1930s. These religious buildings, representing a trio of faiths, successfully bridged the late revivals with the modernism that followed the Second World War.

Father Ruh and Ukrainian churches Another European cleric-architect who came to Canada and used early medieval architectural traditions as the basis for contemporary church-building was the Reverend Philip Ruh (1883-1962). The energetic Father Ruh spent fifty years among the Ukrainian-Canadians of the Prairie Provinces as a missionary and an architect, and left a remarkable legacy of more than thirty Ukrainian Catholic churches from Alberta to Ontario (as well as a smattering of other buildings) that take Byzantine-inspired forms to the limit. Unlike Dom Bellot, Father Ruh would have considered himself a traditionalist and not a modernist.[58]

Born in a district of Lorraine that today forms a part of Belgium, Ruh was accepted into the Oblate order and studied some architecture at an Oblate college in Germany. He was ordained in 1910 and assigned to Galicia in western Ukraine. After spending a year there learning the Ukrainian language and culture, he arrived in Edmonton in April 1911 as a missionary, and was assigned the vast region north of the South Saskatchewan River as his territory. In this architectural milieu of culturally distinctive but small-scaled

Ukrainian-Canadian church-building [9.38-43], Father Ruh assumed the task of designing and overseeing the building of churches throughout the Prairies.

Holy Trinity Church (1921), near Leduc, Alberta, was an early work built under Ruh's direction. It combines features of the twin-towered longitudinal churches built by the Oblates across Canada, with the octagonal onion dome, two smaller onion-shaped cupolas, and detached belltower that are essential parts of the Ukrainian tradition. The interior was decorated several years later by Peter Lipinski, the most prominent Ukrainian church-painter in the Prairies.[59]

In 1924 Father Ruh was transferred from Alberta to Manitoba, where he built a series of large and elaborate churches that reflected the growing establishment of the Ukrainian-Canadian community. The first of these was the cathedral-like **St Mary's Church at Mountain Road** [14.33], Manitoba, built in 1924-5 and tragically burned in 1966. Constructed entirely of wood, the ground plan—based on the Greek cross—rose through many stages to its climax

14.33 St Mary's Church, Mountain Road, Manitoba, 1924-5. PAM/A.S. Mountain Road 1/N10728.

in a large central onion dome. Four smaller cupolas capped the arms of the cross. The complexity of the ground plan, served by ten entrances, suggested that Ruh's ambition as a builder may have exceeded his sophistication as a designer, but the building made a striking impression.[60]

The Church of the Immaculate Conception at Cook's Creek [14.34], Manitoba (originally dedicated to St John the Baptist), begun in 1930 and not consecrated until 1952, goes even further in its scale and its elaboration of forms. The Ukrainian Catholic parish at Cook's Creek had grown to 350 families, and the two small earlier churches in the area were inadequate to serve them. As at Mountain Road, Father Ruh was appointed as the parish priest and worked alongside his parishioners in constructing the church.[61]

Built of brick, the Church of the Immaculate Conception is cruciform in plan, with the base some 140 feet by 100 feet (43 by 30 m)—large enough to accommodate one thousand worshippers. There are nine domes or cupolas—round rather than onion-shaped—one over each arm of the cross, one at each corner of the central crossing, and the central dome itself, which rises 114 feet (35 m) above the ground. The domes are said to symbolize the nine ranks of angels. The complex stacked massing—composed of transepts, apses, chapels, and other protuberances, and inspired by the Byzantine-Ukrainian tradition—creates a remarkable effect. Its dynamism seems more Baroque than medieval in feeling, though it does not lose sight of the source of inspiration: the grand Byzantine churches of Ukraine, such as Santa Sophia in Kiev (begun in 1037). The classical portico, with

14.34 Church of the Immaculate Conception, Cook's Creek, Manitoba, begun 1930. Manitoba Culture, Heritage and Citizenship, Historic Resources.

the wide spacing between the central columns, focuses the attention in a Baroque manner.

Father Ruh returned to Alberta to design **St Josaphat Ukrainian Catholic Cathedral [14.35]** on 97 Street

14.35 Interior, St Josaphat Ukrainian Catholic Cathedral, Edmonton, Alberta, 1939-44. Historic Sites and Archives Service, Alberta Community Development.

in Edmonton (1939-44). Built as a parish church, it was designated a cathedral in 1948, when Edmonton became the seat of a newly formed Ukrainian Catholic Exarchate. The plan is similar to that of the church at Cook's Creek, although when the urbane parishioners objected to the proposed height, Father Ruh lowered the seven cupolas and the roofs. The exterior walls are faced in patterned brick, and the cupolas are roofed in copper. The impressive vaulted and domed interior is painted with a rich decorative program that was added in the 1950s. It includes a *Last Judgment* by J. Bucmaniuk, with Stalin and Hitler among those being cast into Hell, and the artist and his mother among the throng ascending to Heaven.[62]

Though largely self-trained as an architect, Father Ruh made a remarkable contribution to Canadian church building. Using the developing folk tradition of Prairie Ukrainian churches, and introducing his romantic vision of the historic churches of the Old Country, he far exceeded the ambitions and scale of the previous generation of builders. The dynamic compositions of his large 'prairie cathedrals' are as Baroque in spirit as they are Byzantine in inspiration. They stretch traditional forms in a manner that goes far beyond the precedent of history. The result was a unique attempt to create a distinctive—and contemporary—cultural and regional architectural style.

The late-classical revivals

Between the wars, styles inspired by classical antiquity continued to be employed, along with those derived from the Middle Ages. Public buildings, in particular, adopted the language of classicism. The language might be based on the architecture of ancient Greece and Rome (the Neoclassical Revival); or it could be closer to that of the European revival of antiquity in the fifteenth to seventeenth centuries (the Late Renaissance and Baroque Revivals); or to the eighteenth century (Georgian Revival). The differences among these 'dialects' may appear quite distinctly in sophisticated architect-designed buildings; but frequently the classical language was loosely adopted, making precise classification impossible—and inappropriate. This section looks at several buildings in the classical modes, and shows the range of types and styles.

The predominant style was the Neoclassical Revival. It represented a later and more refined version of Beaux-Arts Classicism, similar in historical decorative vocabulary but much simpler in effect and less bombastic in manner. Plain wall surfaces were admissible—indeed favoured—with ornament

focused around entrances. Windows and doors were more often capped by flat lintels than round arches, reflecting a preference for Greek over Roman sources.

As we have seen, Beaux-Arts Classicism had been the preferred style for urban railway stations in the pre-war period. The Union Stations in Winnipeg [**9.12**], Ottawa, and Toronto [**9.13**], and the two stations in Vancouver, were early and successful landmarks in the style. At a symbolic level, these large terminals were the gateways to Canada, associated with the gates and grand public structures of the ancient world; at a utilitarian level they housed complicated circulation plans that accommodated hordes of travellers.

In the twenties and thirties the classical muse continued to inspire urban stations, but in the less-ostentatious attire of the Neoclassical Revival. The second CNR **station in Edmonton [14.36]**—designed by John Schofield, 1927-8—was similar in scale to the earlier Ottawa station, but seemed modest by

14.36 CNR Station, Edmonton, Alberta, 1927-8. PAA/Alfred Blyth Collection/BL.193.

comparison. A pair of Greek Doric columns marked the entrance, the metal canopy featured a row of acroteria, and a succession of pilasters separating the windows along the sides provided a dim echo of Toronto's grand entrance colonnade. The dominant characteristic, however, was not this classical ornament, but rather the plain walls of dark red brick (concealing a reinforced-concrete structure). Simplicity, not complexity, provided the theme. The imagery lacked the conviction of Beaux-Arts Classicism: classical forms were adopted like well-worn clothes—familiar and comfortable, but lacking in impact.

In 1945-6 the Edmonton station was somewhat disfigured by the addition of a third storey. A broad central concourse rose the full height of the two-storey

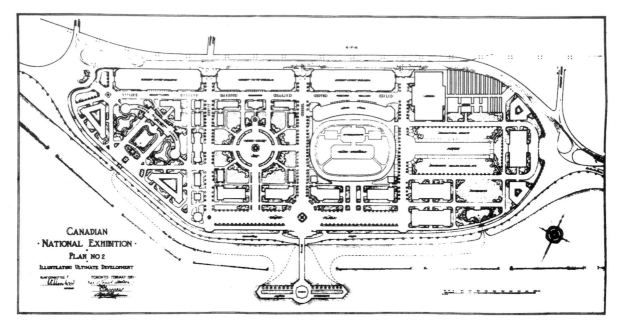

building and was flanked by a restaurant on one side, the ticket window on the other, and offices on the upper floor. Twenty years later it was demolished, to make way for the tall CN Tower and the present third station (Abugov and Sunderland, 1965-6).[63]

Classical forms appeared in several other building-types, including exhibition structures. This is hardly surprising, since the main impetus for the late-classical revivals came from the Chicago World's Fair of 1893, whose ambitious building program aroused the American taste for Beaux-Arts planning and had a lasting influence on North American architecture. In 1915 the Panama-Pacific International Exposition in San Francisco reinforced the link to classical planning and styles—and the association continued during the inter-war period.

The **Canadian National Exhibition [14.37]** in Toronto—the world's largest annual exhibition, founded in 1878—underwent a major building program in the 1920s. The ensuing work clearly reflected the prevailing classicism of the time and the persistence of Beaux-Arts planning after the First World War. Architects Chapman and Oxley—Chapman, it will be recalled, had studied at the École des Beaux-Arts—prepared a series of site plans and designed several new buildings. One plan organized the large site by means of a formal, although not symmetrical, cross-axial system. The principal east-west axis led through the amusement area and a large parterre (called the music court) to the principal grandstand. Parallel roadways served the exhibit buildings, and

14.37 Site plan, Canadian National Exhibition, Toronto, Ontario. 1921. From Howard D. Chapman, *Alfred Chapman: The Man and His Work*, 1978.

the main north-south route terminated in a casino on the Lake Ontario shore. Another formal parterre, arranged on a 45-degree angle, rationalized the irregularities of the western edge of the site.

Chapman and Oxley's plan was only partially realized, and two of the firm's four executed exhibition buildings (the Pure Food and Electrical Engineering Buildings, 1922 and 1928 respectively) have been demolished, but their legacy remains in the Ontario Government Building (1927)—and especially in the **Princes' Gates [14.38]** of 1927, the imposing structure that forms the grand eastern entrance to the site, facing downtown Toronto (it does not appear on the illustrated site plan). Named in honour of two sons of George v, Prince Edward (the Prince of Wales) and Prince George—who in August 1927 officially opened it (as well as Union Station)—the Princes' Gates are a tribute to the continuing domination of imperial classicism. They consist of a central triumphal arch (crowned by a Winged Victory representing progress and advance), flanked on either side by a broad colonnade that terminates at each end in a curved pylon (echoing Bernini's piazza in front of St Peter's in Rome). The entire structure, which is 300 feet (92 m) wide, is built of cement stone provided by Peerless Artificial Stone Limited of Toronto. Despite its overt historicism and sculptural flourishes (cast from moulds by sculptor

14.38 Princes' Gates, Canadian National Exhibition, Toronto, Ontario, 1927. CNE Archives/General Photograph Collection.

Charles McKechnie) atop the central and end features, the design continues the tendency towards restraint. Acknowledging its 'slightly severe character', Chapman explained that his choice of style was motivated by the timelessness of classical design:

14.39 National Research Council, Ottawa, Ontario, 1930-2. Photograph by Hellmut W. Schade, 1985.

The general architectural treatment is in a late Roman character. A more or less classic style was chosen owing to the fact that the Canadian National Exhibition is a permanent Exhibition and it was thought advisable to avoid styles that were liable to become obsolete with the change of fashion or public taste.[64]

Indeed, classicism provided a universal vocabulary that would not quickly go out of date and could be used to express imperial might and solidarity. This belief could be seen in official architecture throughout the British Empire, from the grandiose work of Sir Herbert Baker (1862-1946) in South Africa, which asserted British dominion during the period of the Boer War, to the elegantly monumental buildings in New Delhi, the new capital city of India—designed by Sir Edwin Lutyens (1869-1944), Baker, and others, and built from 1912 to 1929. The Princes' Gates echo some of the refinement of Lutyens' work—a further simplification of form that would blossom in the 1930s, and will be introduced below as Modern Classicism.

The classical language was also adopted by the Canadian government (though the Château Style had its proponents, it never became universal). Sproatt and Rolph, the champions of the Late Gothic Revival, used a version of the Neoclassical Revival (one that might best be described as a Late Baroque Revival) for the **National Research Council [14.39]** in Ottawa (1930-2), the headquarters for scientific research. Presenting a broad façade to Sussex Drive, the building is divided by three pavilions into four wings (with the two central wings having a row of giant engaged Doric columns spanning the first and second floors). While the design looks back to the French Baroque architecture of Louis XIV as it was revived during the nineteenth century (though it lacks the mansard roofs and picturesque skyline of the Second Empire style), the formality and breadth of scale are reminders of the earlier Beaux-Arts Classicism. But the composition (as in the Late Gothic Revival of Hart House) is more restrained: the skyline is uninterrupted, and the treatment approaches monotony.[65]

Eric Arthur, in his review of the 1932 RAIC exhibition, was highly disparaging of the National Research Council building. After praising Hart House, he dismissed the NRC's style as 'archaic' and stated that, rather than expressing the 'light and power and the majesty of science . . . its great façade suggests nothing but the civil service.' He continued: 'One wonders what made Mr Sproatt hitch his Gothic waggon to a 19th century classic star.'[66]

Banks, trust companies, and insurance firms continued to use the classical modes, which inspired confidence among investors and clients by symbolizing wealth, integrity, and—above all—stability. Born in the Romantic Victorian age, these associations continued unabated between the wars. In the major cities new building programs often included large amounts of speculative office space, enabling institutions to build ever higher and larger in their desire to impress by sheer size. As a result, priorities shifted, despite the continued classical vocabulary. Tall towers became the focus of attention, while the temple component was relegated to the base. Columns, pilasters, cornices, parapet ornament, and other bits and pieces from antiquity might be applied liberally, and often with considerable compositional skill, but with far less intensity or conviction than in the previous generation.

Montreal's **Sun Life Assurance Company Building** [14.40] illustrates the trend. One of several Canadian claimants to the title of largest or tallest building in the British Empire, it took shape in stages over the course of a decade and a half. Darling and Pearson were the architects. The first portion, erected in 1914-18 (at the very end of the heyday of Beaux-Arts Classicism), was seven storeys high, dominated by a seemingly endless row of giant Corinthian columns extending to the top of the fourth floor. In this incomplete stage it resembled the familiar temple-bank form that prevailed during the pre-war period.

Immense additions followed. The first enlarged the seven-storey building to fill an entire block of Dorchester Street (now Boulevard René-Lévesque) at Dominion Square. In this form the building won first prize in the financial class of the Ontario Association of Architects' exhibition of 1926. A writer for the *Journal* of the Royal Institute of British Architects called it 'one of the finest *modern* office buildings in America.'[67] Eric Arthur was less generous in his criticism:

> The Sun Life Building is certainly everything that a great company could wish for. It has a certain dignity, but its manners might be improved. The building is a symbol of its boasted millions, and it is a model of efficiency and fire-proof construction. In its colossal temple front it is reminiscent of Imperial Rome. What other company with fewer millions could ever be noticed in its vicinity?

Arthur went on to complain of feeling 'insignificant' and 'mouse-like' when standing in front of the building—the same sensation that so many people have experienced in the shadow of the many high-rises that followed. Arthur described the excessive height of the columns as 'so forbidding', concluding: 'I see no particular merit in mere size.'[68]

By 1931 the Sun Life Building had grown to 24 storeys, its increased height achieved with a tower set-back from the sides. It maintained the classical theme by rising in layers, with windows (having classical proportions and detailing) climaxing in a colonnade of paired Ionic columns; above the cornice the building continues to rise through six attic storeys set back in pairs. The overall impression of the tower portion, however, is no longer temple-like: it is rather one of flat and relatively unornamented wall surfaces that create an effect of verticality. The original block now reads as a sturdy podium rather than as a grandiose temple. The completed building would surely have made Arthur feel even more mouse-like, because he would have been dwarfed not only by the columns at its base, but by the tower.

For the benefit of those who were impressed by statistics, it was noted that the total weight of the structure exceeded a quarter of a million tons, including almost 19,000 tons (17,200 tonnes) of structural steel, 43 tons (39 tonnes) of Stanstead granite (covering the steel frame), and 14 million bricks.[69]

One classical-revival style that was particularly popular in the United States was the Georgian Revival, which reinterpreted buildings of the

14.40 Sun Life Assurance Company Building, Montreal, Quebec, 1914-31. Photograph by Hellmut W. Schade, 1980.

American colonial and federal periods, giving them a new patriotic meaning. Its beginnings have been traced to a pair of houses in Newport and Boston designed in the 1880s by McKim, Mead and White.[70] The style peaked before the First World War, and received a second impetus from the massive restoration and reconstruction of Williamsburg, Virgina, begun in 1926 under the patronage of John D. Rockefeller, Jr. Colonial Williamsburg also aroused Canadian interest in Georgian architecture. In the late 1920s Georgian Revival buildings, for both public and residential use, began appearing right across the country. The **Courthouse in Weyburn [14.41]**, Saskatchewan, is especially impressive. Designed by Maurice Sharon and built in 1928, it is a symmetrical two-storey brick building with stone trim and a gable roof. The Adam-inspired blind arches surrounding the ground-storey windows, the second-floor shutters, the columned portico, the dormers, the cupola, and the heavy parapet walls at the ends all look back to the English Colonial buildings of the American seaboard (particularly those of Virginia)—and, to a lesser extent, to their source, the seventeenth-century architecture of Britain. If it seems unusual that Saskatchewan should follow so American a model, it may be recalled that the Prairie legislative buildings also had American prototypes. But Sharon could have been aware of a source within his own province. The Land Titles Offices in Yorkton and Battleford—built in 1907 and 1908, respectively, to designs by Darling and Pearson—are tidy red-brick buildings with large arched windows, stone quoins, and cornices inspired by the Adamesque strain of Georgian architecture (buildings that would not have been out of place in Niagara-on-the-Lake a century earlier).[71]

Another American-inspired revival whose sources reach back to the classical tradition was the Spanish Colonial Revival. In the first third of the century two closely related strains of Spanish architecture became popular: the simple structures of the Franciscan missions in California, and the more elaborate buildings of the Spanish Baroque in Mexico. Although in California (where they began) the revivals of the two are easily distinguished—the former is called the Mission Style, the latter the Spanish Colonial Revival—by the time they reached Canada there was little to differentiate them.

Buildings in the style are characterized by broad expanses of white stucco wall, red pantile ('Spanish tile') roofs, and the frequent use of arches, columns, wrought-iron railings, and curved gables. The Spanish Colonial Revival was most common in the late 1920s

14.41 Courthouse, Weyburn, Saskatchewan, 1928. Photograph by B. Weston, 1971. SAB/71-219-67.

in British Columbia, which continued to look south for inspiration. The **Besner Block [14.42]** in Prince Rupert, BC—built in 1928—uses Spanish forms on a three-storey downtown retail-and-apartment building named for the sometime bootlegger Olier Besner, who retained Vancouver architect H.H. Gillingham (1876-1930). The distinguishing features are the stucco walls, the decorative tile overhangs of the roof

14.42 Besner Block, Prince Rupert, British Columbia, 1928. Photograph by Harold Kalman, 1982.

14.43 School, Punnichy, Saskatchewan, 1920s. From *JRAIC*, November 1927.

(the actual roof is flat), the stepped and curved gable-like parapets that separate them, and the arched surrounds and colonettes of the top-floor windows. The central feature is an open arch that reveals a deep light well, a feature that we saw being introduced in apartment buildings at the beginning of the century. The nearby Capitol Theatre (W. Dodd and Co., 1926-8) also adopts features of the style.[72]

While each of the classical revivals had archetypes that displayed its characteristic features, many classically inspired buildings are not clear-cut examples of any particular revival style. Sources were frequently blended and diluted. Architects and builders, particularly in the public arena, placed more importance on achieving functional and cost-effective design than on reviving historical models. After the First World War historicism lost much of its intensity and conviction, and so its forms were used to satisfy a lingering need for variety and decoration—and perhaps nostalgia—rather than to create a faithful reflection of a particular style.

The struggle between functionalism and historicism may be seen in the **school at Punnichy** [14.43], Saskatchewan, erected in the 1920s to designs by F.H. Portnall (1886-1976) of Regina. Typical of small schools across Canada, it has four classrooms, with one located on either side of a central hall on each of the two floors. The staircase is enclosed within the central projection, and a teachers' room and library

occupy a smaller projection at the rear. Brick was chosen to reduce the risk of fire; the checkerboard patterns in the spandrels between the windows enliven its surface. The only historical quotations are the stylized Palladian window illuminating the stairs, and the hints of buttresses beside it and at the corners. The former was derived from classical sources and the latter from Gothic, revealing a lack of interest in historical consistency. The overall composition has Georgian overtones (the projecting central gable of an Ontario Georgian house comes to mind), but Portnall would likely have argued that the arrangement best met the needs of the functional program.[73]

Theatres The discipline and restraint that characterized the revivals, and even the design of the Punnichy school, had an antithesis in the extravagance and opulence of the 'picture palaces' that were built between the wars. Impresarios such as Marcus Loew, Alexander Pantages, and B.F. Keith (based in the United States) developed multimillion-dollar empires that circulated moving pictures and vaudeville acts around the continent. A Canadian equivalent were the Allen theatres, which were taken over in 1923 by Famous Players Canadian Corporation. All built chains of movie houses, each striving to construct larger, more ornate, and more memorable showplaces than its competitors'. Many adopted variants of the classical manner, while others favoured exotic styles, producing 'atmospheric' effects inspired by stage sets that transported patrons to a fantasyland that was far away in time and place. 'We sell tickets to theatres,' explained Marcus Loew, 'not movies.'[74]

The first deluxe moving-picture theatre in North America, as well as one of the first cinemas of any scale, was the **Ouimetoscope [14.44]** in Montreal, built in 1907 by L. Ernest Ouimet. Designed with a balcony, boxes, and an orchestra pit, the theatre had 1,000 plush seats [14.45]—the most expensive of which were reserved—that sold for 35 cents in a day when the competition charged only 5 or 10 cents. Six reels of moving pictures alternated with live shows, and a seven-piece orchestra provided music. The brick front on Ste Catherine Street had the appearance of a commercial building, although a crown-like peak over its rounded corner bay was the precursor of the tall marquee. The building survives at 1206 Ste Catherine East and is used as a repertory movie house.[75]

American architects developed this building-type to palatial splendour, and several designed theatres in Canada. Thomas W. Lamb (1871-1942) of New York—the designer of that city's Regent Theatre (1913), which is usually cited as being the first purpose-built deluxe movie theatre (although the Ouimetoscope preceded it), and of several play-houses, including the Ziegfeld, and the second Madison Square Garden—created at least sixteen movie houses in Canada. They included Loew's Yonge Street, Toronto—with two separate houses, one, the Winter Garden, above the other (1913-14, restored and now known as the Elgin and Winter Garden Theatres); Loew's Uptown, Toronto (1920); the Loew's Theatres in Montreal (1917), Ottawa (1919-20, later the Capitol), and London (later the Capitol); the Temple Theatre (later the Capitol) in Brantford; and the Capitol Theatres in Winnipeg, Calgary, Vancouver, and Victoria—the last four built for Famous Players Canadian Corporation. Most of these were theatres intended for vaudeville, but they were adapted for cinema. Lamb's Canadian theatres were decorated in the Adam Style, a variant of the Georgian Revival based on the exquisite motifs popularized by the late-eighteenth-century Scottish architects Robert and James Adam. Lamb explained that he 'felt that this style of decoration most ably reflected the moods and preferences of the American people.' He saw it as having a 'living room' style that was elegant, without being intimidating.[76]

14.44 Ouimetoscope, Montreal, Quebec, 1907. NAC/Moving Image and Sound Archives/Stills Collection/2508.

Lamb's **Pantages Theatre, Toronto [14.46]**, of 1920, was the largest in Canada, with 3,626 seats. The deep, domed auditorium has a gilded proscenium, boxes framed by columns and curtains, and brocaded walls. The plaster dome is composed of

14.45 Interior of the Ouimetoscope, Montreal, Quebec, 1907. NAC/Moving Image and Sound Archives/Stills Collection/2507.

14.46 Auditorium, Pantages Theatre, Toronto, Ontario, 1920. Courtesy Philip B. Jackson.

743

concentric elements interlaced with delicate radiating filigree work. A large chandelier hangs from its centre. The principal entrance is on Yonge Street, a busy commercial artery, whereas the large auditorium is situated on less expensive land facing adjacent Victoria Street. This arrangement, typical of many big-city theatres, was solved by the creation of a long, elegant corridor-like entrance (crossing an alley) that was originally treated as a series of vaulted spaces, with engaged columns along the sides framing murals and mirrors. This leads to a domed elliptical lobby, whose ceiling features cameo-like roundels, and then on to the auditorium. The elaborate colour scheme features gold, ivory, and blue. In 1972 the Pantages (by then called the Imperial) was divided into six cinemas (by Mandel Sprachman, b. 1925)—a fate shared by many large vaudeville and movie houses as television emptied them. In 1988-9, however, it was restored to its original state as a single house and theatre (whose first production was *The Phantom of the Opera*), and the name 'Pantages' was returned to it by Cineplex Odeon Corporation. David K. Mesbur was the architect, and Commonwealth Historic Resource Management Limited acted as restoration consultant.[77]

Another leading theatre architect who worked in Canada was C. Howard Crane (1885-1952) of Detroit, the preferred architect of Allen Theatre Enterprises. The many Allen Theatres included those in Toronto (1917, later the Tivoli), London (1918, later the Capitol), Winnipeg (1919, later the Metropolitan), Vancouver (1919, later the Strand), Calgary (1921, later the Palace), and the Palace in Montreal (1921). Crane's handling of the Adam Revival was more delicate and truer to Georgian sources than Lamb's.

Architect B. Marcus Priteca (1890-1971)—like Lamb, a Scot by birth—caught the eye of Seattle impresario Alexander Pantages and was retained to design almost all the theatres in his large western circuit, which took shape in a Neoclassical manner, with gleaming white terra-cotta façades that came to be known as 'Pantages Greek' (Pantages was Greek by birth).[78] Those in Canada included the Pantages Theatres in Edmonton (1913, later the Strand; demolished), Vancouver (1916-17, later the Majestic; demolished), Calgary, and Winnipeg. The Toronto Pantages, a lone eastern outpost, was likely the only theatre in the chain not designed by Priteca.

In the mid-1920s Priteca turned to a more exotic manner. The 2,800-seat **Orpheum Theatre [14.47]** on Granville Street in Vancouver (with Frederick J. Peters, Associate Architect, 1926-7), operated by the Chicago-based Orpheum Circuit (and opened in the

14.47 Orpheum Theatre, Vancouver, British Columbia, 1926-7. Photograph by Stuart Thomson, 1929. Vancouver Public Library/11036.

year in which talking-pictures were introduced), displays a decorative scheme derived from the Spanish Baroque, with exuberant arches, tiered columns, and interlaced mouldings executed in marble, travertine, cast stone, and plaster. It presents a narrow front to Granville Street, with a corridor leading to the lavishly decorated lobby and auditorium. The decorative work was executed by Anthony B. Heinsbergen, a frequent Priteca collaborator, who painted the allegorical scene in the dome. The auditorium is comparatively intimate in scale for so large a theatre, a result of the balcony's being extended further forward than usual and the omission of boxes, with only a grille concealing the organ pipes inserted between the balcony and the proscenium. In 1975-7 the City of Vancouver restored the Orpheum (Thompson, Berwick, Pratt and Partners, with Paul Merrick as the principal designer), and it is now

14.48 Empress Theatre, Montreal, Quebec, 1927-8. From *JRAIC*, November 1928.

14.49 Fire curtain in the auditorium, Empress Theatre, Montreal, Quebec, 1927-8. From *JRAIC*, November 1928.

the permanent home of the Vancouver Symphony Orchestra. An elderly Tony Heinsbergen supervised the redecoration.[79]

The most exotic theatre in the country was Montreal's 1,550-seat **Empress Theatre** [**14.48**], designed by J. Alcide Chaussé (1868-1944) for Confederation Amusements. Built in 1927-8, it adopted the Egyptian Revival (inspired by the discovery of Tutankhamen's tomb in 1922), which was used for other theatres as well—notably Grauman's Egyptian Theatre in Hollywood (1922, demolished; designed by Meuer and Holler, who also produced the more celebrated Grauman's Chinese Theatre in 1927). At the Empress an Egyptian theme was maintained inside and out. Exterior decorative motifs—lotus columns, sphinx heads, winged scarabs, and bas-relief friezes—were inspired by Egyptian architecture. The conceit was carried much further inside, where the **auditorium** [**14.49**] resembled the courtyard of an Egyptian palace. On the upper walls, painted views of the Nile were framed between pilasters, as if the landscape were seen from a building sited

on its banks. The lower walls simulated the rusticated stone blocks of those of an Egyptian palace. The proscenium was composed of Egyptian columns topped by an elaborate corbelled architrave and a painted frieze. On either side of the opening stood a life-size figure of a woman tipping a vase towards a splashing fountain, and the grille for the organ pipes above the statues was decorated with a lotus motif. Gold, silver, rich blues, and reds provided scrumptious colour. Even the asbestos fire-curtain was painted in false perspective, giving an illusion of the continuation of the courtyard. The Empress was a truly 'atmospheric' theatre, where 'our fancy is free to conjure endless tales of romance'—in the words of the best designer of atmospherics, American architect John Eberson. Another victim of television, the Empress became a cabaret in 1963 and a multiple-cinema in 1968.[80]

The period house

During the affluent years of the late 1920s romance also had a place in the residences of well-to-do Canadians: the free use of historical styles in the search for a desired effect—or a wished-for fantasy—was evident in domestic architecture.[81] Although several period styles used for public buildings appeared in houses, the most popular among those built for affluent Canadians was the Georgian (or Late Georgian) Revival. The style was popular in the US before the First World War, but it became fashionable in Canada only in the 1920s. The principal

sources—particularly in Ontario—were Georgian Britain and the Colonial and Federal styles in the US. The effect achieved a strong sense of formality and a restrained decorative program that used numerous classically derived features.

Vincent Massey, who was Canada's Minister (ambassador) in Washington at that time, used the Georgian Revival for his country estate, **Batterwood House [14.50]**, at Canton, Ontario, designed by the Toronto firm of A.S. Mathers (1895-1965) and Eric W. Haldenby (1893-1971) and built in 1927-9. Massey purchased the property—located east of Toronto and north of Port Hope—in 1919 and immediately began work on a comprehensive series of gardens, which were quite grown by the time the house was completed. The red-brick house, trimmed with Indiana limestone, rises two storeys, with an attic floor contained within the steep roof. The entrance faces south and is framed by a pedimented and pilastered surround; the courtyard in front is defined by two projecting wings, the one at the right containing Massey's fine library. The projections are repeated at the rear in the form of large, curved bay windows that overlook a formal lawn and a picturesque rock garden. Behind the apparent symmetry is a highly irregular plan that responded well to the needs of the household. The entrance-hall is off-centre, reached from a vestibule; a large living-room (panelled in Canadian pine) extends to the

14.50 Batterwood House, Canton, Ontario, 1927-9. From *JRAIC*, December 1929/MTRL.

14.51 Gerald R. Larkin house, Toronto, Ontario, 1926. Photograph by William Dendy.

right (east); and a low kitchen wing projects at the left, hidden behind the plantings. The brick, the small-paned windows and dormers, and the sparse classical detail may owe something to the architecture of Upper Canada; but the principal derivation is from the eighteenth-century architecture of the US, popularized by the reconstruction of Colonial Williamsburg. Historical styles evidently continued to bear strong associations, as they had throughout the previous century, and Massey chose an entirely different source for Batterwood than for Hart House, out of respect for the distinct traditions of domestic and collegiate architecture. He acknowledged his strong feeling for Hart House, however, by taking the humble contractor's shed used in its construction and re-erecting it at Batterwood as a potting-shed beside the greenhouse.[82]

A particularly splendid Georgian Revival residence is the **Gerald R. Larkin house [14.51]** on Castle Frank Road in Toronto's exclusive Rosedale district, which was given the first award and medal of honour by the Toronto Chapter of the RAIC. Larkin was head of the Salada Tea Company; his father, Peter C. Larkin, had founded the firm and served as Canada's first

High Commissioner in London. Gerald Larkin built the house in 1926 to contain his collection of English and European art and furniture (much of which was donated to Trinity College and St Thomas's Anglican Church on his death), and as the setting for a gracious social life. His architects were George, Moorhouse, and King, who were responsible for a number of substantial Toronto-area residences in the 1920s and 1930s. Senior partner Allan George (1874-1961) had been trained in England (before working with Darling and Pearson, and Sproatt and Rolph), and was the son of English architect Sir Ernest George (1839-1922), the designer of fine neo-Georgian houses built at the turn of the century.[83]

The Larkin house is modelled on a moderate-sized English Georgian urban house of the eighteenth century. The principal elevation is two storeys high and seven bays wide, with the three central bays projecting and capped by a sculpted pediment; a balustrade forms a parapet on either side. The exterior is rendered in red brick, with quoins at the corners and a white-painted wood surround with a broken pediment (and hanging lantern) at the entrance. On the right, a more simply treated recessed wing contains the kitchen and bedrooms for four maids—an indication of the lifestyle within. Both inside and out, the craftsmanship is superb. Each of the principal public rooms was modelled on a different phase of English architecture: the library Jacobean in treatment, the living-room dominated by an Adam-style mantel, and the panelling of the dining-room carved in the manner of Grinling Gibbons.

The limited awareness of Ontario's architectural heritage is evident in a 1928 article by architect W.L. Somerville, a prolific designer of houses and president of the Ontario Association of Architects. He illustrated the Larkin house and drew attention to two strains of domestic architecture: 'the romantic or picturesque type of house [e.g. Late Gothic Revival or Tudor Revival] and . . . the formal'. He expressed a strong preference for the latter, claiming that 'the English Georgian and American Colonial are certainly our rightful heritage in Ontario.' He credited the recent publications of Eric Arthur with casting attention on early Ontario houses, which he saw as possessing the same Anglo-American character, but dismissed 'our own [Ontario] architectural heritage [as] meagre.'[84]

Far more attention was paid to regional traditions in Quebec, where they were very strong. The domestic architecture of New France was promoted as a prototype to be emulated. Research on historic buildings—particularly by Pierre-Georges Roy in Quebec

City and Ramsay Traquair at McGill University from the 1920s to the 1940s—led to a new awareness of the province's architectural heritage. However, as cultural and political differences rendered a strictly French model somewhat inappropriate for the English-speaking social élite, many architects working in Quebec developed a blend of French and Anglo-American sources.

The **A.J. Nesbitt house [14.52]** on Forden Crescent in Westmount, the upper-income suburb of Montreal, is a fine example of this peculiarly Quebec synthesis. In designing this residence, which was built in 1926, for a wealthy broker, architects Harold E. Shorey (1886-1971) and S. Douglas Ritchie (1887-1959) combined the steep roof, heavy end gable walls, and randomly coursed stone of the Québécois cottage with the formal two-storey, five-bay façade, low wings at the sides, fan-lighted entrance, and shuttered windows of the Georgian house. They even went so far as to include double chimneys in the end walls, connected by a flat parapet—features that Traquair and others had noted as being characteristic of houses in the Montreal region in the seventeenth and eighteenth centuries. The result may be a curious compromise, but it achieves an appropriate British formality and grandeur, acknowledging the prevailing Georgian Revival, while also making references to the traditional local vocabulary.[85]

A similar stylistic mélange was achieved at the **Geoffrion house [14.53]**, which straddles the Montreal-Westmount boundary on Upper Belmont. This stalwart stone structure was built in 1930-1 for Aimé Geoffrion, a distinguished lawyer—like his father, the Honourable C.A. Geoffrion—and professor of law at McGill University from 1905. It was designed by architects Louis-Auguste Amos (1869-1948) and his son Pierre-Charles Amos (1897-1976). The formal symmetry of the Georgian style is here modified not by Quebec tradition—despite the owner's being French Canadian—but rather by the Late Renaissance Revival. Fifteenth-century Italianate sources are seen in the projecting arched entry, the paired round-arched windows on the second floor, and the balustraded terrace, which address the steeply sloping site whose rear prospect faces the Oratoire Saint-Joseph. The fine detail includes projecting string-courses between the floors and incised colonettes in the corners. The architects' awareness of modernist tendencies is revealed in the simplicity of the massing, taut wall planes, and unifying hipped roof. Enlarged and altered internally over the years, the house is now owned by a religious order and used as a private school.[86]

14.52 A.J. Nesbitt house, Westmount, Quebec, 1926. From *JRAIC*, May 1928.

14.53 Geoffrion house, Westmount, Quebec, 1930-1. Photograph 1982. Communauté urbaine de Montréal.

14.54 Rio Vista, Vancouver, British Columbia, 1930. Photograph by John Roaf, 1973.

In British Columbia the prevailing modes remained the Tudor Revival—which had been popular since before the First World War—and the Spanish Colonial Revival, which was fashionable in California. In 1930 Harry F. Reifel, the son of a pioneer brewer and distiller and himself an alleged rum-runner during the American prohibition, built the sumptuous **Rio Vista** [14.54] on Vancouver's posh Southwest Marine Drive. The architect was the British-born Bernard C. Palmer (1875-1936), a former associate of the talented Samuel Maclure. Rio Vista's stucco walls, round arches, wrought-iron ornament, and red-tile roof are all characteristic of the Spanish Colonial Revival. The extravagantly landscaped grounds contain a bridge crossing a deep ravine, and an immense conservatory with a 'Pompeiian' pool. Reifel's brother George built, nearby, his own neo-Spanish house—called Casa Mia (1932), designed by a former Maclure partner, Ross A. Lort (1889-1968).[87]

The Spanish Colonial Revival also made a somewhat surprising appearance in a number of Ottawa houses designed by W.E. Noffke, a German-born but locally trained architect who returned to Ottawa in 1924 after a brief practice in Los Angeles, where he became infatuated with the California-based style. The best of the group is the Levi W. Crannell House (Noffke, Morin, and Sylvester, 1926) on Clemow Avenue, whose white stucco elevation is enlivened by twisted colonettes, a wrought-iron balcony, and other studied Spanish detail.[88]

Responses to Modernism

Not all Canadian buildings erected between the wars continued the stylistic revivals from the Victorian era. As Canadian architects gradually became aware of new work in the United States and Europe—and reacted to it in periodicals, in teaching, and (conservatively) in design—newer trends had a noticeable impact on building and theory in Canada.

Canadian architects maintained that their work was modern even when it was based on forms from the past. To them the word 'modern' meant 'of its time', or 'contemporary'. A 'modern' architect was therefore one who sought an appropriate expression of the day—whatever that might be—and used up-to-date building technology. In 1920s usage 'modern' was distinct from 'modernism' (or 'modernist'), which referred to a specific architectural doctrine of the European 'modern movement' that turned its back on historical precedent.

John M. Lyle (1872-1945)—a respected Toronto architect, teacher, and self-appointed authority within the architectural profession—expressed moderate views towards the modern movement that were agreeable to his colleagues, in a 1929 address to an RAIC luncheon in Toronto. Recently returned from a trip to France and England, where he spent his time looking at buildings, he had been

> particularly anxious to study the modern movement in architecture which is now sweeping over the world. The modern movement has, in my opinion, much to commend it. It might be described as a revolt against archeology in architecture, and while much of the work that has been done in this manner is thoroughly bad, there is also much that is very sound and very beautiful . . . . It is a movement that we Canadian architects might study to our advantage, and if we are to develop a Canadian note along modern lines, I should be inclined to follow the Swedish architects who are developing their modern architecture along national Swedish traditional lines.[89]

Three years later, in 1932, Lyle returned to the same theme at another talk to the Institute, in which he advocated a form of modernism that was tempered by conservatism—a typically Canadian non-committal approach:

> Nineteenth century eclecticism still has architectural Canada by the throat . . . It is not architecture but archeology, and I am firmly convinced

that future generations will regard the great mass of Canadian work as merely interesting specimens of craftsmanship, and not as creative works of art . . . . We need a tonic . . . .

This new medicine is called 'Modernism' . . . . The extreme modernist is, in my opinion, equally at fault with the extreme traditionalist, in that he is trying to tie up architecture to a definite set of formulas . . . . If, however, you look at the modern movement as a new spirit of design and a release from the historical styles of the past, then I see a germ of greatness which offers rewards to the skilful designer.

While we may agree with the extreme modernist of the engineering view-point, that certain types of buildings lend themselves to a blocky, bald treatment and the elimination of all ornament, we most certainly do not accept this point of view as the last word in the development of a new architecture. If this conception of architecture was to dominate, we would have no national or distinctive architecture, all architecture would look alike. It would become international and the slab-sided box outlines of Germany and France would be identical with those of Canada and the United States.[90]

Lyle was right. We do consider much Canadian architecture of the 1920s to lack creativity, and modernist architecture did lead to an 'International Style'. The term was coined, in that same year of 1932, for an exhibition of the new architecture—held at the Museum of Modern Art in New York—in which the buildings looked alike from one country to another.

This section examines differing Canadian responses to the modern movement. It begins with the Canadian rendition of the Prairie Style; continues with the modified version of the Neoclassical Revival, known as Modern Classicism; and finally turns to the bolder design inspired by Art Deco. Canadian work in the International Style is treated in Chapter 15.

The Prairie Style

A bold new approach to design emerged in the American Midwest in the first decade of the twentieth century. Created primarily by the brilliant American architect Frank Lloyd Wright (1867-1959), and spread beyond Chicago by a number of Wright's colleagues and admirers (collectively known as the Prairie School), the Prairie Style was intended primarily for residences, although the manner was adapted for larger buildings as well. Responding to the flat Prairie landscape, the style was characterized by a dominant horizontality, which was seen in low massing, broad and gently sloping roofs, clearly defined parapets, ribbon windows, belt-courses, and other linear elements. Chimneys, piers, and mullions often provided a perpendicular counterpoint. Wood, plaster, and brick were the most commonly used materials, and plans were more open than previously, with wings often radiating from a central core. Ornament resulted from varying colours or textures, and enriched surfaces—avoiding direct quotations from historical sources. The Prairie Style also brought about significant changes in internal planning, opening up the house in a dramatic new manner.

Wright's work became widely known, through both the American popular press (several designs appeared in the *Ladies' Home Journal*) and the European architectural press (Ernst Wasmuth, of Berlin, published Wright's work in 1910). As a result, his revolutionary manner became an important ingredient of the emerging International Style. Though the Prairie Style brushed Canada gently just before and during the First World War, and its impact was slight, its use marked the first Canadian venture in a decidedly modern expression of design.

Frank Lloyd Wright had a brief Canadian career as a result of his friendship with Francis C. Sullivan (1882-1929), an Ottawa-based architect who trained with Moses Edey and then worked in Wright's office for several months in 1911. The two were associated on a handful of Canadian projects, which Wright exhibited at the Chicago Architectural Club in 1914. Only one seems to have been built: the **Banff Pavilion** [14.55], a recreational facility, on the Bow River in Banff, Alberta (1911-13), that was demolished in 1939. The commission presumably came about as a result of Sullivan's having worked with the Department of Public Works. The drawings, which survive in the National Archives of Canada, are signed by 'Frank Lloyd Wright and Fras. C. Sullivan: Associate Architects: Ottawa: Ontario'.[91]

The Banff Pavilion was 200 feet (60 m) long and quite low, its horizontality emphasized by the massing, the rough-sawn wood siding, the continuous row of leaded-glass windows above the walls, the uninterrupted low hipped roof, and the secondary hipped roof over the clerestory. Stone chimneys and piers provided vertical accents. The **interior** [14.56] was dominated by a row of open wood trusses, with the rustic stonework of the fireplaces and piers forming a handsome contrast with the dominant wood. The plan was based on that of Wright's (Illinois)

14.55 Banff Pavilion, Banff, Alberta, 1911-13. The Frank Lloyd Wright Foundation 1957.

River Forest Tennis Club (1906), and the tiers of broad hipped roofs recall his Robie House in Chicago (1908-9). The Banff Pavilion, therefore, embodied the innovations of Wright's Prairie Style.

Whatever Sullivan's role in the design of the Banff Pavilion may have been, he was an accomplished

14.56 Interior, Banff Pavilion, Banff, Alberta, 1911-13. Whyte Museum of the Canadian Rockies/Peter and Catharine Whyte Collection/v683 NA66-1471.

designer in his own right, adapting the Prairie Style to the greater verticality and massiveness characteristic of Canadian architecture. The **Edward P. Connors house [14.57]**, built in 1914-15 on Huron Street in Ottawa, reveals the kind of synthesis Francis Sullivan could accomplish at his best. The familiar horizontal lines appear in the flat roof over the entrance, in the forceful eaves of the roof and dormer, and in the wood belt-course that divides the brick ground floor from the stucco above. In contrast to Wright's work, the verticals are equally (if not more) emphatic, and are seen in the entrance piers, the stalwart chimneys, and the ends of the side walls,

14.57 Edward P. Connors house, Ottawa, Ontario, 1914-15. Photograph by John Roaf, 1982.

which project forward as brick piers topped by urns. The steep slope of the gable roof follows local tradition. While the Connors house reveals a masterly blending of the new Prairie Style with Ontario's Victorian vernacular, it expresses a 'modern' vocabulary that avoids direct historical references.[92]

This same fusion is seen in Sullivan's elegant, yet eccentric, church of Sainte-Claire de Goulbourne (1915) near Dwyer Hill, just west of Ottawa, in which a steep gable roof is set on low stucco walls, pierced

by a row of windows and punctuated by a tall bell-tower.[93] Sullivan's productive period was short—mainly between 1911 and 1916. Plagued by failing health and other problems, he moved to the US in 1921 and died at Wright's winter camp in Arizona in 1929.

A few other architects of the Prairie School also worked in Canada. Leroy Buffington (1847-1931) of Minneapolis (who encountered the style late in his career), and the Chicago-trained John D. Atchison (1870-1959), both designed houses in Winnipeg—the Canadian city closest in spirit and topography to Chicago—that exemplified the Prairie School manner.[94]

Some architects who had no known contact with the American Midwest also turned to the Prairie Style. One was Marius Dufresne, whom we met as the city engineer and principal designer of the Montreal suburb of Maisonneuve [12.9]. The massing and detail of Dufresne's **Maisonneuve Fire Station [14.58]** of 1914-15 bears a close resemblance to Wright's Unity Temple (1906) in Oak Park, Illinois. The blocky composition (doubled at Maisonneuve, with a hose tower between the two halves), the corner piers, the clerestory windows separated by ornamented piers and capped by assertive flat roofs, and the cubic central mass, all acknowledge Wright's familiar prototype. The Fire Station is constructed of stone (whereas Unity Temple used concrete, then a new material). Dufresne referred to a more traditional vocabulary in the new municipality's other

14.58 Maisonneuve Fire Station, Montreal, Quebec, 1914-15. Photograph 1979. Communauté urbaine de Montréal.

14.59 Alberta Temple of the Church of Jesus Christ of Latter-Day Saints, Cardston, Alberta, 1913-23. Courtesy the Church of Jesus Christ of Latter-Day Saints.

buildings, using Beaux-Arts Classicism for its Public Baths, and a Second Empire hybrid for the Public Market. He presumably turned to the Chicago source for the fire station as a modern means of expression appropriate to its motorized function (fire trucks were a significant innovation at the time), ironically making eclectic use of a decidedly non-eclectic source.[95]

A remarkable religious building that also acknowledges Wright's Unity Temple is the **Alberta Temple of the Church of Jesus Christ of Latter-Day Saints** [**14.59**], built at Cardston, Alberta, in 1913-23—the first Mormon temple to appear outside the US. Cardston had been settled by Mormons in 1887; and by 1912, when the Alberta Temple was proposed by the Church hierarchy in Salt Lake City, some 7,000 Mormons were living in Southern Alberta. An architectural competition among fourteen American firms led to the selection of a boldly modern design by the young American architects Hyrum Pope (1876-1939) and Harold Burton (1887-1969). The Utah press reported, in exasperation, first that 'The architecture of the proposed building cannot be identified exactly with any historically accepted style', and later—

evidently unfamiliar with the Prairie Style sources— that it 'might be termed a strictly "Mormon" style of architecture'.[96]

Work on the Alberta Temple began in 1913 and continued for a decade. The blocky, almost abstract, composition is composed of crisply delineated vertical buttress-like slabs tied together by strong horizontal members. The Temple is cruciform in plan, each arm containing one of the four ordinance (instruction) rooms, with shallow wings containing stairways and minor rooms projecting obliquely from the interior angles. The central core encloses the celestial room at the top. Each room is a few steps higher than its predecessor, reinforcing the idea of progression rooted in the Temple ceremony. The general massing and the treatment of details, such as the narrow windows separated by piers, reveal Pope's and Burton's admiration for Wright's Unity Temple. The upper portions of some piers bear decoration reminiscent of Central American aboriginal temples, which Burton (and Wright) admired. The Temple has a structural steel frame, concrete slabs, and is faced with unpolished white granite. It is superbly sited at the crest of a gentle hill. In 1986 91 the Temple was renovated, some rooms were restored, and a new entry was built by Gowling and Gibb of Calgary.

The Prairie Style episode was important for Canadian architecture because it marked the first determined departure from historical precedent. However, the style never became widespread in Canada, nor did it appear in as aggressively a 'modern' mode as in the US. Nevertheless, it opened Canadian eyes to the possibilities of new forms of expression.

Modern Classicism

Most Canadian architects—including John Lyle—searched for ways of achieving modernity within a framework that would still accept tradition. Lyle's solution lay in

> new combinations of old forms and a new language of ornament . . . . [with] symbolism in the form of fresh, vital, contemporary decoration.... While we cannot claim, as yet, a distinctive Canadian style, may we not hope that this new freedom for the designer will sweep us along towards a national architecture.[97]

This focus on ornament within a classical framework was consistent with Lyle's background. Born in Belfast, he came to Hamilton, Ontario, as a child. His father was an energetic and cultured minister who rose to become moderator of the Presbyterian Church in Canada. The young John Lyle showed considerable talent for design, and nurtured this with an intense program of education. He followed his studies at the Hamilton Art School with a year at Yale University, and four years at the École des Beaux-Arts in Paris, where he was enrolled initially in the *atelier* of Jules Godefroy and Jacques Freynet, and then with Paul Blondel. He spent the years from 1896 to 1906 working with several leading classicist architectural firms in New York, first in the office of Howard and Cauldwell, and subsequently as a renderer for Carrère and Hastings, and for Warren and Wetmore.[98]

On Lyle's arrival in Toronto in 1906 his talents, training, and social background ensured his rapid rise in the profession. His early work in Toronto included the Royal Alexandra Theatre (1907); and participation in the Union Station [**9.13**, **14**] and the Toronto Stock Exchange (1912, demolished)—all examples of Beaux-Arts Classicism.

Among his many private and institutional clients, Lyle counted a number of banks. In his designs for a series of buildings for the Bank of Nova Scotia, we can see the transition to the style that we call Modern Classicism. The small branch of the Bank of Nova

14.60 Bank of Nova Scotia, Ottawa, Ontario, 1923-4. Photograph by Harold Kalman.

Scotia (1920) at St Andrews, New Brunswick, adopts the Georgian Revival—reflecting the Georgian tradition of St Andrews and the Maritimes—with red brick walls, white stone trim, a pedimented doorway, and tall arched windows.[99]

The **Bank of Nova Scotia in Ottawa [14.60]**, built in 1923-4 on Sparks Street, is a grander and more explicitly historicist exercise that blends the temple-bank of the Neoclassical Revival with the Georgian Revival (seen in the elevated first floor) and Beaux Arts Classicism (seen in the emphasis on the extremities). The ground floor is faced with rusticated masonry, and supports a powerful grouping of four Doric columns set *in antis* between bays,

14.61 Bank of Nova Scotia, Calgary, Alberta, 1929-30. Photograph 1930. Bank of Nova Scotia Archives.

with niches on either side containing bronze braziers and a cornice and parapet surmounting them. Over the entrance a frieze of ox skulls, joined by festoons, is taken from antiquity; on the other hand, the Doric frieze over the columns contains (in the metopes) symbols of Canadian history and prosperity, such as a log cabin and a wheat sheaf. (Here Lyle was beginning his search for a national architecture by using distinctly Canadian images in his decoration.) The muscular quality of Lyle's classical forms is complemented by the delicacy of detailing in carved stone (the friezes) and cast bronze (the grilles below the windows). Pleased with this design, Lyle used it as his diploma piece for admission to the Royal Canadian Academy.[100]

He was less pleased, however, when his friend

Omer Marchand, a fellow student at the École des Beaux-Arts, said of the bank: *'C'est très bien, mais c'est le goût anglais'* (it is English in taste); and when his colleague Mackenzie Waters said that the bank 'looks like a London street façade.' These comments made Lyle realize that the Georgian and Classical elements were more evident than he had intended, and set him thinking about the nature of 'modern Canadian architecture'.[101]

Some of the results of that thinking can be seen in the **Bank of Nova Scotia in Calgary [14.61]** on 8 Avenue sw, designed by Lyle shortly after his return from Europe, and built in 1929-30. Although the

755

elevations of the Ottawa and Calgary banks may appear similar in an outline drawing, they are worlds apart in execution and effect. The Calgary building is very flat, looking as if it had been pressed with an iron (or perhaps a steam-roller). The classical forms seem to be engraved in bas-relief. Columns have become pilasters, cornices project inches rather than feet, and the niches have gone. The banking hall, too, is severe in its rectilinearity, and its walls feature flat pilasters textured with incised reeding rather than traditional flutes. The low-relief wall—where the classical details are simplified and almost streamlined—is a vital characteristic of Lyle's approach to modernism, yet Lyle's bank has captured this essential quality without actually producing a modernist building.[102]

Another new feature of the Calgary bank is its almost complete reliance on a Canadian—and specifically Western—decorative vocabulary. The surround of the entrance door features prairie flowers; the ground-storey window reveals show Indians, Mounties, horses, and buffalo; the decorative panels over the windows of the *piano nobile* offer a wheat sheaf, a saddle, and gushing oil (oil had recently been discovered in Alberta); the window grilles are based on wheat tassels; and the capitals of the pilasters include anvils and gears. The iconography was contemporary and regional, but its didactic use to communicate cultural values was the method Lyle had learned at the École des Beaux-Arts. The architect explained that the bank

> is an attempt to . . . design a building in the modern manner with tradition as a background. While many of the forms used are reminiscent of the classical school, they vary greatly in form, proportion, and detail treatment.[103]

The Calgary bank represents a seminal example of an emerging style that we call Modern Classicism. Lyle was groping for a route that would take him from Beaux-Arts Classicism to modernism, and found it by reducing substantiality and emphasizing surface rather than bulk. As architectural critic and historian Trevor Boddy has noted: 'Lyle brought modernism, nationalism, and regionalism in architecture together in a synthesis all the more exciting for its instability.'[104] The building was recently sold by the Bank of Nova Scotia and—sadly—is now a disco.

In Lyle's **Head Office of the Bank of Nova Scotia in Halifax [14.62]**, designed in association with Andrew R. Cobb (1876-1943) of Halifax, Lyle repeated these innovations on a larger scale in a program that called for four storeys of offices above the bank-

14.62 Perspective of the Bank of Nova Scotia, Halifax, Nova Scotia, 1930. Bank of Nova Scotia Archives.

ing premises. A single entrance vestibule leads to both the splendid banking hall and the office elevators—now a common arrangement, but an innovation at the time. Built in 1930, it has the gracious elegance associated with Georgian architecture and that was expected of Lyle. As he explained:

> In designing the exterior we were anxious to strike a modern note but owing to the fact that the Parliament Building [Province House, 3.53] was just across the street we felt that certain characteristics of this very fine building should be echoed in the new building.[105]

The principal elevation on Hollis Street expands the composition seen at Calgary, so that the rusticated level rises the full height of the banking hall, and the pilasters frame the office bays below the cornice. The central portion of the elevation projects slightly forward. The grooves in the pilasters, the channels in the masonry, and indeed all of the edges appear to be razor-cut in the Bedford limestone, like the richly decorated octagonal coffers in the banking hall. The building's debts to tradition, however, were recognized, the Halifax *Star* noting that 'it fits gracefully into its surroundings'.[106]

The ambitious decorative program, executed with the help of sculptor Ira Lake, treated three themes: history, economic development, and floral, faunal, and marine motifs. No fewer than 86 of the last group appear, as Lyle noted:

. . . from the small trailing arbutus—the floral emblem of Nova Scotia—to the sunflower, and from the sea-gull to the Canada goose, the bear, the silver fox, the codfish and crab . . . . In every case we studied the natural forms, translating them into conventionalized ornament for wood, stone, plaster, bronze or iron. The ornament on the exterior stone work was treated in the modern manner, quite flat with softened arrises with occasional crisp, sharp notes as accents. The effect of this treatment in the wall is to make the ornament plastic in character and married to the wall surface without undue play of light and shade.[107]

Some decorative panels depict regional scenes, including one of the smelter at Sydney, rendered in a stylized expressionistic manner.

The significance of the building, and of Lyle's abundant and rather synthetic application of Canadian decorative motifs, has been well summarized by Alan Gowans:

It is perhaps appropriate that here, across the street from Province House where . . . the British classical tradition began, we should see it in a sense coming to an end. For the classical forms here are vestigial; they do not articulate the building or define its form, but are simply and obviously applied decoration—the classical spirit, in short, is gone, and its forms will soon follow.[108]

During the twenties John Lyle's buildings had developed from the Georgian and Neoclassical Revivals to Modern Classicism. The work of many other architects was evolving in much the same way, and by the early and mid-1930s buildings across the country displayed features of the new style. It has been called by many names, in addition to Modern Classicism—including 'Stripped Classicism', 'International Stripped Classicism', and 'Starved Classicism' (all references to its apparent insubstantiality). In the United States it is sometimes called the 'WPA Style' because it was used in many buildings constructed by the Works Progress Administration, a federal public agency established under the New Deal. (The terms 'Moderne' and 'Modernistic' are also used to describe the manner, but these words are more general in scope and refer also to distinct tendencies that are discussed below.) The principal features of Modern Classicism are the continuing use of a decorative vocabulary derived from classical antiquity, the apparent thinness of the wall in a manner expressing volume rather than mass, and the frequent reduction of form to its bare essentials—a reduction that was in part driven by cost-cutting measures of the Depression years.

Another talented architect whose work reflects the styles that were evolving between the wars was Montreal's Ernest I. Barott (1884-1966). His early work—produced in partnership with Gordon Blackader (1885-1916) and Daniel T. Webster (d. 1939?)—included the CPR Vancouver Station (1913-15), a fine example of Beaux-Arts Classicism. After Blackader died in action in the First World War, Barott continued to practise under the firm name Barott and Blackader.

His most accomplished exercise in Modern Classicism was the regional office of the **Bank of Montreal in Ottawa [14.63]** on Wellington Street, directly across from the Parliament Buildings. Barott won the commission in a competition whose principal assessor was Alexander B. Trowbridge of Washington, DC, a city that boasted fine examples of the classical style. The Ottawa bank, built in 1929-32, presents a modern rendition of the temple bank wrapped in a sublimely simple package. The severely cubic building is reminiscent of the late-eighteenth-century French 'Revolutionary' architecture of Étienne-Louis Boullée (1728-99) and Claude-Nicolas Ledoux (1736-1806). Described by Barott as 'a modern interpretation of Greek design', the bank presents façades to three streets, each articulated with a ribbon-thin cornice and pilasters that appear to be engraved in the Queenston limestone walls. Stanstead granite is used for the basement. Panels above the windows on all the façades are filled with exquisite allegorical scenes in low relief, carved by New York sculptor Emil Siebern, representing aspects of Canadian industry and commerce and the role of the Bank of Montreal in the community. The bronze and iron window grilles are equally elegant. Almost the entire building—except for the basement—is taken up by the grand, finely proportioned, and column-free (an admired stuctural achievement) **banking hall [14.64]**, which is covered by a gently coved coffered ceiling from which elongated chandeliers are suspended. The design was much praised by the architectural profession, and received the Royal Architectural Institute of Canada's Gold Medal for 1932.[109]

Modern Classicism became the preferred style of the corporate and government establishment. The route to its acceptance was led by the nation's staunchly conservative chartered banks, and was soon followed by other financial institutions, blue chip companies, and the public service. The style represents the conservative strain of modernism. Those clients who had long favoured one or anoth-

14.63 Bank of Montreal, Ottawa, Ontario, 1929-32. Photograph by John Roaf, 1982.

14.64 Banking hall, Bank of Montreal, Ottawa, Ontario, 1929-32. Collection Centre Canadien d'Architecture/ Canadian Centre for Architecture, Montreal. Copyright Phyllis Lambert and Richard Pare.

er brand of classicism as an expression of power and stability continued to do so in this modified vocabulary. Perhaps because many were located in the Toronto-Ottawa-Montreal triangle, the best examples of the style are seen in those cities.

The *ne plus ultra* of the manner was the **Bank of Canada [14.65]** in Ottawa (1937-8), the nation's central bank, located on Wellington Street across from the châteauesque Confederation and Justice Buildings. It was designed by the Toronto firm of Marani, Lawson and Morris, in association with S.G. Davenport (1877-1956), who for a time had been chief architect for the Royal Bank of Canada. Built nearly a decade after Barott's Bank of Montreal nearby, it reflected and developed upon its predecessor. The architects described the Bank of Canada as being 'of a simplified modern classical architecture'. The austere and planar façade, its rigid geometry accentuated by the hardness of the light-grey Quebec granite, is composed of a pristine base and an equally bare parapet (ornamented by a coat of arms), joined by flat corner piers and six grooved pilasters that

14.65 Bank of Canada, Ottawa, Ontario, 1937-8 and 1974-9. Photograph by Hellmut W. Schade, 1991.

define seven tiers of windows. A row of understated notches at the top are vestiges of a dentilled cornice. The wall surface is treated like a taut membrane, with the only hint of mass seen in the crisp window reveals, whose spandrels contain seven bronze figures, by sculptor Jacobine Jones, representing major Canadian industries. The bronze doors display replicas of Greek coins, and huge Greek-inspired urns (symbolizing the storage of wealth) are placed at some distance from either side of the entrance, standing on a pierced balustrade. The build-

ing program anticipated future expansion, and so the site was large enough for additions at the sides and in the rear. These additions occurred four decades later when twin 12-storey towers (1974-9) were wrapped around the original building, which acquired a château-type copper roof. They were designed—in a comparably austere vocabulary of their own day—by Arthur Erickson Architects in association with Marani, Rounthwaite and Dick.[110]

While the Bank of Canada continues the temple allusions of the classical banks built at the beginning of the century, the treatment seems worlds apart from the bulk and bombast of Beaux-Arts Classicism or the calmer and reduced compositions of the Neoclassical Revival. It displays a vestigial classicism, frozen in time and space; but in its emphasis on volume and line, rather than mass, the treatment is truly modern.

The distinctions between the different phases of twentieth-century classicism are not always cut-and-dried. Characteristics of both the Neoclassical Revival and Modern Classicism often appear in a single building, as in the **Automotive Building** (1929) at Toronto's Canadian National Exhibition [14.66]. The commission was won in a competition by Douglas E. Kertland (1888-1982), a former member of Lyle's office. An imposing structure located a short distance from the Princes' Gates, its symmetrical rectangular plan has six large display areas surrounded by a concourse on two levels that is entered in the centre of the two long sides and at the four corners. The main entrances on the north and south sides (the latter facing Lake Ontario) are similar: loggias of three round arches set between

14.66 Automotive Building, Canadian National Exhibition, Toronto, Ontario, 1929. CNE Archives/Pringle and Booth Photograph Collection/x57386.

monumental piers. Above each of the three doors is a tall window fitted with grille-work; in each bay hangs a long lantern-like chandelier (reminiscent of the chandeliers in the banking hall of the Bank of Montreal in Ottawa). The walls—of cast artificial stone that imitates light Indiana limestone—display the visual thinness, the crisp edges, and reduced ornament of Modern Classicism on the one hand; yet the handling of the composition, with its climactic build-up of forms at the centre and the corners, has more in common with the earlier and more traditional revivals. This may be seen particularly well in the treatment of the two central pavilions, which are inserted between broad, lower wings and feature a pair of flat, buttress-like piers that flank a recessed triple doorway. This common organizational device appears, for example, at Chapman and Oxley's Royal Ontario Museum [14.24], a work whose style is best described as Romanesque Revival—demonstrating how the compositional pattern characteristic of an era transcended the choice of historical sources.

An appreciative colleague, likely architect Herbert Harold Kent (1900-72), described the dual character of the Automotive Building when he wrote that

> the general impression one gathers [is] of classical dignity and almost Grecian restraint; the other, paradoxically enough, is the effect of modernity. The architect skillfully, or rather spontaneously, has harmonized these two principles to a far greater extent than we have yet seen in work tha[t] can be classed as 'Modern.'[111]

During the 1930s Modern Classicism became the preferred mode for urban federal architecture. The large 'dominion buildings' that were built in many cities across the country to accommodate government offices, using funds released by the Public Works Construction Act, show the manner well (and stand in contrast to the Château Style government buildings of the same era). Most were designed by local private architectural firms, although guidance would have been provided by the Department of Public Works and its Chief Architects, Thomas W. Fuller and Charles Sutherland. As architectural historian Janet Wright has noted, 'the new federal architecture of the mid and late 1930s was not the revolutionary modernism of the International Style, but represented a reinterpretation of established building types in the light of current values of modernism and nationalism.'[112]

The **Dominion Building in Hamilton [14.67]**, Ontario, designed in 1934 by G.J. Hutton (1881-

14.67 Dominion Building, Hamilton, Ontario, 1935-7. Photograph 1984. PC/Heritage Recording Services.

1942) and W.R. Souter (1893-1971) of that city, and built between 1935 and 1937, is typical. It is one block long, six storeys high, and traditionally composed with a giant order of shallow pilasters uniting the top four floors. The main entrance is highlighted by a three-level frontispiece that steps forward slightly and is crowned by a carved sculptural frieze. The deep recess in which the entrance is set is repeated in elongated form to enhance the floor above. The decoration is reductionist rather than additive; openings for windows and doors have been pared away from the wall, and the customary window frames have been omitted to emphasize the edges. Above the lower two floors—the public spaces—a shallow moulding has been substituted for the cornice. The sculpted frieze over the main entrance features a row of active figures representing the nation's industries. Conceived in the tradition of Greek relief sculpture, these representations are carved into the wall plane in low relief.[113]

Greater height is achieved in the **Dominion Building in Winnipeg [14.68]**. Built in 1934-7 to designs by George W. Northwood, it displays a tower-like projection over the entrance that rises in two stages and culminates in a tall flagpole. Its round-arched entrance adopts somewhat Romanesque detail, whereas the parapet (and the upper stage of the tower) exhibits the zig-zag ornament characteristic of the Art Deco style, which will be discussed shortly. Cream-coloured Tyndall stone gives it its 'white' appearance.[114]

Both abstract and figurative sculptural decoration appears on government buildings of the time. Particularly notable are the naturalistic relief panels on the Toronto Postal Delivery Building (1939-41), behind the Union Station, which depict the history of transportation with images that include smoke signals, canoes, a clipper ship, a train, and an airplane. Designed by Charles Brammall Dolphin (1888-1969), the building was described by the Department of Public Works as 'Modern Classic in style'. Its bulkless stone walls feature tall grooved pilasters that separate the windows along much of the building, contrasting with the ribbon windows that wrap around the corners in the manner of the more progressive International Style.[115]

14.68 Dominion Building, Winnipeg, Manitoba, 1934-7. Photograph 1982. PC/Heritage Recording Services.

So customary was Modern Classicism for government building that the massive six-column Greek Doric portico that forms the frontispiece of the Dominion Building at Amherst, NS (1935-6), seems conspicuously *retardataire*. It was designed by the talented, but conservative, Halifax architect Leslie R. Fairn (1875-1971), who was born a decade or two before the designers of the other federal buildings, and was affected by the Atlantic provinces' tenacious grip on tradition. (The more progressive Bank of Nova Scotia in Halifax, it will be recalled, was designed by an Ontarian.) Fairn's other work admitted features of Modern Classicism only in the 1940s and 1950s. In 1965, as a man of ninety, he finally recognized that change was inevitable: 'Trends are away from the traditional type of architecture to the more functional. I'm not criticizing it, we're living in a changing world and we have to go along with it.'[116]

Between the wars the classical language was adopted for official government building throughout the British Empire—and indeed universally. As it provided an unrivalled statement of authority, it achieved notorious prominence in the architecture of the dictatorial regimes of the thirties. Modern Classicism appeared, in particulary unrelenting versions, in the architecture of Hitler's Germany, Mussolini's Italy, and Stalin's Russia—forming a style that has been called Totalitarian Classicism (or Fascist Modern). It goes without saying that Canada's rendition of the style was comparatively gentle in scale, and restrained in manner.

Art Deco and Moderne

Art Deco is a decorative style—the culmination of a modern aesthetic that began to develop after the turn of the century, notably in France—that reached its peak in the twenties and early thirties. It was officially introduced at the huge Exposition des Arts Décoratifs et Industriels (whose popular abbreviation, les Arts Déco, gave its name to the style) that was held in the centre of Paris in 1925. Embracing furniture, jewelry, graphics, bookbinding, glass, ceramics, fashions, textiles, and architecture, it displayed the work of mainly French artists in a dazzling exhibition. It combined opulence of materials with elegant simplicity of design that featured geometric forms made up of predominantly angular elements, like chevrons and zig-zags, as well as curvilinear forms—all highly stylized. While designs were partly inspired by the classical past, the resulting decoration did not adopt historical forms. Beauty was found in Cubism, the machine aesthetic, jazz, streamlining, and twenties' costume—all of which contributed to produce a new kind of decoration. Palettes were light and bright, and included pastel tones.

John Lyle used the new decoration in his banks of the time, and described it in his 1929 lecture:

> Speaking generally, its characteristics are a simplicity of wall surface, both of exterior and interior, a use of parallel lines or concentric curves, a use of incised relief ornament with semi-flat surfaces, a daring use of modern materials, . . . [and] an altogether charming use of what might be termed sunshine colours.[117]

The term Art Deco is often used to describe an architectural style that all but broke with the traditional revivals, and achieved a popular, non-revolutionary modernism, primarily through the application of the new decoration. Art Deco office buildings stress verticality, have a multiplicity of planes and angles and decorated flat surfaces, and sometimes appear to have been sculpted from a large slab of a plastic material. Several writers have preferred the terms 'Modernistic', 'Moderne', or 'Streamlined Moderne' to describe this style of architecture, reserving 'Art Deco' for the ornament.

E.I. Barott designed a paradigm of the style in a Montreal office tower, the 23-storey **Aldred Building** [14.69] on Place d'Armes, which shares the historic square with four earlier architectural landmarks: the Séminaire [2.39], the Church of Notre-Dame [6.9], the Bank of Montreal [10.49], and the New York Life Insurance Co. Building [10.38]. The Aldred building (built in 1929-31) rises from the street by means of a series of setbacks, its verticality emphasized by the diminishing floor area as well as by the continuous vertical articulation of the alternating wide and narrow piers that separate the windows.

Setbacks—as distinct from a monolithic slab like the adjacent New York Life Insurance Co. Building—had been introduced in Montreal earlier in the twentieth century to allow light to reach the street. They were first required by New York City's innovative and influential zoning ordinance of 1916 and confirmed in a Montreal by-law passed in 1924. The first truly elegant setback design appeared in Finnish architect Eliel Saarinen's widely praised second-prize competition entry for the Chicago Tribune Tower (1922), and Saarinen's treatment is clearly reflected in Barott's scheme.

14.69 Aldred Building, Montreal, Quebec, 1929-31. Photograph by Hellmut W. Schade, 1992.

The Aldred Building made a distinct break from Barott's slightly earlier Beaver Hall Building (1928-9), on Beaver Hall Hill in Montreal, which—like the Sun Life Building—places a tower (with only minor setbacks) on a large podium. The Beaver Hall Building bears comparison with an entry submitted by John Lyle for the celebrated international competition for the Chicago Tribune Tower. Both use a wholly classical decorative vocabulary, with the top stage consisting of a giant order capped by a stepped pyramid in the manner of the ancient Mausoleum at Halicarnassus. The Aldred building, on the other hand, replaces classicism with the new language of Art Deco. Decoration appears in the spandrels below the windows and on the piers at the top of every stage.[118]

Barott's client was the dynamic John Edward Aldred, whose diversified business interests ranged

14.70 Ground-floor corridor, Aldred building, Montreal, Quebec, 1929-31. Collection Centre Canadien d'Architecture/Canadian Centre for Architecture, Montreal. Copyright Phyllis Lambert and Richard Pare.

from the Gillette Safety Razor Company to the Shawinigan Water and Power Company (he was president of both). Born in the milltown of Lawrence, Massachusetts, Aldred was a director of several power, railway, and real-estate firms, and built the Technical School in Shawinigan as a gift to that community.[119] Just as many of the clients of the progressive architecture of the Prairie School have been shown (by architectural historian Leonard K. Eaton) to have been aggressive individualists with a technological bent, who were not supported by a strong organized institutional network,[120] we may hypothesize that the patrons of the new commercial architecture, like Aldred, had a similar profile. He took strong control over the design of his speculative office building, and steered Barott from Modern Classicism to Art Deco.

The decoration and materials of the Aldred Building made an important new statement. Abstract geometrical forms replaced classical motifs, which remain only in the most vestigial form. Externally the Indiana limestone walls are complemented by aluminum and black glass spandrels. In the **ground-floor corridor [14.70]**, marble, brass, and terazzo are combined in colourful and non-historical patterns, with a strong geometric basis. Naturalistic ornament occurs as well, such as the birds sitting on telegraph wires—seen in the arch above the main lobby—but octagons, diamonds, scallops, and straight lines predominate.

Another accomplished Art Deco commercial tower is the **Marine Building [14.71]** at Burrard and Hastings Streets in Vancouver, developed and built in 1929-30 by Toronto's upstart (and short-lived) Stimson Developers to accommodate commercial shipping interests and the Vancouver Merchants' Exchange. The description by architects McCarter and Nairne—J.Y. McCarter (1886-1981) was a hard-nosed pragmatist and George C. Nairne (1884-1953) a romantic artist—shows that the partners thought of building and ornament as one:

> The building in its architectural conception suggests some great crag rising from the sea, clinging with sea flora and fauna, tinted in sea-green, touched with gold, and at night in winter a dim silhouette piercing the sea mists.[121]

The tower of the 21-storey building rises above a four-storey podium (with a narrow setback on the Hastings Street side) and a ten-storey wing along Burrard Street; and a striking sense of verticality is expressed in the repeated motif of tall, thin, buttress-like piers. Gradual setbacks in the highest stages are crowned by the hip-roofed penthouse. The cur-

14.71 Marine Building, Vancouver, British Columbia, 1929-30. Photograph by Leonard Frank, 1930. Vancouver Public Library/12009.

tain walls (which cover a steel frame with concrete floor slabs) are mainly pinkish-buff brick, combined with terra cotta, and are heavily loaded with terra-cotta bas-relief ornaments (in pink and green, with gold highlights) designed by the firm's 'Doc' Watson, C. Young, and J.D. Hunter. Rich terra-cotta ornament also decorates the higher reaches of the building along the parapets at every setback. Terra-cotta panels near the base depict the history of transportation and the discovery of the Pacific Coast, and a frieze with waves, sea horses, and marine fauna appears above the ground floor around both fronts of the building. Over the main entrance on Burrard Street—the doorway is contained within a series of receding arches in a manner inspired by Romanesque or Gothic design—a ship's prow sails out of the sunset and Canada geese fly across the rays; and growing out of the arched surround is a burst of marine growth. Scallops, swirls, and zig-zags continue the Art Deco treatment in the bronze grilles. The theatrical treatment extends into the **lobby** [14.72], in which a striking effect is achieved by green and blue tiled walls; a beamed ceiling; exquisite brass elevator doors; abstract floor tiles chosen for their

colours; and indirect lighting concealed behind ships' prows. (All these lobby details were somewhat compromised in a 1989 renovation.)

The podium fills the irregular site. The principal ground-floor spaces are the lobby and, beyond it, the Merchants' Exchange, which in 1989 was converted to an elegant Chinese restaurant. The office floors in both the Burrard Street wing and the attached main tower are notable for their open plan and central service core (containing elevators, stairs, and toilets), which deviated from the then-standard layout of corridors and small offices—as at the Aldred Building—and anticipated the arrangement that has prevailed in office buildings since the 1960s [**14.73, 74**].

At the end of the economic boom of the 1920s, high-rises with similar aspirations were developed in all large cities—particularly in Toronto—although none were quite so spectacular as the Marine Building. Most, like the Aldred Building, seem to have been produced by non-establishment developers. The sixteen-storey Concourse Building on Adelaide Street West in Toronto (Baldwin and Greene, 1928) is particularly notable for its tile decoration,

14.72 *(right)* Lobby, Marine Building, Vancouver, British Columbia, 1929-30. Photograph by Leonard Frank, 1930. Vancouver Public Library/12011.

14.73 Ground-floor plan, Marine Building. Drawing by David Byrnes.

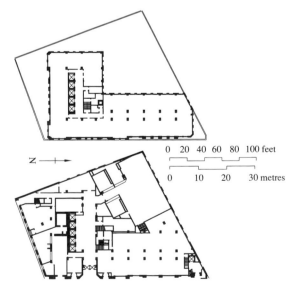

14.74 Typical office floor-plan, Marine Building. Drawing by David Byrnes.

particularly the tile mosaics at the entrance designed by painters J.E.H. MacDonald and Thoreau MacDonald.[122] The Toronto Star Building (Chapman and Oxley, 1927-9; demolished), on King Street West, placed considerable emphasis on granite carvings, terra cotta, and bronze near the six-storey reinforced-concrete base, but its steel-framed shaft rose somewhat staidly above it.[123] The *Toronto Star* was then a relatively young and maverick paper, having been founded by labour in 1896 and reorganized by Liberal-leaning business interests in 1899.

Setback towers were also erected by establishment clients, but they tended to base the decorative scheme on historical themes and not Art Deco ornament. The **Canadian Bank of Commerce** [**14.75**] on King Street West in Toronto (York and Sawyer of New York, with Darling and Pearson associate architects, 1929-31)—when completed, the tallest building in the British Empire at 34 storeys—expresses verticality very well through its setbacks, and the piers that soar beyond the parapets at each stage. The decorative scheme is Romanesque Revival, with arched doors and window heads on the base echoed by arched corbels at the top of each tier.[124] In 1931 the design received the RAIC's first award for office buildings, whereas the Aldred Building received only an honourable mention in the same competition—revealing the conservatism of the architectural pro-

fession as a whole. After the amalgamation of the Bank of Commerce with the Imperial Bank of Canada in 1961, the 1931 building was fortunately retained—and renovated—to become part of the scintillating Commerce Court development (pages 800-1) whose tower appears at the left of the photograph.

Art Deco ornament appears in Canada at its purest in the interior design work done for the **T. Eaton and Company** by Jacques Carlu (1890-1976). Born in France and trained at the École des Beaux-Arts, he was introduced to Canada in 1913 when he worked with planner Thomas H. Mawson on the designs for Calgary [**12.7**]. In 1924 Carlu accepted a teaching post at the Massachusetts Institute of Technology, and he continued to teach in the United States and France while carrying on an architectural practice.[125]

In 1930 Carlu designed the interiors for the new Eaton's department stores in Montreal and Toronto. Ross and Macdonald were the architects for both buildings, associating in each case with Sproatt and Rolph. At the Montreal **Eaton's store** (1925-7), the ninth-floor suite consisted of elevator lobbies, hallway, a foyer, and the sleek 500-seat **dining-room** [**14.76**]—131 by 75 feet (40 by 23 m) in size—that was treated as a nave, 35 feet (11 m) high, with lower aisles along the sides. Controlled natural and artificial light enter through the windows of opal glass

14.75 *(left)* Canadian Bank of Commerce, Toronto, Ontario, 1929-31, with Commerce Court (1968-72) on the left. Photograph by William Dendy.

14.76 Dining room, Eaton's store, Montreal, Quebec, 1930. Archives of Ontario/AO1950.

14.77 Foyer of the Eaton Auditorium, Eaton's College Street, Toronto, Ontario, 1930. Archives of Ontario/AO1459.

14.78 Perspective of the proposed Eaton's College Street, Toronto, Ontario, 1928. Archives of Ontario/AO110.

in the clerestory. The walls are covered with horizontally striped fabric in beige and pink, and square columns of pink and grey marble support the clerestory. At either end is a black marble fountain and a large mural in black, silver-grey, and pink painted by Natacha Carlu, the wife of the designer. Although the plan was determined along Beaux-Arts lines—the nave-and-aisle treatment derives from a church, and the column-and-entablature has classical origins—the sources have been translated into something entirely contemporary. The room's geometric—and gracious—elegance was unlike anything seen before in Canada.[126]

A similar streamlined and French Art Deco elegance characterized the seventh floor (as well as the other public areas) of the **Eaton's College Street store** (1928-30) in Toronto. Here the suite consisted of the Round Room (a restaurant), the Eaton Auditorium (a concert hall that could be converted quickly into a ballroom), and a long **foyer [14.77]**

---

between the two. The decorative vocabulary and colours were not unlike those in the Montreal store: silvered shades of beige and grey with black, with horizontally striped walls and exposed fluorescent tubes in the foyer. For the Auditorium (and its gallery) Carlu employed (as elsewhere on the floor) solid shapes—in the tiled floor and in the lines that swept around three sides of the Auditorium to focus on the stage, which was framed by panels of translucent glass and had a gold curtain with black and silver horizontal stripes. Light was provided by the glass-and-metal ceiling over the vestibule and the glass fixtures over the exits and marking the stairways. The Round Room—which was entered from the foyer through glass and Monel-metal doors—

14.79 Toronto Stock Exchange, Toronto, Ontario, 1936-7. Photograph by Hellmut W. Schade, 1986.

14.80 Trading floor, Toronto Stock Exchange, Toronto, Ontario, 1936-7. Hugh Robertson.

was a circle within a square: the corners were filled by raised alcoves and the circular shape was reflected in the round mouldings of the coved and domed lighted ceiling, and in the circles of the floor tiling. On the curved walls between the alcoves Natacha Carlu painted murals. In the centre of the room was a fountain that rested on tiers of black and white frosted glass in a circle of water lighted from below. The retail portions of the store were the responsibility of French-born architect René Cera (1895-1992), a member of Eaton's staff, and were complementary in design.[127]

The College Street store—which was intended to be the podium of a skyscraper—was originally conceived as part of a mammoth project intended to contain over 4 million square feet (370,000 m²) of floor space and to cover an entire city block [14.78]. But the Depression prevented its completion. Ross and Macdonald's scheme, with modern classical features on the base and no historical references above, remained the most ambitious of all setback towers of the time.

Carlu's decorative work at the two Eaton stores—which has often been favourably compared with the elegant Art Deco design in the great ocean liners of the 1920s, the *Normandie* and the *Île de France*—brought state-of-the-art French design to Canada in two very accessible interiors. They were much admired, and the decorative vocabulary filtered into other Canadian work, but rarely with the *tout ensemble* of the prototypes.

The **Toronto Stock Exchange** [14.79], built in 1936-7, is the most elegant subsequent design in the Carlu spirit. The architects were George and Moorhouse, with S.H. Maw (1881-1952) as associate architect. The 39-foot-high (12-m) **trading floor** [14.80], which begins one storey above the ground, is the dominant space, and its tall, narrow windows achieve an equivalent importance on the façade. The lower 6 feet (1.8 m) of the walls are pale marble, with the walls above faced in acoustic tile horizontally striped with silver metal bands and wood strips. This striped theme is continued in the ceiling, where bands of acoustic panels and discs alternate with bands of illuminated opal glass. Eight murals by Charles Comfort represent the principal industries of Canada.

The granite-and-limestone façade on Bay Street—rising flush with the streetline on a relatively small site—is composed somewhat like a traditional temple bank (the Bank of Canada comes to mind), but gone are all vestiges of classical detail, except for the piers between the windows that support a cornice-

like moulding across the façade. The horizontal pattern on the recessed end bays rejects the traditional vertically fluted pilaster, and the cut-stone frieze—a striking angular depiction of workers and their machines designed by Comfort—is placed below rather than above the piers, above the main entrances. However, lest the building's being 'the last word in modern achievement' made people forget that the Exchange 'has as its background the sound tradition of British financial institutions', the executive offices on the third level were designed in the traditional Queen Anne and Georgian styles. The conservatism of the Canadian financial establishment would not be denied![128] The Toronto Stock Exchange moved to First Canadian Place in the early 1980s, and the present building has been incorporated, as the Toronto Design Centre, into the fifth Toronto-Dominion tower (pages 800-2).

Canadian Art Deco more usually followed not so much Carlu and France as the stylized form of ornament popularized in the United States. **Vancouver City Hall** (Townley and Matheson, 1935-6) is particularly interesting both for this kind of ornament and for the dynamic cubic massing of its setbacks [14.81]. The hard-edged geometry and column-like shafts between the recessed windows show the influence of Modern Classicism, while the geometric ornament in the spandrels and on the friezes atop each block are vintage Art Deco, revealing the positive fusion that could be achieved between these two contemporaneous styles. The term 'Moderne' (or 'Modernistic') is perhaps more apt for a building of this nature than 'Art Deco', expressing the architects' use of surfaces and volumes to provide a futuristic impression. This image was particularly important to Vancouver Mayor G.G. McGeer, an ardent unionist who forged the amalgamation of Vancouver with its two largest suburbs and envisioned the new city hall as a vital symbol of his forward-looking office.[129]

A similar image was created nearly two dozen years later, and at the other end of the country, in the **Confederation Building** [14.82], built in 1958-60 in St John's, Newfoundland, the home of the young province's legislature and its executive and administrative offices. Premier Joey Smallwood, who brought Newfoundland into Confederation, held a notion of 'progress' that was not unlike McGeer's. He commissioned a building designed by A.J.C. Paine (1886-1965), a former Newfoundlander practising in Montreal, in association with Lawson, Bettes, and Cash. The broad façade, an impressive 650 feet (200 m) wide, rises in steps from two storeys at the

14.81 City Hall, Vancouver, British Columbia, 1935-6. Photograph by John Roaf, 1973.

14.82 Confederation Building, St John's, Newfoundland, 1958-60. Newfoundland Tourism.

extremities to a 12-storey central tower capped by a hipped roof and a beacon. Clean, continuous white (concrete) piers emphasize the verticality. The premier's oak-panelled suite, the Cabinet Chamber, and the House of Assembly are all located high in the tower. Gordon Pushie, Director General of Economic Development, expressed the provincial government's pride in it as an architectural symbol when he wrote:

> Pointing its stately tower skyward, it also points up a whole new concept of centralized administration of government. The new Confederation Building . . . is both a splendid twelve-storey monument to Newfoundland's union with Canada and an interesting experiment in efficiency in government . . . . [The functions of government] have been brought together in a building of such truly fine proportions that it strikes admiration in the visitor and pride in the hearts of all Newfoundlanders.[130]

The Confederation Building's Moderne design was startling in Newfoundland, although the style had long abandoned centre stage in the rest of Canada.

'Moderne' and 'Art Deco' are often used interchangeably (with the former being the more appropriate) to describe a type of relatively small commercial, public, or domestic building that proliferated across the country in the late thirties and early forties. Their distinguishing features are plain, white exterior surfaces (usually painted stucco or concrete); compositions that are divided into rectangular planes, or portions, by hard-edged projecting (or recessed) vertical and horizontal elements; a sometimes capricious placement of windows; an overall balanced asymmetry that recalls the paintings of Piet Mondrian and his Dutch colleagues who founded the influential journal De Stijl ('The Style', 1917-28); and the frequent use of modernistic lettering and relief sculpture. The whiteness and plainness of the wall surfaces suggest a link with the classical revivals, particularly the Spanish Colonial Revival. (Interestingly, the Moderne and the Spanish Colonial Revival were both styles beloved and promoted by Hollywood.)

An early house of this kind that marks the transition, by way of classicism and Art Deco, to the Moderne—and one with a particularly interesting history—is the **Lawren Harris house [14.83]** on Ava Crescent in Toronto. Harris, who was instrumental in founding the Group of Seven and served as the first president of the Canadian Group of Painters, was the son of the successful farm-implement manufacturer who entered into partnership with Hart Massey to form the Massey-Harris Company. The young Harris's private income gave him the oppor-

tunity to become an enlightened architectural patron. In 1913 he commissioned Eden Smith to design the remarkable, factory-like Studio Building on Severn Street in Rosedale Valley. For his house on Ava Crescent he chose the Russian-emigrée architect Alexandra Biriukova (1895-1967), who trained in St Petersburg and Rome—where she would have been exposed to leading-edge Art Deco design—before coming to Toronto in 1929. Biriukova was the first woman to join the Ontario Association of Architects. (One person who endorsed her application was architect Douglas Kertland, designer of the Automotive Building at the CNE, with whom she may have worked when she arrived in the city.) The Harris house was to be her only commission. The reason is not known, but one wonders whether conservative Toronto rejected her modern design; or if it was simply too difficult—particularly for a woman—to break into practice during the lean Depression years. She resigned from the profession in 1934 and spent the rest of her working life as a tuberculosis nurse in a Toronto-area hospital.[131]

Designed and built in 1930-1, the house reflects the movement towards abstraction that characterized Harris's magnificent landscape paintings of the 1920s. Harris evidently participated in the design, since he wrote to the painter Emily Carr in June 1930, before retaining Biriukova, saying that he had gone to Stuttgart (site of the German Werkbund's strikingly modernist housing exhibition of 1927) to see examples of modern architecture.[132] The smooth, white, stucco-clad house is severely geometrical in form, reflecting Canadian Modern Classicism, contemporary European ideas (which will be discussed in the next chapter), and Harris's own interest in pure forms (inspired by his commitment to Theosophy). His house may well be the first Moderne building in Canada.

A pair of two-storey wings with chamfered corners project at angles from a three-storey square central block, each component covered with a flat roof—a virtually unknown feature in Canadian houses of the time. The arched central window, with finely incised mouldings and a wrought-iron balcony, echoes similar motifs in Spanish Colonial Revival designs (and on the Automotive Building), and the symmetry is strongly classical in spirit. Even with its links to the other styles, the ensemble is best defined as Moderne. The interior spaces are quite varied, with a rectangular living-room (in the right wing), an octagonal dining-room (at the left), a five-sided library accessible from the oval entrance hall, and a semicircular staircase in the main block. The high, light, and sim-

14.83 Lawren Harris house, Toronto, Ontario, 1930-1. Photograph by William Dendy.

ply detailed rooms showed Harris's paintings to their best advantage. The metal-framed windows and chromed-steel balustrades conveyed an interest in new materials. The house was subsequently owned by Beatrice Centner Davidson, who graduated in architecture from the University of Toronto in 1930 and, with her husband Harry, was a leading supporter of contemporary art and architecture in Toronto.[133]

The **Varscona Theatre** (Rule, Wynn, and Rule, 1940; demolished 1987), at Whyte Avenue and 109 Street in Edmonton, showed the more developed Moderne manner well [**14.84**]. The façade was dom-inated by a tall element intersected by horizontal fins (actually the intake tower for the air-condi-tioning system) and by the broad marquee. The bright red and black trim and the stylized lettering contrasted with the gleaming white of the walls. Glass blocks and a circular window were also uti-lized. The plain auditorium wall was interrupted only by vertical piers that responded to the internal steel structure and a continuous horizontal course that was a vestigial cornice. The interior of the cin-ema had a tapered, parabolic plan and was deco-rated only by vertical stripes near the screen and a striped pattern in the acoustic tiles of the ceiling. Similar to the Varscona is the rival Garneau Theatre, designed by William George Blakey (1885-1975) and

14.84 Varscona Theatre, Edmonton, Alberta, 1940. PAA/Alfred Blyth Collection/BL. 254/1.

also built in 1940—located only a few blocks away and still in use.[134]

Many other houses of the time, besides the Harris house, manifested a similar search for a modern expression. The **H.G. Barber house [14.85]**, on West 10th Avenue in Vancouver, is representative. Built in 1936 to designs by Ross A. Lort, it features sheer concrete walls relieved by asymmetrically placed windows and sparse vertical articulation. Far more rectilinear than that of the Harris house, the façade is a fine abstract composition on its own, enlivened by the step in the parapet and the slight recess of the entrance bay.[135]

The Moderne style was used superbly at the **Garden Court Apartments [14.86]** on Bayview Avenue in Toronto, built in 1939-42 to designs by Forsey Page and Steele (who will be introduced in the next chapter). The courtyard apartment plan—seen three decades earlier at Eden Smith's Riverdale Courts [11.60]—is used here effectively. A series of two- and three-storey blocks is arranged on the perimeter of the large centre court, which was designed by landscape architect H.B. Dunnington-Grubb and presents ordered plantings of trees, shrubs, and flowers. Pairs of one- and two-bedroom apartments on each floor are accessed by a common hall and stairs, most of which open onto the court and thereby avoid the need for corridors (as at the much earlier Bishop's Court Apartments [11.58] in Montreal). The ground-floor apartments have direct access to the grounds, and the suites on the upper floors all have balconies (some on top of projecting ground-storey window bays and others recessed into the

plane of the wall). The clean and crisp Moderne exterior features yellow-brick walls with projecting band-like horizontal courses occurring at the corners (like classical quoins), near the top (a vestigial cornice), and between pairs of windows—providing associative links with the Georgian Revival. Simple projecting canopies, some square and others curved, protect the entries from the weather. This residen-

14.85 H.G. Barber house, Vancouver, British Columbia, 1936. Photograph by Robin Ward, 1992.

14.86 Garden Court Apartments, Toronto, Ontario, 1939-42. Photograph by William Dendy.

tial complex provides a good compromise between relatively inexpensive apartment living and the privacy of the detached house, and it remains a popular address.[136]

The architect who best combined the progressive aspects of the classical, Art Deco, and Moderne manners was the gifted Ernest Cormier (1885-1980). Initially trained as an engineer at the École Polytechnique in Montreal, he worked for a period with the Dominion Bridge Company. In 1908 he decided to study architecture and attended the *atelier* of Jean-Louis Pascal at the École des Beaux-Arts in Paris. After spending two years in Rome with a scholarship from the Royal Institute of British Architects, Cormier returned to Montreal in 1918. Soon afterwards architects Louis-Auguste Amos and Charles S. Saxe (1870-1943) invited Cormier to be their designer for the new Court House (Palais de Justice) on rue Notre-Dame est in Montreal (1922-6). This severely Neoclassical building (now known as the Centre administratif Ernest-Cormier), marked by a row of fourteen Doric columns along the façade, is an early precursor of Modern Classicism, since the classical language has been simplified somewhat, particularly in the omission of window surrounds and the stripped pilasters of the side elevations.[137]

Cormier's most important commission was the main pavilion of the **Université de Montréal [14.87]**. After fires in 1920 and 1922 destroyed the former principal building of the university, which had begun as an offshoot of Quebec City's Université Laval, a

decision was made to build an entirely new campus on a spacious site on the north-east slope of Mont Royal. Cormier initiated design development in 1924 and construction began in 1928. Work was delayed by the Depression, and the main building was not opened until 1943. Much construction followed, and the university is now the largest in Quebec, with more than 50,000 students.[138]

Cormier's building complex was planned on Beaux-Arts principles: linked wings grouped symmetrically and rationally on either side of a central court of honour, forming six smaller courts, each about 100 feet (30 m) square. The wings on the right-hand side were designed to serve as a teaching hospital, the other wings as classrooms. In the centre the administration building—containing offices, a large amphitheatre, lecture halls, and the library—is surmounted by a 245-foot-high (75-m) tower containing the library stacks. The chapel, indicated by a somewhat Scandinavian stepped gable (seen at the right rear), was located on one side to symbolize the secularization of the university (which had been founded with the sanction of the Vatican). The exterior walls of beige brick, which cover a reinforced-concrete structure, are articulated with elegant vertical piers that are amplified on the administration building and its tower. This slender shaft, which terminates in a cubic stage and a small dome (intended as an observatory), reflects the composition of the Nebraska State Capitol (1920-32), designed by Bertram Grosvenor Goodhue.[139]

The architect of All Saints Cathedral in Halifax [14.9], Goodhue left Ralph Adams Cram in 1913 and abandoned the Gothic Revival. He spent the decade left to him searching for a modern style that was free of historical precedent. His celebrated Nebraska Capitol shows an awareness of European developments, particularly the work of Eliel Saarinen and his railway station at Helsinki (1905-14), although its plan and composition are rooted in Beaux-Arts formalism.

The Université de Montréal similarly offers a fusion of classicism and modernism, displaying a design that is neither historical nor revolutionary. As Cormier explained: '. . . the buildings are modern in design yet not modernistic. They have been designed from the point of view of practicability, and nothing has been done purely for the sake of aspect.'[140] He praised the client for not imposing a historical style—presumably alluding to Collegiate Gothic, which dominated university design at this time.

The house that Cormier built for himself in Montreal offers a remarkable statement of the Art

14.87 Université de Montréal, Montreal, Quebec, begun 1928. Collection Centre Canadien d'Architecture/Canadian Centre for Architecture, Montreal. Copyright Phyllis Lambert and Richard Pare.

14.88 *(right)* Cormier house, Montreal, Quebec, 1930-1. Photograph by Brian Merrett.

Deco/Moderne aesthetic. Located on a narrow and steeply sloping site, the **Cormier house [14.88]** built in 1930-1, has a single-storey principal entrance—at the upper level on avenue des Pins. It consists of two rectangular masses, faced in grey composition granite, that step up to the taller adjacent house. At street level the lower block contains the entrance hall and kitchen, stairs, dining-room; on the higher level are Cormier's **studio [14.89]** and a terrace. The walls are vertically articulated, with relief sculpture over the door and window. The structure is reinforced concrete throughout. The stuccoed rear façade is five floors high, its modernist elevation contrasting with a historicist turret in the garden. The interior spaces have a severely Art Deco character—created by the furnishings, colours, textures, and patterns that were all designed by Cormier. Recurrent

14.89 Studio, Cormier house, Montreal, Quebec, 1930-1. Collection Centre Canadien d'Architecture/ Canadian Centre for Architecture, Montreal. Copyright Phyllis Lambert and Richard Pare.

themes are horizontal bands, checkerboards, and—in the studio—interlocking circles. The Cormier house has been classified as a historic monument by the Province of Quebec. In 1981 it was purchased by former prime minister Pierre Elliott Trudeau to be his residence.[141]

Cormier's stately Supreme Court of Canada of 1938-9 was introduced above [**14.17**]. Despite its imposed Château Style roof, the Modern Classical façade indicates that Cormier was once again seeking modernism within the classical Beaux-Arts tradition, rather than independently of historical precedent. In this he paralleled the French-born American architect Paul Philippe Cret (1876-1945), another graduate of the *atelier* Pascal, whose best-known work in the manner is the Folger Shakespeare Library in Washington (1928-32).

Cormier's considerable skill as an engineer was revealed in the Seaplane Hangar that he designed in 1928 (demolished 1987) for the Compagnie aerienne franco-canadienne at Pointe-aux-Trembles, near Montreal—the first reinforced concrete arched hangar in North America. His last major work, the National Printing Bureau in Hull, Quebec (1950-58), is a glass curtain-walled industrial building in the International Style, showing that he continued to search for a modern expression even in his sixties.[142] His greatest satisfaction came from the international recognition he received for designing the doors of the United Nations General Assembly building (1947) in New York.

For all their formal and stylistic inventiveness, Canadian architects between the wars had little interest in what they called 'modernism'. Though they were decisively influenced by European and American developments, their greatest interest lay not in architectural polemics but in their attempt to create a Canadian style that would illustrate the country's varied history and imagery: significant and meaningful decorative detail, combined with high-quality and time-tested forms. The development of a true modernist architecture is credited to a group of Europeans who were born in the same decade as Ernest Cormier. It was left to a younger generation of Canadians to integrate the manner into the architecture of this country.

CHAPTER 15

MODERN ARCHITECTURE AND BEYOND

'MODERN' IS a term that has been used for centuries to describe what was perceived as belonging to the present or the recent past. The reader may recall that Anthony Trollope praised the 'modern gothic' of the Parliament Buildings in Ottawa (page 541), and that Percy Nobbs admired the 'modern Free Classic' of early-twentieth-century public buildings in England (page 556). The 'modern' period might be seen as being of either long or short duration. The former is the case with James Fergusson, the author of the first comprehensive history of architecture, who devoted his last volume (of three) to the five centuries from the Renaissance to his own day and entitled it *A History of the Modern Styles of Architecture* (1862, 3rd ed. 1891). All these observers used the word 'modern' as a chronological term without implying any particular characteristics or values.

In the second quarter of the twentieth century the word 'modern' acquired a more specific meaning, describing styles and values that made a decisive rupture with the buildings of the past. Architects of the 'modern movement', as it was called, believed that they were turning their backs on history and developing a new order. An act that symbolized the intended break with precedent was the decision of German-American architect and teacher Walter Gropius, a leader of the new movement, to remove architectural history and Beaux-Arts principles from the curriculum at Harvard University's Graduate School of Design, of which he became chairman in 1938.

The buildings discussed at the end of the last chapter made preliminary steps towards letting go of the past. Their architects sought to be current by adopting new programs, structural systems, materials, compositions, and ornament. Nevertheless, all retained tangible and conscious links with tradition. Not so the architects who are discussed in the first part of this chapter. Most of them passionately embraced truly modernist principles—espousing a deliberate anti-historicism—in their search for new means of expression.

Modernism (the '-ism' affirms it as a doctrine) reached Canada tentatively in the 1930s and became firmly entrenched in the 1950s. Over the period of three decades, coincident with the post-war economic boom, it caused massive changes in the appearance of Canadian cities. Its ascendancy, however, was not permanent. As early as the 1960s, architects and the general public began to find fault with the buildings and theories of the modern movement.

A decided shift in values since that time has brought about a greater respect for the physical and historical context of architecture. Buildings from this recent past, often called the 'Post-Modern' period (here the word 'modern' refers to a style rather than to being up-to-date), conclude this look at new architecture.

Modern Architecture

The International Style: prototypes

In the first decades of the twentieth century, a group of European architects—influenced in part by recent work in the US—developed a new means of expression that came to be known as the 'International Style'. The name was proposed by Alfred H. Barr, Jr, director of New York's Museum of Modern Art, to its first chroniclers, architectural historian Henry-Russell Hitchcock and architect Philip Johnson (b. 1906), who exhibited photographs of the new architecture at the Museum in 1932. Hitchcock and Johnson defined the basic characteristics of the style as an emphasis on volume and not mass, a sense of regularity (as opposed to symmetry), and a reliance

on the intrinsic elegance of materials (rather than on applied decoration). They identified the leaders of the new movement as the Swiss-French architect Le Corbusier (1887-1965), the Germans Walter Gropius (1883-1969) and Ludwig Mies van der Rohe (1886-1969), and the Dutch architect J.J.P. Oud (1890-1963). Gropius and Mies were both directors of the Bauhaus, the influential school of art and architecture in Dessau, Germany—Gropius from its founding in 1919 until 1928 and Mies from 1930 until it was closed by the Nazi government in 1933. Hitchcock and Johnson noted, as well, that in the process of designing their buildings, these architects sought to sever ties with the past and abandon historical forms.[1]

Canadian architects became increasingly aware of the International Style through the 1920s, but were generally skeptical or negative towards it. We have seen that John Lyle described with interest to his Canadian colleagues his observations of the new European buildings, but rejected the total break with the past (Chapter 14). Percy Nobbs was even less receptive. In 1930 he illustrated a selection of recent German and Dutch work in the *Journal of the Royal Architectural Institute of Canada* and dismissed most of it as an 'adverse influence', although he conceded that

. . . the architectural realists of Europe may have an enormous influence for good on our future work, that is, if we keep our heads, accept so much of their doctrine as will help us, and solve our own problems in our own way, with a weather eye on our climate.[2]

The conservative *Journal* admitted the voices of modernism very cautiously, with an article by Jacques Carlu in 1931; one, on houses, by Émile Venne, professor at Montreal's École des Beaux-arts, four years later; and a piece by American William Lescaze in 1937.[3]

The International Style made only a tentative entry into Canadian architecture during the 1930s. The earliest identified building in the style is the **Toronto, Hamilton and Buffalo Railway Station [15.1]** on Hunter Street in Hamilton, Ontario, built in 1931-3. The TH&B was a small, but strategically located, regional line financed by a consortium that included the New York Central Railroad and the Canadian Pacific Railway (it is now wholly owned by the latter). The architects were Fellheimer and Wagner of

New York, successors to Reed and Stem (the architects for Grand Central Station) and the designers of the line's large station-office building in Buffalo, New York (1927-9).

The original design, proposed in 1930, was for a 10-storey Art Deco setback tower, similar in its massing and articulation to the taller Aldred Building in Montreal [14.69] and Canadian Bank of Commerce in Toronto [14.75], both begun a year earlier. Whether in response to the worsening economy, to new architectural tastes, or—more likely—to both, the Hamilton station was built to a revised design, only seven storeys high, that went far beyond the Art Deco and Moderne styles, and introduced the International Style to Canada. All features of the style (as defined first by Hitchcock and Johnson, and subsequently by other architectural historians) are present: smooth curtain walls (Queenston limestone and glass, the stone backed with hollow tile and supported by a structural steel frame) that are treated as thin membranes and express the volumes that they enclose; windows that appear as a continuation of the wall and turn around the corner without any apparent support at the angle; a flat roof; and a total absence of historical references. These same characteristics are seen, for example, at Gropius's school building for the Bauhaus in Dessau (1926), and at the Philadelphia Savings Fund Society Building (1931-2), a prototype office tower by architects Howe and Lescaze. The Hamilton station may lack the magnificence or the grace of the German and American prototypes, but it nevertheless provides a bold statement of the new design values. Observers recognized the link between economy and aesthetics. *Canadian Railway and Marine World* described the station as being 'distinctly utilitarian in design, including chaste lines and dispensing with ornamentation.'[4]

As at Buffalo, the TH&B's Hamilton building combines station and office uses. A two-storey base containing the station concourse is surmounted by four floors of offices and a penthouse (originally used as a conference room). The handsome concourse—semicircular in plan and overlooked by a mezzanine gallery—is brightly finished in modern materials and colours: a beige-and-brown terrazzo floor, ox-blood ceiling with aluminum light fixtures, stainless-steel wainscotting finished in red, steel-faced columns, and brown-leather banquettes. Noting the use of stainless steel, the trade magazine *Construction* remarked: 'We believe this is the first comprehensive installation of this kind in Canada.'[5]

Some of the features of the Hamilton station could be seen separately (but not integrated so effective-

15.1 *(left)* Toronto, Hamilton and Buffalo Railway Station, Hamilton, Ontario, 1931-3. Photograph by Hellmut W. Schade, 1985.

ly) in other Canadian buildings of the time. One was the **Jewish General Hospital [15.2]** on rue Côte Ste-Catherine in Montreal (1929-34), by J. Cecil McDougall (1886-1959), in association with C. Davis Goodman (1894-1962). It features ribbon corner windows with cantilevered spandrels illuminating the solaria at the ends (a feature inspired by the Bauhaus building [1925-6] in Dessau, designed by Gropius). The principal elevation, however, features the thinly fluted giant pilasters of Modern Classicism, and the chevrons in the façade spandrels derive from Art Deco, marking this as a transitional design.[6] The different 'modern' styles were frequently intermixed in this way, and the lines between them remained blurred.

A similar ambiguity is seen in the **William H. Wright Building [15.3]**, the former headquarters of the Toronto *Globe and Mail*, designed by Mathers and Haldenby and built in 1937 (demolished). The pier-and-spandrel treatment, and the relief sculpture of the façade on King Street West (at the right

15.2 Jewish General Hospital, Montreal, Quebec, 1929-34. Courtesy the Jewish General Hospital.

15.3 William H. Wright Building, Toronto, Ontario, 1937. John McNeill/*The Globe and Mail*/69329-13.

15.4   Canada Packers Plant, Edmonton, Alberta, 1936.
PAA/BL.1812/3.

in the photograph), were within the Modern Classical tradition. In contrast, the elevations on the York Street side (at the left) and the rear (Pearl Street, not visible) abandoned classical references and used ribbon windows set without reveals at the plane of the wall, which appeared as a taut skin stretched over the reinforced-concrete structural frame that was only slightly visible behind the glass. A hierarchy of values was evident: the modernist treatment was seen as being less genteel and was therefore relegated to the secondary elevations.[7]

This attitude encouraged architects to use the International Style with impunity for industrial buildings—the building-type for which the style had first been adopted in Europe. At the **Canada Packers Plant** [**15.4**] in Edmonton (1936)—used for slaughtering, curing, and packing meats—a balanced asymmetry is composed of abstract cubes constructed with a reinforced-concrete frame and unrelieved brick curtain walls (ironically laid in the pattern called *German garden bond*).[8] The architect was Eric R. Arthur (1898-1982), whom we have already met as a historian and critic. From his position as professor of architecture at the University of Toronto, the New Zealand-born Arthur championed international modernism to a generation of students. It was appropriate that this influential teacher should also have distinguished himself as an architectural historian, presenting old

buildings as artifacts from the past so as to clear the way for the new order. Arthur's book, *The Early Buildings of Ontario* (1938), which contains measured drawings by his students, was the first serious look at the subject; and his *Toronto: No Mean City* (1964) was the first professional history of that city's architecture. At the same time—as Blanche van Ginkel, the former dean of architecture at the University of Toronto, noted—'He was the first, or one of the few, who wanted to introduce into Toronto a sense of the twentieth century in architecture.' This was notably expressed in Arthur's role in the choice of designer for Toronto's new City Hall [**15.32**].[9]

Domestic architecture played an important role in leading the way towards the acceptance of modernism. In the 1930s a small group of architects who had been exposed to European modernism found understanding clients who encouraged their innovations. In Quebec, architects Robert Blatter (b.1899) and Marcel Parizeau (1898-1945) designed a number of interesting houses that revealed their fluency with the International Style. The **Bourdon house** [**15.5**] on chemin Saint-Louis in Sillery, near Quebec (1934, demolished), by the Swiss-born Blatter—who had associated with the likes of Picasso, Utrillo, and Le Corbusier before coming to Quebec in 1926—offered a pleasing play of abstract shapes and volumes. The two-storey semi circular bay, with a ribbon window at the ground-floor level, was counterbalanced by the lower wing on the right, whose entrance porch and upstairs balcony could

15.5 Bourdon house, Sillery, Quebec, 1934. Ministère de la Culture, Fonds photographique/FM15123-N-1.

15.6 Paul Laroque house, Montreal, Quebec, 1936. From *JRAIC*, September 1939.

be read as voids. The brick walls were painted white and the windows were located close to the outer plane, denying the walls any sense of mass; and the roof was flat.[10]

The Quebec-born Parizeau studied at the École Polytechnique de Montréal and then, from 1923, spent ten years in Paris—much of the time attached to the *atelier* Héraud at the École des Beaux-Arts—and travelling around the Continent. His short career was marked by a number of fine houses, including the **Paul Laroque house** [15.6] on Ainslie Avenue in the Montreal suburb of Outremont (1936), whose geometry and details recall those of the Bourdon house. (The house was built for Laroque's father-in-law, businessman and banker J.-B. Leman, and is sometimes called the Leman house.) Parizeau taught at the progressive École du Meuble in Montreal, as did painter Paul-Émile Borduas, who introduced international modernism to Quebec painting.[11] Another Montreal architect who was quick off the mark was Henri S. Labelle (1896-1989), whose Outremont house for J. Donat Langelier (1931) combined features of Modern Classicism (pilaster-like strips flanking the frontispiece) with the International Style (corner windows flush with the membrane-like brick walls).[12]

These houses, and others like them, display the design vocabulary associated with the International Style, but when they are compared to a European house in the style—such as Le Corbusier's seminal Villa Savoye in Poissy, France (1928-31)— they seem heavy and clumsy, and express a characteristically Canadian avoidance of elegance, much in the way that Francis Sullivan's houses in the Prairie Style appear far more massive than those of Frank Lloyd Wright [14.57]. Indeed, rather little separates the Bourdon or Laroque house from a less modernist design, such as Alexandra Biriukova's Lawren Harris house in Toronto (1930-1, 14.83) or Ross Lort's Barber house in Vancouver (1936, 14.85), which are better described as Moderne (rather than International Style)—the former for its more mannered plan and details, and the latter because of its vertical fins, flute-like ribs, and other decorative features.

Vancouver and the West Coast Style

The first blossoming of modernism in Canada occurred in Vancouver, the youngest of Canada's metropolises. This section gives an overview of the city's development before focusing on buildings erected from the late 1930s to the early 1970s. Over the next two decades Vancouver architects continued to take a leading role: some of their more recent buildings are examined later in this chapter, together with those of other architects across the country.

Modern ideas have always found a fertile breeding ground in Vancouver. The city was formed by industry and technology—in the 1860s because of (exaggerated) reports of coal reserves, and as a service centre to the infant forest industry; and two decades later as the western terminus of the transcontinental railway. As a consequence it has continually welcomed new trends in architecture and planning. Complementary environmental factors are the benign climate, which permits technical innovation in building; and the spectacular setting, between the mountains and the ocean, that challenges good designers and forgives poor ones.[13]

The City of Vancouver—the name (that of the explorer George Vancouver) is said to have been chosen over 'Granville' by CPR General Manager William Van Horne—was incorporated in April 1886, and only a month later a fire, caused by crews clearing the forest, destroyed virtually all the community's flimsily constructed wood buildings. The disaster was a blessing in disguise, since it permitted rebuilding on a grander scale. Helped by the expanding economy and by experienced architects who came to Vancouver from elsewhere in Canada (many from Winnipeg) and from Britain, the new buildings displayed the latest North American styles, including Victorian Italianate and Richardsonian Romanesque for commercial buildings, and Queen Anne for domestic.

Vancouver experienced strong growth in the decade leading up to (and immediately following) the First World War. Major public and commercial buildings adopted the fashionable classical styles, while housing embraced the Craftsman Bungalow, aggressively marketed as a 'modern' house with all the latest conveniences and affordable by every working family. Street after street in Vancouver's expanding streetcar suburbs featured rows of these developer-built gable-roofed wood houses [11.41].

The boom years of the late 1920s saw the enthusiastic introduction of early modernist tendencies—the best example of which is the Art Deco Marine Building (1929-30, 14.71). Planning, considered to be a progressive activity, became a serious endeavour. We have seen that the affluent suburb of Point Grey was the first Canadian municipality to enact a zoning by-law, in 1924 (Chapter 12). In 1929 the City of Vancouver amalgamated with Point Grey and South Vancouver and promptly commissioned planners Harland Bartholomew Associates of St Louis, Missouri, to produce a comprehensive plan. A new City Hall was built (1935-6, 14.81), symbolically located at 12th Avenue and Cambie Street, near the point where Vancouver, South Vancouver, and Point Grey met. A Moderne building, the City Hall effectively expressed the community's progressive attitude. A handful of residences, such as Ross Lort's Barber house, also adopted the Moderne style.

Other British Columbia architects, a decade or two younger than Lort, were making even more important modernist statements. The first of the visionaries was Charles B.K. Van Norman (1907-75), a native of Ontario who studied at the University of Manitoba and settled in Vancouver. His domestic work in the 1930s was relatively gentle in its modernity. Van Norman chose to simplify house-forms through the vehicle of the Cape Cod Cottage—a variant of Georgian that was inspired by revivals of American Colonial building—rather than by turning to the Moderne. Although he retained some period-inspired elements—such as clapboard siding, shuttered windows, and gabled roofs—he did it without direct historical quotations. One of many Vancouver examples of his manner is the **Halterman house** [15.7], built in 1937 on Angus Drive, on the south edge of expanding Shaughnessy Heights. This understated essay in brick and wood is treated as a single storey, with dormer windows penetrating the roof, and its asymmetrical composition is dominated by a gable at the left-hand side.[14]

Van Norman's early public buildings, on the other hand, are more uncompromisingly modern. The small City Hall in Revelstoke, BC (1939), is a modest yet startling exercise in the International Style, with white walls, a flat roof, and an abstract cubic massing punctuated by the fire department's tall hose tower.[15] Despite—or, more likely, because of—his advanced ideas, Van Norman received few large-scaled commissions until the 1950s, by which time other architects had caught up to him. He designed

15.7   Halterman house, Vancouver, British Columbia, 1937. Photograph by Robin Ward, 1992.

15.8   B.C. Binning house, West Vancouver, British Columbia, 1939-42. Photograph by Hellmut W. Schade, 1992.

many office, apartment, and public buildings in the 1950s and 1960s, a few of which are described below.

Another leading participant in the acceptance of the International Style and the development of an early and important regional variant, the West Coast Style, was not an architect at all, but a painter and educator, B.C. Binning (1909-76). In 1934 he began to teach at the Vancouver School of Art (where he had been a student; it is now known as Emily Carr College of Art and Design). Committed to formal abstractionism in painting, Binning subscribed to similar values in architecture. He revealed his approach in his own residence, the **B.C. Binning house [15.8]** in West Vancouver, which he designed and built incrementally between about 1939 and 1942. Based on a standard wood-frame structure consisting of vertical posts and horizontal beams, it was one of the first flat-roofed houses in the Vancouver area. The rectangular plan is arranged as two parallel strips, joined by a gallery. The southern exposure, facing the sun and a view of the Strait of Georgia, is mostly glazed with floor-to-ceiling glass.[16]

Binning invited a number of celebrated architects and artists to Vancouver, one of whom was the Viennese-born modernist Richard Neutra (1892-1970), then practising in Los Angeles. The young Ron Thom and Arthur Erickson (both are discussed below) were among the students Binning invited to his home to meet Neutra. Thom later exclaimed: 'Did Neutra ever turn me on!'[17] In 1949 Binning joined the faculty of the School of Architecture at the University of British Columbia, whose director was the Swiss-born Frederic Lasserre (1911-61), a devoted advocate of the International Style who had worked with the modernist Tecton group in London in the late 1930s and may also have been associated briefly with Le Corbusier. (He was the designer of the building at UBC that bears his name.) Like many modernists, Lasserre argued that the new architecture had objectivity on its side— that good design was 'the simple spontaneous expression of a building solution.'[18]

Vancouver was home as well to Robert A.D. Berwick (1909-74) and Charles Edward (Ned) Pratt (b. 1911), two graduates of the University of Toronto who were deeply affected by the European modernism introduced to them by Eric Arthur and his colleagues. In 1945 they joined the firm of Sharp and Thompson (Chapter 14) and soon transformed this thirty-year-old partnership—which became known as Sharp and Thompson, Berwick, Pratt— into the most dynamic firm in the West, as well as the principal training-ground for countless younger

architects (including both Erickson and Thom, as well as others who will be introduced below). After having been in business for 84 years, the firm wound up its affairs only in 1990, and it has been succeeded by the partnership known as Hemingway Nelson.[19]

Their approach is illustrated in the **C.E. Pratt house [15.9]** on Lawson Avenue, West Vancouver, designed by Pratt for his family around 1946. The two-storey frame house is sublimely simple in concept and execution. The plan is a rectangle, with hall, living, and dining spaces occupying most of the **ground floor [15.10]**, all illuminated by a continuous row of floor-to-ceiling windows that look out to the southern panoramic view. The kitchen and laundry occupy separate rooms along one end. On the **upper floor [15.11]** a corridor connects the three bedrooms, whose smaller windows also look south. The staircase breaks out of the rectangular plan, and the car-port is separate, linked by a covered walkway. The exterior walls are faced with broad bevelled siding, except for the lower level at the chimney end, which is brick. The roof slopes very gently up to the south.

Describing the factors influencing his design, Pratt combined an explicit pragmatism (similar to Lasserre's) with an implicit devotion to the work of international modernists in explaining that the roof overhang (pronounced on the garden side) was dictated by the need for protection against rain; the nearly flat tar-and-gravel roof followed from the overhang as well as from the rising cost of cedar shakes; the wide glass area on the southward-facing garden side responded to the summer sunshine; and the open planning of the ground floor arose, in part, by conditions imposed by radiant heating.[20]

This direct response to climate, materials, and technology was critical to the new domestic architecture. In 1951 Pratt built a second house for himself, in the British Properties of West Vancouver, in which the vertical posts were spaced four feet apart and filled with 'sandwich panels' consisting of two standard sheets of plywood filled with a layer of insulation. This four-by-eight-foot (1.2 x 2.4 m) factory-produced module became the basis for many subsequent houses designed by Pratt's firm and by other Vancouver architects.

By the 1940s Vancouver had acquired a significant community of architects with similar points of view. Most built houses of this kind for themselves, and for courageous clients, on the mountainous North Shore. In the main these houses were based on a clearly articulated structure of vertical posts and horizontal beams (the system to which lumber

15.9   C.E. Pratt house, West Vancouver, British Columbia, *c.* 1939-42. Photograph by John Roaf, 1973.

15.10, 15.11   *(below)* Ground-floor and upper-floor plans, C.E. Pratt house, West Vancouver, British Columbia, *c.* 1946. Drawing by David Byrnes.

naturally lent itself), with flat roofs and large expanses of glass. In addition to Pratt's, the houses designed by architects for their families' own use included those in Vancouver by C.B.K. Van Norman (1938; demolished); in West the Vancouver region by Robert Berwick (his first, begun in 1937, was financed by the first mortgage in the Vancouver region issued under the National Housing Act, and the second was built in 1939); Peter Thornton (by Gardiner and Thornton, 1939); John C.H. Porter (built 1948-9); as well as a pair in North Vancouver by Fred Hollingsworth (built 1948) and Ron Thom (built 1957). The most attractive is **J.C.H. Porter's creekside house [15.12]** on Ottawa Avenue in West Vancouver, which (like Pratt's and most of the others) is situated south of the street so that only the parking area and entrance face the roadway, and the open living spaces are oriented southwards for the view and for privacy. Cedar is used for the structural members, exterior siding, and the low-pitched V-shaped tongue-and-groove roof. Open planning without full partitions allows rooms to flow into each other, and glass walls with sliding glass panels on the garden front break down the traditional distinction between inside and out.[21]

The work of Ronald J. Thom (1923-86) reveals the more picturesque aspect of the West Coast Style. A

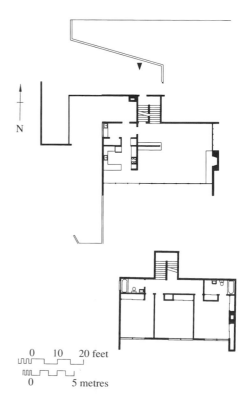

0   10   20 feet

0   5 metres

painter and a pianist who turned to architecture, with the encouragement of Binning and Pratt, Thom learned the profession by apprenticing with Pratt's firm. (He did not become a registered architect until 1957, when he was 34.) His most important work at the time consisted of single-family houses that were superbly integrated into the landscape—Thom had studied the work of Frank Lloyd Wright intensively. As Dick Mann, a partner in the firm, recalled: 'He *understood* Wright. He knew the secret to his geometry.' Mann says that Thom was 'hopelessly romantic' and 'collected around him people who were bored with the European [International] style, as we are today.' Thom rejected the International Style even before it had been accepted by most other Canadian architects.

One of Thom's best, and earliest, houses, designed while he was still apprenticing (Pratt was also involved), was the **D.H. Copp House** [**15.13**] on Belmont Avenue, Vancouver (Sharp and Thompson, Berwick, Pratt, 1951), which is located on a steep hillside site with a view of both the water and the mountains. All that was visible from the higher (street) side was a series of horizontal roof planes floating above the shrubs and trees (the landscaping was also designed by Thom) and a brick chim-

15.12 J.C.H. Porter house, West Vancouver, British Columbia, 1948-9. Photograph by Robin Ward, 1992.

15.13 D.H. Copp house, Vancouver, British Columbia, 1951. Photograph by John Roaf, 1973.

15.14   Vancouver Vocational Institute (now Vancouver Community College), Vancouver, British Columbia, 1948-9. Photograph by John Roaf, 1973.

15.15   *(right)* BC Electric Building, Vancouver, British Columbia, 1955-7. Photograph by Hellmut W. Schade, 1992.

ney that serves as an anchor, and now even they are hidden by the greenery. 'It's one of his masterpieces, that sense of the horizontal and the land,' according to Barry Downs, another talented architect who worked in Berwick and Pratt's office in the 1950s and was a chronicler of the new movement. 'Always the hearth and big fire, the informality. No worry about insulation or double glazing. The four-by-four sheet of plywood was Ron's *tatami* mat'—a reference to the use of industrial plywood and the Japanese features and flavour of this and other houses by Thom and his peers that were adopted by way of Frank Lloyd Wright.[22]

Sharp and Thompson, Berwick, Pratt (renamed Thompson, Berwick, and Pratt in 1955, ten years after the retirement of G.L.T. Sharp; and subsequently Thompson, Berwick, Pratt, and Partners) made countless important contributions to commercial and public, as well as residential, architecture. The firm's **Vancouver Vocational Institute [15.14]**—built in 1948-9, and which housed the Vancouver School of Art—introduced modernism to downtown Vancouver. Ribbon windows with stucco spandrels are set off against blank red brick walls in a clean, crisp, rectilinear composition. Columns are frankly exposed bchind windows, and the staircases are revealed behind sheer glass walls.[23]

The firm's biggest triumph was the Vancouver head office (1955-7) of the British Columbia Electric Company (as the formerly private utility was then called), the **BC Electric Building [15.15]**, on Burrard Street (subsequently known as the BC Hydro Building), which was recognized internationally as having broken important new ground in office planning and structural design. BC Electric chairman Dal Grauer worked closely with C.E. Pratt, the partner in charge of the project, and with Ron Thom. One of Grauer's requests was that every one of the thousand employees might be able to look out a window and benefit from natural light. The plan of the typical office floor is therefore a thin, tapered, lozenge-shaped rectangle, wider beside the central service core (which projects above the roof as a penthouse) and narrower at the ends, allowing every desk to be located no farther than 15 feet (4.6 m) from a window. (A similar shape was adopted, although using reinforced concrete, in the contemporaneous Pirelli Building in Milan, by Gio Ponti and Pier Luigi Nervi, 1955-6.) The floors are cantilevered from the bearing walls of the core like branches from a tree, and are supported only slightly by slender perimeter columns. The exterior skin is a curtain wall of porcelain, steel, and glass. The sleek 22-storey tower is colourful, decorated with blue, green, and black

15.16 Vancouver Public Library, Vancouver, British Columbia, 1956-7. Photograph 1958. Vancouver Public Library/29956.

mosaic tiles designed by B.C. Binning. Adjacent is the low Dal Grauer Substation, built a few years earlier (1953-4), whose brilliantly coloured mechanical works are exposed behind a transparent glass wall. Both the BC Electric Building and the substation follow the tenets of international modernism—although their individuality and the use of colour and texture are decorative features associated with the West Coast. BC Hydro abandoned its building for a new head office on Dunsmuir Street (Musson Cattell Mackey Partnership, 1991-2), and in 1993-4 the 1950s landmark was adapted as condominium residences and renamed The Electra (Paul Merrick Architects).[24]

During the mid-1950s a number of other Vancouver firms produced fine modernist buildings. Among them was the talented and successful, but short-lived, partnership of Harold N. Semmens (1914-65) and Douglas Simpson (1916-67), both trained at the progressive School of Architecture at the University of Manitoba. Their most important public commission was the new central facility for the **Vancouver Public Library** [15.16] at Burrard and Robson Streets, built in 1956-7 only a few blocks north of the BC Electric Building. In this reinforced-concrete structure that is strictly rectilinear, wide column-spacing allows clear interior spaces and flexibility for expansion. Non-load-bearing exterior walls of glass, aluminum, and granite are combined in a handsome pattern that distinguishes between administrative offices (on the top floor) and stacks (the two middle floors). The large expanse of glass at street level provides a public image of accessibility, inviting passers-by to enter. The plans for expansion could not foresee the enormous growth of Vancouver and its library system, and so the building has been succeeded by a new Vancouver Public Library further east on Robson Street (Moshe Safdie and Associates and Downs, Archambault and Partners, 1992-4). The fate of the 1950s modernist landmark remains uncertain— although, like the BC Electric Building, it may be adapted for a new use.[25] The same precarious situation exists with many other commercial and public buildings of the period. Most have reached a critical stage in their lives, having served their original uses for more than a generation, and have now begun to look old-fashioned. They must either be upgraded with a significant reinvestment, or demolished and replaced with new construction better suited today's technical requirements. The high real-estate prices in Vancouver tend to favour the latter course.

C.B.K. Van Norman also produced some early International Style public and commercial buildings. His Customs Building (1950-4; demolished 1992), at Burrard and West Pender Streets, was a very early venture into the International Style. The **Burrard Building [15.17]** at Burrard and West Georgia Streets (1955-6—the first office tower built since the Art Deco landmark Marine Building [**14.71**])—was the first tall curtain-walled building in the city. Unlike the BC Electric Building, which it preceded by a few months, it has a conventional corridor plan, with a staircase at each end, rather than a central core. (The curtain wall was replaced in renovations by Musson Cattell Mackey Partnership in 1988-90. The photograph shows the building with its original exterior cladding.)[26]

McCarter, Nairne and Partners, who had designed the Marine Building, were also responsible for several important modernist public and commercial buildings. One was the large General Post Office (1953-8) on East Georgia Street, designed in association with the Department of Public Works. It remains

15.17   Burrard Building, Vancouver, British Columbia, 1955-6. Photograph by John Roaf, 1973.

in use, although its future also is in question.[27]

In the 1940s and 1950s Pratt, Van Norman, and the other first-generation modernists cleared the tables of historicism, creating a distinctive modern and Western idiom and opening the door for a younger generation of architects who adopted a freer, and more expressive, manner. Once again, buildings in the Vancouver region led the way. A primary monument of this later West Coast manner is **Simon Fraser University**, on Burnaby Mountain in nearby Burnaby, which was intended eventually to accommodate 18,000 students and to attract them with popular programs. The ensuing competition, held in 1963, was won by Erickson/Massey Architects of Vancouver—a partnership, formed in 1953, of Arthur Erickson (b. 1924) and Geoffrey Massey (b. 1924; the nephew of Vincent Massey and cousin of Hart Massey), with the Vancouver-born and McGill-educated Erickson the principal designer. Simon Fraser was the firm's first major commission.

Rather than providing independent clusters of buildings for each college or faculty, as at most other universities, new and old, Erickson devised a linear scheme along a strong central axis (following the mountain ridge), forming a spine to which all buildings would be connected. The changing levels are addressed by terracing. Simon Fraser was organized by use (academic, social, recreational, and residential) and discipline (science and humanities), rather than by departments or colleges. This treatment, and the scope for interdisciplinary studies, are expressed in the linked arrangement of the buildings. Erickson/Massey, who were appointed design co-ordinators, received the commission for the Central Mall and Transportation Centre, while a number of other architects designed the other buildings. The first phase was completed in 1965, and construction has been ongoing since then. Concrete is the primary building material.[28]

The multi-storey **Central Mall [15.18]** is the principal walkway and meeting-place of the university, and shares the characteristics of both outside and inside spaces. Built in 1963-5, it is flanked by what are perceived as the exterior walls of buildings, yet the mall is covered by a glazed roof, 297 by 133 feet (91 by 41 m), built up of deep girders fabricated from fir beams and steel tie-rods. Automobiles enter the transportation centre on a lower level. The photograph looks along the axis of the mall, with the Academic Quadrangle (by Zoltan S. Kiss, 1963-5) beyond it. The mall became a prototype for countless other internal malls and atriums built over the next few decades.

15.18   Central Mall, Simon Fraser University, Burnaby, British Columbia, 1963-5. Photograph by John Roaf, 1973.

The widely travelled Erickson—acknowledging that he had been influenced by historical architecture around the world— noted that Greek palaestras, Buddhist temples, and Christian monasteries all yielded ideas for the new complex, and concluded that Simon Fraser 'casts the contemporary university as an appropriate Acropolis for our time.'[29]

Its spatial planning, which forces student interaction, was blamed for student unrest in the late 1960s. Architect Henry Elder, who was chairman of the competition and the head of the School of Architecture at the University of British Columbia, recalls:

> When they had their revolution there, the president rang me up and said: 'Your building has caused a revolution.' I said: 'Goody, goody!' If architecture can prompt action, then it has succeeded. When it gets no response, it's a failure.[30]

Simon Fraser University is more than just a group of buildings; it is an attempt to redefine the way in which architecture accommodates the needs of university education.

The hallmark of much of Erickson's work through the 1960s and 1970s was the interpenetration of exterior and interior spaces within a post-and-beam framework that is tightly controlled, but not fixed to a rigid grid. It is seen in his exquisite houses as well as in his public buildings. The **Smith house** [15.19] on

The Byway in West Vancouver (Erickson/Massey, 1965)—the second house that Erickson designed for artist-couple Gordon and Marion Smith—is closely integrated into its treed and rocky waterfront site. Erickson stated: 'I wanted the Smith house to

15.19   Gordon Smith house, West Vancouver, British Columbia, 1965. Photograph by John Fulker, *c*. 1966. Courtesy Arthur Erickson Architectural Foundation.

15.20 Museum of Anthropology, University of British Columbia, Vancouver, British Columbia, 1973-6. Photograph by Simon Scott, *c.* 1974. Courtesy Arthur Erickson Architectural Corporation.

reveal the site in the same way that I had found it revealed to me when I first walked onto it.' He used cedar posts and overlapping beams, with large expanses of glass, in an organic manner that grows upward around a central timber-paved courtyard in the manner of a 'square spiral'. It combines the minimalist structures associated with Mies (compare the Hart Massey house, **15.36**) with the more natural and site-specific houses inspired by Frank Lloyd Wright (compare the Copp house, **15.13**). Columns and beams were made the same thickness 'to achieve the greatest possible sense of repose'. As Erickson explained: 'To the horror of my colleagues, I never let structural veracity interfere with aesthetic purpose.'[31]

The **Museum of Anthropology [15.20]** at the University of British Columbia (Arthur Erickson Architects, 1973-6) renders the post-and-beam form in reinforced concrete. A series of graduated frames—inspired by the structural members of the Kwakwaka'wakw (Kwakiutl) longhouse **[8.6]** and consisting of precast posts as high as 50 feet (15 m), and projecting post-tensioned cross-beams up to 180 feet, (55 m) long—enclose both the entrance

and the glass walls of the Massive Carving Gallery, facing the Strait of Georgia, whose exhibits include huge totem poles. Seen from the rear of the museum—outside the Massive Carving Gallery, as in the photograph—the sensitive and dramatic proportioning of the sequence of frames is immediately evident; from within, they create a dramatic setting for the carvings, which are displayed against a spectacular backdrop of water and mountains. The other galleries (on the left) are contained within an extensive, but low, flat-roofed structure that blends into the landscape. More totem poles, log houses, and native flora fill the site around the museum building. (The Koerner Ceramics Gallery, designed by Erickson, was added in 1990.)[32]

The effective linking of exterior and interior spaces, the creation of striking forms—and, where appropriate, a sense of occasion—are Erickson hallmarks that have helped to earn him an international reputation. He has designed a number of other important buildings in Canada and abroad, including the pyramidal wood 'Man and His Community' pavilion at Expo 67 in Montreal (1966-7); the angular and reflective Canadian pavilion at Expo 70 in Osaka, Japan (1968-70); the MacMillan Bloedel Building in Vancouver (1968-9, with Francis Donaldson), a corporate headquarters with poured-in-place concrete walls and deeply recessed windows

15.21 Robson Square, Vancouver, British Columbia, 1974--9. (The BC Electric Building is in the centre background.) Photograph by Ezra Stoller/Esto, 1980. Courtesy Arthur Erickson Architectural Corporation.

that create a powerful image; and the University of Lethbridge (1970), a long, low-slung complex that nestles into the side of a coulee.

Erickson's **Robson Square** [15.21] in Vancouver (1974-9) combines the glass-roofed Law Courts with a landscaped public square that accommodates public activities on several levels inside and out (the extensive landscape design was by Cornelia Hahn Oberlander and Raoul Robillard). Erickson's buildings adopt bold, unique shapes that show sensitivity to their site and context.[33] An exception is Roy Thomson Hall (Arthur Erickson Architects with Mathers and Haldenby, 1979-82), located on King Street West, at Simcoe, in a historic area of downtown Toronto. While its almost circular glass-sided (and flat-topped) roof, glass walls, and mirrored panels bring the cityscape into the foyer and other circulation areas, the building itself is strangely isolated from its setting.[34]

A more recent Erickson building, the Canadian Chancellery in Washington, DC (1986-9), fills a large and irregular site—the last remaining property on Pennsylvania Avenue, across from I.M. Pei's East Building of the National Gallery—by placing the offices along two sides and erecting the stick-like bare frame of a classical building (having corner posts and a 'hanging architrave', but lacking walls) along the other two, more visible, sides, causing interior and exterior spaces to merge. This, and other historically associative allusions (including a columned rotunda), met Washington's design requirements for a neoclassical vocabulary without resorting to any imitative forms—in much the same way that Ron Thom suggested a Gothic building at Massey College [15.43, 44], and as younger Post-Modern architects would later do (see below).[35]

Other Vancouver architects also worked with post-and-beam construction and wood, and contrived a smooth flow of space inside and outside. Barry Downs (b. 1930)—a close associate of Ron Thom who also worked at Thompson, Berwick, and Pratt in the fifties and sixties, and has been in partnership since 1969 with Richard Archambault in the firm Downs/ Archambault—is best known for his residences, which are intimately related to the landscape. Two of the best are the Bowker house (1968) and Caine house (1971), both in West Vancouver.[36] Downs transferred his residential idiom to public buildings in the sensitive and serene **North Vancouver Civic Centre** (**15.22**, Downs/Archambault, 1974). A city hall and a library are rendered as separate, but related, buildings—low, reinforced-concrete structures, partly clad in cedar, that nestle in the hillside and look as if they had grown out of it. Both buildings are partially underground, allowing pedestrians to see into the Council Chamber of the City Hall through a clerestory window (the windows have since been covered). As Downs explained: 'We wanted the new buildings to look comfortable on their site, and offer most of their ground to civic park space.' This they did— with the result that the City Hall lacks visibility, and is difficult for visitors to find.[37]

Downs and his contemporaries adopted a strong regional style that is rooted in the rugged, wooded landscape of British Columbia, working in harmony with the land rather than trying to dominate it.

15.22 North Vancouver Civic Centre, Vancouver, British Columbia, 1974. Photograph courtesy John Fulker and Associates Ltd.

In this respect their manner parallels that of the aboriginal builders of earlier times, and openly acknowledges a reverence for native structures. Their conscious regionalism was paralleled in other areas of Canada at the time (this is discussed in a later section). These architects admired the contemporaneous wood architecture of the Bay Area of California, such as the vernacular-inspired Sea Ranch Residential Resort north of San Francisco (1965), designed by Charles Moore (b. 1925-93) of Moore, Lyndon, Turnbull, Whitaker. In both British Columbia and California, modern architecture has developed out of a long tradition of wood building, in which the Craftsman Bungalow formed a common experience. In the words of Downs: 'There is a West Coast need for a sense of containment, stability and joy of place in what is often a rugged, brooding environment.'[38]

The mature International Style

Toronto and Montreal—Toronto also took a leading role in the spread of the International Style during the 1950s, starting more slowly than Vancouver but ultimately surpassing it. The leading firm was unquestionably John B. Parkin Associates. A resourceful and aggressive businessman, John B. Parkin (1911-75) graduated from the University of Toronto and worked in London before setting up a practice in Toronto in 1937. Ten years later he took on as a partner the younger—and unrelated— John C. Parkin (1922-88), a graduate of the

15.23 Headquarters of the Ontario Association of Architects, Toronto, Ontario, 1953-4. Photograph by Panda Associates. Courtesy Hugh Robertson.

University of Manitoba and the Harvard Graduate School of Design, where he studied under Gropius. John C. Parkin immediately became the partner in charge of design and led the firm to a stunningly successful practice that became known for its un-compromisingly rectilinear buildings in the International Style. By 1960 John B. Parkin Associates was the largest firm in Canada, with about 180 staff, fulfilling John B.'s dream of offering architectural, engineering, landscape architecture, and interior-design services, under one roof after the model of European and American offices. This new approach—then radical but now standard among the larger practices—made design the product of a corporate entity rather than of an individual architect.[39]

An early Parkin landmark was the elegant **Headquarters of the Ontario Association of Architects** [15.23] on Park Road in Toronto, only a few hundred feet away from the Studio Building— constructed in 1913-14 and designed by Eden Smith for co-owner Lawren Harris; it was used by an earlier generation of artists, including some members of the Group of Seven. The firm won the commission in a competition, announced in 1950, which was decided by a three-man jury that included Eric Arthur. The jury declared that it 'expects a design that represents the aspirations and the ideals of the association.' More than ninety per cent of the 37 competitors submitted a modern design; in theory, at least, Ontario's

architects (and not only John B. Parkin Associates) had accepted the advent of modernism.[40]

Constructed in 1953-4, the clubhouse (its main function) is a lucidly planned, exquisitely detailed, and pristinely finished jewel—a showpiece of International Style design. The clarity is revealed in the plan, and its simple mathematical basis: every dimension is a multiple of a 5-foot (1.5-m) module, and the ensemble is a two-storey rectangle, 40 feet wide, 80 feet deep, and 20 feet high (12.2 × 24.4 × 6.1 m). Everything is open and transparent, aided by the few partitions and the many windows that allow internal and external spaces to flow together. The upper floor is entered from a broad staircase through a deep portico, intended to exhibit sculpture; this level contained a library, two offices, and a boardroom, all located around services placed within an enclosed central core. The ground floor had dining and lounge facilities. The two levels are joined by a kind of vertical open space—a ramp set within a high and narrow exhibition hall, with the kitchen and furnace room contained in the lower part of the same central service area. The exterior materials are white-painted exposed steel columns and beams and buff brick; one wall is entirely open with windows that look out on Rosedale valley. Interior materials include

15.24 Ortho Pharmaceutical plant and office, Don Mills, Ontario, 1955-6. NAC7690.

teal cork, purple brick (around the service core), oiled walnut, polished nickel hardware, acoustic-tile ceilings, and terrazzo floors. Every item in the building, from furniture to tableware, was designed by the project architects, and most were manufactured in Canada. In order to raise money for the new pieces, the Association sold the antique furniture from its previous headquarters—in their enthusiastic embrace of modernism, dispensing with traditional design literally as well as symbolically.

Somewhat ironically, the OAA enjoyed its modernist gem only as long as the style remained in vogue. In the early 1990s, as Post-Modernism achieved popularity, Ontario's architects abandoned their Parkin masterpiece in favour of a new headquarters building in Don Mills (Ruth Cawker, 1992). The Parkin building, much changed inside, now houses the offices of Roger du Toit Architects Limited and du Toit, Allsopp, Hillier.

In 1954 the building was opened by the Governor General, the Rt-Hon. Vincent Massey—who remained an important patron of architecture, as he had been a generation earlier in directing the commission for Hart House [**14.1**]. At the suggestion of Eric Arthur, who was then editor of the *Journal* of the Royal Architectural Institute of Canada, Vincent Massey (through the Massey Foundation) and the RAIC joint-

ly established the Massey Medals for Architecture in 1950. These awards, which were given periodically for several decades, were important for recognizing excellence in Canadian architectural design.[41] Massey subsequently became the client for Massey College at the University of Toronto [**15.43**].

The Parkin manner is represented well by the elegant **Ortho Pharmaceutical plant and office** [**15.24**] on Greenbelt Drive in Don Mills (1955-6), one of many well-designed light-industrial complexes built in this planned new community. The office wing features a reinforced-concrete structural frame that is painted white and pulled away from the dark glass and dark-blue spandrel panels of the curtain wall framed in black steel, clearly expressing the structure as being independent from the curtain wall. (A curtain wall is a non-load-bearing exterior skin supported by the structural frame.) The plant wing, in contrast, is finished in white glazed brick set flush with the columns and pierced only by a narrow ribbon window. The administrative and manufacturing functions are clearly distinguished from each other, yet they combine in a harmonious ensemble that is greater than the sum of the component parts. The building is formal, precise, technological, and abstract.[42]

Nearly thirty years later John C. Parkin reflected on the significance of these two early commissions, alluding to the battles that he and other modernists had to wage to gain acceptance:

The Ontario Association of Architects building, completed in 1954, . . . proved pivotal in the acceptance of contemporary architecture in Ontario. The Association, through its choice of a design in the contemporary style, gave its official imprint of approval to the movement and thus, symbolically, a respectability to contemporary architecture. The Ortho Pharmaceutical building, completed in 1956, with its clear, classic, contemporary design influenced building not only in Ontario but throughout Canada and the United States. Victory had clearly been won for the progressive modern movement, and contemporary design became the 'mainstream' of Canadian architecture.[43]

Many commissions, large and small, followed quickly for the Parkin firm, most of them in the Toronto region. An important federal project was Toronto International Airport (now Lester B. Pearson International Airport): between 1957 and 1965 John B. Parkin Associates (in association with W.A. Ramsay, Chief Architect of Air Services for the Department of Transport) designed the Passenger Terminal (or 'Aeroquay'; now called Terminal 1), the Adminstration Building, and the Control Tower. The circular passenger terminal provided new functional as well as aesthetic solutions to airport design—and parking within 300 feet (92 m) of the ticket lobby.[44]

The Parkin firm is equally well known for its involvement in the design of tall office buildings. 'The "glass" skyscraper', wrote American architectural historian William Jordy, 'was, indeed, the consummate vision of the International Style.'[45] Indebted in part to the Chicago school of the late nineteenth century (page 571), the 'crystal tower' became the symbol of futurism among Europeans in the second and third decades of the twentieth century: Mies van der Rohe proposed glass office towers in famous unexecuted projects of 1919-20. Only after he came to America did Mies have the opportunity to develop the genre, first in a pair of apartment towers at 860-80 Lake Shore Drive, Chicago (1948-51), and then at the Seagram Building in New York (1954-8), in which Philip Johnson (whose earlier involvement with Mies was as a curator) was his collaborator. Mies achieved a severity and a discipline that are best expressed in his much-quoted dictum, 'less is more'. Since the immediate successors to these buildings embody the second generation of modernist design, American architectural historian John Jacobus refers to an 'International Style Revival' occurring around 1950. But in Canada the International Style did not reach its full flowering until the 1950s and

1960s: 'revival' is therefore an inappropriate word to use in the Canadian context.[46]

The climax of the Parkin work and the project with the highest profile was **Toronto-Dominion Centre [15.25]**, a cluster of tall office buildings on King Street West in the heart of downtown Toronto. The initial program (subsequently expanded considerably) was unprecedented in its scale: it called for 3.1 million square feet (288,000 m²) of office space, considerable banking space, 154,000 square feet (14,300 m²) of retail shops, and underground parking for 700 cars. The first phase of the development [15.26], undertaken between 1963 and 1969, produced two towers—46 and 56 storeys high—and a low banking pavilion, all arranged in a balanced, but asymmetrical, composition much like a three-dimensional rendition of a painting by the Dutch abstractionist, Piet Mondrian. The retail concourse is below grade. A third tower (not conceived by Mies) was added in 1974, a fourth tower in 1985-6, and a fifth in 1990-1—the last incorporating the half-century-old Stock Exchange building [14.79]. The radical intrusion of this complex into the downtown fabric precipitated a wave of development that transformed the city and its skyline and inspired similar construction across Canada.[47]

The Toronto-Dominion Centre was designed primarily by Ludwig Mies van der Rohe. The German-born visionary, who was an initiator of the International Style and had immigrated to the US in 1937 at the age of fifty, was head of the architectural school at Chicago's Illinois Institute of Technology (IIT). Since Mies was not registered in Ontario as an architect, John B. Parkin Associates and Bregmann and Hamann, a Toronto partnership that was to become a leader in office-tower design, were the 'architects of record', producing the working drawings and supervising construction respectively. Mies and his co-designers remained deeply committed to the project, giving every detail their fullest attention.

The Toronto-Dominion Centre carried Mies's earlier achievements a step further in the search for a classic solution to the glass skyscraper. The elegant black towers are faced in a curtain wall consisting of bronze-tinted glass supported by a steel frame. Attached to the outside of the structural columns and the mullions are exposed steel I-beams (so called because in section their shape is that of the letter 'I') painted matte black [15.27]. These verticals, seen together with the horizontal lines of the spandrels, overlay the surface with a delicate web-like grid. (Mies also used external I-beams in this way at Lake

15.25 Aerial view of the financial district, Toronto, Ontario, including the Toronto-Dominion Centre. Photograph 1989. Industry, Science and Technology Canada.

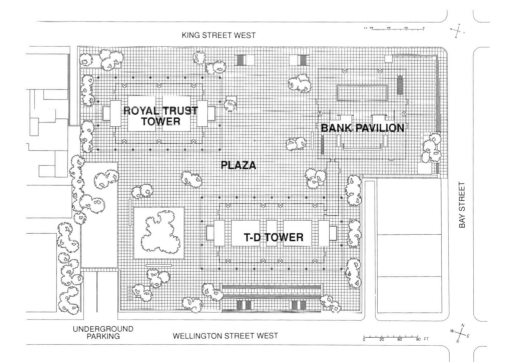

15.26 Site plan of the first phase, Toronto-Dominion Centre, Toronto, Ontario, 1963-9. Courtesy NORR Partnership Limited.

Shore Apartments and the Seagram Building.) Although they perform a minor structural function by stiffening the walls, their real purpose is aesthetic. They run the full height of the window walls and are abruptly severed at the top and bottom, indicating that they do not provide support. The I-beams offer relief to the otherwise flat façade, blur the differences between the widths of the mullions and the columns, and conceal partitions behind some mullions; also—and most important—the I-beam is the fundamental component of steel-frame construction and therefore the ultimate symbol of modern technology.

A mathematical order overlies the entire composition of the T-D Centre, not only in the proportions of the external grid but also in the planning of all elements, large and small. The height of each tower is proportioned to its width and depth. The granite plaza (often criticized for its windy bleakness) is paved in five-foot-square (1.5-m) modules. The banking pavilion, which is treated as a single interior space, is 15 modules (i.e. 75 feet or 22.9 m) square and expresses the grid on its granite floor and in the lighting baffles of its ceiling. English oak and green marble provide an understated richness that relieves the blackness of the enclosing box. All the furniture and fixtures in the banking pavilion and the public spaces of the towers were designed by the architects. (Mies frequently designed furniture. His most famous creation was the 'Barcelona Chair', first made for the German pavilion at the international exposition in Barcelona, 1929.)

The exquisite, clear, crisp linearity and the abstract formalism of the T-D Centre achieved a classic statement of the International Style aesthetic, much in the same way that the Parthenon was a classic statement of Greek architecture. It is a design solution that is independent from issues of use, geography, and context: the Toronto office towers were a refinement of a pair of Chicago apartment buildings erected two decades earlier. Toronto architect Macy DuBois recognized this in a perceptive critique of 1967: he questioned Mies's having used a 20-year-old 'lesson of simplicity', accused him of ignoring functional problems, and dismissed the style as 'an architecture offering *general solutions*'.[48]

Hindsight has led some observers to wish that the Toronto-Dominion Centre could have been allowed to remain the final 'lesson of simplicity'. Unfortunately its 'general solution' became regarded as a formula that could be imitated by architects lacking the design skills, attention to detail, or perfectionism of Mies or Parkin. Boxy steel-and-glass tow-

15.27 Detail of elevation, Toronto-Dominion Centre, Toronto, Ontario, 1963-9. Photograph by Steven Evans.

ers rose again and again, with limited variety and ever-diminishing quality, as a symbol of corporate building. Some of the progeny are fine buildings in their own right, but the insertion of a myriad of tall, unrelieved boxes into the heart of every city in Canada incited a disdain that would hasten the end of international modernism.

The seventies saw the erection of two of the better such bank towers in downtown Toronto that entered the sweepstakes for the title of tallest building in the British Commonwealth. Both were designed by consortia of talented American and Canadian architects. While neither looks like the T-D Centre, both are 'point towers' (tall, narrow buildings whose profiles are uniform from bottom to top) that aggressively competed with it for architectural and corporate recognition. The 57-storey Commerce Court (1968-72; to the right of centre in **15.25**), designed for the Canadian Imperial Bank of Commerce by the American firm I.M. Pei and Associates (introduced below) with Page and Steele, is a stainless-steel-and-glass-clad building that has been set back from King Street so that it both displays, and forms a silvery sleek contrast to, the handsome 1929 Canadian Bank of Commerce [**14.75**] next to it. Across King Street from these buildings (left of centre in **15.25**) is the 72-storey

First Bank Tower (1972-5), a part of First Canadian Place, designed for the Bank of Montreal by Edward Durell Stone (1902-78) Associates, also an American firm, with Bregmann and Hamann. Like Commerce Court, it is faced in light materials (in contrast to the dark T-D Centre), in this case Carrera marble—requiring more of the elegant Italian stone than any other building in the world.[49]

The aggressive competition among the chartered banks for the distinction of having the tallest building was inspired in part by the Royal Commission on Banking and Finance (the Porter Commission) of 1961-4, which encouraged 'a more open and competitive banking system',[50] and also by the attitudes of the private developers with whom the banks formed partnerships. The Toronto-Dominion Centre, for example, was developed jointly by the Toronto-Dominion Bank and CEMP Investments Ltd., a company controlled by the Bronfman family of Montreal, who own the beverage empire that erected the Seagram Building. In 1954 architect and arts patron Phyllis Lambert (represented by the 'P' in 'CEMP') had convinced her father, distillery president Samuel Bronfman, to retain Mies as architect of the Seagram Building, and that successful relationship led to Mies's commission for the T-D Centre.[51]

The severity of the T-D Centre and the other Toronto bank towers provide a contrast to the warmer, more colourful, and more decorative use of modern forms in the BC Electric Building and other West Coast architecture. Such regional differences are not new. The classical discipline of the Toronto buildings recalls the order that characterized Ontario's Georgian Classicism of a century and a half earlier, while the relative decorativeness and freedom of the Vancouver school continues the love for colour, texture, and richness seen in the Queen Anne Revival and Tudor Revival buildings that were so important a part of the early architecture of British Columbia.

The Miesian skyscraper did not represent the only available modern vocabulary. Other architects produced glass towers with different design elements. Three important office buildings in Montreal—all earlier than, or contemporaneous with, the Toronto-Dominion Centre—offered variations on the modernist theme. All three, like their Toronto counterparts, were designed by foreign firms working with local architects, revealing the perception among developers that Canadian firms were not yet capable of designing and executing large office buildings.

The 33-storey **C.I.L. House [15.28]**—built in 1960-2 on Boulevard René-Lévesque (formerly Dorchester Boulevard) in Montreal—was initially designed by Montreal architects Greenspoon, Freedlander, and Dunne as a conventional stepped tower; but American architects Skidmore, Owings, and Merrill reworked it into their own formula for office towers—one that had received wide recognition with the Lever House building in New York (1952), a

15.28 C.I.L. House, Montreal, Quebec, 1960-2. Photograph by Hellmut W. Schade, 1992.

distinguished neighbour of the Seagram Building. The scheme consists in part of a 20,000-square-foot (1,860-m²) typical office floor with a central service core (an area that provided maximum operating efficiency and was easily rentable to large corporations); dedicated 'mechanical floors' (containing machinery for the mechanical services) on an intermediate storey and at the top; and an exterior treatment with a curtain wall of glass, black anodized aluminum spandrels, and continuous aluminum mullions that produce a similar effect, but in lower relief and a contrasting colour, to Mies's I-beams. The effect is one of cold, crisp, geometrical purity, quite similar to—although less sombre than—that of the T-D Centre.[52]

Across the street is **Place Ville Marie** [**15.29**], a 7-acre (2.8-hectare) multi-building development that filled in the gaping hole between the south end of the Canadian National Railways' Mount Royal Tunnel (page 657) and its modernist Central Station (John Schofield, 1938-43). The principal component of Place Ville Marie (1958-66) is a 45-storey aluminum-and-glass-clad tower, whose cruciform shape (with a central service core) allows natural light to reach every part of the large 38,000-square-foot (3,530-m²—nearly an acre) floor-plate. When it was built it had the largest area of any office building in the world. Two low-rise buildings frame the tower. The complex also includes an underground parking garage and a large shopping concourse, containing about 150,000 square feet (14,000 m²). This, the first extensive below-grade retail development in Canada, was linked to the station, the Canadian National Railways' new Queen Elizabeth Hotel, and, over time, to other downtown developments, creating an extensive pedestrian network that has come to be known as the 'underground city' ('*ville intérieure*'). The developer (then called a 'promoter') was the visionary William Zeckendorf of Webb and Knapp, Inc., a New York contracting firm, who called his development 'a city within a city'. I.M. Pei and Partners worked in association with the distinguished Montreal firm of Affleck, Desbarats, Dimakopoulos, Lebensold, Michaud, and Sise (see below) and urban designer Vincent Ponte. Ieoh Ming Pei (b. 1917), a graduate of the Massachusetts Institute of Technology and Harvard (where he studied with Gropius), was the architect for Webb and Knapp at the time; the partner in charge was Henry N. Cobb. Like Pei's later Commerce Court, Place Ville Marie is bright and shiny, although its bulk gives it a far heavier appearance than the slender Toronto tower. As was the case with T-D Centre in

15.29 Place Ville Marie, Montreal, Quebec, 1958-66. Courtesy Propriétés Trizec Ltée.

Toronto, Place Ville Marie incited a wave of speculative high-rise building that utterly changed Montreal's downtown core.[53]

A slightly later Montreal project, **Place Victoria** [**15.30**], built in 1962-6 on historic Square Victoria, also looked abroad for design assistance, this time to Italy. (The developer was a corporation based in Rome.) Greenspoon, Freedlander, and Dunne teamed up on this occasion with architect Luigi Moretti (1907-73) and structural engineer Pier Luigi Nervi (1891-1979), a pioneer in the daring use of concrete. Originally conceived as three huge towers set on a podium, it was scaled down to two lower towers. The initial phase of work saw the construction of only one, the 47-storey Stock Exchange Tower (*La tour de la Bourse*), hailed as the tallest reinforced-concrete office building in the world. Four mammoth columns—one at each corner, clad in white precast concrete panels—and the central core provide the primary support. The dark bronze-coloured aluminum-and-glass curtain walls, which bulge at the centre and taper slightly towards the top, form a nice contrast with the light corner columns. The office floors are neatly divided into three equal blocks, separated by recessed mechanical floors. The dis-

15.30 Place Victoria, Montreal, Quebec, 1962-6. Courtesy Corporation Immobilière Magil Laurentienne.

tinctive composition is far bolder and more plastic than the relatively flat and linear American designs seen in the buildings discussed above. The second tower at Place Victoria was eventually built to a different design as the smaller Hyatt Regency (now Grand) Hotel (1976-7).[54]

Another European approach to modernism is seen in the work of Peter Dickinson (1925-61), a driven designer who crammed his prolific career into eleven years before his tragic death from cancer at the age of 36. Raised in London and trained at the Architectural Association—which had 'gone modern' in the late 1930s—Dickinson was recruited sight unseen by Forsey Page (1885-1970) of Page and Steele who, with his younger partner W. Harland Steele, had an established practice that occasionally ventured into modern design (as at the Moderne Garden Court Apartments, **14.86**). Dickinson arrived in Toronto in 1950 and immediately became the chief designer at Page and Steele, a position he retained for eight years before establishing his own firm. Much of his work consisted of apartment and office buildings for independent Toronto developers, many of them European and/or Jewish, whose separateness from the conservative Toronto 'WASP' establishment allowed them to free Dickinson to design as he wished. This policy contrasted with that of the rival Parkin practice, most of whose clients were from the public, institutional, and big-business sectors.[55]

Dickinson's manner is seen at **Benvenuto Place** [**15.31**], on the edge of the escarpment off Avenue Road in Toronto, built in 1955 for Leon S. Yolles. (It was built in the former gardens of 'Benvenuto', the home of S.H. Janes, the developer of Toronto's Annex. The garden wall can be seen in the photograph.) The large, rambling seven-storey building is faced in a curtain wall of cream-coloured brick enclosing a structure of reinforced concrete columns and innovative flat slabs (or 'plates') that permitted larger spans between columns than had been achievable before. (The structure was designed by engineers Hooper and Yolles, whose partner, Morden Yolles, was the developer's son and a frequent collaborator of Dickinson. 'Flat-plate' construction had been introduced earlier in Vancouver, in apartment buildings in the West End designed from 1949 onwards by engineers Read Jones Christofferson.) The brick (sometimes framing metal-sash windows, sometimes creating patterns of small decorative openings), the projecting balconies (whose edges are exposed concrete), and the flamboyant canopies (removed during renovations in 1977-8, at which

15.31 Benvenuto Place, Toronto, Ontario, 1955. Panda Photography. Courtesy Morden Yolles.

time the apartment-hotel was converted entirely to apartments), produce a lively, rhythmic composition that appears uncontrolled when contrasted with the severity of a disciplined Parkin creation. The Benvenuto has stood the test of time well; in 1990 it became the first 1950s building in Toronto to be designated under the provisions of the Ontario Heritage Act as having architectural significance.[56]

Dickinson liked colour, texture, and variety, yet used them within a wholly modernist language. His first major office building—111 Richmond Street West, Toronto (for Yolles and Kenneth Rotenberg, c. 1954)—presents an expanse of horizontal bands of limestone and glass, with an angled entrance canopy, and, on the west side, a twelve-storey wall of green-glazed brick (of which there is now hardly a sign because of the building that abuts it); and the 12-storey north wing (1955-6) of the Park Plaza Hotel in Toronto (also for Yolles and Rotenberg) is noted for its colour and patterning. He left Page and Steele in January 1958 and formed Peter Dickinson Associates, quickly building it into a large, multi-talented firm with seventy architects working out of offices in Toronto, Ottawa, and Montreal. In the hectic three years left to him, Dickinson received

many commissions, the largest of which was the tall and slender Canadian Imperial Bank of Commerce Building in Montreal (1958-63, in association with Ross, Fish, Duchenes and Barrett of Montreal), the only one of the major bank towers in Toronto or Montreal to have been designed entirely by Canadian architects.[57] Another large commission was the Four Seasons Motor Hotel (1959, demolished) on Jarvis Street, Toronto (for Isadore Sharp), a sleek, handsome low-rise building of fieldstone, white-painted brick, and California redwood trim, in which the rooms were arranged around an interior landscaped court.[58]

The Montreal Stock Exchange Tower of Place Victoria, and the work of Peter Dickinson, pointed the way to the future. From the mid-1960s on, the better new office towers (and other building types as well) were packaged in ever more interesting and varied shapes, while concrete and other solid materials began to replace transparent steel and glass. This came in part as a reaction to the discipline and sameness of the International Style and from a desire to give vent to individual expression.

The new approach first came into prominence with **Toronto City Hall [15.32]**. Public criticism of a dull design for a new city hall—commissioned in 1953 from a group of established Toronto firms—led to Eric Arthur's being directed to organize a com-

15.32   Toronto City Hall, Toronto, Ontario, 1961-5. City of Toronto Archives/1983-120.

petition, which attracted submissions from around the world; some 520 architects from 42 countries submitted drawings and models in April 1958. Among the six jurors were C.E. Pratt, noted Finnish-American modernist Eero Saarinen, and Arthur himself. The winner was Viljo Revell (1910-64) of Finland, working with three compatriots; he affiliated with John B. Parkin Associates for the construction.[59]

Revell's landmark building of 1961-5 is a bold, sculptural design that features two thin concave freestanding towers of unequal heights (20 and 27 storeys) that embrace the saucer-shaped Council Chamber. The inner faces of the towers are glazed; the outer faces are covered with a ribbed veneer of precast concrete panels inlaid with strips of marble. The towers represent the separateness of the two municipal governments that were to use the building, the City of Toronto and Metropolitan Toronto. The towers and the Chamber (whose handsome interior has some of the qualities of a Greek amphitheatre) rest on a broad podium that contains public facilities and offices for the mayor, Metro chairman (now used solely to receive dignitaries—the Metro Toronto offices are in a new building elsewhere), and councillors. The two entrances are situated beneath an overhanging roof supported by columns. Inside, the square low-ceilinged foyer is dominated by a huge white column that mushrooms into the broad base of the Council Chamber.

The City Hall stands as a daringly expressionist conceit— the antithesis of the 'general solution' (Macy DuBois's phrase) that was then favoured for office buildings, such as the contemporaneous Toronto-Dominion Centre (although both complexes feature towers of uneven height, with a pavilion between). Its strikingly plastic quality—made possible by the use of concrete—was commented on by James Murray, a Toronto architect and champion of the International Style who founded *The Canadian Architect* in 1955. He noted (in 1965): 'It is undoubtedly among the world's most consciously contrived, sculpturally derived architectural forms—and so calls to judgment the separateness of architectural and sculptural values.'[60]

The architectural community heaped praise on the new City Hall. Ron Thom, for one, wrote that 'It has avoided eclecticism completely, and yet is in no danger of being mistaken for a commercial office complex. It is a convincing and poetic expression of the various parts of the living function it houses.'[61]

The new City Hall quickly became a civic symbol, as Revell intended, and with the open space in front of it—named Nathan Phillips Square after the mayor

who had battled for a modern design—became the living centre of a new and dynamic Toronto. The square is both a setting for the buildings and a popular place for assembly. Flanked by a defining colonnade, it features a reflecting pool that becomes a skating rink in winter. Parking for 2,350 cars is provided below ground.

The building and the square occupy the site, on Queen Street West, that had been earmarked for a civic centre in John Lyle's City Beautiful plan of 1911 [12.20], between the Georgian Osgoode Hall [4.38] and Lennox's Romanesque Revival City Hall [10.31]—which, after once being threatened with demolition, has been adapted as a courthouse. The three neighbouring buildings provide a stimulating contrast of masterpieces from three eras of architecture.

Beyond the Metropolises The buildings discussed above were built in or near the cities of Vancouver, Toronto, and Montreal—urban centres that certainly led the way in the acceptance and promotion of the International Style. But parallel efforts occurred elsewhere in Canada as well.

Alberta, a province with a relatively short building tradition, was particularly receptive to the new style. Several architects in Calgary and Edmonton had experimented with modernism in the 1930s and 1940s, as at the Varscona [14.84] and Garneau Theatres in Edmonton, both built in 1940. A more important event was the construction of the **Barron Building** [15.33] on 8 Avenue sw in Calgary (1949-51), a combined office building and cinema designed by John A. Cawston (1911-66) of Cawston and Stevenson. Built by lawyer and developer J.B. Barron, the building was the first one in Calgary to respond to the need for oil-company offices that resulted from the discovery in 1947 of the Leduc oil field, 30 km south of Edmonton. The original tenants of the Barron Building included the Sun Oil Company, the Shell Oil Company, and the Socony Mobil Oil Company—which helped to keep petroleum industry headquarters in Calgary, rather than Edmonton. The office district that subsequently developed, in this western end of downtown Calgary, became known as the 'oil patch'. The 11-storey Barron Building—clad in yellow brick, Tyndall limestone, and ornamental aluminum—combines Art Deco straight lines, sleekness, and ornament with the ribbon windows and cubic massing of the International Style.[62]

Other buildings in the oil patch continued the modern theme. The Petroleum Building (1951)—with hard, rectilinear lines, and six tiers of ribbon

windows along the façade framed by textured piers—was designed by Rule, Wynn, and Rule, an important Alberta firm that helped to prepare the way for modernism. The principals were John U. Rule (1904-78), Gordon Wynn, and Peter L. Rule (1913-64), three graduates of the short-lived architecture program at the University of Alberta who joined in practice in 1938.[63]

Toronto was not the only city to build a new city hall as a symbol of a rejuvenated, forward-looking municipality; others included Edmonton and Ottawa. The **Edmonton City Hall** [**15.34**] by Dewar, Stevenson, and Stanley, with Hugh W. Seton the principal designer (1955-7, demolished), brought a fussy version of the International Style to the Alberta capital. Kelvin Stanley was the partner in charge. The horizontally composed structure, with *de rigueur* ribbon windows, bulged at the centre (somewhat like

15.33 *(left)* Barron Building, Calgary, Alberta, 1949-51. Photograph by Lorne Simpson, 1994.

15.34 Edmonton City Hall, Edmonton, Alberta, 1955-7. Photograph *c.* 1960. City of Edmonton Archives/EA-20-990.

15.35 Ottawa City Hall, Ottawa, Ontario, 1958. Photograph by Harold Kalman, 1965.

the BC Electric Building), had solar fins over the windows to control sunlight (a device often used by Le Corbusier), and was topped by a penthouse cafeteria with a sculpted roof. To the left of centre in the photograph, the Council Chamber protruded from the ground as a rectilinear block on stilts, and the public counter-service areas were on the right. Rich materials were used throughout: travertine for the spandrels, red granite for the end walls, and green marble in the lobby. Mayor William Hawrelak and his Council intended that the new City Hall should be a symbol of modernism and progress. Unfortunately, the reliance on borrowed clichés, rather than on creative new design solutions, determined that its image would soon become dated. By the 1970s the building looked distinctly un-modern, and in 1980 a competition was held to design its replacement—which did not produce a new building. But a decade later (after barely more than 30 years in service) the City Hall was demolished, and its successor was finally built (Gene Dub, 1992-3).[64]

Similar in conception, but far more accomplished in design, and pristine in its perfection, was the **Ottawa City Hall [15.35]**, designed by Rother, Bland, Trudeau of Montreal and built in 1958 after a nation-

al competition. Vincent Rother had practised in England; John Bland (b. 1911) was the passionate advocate of modernism at the School of Architecture of McGill University; and Charles Trudeau was a talented designer and the brother of Pierre Elliott Trudeau. The composition is nearly identical to Edmonton's, with the Council Chamber projecting from an office block and a penthouse on top; but all is treated in a well-proportioned and disciplined manner that expresses the nature of the structure, which is clad in limestone, aluminum, and glass curtain walls. As at Edmonton, the municipal functions outgrew the building, but Ottawa's pride in its modern masterpiece determined that the new work (by Moshe Safdie, 1992-3) should complement, rather than replace, the earlier building. It does this by being wrapped around its predecessor in a way that allows unobstructed views of it from both the front and the back.[65]

Ottawa architect Hart Massey (b. 1918)—the son of Vincent Massey—had a short but important career, from 1953 until his early retirement in 1970. His own striking **Hart Massey house [15.36]**, built in

15.36 Hart Massey house, Ottawa, Ontario, 1959. Photograph by John Roaf, 1982.

1959 on Lansdowne Road in the well-to-do Ottawa suburb of Rockcliffe Park, is a minimalist structure consisting of a delicate steel frame that contains a series of modular 'boxes', some glazed, others with opaque walls. It recalls the two famous 'glass houses' built a decade earlier by the masters of modernism: Mies van der Rohe's Farnsworth House in Plano, Illinois (1946-50), and Philip Johnson's house for himself in New Canaan, Connecticut (1947-9). Whereas the two American houses are set on tidy flat grassed clearings, with trees as a backdrop, and dominate their surroundings, the Massey house is integrated into a less-disciplined sloping site among trees on the shore of MacKay Lake. By raising the house free of the ground on thin columns, Massey left the site virtually untouched (a characteristically Canadian acceptance of the natural landscape), and the structure floats within this setting. The steel members were originally painted white, but Massey later coloured them black to provide a better contrast with the trees. Hart Massey was awarded a Massey Medal for his design—which his neighbour, the distinguished landscape architect Humphrey Carver, described as 'a beautiful and very cerebral house'.[66]

Modernist houses—with rectilinear compositions, flat roofs, and broad expanses of windows—appeared across the country. One of the countless competent designs is Six Acres (1954-7) in Edmonton, the home and office designed for themselves by architects Jean Wallbridge (1912-67) and Mary Imre (1918-88), both of whom had worked in the office of Rule, Wynn, and Rule.[67]

Winnipeg also acquired some good modern buildings in the years around 1960. An example was set by the Faculty of Architecture in the University of Manitoba, which taught progressive principles and erected a new classroom and office building, the **J.A. Russell Building** [15.37] (Smith, Carter, Parkin, 1959). The two principal storeys appear to float above the ground; but in fact they are cantilevered to overhang beyond the basement. The exposed structural columns stand proud of the curtain wall (as at the Ortho plant in Toronto), creating an analogy with a classical Greek temple—except that there is no support at the corners here. The mullions are continuous through the two storeys, creating a persistent grid as they cross the horizontal lines of the win-

15.37 J.A. Russell Building, University of Manitoba, Winnipeg, Manitoba, 1959. Photograph by Henry Kalen.

dows and spandrels. A similarly symmetrical, formal, and precious temple-like effect occurs at the Winnipeg Civic Centre (Green, Blankstein, Russell Associates, 1962-5), in which white free-standing columns set up a syncopated rhythm across the façade. It replaced the eccentric old City Hall [**7.37**].[68]

By the mid-1960s international modernism was firmly established in most regions of Canada. What had begun as experimentation among a handful of Vancouver architects and artists, and by a few buildings in central Canada designed by American architects, was now the accepted language of Canadian businesses, public institutions, and municipalities. The buildings of the modern movement were reduced to a series of universal designs—one for offices, one for houses, one for city halls, and so on—that could be used and re-used with variations. In the hands of the best designers, the results were objects of considerable beauty and utility; in those of lesser talents, they could be banal. In either case, the future of the style was limited. It could progress only to the point of near-perfection and did not permit sufficient vari-

ety to go on pleasing indefinitely. Buildings in the International Style were seen by many observers as being cold, impersonal, and unaccepting of the idiosyncracies of time and place. These limitations led first to variants that were more personally and regionally expressive, and ultimately to the complete fall from favour of the International Style.

Late Modernism, Expressionism, and Regionalism

The limitations of the International Style were recognized by a second group of architects, most of them somewhat younger people who grew up with modernism and recognized the limitations of the International Style. Many pursued directions that were similar to those seen in the Toronto City Hall. They extended and exaggerated the modernist vocabulary beyond the glass curtain wall; developed bolder, more sculptural shapes; used structural components in a more ornamental manner; and sought a more aggressive expression of function, individualism, and structure. This phase of modern architecture, which was prevalent in Canada from the mid-1960s through the 1970s, corresponds to some extent to what Charles Jencks and other European and American writers have described as 'Late-Modernism'.[69]

A fine example of Late-Modernism is **Crown Life Place** [15.38] on West Georgia Street in Vancouver, built in 1976-8 and designed by the firm of William Rhone and W. Randle Iredale. The principal designer was Peter Cardew (b. 1939), who had come to Canada from England, where he studied at the Kingston School of Art. Rather than imposing the International Style's 'general solution', Cardew

15.38 Crown Life Place, Vancouver, British Columbia, 1976-8. Photograph by Robin Ward, 1992.

responded thoughtfully to the particular site and environmental conditions. The V-shaped office tower is oriented to present window walls facing the mountains and the water to the north and west, and concrete walls to the south—a direction that lacks scenery and produces the greatest heat-gain from the sun. The window walls are sheathed in a somewhat Miesian curtain wall of green-tinted glass and aluminum mullions; but the aggressive angular shape, concrete 'pilotis' (stilts, popularized in the 1920s by Le Corbusier), and the exposed concrete elevator tower deviate from the lessons of Mies and introduce ideas from the new 'Brutalist' style associated with the Scottish architect James Stirling (b. 1926). The spacious brick plaza features a cascade of water and a single-storey retail block.[70] Somewhat ironically, the construction of Crown Life Place required demolishing the generation-old Marwell Building (Semmens and Simpson, 1952), an early landmark of international modernism that had been awarded the first Massey Gold Medal for Architecture. Only a handful of architects raised a fuss: the International Style evidently had a short life in Canada.

The Toronto firm of Diamond and Myers (the former partnership of A.J. Diamond, b. 1932, and Barton Myers, b. 1934) produced a number of stunning Late-Modern designs. Myers, a native of Virginia who worked with the American architect Louis Kahn (1901-74) before immigrating to Toronto in 1968, and whose principal office is now in Los Angeles, was the partner in charge for the much-admired **Wolf house** [15.39] on Roxborough Drive in Toronto (1975). Conceived as a prototype for what Myers called a ' "shoe-box" row house', the long and relatively narrow plan (79' by 36'-6", or 24 by 11 m) has no windows along the side walls, but is opened up by a light-court mid-way along the west side— here facing parkland and a ravine, since there is no adjoining house in the 'row'. The front elevation consists of a recessed parking area and entry ramp (flanked by industrial handrails) on the ground floor and three bedrooms on the second floor (with steel 'Dutch doors' beside the plate-glass windows to provide ventilation). The living- and dining-rooms (below) and master bedroom suite (above) are placed at the rear, looking out at the lush garden [15.40, 41]. In his selection of materials and finishes, Myers 'explored the potential for achieving an elegant architecture (in both the mathematical and aesthetic sense) out of the more common building products used today.' The structure is assembled from a steel frame, with metal decking and open-web steel joists of the type commonly used for warehouses, all detailed to

15.39 Wolf house, Toronto, Ontario, 1975. Barton Myers Associates, Inc.

15.40, 15.41 *(below)* Ground-floor and second-floor plans, Wolf house, Toronto, Ontario, 1975. Drawing by David Byrnes.

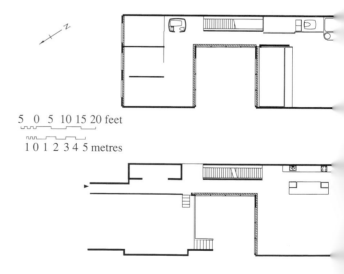

5 0 5 10 15 20 feet

1 0 1 2 3 4 5 metres

industry standards. The side walls are finished with horizontal aluminum siding. Sliding doors and sliding wall-sections within the house (reminiscent of J.C.H. Porter's Vancouver house of 1948) increase the flexibility of the space. The Wolf house indeed achieves its intended elegance. Its tasteful use of industrial materials impressed a generation of architects and foreshadowed the 'high-tech' trend of a decade later. The house is Late-Modernist in its somewhat ornamental use of structural members (a characteristic, it will be recalled, of Mies's earlier use of applied I-beams at the Toronto-Dominion Centre) and in the variety of its surface finishes.[71]

Diamond and Myers, in association with Edmonton architect Richard L. Wilkin, produced the equally sophisticated **Citadel Theatre** [15.42] on Winston Churchill Square in Edmonton (1976). The lobby is enclosed in walls and skylights of glass, allowing theatre-goers to see out, as they are seen by outsiders during intermissions. The stepped reinforced-concrete underside of the seating of the 685-seat Shoctor Theatre, the largest of the three original auditoriums, forms the ceiling of the lobby. A second phase of construction in 1983-4 (by the Chandler Kennedy

15.42   Citadel Theatre, Edmonton, Alberta, 1976.
Photograph by Daryl Benson, 1994.

Architectural Group) created two additional stages
and the large Lee Pavilion—an indoor garden, with
a large pond and waterfall, that is available to both
patrons and the general public. Entered at ground
level, the public amenity is a 24-hour public space
that is an extension of the sidewalk, forming a part
of the city's Pedway system (addressed below).[72]

Late-Modernism did not flourish in Canada as it
did in Europe and the US. As Canadian architects
were never completely sold on the International
Style, they showed less respect for it and its variants
than their counterparts in other countries. Instead,
many chose to deviate from international modernism in order to express a regional character and
a personal vision, while also employing a wholly
modern vocabulary and technology. For this second
phase of modernism in the Canadian context, the
term 'Modern Expressionism' may therefore be more
appropriate than Late-Modernism, because it emphasizes the architects' new expressive directions.
Whatever name is preferred, the buildings described
in the remainder of this section combine aspects of
European and American Late-Modernism with a very
Canadian emphasis on regionalism and expressionism.

An important early project that anticipated aspects
of Late-Modernism—and one that brought together the architecture of western and central Canada—
was **Massey College [15.43]**, a graduate college at
the University of Toronto that provides living and
common space for 95 'fellows'. The facility was built
in 1960-3 by an endowment of the Massey
Foundation, represented by the Right Honourable
Vincent Massey—the same client who had sponsored Hart House [14.1] at the University a half-century earlier. In a memorandum of 1960, Massey
explained that the new graduate college

should, in its form, reflect the life which will go on
inside it, and should possess certain qualities—dignity, grace, beauty and warmth. Such a college as
we have in mind possesses antecedents in various
countries, and whatever their physical forms may
be or the date of their erection, they have a character in common. What we wish is a home for a

15.43 *(above)* Massey College, Toronto, Ontario, 1960-3. Courtesy the Master and Fellows of Massey College.

15.44 Dining-hall, Massey College, Toronto, Ontario, 1960-3. Courtesy the Master and Fellows of Massey College.

community of scholars whose life will have intimacy, but at the same time academic dignity.[73]

The competition for the college was won by Thompson, Berwick and Pratt, with Ron Thom—who had become a partner in 1958—the designer and architect in charge. Thom moved to Toronto to supervise construction and remained in that city, establishing his own firm, R.J. Thom Architects (later changed to The Thom Partnership).

Thom's brilliant solution was at once modern and traditional. Massey College consists of a three-storey brick quadrangle arranged around the edges of a compact one-acre (0.4-hectare) site on a busy street corner within the grounds of the University of Toronto. The residential suites—organized in clusters, each with a common entry and staircase—and the communal rooms all open onto the landscaped interior courtyard, satisfying the requirement for intimacy, while also shutting out traffic noise.

Every surface, and every element of the plan, is broken up into small elements; all are dynamic, shifting, varied. Rather than the clarity and rationalism of the International Style (at which Thom showed himself to be a leader with the BC Electric Building), we see a far greater complication of form and a more decorative use of structural elements. The elevations constantly advance and recede, establishing an irregular rhythm of vertical units of windows and solids—the latter consisting of warm umber brick load-bearing walls. The window mullions and spandrels are fashioned from limestone. (Thom had wanted concrete, but the contractor pointed out that stone was cheaper.) The spandrels are filled with carved geometric forms that recall, without ever imitating, Gothic trefoils; and the mullions project, pinnacle-like, above the parapet, to form a picturesque silhouette that is emphasized by the lace-like openwork above the entrance, the dining-hall, and the tall belltower. Thom showed meticulous care for detail inside as well as out. The magnificent 25-foot-high (7.6-m) **dining-hall [15.44]** is illuminated by clerestory windows by day, and at night by light fixtures that were designed by Thom (as was all the furniture). The tiny chapel is covered by low ribbed vaults.

Every element of Massey College relates closely to the centuries-old 'Oxbridge' tradition—as well as to the more recent Gothic-inspired colleges at the University of Toronto—and therefore meets Massey's requirement that the building should follow its antecedents. It suggests all the features of a Collegiate Gothic quadrangle (such as Hart House) without displaying a single direct quotation from the Gothic, since the design vocabulary is entirely modern and non-historical. Massey College is Gothic only by *association*, in much the same way that the Gothic Revival churches of the nineteenth century were associated with those of the Middle Ages, or as the architects of the Arts and Crafts Movement intended that their houses should be associated with English vernacular dwellings. Indeed, the question of whether Massey College is a *survival* or a *revival* of the Late Gothic Revival (i.e. the Gothic Revival third time around) surfaces in the same way in which architectural historians ask whether English builders who used Gothic forms in the seventeenth century were continuing or reviving the medieval Gothic style. At Massey College, the decorative qualities, natural materials, and respect for the site are all characteristics of the British Columbia modernism that Thom brought to Toronto, and are directly descended from the Arts and Crafts Movement, which had so strong an impact on that western province. Many critics of the 1960s, however, regarded Massey College as retrograde. One writer, evidently sympathetic to the International Style (then at the peak of its popularity), denounced these associative forms as historicist impurities, and maintained that the building 'set Canadian architecture back fifty years.'[74] Now, at a distance of several decades, we are able to recognize Massey College as inspired contextual architecture that used the architectural heritage and the surroundings as inventive springboards to a new, wholly modern expressionist architecture. It not only satisfies Vincent Massey's desire for a building possessing 'dignity, grace, beauty and warmth', but continues to be a happy domain for countless students and scholars.

In 1963 Thom received a second, and much larger, collegiate opportunity when he was appointed co-ordinating architect and phase-one designer for an entirely new campus, **Trent University**, on a lovely 1500-acre (600-hectare) site along the Otonabee River near Peterborough, Ontario. The program explicitly requested that the buildings share the spirit of other outstanding universities, citing the University of York in England as an example. The buildings of the first phase, erected between 1964 and 1968, are constructed primarily of grey concrete, using granite aggregate from the region and therefore yielding the colour of local stone. Cedar and pine warm the interiors. The view of **Champlain College [15.45]**, designed by Thom (but officially a work of Thompson, Berwick and Pratt), shows his highly picturesque and abstract composition of forms that succeed in achieving a Collegiate Gothic feeling.[75]

15.45 Champlain College, Trent University, Peterborough, Ontario, 1964-8. Photograph © Steven Evans.

Thom continued his Toronto practice for two decades, maintaining a happy marriage of central-Canadian and West Coast architecture in buildings such as the Shaw Festival Theatre at Niagara-on-the-Lake (1973) and the plan and some buildings for the Metro Toronto Zoo (1970-4).[76]

Among the other architects from the West who worked in this new regional and expressionist mode, the most celebrated is Arthur Erickson, whose buildings were discussed above in the context of Vancouver.

Prairie regionalism. The prairie environment inspired a very different architectural response: the land is flat, the climate hostile, and the society rigid—in contrast to the mountains, the benign climate, and the flexible lifestyles of the coast. Edmonton architect Peter Hemingway maintains that because of these factors,

> the most powerfully original buildings in the post-war era have come from here. I would go further and say that perhaps the only truly Canadian—as against adopted—architectural images have been created on the Prairies, out of this harsh necessity for strong forms in a landscape wide as Heaven or Hell.[77]

A number of architects have contributed to the creation of these strong forms, among them Étienne Gaboury in Manitoba, Clifford Wiens in Saskatchewan, and Hemingway and Douglas Cardinal in Alberta.

Étienne-Joseph Gaboury (b. 1930) is a native of Manitoba and a graduate of the University of Manitoba, whose excellent architectural program, directed by John Russell, was linked to the Bauhaus-derived curriculum at Gropius's Harvard.[78] Gaboury spent a year in Paris at the École des Beaux-Arts, where he was impressed by the work of Le Corbusier and other early modernists, and then returned to practise in his home province. Writer Carol Moore Ede paid him tribute for having

> a deep understanding of his native geography. Each of his buildings pays homage to the vast flat expanses of the Prairies, and his subtle use of materials and light gives rise to a special and personal regionalism.[79]

His **Église du Précieux Sang** (Church of the Precious Blood) [15.46] in St Boniface, Manitoba, was built in 1967-8 for a predominantly Métis congregation, when Gaboury was in partnership with Denis Lussier and Frank Sigurdson. (Since 1976 he has been the principal of his own firm.) The tipi provided a source of inspiration for the bold, sculptural design, but the prototype has been twisted to

15.46 Interior, Église du Précieux Sang, St Boniface, Manitoba, 1967-8. Photograph by Henry Kalen. Courtesy Gaboury Associates.

produce a dynamic, spiral plan and a swirling super-structure. Within the church twenty-five glued-laminated beams, the largest one 100 feet (30 m) long, support the roof of rough cedar shakes in the same way that poles provide a frame for a tipi. The smoke hole is implied by the dramatically contorted sky-light, which allows the controlled entry of light to accentuate the sculptural building-form. Below the roof structure is an undulating glazed-brick base that bulges to accommodate chapels and confessionals. The circular seating focuses on a freestanding altar, following the reforms introduced by the Second Vatican Council (1962-5) that encouraged the con-gregation to participate more actively than before in the mass. The expressionist approach to creating a devotional space seems to offer homage to Le Corbusier's renowned Chapel of Notre-Dame-du-Haut at Ronchamp, France (1951-5), although the forms, materials, and appearance are worlds apart—Gaboury's vocabulary in his church is entirely Canadian. Both architects, however, turned their

15.47   Église du Précieux Sang, St Boniface, Manitoba, 1967-8. Photograph by Henry Kalen. Courtesy Gaboury Associates.

backs on the rationalist principles on which the mod-ern movement had been based in order to create reli-gious buildings that use space, form, and light to evoke a strongly visceral reaction.[80]

Gaboury was involved in a number of other build-ings in St Boniface, including the St Boniface Civic Centre (1965), which also suggests an admiration for Le Corbusier; and a new St Boniface Cathedral (1970-2) within the stabilized ruins of Omer Marchand's Beaux-Arts cathedral [**10.58**], which had been gut-ted by fire in 1968.[81] Gaboury was subsequently award-ed two important federal commissions: the Canadian Embassy in Mexico (1980-1) and the **Royal Canadian Mint** [**15.48**] near Winnipeg (1978). The latter retains the architect's bold sense of form, and is construct-ed of slick, gleaming, high-tech materials. A land-mark on the eastern approach to Winnipeg, the prin-cipal glass-clad triangular mass soars above the flat prairie.[82]

Clifford Wiens (b. 1926) has worked in a paral-lel manner in his native Saskatchewan. His **Heating and Cooling Plant at the University of Regina** [**15.49**] dominates its environment with its strong A-frame constructed (in 1967) of precast, post-ten-

15.48 Royal Canadian Mint, near Winnipeg, Manitoba, 1978. Photograph by Henry Kalen. Courtesy Gaboury Associates.

15.49 Heating and Cooling Plant, University of Regina, Regina, Saskatchewan, 1967. Photograph by Henry Kalen. Courtesy Clifford Wiens.

sioned concrete arches 40 feet (12.2 m) high at the peak and surmounted by a horizontal cooling tower. The unpainted steel roof was designed to oxidize so that its rich, brown patina gradually weathered to bluish grey. With this building Wiens, who was raised on a Mennonite farm, revealed his devotion to the prairie vernacular, and particularly to grain elevators—'one of the very few successful Prairie buildings'—whose aggressive profiles made them function 'as symbols and beacons, giving scale and a sense of place.'[83] His newer work, such as the regional offices of the Royal Bank of Canada (1980) and the Canadian Broadcasting Corporation (1982) in

15.50 Muttart Conservatory, Edmonton, Alberta, 1977.
Photograph by James Dow.

15.51 Winnipeg Art Gallery, Winnipeg, Manitoba, 1971.
Photograph by Hellmut W. Schade, 1986.

Regina, reflect urban corporate architecture without
sacrificing his dedication to Prairie expressionism.

The **Muttart Conservatory [15.50]** in Edmonton
(1977), by the English-born Peter Hemingway (b.
1929), with Paul Chung the designer-in-charge, faced
the challenge of providing controlled environments
in a climate of extremes by burying the concrete walls
of four linked conservatories and roofing them with
glass pyramids of prefabricated steel-and-aluminum
greenhouse framing. The four pyramids vary in size,
the largest being the 78-foot-square (23.8-m) Tropical
House, and are arranged around a central reception
and service area. Hemingway's Giza-on-the-
Saskatchewan—which perhaps also foreshadows I.M.
Pei's glass pyramid in the Louvre's central courtyard (completed 1989)—reflects both the summer
and the winter sun, providing welcome relief to the
bleak river bank.[84]

Other buildings in the Prairie Provinces have shown
a similar propensity for assertive forms. The **Winnipeg
Art Gallery [15.51]**, built in 1971, responded to its
triangular site—and to a preference for exhibition
galleries without windows—with an austere wedge:
its sheer walls of light-grey Tyndall limestone (placed
over reinforced-concrete bearing walls), with a chunk
taken out of the top (to provide a view from the restaurant's outdoor eating area), converge at a knife-edged
point. Associated architects Gustavo da Roza (b.
1933) and the Number Ten Architectural Group

(with Isadore Coop leading his firm's team) won a competition whose jury described the design as a 'brilliant symbolization of progressive Winnipeg'—an attribute that is commonly claimed by modern municipal buildings. (The Winnipeg Art Gallery was completed several years before the widely praised and similarly conceived East Building of the National Gallery of Art in Washington, DC, designed by I.M. Pei and built in 1974-8.)[85]

Ukrainian churches, which were so conspicuous a feature of earlier Prairie architecture [9.39-44], continued to be impressive in recent years, largely through the work of Radoslav Zuk, a European-born professor of architecture at McGill University who designed numerous Ukrainian churches in Canada and the US in association with various local firms.

15.52   St Stephen's Byzantine Ukrainian Catholic Church, Calgary, Alberta, 1979-82. Photograph by Radoslav Zuk.

His **St Stephen Byzantine Ukrainian Catholic Church** [15.52] on 45 Street sw in Calgary (1979-82)—in which Hugh McMillan Architect Ltd executed Zuk's concept—has a brick-and-cedar rectangular nave (scaled to harmonize with the residential neighbourhood) out of which spring five cedar-clad towers topped with stylized segmented domes.[86]

The most intense of this group of expressionist Prairie architects is Douglas Cardinal. Born in 1934 in Red Deer, Alberta, to Métis parents, Cardinal enrolled in the School of Architecture at the University of British Columbia, but reacted badly to the curriculum: 'You were supposed to be interested in early Le Corbusier and the Bauhaus School', he wrote, '[but] that left me cold. Corb's Ronchamp—now that's what I'm interested in.'[87] Cardinal failed his design studio and was told by Fred Lasserre that he had 'the wrong family background' to become an architect.[88] He subsequently graduated with honours in architecture from the University of Texas, and returned to Canada.

Cardinal revealed his highly individual architectural approach in his first public commission, **St Mary's Roman Catholic Church** [15.53] at Red Deer (1965-8), a complex curvilinear building. Father Werner Merx, the newly appointed parish priest of the young congregation, was a liberal Oblate who saw Cardinal's deviations from orthodoxy as being compatible with the reforms of Vatican II. In developing the spatial organization of the sacraments, and other building components, Cardinal used schematic models that were the three-dimensional equivalents of 'bubble' diagrams. When he was satisfied with the arrangement, he translated these bubbles into space, which yielded a complex, curvilinear form [15.54]. The focus is the altar, a six-ton block of Tyndall limestone that is raised on a stepped podium and illuminated from above by a cylindrical skylight; around it the church grew 'in the manner of a seashell around its soft creature.' The space is enclosed within a double red-brick wall, with reinforced concrete in the cavity, and is covered by an amorphous post-tensioned concrete roof, slung like a hammock with a 120-foot (36.6-m) span—similar to Mexican structures that Cardinal had seen while living in Texas. Calgary engineer Henry Ricketts (of the firm Ricketts and Evers) recognized that the structure was too complex to calculate manually, and so he resorted to a computer at a major American university—an early use of computers for structural design. The tops of the walls (one can hardly speak of a roof-line) undulate as freely as the plan. Three voids in one parapet wall were created as a cam-

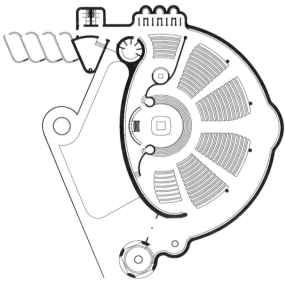

15.53 St Mary's Roman Catholic Church, Red Deer, Alberta, 1965-8. Photograph by Hu Hohn. Courtesy Douglas Cardinal Architect Ltd.

15.54 Plan of St Mary's Roman Catholic Church, Red Deer, Alberta, 1965-8. Drawing by David Byrnes.

panile, to accommodate bells (when the parish could afford them).[89]

Cardinal thought his design was appropriate in the context of the recurring curvilinear theme in Catholic religious architecture, seen in the Baroque churches of Italy and Mexico and in the Art Noveau work of Barcelona architect Antonio Gaudi (1852-1926). St Mary's also recalls the 1920s expressionism of German architect Erich Mendelsohn (1887-1953). As Cardinal explained:

> I thought I was in step with what Corb and [Finnish architect] Alvar Aalto and [Spanish-Mexican architect] Felix Candela were doing. I felt they were

taking shapes and forms and providing a sense of drama and excitement.... With my church, I tried to evolve a form growing out of the functional requirements and to show respect for materials, much in the same thinking as the International Style—form follows function, less is more, all that jargon. But instead of using rectilinear forms, I used curvilinear forms. I think in curvilinear forms. My sketches are all curved forms, amorphous shapes. That's the way I think, the way I'm made. Even music I see in pictures.[90]

This way of thinking, and designing, revealed itself clearly in Cardinal's subsequent work. His principal public buildings in the 1970s were Grande Prairie Regional College in Grande Prairie, Alberta (1972-6), the Alberta Government Services Building at Ponoka (1977), and the St Albert Civic and Cultural Centre at St Albert, Alberta (1983), all of which adapted the architectural language of curved brick walls to programs of greater complexity. He also designed a number of schools, one of which, the Diamond Jenness School at Hay River, NWT, has deep purple steel-clad walls—the colour was chosen by the students—whose curved corners and stairwells make the plan appear freer than it actually is. His architectural office became one of the earliest to rely entirely on computer-aided drafting and design (CADD).[91]

Cardinal's first project outside Alberta and the Northwest Territories brought Prairie expressionism to Central Canada amidst a great deal of fanfare: the striking **Canadian Museum of Civilization [15.55]** in Hull, Quebec, built between 1983 and 1989 in association with Tétreault, Parent, Languedoc et Associés of Montreal. Situated directly across the Ottawa River from the Parliament Buildings, the museum consists of two curved blocks, intended to appear like rugged rock outcrops rising at the river's shore. In his competition proposal for the building,

Cardinal wrote that architecture 'is living sculpture . . . [intended] to symbolize the goals and aspirations of our culture';[92] he explained elsewhere that:

The Museum is a symbolic form. It speaks of the emergence of this continent, its forms sculptured by the winds, the rivers, the glaciers. . . . [It] truly aspires to be ... a celebration of man's evolution and achievement.'[93]

The buildings stand, then, as metaphors of the natural landscape. Seen from the grounds, the one on the right or east (called the Canadian Shield Wing) contains the public exhibition galleries and is identified by the tall columns and the glazing, which illuminates the Grand Hall; and by a series of copper vaults, beneath the highest of which is the large, curved History Hall. Both galleries overwhelm the visitor with their immense scale. The left-hand building (called the Glacier Wing) accommodates the conservation and administration functions and is enclosed within horizontally articulated undulating walls faced in rusticated and smooth-dressed Tyndall limestone. Seen from the entrance in Hull, the blocks frame a magnificent view of the Parliament Buildings. Because it represents both a very personal and a regional expression of architectural form, the Canadian Museum of Civilization has inspired considerable praise, along with some criticism.

The Museum of Civilization forms a nice contrast with its sister institution across the Ottawa River, the **National Gallery of Canada [15.56]**. The nation's art gallery was built at the same time (1983-8), to designs by Parkin/Safdie, a joint venture of Parkin Associates (which in 1977 had won a competition for a National Gallery on another site) and

15.55 Canadian Museum of Civilization, Hull, Quebec, 1983-9. Canadian Museum of Civilization.

15.56 National Gallery of Canada, Ottawa, Ontario, 1983-8. Photograph by Claude Lupien. National Gallery of Canada.

Moshe Safdie, the building's designer. The Israeli-born, McGill-educated Safdie (b. 1938) creates a geometry of rectilinear surfaces and hard edges where Cardinal indulges in sensuous curves; his granite-faced exterior walls are cool and smooth where the other's limestone walls are warmly textured. Safdie's Gallery is immaculately ordered, while Cardinal's museum is flamboyantly expressionistic. The National Gallery is laid out in the manner of a classical museum, as a series of linked and humanly scaled picture galleries, many illuminated with natural light from above. The *pièce de résistance* is the Great Hall, a glazed pavilion whose shape reflects that of the nearby Library of Parliament, and which is reached by a long, sloping entrance corridor that Safdie has acknowledged was inspired by Gianlorenzo Bernini's Baroque masterpiece of interior design, the Scala Regia in the Vatican.[94]

Quebec and Expo 67 It is appropriate that the Museum of Civilization should be on the Quebec side of the National Capital Region, since the architecture of Quebec, much more than that of Ontario, has shown expressionist tendencies akin to the work of Prairie designers. Here, too, some of the most exciting buildings have been churches, again a response to the wave of construction inspired by Vatican II and a new progressive spirit in the Catholic church—and as well reflecting the earlier innovations of Dom Bellot (pages 728-32). The

1960s were also the years of the Quiet Revolution, and French-Canadian architects may have been seeking a new national expression that was distinct from the International Style mainstream of Ontario and corporate Montreal. (It is likely that they remained unaware of the parallel—although somewhat later—work on the Prairies, and that the Prairie architects were equally uninformed about the activity in Quebec.) The outcome was a variety of innovative buildings, many based on abstract forms, that display an exuberance and animation probably best described as Gallic.

One of the most inventive among the new generation of architects was Montrealer Roger D'Astous, who spent time at Taliesin with Frank Lloyd Wright. His first commission, the church of Notre-Dame-du-Bel-Amour in Montreal (1955-7), is the only building he has designed that resembles Wright's work—in this case the First Unitarian Church at Madison, Wisconsin (1950).[95] D'Astous's subsequent buildings, most of them undertaken in partnership with Jean-Paul Pothier, took off in a very individual manner. At the innovative church of **Notre-Dame-des-Champs, Repentigny** [15.57], built in 1962-3, the walls and roof are one and the same cedar-shingled, counter-curved surface that envelops the nave and is pierced at the top with skylights— giving worshippers the illusion that the roof opens onto the heavens, like the vault of a Baroque church. The shingled semi-hemispherical choir protrudes from the end wall and a freestanding frame serves as a belltower by the entrance end.[96] The approach to space and form have an affinity with Clifford Wiens's Heating and Cooling Plant at Regina, built five years

15.57   Notre-Dame-des-Champs, Repentigny, Quebec, 1962-3. Office du film du Québec/65-1755.

15.58   Château Champlain, Montreal, Quebec, 1967. Collection of Harold Kalman.

later, although the shapes, structure, and materials are entirely different.

D'Astous and Pothier were the architects of the **Château Champlain [15.58]** in Montreal (1967), an addition to the Canadian Pacific Railway's chain of landmark hotels. It was the first stage of what was to have been a major redevelopment called Place du Canada, but that was abbreviated because, under immense pressure, CP Rail undertook to preserve, rather than demolish, the adjacent Windsor Station [9.9]. The 38-storey hotel has a reinforced concrete foundation and a structural steel frame, but rather than being clad in the glass-and-metal curtain wall characteristic of the International Style, it is covered with curved precast concrete units that provide every room with a semicircular bay window—presumably an allusion to the prevalent bay windows of earlier eras, and therefore intended as a modern expression of the Château style. It was the first tower in Montreal to be designed by francophone Quebeckers, and its sculptured quality reflects Quebec regionalism in contrast to the rectilinearity of the prevailing international modernism.[97]

A comparison similar to that between the buildings at Regina and Repentigny may be made between Gaboury's Église du Précieux Sang and the earlier **Notre-Dame-de-Fatima at Jonquière [15.59]**, in the Saguenay/Lac-Saint-Jean region north of Quebec City. Built in 1962-3, it was designed by the partnership of Léonce Desgagné, who began his career as a follower of Dom Bellot, and Paul-Marie Côté. The form of Notre-Dame-de-Fatima suggests a tent or a tipi, and also the loosely clasped praying hands of Rodin's sculpture, *La Cathédrale* (1908, admired by Desgagné). It is composed of a cone that has been sliced in two, the segments offset; their overlapping edges are connected by a band of glass that lies beyond the view of the worshippers, allowing the dramatic, Baroque-like entry of light. One segment rises to become a slender spire. The building is a thin concrete shell (designed by structural engineer Louis Lemieux) consisting of 4 inches (10 cm) of Gunnite covered on the inside with a layer of asbestos (the hazards of the material had not yet been recognized) for thermal and acoustic insulation. The result is a *tour de force* of expressionism that recalls the chapel of the presidential palace at Brasilia (1958) by Oscar Niemeyer (b. 1907).[98]

Paul-Marie Côté had earlier distinguished himself—while a young architect in the office of Desgagné and Boileau—with **Église Saint-Marc de La Baie** (formerly Bagotville, 1955-6) [**15.60**], an accordian-pleated A-frame (also formed in concrete) whose façade is reduced to a simple triangle of glass. Architectural historian Claude Bergeron has declared that Saint-Marc 'introduced modernism to Quebec religious architecture in a spectacular manner.'[99]

Another architect with a bold design vocabulary is Jean-Marie Roy (b. 1925), who studied at the École des Beaux-Arts in Montreal. He opened a practice in Quebec City 1955, receiving many ecclesiastical commissions, and in 1966 joined in partnership with Paul Gauthier and Gilles Guité. Among the more interesting secular works by Gauthier, Guité, Roy Architectes that were directed by Roy are the Centre culturel at Rouyn (1967), a theatre in which the metal-clad trapezoidal blocks of the auditorium and the stage house intersect each other in an uncompromising manner; and the interpretative structures at Les Forges du Saint-Maurice near Trois-Rivières [**5.44**]. At the **Pavillon d'éducation physique et des sports** (PEPS) [**15.61**], built in 1969-71 at Université Laval, Sainte-Foy, the large interior spaces are enclosed by a post-and-beam frame clad with precast concrete panels to produce a strongly horizontal expression in which the planes advance and retreat in three dimensions in an elegant sculptural abstraction. Triangular projections at the top are the intakes and exhausts for the mechanical system in the upper central portion.[100]

Montreal architect, sculptor, teacher, and critic Melvin Charney (b. 1935) has contrasted the work

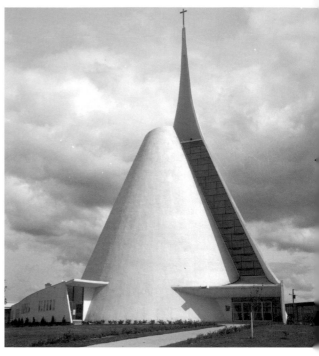

15.59   Notre-Dame-de-Fatima, Jonquière, Quebec, 1962-3. Ministère de la Culture, Fonds photographique/FM1454-55-B-1.

15.60   Église Saint-Marc, La Baie, Quebec, 1955-6. Ministère de la Culture, Fonds photographique/FM1407-D-9.

15.61 Pavillon d'éducation physique et des sports, Université Laval, Sainte-Foy, Quebec, 1969-71. Courtesy Gauthier, Guité, Roy Architectes.

of Roger D'Astous and Paul-Marie Côté with that of Jean-Marie Roy, noting that the first two attempted 'to create an indigenous vocabulary by delving into modes of self-expression', while the latter moved from an 'overwrought formalism' to 'an abstract figuration of geometric forms' that was 'an authentic, Modern, avant-garde expression', comparable to the work of the painters known as *Les Plasticiens*. Charney explains that these were alternative ways in which Quebec architects could acknowledge the Quiet Revolution and attempt to distinguish their work from that being done in the rest of Canada.[101]

The dominant architectural firm in Montreal throughout this period—and a firm whose principals represented a variety of cultural backgrounds and was less involved with Quebec's concerns—was Affleck, Desbarats, Dimakopoulos, Lebensold, and Sise, which practised under that name between 1955 and 1970 (Jean Michaud was also a partner until 1958); and from 1970 as ARCOP Associates ('ARCOP' being a contraction of 'architects in co-partnership', indicating the principals' relative independence). The firm came together with the competition for the Queen Elizabeth Theatre in Vancouver (1957-9, 1962), and this led to other commissions for arts complexes: Salle Wilfrid Pelletier at Place des Arts in Montreal (1963), the Confederation Centre in Charlottetown (1964), the Arts and Culture Centre in St John's (1964-7), and the National Arts Centre in Ottawa (1964-7).

The **Confederation Centre of the Arts [15.62]** was a project of Dimitri Dimakopoulos (b. 1929), who was born in Athens and studied architecture at McGill. It was built in 1964 on and under Queen Square in Charlottetown, adjacent to historic Province House [3.54] and occupying the space of the last market house (which burned in 1958) and other former public buildings. The visitor descends a flight of steps from the Square into skylighted Memorial Hall, a shrine to the Fathers of Confederation. Broad underground walkways lead from there to three other buildings arranged in a horseshoe around Memorial Hall: a library, a theatre, and an art gallery and museum. Each is expressed as one or more cubes that rise above grade, achieving regularity without symmetry. Reinforced-concrete frames are faced with Wallace sandstone, the same material that had been used for Province House. The walls seem to float in space, allowing light to enter at the corners. In its serenity, clarity of form, abstract composition, and curtain-wall construction (albeit they are stone walls),

15.62 Confederation Centre of the Arts, Charlottetown, Prince Edward Island, 1964. Courtesy the ARCOP Group.

the Centre displays the features of the International Style. The assertiveness of the cubes and their somewhat mannered details look forward to the expressionism of Late-Modern design.[102]

This tendency was evident in the firm's work for **Expo 67**, the 'first-category' international exhibition held in Montreal during Centennial Year. At the initiative of Montreal's Mayor Jean Drapeau, Expo was developed on Île Sainte-Hélène, an island park in the St Lawrence River, and on a newly created artificial island adjacent to it, Île Notre-Dame. The theme, selected in 1963, was *Terre des Hommes* (rendered in English as 'Man and His World'), the title of a book by Antoine de Saint-Exupéry. Although in architectural terms Expo was intended to demonstrate Canada's international stature, many of the Canadian buildings ironically promoted expressionism and architectural distinctiveness, largely at the expense of the International Style.[103]

Affleck, Desbarats, Dimakopoulos, Lebensold, and Sise designed two of the four theme pavilions: Man the Producer and **Man the Explorer [15.63]**. (These and all other buildings at Expo were built between 1965 and 1967; most were demolished a few years after the fair.) The two theme buildings were constructed from modular components: massive tetrahedrons of exposed structural steel that functioned as space frames and could be assembled in a variety of configurations. Where protection from the weather was required, the cladding was a glass-fibre blanket sandwiched between two layers of expanded metal mesh and protected on the outside by stained plywood. The idea of a modular system based on prefabricated parts produced a kind of universal solution, which was an objective of the International Style; but the theme-buildings' overpowering scale and mass had an emotive power that was entirely inimical to that style.

Modular systems were also adopted elsewhere at Expo 67—most notably in **Habitat 67 [15.64]**, an experimental housing project by Moshe Safdie (conceived as a student project while he was at McGill), with David, Barott, Boulva as associates. Habitat was intended as a prototype solution for high-density housing that would achieve both privacy and economy. Each housing unit was a precast elongated cube that could be fabricated at the site, lifted into place by a crane, and arranged in such a manner that the windows of one unit would overlook those of an adjacent one. The basic module (about 600 square feet, or 55 m²) could stand alone to form a bachelor apartment, or it could be combined with others to make up a larger suite. Plastics were considered

as a potential building material, but the more familiar concrete was adopted, despite its greater weight and low tensile strength. Safdie intended that Habitat should contain between 800 and 1,000 units, including a small retail area, but technical problems, rising costs, and the pressures of time reduced it to 158 units—far too small to realize any economies of scale. Although intended as a prototype for low-cost housing, of necessity it ended up providing expensive suites, which remain in use. Nevertheless, many people have defended the validity of the system, and it remains a viable, yet still undeveloped, option for mass-produced low-cost housing. From a design point of view, Habitat looks like a mountain of randomly placed building blocks whose multiplicity of units and complicated forms abandon modernist principles.[104]

The two international pavilions at Expo 67 that aroused the greatest interest were prototype solutions for multi-purpose buildings. These were the West German Pavilion, a gigantic tent consisting of a steel-mesh-reinforced fabric draped over eight supports (by R. Gutbrod and the celebrated Frei Otto [b. 1925], in association with O. Tarnowski and George F. Eber); and the American Pavilion, a geodesic sphere 250 feet (76 m) in diameter, composed of countless sections of metal piping and glass (by R. Buckminster Fuller [1895-1983], Geometrics Inc., and Cambridge Seven Associates Ltd., in association with John B. Parkin Associates). Like Habitat, neither has been reproduced with particular success. Among the better Canadian-designed structures that followed international trends were the Quebec Pavilion (by Papineau, Gérin-Lajoie, and Leblanc) and the Musée des Beaux-Arts (by Gauthier, Guité, and Côté, with John Bland as consultant).

Mayor Jean Drapeau intended that Montreal would be showcased to the world through Expo 67, and the frenzied construction activity that preceded the opening included the construction of the first three lines of the Métro, the city's subway system (which connected with Expo's own sophisticated transportation system). Rather than using variations of a standard design for each of the original twenty-six stations, the city wisely chose to involve a number of separate architectural firms, bringing together architects in the public and private sectors on the same team. The quality and variety of design among the stations are still appreciated by harried commuters.[105]

The monument most closely associated with Jean Drapeau's obsessive desire for Montreal to be noticed by the world is the **Olympic Stadium [15.65]**, the

15.63 Man the Explorer, Expo 67, Montreal, Quebec, 1965-7. Collection of Harold Kalman.

15.64 Habitat 67, Expo 67, Montreal, Quebec, 1965-7. Collection of Harold Kalman.

15.65 Olympic Stadium, Montreal, Quebec, 1973-87.
Courtesy Régie des installations olympiques.

principal structure erected (in 1973-87) for the 1976 Summer Olympic Games. Drapeau personally selected French architect Roger Taillibert (on the basis of his Parc des Princes stadium complex in Paris) to plan and design the large Olympic Park, which included the 60,000-seat Stadium and several other sports facilities (most notably the elegant Vélodrome, seen in the right foreground). Taillibert (in association with architect André Daoust) produced a technically complex structure looking not unlike a gigantic clam shell and composed of 12,000 prefabricated concrete components. The principal frame is made up of 38 tubular 'consoles' that support the stands and roof. Because Olympic regulations require that the Games be played in the open air, though the Stadium was intended to be used subsequently for professional sport in the unpredictable Montreal climate, Taillibert attempted the world's first retractable domed stadium. A tower that rises 556 feet (170 m) and leans at a dramatic angle supports the woven synthetic fabric of the 200,000-square-foot (18,500-m²) roof, which retracts somewhat like an umbrella with the help of 46 synchronized winches. The tower and roof were not completed until the Montreal Expos' 1987 baseball season, and after a few frustrating years of enduring tears and technical failures while opening and closing the roof, the

authorities decided to keep it permanently closed.[106]

Returning to the work of Affleck, Desbarats, Dimakopoulos, Lebensold, and Sise, it is timely to

15.66 Place Bonaventure, Montreal, Quebec, 1964-8.
Courtesy Place Bonaventure.

introduce Raymond Affleck (1922-89), a native of Penticton, British Columbia, who trained at McGill under Frederic Lasserre (before Lasserre took up his appointment at UBC) and did graduate work at Lasserre's former school, the Zurich Polytechnic. Among the firm's buildings, those associated most closely with Affleck include Place Ville Marie [15.39] and the nearby **Place Bonaventure** [15.66], for which Affleck worked closely with design architect Eva Vecsei. Built in 1964-8, and an early experiment in multi-purpose building, it contains, from bottom to top, a two-level retail arcade; a 250,000-square-foot (23,000 m²) exhibition area ('Concordia Hall'—likened by teacher and writer Jean-Claude Marsan to the hypostyle hall of an Egyptian temple because of the huge concrete columns and beams that support the upper storeys); five levels of merchandising mart; an international trade centre; and a 400-bedroom hotel. The internal courtyards of the hotel are attractively landscaped (and, surprisingly, populated by squirrels), and hotel guests are barely aware of being in a city. Underground pedestrian walkways connect the complex to Central Station—the building fills an entire city block over the tracks—as well as to the Bonaventure Métro station, Place Ville Marie, and the Queen Elizabeth Hotel, making it a link in Montreal's 'underground city'. Place Bonaventure was also daring in its construction management as an early example of 'fast-tracking'—Affleck was designing the upper floors as the lower ones were being built.[107]

The exterior walls consist of cast-in-place concrete panels suspended on the reinforced concrete frame and displaying a variety of sandblasted finishes. They are relieved by few windows, other than those of the hotel at the top. Its weighty and massive appearance, and the textured, monolithic surfaces, make Place Bonaventure a representative of 'Brutalism', a style associated with the work of Scottish architect James Sterling, American architect Paul Rudolph (b. 1918), and the English husband-and-wife architectural team of Peter Smithson (b. 1923) and Alison Smithson (b. 1928).

Planning for commerce:
The shopping centre and the atrium

The complexities of late-twentieth-century society have forced architects to address issues that are far broader than the simple design of an individual building. The increasing scale of commercial activity and the growth of suburban communities are two developments that have created at least as many

problems as they have solved. The emergence of landscape architecture and planning as professions (see Chapter 12) were attempts to grapple with these new intricacies, but at first they served only to create more specialized disciplines and to isolate architects from these matters. Architects came to realize that they must address these issues in concert with the planners, rather than design buildings in isolation from them.

We have cited a few of the new problems and attempts at solving them. For example, the design of Toronto's new City Hall included that of Nathan Phillips Square, an important civic open space. The multi-functional program at Place Bonaventure created a city within a city, providing a variety of uses that serve different markets and linking it to transportation services.

This section looks at additional ways in which Canadian architects have attempted to come to grips with the challenges and the acknowledged problems of architecture and the city. A significant mid-century development that responded to the growth of suburbia within the context of regional planning was the shopping centre. However, it soon became evident that shopping centres were victims of their own success and were sucking the life out of city centres.

From the 1960s on, working within the framework of Late-Modernism, architects began to look at such fundamental issues as liveability in the urban core. They were motivated by a number of factors, including increasingly large-scaled and multi-use building programs and the consequent restrictions and guidelines set by municipal planners, who began to heed the voices of community residents. There was also a widespread feeling that mainstream modern architecture and planning had been a failure. Author Jane Jacobs—who has lived in Toronto since 1967—set the profession on its heels with *The Death and Life of Great American Cities* (1961), a convincing attack on contemporary city planning (in particular the separation of land uses) that focused on how people use cities.[108] Planners and architects responded by building retail complexes within downtown commercial developments, generally entered by way of large internal spaces known as atriums. This section looks at both of those developments: shopping centres and atriums.

Shopping centres The suburban shopping centre—usually thought of as a group of retail and service establishments constructed and managed as a single unit—was, like the post-World-War-II suburb, an

American creation. A number of small community shopping centres were built in the US before the Second World War, and after the war they developed rapidly to serve large regional markets. In Canada, planner Eugenio Giacomo Faludi (b. 1899), a Hungarian-born and Italian-trained architect and planner who moved to Canada in the 1940s, was an active promoter of the regional shopping-centre concept. In 1949 he wrote an important article, directed at architects, describing its enticing possibilities.[109]

The first in Canada was the **Norgate Shopping Centre** [15.67] in Ville de Saint-Laurent (a Montreal suburb), designed in 1949 by architect Maxwell M. Kalman (b. 1906) as part of a large residential apartment development ('Norgate'), which was intended for veterans with families and was generously financed by the Central Mortgage and Housing Corporation. This was followed quickly by the larger Dorval Shopping Centre, also in suburban Montreal (Eliasoph and Bercowitz, with M.M. Kalman, 1950), and the Park Royal Shopping Centre in West Vancouver (C.B.K. Van Norman and J.C. Page, 1950). The Montreal architects and developers were inspired by suburban New York models, while those in Vancouver followed comparable work in Seattle—particularly Northgate (by John Graham and Company of that city, completed 1950)—but the results were similar. All were simple, rectangular, no-frills buildings intended to sell merchandise, not to win design awards. Most (including Norgate) were arranged in an L-shaped configuration, facing a large parking-lot, with the stores entered directly from the lot (much like the countless small 'strip malls' outside every Canadian city that have been

built since then). Early shopping centres near Toronto, built on the same general plan, were Sunnybrook Plaza (1951) and York Mills (c. 1952). All used the concept of having two or more 'anchor' tenants (usually a department store and a supermarket), with smaller specialty shops between them. The anchors often participated in the development, as did Steinberg's supermarket chain in the early Montreal-area centres.[110]

In the next stage of design, the stores were accessed from sheltered walkways in internal landscaped courtyards rather than from the parking-lot on the periphery, creating a friendlier and vehicle-free environment. The Don Mills Shopping Centre (originally called the Don Mills Convenience Centre) in suburban Toronto (John B. Parkin Associates, 1955) and the **Rockland Shopping Centre** [15.68] in the Town of Mount Royal, near Montreal (Ian Martin and Victor Prus, 1958-9), were early examples. Both featured modernist designs far more distinguished than their first-generation predecessors. At Rockland, a series of covered arcades (some arched and others with flat roofs) linked five separate building blocks. The architectural treatment was varied, using stone, concrete, wood, plastics, and brick in a number of colours and textures, creating an eclectic effect that recalled the main streets that shopping centres were replacing. The two shopping centres remain in use, although they have been altered considerably over the years.[111]

From here it was a short step for the shopping centre to evolve into the shopping 'mall'—a name derived from 'pall-mall', which refers to both a game and the long grass field on which it was played. Walkways were enclosed under roofs to create an entirely weather-protected, climate-controlled space, after the example of Southdale Center (1954-6)—designed by Victor Gruen (1903-80) in Edina,

15.67 Norgate Shopping Centre, Ville de Saint-Laurent, Quebec, 1949. Photograph 1964. Ville de Saint-Laurent.

15.68 Rockland Shopping Centre, Mount Royal, Quebec, 1958-9. Photograph by Victor Prus.

Minnesota—which in turn explicitly followed the models of the nineteenth-century European galleries (discussed below). Gruen's earlier Northland Center (1954) in Detroit, Michigan, had provided a model for the separation of cars and pedestrians.[112]

Yorkdale Shopping Centre in North York, Ontario (John B. Parkin and Associates, with John Graham and Company, 1960-4) was an early example of the enclosed mall, and by far the largest mall to date in Canada. Developed by Webb and Knapp (later Trizec Corporation), with the participation of Eaton's and Simpson's, it was built as a regional shopping centre, located on a 99-acre (40-hectare) site at the intersection of two expressways. As originally built, it contained the two department stores, a Dominion supermarket, 90 smaller shops (including restaurants), a 'bazaar' for temporary stalls, two movie theatres, and professional offices; it enclosed 1.28 million square feet (119,000 m²) and provided parking

spaces for 6,500 automobiles. Yorkdale was a model for a self-sufficient 'controlled' shopping centre, in which the developer selects the tenants, decides on the extent of competition, and co-ordinates all advertising. The plan was arranged in an 'L', with Eaton's at the intersection and Simpson's and Dominion at the ends, and with shops along either side of the connecting malls. Benches and internal landscaping break up the 1,600-foot (490-m) length of the malls, and different ceiling treatments provide variety—which, however, the exterior elevations carry to an unhappy extreme because each of the major stores chose its own distinctive design.[113]

The largest suburban shopping centre in Canada—and, for a period, in the world—is the **West Edmonton Mall** [15.69], developed by the Ghermezian brothers' Triple Five Corporation, designed by Maurice Sunderland, and built in 1981-6. This gigantic mall contains 800 retail stores (including eight department stores) and 100 food outlets on three levels, comprising an amazing 5.2 million square feet (484,000 m²). Architecturally and structurally it is

15.69 Europa Boulevard, West Edmonton Mall, Edmonton, Alberta, 1981-6. Courtesy West Edmonton Mall.

unambitious, with frame structures, brick exterior walls, and arched and glazed galleria roofs. The stores are likewise unexceptional, simply providing more of what is found in most other regional malls. Remarkable are the scale and the animation, which have made it a major travel destination for all of western Canada. (Its promoters call it 'a worldwide tourist attraction' and 'the eighth wonder of the world'.) In order to retain the 6 million people who are drawn there every year (and are necessary to keep the stores—and Edmonton's economy—solvent), the West Edmonton Mall is an entertainment as well as a shopping centre. It features an amusement park ('Fantasyland') that includes a roller coaster, a 7-acre (2.8-hectare) wave pool ('World Waterpark'), a professional hockey rink, the Deep Sea Adventure Area (which offers submarine rides and a porpoise pool), a large bingo hall ('Caesar's Palace'), a miniature golf course ('Pebble Beach'), and 19 motion-picture screens. It is so big that it has attracted its share of social problems and services, which range from pros-

titutes in the one case to an evangelical chapel in the other. The mall is connected directly to its own Fantasyland Hotel, promoted for its 'theme' rooms. Architect Peter Hemingway writes that 'by architectural standards, it is vulgar, crass, and fey, but it does seem to strike a chord with visitors. What a world away from the spartan Miesian interiors that we accepted as sacred in the 1950s!' The Ghermezians have turned to bigger markets yet in building the even larger Mall of America in Bloomington, Minnesota, which was completed in 1992.[114]

Shopping malls are continually renovating and updating their appearance and adjusting the 'mix' of stores as market techniques alter with the times. Regional shopping centres have had a deleterious impact on city centres, since they encourage their patrons to abandon the established urban retail infrastructure. Nova Scotia, Prince Edward Island, and New Brunswick all reacted in the 1970s by introducing legislation intended to combat regional malls. Canadians, more than Americans, maintained their commitment to downtown business districts. This was demonstrated by the construction of a series of large urban malls. Wellington Square in London,

Ontario (1958-60), was claimed as the first downtown shopping centre in North America; developed by Webb and Knapp, it was designed by John Graham and Company. In Ottawa, Sparks Street was closed to vehicular traffic (temporarily in 1960 and permanently in 1967), creating a shopping precinct known as the Sparks Street Mall and becoming a prototype for a number of other street closures.

The underground retail facility at Place Ville Marie in Montreal, also a Webb and Knapp development, was heralded for reinforcing the vitality of the downtown core. So too were Pacific Centre in Vancouver (Victor Gruen and Associates, with McCarter, Nairne, and Partners, 1969-76), where the shopping is also located below grade, over a large underground parking garage; and others such as Scotia Square in Halifax (Allward and Gouinlock, 1969) and Midtown Plaza, Saskatoon (Gordon R. Arnott and Associates, 1969-70), where the retail activity is at and above grade.

Internal circulation and the atrium Office development in the large cities mushroomed as a result of the buoyant economy of the 1960s and 1970s, inspiring a rivalry among financial institutions and other corporate builders to create the tallest, largest, and sleekest towers in town. We have seen how, in Toronto, the Toronto-Dominion Bank's T-D Centre was quickly challenged by the Canadian Imperial Bank of Commerce (at Commerce Court) and the Bank of Montreal (at First Canadian Place). The same mindless race occurred in virtually every other Canadian city, with less-distinguished clones of the Toronto (and American) International Style prototypes creating aggressively higher skylines. The result was massive density in a relatively small area that led to an increasing strain on the urban infrastructure, including ever-worse traffic problems and overworked municipal services.

In the heat of this competition, the Royal Bank of Canada required a new Toronto headquarters, partly to accommodate central services that were being relocated from Montreal during Quebec's politically troubled 1970s. It decided not to enter the competition for the tallest tower, nor to bring in a prestigious American architect (as had the other three banks). The Royal Bank chose instead to concentrate on providing a gateway (from Union Station and the subway) to the financial district that would respond to—rather than create—circulation problems. The result is seen in **Royal Bank Plaza [15.70]** at Front and Bay Streets, a work of the Webb Zerafa Menkès Housden Partnership (WZMH) that was built

in 1972-6. The architects chose to achieve a dramatic exterior appearance and friendly internal spaces. Two triangular towers, 41 and 26 storeys tall, rise at either side of a 130-foot-high (40-m) banking hall, which is set on a diagonal grid in order to respond to pedestrian patterns (people on foot seek a diagonal 'shortcut'). Between the towers is a high public space— called an atrium—containing the banking hall and providing access to two levels of shopping below, visible through a cutaway portion of the floor. The structural frame of reinforced concrete is clad in zig-zag curtain walls of aluminum, steel, and, most strikingly, golden mirror-glass— gold leaf was laminated into the glass panels. The resulting coloration enlivens the towers quite remarkably as their colour changes under the changing light of day, and because the faceted metallic surfaces create brilliant reflections. The building is not only an ornament in the Toronto skyline (it can be seen on the right in **15.25**), but it also makes a bold statement that differs greatly from that of other bank towers in breaking away from the four-square clar-

15.70 Royal Bank Plaza, Toronto, Ontario, 1972-6. Photograph by William Dendy.

ity of the International Style into the ambiguity of Late-Modernism.[115]

Architects Peter Webb (b. 1927), Boris Zerafa (b. 1933), René Menkès (b. 1932), and Warwick (Rick) H.G. Housden (b. 1931) all worked at Peter Dickinson Associates during the firm's last frantically busy years. They (and three other colleagues) formed a partnership that completed some of the projects left unfinished at Dickinson's death in 1961 and went on to become the third-largest architectural practice in North America (and the largest in Canada), with offices in Toronto, Montreal, Calgary, Vancouver, and five American cities; in 1983 WZMH boasted 16 principals, 10 associates, and a staff of 400. Under the dynamic leadership of Zerafa, the partners have continued Dickinson's inclination to seek work primarily from private developers rather than public-sector and institutional clients (the Royal Bank was an exception), and have therefore sometimes been unfairly denigrated as 'architects of commerce'. The firm took Dickinson's modernist manner as a point of departure, and has worked in an idiom that is best described as Late-Modern. As Zerafa explains: 'We're content to stay just this side of "leading edge". Let other architects experiment; we won't treat clients as guinea pigs.'[116]

Petro-Canada Centre [15.71] in Calgary is representative of WZMH's high-rise office buildings in the way it builds on previous achievements without seeking novelty. Erected by a private developer (PEX/ARCI Joint Venture), with Petro-Canada (the Crown corporation created in 1975, which acquired four foreign-owned multi-national oil companies) the major tenant, it was planned in 1979, near the end of Calgary's oil-fueled economic boom, but was not completed until 1984, when that city was suffering from a serious recession. (In 1979 Calgary built more office space than New York and Chicago combined.) The complex consists of two Late-Modernist towers, 56 and 35 storeys high, set on a 45-degree axis with a large atrium between them. The tops of the towers are sloped, a cliché during the 1980s. The exterior is clad in red polished granite and copper reflective glass, giving it a distinctive red colour. The basic components—towers of uneven heights set obliquely to the street grid embracing a lower pavilion—follow the precedent of the Royal Bank Plaza, which can be traced back in turn to Toronto City Hall and Toronto-Dominion Centre—indicating a strong thread of continuity from the Miesian prototypes through the freer and more expressionistic buildings of the succeeding decades.[117]

Petro-Canada Centre includes raised gardens on

both sides of its city block, which form an integral part of Calgary's innovative 'Plus 15' (+15) system. This is a network of elevated and environmentally controlled walkways, corridors, and mid-block bridges 15 feet (4.6 m) above the city streets (hence the name) that link most downtown building complexes. The system was conceived in 1967 by Affleck, Desbarats, Dimakopoulos, Lebensold, and Sise, working together with members of the City of Calgary's Planning Department. The intention was to separate pedestrian from vehicular traffic, provide protection from the weather, and create a pleasant environment—all features introduced in the suburban shopping centres of the late 1950s. The principal feature is the Devonian Gardens in Toronto-Dominion Square (J.H. Cook Architects and Engineers, in association with Skidmore, Owings, and Merrill, 1972-7), a 3.5-acre (1.4-hectare) landscaped space with fountains and children's play areas. Developers who contribute to Plus 15 are rewarded with bonuses that allow them additional building density. The weaknesses of the system are the loss of street activity and the sterility of the internal spaces that have been created, in terms of the common mediocrity of design and the regulation disallowing retail, entertainment, or service facilities. Older buildings and street-level shops have been unable to link in to the system, putting them into a competitive position with new developments.[118]

Plus 15 is one of several solutions that architects and planners have proposed as ways of coping with the Canadian winter (or, in planning jargon, of creating a more 'liveable' winter city). Montreal's 'underground city' (page 802) is another; its objectives are similar to those of Calgary's Plus 15—although it is below, rather than above, grade. Toronto also has a network of underground walkways and Edmonton is developing a 'Pedway' system that is partly above and partly below street level.

Another answer has been the development of the atrium—a high internal skylit space of the kind that emerged in buildings designed by a number of (mostly Toronto) firms during the 1970s and is seen in Royal Bank Plaza and Petro-Canada Centre. It was encouraged by a study—done in 1976 by Robert Tamblyn of Engineering Interface Ltd of Willowdale, Ontario—that showed that a 10-storey doughnut-shaped office building with a central roofed atrium extending the full height of the building has lower construction and energy costs than a 31-storey cen-

15.71 Petro-Canada Centre, Calgary, Alberta, 1979-84. Courtesy WZMH Partnership.

tral-core tower with the same floor area. Named after its unroofed Roman prototype, the Canadian atrium has the added advantages of providing not only a space for social interaction and circulation, but also shelter from the weather.[119]

One of the largest and most successful atriums is the **Eaton Centre** [15.72] in Toronto (1973-81), a 900-foot-long (275-m) glass-roofed building that stretches from Queen Street West to Dundas, along Yonge Street. Providing access to multiple levels of retail shopping and a large Eaton's department store, it is flanked by three office towers—the Cadillac-Fairview Tower on Queen, the Eaton Tower on Yonge, and Eaton's own offices on Dundas—and a parking garage. The most dramatic entrance is on Dundas— a large, high, glass-covered space that leads, by way of escalators and stairs, to an array of shops and restaurants, the Eaton's store, and the subway. Covering five city blocks, the Eaton Centre reverses conventional ideas of interior and exterior space. The 'street' is an elongated atrium—the 'galleria' south of Eaton's housing more than 300 shops. It has the trappings of an external roadway: trees, awnings, abundant natural light, and even a flock of sculpted Canada geese (by Michael Snow) overhead. The exuberant detailing combines metals and glass in a manner that exposes structural and mechanical functions. Staircases and escalators direct the constant flow of people. On Yonge Street—a thoroughfare with considerable pedestrian and vehicular activity—the **exterior** [15.73] is presented as a mirror-glass elevation with exposed 'high-tech' structural elements above shop-fronts at ground level, and to the north a buff enamelled-metal wall.[120]

The Eaton Centre was designed by the Zeidler Partnership with Bregman and Hamann, and the Eaton's store by E.L. Hankinson and Parkin Millar Associates. The chief designer of the Centre was Eberhard Zeidler (b. 1926), who immigrated to Canada from his native Germany in 1951. Zeidler explained his intentions:

It has been my attempt here to create an architecture that rises beyond its economic function and its structural necessity and created space that people enjoy, yet has resolved all of the issues of content. It is beyond a 'modern' approach that only searches for a constructional formal expression, yet it also rejects a 'post-modern' approach that uses forms for forms' sakes. . . . The galleria was discussed as an urban street that had an independent right within the grid pattern of Toronto.[121]

The scheme continues a long European tradition of enclosed galleries (arcades in England, *passagen*

in Germany) that provided a roofed street for pedestrians, often on multiple levels, giving direct access to shops. Although prototypes are found centuries earlier (one of the most elaborate being The Rows in Chester, England, begun in the 13th century), a number of remarkable galleries were built in the second half of the nineteenth century. Two are the Galleria Vittorio Emanuele II in Milan (Guiseppe Mengoni, 1865-7), a cross-shaped structure 96 feet (29.3 m) high that is vaulted in glass; and the Cleveland Arcade in Cleveland, Ohio (John Eisenman and G.H. Smith, 1888-90), that has shops on five levels and is also covered by a glass roof.[122]

In the Royal Architectural Institute of Canada's *Metropolitan Mutations*, an exhibition and symposium on 'the architecture of emerging public spaces', the Eaton Centre was described (somewhat effusively) as

a metropolitan-scale interior street, a modern baroque of grand volumes, changing levels, theatrical overlooks and vistas containing a phantasmagoria of displayed goods and people. With its connections to the regional subway system, its massive parking garages and department stores, this quasi-public street has become the principal shopping precinct in the downtown. Like the arcades of European cities, it is descended from the urban street yet is radically different in scale, specialization and ownership.[123]

The ownership issue is significant, since the galleria blurs the line between public and private space, raising broad issues of accessibility (controlled by the Centre), liability, and human rights that have yet to be resolved. Nevertheless, the Eaton Centre has revitalized Toronto's downtown core, attracting some twenty million shoppers (many of whom would have patronized regional malls) and tourists a year.

Zeidler has consistently shown an interest in designing for the movement and interaction of people. He was the principal designer of Ontario Place, an entertainment-oriented waterfront urban park that was Toronto's response to Expo 67 (Craig, Zeidler, and Strong, 1968-70). He was also the principal designer for **Canada Place** [15.74], the Canadian government's pavilion for Expo 86 in Vancouver (by Zeidler Roberts Partnership, with Musson Cattell Mackey Partnership and Downs/Archambault and Partners, 1983-6). Unlike most of the other pavilions at Expo

15.72   Interior, Eaton Centre, Toronto, Ontario, 1973-81. Photograph by Balthazar Korab. Courtesy Zeidler Roberts Partnership/Architects and Bregman and Hamann.

15.73 Yonge Street elevation, Eaton Centre, Toronto, Ontario, 1973-81. Photograph by Ian Samson. Courtesy Zeidler Roberts Partnership/Architects and Bregman and Hamann.

15.74 Canada Place, Vancouver, British Columbia, 1983-6. Photograph by Peter C. Powles, 1992.

86, which (despite their consistent architectural excellence) were intended only for temporary use, Canada Place is a permanent building located in downtown Vancouver, along Burrard Inlet. Its primary use is as a trade and convention centre. The exterior of the large exhibition and meeting halls is covered by striking fabric roofs in the form of sails. They enliven the Vancouver waterfront in a manner that suggests the famous Sydney Opera House and alludes to the secondary role of the complex as a cruise-ship terminal. Canada Place also contains the streamlined Pan-Pacific Hotel, Vancouver's World Trade Centre, and an IMAX theatre.[124]

A number of Zeidler's other buildings have, like Eaton Centre, been built around a large atrium. The Walter C. Mackenzie Health Sciences Centre at the University of Alberta, Edmonton (1980-82, by the Zeidler Roberts Partnership, in association with Groves Hodgson Palenstein and with Wood and Gardener) is built around a five-level internal space that enables both patients and staff to shed the sense of isolation that is so often inherent in a hospital.[125]

The Health Sciences Centre responded to the master plan for the University of Alberta undertaken in 1969-72 by Diamond and Myers. Myers, the partner in charge, suggested that new additions to the campus be linear and provide a continuous covered atrium (at ground level) that would connect all the buildings. The first application of this principle was the University's **Housing Union Building** (HUB) [**15.75**], built in 1972 to designs by Diamond and

Myers in association with Richard L. Wilkin. The long, narrow building contains student housing on either side of a linear atrium—also called a galleria by its architects—that contains shops and lounges. The colourfully shuttered windows of the residences open onto the atrium, as well as to the out-of-doors, and the shops have angled canopies, giving the atrium many of the features of a conventional street; whereas the exposed air ducts are clearly interior devices, deliberately confusing perceptions of inside and outside space. Service vehicles use a lower level, beneath the mall; this right-of-way was originally intended to have been a city street open to all traffic—revealing the architects' acceptance of the existing urban fabric as a determinant in their design.[126]

Other architects have created effective atriums with a different character. Raymond Moriyama (b. 1929), a native of Vancouver who studied at the University of Toronto and McGill before entering private practice in Toronto in 1958, is highly adept at manipulating both exterior and interior spaces, as he first

15.75 Housing Union Building, University of Alberta, 1972. Photograph by Hellmut W. Schade, 1980.

15.76 Scarborough Civic Centre, Scarborough, Ontario, 1973. Photograph by Lenscape Inc. Courtesy Moriyama and Teshima Architects.

showed in his design for the Ontario Science Centre, which opened in 1969. The natural surroundings of this three-building complex, set in a 180-acre (72-hectare) park on the slopes of the Don Valley, at Eglinton Avenue and Don Mills Road, are brought inside through the many glass walls. Moriyama's **Scarborough Civic Centre [15.76]** was built in 1973 as the centrepiece of the new town centre of the Borough (now City) of Scarborough, just east of Toronto. The core is a circular atrium (called the 'central space') 80 feet (24 m) in diameter and 67 feet (20 m) high, on either side of which are segments of a larger circle: one containing the municipal offices and the other those of the Board of Education, both with balconies at each level opening onto the atrium, which serves as an arrival area for visitors as well as an unstructured common space. The Council Chamber (called the 'meeting hall') occupies a smaller circle at one side of the central space. The two office wings embrace a core building in a similar manner to the towers of Toronto City Hall, but here the focus is a social space rather than an official one, reflecting the increasing democratization of civic government. Seen from the exterior, the cylinder with wedges cut out of it—the edges marked by white aluminum siding cut at an angle to reveal a membrane of dark reflective glass—makes a bold and sculptural statement similar to that of Gaboury's Royal Canadian Mint [15.48].[127]

Moriyama's best-known atrium—observed and enjoyed by hundreds of people every day of the week as they rise five storeys in one of two glass-enclosed elevators—is in the Metropolitan Toronto Reference Library (1973-7) on Yonge Street at Asquith. They are made aware of the activity of the entire library by being able to view the facilities that surround the atrium from every floor. Whatever objections the staff may have to this huge, empty central space (relieved at every floor by banners announcing the subject classifications), users young and old have no complaints and are very much at home in the light-filled environment.[128]

Atrium and high-rise towers have been combined in **Complexe Desjardins [15.77]** at rue Sainte-Catherine and rue Jeanne-Mance in Montreal, a large development financed by the associated *caisses populaires* (credit unions) of Quebec and the provincial government (1972-6). It was intended as an architectural statement that declared that the prosperity of Quebec was based on the savings of ordinary people (in the words of newspaper editor and sometime leader of the Quebec Liberals, Claude Ryan, 'les petits gens'). The developers pledged to create 'the

15.77   Complexe Desjardins, Montreal, Quebec, 1972-6. Courtesy Place Desjardins Inc.

concrete symbol of a fierce determination to remodel the city, and thereby, the man on the street.' The 8-acre (3.2-hectare) site, across the street from Place des Arts, is covered with a three-storey podium (the *basilaire*), in the centre of which is a large atrium (called Place Desjardins), the size of a city block, that contains shops and restaurants, wider in the centre and narrower at either end where it meets the street. It is aggressively animated with concerts, exhibitions, and other popular programming. Above the *basilaire* rise three office towers (the tallest of which has 41 storeys) and the Méridien Hotel—the four composed somewhat clumsily to make a complex, and faced in precast concrete. They form a nice contrast with the sleek elegance of the corporate imagery in the primary business district, a short distance west. The project was as complex as its name, having been created by a large consortium of design firms. The master planning was by La Société La Haye-Ouellet; the podium by Longpré, Marchand, Goudreau; the office towers by Blouin Blouin and Gauthier, Guité, Roy; and the hotel by Jean Ouellet and Jacques Reeves of La Haye-Ouellet. Despite its relative isolation, Complexe Desjardins is large enough to ensure the liveliness of its voluminous atrium. Like the Eaton Centre, it is important not only for having advanced the development of the atrium, but also for its place in the migration of the shopping centre from the suburbs to the central city.[129]

Complexe Desjardins and many of the other buildings considered above used the design vocabulary of Late-Modernism and its variants. The modernist manner has continued into the 1990s, although with diminishing popularity.

Beyond Modernism

The drive to revitalize established city centres was part of a broader tendency to respect the past and to retain (and enhance) existing buildings and communities. The causes of this new attitude—which go far beyond architecture and urban design—have yet to be understood fully, but they are related to broad sociological changes that include a fear of 'future shock' (a term coined by American futurist Alvin Toffler to describe the stressful reaction to too much change) and to the environmental, or 'green', movement, which attempts to stop the widespread destruction of the earth's ecological systems. The principal architectural responses to this new spirit of the times have been Post-Modernism and heritage conservation. Both reveal an interest in the history of architecture, which has been reintroduced into the architectural curriculum at many universities. Exhibitions of historical architecture have become more common; one blockbuster show that attracted a considerable amount of attention was *The Architecture of the École des Beaux-Arts*, organized by Arthur Drexler of the Museum of Modern Art, and shown at that New York museum and at the National Gallery of Canada in 1975-6.[130] The exhibition tantalized younger architects but puzzled older ones. John C. Parkin may have spoken for many mature modernists when he linked it to Post-Modernism:

> Post-Modernism—or as I prefer to call it, neo-conservatism—is not going anywhere. . . . What Arthur Drexler . . . has attempted to do, in terms of reviving an interest in the Beaux-Arts, is regarded by many at the Museum with great academic interest. The quality of the drawings is interesting. But there isn't one of them—I do not believe— who would build a building in that ideology.[131]

Quoting Philip Johnson, Parkin called the new trends 'foggy chaos' and 'digressions which I just don't think are going to last.' History will tell whether he was right.

This final section considers the two phenomena of Post-Modernism and heritage conservation, providing a glimpse of the state of Canadian architecture as the twentieth century comes to a close.

Post-Modern architecture

Modernist buildings had come to be seen as cool and aloof, increasingly sterile in design, and indifferent to both their users and their surroundings. Among the architects who criticized the International Style and the fundamentals of modernism were the American Robert Venturi (b. 1925), whose *Complexity and Contradiction in Architecture* (1966) and *Learning from Las Vegas* (written with Denise Scott Brown and Steven Izenour, 1972) emphasized the roles of history and popular art (and restated Mies's 'Less is more' as 'Less is a bore'!); and Toronto's George Baird (b. 1939), who co-edited *Meaning in Architecture* (with Charles Jencks, 1969), which explored the ways in which buildings affect people who use them. Jencks defined a new order in *The Language of Post-Modern Architecture* (1977 and subsequent editions), in which he dates 'the death of modern architecture' to 15 July 1972, when the Pruitt-Igoe housing development in St Louis, Missouri (1952-5), was blown up because of uncontrollable vandalism attributed to flaws in its design. Anthony Jackson (b. 1926), a teacher at the Nova Scotia Technical University, wrote polemics criticizing modernism and seeking the way to a more socially relevant architectural style. The attack on International modernism finally went popular with American bestselling author Tom Wolfe's *From Bauhaus to Our House* (1981).[132]

Late-Modern expressionism constituted an initial response to the austerity of the International Style. A second group of architects—usually called Post-Modernists—sought a solution not so much in a personal expression through individual shapes and spaces, but rather by turning to the physical context and buildings of the past from which they gleaned a new-old architectural vocabulary. Historical features began to be used for both their form and their meaning, setting up deliberate associations, often wittily, with buildings of the past—in much the same manner as the nineteenth-century revivalists. These architects recognized (as had their predecessors in the pre-modern era) that their own buildings were no more than the newest productions in a centuries-long tradition, whereas modernists had perceived their buildings as being fundamentally different from those of their predecessors. Ron Thom anticipated the Post-Modernist attitude at Massey College in the 1960s, but he emulated Gothic in a proper modernist manner without actually using any historical detailing.

In the 1970s architects began to reuse historical forms and programs as well. Ironically, it was Philip Johnson—a leading figure in the development of the International Style and a man to whom Parkin looked for support in his attack on Post-Modernism—who fired one of the first salvoes announcing the new movement. His American Telephone and Telegraph Building in New York City (Philip Johnson and

15.78 Bradley house, North Hatley, Quebec, 1977-9. Photograph by Cedric Pearson. Courtesy Peter Rose.

John Burgee, 1978-82) has a base derived from a Renaissance frontispiece and a sloping top that resembles a broken pediment; sheathed in pink granite, the building has been likened to a Chippendale highboy, a grandfather clock, and a Rolls Royce radiator.

Post-Modern values are seen clearly in the **Bradley house [15.78]** near North Hatley, in the Eastern Townships of Quebec (1977-9), designed by Peter Rose (b. 1943), a Montrealer who studied architecture at Yale University with the innovative Charles Moore. The house is the year-round residence of a client who had vacationed in the scenic area for years. Set on a hill with a superb view, it is sited just beyond the knoll to shelter it from the wind and drifting snow. A three-storey-high octagonal central hall capped by a tower forms a hollow core around which the rooms radiate (in a kind of domestic version of the central space at the Scarborough Civic Centre). The perimeter wall is nearly square, except for a V-shaped segment that has been removed from the south elevation and an entrance arcade that extends to the southwest.[133]

Rose recognized that the program for the Bradley house resembled that of many of Palladio's sixteenth-century clients, who wanted both a modestly scaled week-end retreat and a principal residence within reach of the city (Venice rather than Montreal); and so he created a new building in the spirit of a Palladian villa. Several of Palladio's villas are square houses organized around a high central hall with one or more colonnaded entrances; two examples are the Villa Foscari and the famous Villa Rotonda. Rose has adapted these features in a distinctly non-historicist design. The arched window of the tower vaguely alludes to a Palladian window, but more as a pun than a borrowed form. Rose's office immersed itself in sixteenth-century Italian architecture during this time—so much so that his colleague, Erik Marosi, acquired the nickname 'Michelangelo'. The Bradley house is not, however, an *imitation* of an Italian villa (it doesn't look like one; for starters, Palladio's houses were stuccoed masonry); it is a *metaphor* of one, a kind of visual code, built up of words (or signs) that are legible to a person who is familiar with Palladian architecture. Since not everybody is an architectural historian, the house also conveys a more popular meaning: it offers a metaphor of another, more familiar, historical building-type as well. The wood clapboard siding, sloped roof, and picturesque asymmetry relate just as strongly to the Queen Anne Revival

15.79 Aerial view of the Centre Canadien d'Architecture/
Canadian Centre for Architecture, Montreal, Quebec,
1985–9. Photograph by Alain Laforest, 1990. Centre
Canadien d'Architecture/Canadian Centre for Architecture.

frame houses that dominate North Hatley and are
recognizable to any local observer as evocative symbols of comfortable country living.

Through its siting, plan, massing, materials, and
details, the Bradley house responds to the context
of its site, its region, and the wider heritage of Western
architecture. This contextualism and coding are basic
principles of Post-Modern architecture—particularly the 'double-coding' that conveys one level of
meaning to architects and another to the public.
(This vocabulary is derived from semiotics, the study
of signs.) A similar solution to a parallel program is
seen at the Osborn House on Fishers Island, New
York (1972–3), by James Righter, a colleague of Rose
and a fellow student of Moore.[134] Rose adopted the
idiom at another house in North Hatley, built for
Marosi in 1977, and (working with Righter and Peter
Lanken) at Pavillon Soixante-Dix (1977), a ski pavilion at St-Sauveur, Quebec.[135]

A deep respect for both the local and the broader historical contexts is evident as well in Rose's
largest and best work to date, the **Centre Canadien
d'Architecture / Canadian Centre for Architecture**
(cca) **[15.79]** in Montreal (Peter Rose Architect, with

Phyllis Lambert consulting architect, and Erol Argun
associate, 1985–9). Founded in 1979 as an architectural study centre and museum (and a manifesta-
tion of the renewed interest in architectural history), the cca is the creation of Phyllis Lambert (b.
1927). As we have seen, she first earned a niche in
history in 1954 by persuading her father, Samuel
Bronfman, the president of Joseph E. Seagram and
Sons, to retain the best possible architect for the
Seagram Building in New York. With the help of
Philip Johnson, she selected Mies van der Rohe; she
later graduated from Mies's school of architecture
at the Illinois Institute of Technology. Lambert's
own design work has included the Miesian Saidye
Bronfman Centre in Montreal (with wzmh, 1968).
Her interests subsequently turned from modernism
to conservation and history (just as Johnson turned
to Post-Modernism), as she organized the advocacy
group Héritage Montréal (1975) and then created
the cca.[136]

In 1974 Lambert bought the Shaughnessy house
on Boulevard René-Lévesque, a Second-Empire dou-
ble-house (W.T. Thomas, 1874)— once the residence
of cpr president Sir Thomas Shaughnessy and threatened with demolition—and it became the centre-
piece of the cca. A preliminary scheme would have
doubled the house in size and placed all additional
construction underground, but in the final design

Rose wrapped a large new stone building around three sides, creating an E-shaped plan (the down-stroke running east-west), with the Shaughnessy House forming the middle leg of the 'E'. The old house dominates the south elevation, facing Boulevard René-Lévesque (at the rear in the photograph); the scale and the repetitive full-height bay windows (on both the new and the old buildings) reflect the features of the many Victorian row houses in the neighbourhood. The CCA is entered not on this side but from rue Baile on the north, since the city would not permit access from the busy arterial road. The broad north wing, scaled like an institution and not a house, is blank in the centre and focuses its window openings at the ends, in the tradition of Beaux-Arts Classicism. It contains the museum and library reading room, the west wing contains the Théâtre Paul-Desmarais, and the east wing provides study facilities for visiting scholars (set around a three-storey atrium). A mezzanine and three lower levels are used for offices and storage. The ground floor of the Shaughnessy house (restored by Denis St-Louis, of Bilodeau St-Louis Architectes) is used as a reception facility, and offices are located upstairs. The total floor area is a generous 150,000 square feet (14,000 m²). Across the Boulevard, in the distance, is the CCA Garden, a landscaped park and sculpture garden designed by Melvin Charney, which contains fanciful architectural elements that relate to the past and to the transience of things.

The reinforced-concrete structure of the new CCA building is enclosed in walls of self-supporting (i.e. not a curtain wall) limestone, windowless outside the museum and opened up elsewhere with a carefully orchestrated hierarchy of windows. The sparse ornament alludes to classical prototypes: a convex bull-nose moulding separates the smooth main floor from the channelled masonry of the 'basement' (the curatorial level), and a projecting, perforated cornice fabricated from anodized aluminum enlivens the walls with its play of shadow patterns. The elegantly detailed interior finishes include black granite floors, limestone walls, and panels of Canadian maple. The building possesses a strong sense of classical order, which is felt particularly forcefully in the sequencing of spaces and the controlled natural illumination. The CCA is a museum in the grand classical manner and fits self-consciously into the post-Renaissance tradition of European and American institutions. It offers something of a revival of Beaux-Arts Classicism—a decade after the Beaux-Arts exhibition.

Classical sources are used as well, although in a somewhat different way, in the **Mississauga City Hall and Civic Square** [15.80], which is sometimes cited as the prime Canadian example of Post-Modern ('PoMo') architecture, although its architects ironically have tenuous links with Canada. The large architectural complex was built in 1982-6 to designs by Jones and Kirkland—a partnership formed for the occasion by Edward Jones (b. 1939) and Michael Kirkland (b. 1943), born and trained in England and the US respectively (Jones has since returned to Britain). They won a national competition whose professional adviser was George Baird. Mississauga, like Scarborough, is a newly incorporated city near Toronto, made up of many former towns and rural communities and therefore lacking an urban centre. The City Hall, its civic square, and the surrounding town centre have been planted on former agricultural land adjacent to a new expressway and near a number of new residential subdivisions.[137]

The City Hall was designed to provide a strong, emphatic image of simple forms in a nondescript landscape. With seemingly weightless walls of buff brick and white banding, perforated by rows of small windows, the geometrically distinct blocks are composed of a broad gabled (or pedimented) building that presents a ceremonial façade to the civic plaza; a high square clock tower (a segment of which is exposed steel), containing a viewing platform and restaurant; and behind (to the north) a cylindrical Council Chamber and a 14-storey office block covered with a hipped roof. The separate blocks are joined by the three-storey-high Great Hall, a somewhat overwhelming indoor square finished in green marble with black granite bands [15.81]. The domed Council Chamber is lighter in colour and mood, ringed with paired columns over which are inscribed the names of the municipalities that constituted Mississauga (just as the names of major Canadian cities served by the railway are inscribed in the concourse of Toronto's Union Station, **9.14**). The civic square or plaza is filled with arcades, pavilions (that conceal ramps leading to an underground garage), and a 300-seat semicircular amphitheatre. Unlike Toronto's Nathan Phillips Square, this square is underused, partly because the entrance is located on the other side, and also because suburban Mississauga lacks the pedestrian activity of downtown Toronto.

Observers enjoy reading the visual codes embedded in the building forms, a practice that has not been discouraged by the architects. In an attempt to explain how the complex grows out of its agricultural context, they see the group as representing an Ontario farmstead: the façade building becomes a gable-roofed barn, the council chamber a silo, the clock tower a

15.80 Mississauga City Hall and Civic Square, Mississauga, Ontario, 1982-6. Photograph © Steven Evans.

15.81 Interior, Mississauga City Hall, Mississauga, Ontario. Photograph © Steven Evans.

wind-charger, and the office block a house. The banded walls recall Ontario Victorian polychromatic brickwork. These are all popular, readily accessible metaphors based on the common experience of Ontarians. Observers with broader architectural experience may see sources in other architecture of the past. Some argue that the office tower alludes to the Château Style or that the entire complex is derived from a pedimented Italian public building and its *campanile*, facing a large *piazza*. Whatever may have been intended—and these multiple levels of meaning (the double-codes) are all plausible—it is significant that the City Hall lends itself to such interpretations. It draws on a rich vocabulary of traditional motifs with which we and our experiences can easily identify. This is in part popular architecture, analogous to 'pop' imagery in the visual arts, and in part erudite design—its full scope of meanings legible only to other architects. The former ensures that it is approachable, not aloof—a marked contrast to the distancing qualities of modernism.

Other architects have produced engaging buildings with qualities that may be loosely characterized as Post-Modern; several of them practise in Vancouver. One is Paul Merrick (b. 1938), who excelled as a designer with Thompson, Berwick, Pratt and Partners in Vancouver (e.g. for the Curt Latham house, 1968, and the CBC Broadcasting Centre, 1973-5), with R.J. Thom Architects in Toronto (for the Chemistry Building at Trent University), and with the Chandler Kennedy Architectural Group of Calgary (for Phase 2 of the Citadel Theatre, Edmonton), before forming his own firm, Paul Merrick Architects. In the late 1980s Merrick was responsible for a number of high-profile buildings in Vancouver that revealed his facility in the Post-Modern mode. **Cathedral Place [15.82]**, on West Georgia Street, was controversial even before it was begun, since the much-admired Georgia Medical Dental Building (McCarter and Nairne, 1929) was demolished—blasted by a spectacular 'implosion'—to clear the site. Merrick's design of the high-rise office tower, built in 1989-91, reflects many of the features of the historic buildings around it, as well as the one that it replaced. The setbacks, brick facing, and entrance arch of Cathedral Place are all drawn from the Georgia Medical Dental Building, and casts of some of its terra-cotta Art Deco ornament (including three larger-than-lifesized nurses) are incorporated into the elevations and the lobby. The height of the building and the steep hipped roof reflect the Hotel Vancouver across the street, and a few Gothic features—such as the perforated para-

15.82 Cathedral Place, Vancouver, British Columbia, 1989-91, with the Hotel Vancouver in the background. Photograph by Danny Singer Animation Inc. Courtesy Paul Merrick Architects Limited.

pets and repeated finials— are inspired by the design of Christ Church Cathedral next door. Behind the office building, and linked by a tranquil landscaped courtyard (by Christopher Phillips and Associates), is the low Canadian Craft Museum, with a similar hipped roof. In Merrick's skilled hands the building works, and produces a truly site-specific contextual architecture that embraces its environment.[138]

Richard Henriquez (b. 1941) has also designed some distinctive buildings, mostly in Vancouver,

15.83 Annex to the Sylvia Hotel, Vancouver, British Columbia, 1985-6. Photograph by Robin Ward, 1992.

15.84 Environmental Sciences Centre, Trent University, Peterborough, Ontario, 1990-1. Photograph © Steven Evans. Courtesy Henriquez Partners.

at the University of British Columbia (1971-2), which respected the campus landscape by going underground and revealing itself only by means of skylights and a sunken courtyard. His Gaslight Square on Water Street (Henriquez and Todd, 1974-5), designed with Robert Todd, captured the spirit of historic Gastown with its bay windows, brick walls, awnings, and modest scale. His condominium **annex to the Sylvia Hotel [15.83]** at 1861 Beach Avenue (Richard Henriquez and Partners, 1985-6) is built partly in imitation of the Edwardian style of the 1912 brick hotel, but on the waterfront side it presents a large expanse of glass that gives the impression that a brick wall has been peeled away to reveal the glazing. It relates to both its historical context (the original Sylvia and the Edwardian commercial buildings of the city) and its contemporary context (the glazed condominium towers that dominate this English Bay neighbourhood).[139]

Henriquez's most important building east of British Columbia is the **Environmental Sciences Centre [15.84]** at Trent University (1990-1), across the Otonabee River from Champlain College and Ron Thom's other early Trent buildings (and near Paul Merrick's Library for the campus). This large addition to the campus is composed of a number of seemingly organic and disparate components, each with its own story to tell. The main block, horizontally articulated and finished in concrete and brick, is difficult to see in isolation, since its form is interrupted by numerous idiosyncratic elements. Architectural critic Adele Freedman has described the complex arrangement:

> What seemed a row of spires are fumehood stacks. That cone pointing at a strange angle is a skylight. The half-finished structure over on the left is an animal-holding facility masquerading as a barn. The field receding into the horizon is a sodded roof. The sturdy tower rising directly ahead belongs to the heating system. . . it's a tangle of reinforcing rods emerging from a concrete beam that supports a large wooden fan, the gateway roof.[140]

Many of these features have specific meanings that relate to the land and to history. The sod roof is intended as a refuge for groundhogs who lost their homes to construction. A wedge was driven through the building at one point to commemorate a railway that once traversed the site. The cylindrical 'Envirosphere' that links the two principal wings is an eccentric concrete staircase that leads to a mast, inclined at the same angle as that of the earth to the sun; and above it is a white cupola whose skylight an eccentric concrete staircase that leads to a mast, inclined at the same angle as that of the earth to the sun; and above it is a white cupola whose skylight (referred to by Freedman) Henriquez calls the 'eye of the universe'. Wood trellises and other features pay homage to Ron Thom, and the barn and the sloped groundhog ramp were taken by Henriquez from sketched ideas in Thom's master plan for the campus. As Freedman concludes: 'Trent University got a lot more than a science building: Henriquez delivered a piece of landscape.'

A similarly organic approach to architecture is seen at the **Newton Library** [**15.85**] in Surrey, BC. It was designed in 1991 by Patkau Architects, the distinguished Vancouver-based wife-and-husband team of Patricia Patkau and John Patkau, both of whom came to British Columbia from Manitoba. Surrey is a rapidly expanding suburban community (not unlike Mississauga in southern Ontario) characterized by tract housing, strip development, shopping malls, and rapidly disappearing farms. The library, the adjacent senior citizens' centre, and other intended public and commercial buildings in the former village centre of Newton are set within a sea of parking lots and will be connected by a pedestrian spine. The library itself is a boldly angular structure, with a V-shaped (inverted gable) roof supported by an assertive series of glued-laminated wood columns and beams, all angled, like the roof and the glazed curtain walls. Two of these wood structural units emerge at the entrance to form a portal. A contrapuntal rhythm is created by the rectilinear mustard-coloured concrete walls that enclose the offices, activity room, and washrooms. Perched on the roof is a large aluminum-faced canted box that contains the air-conditioning equipment. The interior is dominated by a large, open, and naturally illuminated reading room—public where the roof rises high, and intimate where it dips low.[141]

The historical context of the library is somewhat elusive, since few components of the original Newton town centre survive, and the modern environment is too chaotic and undefined to merit emulation. The Patkaus, therefore, made few references to the setting, although they describe the timber frame and its concrete foundations (conspicuous elements within the library) as a metaphor for the natural 'sticks and stones' of the region. Their main approach has been to rely on the abstract assertiveness of their design to define the library as a public building, and to set it apart from the dull sameness of the Surrey townscape.

The Newton Library has some similarities with

15.85 Newton Library, Surrey, British Columbia, 1991. Photograph by James Dow, 1992.

the Patkaus' **Seabird Island School** [**15.86**], near Agassiz, BC, built in 1990-1 for a Salish band on their reserve in the Fraser Valley, about 75 miles (120 km) east of Vancouver. This is one of a number of stunning new school buildings in First Nations communities across British Columbia, all designed by talented architects (who are selected by the bands) and largely built by band members, who also control the curriculums. (Other schools in this group have been designed by Hughes Baldwin [see page 683] and Peter Cardew, whom we met earlier.) The innovative building program was developed by the federal Department of Indian Affairs and Northern Development, and managed by architects Marie-Odile Marceau and Richard Evans, as a new approach to native education that would counteract the negative images and memories of the old federally controlled Indian residential schools.

The Seabird Island School was the first of this group. Its organic form seems to grow out of the ground, its seemingly free-form roof reflecting the mountains that surround the flat site and also deflecting the fierce winter winds. The Patkaus decided that the school 'needed to be a figure in space. A thing rather than a building—somewhat zoomorphic.' The north side (to the left in the photograph) contains the gymnasium, and is fully enclosed (and protected) by the dominant shingled roof-walls, whose assertive forms recall the Prairie regionalism in which the Patkaus were educated. Along the south façade

ipating the oblique frame of the Newton library. The school is entered in the centre of this south façade, with a common area leading to the elementary school on one side, and the secondary school on the other.[142]

While the Newton and Seabird Island buildings retain the posts and beams that were characteristic of the West Coast style since the 1940s, their angular orientation has distorted the rectilinearity that was so central a feature of early modernism. The first building to focus attention on the Patkaus, their Pyrch house in Victoria (1984)—winner of the Governor-General's Award for Architecture—likewise changed the nature of the post-and-beam house with its V-shaped plan. The windowless stucco elevation that faces the street, dominated by the door to the garage, has a notched parapet and is topped by a hipped copper roof, whose castlelike allusions symbolize the owners' desire for privacy.[143]

The Patkaus are among the many architects whom it is difficult to classify as Post-Modernists, though they have flirted with PoMo and adopted some of its principles as a consequence of the general loss of faith in modernism. This is true, as well, of the recent work of Barton Myers (whom we earlier saw as a Late-Modernist), in his **Unionville Library** [15.87] at Markham, Ontario. The architectural and urban design of the library, built in 1985, recalls the Victorian origins of Unionville, now amalgamated with Markham, and its many period survivors (unlike Newton, now a part of Surrey, which retains little from the past). Composed to emulate a historic village centre, the dominant feature is a seemingly half-completed tower—reminiscent of the one at the Mississauga City Hall—whose top portion consists

lage centre, the dominant feature is a seemingly half-completed tower—reminiscent of the one at the Mississauga City Hall—whose top portion consists of an open steel frame without a veneer of brick. The library is covered by a barn-like copper roof, and gables along the sides are finished with patterned brickwork, both characteristic of the nineteenth-century Ontario vernacular (which was also a source at Mississauga). Architect Eberhard Zeidler praised the building and its tower, saying that the Unionville Library 'creates the symbol [of the Victorian period] without the tiresome and heavy imitation required of outlining the whole form in brick', and noted that it uses new technology (as Myers had done at the Wolf house and the Citadel Theatre) to evoke a historic memory.[144]

Myers' recent work has been described by British architecture critic E.M. Farrelly (referring specifically to his Seagram Museum in Waterloo, Ontario, 1984-5) as 'stand[ing], well meaning but undecided, with one tentative toe in each of many camps'; and as one of many 'curious buildings—neither modern, nor Post-Modern nor yet traditional, but caught somewhere, not quite comfortably, between.'[145] A parallel malaise was detected by the jury that selected the 1990 Governor-General's Awards for Architecture, who noted a want of enthusiasm, conviction, passion, and freshness in entries from across the country. As jurist Arthur Erickson declared: 'It is now time for a serious, soul-searching reappraisal and a critical assessment of the impact of the American influence on Canadian work.'[146] This search for a platform and a vision is a situation in which many sensitive architects of the 1980s and 1990s find themselves. Yet regardless of which 'camp' their buildings may be placed in, the work of most architects has certainly progressed far beyond modernism.

A number of skilled architectural firms have avoided Post-Modernism almost entirely, continuing the forms of Late-Modernism, although often enriching them—in a decorative, as well as a structural, way—with the enthusiastic use of industrial and technological components. This 'high-tech' manner has been inspired to a large extent by the work of British architects Richard Rogers and Norman Foster, which was exalted in Paris's Centre Pompidou (Renzo Piano and Richard Rogers, 1977), a major art gallery that is a building turned inside out, with its conspicuous structural frame and escalators placed outside, rather than inside, the 'exterior' walls. We have seen this approach in Canadian buildings, such as Zeidler's Yonge Street elevation of the Eaton

Centre and Diamond and Myers' Wolf house. In many ways the high-tech manner romanticizes the idea of industrialization by using structural elements in a decorative way, just as Mies had used structural I-beams on the elevations of the Toronto-Dominion Centre.

The IKOY Partnership of Winnipeg has designed some fine Late-Modern buildings with strong high-tech flavour. One is their strikingly attractive **Northwest Leisure Centre [15.88]** in Regina, Saskatchewan (built in 1984, in association with R.E. Hulbert and Associates, architect for the Saskatchewan Housing Corporation). It consists of three independent blocks—a general-purpose hall, a pool, and an ice rink (proposed for a later phase of construction)—connected by an 'interior street', which is a walkway (partly outdoors and partly indoors) covered by a gable roof supported by steel columns. The Leisure Centre is largely composed of off-the-shelf industrial components, with both the exterior and interior cladding consisting of standard industrial steel panelling, chosen for reasons of economy. The materials and components are celebrated with colour. The exterior cladding is bright yellow, and within the space occupied by the pool the ceiling and walls are yellow ribbed steel, the open-web roof truss is blue, and the ventilation ducts are red, with the grey concrete of the retaining walls clearly visible. The bold treatment continues the strong statements seen in Prairie regionalism in the 1960s and 1970s.[147]

Despite the work of Late-Modernist 'holdouts' such as the IKOY Partnership, Post-Modernism remains the dominant trend in the 1990s. And the two trends share common roots in a romanticized gaze at the past—be it the historical symbolism of Post-Modernism or the technological symbolism of high tech. This same romanticism becomes nostalgia in the hands of populist designers. If the visual puns and codes embodied in a building such as the Mississauga City Hall (the references to a barn and a silo) are somewhat esoteric, those used by the builders of houses in residential developments directed at a popular market—the vernacular housing of today—are very easy to read. Certain elements are clearly indicative of comfortable living because people associate them with houses that they see as desirable: such as sloped roofs, chimneys, and dormer windows, which express 'home' without relating to any particular styles from the past. Others have specific stylistic associations: for example, Georgian fanlights and shutters; Tudor Revival mock half-timbering (a potent British-

15.88 Northwest Leisure Centre, Regina, Saskatchewan, 1984. Photograph by Gerry Kopevon. Courtesy IKOY Architects.

adians as a symbol of luxury. The names given to the house-types by the developers reinforce the association.

The potency of such traditional design elements should not be underestimated. This was clearly understood by the architects of the nineteenth and early twentieth centuries—the pediment of a Georgian building connoted British imperial loyalty, and a pointed arch was a symbol of Christianity—but the allusions lost all meaning for architects who were captivated by the first flush of enthusiasm for modernism. It took the semiologists to remind architects of the relevance of cultural imagery. Advertising agencies understood this well; in the 1970s the Château Style Hotel Vancouver was promoted with pictures of its steep roof and the caption 'Put a Roof over your Head'. Modernist houses with flat roofs never achieved popularity simply because they lacked an identifiable roof pitch. Architects David Crinion, of the Canada Mortgage and Housing Corporation, and Downs/ Archambault of Vancouver learned this in 1972 when they were designing an affordable rental housing project in Champlain Heights, a Vancouver subdivision. They turned to architectural programmers from California, and the American architect and teacher Christopher Alexander, to determine what features would be important. The first reponse was 'the roof is home', leading the architects to place vestiges of sloping roofs over the entrances, even though flat roofs provided the most cost-effective solution.[148]

At their most mundane, Post-Modern buildings, like modernist buildings, can degenerate into empty clichés—as is seen in the countless commercial buildings with false gables, hipped roofs (often called 'party hats'), and masonry skins 'peeled' away to reveal glass walls. At their best, Post-Modern buildings can be great architecture. PoMo's defenders hail the style as a return to the mainstream of architectural tradition after the modernist interlude; its detractors criticize it as being nothing more than one arbitrary vocabulary of forms replacing another. But the best Post-Modern architects today are inspired by the same ideals that drove the first Post-Modernists: they respond to geographical and functional contexts, favour variety and diversity over sameness, infuse buildings with witty allusions, and respect historical tradition. The ultimate question is whether PoMo is a brief interlude in the course of twentieth-century modernism, or whether modernism itself was a brief interlude in the centuries-long European-American tradition of architecture. We may know the answer in a few decades.

Heritage conservation

Post-Modern architecture, at its best, reveals a deep respect for historic architecture, relying on an observer's familiarity with the architecture of the past to convey its codes and metaphors. But the fullest respect for the past comes in retaining and using it—not just alluding to it. The last few decades have witnessed a remarkable increase in the conservation of Canada's built heritage, a trend that continues as the century draws to a close.

The retention of historic buildings began as a cultural endeavour. Until recently, the main motivation for preserving a historic building was usually its historical or architectural significance—because it had exceptional historical associations or was considered to be a particularly good example of a past style. More often than not, it was left to a public agency to acquire a building of this stature, and to preserve it—usually as a museum, or as an interpreted historic site. Since 1919 the federal government's Parks Canada (originally called the National Parks Branch) has maintained a program of commemorating national historic parks and sites on the advice of the Historic Sites and Monuments Board of Canada. Buildings and sites of particular importance would often be acquired and restored, and not just marked with a plaque; in this way places such as York Factory on the west coast of Hudson Bay, Bellevue at Kingston, Ontario, and some buildings in Dawson City in the Yukon have been preserved (and in some cases reconstructed—i.e. built to replicate lost buildings).[149]

The federal government has not been alone in preserving Canada's past. Similar activities have been undertaken—sometimes persuaded by community pressure—by provincial governments (for example, Acacia Grove in Nova Scotia, Place Royale in Quebec City, Sainte-Marie Among the Hurons in southwestern Ontario, and the Richard Carr house in Victoria); by municipal governments (the Nanaimo Bastion and Craigdarroch Castle on Vancouver Island); and non-government institutions (The Grange and the Campbell House in Toronto). Common to most of these projects has been the desire to restore (or reconstruct) a building, or a group of buildings, to resemble their appearance at a particular period in the past. Most have become artifacts to be observed and appreciated, as in a museum.

This kind of preservation activity continues. A recent project of considerable interest for the beauty and significance of its architecture, as well as its technical challenges, was the restoration of the

Rideau Street Convent Chapel [15.89] by Parks Canada and Commonwealth Historic Resource Management Limited (1987-8). The Gothic Revival chapel—designed by Georges Bouillon (1841-1932) and built in 1887-8 as part of the Convent of Our Lady of the Sacred Heart in Ottawa—features large wood fan vaults supported by cast-iron columns. The convent was demolished in 1972, and the architectural components were dismantled and stored. But they were subsequently reassembled, as in a gigantic jig-saw puzzle, and the chapel is now a central feature of the new National Gallery of Canada [15.56].[150]

In the 1970s, as the 'heritage movement' gained momentum, the basis for preservation broadened beyond museum-type activities. It was fuelled in part by a new attitude that resulted from the changing social, environmental, and economic conditions alluded to at the beginning of this section. Historical architecture began to be appreciated not only for its historic value or artistic excellence, but also for its economic and contextual values. The oil crisis of 1973 contributed to the new view, since rehabilitation was recognized as being more energy-efficient than demolition and new construction. It was realized that old buildings could be conserved ('conserve' and 'preserve' have much the same meaning, but the former implies change and the latter a more static situation), while being put to a new and economically productive use.

New legislation backed this perception. Provincial governments assumed the power to require property owners to preserve buildings without the government's acquiring them. Every province enacted heritage legislation, giving them powers to designate and protect privately owned buildings; Quebec was the first, with its Cultural Property Act (*Loi sur les biens culturels*) of 1972. A year later Heritage Canada was founded, under federal-government sponsorship, as an independent non-profit foundation that would, among other things, fight for stronger heritage legislation and acquire certain buildings to preserve them.[151]

The proper way to the future was seen as controlling and managing (not preventing) change—or by achieving 'continuity with change', in the words of Mark Fram and John Weiler, who were then on the staff of the Ontario government's heritage branch:

. . . continuity and change are not antagonistic. They are essential to one another. . . . The quality of the lives we lead depends heavily on our abil-

15.89 Rideau Street Convent Chapel, National Gallery of Canada, Ottawa, Ontario, 1887-8, restored 1987-8. Photograph by Malak. National Gallery of Canada/17.625.0.16.

ity to maintain, in the context of continuing change, a sense of place, a sense of time, and a sense of propriety.[152]

The sense of place and time were to be derived from understanding, and responding to, the physical, natural, and cultural context—just as Post-Modern architects try to reflect context in their buildings.

Raymond Moriyama expressed similar sentiments with respect to a natural landscape in the late 1970s: his conceptual 100-year master plan for land use, conservation, and development of the Meewasin Valley, in and near Saskatoon:

> The South Saskatchewan River, with all its subtle and sometimes violent voices, speaks a unique and special language in this Prairie environment. It would be wise to learn that language, and listen to it, before acting.[153]

Area conservation Moriyama was planning for a broad area in Saskatchewan, and, indeed, it is in area conservation that some of the more enlightened attitudes can be found. But several early and important initiatives came out of the Maritime Provinces and Quebec, which have a stronger sense of history than the younger provinces. Fortress Louisbourg [2.6,7] on Cape Breton Island and Place Royal [2.2] in Quebec City have both been described. The former is an isolated reconstructed museum-village, whereas the latter is a partially restored and reconstructed historical vignette that functions within the context of a larger city (whose historic area has been named a World Heritage Site). Both were government initiatives.

A seminal conservation project that used both private and government capital in a commercial context was **Historic Properties** [15.90], built on the Halifax waterfront in 1972-6. What began in 1969 as a community protest against a proposed harbour expressway that would have destroyed a number of early warehouses, led to Halifax City Council's calling for proposals for their restoration. The task was awarded to John Fiske, of Stevens and Fiske Construction, who created Historic Properties Limited to do the work, and retained Halifax architects Duffus Romans Kundzins Rounsefell, led by partner Allan F. Duffus. The immediate objective was to retain seven stone and wood buildings on the east side of Lower Water Street, which had been built in the early nineteenth century to serve the city's booming sea trade—buildings with names like Simon's Warehouse, the Old Red Store, and the Privateers' Warehouse

(which was once used to store booty taken from enemy ships during the Napoleonic wars). These were carefully restored to their nineteenth-century appearance on the basis of intensive research by Parks Canada, whose staff became involved—and federal funding assistance was provided—because the complex was commemorated as a National Historic Site. With the addition of three new buildings, the development is now used for retail and office use.[154]

Fiske recognized that in order to create a sufficient 'critical mass' to attract business to the waterfront, it would be necessary to include historic buildings further from the water; he therefore acquired many of the fine commercial buildings on Granville Street that had been built after the 1859 fire [10.34]. Commercial viability was assured when the Nova Scotia College of Art and Design became the major tenant in the area (the College's architects were C.A. Fowler, Bauld, and Mitchell). Duffus planned to link the two portions of the development, and the new shopping facilities at Scotia Square, with a pedestrian promenade, although the construction of the Barrington Inn on the south side of Granville Street in 1977-9 (Page and Steele), which incorporated the dismantled and rebuilt façades of additional historic Granville Street buildings, did not allow the entire scheme to be fully realized. The result is nevertheless a large and vibrant development that is dominated by old buildings and animated by shoppers, students, and special events.

Scholarly restoration, seen at Historic Properties, is often not the appropriate approach. Rehabilitation (a type of conservation activity that permits more liberal changes to enable an efficient new use) was the approach adopted at Vancouver's **Granville Island** [15.91], a landfill site in False Creek, in the shadow of the Granville Street Bridge, that was created in 1915 for industry and is now a very popular commercial and recreational precinct. The freer approach was justified because the individual buildings possessed relatively little historical significance; indeed, preservation on grounds of their architectural or historical value alone may have been inappropriate. The developer, Canada Mortgage and Housing Corporation, acquired the 38-acre (15-hectare) site (which had always been federal property) in 1975, and determined to learn from its experience at Toronto's Harbourfront (see page 865). The

15.90 Historic Properties, Halifax, Nova Scotia, restored 1972-6. Photograph by Harold Kalman, 1978.

15.91 Granville Island, Vancouver, British Columbia, rehabilitation begun 1977. Courtesy Hotson Bakker Architects.

five-member Granville Island Trust decided that development should respect and retain existing industrial buildings and themes. A few industries have remained—most conspicuously a large concrete-mixing plant—but the working sites are being converted to other uses as their leases expire.[155]

Architects Norman Hotson and Joost Bakker, now partners in Hotson Bakker Architects, produced a master plan in 1977 that provided guidelines for rehabilitation and encouraged the mixture of uses. Work has been ongoing since that time. Old buildings have been refitted and reclad while retaining their original structure and rooflines—using industrial materials and devices such as corrugated metal siding, external metal staircases, and exposed light bulbs—and enlivened with metal canopies and bright colours. Some compatible new infill has been permitted. The confusing array of streets, many of which retain railway tracks, are defined by a Hotson-designed system of timber posts connected by bright blue metal pipes that contain electrical services; there are no sidewalks, forcing pedestrians and automobiles to share the same roadways. As Hotson explained, revealing that he had absorbed the lessons of Jane Jacobs:

We wanted to create a public amenity, not a park. . . . In today's cities, all land uses are segregated. Our idea was to return to the original roots of settlement, to create something more village-like where all land uses are in one place.[156]

The commercial anchor is the Granville Island Public Market, a large food and craft emporium contained in a group of interconnected factories once occupied by BC Equipment and Wright's Ropes (rehabilitated by Hotson and Bakker, 1979-80) that retain pulleys and derricks hanging from the ceilings. Other businesses include marine industries, marinas, restaurants, a brewery, a hotel, design offices, theatres, art and craft galleries and workshops, and the Emily Carr College of Art and Design (formerly the Vancouver School of Art)—the College accommodated in the former British Ropes and Westex buildings, which were joined by new construction and clad in metal (by Ron Howard of Howard/Yano, 1979-80). The new Granville Island is busy, vibrant, and joyous—realizing the intent that it should create an atmosphere of 'randomness, curiosity, delight, and surprise', in the words of Hotson. The wares and the ambiance draw hordes of shoppers, despite traffic jams and insufficient parking. The mixture of old and new has proved to be an unmatched commercial success. The balance between the two is changing, however, with the construction of a large new annex to Emily Carr College (Patkau Architects and Toby Russell Buckwell and Partners, 1993-4), which is the most massive structure on the Island.

A comparable desire to retain the continuity of the historic urban fabric, even where individual structures are not distinguished—but when the whole is appreciated as being greater than the sum of the parts—is seen in the many other downtown revitalization initiatives that have occurred during the last generation. One of the first to put new life into an old town centre was the fixing-up of buildings along Magdalen Street in Norwich, England, in 1955 under the leadership of the Civic Trust. The Norwich Union Life Insurance Society subsequently assisted downtown rehabilitation schemes in Oakville and Niagara Falls, Ontario, and other Canadian communities. The Devonian Group of Charitable Foundations funded a program called Main Street Alberta, assisting towns in that province between 1973 and 1980. This kind of activity was particularly relevant in North America, where regional shopping centres were sapping the life from established Main Streets. In the US, the National Trust for Historic Preservation's Main Street Program demonstrated that preservation and economic revitalization are entirely compatible.[157]

Following these leads, a number of provincial governments began in the 1970s to offer funding and technical assistance by means of downtown revitalization programs, and many municipalities began to recognize that conservation was a valid approach to urban renewal. In 1981 Heritage Canada initiated its own Main Street Program, which placed project coordinators in selected towns to work with local business and community leaders. The first demonstration project was begun in **Perth [15.92]**, Ontario, in 1981, with restoration landscape architect John J. Stewart (b. 1947) as the co-ordinator (and subsequently national program director). Under Stewart's guidance incremental improvements by individual merchants—removing an unsightly sign, replacing inappropriate modern shopfronts, repainting with sensitive colours, planting a tree—made the nineteenth-century stone commercial buildings of Gore and Wilson Streets come to life and increased retail sales significantly. Parallel projects in a number of Canadian cities—including Nelson, British Columbia (supported by both Heritage Canada and the provincial government)—had equally positive architectural and economic results. As a result of these and similar initiatives, Main Street began to challenge the regional mall by imitating it—that is, by co-ordinating design, retail activity, and marketing.[158]

15.92 Wilson Street, Perth, Ontario, rehabilitation begun 1981. Photograph *c.* 1983. Collection of Harold Kalman.

Individual building projects The conservation movement has not been restricted to broad areas. Many individual buildings, and closely related groups of them, have also been restored or rehabilitated for purposes other than solely preserving a significant historic structure. A celebrated example is **Maison Alcan [15.93]** in Montreal (1980-3), the world headquarters of the Aluminum Company of Canada, by Raymond Affleck of ARCOP Associates and Julia Gersovitz. Conceived by Alcan president David Culver, who foresaw that the scheme would benefit the corporation's public image, the project conserved and rehabilitated three greystone mansions (built between 1871 and 1895) and the 10-storey Berkeley Hotel (1928) on Sherbrooke Street West, and used a glazed atrium to link them 'and a new Late-Modern low-rise office building'. Interior bridges join the

old and new buildings. The renovated interiors include exquisitely finished offices. The older masonry buildings are purposely contrasted with the 'high-tech' anodized aluminum wall of the new construction. 'This contrast', wrote Affleck, 'was, however, developed within an overall unity of scale, height and response to urban context.'[159]

Affleck had previously created **Market Square [15.94]** in Saint John, New Brunswick (ARCOP Associates, in association with Mott Myles and Chatwin, 1978-83). This large project involved the integration of seven rehabilitated nineteenth-century brick warehouses on Market Slip with a new trade and convention centre, a library, office space, retail complex, and underground parking. (A separate hotel and residential complex was built adjacent and also integrated into Market Square.) A large three-storey atrium forms an internal connection between the different components. The old red brick buildings set the tone for the design of the new facilities, which are mostly three-storey brick buildings

whose plainness allows the old façades to assume a disproportionate but handsome prominence. This is good contextual design: allowing the local style and materials to provide inspiration for the new work.[160]

Old and new were also combined in the **Pacific Heights Housing Co-operative** [15.95] on Pacific Avenue in Vancouver (1983-5). Architect Roger Hughes (b. 1944) was motivated partly as an activist who wanted to preserve an intact and highly visible group of early-twentieth-century frame houses adjacent to the downtown end of the Burrard Street Bridge (near Granville Island). His solution was to incorporate them into a project offering family-oriented non-profit housing. Hughes and his partner, Nigel Baldwin (b. 1946), converted the eight houses into duplexes and erected a new building behind them. The houses were moved: first backwards, while garages were built beneath them; then forward (closer to the

street than originally) and sideways to read as four pairs with entries between them. (One house had to be demolished and rebuilt because of its condition.) The new medium-rise infill building contains stacked two-storey apartments whose units are entered from a 'street' between the old houses and the new building and a 'street in the sky' on the fourth storey of the new building. It is faced in brick below the entry level and in beige (formerly blue) metal siding above it. Ninety-one units have been created, the result of additional density provided by the city as an incentive for preserving the historic structures. The flat façade and cut-out quality of the new building make it read as a backdrop to the old houses; with its undulating silhouette (punctuated by a PoMo-inspired elevator tower) it can also be read metaphorically—in good Post-Modern fashion—as a city skyline.[161]

Many municipalities have adopted measures that give their planners the flexibility to encourage preservation with financial incentives. One such technique, the density bonus (used at Pacific Co-op), is given to a developer in return for providing the city with an amenity—which may be preserving a significant building, including a cultural facility, or creating another public benefit (as was done in Calgary for

15.93 *(left)* Atrium, Maison Alcan, Montreal, Quebec, 1980-3. Photograph by Fiona Spalding-Smith. Courtesy the ARCOP Group.

15.94 Market Square, Saint John, New Brunswick, 1978-83. Courtesy the ARCOP Group.

15.95 Pacific Heights Housing Co-operative, Vancouver, British Columbia, 1983-5. Photograph by Gary Otte, 1985.

buildings that plugged into the Plus 15 system); additional density provides the developer with additional revenue. Alternatively, the municipality may permit a new infill building on a lot intended for only a single house; an infill residence (by Robert G. Lemon, in 1990) allowed the preservation of the Barber house in Vancouver [**14.85**]. Another, less-creative, method of encouraging preservation is a cash grant or tax abatement: the City of Edmonton has given this to the Hudson's Bay Company for the retention and rehabilitation of its retail store (Moody and Moore, 1938-9) on Jasper Avenue.

Perhaps the most equitable preservation technique is the transfer of density rights (TDR), in which floor space (density) that is permitted by the zoning by-law but not actually used in a historic building may be transferred to a nearby development site. (This generally works only in urban centres, where land values are high.) Two Gothic Revival churches on downtown sites with high permitted densities have been preserved by this technique. One is Christ Church Cathedral (C.O. Wickenden, 1889-95) at Burrard and Georgia Streets in Vancouver, whose unused density was purchased by the large adjacent Park Place office tower (Musson Cattell Mackey Partnership, 1984): Park Place and the Cathedral

are seen in the foreground of **15.82**. The other is the **Church of the Redeemer** (Smith and Gemmell, 1879) at Bloor Street and Avenue Road in Toronto, whose density was sold for more than $3 million and other benefits to the developers of the mixed-use **Renaissance Centre** [**15.96**] that envelops it (Webb Zerafa Menkès Housden with Page and Steele, 1982).[162]

The construction of new buildings need not necessarily be an ancillary activity. Many individual structures have been restored for reasons that were primarily financial. The **Pantages Theatre** in Toronto [**14.46**] was restored in 1988 (David K. Mesbur, architect; Commonwealth Historic Resource Management Limited, restoration consultant) for commercial productions because owner Garth Drabinsky of Cineplex-Odeon Corporation (now Live Entertainment Canada) recognized that to do this was less expensive—and far more spectacular—than to construct a new theatre of similar size. The **entrance lobby** [**15.97**] was restored with only minor alterations; and the auditorium, which had been broken into six cinemas, regained its original volume. Many of the components (including an exquisite dome) had survived largely intact, but others (such as the boxes) had to be reconstructed. The theatre is entered from Yonge Street through the long entrance lobby and an elliptical lobby, both of which have magnificent plasterwork that features classical ornament inspired by the eigh-

15.96   Church of the Redeemer (1879) and Renaissance Centre, Toronto, Ontario, 1982. Photograph by Harold Kalman, 1992.

15.97   Entrance lobby, Pantages Theatre, Toronto, Ontario, restored 1988. Photograph by Fiona Spalding-Smith. Courtesy Live Entertainment Canada.

teenth-century work of Robert Adam. The restoration of the Pantages was followed closely by that of the Elgin and Winter Garden Theatres, a few dozen yards further south on Yonge Street, which had been acquired by the Ontario Heritage Foundation.[163]

At **Sinclair Centre** [15.98] in downtown Vancouver (1983-6), the federal Department of Public Works preserved four large historic buildings that fill a city block; one is the former Central Post Office [10.13]. The four buildings were restored externally and rehabilitated internally to provide more efficient government office space (the reason Public Works undertook the work), as well as retail and food-service establishments on the lower floors. Associated architects Richard Henriquez and Toby Russell Buckwell and Partners inserted an attractive atrium, spanned by light steel trusses that resemble the ribs of a Gothic vault, in the space between the buildings and in space created by the removal of part of the former Post Office Annex. The level of intervention was relatively low, however, which is considered preferable from a conservation perspective.[164]

The degree of alteration caused by rehabilitating a historic building is often more considerable than at Sinclair Centre, as at **Queen's Quay Terminal Warehouse** [15.99] (Zeidler Roberts Partnership, 1981-3) at Toronto's Harbourfront, a large waterfront development initiated by Canada Mortgage and Housing Corporation. Eberhard Zeidler was the designer for this adaptive re-use of the Toronto Terminal Warehouse (Moores and Dunford of New York, 1926-7) as a retail-office-residential-theatre complex. The mammoth eight-storey reinforced-concrete building—its exterior a simple design of horizontals and verticals with Art Deco detailing—originally provided warehouse and cold-storage facilities. For the renovation, the building was gutted to provide two atriums and shopping concourses on two levels with escalators joining them. This transformation was made with considerable sensitivity to the building's original structure, the columns of which were retained (some shorn of their walls and floors) in the creation of an attractive commercial environment. The creamy-white finish, skylights, and large windows allow the interior to be suffused with light and, on the south, for the Toronto harbour in Lake Ontario to form part of the overall visual composition. Four additional storeys placed on top, containing 72 condominium units, were recessed so as to remain clearly distinguishable from the original building mass.[165]

One successful conservation project inspires anoth-

15.98 Atrium, Sinclair Centre, Vancouver, British Columbia, 1983-6. Photograph by Gary Otte.

15.99 Queen's Quay Terminal, Toronto, Ontario, rehabilitation 1981-3. Photograph by Fiona Spalding-Smith. Courtesy Zeidler Roberts Partnership/Architects.

er, as renovated and reconstituted buildings are published and ever more architects and developers recognize the economic, cultural, and environmental advantages of preservation. Happily such projects are ongoing throughout the country.

Conservation and Post-Modernism come together in a number of recent buildings whose forms and materials are directly inspired by—and may even replicate— buildings of the past. Such construction requires a close study of architectural history, and a sincere respect for the past. The more superficial side of this trend is seen in domestic architecture, where builders' pastiches of historic forms appeal to nostalgia. But the new revivalism also appears in a more serious vein, in some fine buildings for cultural groups

that seek to establish an association with their traditional architecture. Aboriginal organizations are responsible for many. For example, at the Round Lake Treatment Centre in Armstrong, BC (Collins Fulker McDonell Maltby, 1984), the central structure is the circular counselling building, whose form is derived from the historic pit house [8.9, 10, 11].[166]

This new direction in architecture is well illustrated by the **First Nations House of Learning** [**15.100**] at the University of British Columbia, designed by Larry McFarland Architects and built in 1991-2, and providing a meeting-place and support facility for aboriginal students. Its shape and structure have been inspired by the longhouses of the Coast Salish; and the gabled roof, supported by massive cedar logs, also recalls aspects of the cedar houses of the Haida, Kwakwaka'wakw, and Nuu-chah-nulth (pages 365-71). The 3,000-square-foot (280-m²) Great Hall features carved house posts supporting massive 3-foot (1-m) roof beams. Nothing is directly imitative of (yet everything is clearly inspired by) the historical sources.[167] Much the same might be said of Arthur Erickson's nearby Museum of Anthropology [15.20], but where the Museum is a brilliantly creative reinterpretation in new materials (primarily reinforced concrete and glass), the House of Learning is more derivative, more academic. The 1990s' greater respect for history may to some extent reveal a failure of nerve—a lost ability to create a great, visionary, architectural statement.

The Round Lake Treatment Centre and the First Nations House of Learning (and, more generally, the many buildings we have seen emanating from the Post-Modern and conservation movements) bring architecture back to its roots in history—in these instances, to a sensitive reinterpretation of the buildings

15.100 First Nations House of Learning, University of British Columbia, Vancouver, British Columbia, 1991-2. Photograph by Steven Evans. Courtesy Larry McFarland Architects.

of the First Nations and to a renewed regionalism.

Within the space of only a few centuries, Canadian architecture has evolved full circle. The first generations of non-native Canadians built structures and communities that were vernacular variants—both regional and ethnic—of external prototypes. We have seen how the early settlements and buildings of Quebec looked towards France, how those of Nova Scotia and Upper Canada echoed their predecessors in England and New England, and how British Columbia reflected the influence of both England and the American West Coast—yet in each case producing something new and distinctive from the sources. Post-Confederation architecture was likewise based on the centuries-old European legacy, yet showed a new national awareness that helped to unite the young Dominion. In the mid-twentieth century an optimistic modernism turned its back on this historical tradition. The vision of a brave new world, epitomized by Henry Ford's much-quoted 'History is bunk!', was taken quite literally by the

architects of the International Style, who abandoned historical forms and abolished architectural history from the university curricula. And today architects have turned to a contextual mode that once again respects the continuity of past and present— either alluding to, or actually restoring, the familiar buildings and communities of the past. It has been said that the more things change, the more they remain the same. The architecture of the 1980s and 1990s bears out this aphorism.

It is evident that a familiarity with the past is needed in order to address the present and the future. Although the modernists created many buildings of great beauty and utility, their work ultimately alienated people more than they pleased them. Today's architects' renewed appreciation of history seems to parallel North American society's passion to rediscover its roots, and the production of buildings and spaces that are more 'user-friendly' than ever before.

Architecture, above all, is an expression of society's values, and it is in our buildings that we discover much about our distinctively Canadian nature. At the same time, by searching for common threads in the architecture of all periods, we can begin to identify a specifically Canadian point of view. One key Canadianism is the tendency to simplify prototypes, to absorb ideas from abroad and modify them into something more restrained and less ostentatious. This is seen throughout Canada's building history, from the relative plainness of Canadian Georgian (compared with the more consistent use of classical ornament in the British and American models); in the reluctance to emulate the pomposity and bombast of American and French buildings in the Second Empire and Beaux-Arts styles; to the crisp austerity of the proto-modernist work of John Lyle and Ernest Cormier. These architectural directions mirror the modesty, self-deprecation, and avoidance of the spotlight that are so characteristic of Canadians. The Canadian penchant for compromise can be seen, as well, in the many resolutions that were found between conflicting influences— as expressed by John Lyle, when he remarked, 'The extreme modernist is, in my opinion, equally at fault with the extreme traditionalist. . . .',[168] and sought instead a comfortable middle ground.

Other common features in Canadian architecture include the respect shown to nature, natural forms, and local materials (seen, for example, in the organic nature of the *habitant* farmstead of the seventeenth century, and the curvilinear splendour of the Canadian Museum of Civilization of the twentieth); and in the retention of distinctive regional differences (see the Late-Modernist buildings in British Columbia, the Prairies, Ontario, and Quebec), just as the national political stage fosters strong regionalist parties and points of view. The design of Canadian buildings and towns has frequently attempted to be innovative in addressing social issues—as in garden apartments, northern housing, Habitat 67, new towns such as Kitimat, and the development of the atrium and internal circulation spaces.

Despite these innovations, Canadian architecture has had relatively little impact beyond Canada's borders— although many Canadian architects have been admired abroad. It may be the primary strength, rather than the weakness, of Canadian architecture that most architects are more interested in solving problems at home than in grandstanding abroad. In this context the outlook is good for Canadian architects to continue to solve issues of building and planning in order to provide a better built environment.

NOTES

Abbreviations

REFERENCE BOOKS

CE   *Canadian Encyclopedia: Second Edition*

CUM   Répertoire d'Architecture traditionelle sur le territoire de la Communauté urbaine de Montréal

DCB   *Dictionary of Canadian Biography*

REPOSITORIES

NAC   National Archives of Canada

PERIODICALS

APT Bulletin   *Bulletin of the Association for Preservation Technology*

CAB   *Canadian Architect and Builder*

JCAH   *Journal of Canadian Art History*

JRAIC   *Journal, Royal Architectural Institute of Canada*

JSAH   *Journal of the Society of Architectural Historians*

RACAR *Revue d'art canadienne/Canadian Art Review*

SSAC Bulletin *Bulletin of the Society for the Study of Architecture in Canada*

CHAPTER 9 The Railway and the Opening of the West

1 For the CPR, see Harold A. Innis, *A History of the Canadian Pacific Railway,* Toronto: McClelland and Stewart, 1923; John Murray Gibbon, *Steel of Empire: The Romantic History of the Canadian Pacific, the Northwest Passage of Today*, Toronto: McClelland and Stewart, c.1935; J. Lorne McDougall, *Canadian Pacific: A Brief History*, Montreal: McGill University Press, 1968; Pierre Berton, *The National Dream: The Great Railway, 1871-1881*, Toronto: McClelland and Stewart, 1970; Pierre Berton, *The Last Spike: The Great Railway, 1881-1885*, Toronto: McClelland and Stewart, 1971; Omer Lavallée, *Van Horne's Road*, Montreal: Railfare, 1974; W. Kaye Lamb, *History of the Canadian Pacific Railway*, New York: Macmillan, 1977; and David Cruise and Alison Griffiths, *Lords of the Line: The Men Who Built the CPR*, Markham: Viking, 1988.

2 Robert F. Legget, *Railroads of Canada*, Vancouver: Douglas, David & Charles, 1973; G.R. Stevens, *History of the Canadian National Railways*, New York: Macmillan, 1973; T.D. Regehr, *The Canadian Northern Railway: Pioneer Road of the Northern Prairies, 1895-1918*, Toronto: Macmillan, 1976.

3 John Witham, 'Canadian Pacific Railway Stations, 1874-1914—Historical Report', *Inventory of Railway Station Buildings in Canada*, Screening Paper, Historic Sites and Monuments Board of Canada, ed. H.E. MacNeil, Ottawa, 1974, pp. C.2-C.3; Lavallée, *Van Horne's Road*, p. 42.

4 Commonwealth Human Resource Management Limited, *A Study of Canadian Pacific's Heritage Railway Properties*, Perth, 1989, p. 29; David Butterfield, ed., *Railway Stations of Manitoba*, rev. ed., Winnipeg: Manitoba Culture, Heritage and Recreation, 1984, p. 145; Charles W. Bohi and Leslie S. Kozma, *Canadian Pacific's Western Depots: The Country Stations in Western Canada,* David City, Nebraska: South Platte Press, 1993.

5 *The Canadian Pacific Railway*, Montreal, 1887, p. 27; cited in Mathilde Brosseau, 'Canadian Pacific Railroad Stations, Past and Present—Architectural Report', *Inventory of Railway Station Buildings in Canada*, Screening Paper, Historic Sites and Monuments Board of Canada, ed. H.E. MacNeil, Ottawa, 1974, p. C.37.

6 The Yahk and Exshaw stations are illustrated in Julian Cavalier, *North American Railroad Stations*, South Brunswick, NJ: A.S. Barnes, 1979, p. 97 and plate opposite; the Mortlach station is illustrated in H. Roger Grant and Charles W. Bohi, *The Country Railroad Station in America*, rev. ed., Sioux Falls, SD: Centre for Western Studies, 1988, p. 164. Standard plans for CPR stations are illustrated in J.W. Orrock, *Railroad Structures and Estimates*, New York: John Wiley & Sons, 1909, 1918; and CPR Co. *Standard Plans*, Montreal: Chief Engineer's Office, CPR, 1916.

7 Edwinna Von Baeyer, *Rhetoric and Roses: A History of Canadian Gardening 1900-1930*, Markham: Fitzhenry & Whiteside, 1984, p. 17; the discussion of CPR Gardens is found on pp. 14-33.

8 Charles Bohi, *Canadian National's Western Depots: The Country Stations in Western Canada*, Don Mills: Railfare and Fitzhenry & Whiteside, 1977; J. Edward Martin, *Railway Stations of Western Canada*, [White Rock, BC:] Studio E, 1980; Grant and Bohi, *Country Railroad Station*, pp. 147-8; Butterfield, *Stations of Manitoba*; David McConnell, 'The Stations of the Canadian Northern Railway—Historical Report', *Inventory of Railway Station Buildings*, pp. 4C.1-9; Mathilde Brosseau, 'Stations on the Canadian Northern Railway, Architectural Report', *Inventory of Railway Station Buildings*, pp. 4C.10-12. Pratt is identified in McConnell, 'Stations', p. 4C.4, and in Martin, *Stations of Western Canada*, p. 56.

9 Bohi, CN's *Western Depots*, pp. 46-9.

10 Most are listed and some illustrated in Orrock, *Railroad Structures*.

11 Edward Forbes Bush, *Engine Houses and Turn-Tables on Canadian Railways 1850-1950*, Microfiche Report Series, 209, Ottawa: Parks Canada, n.d; David Smyth, *Extant Engine Houses in Canada: A Report Presented to the Historic Sites and Monuments Board of Canada*, Ottawa: [Canadian Parks Services], 1992. Gregg Brown and Linda Moore, *The Story of CPR Roundhouses in British Columbia*, University of British Columbia, School of Architecture, 1978.

12 Smyth, *Engine Houses*, pp. 219-55.

13 *Canadian Railway and Marine World*, December 1929, pp. 733-4, 740-3; Historica Research Limited, 'Heritage Assessment of Built Features...Southtown Development, Toronto', London, March 1989; Bush, *Engine Houses*, pp. 68-70; Smyth, *Engine Houses*, pp. 43-59.

14 Lavallée, *Van Horne's Road*, pp. 44-5; Harold Kalman and Douglas Richardson, 'Building for Transportation in the Nineteenth Century', *JCAH*, 3, 1-2, Fall 1976, pp. 31-2. Information on the relocation was provided by Robert Turner.

15 Lavallée, *Van Horne's Road*, pp. 191-3; Berton, *Last Spike*, pp. 187, 206-7.

16 Kalman and Richardson, 'Building for Transportation', pp. 34-5; Norman R. Ball, '*Mind, Heart, and Vision': Professional Engineering in Canada 1887 to 1987*, Ottawa: National Museum of Science and Technology, 1987, pp. 22, 44-8; R.F.P. Bowman, *Railways in Southern Alberta*, Occasional Paper No. 4, Lethbridge: Whoop-up Country Chapter, Historical Society of Alberta, 1973, pp. 18-23.

17 Kalman and Richardson, 'Building for Transportation', p. 37 and fig. 25 (a drawing of the Port Arthur station by Sorby); Harold Kalman, 'The Canadianization of Thomas Charles Sorby', lecture, Concordia University, Montreal, 29 March 1979; Peterborough Architectural Conservation Advisory Committee, 'The Canadian Pacific Railway Station...Peterborough, Ontario', unpublished paper, Peterborough, 1987; Commonwealth, *Heritage Railway Properties*, pp. 30-1, 173-4.

18 Martin P. Eidelberg, 'E. Colonna: Essay', in *Edward Colonna, 1862-1948*, Dayton, Ohio: Dayton Art Institute, 1983, Martin Eidelberg, 'The Life and Work of E. Colonna, Part 1: The Early Years', *Decorative Arts Society Newsletter*, 7:1, March 1981, pp. 4-7, with additional information provided by Eidelberg; John Bland, 'E. Colonna's Contribution to the Château Style in Canadian Architecture', *AIBC Forum*, 2:1, January-February 1978, pp. 14-15.

19 Saumuel H. Graybill, Jr., 'Bruce Price, American Architect, 1845-1903', Ph.D. thesis, Yale University, 1957; Russell Sturgis, 'A Review of the Works of Bruce Price', *Architectural Record*, Great American Architects Series, 5, June 1899. Price subsequently opened a Montreal office, which was managed by Frederick Bullock Marvin; see Susan Wagg, 'The McGill Architecture of Percy Erskine Nobbs', MFA thesis, Concordia University, 1979, p. 129.

20 Harold Kalman, *The Railway Hotels and the Development of the Château Style in Canada*, University of Victoria Maltwood Museum Studies in Architectural History, 1, Victoria, 1968, pp. 7-9; Kalman and Richardson, 'Building for Transportation', pp. 38-9; Peter Lanken, ed., *Windsor Station, La Gare Windsor*, Montreal: Friends of Windsor Station, 1973; Omer Lavallée, 'Windsor Station 1889-1964', *Canadian Rail*, 152, February 1964, pp. 27-37. Price's earlier schemes for Windsor Station were published in *Building*, 8, 10 March 1888, p. 81 and plates.

21 Cited in Brosseau, 'Canadian Northern', p. 4C.10; see also *1980: The Year Past: Report of the City of Winnipeg Historical Buildings Committee*, Winnipeg: City of Winnipeg, 1981, pp. 37-9.

22 Douglas Richardson, '"A Blessed Sense of Civic Excess": The Architecture of Union Station', in Richard Bébout, ed., *The Open Gate: Toronto Union Station*, Toronto: Peter Martin Associates, 1972, pp. 69-75; William Dendy and William Kilbourn, *Toronto Observed: Its Architecture, Patrons, and History*, Toronto: Oxford University Press, 1986, pp. 209-13.

23 Gibbon, *Steel of Empire*, p. 304. John Murray Gibbon was a talented publicist in the employ of the CPR.

24 Kalman, *Railway Hotels*, pp. 5-6; E.J. Hart, *The Selling of Canada: The CPR and the Beginnings of Canadian Tourism*, Banff: Altitude Publishing, 1983, pp. 11-14. See also Abraham Rogatnick, 'Canadian Castles: Phenomenon of the Railway Hotel', *Architectural Review*, 141, May 1967, pp. 364-72; Bill McKee and Georgeen Klassen, *Trail of Iron: The CPR and the Birth of the West, 1880-1930*, Calgary: Glenbow-Alberta Institute and Vancouver: Douglas & McIntyre, 1983, pp. 172-83; Catherine Donzel, Alexis Gregory, and Marc Walter, *Grand Hotels of North America*, Toronto: McClelland and Stewart, 1989, pp. 191-208.

25 Mrs Arthur Spragge, 'Our Wild Westland', part 10, *Dominion Illustrated*, 3, 7 September 1889, p. 155, cited in Kalman, *Railway Hotels*, p. 6; David A.A. Finch, *A History of the Canadian Pacific Railway in Glacier National Park, British Columbia, 1884-1930*, Microfiche Report Series, 292, Ottawa: Environment Canada-Parks, 1987; W.L. Putnam, *The Great Glacier and Its House*, New York: American Alpine Club, 1982; Hart, *Selling of Canada*, pp. 14-16.

26 Hart, *Selling of Canada*, p. 55.

27 Bart Robinson, *Banff Springs: The Story of a Hotel*, Banff: Summerthought, 1973; Kalman, *Railway Hotels*, pp. 9-10; Hart, *Selling of Canada*, pp. 17-19; *Dominion Illustrated*, 1, 21 July 1888, p. 38.

28 Walter Vaughan, *The Life and Work of Sir William Van Horne*, New York, 1920, p. 151.

29 *Dominion Illustrated*, 1, 21 July 1888, p. 38; ibid., 7, 19 September 1891, p. 276; Gibbon, *Steel of Empire*, p. 316; *Banff Springs Hotel in the Heart of the Canadian Rockies*, brochure, n.d.

30 Kalman, *Railway Hotels*, pp. 11-14, 17, 32-7; Joan Elson Morgan, *Castle of Quebec*, Toronto: Dent, 1949; France Gagnon Pratte and Eric Etter, *Le Château Frontenac*, Quebec: Éditions Continuité, 1993; Luc Noppen, Claude Paulette, and Michel Tremblay, *Québec: trois siècles d'architecture*, n.p.: Libre Expression, 1979, pp. 386-91.

31 Vaughan, *Van Horne*, p. 199; Gibbon, *Steel of Empire*, p. 336.

32 Victor Petit, *Châteaux de la vallée de la Loire des XVᵉ, XVIᵉ et XVIIᵉ siècles*, 2 vols, Paris, 1861; reproduced in Kalman, *Railway Hotels*, fig. 7.

33 Barr Ferree, 'A Talk with Bruce Price', *Architectural Record*, Great American Architects Series, 5, June 1899, pp. 69-70, 82.

34 Henry-Russell Hitchcock, *The Architecture of H.H. Richardson and His Times*, 3rd ed., Cambridge: MIT Press, 1966, pp. 221 ff. and figs 71-3.

35 CPR *Annual Report*, 1898, p. 7.

36 Kalman, *Railway Hotels*, pp. 17-19; Martin Segger and Douglas Franklin, *Victoria: A Primer for Regional History in Architecture*, Watkins Glen, NY: American Life Foundation, 1979, pp. 136-9; Terry Reksten, *Rattenbury*, Victoria: Sono Nis, 1978, pp. 76-86; Anthony A. Barrett and Rhodri Windsor Liscombe, *Francis Rattenbury and British Columbia*, Vancouver: University of British Columbia Press, 1983, pp. 150-60; Godfrey Holloway, *The Empress of Victoria*, Victoria: Pacifica Productions, 1968.

37 *Victoria Colonist*, 21 January 1908; cited in *Hotel News*, January 1933, p. 14.

38 Shaughnessy to R. Marpole, 1 June 1906; cited in John A. Eagle, *The Canadian Pacific Railway and the Development of Western Canada, 1896-1914*, Kingston: McGill-Queen's University Press, 1989, p. 166.

39 Harold Kalman, 'The CPR Buildings', lecture, CPR West Conference, Glenbow Museum, Calgary, 23 September 1983; for Painter, see also Eagle, *Canadian Pacific*, p. 153. Painter's papers are preserved at the Archives, Whyte Museum of the Canadian Rockies.

40 Cited in Gerald Friesen, *The Canadian Prairies: A History*, Toronto: University of Toronto Press, 1984, pp. 302-3.

41 Cited in Hugh Durnford, ed., *Heritage of Canada*, n.p: Canadian Automobile Association and Reader's Digest Association, 1978, p. 325.

42 Van Horne to Harry Moody, 9 November 1897; cited in Eagle, *Canadian Pacific*, p. xi.

43 Lamb, *Canadian Pacific*, p. 216; cited in Eagle, *Canadian Pacific*, p. 174.

44 Eagle, *Canadian Pacific*, pp. 175-8, 185.

45 Ibid., pp. 201-2. See also Renie Gross and Lea Nicoll Kramer, *Tapping the Bow*, Brooks, Alberta: Eastern Irrigation District, 1985, pp. 6-8, 15, 137-9.

46 F.H. Leacy, ed., *Historical Statistics of Canada*, 2nd ed., Ottawa: Statistics Canada, c. 1983, Table A2-14.

47 Heather Robertson, *Salt of the Earth*, Toronto: James Lorimer, 1974, p. 28. See also Donald G. Wetherell and Irene R.A. Kmet, *Homes in Alberta: Building, Trends, and Design 1870-1967*, Edmonton: University of Alberta Press and Alberta Culture and Multiculturalism, 1991, pp. 15-41; Thelma B. Dennis, *Albertans Built: Aspects of Housing in Rural Alberta to 1920*, privately printed, 1986; Kathleen M.

Taggart, 'The First Shelter of Early Pioneers', *Saskatchewan History*, 11:3, Autumn 1958, p. 81-93.

48 David K. Butterfield and Edward M. Ledohowski, *Architectural Heritage: The MSTW Planning District*, Winnipeg: Historic Resources Branch, Department of Culture, Heritage and Recreation, 1984, p. 21.

49 James Rugg manuscript, Saskatchewan Provincial Archives; cited in Robertson, *Salt*, p. 32.

50 Mrs Ed Watson memoir, Manitoba Provincial Archives; cited in Robertson, *Salt*, p. 44.

51 John de Visser and Harold Kalman, *Pioneer Churches*, Toronto: McClelland and Stewart, 1976, p. 167. See also William C. Wonders and Mark A. Rasmussen, 'Log Buildings of West Central Alberta', *Prairie Forum*, 5:2, Fall 1980, pp. 197-217.

52 John Warkentin, 'Time and Place in the Prairie Interior', *Artscanada*, 169/170/171, Autumn 1972, p. 20; Dennis, *Albertans Built*, pp. 43-4.

53 Quotations from Sarah Ellen Roberts, *Alberta Homestead: Chronicle of a Pioneer Family*, ed. by Lathrop E. Roberts, Austin: University of Texas Press, 1968. Roberts' manuscript, 'Of Us and Oxen', is in the Glenbow Museum; it was published in Canada as *Us and the Oxen*, Saskatoon: Modern Press, 1968.

54 Chester Martin, *'Dominion Lands' Policy* (1938); cited in Friesen, *Prairies*, p. 309.

55 G.E. Mills, *Buying Wood & Building Farms: Marketing Lumber and Farm Building Designs on the Canadian Prairies, 1880 to 1920*, Studies in Archaeology, Architecture and History, Ottawa: Parks Service, Environment Canada, 1991. See also *Architectural Heritage*, the series of reports on selected planning districts issued by the Manitoba government (1983 ff.); and Dennis, *Albertans Built*.

56 Mills, *Buying Wood*, pp. 54.

57 Eagle, *Canadian Pacific*, pp. 173-212; Lyle Dick, *A History of Prairie Settlement Patterns, 1870-1930*, Microfiche Report Series, No. 307, Ottawa: Canadian Parks Service, 1987, pp. 8-10, 124-7; Mills, *Buying Wood*, pp. 54-61.

58 Mills, *Buying Wood*, pp. 51-4; G.E. Mills and D.W. Holdsworth, 'The B.C. Mills Prefabricated System: The Emergence of Ready-Made Buildings in Western Canada', *Canadian Historic Sites: Occasional Papers in Archaeology and History*, 14, Ottawa: Parks Canada, 1975, pp. 127-69; Thelma B. Dennis, '"Ready-made" Houses in Rural Alberta 1900-1920', *Alberta History*, 34:2, Spring 1986, pp. 1-8.

59 Mills, *Buying Wood*, pp. 61-9; Dennis, *Albertans Built*, pp. 64-5; Alan Gowans, *The Comfortable House: North American Suburban Architecture 1890-1930*, Cambridge: MIT Press, 1986, pp. 41-55.

60 Mills, *Buying Wood*, pp. 71-86.

61 S.A. Bedford, *Province of Manitoba: Plans and Specifications for Rural Schools...*, Winnipeg: Government Printer, 1903; cited in Ivan J. Saunders, 'A Survey of Manitoba School Architecture to 1930', *Research Bulletin*, No. 222, Ottawa: Parks Canada, 1984, pp. 6-7. See also John C. Charyk, *The Little White Schoolhouse*, I, Saskatoon: Western Producer Prairie Books, 1968.

62 Ivan J. Saunders, 'A Survey of Saskatchewan Schoolhouse Architecture to 1930', *Research Bulletin*, No. 223, Ottawa: Parks Canada, 1984, pp. 7-8; Mills and Holdsworth, 'B.C. Mills', p. 141. See also Saunders, 'A Survey of Alberta

School Architecture to 1930', *Research Bulletin*, No. 224, Ottawa: Parks Canada, 1984; Saskatchewan Association of Architects, *Historic Architecture of Saskatchewan*, Regina: Focus, 1986, pp. 138-41.

63 William Naftel, 'Lanark Place, Abernethy, Saskatchewan: Structural History', Manuscript Report No. 164, Ottawa: Parks Canada, *c.*1975; *Historic Architecture of Saskatchewan*, pp. 160-1; see also Sarah Carter, 'Material Culture and the W.R. Motherwell Home', *Prairie Forum*, 8:1, 1983, pp. 99-111; Allan R. Turner, 'W.R. Motherwell: The Emergence of a Farm Leader', *Saskatchewan History*, 11:3, Autumn 1958, pp. 94-103; Lyle Dick, 'A Social and Economic History of the Abernethy District, Saskatchewan, 1880-1920', Ottawa: Parks Canada, 1983; Friesen, *Prairies*, pp. 315-16.

64 For the landscape, see Nancy Ellwand, 'A Homestead Restored', *Landscape Architectical Review*, May 1986, pp. 10-12; Greg Thomas and Ian Clarke, 'The Garrison Mentality and the Canadian West: The British Canadian Response to Two Landscapes: The Fur Trade Post and The Ontarian Prairie Homestead', *Prairie Forum*, 4:1, September 1979, pp. 83-109.

65 Vladimir J. Kaye, *Early Ukrainian Settlements in Canada, 1895-1900*, Toronto: University of Toronto Press, 1964; Michael H. Marunchak, *The Ukrainian Canadians: A History*, 2nd ed., Winnipeg: Ukrainian Academy of Arts and Sciences in Canada, 1982. Friesen, *Prairies*, pp. 265-7.

66 John Lehr, 'The Landscape of Ukrainian Settlement in the Canadian West', *Great Plains Quarterly*, 2:2, Spring 1982, pp. 96-7; Andy Nahachewsky, 'Ukrainian Dug-out Dwellings in East Central Alberta', Research paper, Alberta Culture, Edmonton, 1985; Dick, *Prairie Settlement Pattern*, pp. 146-7.

67 The authority on Ukrainian-Canadian houses, particularly in Alberta, is John C. Lehr: see Lehr, 'Ukrainian Houses in Alberta', *Alberta Historical Review*, 21:4, Autumn 1973, pp. 9-15 (with earlier bibliography); Lehr, 'Changing Ukrainian House Styles', *Alberta Historical Review*, 23:1, Winter 1975, pp. 25-9; Lehr, 'Ukrainian Vernacular Architecture', *Canadian Collector*, 11:1, January-February 1976, pp. 66-70; Lehr, *Ukrainian Vernacular Architecture in Alberta*, Historic Sites Service, Occasional Paper No. 1, Edmonton: Alberta Culture, 1976; Lehr, 'The Process and Pattern of Ukrainian Rural Settlement in Western Canada, 1891-1914', Ph.D. dissertation, University of Manitoba, 1978; Lehr, 'The Log Buildings of Ukrainian Settlers in Western Canada', *Prairie Forum*, 5:2, Fall 1980, pp. 183-96; Lehr, 'Colour Preferences and Building Decoration Among Ukrainians in Western Canada', *Prairie Forum*, 6:2, 1981, pp. 203-6; Lehr, 'Ukrainian Pioneer Architecture in the Prairie West', *Selected Papers from the Society for the Study of Architecture in Canada*, [I,] Ottawa, 1981, pp. 8-21; Lehr, 'Landscape of Ukrainian Settlement' (1983). For a discussion of houses and farm buildings in Manitoba, see Ledohowski and Butterfield, *Eastern Interlake*, pp. 55-71. Two articles that compare Ukrainian and Mennonite houses are Gwendolyn Dowsett, 'The Vernacular Architecture of Two Ethnic Groups in Manitoba: A Comparative Study', *SSAC Bulletin*, 12:3, September 1987, pp. 7-13; and John C. Lehr, 'Folk Architecture in Manitoba: Mennonites and Ukrainians', *SSAC Bulletin*, 11:2, June 1986, pp. 3-5. See also Radomir Bilash, 'A Century of Settlement:

The Ukrainians of Alberta', *Alberta Past*, 7:1, Spring/Summer 1991, pp. 6-7; William C. Wonders and Mark A. Rasmussen, 'Log Buildings of West Central Alberta', *Prairie Forum*, 5:2, Fall 1980, pp. 209-12.

68 Ledohowski and Butterfield, *Eastern Interlake*, pp. 60-7.

69 Lehr, 'Log Buildings', p. 186.

70 Ukraininan churches in Alberta are introduced in Diana Thomas Kordan, 'Tradition in a New World: Ukrainian-Canadian Churches in Alberta', *SSAC Bulletin*, 13:1, March 1988, pp. 3-7; Diana Thomas Kordan, *Divine Architecture: A Stylistic Survey of Church Architecture in Alberta*, Edmonton: Alberta Culture, 1988; and Diana Thomas Kordan, *Historical Driving Tour: Ukrainian Churches in East Central Alberta*, Edmonton: Canadian Institute of Ukrainian Studies, n.d. For churches in Saskatchewan, see Anna Maria Baran, *Ukrainian Catholic Churches of Saskatchewan*, translated by Christine T. Pastershank, Saskatoon: privately printed, 1977; Savelia Curniski, 'Icons and Banyas: Ukrainian Orthodox Churches in Saskatchewan', *Selected Papers from the Society for the Study of Architecture in Canada*, [I,] Ottawa, 1981, pp. 1-7; also, an inventory of Saskatchewan Ukrainian churches was produced by the Church Historical Information Research Project (CHIRP), Canadian Centre for Folk Culture Studies, Ottawa, 1971-4. For Manitoba, see M.C. Kotecki and R.R. Rostecki, *Ukrainian Churches in Manitoba: An Overview Study*, 2 vols, Winnipeg: Department of Culture, Heritage and Recreation, 1984; churches in the Lake Winnipeg area of Manitoba are discussed in Ledohowski and Butterfield, *Eastern Interlake*, pp. 97-8, 172-4.

71 *St Michael's Ukrainian Greek Orthodox Church*, 2nd ed., Winnipeg: Manitoba Culture, Heritage and Recreation, 1985; de Visser and Kalman, *Pioneer Churches*, pp. 154-5, 171-3.

72 de Visser and Kalman, *Pioneer Churches*, pp. 156-7, 173.

73 The inventory produced by CHIRP; Baran, *Ukrainian Catholic Churches*, pp. 134-5; Rev. I.A. Holowka, ed., *Jubilee: 25th Anniversary of the Parish of the Nativity of the Blessed Virgin Mary, Dobrowody, Sask.*, Dobrowody: Parish Council, n.d. (in Ukrainian); de Visser and Kalman, *Pioneer Churches*, pp. 158, 173. Michael Tatarniuk kindly assisted with translation and interpretation.

74 Diana Thomas Kordan, *Historical Driving Tour*, No. 3; Diana Thomas Kordan, 'Tradition', pp. 5-6. See also Radomir B. Bilash, 'Peter Lipinski, Prairie Church Artist', *SSAC Bulletin*, 13:1, March 1988, pp. 8-14.

75 Donald T. Gale and Paul M. Koroscil, 'Doukhobor Settlements: Experiments in Idealism', *Canadian Ethnic Studies*, 9:2, 1977, pp. 53-71; F. Mark Mealing, 'Doukhobor Architecture: An Introduction', *Canadian Ethnic Studies*, 16:3, 1984, pp. 73-88; Dick *Prairie Settlement Patterns*, pp. 136-40. See also George Woodcock and Ivan Avakumovic, *The Doukhobors*, Toronto: Oxford University Press, 1977; Koozma Tarasoff, *In Search of Brotherhood*, Vancouver: privately printed, 1963.

76 *Historic Architecture of Saskatchewan*, pp. 118-21, with illustrations of other 'prayerhouses'.

77 Gale and Korosch, 'Doukhobor Settlements', pp. 65-8; Mealing, 'Doukhobor Architecture', pp. 79-81.

78 William P. Thompson, 'Hutterite Community: Its Reflex in Architectural and Settlement Patterns', *Canadian Ethnic Studies*, 16:3, 1984, pp. 53-72; Dick, *Prairie Settlement*

Patterns, pp. 154-6; John Ryan, 'Hutterites', *Canadian Encyclopedia (CE)*, 2nd ed., Edmonton: Hurtig, 1988, II, pp. 1031-2. See also John A. Hostetler, *Hutterite Society*, Baltimore: Johns Hopkins University Press, 1974; and Bertha Clark, 'The Hutterian Communities', Part 1, *Journal of Political Economy*, 32, June 1924, pp. 357-74.

79 Cyril Edel Leonoff, *The Jewish Farmers of Western Canada*, Vancouver: Jewish Historical Society of British Columbia and Western States Jewish History Association, 1984; Cyril Edel Leonoff, *The Architecture of Jewish Settlements in the Prairies: A Pictorial History*, privately printed, 1975; Cyril Edel Leonoff, *Wapella Farm Settlement: A Pictorial History*, Supplement to Transactions, Manitoba Historical and Scientific Society, ser. 3, no. 27, 1970-1; Benjamin Smillie, ed., *Visions of the New Jerusalem*, Edmonton: NeWest Press, 1983, pp. 91-107.

80 Cited in Leonoff, *Wapella*, p. 11.

81 Leonoff, *Jewish Farmers*, pp. 47-63; *Rural Municipality of Willow Creek No. 458: Jubilee Year 1912-1962*, n.p: n.d., pp. 53-61; De Visser and Kalman, *Pioneer Churches*, pp. 154, 171.

82 Lily Pierce Page, 'The Settlement of Cannington Manor', in John Hawkes, ed., *The Story of Saskatchewan and Its People*, II, Chicago and Regina: S.J. Clark, 1924, pp. 787-92; Mrs. A.E.M. Hewlitt, *A Saskatchewan Historic Site: Cannington Manor Historic Park*, n.p., n.d.; Hewlitt, *All Saints Cannington Manor*, brochure, Wawota, Sask., n.d.; *Cannington Manor Historic Park*, Regina: Department of Natural Resources, n.d.; Jane McCracken, 'Cannington Manor', *CE* I, pp. 354-5.

83 Stevens, *Canadian National Railways*, p. 224. London: Seeley Service, 1912, pp. 153-7; cited in Bohi, CN's *Western Depots*, p. 47. See also, John Gilpin, 'International Perspectives on Railway Townsite Development in Western Canada 1877-1914', *Planning Perspectives*, 7, 1992, pp. 247-62.

84 Friesen, *Prairies*, pp. 320-1.

85 Harold Kalman, 'Canada's Main Streets', in Deryck Holdsworth, ed., *Reviving Main Street*, Toronto: University of Toronto Press, 1985, pp. 14-15.

86 *Historic Architecture of Saskatchewan*, pp. 34-7.

87 Deryck Holdsworth and Edward Mills, 'Pioneer Prefab Banks on the Prairies', *Canadian Geographical Journal*, 96:2, April-May 1978, pp. 66-9; Mills and Holdsworth, 'B.C. Mills', pp. 144-8.

88 Norman Tucker, *Handbook of English Church Expansion*, Toronto: Mission Books, 1907, p. 124; W.F. Payton, *An Historical Sketch of the Diocese of Saskatchewan of the Anglican Church of Canada*, [Prince Albert: Diocese of Saskatchewan, *c*. 1974], p. 67.

89 Gillian Moir et al., *Early Buildings of Manitoba*, Winnipeg: Peguis, 1973, pp. 45-7; T. Ritchie, *Canada Builds 1867-1967*, Toronto: University of Toronto Press, 1967, pp. 106-7; Robert C. MacKenzie, 'Prairie Grain Elevators "Go to Town"', *Canadian Geographical Journal*, 98:1, February-March 1979, pp. 52-7; Richard J. Friesen, 'Country Grain Elevators of Alberta, 1896-1940', research paper, Alberta Culture, 1983; Harold Kalman, 'This Elevator Is Coming Down', *Canadian Heritage*, 10:1, February-March 1984, pp. 18-24; Commonwealth Historic Resource Management Limited, 'Grain Elevator', research paper prepared for the History Hall, Canadian Museum of Civilization, Perth, 1988.

90 Drawings are in the Manitoba Archives.

91 Marylu Antonelli and Jack Forbes, *Pottery in Alberta: The Long Tradition*, Edmonton: University of Alberta Press, 1978; Robert Bailey, Keith Wagland, and Harold Kalman, *Medalta: A Study for the Rehabilitation and Re-use of the Medalta Potteries, Medicine Hat, Alberta*, Toronto, 1978, pp. 57-63.

92 Alan F.J. Artibise, *Prairie Urban Development 1870-1930*, Historical Booklet No. 34, Ottawa: Canadian Historical Association, 1981.

93 Janice P. Dickin McGinnis, 'Town Growth Study, Calgary, Alberta, 1875-1914', in McGinnis and Frank Donnelly, *Reports on Selected Buildings in Calgary, Alberta*, Manuscript Report Series, No. 391, Ottawa: Parks Canada, 1974-6, pp. 8-32. See also J.W. Grant MacEwan, *Calgary Cavalcade*, Edmonton: Institute of Allied Arts, 1981; M.J. Forhan, *Calgary*, History of Canadian Cities Series, Toronto: James Lorimer, 1978; Max Forhan and Heather MacEwan Foran, *Calgary: Canada's Frontier Metropolis*, Calgary: Windsor Publications, 1982.

94 McGinnis and Donnelly, *Reports*, pp. 22-3, 71-9; Richard Cunniffe, *Calgary—in Sandstone*, Calgary: Historical Society of Alberta, 1969.

95 Research undertaken by the Planning Department, City of Calgary, *c*. 1980-83; McGinnis and Donnelly, *Reports*, *passim*; Cunniffe, *Calgary*, pp. 11-13.

96 McGinnis and Donnelly, *Reports*, pp. 325-31.

97 Cunniffe, *Sandstone*, p. 6; McGinnis and Donnelly, *Reports*, p. 76.

98 Bryan P. Melnyk, *Calgary Builds: The Emergence of an Urban Landscape 1905-1914*, Edmonton: Alberta Culture and Canadian Plains Research Center, 1985.

99 Calgary *Albertan*, 28 February 1913; cited in Alexander Calhoun, 'The Calgary Public Library, 1911-1942. Its Early History, Growth and Place in the Community', unpublished paper, Calgary Public Library, 1942; and in McGinnis and Donnelly, *Reports*, p. 252. See also David R. Conn and Barry McCallum, 'Heritage to Hi-Tech: Evolution of Image and Function of Canadian Public Library Buildings', in Peter F. McNally, ed., *Readings in Canadian Library History*, Toronto: Canadian Library Association, 1986, pp. 123-48, esp. pp. 128-30.

100 Melnyk, *Calgary Builds*, pp. 57-69, 136-41.

101 David Chuenyan Lai, *Chinatowns: Towns Within Cities in Canada*, Vancouver: University of British Columbia Press, 1988; Ban Seng Hoe, 'The Chinatown in Alberta: Architectural Adaptation, Urban Renewal, and Community's Needs', *Selected Papers from the Society for the Study of Architecture in Canada*, [I,] Ottawa, 1981, pp. 22-31; Paul Voisey, 'Chinatown on the Prairies: The Emergence of an Ethnic Community', ibid., pp. 33-52. Harold Kalman, Ron Phillips, and Robin Ward, *Exploring Vancouver: The Essential Architecural Guide*, Vancouver: University of British Columbia Press, 1993, pp. 33-9.

102 Melnyk, *Calgary Builds*, pp. 150-2; Forhan and Forhan, *Calgary*, pp. 76-7.

103 *The Architecture of Edward and W.S. Maxwell*, Montreal: Montreal Museum of Fine Arts, 1991, pp. 94-6.

104 Eagle, *Canadian Pacific*, pp. 224-5.

CHAPTER 10 **Building the Young Dominion**

1 Cited in Wilfrid Eggleston, *The Queen's Choice*, Ottawa: National Capital Commission, 1961, p. 102.

2 For the competition and the construction of the Parliament Buildings, see Alan H. Armstrong, 'Profile of Parliament Hill', *JRAIC*, 34: 9, September 1957, pp. 327-31; T. Ritchie, *Canada Builds 1867-1967*, Toronto: University of Toronto Press, 1967, pp. 16-35; Eggleston, *Queen's Choice*, pp. 125-38; J. Daniel Livermore, *Departmental Buildings, Eastern Block, Parliament Hill, Ottawa*, Ottawa: Department of Public Works, 1974 (the results of the evaluation are reproduced on p. 2a); Douglas Owram, *Building for Canadians: A History of the Department of Public Works 1840-1960*, Ottawa: Public Works Canada, 1979, pp. 83-7; Carolyn Ann Young, '"Odahwah": The Competition of 1859 for the Canadian Parliament Buildings', Phil.M. thesis, University of Toronto, 1989; Geoffrey Simmins, ed., *Documents in Canadian Architecture*, Peterborough: Broadview Press, 1992, pp. 59-76. For the buildings, see National Film Board of Canada, *Stones of History: Canada's Houses of Parliament*, Ottawa: Queen's Printer, 1967; R.A.J. Phillips, *The East Block of the Parliament Buildings of Canada*, Ottawa: Queen's Printer, 1967; J. Daniel Livermore and Leslie Maitland, 'Architectural Heirloom: the East Block', *Canadian Geographic*, 101: 4, August-September 1981, pp. 62-7; Kenneth Binks, *Library of Parliament*, Ottawa: KCB, n.d; R.H. Hubbard, 'Canadian Gothic', *Architectural Review*, 116: 692, August 1954, pp. 102-8; Mathilde Brosseau, *Gothic Revival in Canadian Architecture*, Canadian Historic Sites: Occasional Papers in Archaeology and History, No. 25, Ottawa: Parks Canada, 1980, pp. 20-1, 120-5; Christina Cameron and Janet Wright, *Second Empire Style in Canadian Architecture*, Canadian Historic Sites: Occasional Papers in Archaeology and History, No. 24, Ottawa: Parks Canada, 1980, pp. 12-13, 42-5; Christopher A. Thomas, 'Thomas Fuller (1823-98) and Changing Attitudes to Medievalism in Nineteenth-Century Architecture', *SSAC: Selected Papers*, 3, Ottawa: SSAC, 1982, pp. 103-47 (n. 17 lists the principal manuscript sources); Courtney C.J. Bond, *City on the Ottawa*, Ottawa: Queen's Printer, 1965, pp. 122-5; Harold Kalman and John Roaf, *Exploring Ottawa*, Toronto: University of Toronto Press, 1983, pp. 5-8; Jane Varkaris and Lucile Finsten, *Fire on Parliament Hill!*, Erin: Boston Mills, 1988; Bhabes Chandra Chattopadhyay, 'Government Buildings in Canada and U.S.A.', M. Arch. thesis, University of Toronto, 1964. For further bibliography, see *A Bibliography of History and Heritage of the National Capital Region*, rev. ed., Ottawa: National Capital Commission, 1978, pp. 258-68. Two interpretive articles that focus on the Parliament Buildings are Alan Gowans, 'The Canadian National Style', in W.L. Morton, ed., *The Shield of Achilles: Aspects of Canada in the Victorian Age*, Toronto: McClelland and Stewart, 1968, pp. 208-19; and Douglas Richardson, 'The Spirit of the Place', *Canadian Collector*, 10: 5, September-October 1975, pp. 27-9.

3 Thomas, 'Thomas Fuller', with bibliography; Christopher A. Thomas [misattribution], 'The Parliament Builder: Thomas Fuller's Gothic Vision', *Canadian Heritage*, December 1979, p. 18; obituary of Thomas Fuller, *Canadian Architect and Builder* (*CAB*), 11: 10, October 1898, pp.

168-9; Eric Arthur, *Toronto: No Mean City*, 3rd ed., revised by Stephen A. Otto, Toronto: University of Toronto Press, 1986, pp. 247, 252-3; Harold Kirker, *California's Architectural Frontier: Style and Tradition in the Nineteenth Century*, rev. ed., Santa Barbara: Peregrine Smith, 1973, pp. 89, 97, 210.

4 For the disputes and their resolution, see Eggleston, *Queen's Choice*, pp. 129-31; Livermore, *Eastern Block*, pp. 8-23; Christina Cameron, *Charles Baillairgé, Architect & Engineer*, Montreal: McGill-Queen's University Press, 1989, pp. 84-5, 94-107; John Page, 'Report on the Public Buildings at Ottawa', *General Report of the Commissioner of Public Works for the Year Ending 30th June 1867*, app. 21, Ottawa: Hunter, Rose, 1868, pp. 201-48; J.E. Hodgetts, 'Constructing the Ottawa Buildings: A Case Study', *Pioneer Public Service: An Administrative History of the United Canadas, 1841-1867*, Toronto: University of Toronto Press, 1955; Maxwell M. Kalman, 'Unrecorded Major Changes in the Construction of the Original Centre Block, Ottawa', unpublished manuscript, *c*. 1984, pp. 2-4.

5 Fuller and Jones, competition entry, National Archives of Canada; cited in Richardson, 'Spirit', p. 28. The written statement accompanying their entry is in NAC, Public Records Division, R.G. 11; other important sources are *Documents Relating to the Construction of the Parliamentary and Departmental Buildings at Ottawa*, Quebec: Department of Public Works, 1862; and *Report of the Commission Appointed to Inquire into Matters Connected with the Public Buildings at Ottawa*, Quebec: Blackburn, 1863.

6 *Idem*.

7 Young, 'Odahwah'; J. Mordaunt Crook, *The British Museum*, New York: Praeger, pp. 151-93.

8 Mary Cullen, *Slate Roofing in Canada*, Studies in Archaeology, Architecture and History, Ottawa: Environment Canada, 1990, p. 32.

9 Thomas, 'Thomas Fuller', p. 108; see also Malcolm Thurlby, 'Ottawa Gothic', *Rotunda*, Summer 1988, p. 31.

10 Stefan Muthesius, *The High Victorian Movement in Architecture 1850-1870*, London: Routledge and Kegan Paul, 1972, pp. 160-81; Kenneth Clark, *The Gothic Revival*, rev. ed., Harmondsworth: Penguin, 1964, pp. 168-72, 192-3 (concerning the Foreign Office controversy); Roger Dixon and Stefan Muthesius, *Victorian Architecture*, London: Thames and Hudson, 1978, pp. 155-64 (quotation from p. 164); George L. Hersey, *High Victorian Gothic: A Study in Associationism*, Baltimore: Johns Hopkins University Press, 1972, pp. 183-209 (arguing that these English buildings mark the *end* of High Victorian Gothic).

11 Brown to his wife, 15 August 1864; reproduced in Eggleston, *Queen's Choice*, pp. 132-3. The connections are discussed in Alan Gowans, *Looking at Architecture in Canada*, Toronto: Oxford University Press, 1958, pp. 149-50; Arthur/Otto, *No Mean City*, pp. 144-5; and Douglas Richardson, *A Not Unsightly Building: University College and Its History*, Toronto: Mosaic Press, 1990, pp. 61, 73-6.

12 *Documents Relating to the Construction of the Parliamentary and Departmental Buildings at Ottawa*, pp. 21-2.

13 Livermore and Maitland, 'East Block'. The work was carried out in 1975-81.

14 John J. Stewart, 'Notes on Calvert Vaux's 1873 Design for the Public Grounds of the Parliament Buildings in Ottawa', *APT Bulletin*, 8: 1, 1976, pp. 1-27; Common-

wealth Historic Resource Management Limited, *The Land-scape of Parliament Hill: A History and Inventory*, prepared for Public Works Canada, Perth, 1990. Quotation from Ottawa *Times*, 5 November 1872; cited in Stewart, 'Public Grounds', n. 14.

15 Vaux to Scott, 21 June 1873, NAC; cited in Stewart, 'Public Grounds', pp. 3-4. See the entry on Vaux by Dennis Stead-man Francis and Joy M. Kestenbaum in the *Macmillan Encyclopedia of Architects*, IV, New York: The Free Press, 1982, pp. 303-4.

16 Vaux, letter to the editor of the New York *Times*, 8 August 1885; cited in Stewart, 'Public Grounds', p. 2.

17 Stewart, 'Public Grounds', pp. 2-7; Commonwealth, *Landscape*, pp. 69-72.

18 Anthony Trollope, *North America*, 1862; cited in Binks, *Library of Parliament*, p. 18, and Eggleston, *Queen's Choice*, p. 128.

19 Henry-Russell Hitchcock, *Architecture: Nineteenth and Twentieth Centuries*, 2nd ed., Baltimore: Penguin, 1977, p. 195.

20 William Westfall, *Two Worlds: The Protestant Culture of Nineteenth-Century Ontario*, Kingston: McGill-Queen's University Press, 1989, p. 139.

21 Wilfred Campbell, *Canada: Painted by T. Mower Martin R.C.A., Described by Wilfred Campbell LL.D.*, London: A. and C. Black, 1907, pp. 104-5; cited in Hubbard, 'Canadian Gothic', p. 108, and Westfall, *Two Worlds*, p. 140.

22 Gowans, 'The Canadian National Style', pp. 208-19.

23 See Margaret Archibald, *By Federal Design: The Chief Architect's Branch of the Department of Public Works, 1881-1914*, Ottawa: Parks Canada, 1983; Owram, *Building for Canadians*; Janet Wright, 'Thomas Seaton Scott: The Architect versus the Administrator', *JCAH*, 6: 2, 1982, pp. 202-19; Mark Fram and Jean Simonton, 'Public Buildings', in Norman R. Ball, ed., *Building Canada: A History of Public Works*, Toronto: University of Toronto Press, 1988, pp. 262-85; Deryck Holdsworth, 'Architectural Expressions of the Canadian National State', *Canadian Geographer*, 30: 2, 1986, pp. 167-71.

24 Lawrence Wodehouse, 'Alfred B. Mullett and His French Style Government Buildings', *JSAH*, 31: 1, March 1972, pp. 22-37.

25 Dewe to Department of Public Works, 4 March 1870; cited in Wright, 'Scott', pp. 207-8.

26 William White, Secretary to the Post Office, to F. Braun, Secretary of the Department of Public Works, 3 June 1870; cited in Wright, 'Scott', p. 208.

27 Wright, 'Scott', pp. 207-9; Cameron and Wright, *Second Empire*, pp. 50-1; Arthur/Otto, *No Mean City*, p. 170; William Dendy, *Lost Toronto: Images of the City's Past*, Toronto: McClelland and Stewart, 1993, pp. 110-11.

28 Saint John *Globe*, 19 June 1878, p. 4, and Saint John *Daily Telegraph*, 26 April 1881, p. 1; both cited in C. Anne Hale, *The Rebuilding of Saint John, New Brunswick, 1877-1881*, Fredericton: Queen's Printer, 1990, p. 29; see also Cam-eron and Wright, *Second Empire*, pp. 48-9; Wright, 'Scott', pp. 210-11. For the earlier Custom House, see Leslie Mait-land, *Neoclassical Architecture in Canada*, Studies in Archaeology, Architecture and History, Ottawa: Parks Canada, 1984, p. 56.

29 Cameron and Wright, *Second Empire*, pp. 58-9, 64-5; Wright, 'Scott', pp. 212-14.

30 Christopher Thomas, 'Architectural Image for the Domin-ion: Scott, Fuller and the Stratford Post Office', *JCAH*, 3: 1-2, Fall 1976, pp. 83-94.

31 Fuller to Keefer, 5 October 1881, and Keefer to Macdonald, 13 October 1881, NAC; both cited in Owram, *Building for Canadians*, p. 146.

32 Fuller obituary, *CAB*, p. 169; Wright, 'Scott', p. 207.

33 Archibald, *By Federal Design*, pp. 35-6.

34 Christopher Alexander Thomas, 'Dominion Architecture: Fuller's Canadian Post Offices, 1881-96', M.A. thesis, Uni-versity of Toronto, 1978; Thomas, 'Fuller and Changing Attitudes'; Thomas, 'Architectural Image'; Archibald, *By Federal Design*; Ralph Greenhill, Ken Macpherson, and Douglas Richardson, *Ontario Towns*, Ottawa: Oberon, 1974, unpaginated. All the buildings are illustrated in Thomas, 'Fuller and Changing Attitudes', except the one at Baddeck, Nova Scotia, which is in Harold Kalman, Keith Wagland, and Robert Bailey, *Encore: Recycling Public Build-ings for the Arts*, Don Mills: Corpus, 1980, pp. 122-7.

35 *CAB*, 8: 2, February 1894, p. 22.

36 Thomas, 'Fuller and Changing Attitudes', p. 109; Kalman and Roaf, *Exploring Ottawa*, p. 8.

37 Dendy, *Lost Toronto*, p. 184.

38 'Information on the Late David Ewart, I.S.O.' NAC, R.G. 11, Vol. 2922, File 5805.

39 Edward Mills and Warren Sommer, *Vancouver Architecture, 1886-1914*, Manuscript Report No. 405, Ottawa: Parks Canada, 1975, 1, pp. 22, 292-6; Harold Kalman, Ron Phillips, and Robin Ward, *Exploring Vancouver*, Vancouver: University of British Columbia Press, 1993, p. 84.

40 Alastair Service, *Edwardian Architecture: A Handbook to Building Design in Britain 1890-1914*, London: Thames and Hudson, 1977, pp. 140-57; the War Office is illustrated on p. 149.

41 Warren Hall and Barb Goodman, *Reflections—Lethbridge Then and Now*, Lethbridge: Whoop-Up Country Chapter, Historical Society of Alberta, 1980, not paginated; *Heritage Structures Alberta...Assessment*, Public Works Canada, 1982, pp. 75-9; [Bob Longworth,] 'Alberta Heritage Struc-tures', *SSAC Bulletin*, 7: 5, April 1982, p. 3.

42 Archibald, *By Federal Design*, pp. 37-8; Harold Kalman, 'Crisis on Main Street', in Deryck Holdsworth, ed., *Reviv-ing Main Street*, Toronto: University of Toronto Press, 1985, pp. 50-3.

43 Kalman and Roaf, *Exploring Ottawa*, pp. 29, 34-5, 52, 164. For the competition, see Kelly Crossman, *Architecture in Transition: From Art to Practice, 1885-1906*, Kingston: McGill-Queen's University Press, 1987, pp. 137-42.

44 'Information on the Late David Ewart'.

45 Michel Desgagnés, *Les Édifices parlementaires depuis 1792*, 2nd ed., Quebec: Les Publications du Québec, 1992, pp. 51-79. *L'Hôtel du Parlement*, Quebec: L'Assemblée Nationale du Québec, 1981; Gérard Morisset, 'Le Parle-ment de Québec', *Habitat*, 3: 6, November-December 1960, pp. 24-8; Luc Noppen and Gaston Deschênes, *Que-bec's Parliament Buildings: Witness to History*, translated by R. Clive Meredith and Audrey Pratt, Quebec: Assemblée nationale, c. 1986; Cameron and Wright, *Second Empire*,

pp. 68-9; Luc Noppen, Claude Paulette, and Michel Tremblay, *Québec: trois siècles d'architecture*, n.p; Libre Expression, 1979, pp. 268-70. The provincial legislative buildings are illustrated in 'Old Provincial and Territorial Legislative Buildings', *Canadian Geographic*, 103-6, December 1983-January 1984, pp. 39-50.

46 Quoted in E. Gagnon, *Le Palais législatif de Québec*, Quebec: C. Darveau, 1897, p. 109; cited in Crossman, *Architecture in Transition*, p. 113.

47 *New Brunswick Reporter and Fredericton Advertiser*, 9 February and 31 March 1880; cited in Mary Peck, 'Construction of the New Brunswick Legislative Building at Fredericton', *Selected Papers from the Annual Meetings 1975 & 1976*, Ottawa: Society for the Study of Architecture in Canada, 1981, p. 82, and Cameron and Wright, *Second Empire*, p. 70. See also *The Legislative Tradition in New Brunswick*, Fredericton: Province of New Brunswick, 1985; C. Ann Hale, 'The Legislative Building, 750 Queen Street, Fredericton: CIHB Report', manuscript on file, National Historic Parks and Sites Branch, Parks Canada.

48 Cameron and Wright, *Second Empire*, pp. 66-7.

49 Tully's Report of January 1880 is cited in Eric Arthur, *From Front Street to Queen's Park: The Story of Ontario's Parliament Buildings*, Toronto: McClelland and Stewart, 1979, p. 50.

50 Tully's report of 12 February 1880 is cited in Arthur, ibid., pp. 52-3.

51 Arthur, ibid., pp. 48-125; Crossman, *Architecture in Transition*, pp. 11-17; Frank Yeigh, *Ontario's Parliament Buildings; or A Century of Legislation, 1792-1892. A Historical Sketch*, Toronto: Williamson, 1893; 'Ontario's Queen's Park', *Habitat*, 3: 4, July-August 1960, pp. 18-21; William Dendy and William Kilbourn, *Toronto Observed: Its Architecture, Patrons, and History*, Toronto: Oxford University Press, 1986, pp. 134-6. See also Geoffrey Simmins, *Ontario Association of Architects: A Centennial History 1889-1989*, Toronto: Ontario Association of Architects, 1989; Raymond Card, *The Ontario Association of Architects 1890-1950*, Toronto: OAA, 1950.

52 Margaret McKelvey and Merilyn McKelvey, *Toronto: Carved in Stone*, Toronto: Fitzhenry & Whiteside, 1984, pp. 22-3 and *passim*.

53 Victoria *Daily Colonist*, 16 March 1893; cited in Terry Reksten, *Rattenbury*, Victoria: Sono Nis, 1978, p. 17.

54 Martin Segger, ed., *The British Columbia Parliament Buildings*, Vancouver: Arcon, 1979; Anthony A. Barrett and Rhodri Windsor Liscombe, *Francis Rattenbury and British Columbia: Architecture and Challenge in the Imperial Age*, Vancouver: University of British Columbia Press, 1983, pp. 28-60; Reksten, *Rattenbury*, pp. 14-28; Peter Cotton, 'The Stately Capitol', *JRAIC*, 35: 4, April 1958, pp. 116-18; Dorothy Blakey Smith, 'The Parliament Buildings, Victoria', *Habitat*, 3: 5, September-October 1960, pp. 6-10; Martin Segger and Douglas Franklin, *Victoria: A Primer for Regional History in Architecture*, Watkins Glen: American Life Foundation, 1979, pp. 156-9; Douglas Bogdanski [Franklin], 'The Restoration of British Columbia's Parliament Buildings', *Canadian Collector*, 11: 3, May-June 1976, pp. 56-8.

55 Victoria *Colonist*, 10 February 1898, cited in Cotton, 'Stately Capitol', p. 116. For British precedents, see Dixon and Muthesius, *Victorian Architecture*, pp. 172-80; Barrett

and Liscombe, *Rattenbury*, p. 33. Vancouver architect G.T. Sharp (1880-1974), a slightly younger contemporary of Rattenbury who immigrated to British Columbia in 1906, noted the similarities between the Legislative Buildings and the Imperial Institute (interview with Harold Kalman, 26 October 1972; Canadian Architectural Archives, University of Calgary).

56 See Edward Gibson and Patricia Guest, 'British Columbia Architectural Carver George Gibson', *Canadian Collector*, 15: 1, January 1979, pp. 44-6.

57 See Diana L. Bodnar, 'The Prairie Legislative Buildings', *Prairie Forum*, 5: 2, 1980, pp. 143-56; Bodnar, 'The Prairie Legislative Buildings of Canada', M.A. Thesis, University of British Columbia, 1979.

58 Barrett and Liscombe, *Rattenbury*, pp. 168-9.

59 Edmonton *Bulletin*, 5 May 1906; cited in Crossman, *Architecture in Transition*, p. 145; Bodnar, 'Prairie Legislative Buildings of Canada', p. 24.

60 Regina *Leader*, 9 January 1907; cited in Bodnar, 'Prairie Legislative Buildings of Canada', p. 39.

61 Arthur Drexler, ed., *The Architecture of the École des Beaux-Arts*, New York: Museum of Modern Art, 1977; *The Architecture of the École des Beaux-Arts*, Ottawa: National Gallery of Canada, 1976; Harold D. Kalman, 'The École des Beaux-Arts and Canadian Architecture', Script for Slide Exhibition, Ottawa: National Gallery of Canada, 1976; Jean-Claude Marsan, 'L'Apport de l'École des Beaux-Arts de Paris à l'architecture du Québec', *Habitat*, 20: 1, 1977, pp. 12-15; Donald Drew Egbert, *The Beaux-Arts Tradition in French Architecture, Illustrated by the Grands Prix de Rome*, Princeton: Princeton University Press, 1980; Crossman, *Architecture in Transition*, pp. 95-102.

62 Henry-Russell Hitchcock and William Seale, *Temples of Democracy: The State Capitols of the USA*, New York: Harcourt Brace Jovanovich, 1976, p. 218.

63 Nobbs to John Stocks, 12 August 1907, Saskatchewan Archives Board; cited in Crossman, *Architecture in Transition*, pp. 145-6.

64 Scott to F.M. Rattenbury, August 1907, Saskatchewan Archives Board; cited in Crossman, *Architecture in Transition*, p. 144.

65 'Legislative Buildings, Regina, Sask., E. & W.S. Maxwell, Architects, Montreal', *CAB*, 22, Feburary 1908, pp. 11-14; 'Saskatchewan Legislative Buildings, Regina', *JRAIC*, 1: 2, April-June 1924, pp. 41-6; Lewis H. Thomas, 'The Saskatchewan Legislative Building and its Predecessors', *JRAIC*, 32: 7, July 1955, pp. 248-52; *The Architecture of Edward and W.S. Maxwell*, Montreal: Montreal Museum of Fine Arts, 1991, pp. 170-4; Bodnar, 'Prairie Legislative Buildings of Canada', pp. 73-116.

66 Thomas, 'Saskatchewan Legislative Building', p. 251. The competitive designs are illustrated in Bodnar, 'Prairie Legislative Buildings of Canada', pp. 95-100.

67 Crossman, *Architecture in Transition*, p. 175, n.47.

68 'New Legislative and Executive Building Winnipeg', *Construction*, 5, November 1912, pp. 69 ff; Donald A. Ross, 'Manitoba Legislative Buildings, Winnipeg', *JRAIC*, 1: 3, July-September 1924, pp. 75-80; Thomas W. Leslie, *The Legislative Building of Manitoba*, Winnipeg: Government of Manitoba, 1925; 'Manitoba's Legislative Building', *Habitat*, 3: 4, May-June 1960, pp. 2-6; Bodnar, 'Prairie

Legislative Buildings of Canada', pp. 117-70; Marilyn Baker, *Manitoba's Third Legislative Building*, Winnipeg: Hyperion, 1986; *Edward and W.S. Maxwell*, pp. 175-6.

69 Marc de Caraffe, C.A. Hale, Dana Johnson, G.E. Mills, and Margaret Carter, *Town Halls of Canada: A Collection of Essays on Pre-1930 Town Hall Buildings*, Studies in Archaeology, Architecture and History, Ottawa: Environment Canada—Parks, 1987. See also Fram and Simonton, 'Public Buildings', pp. 268-70. For Mont-Saint-Hilaire and Newborn, see de Caraffe et al., *Town Halls*, pp. 165-6, 158.

70 Commonwealth Historic Resource Management Limited, *Kenyon Township Hall: Heritage/Conservation Report*, prepared for Kenyon Township Council, Perth, 1988; de Caraffe et al., *Town Halls*, pp. 95-6.

71 Municipal Minutes, 17 January 1881, Surrey Centennial Museum and Archives; de Caraffe et al., *Town Halls*, pp. 101-2.

72 de Caraffe et al., *Town Halls*, pp. 134-5.

73 Greenhill et al., *Ontario Towns*, no. 66; de Caraffe et al., *Town Halls*, pp. 46-7, 173-4; P.J. Stokes, 'The Preservation of Victoria Hall', in Jaroslov Petryshyn, ed., *Victorian Cobourg: A Nineteenth Century Profile*, Belleville: Mika, 1976.

74 de Caraffe et al., *Town Halls*, pp. 120-1; Greenhill et al., *Ontario Towns*, no. 73; Nick and Helma Mika, *Belleville: Portrait of a City*, Belleville: Mika, 1983; Avril Flather, ed., *Surrey's Heritage*, Surrey: Corporation of the District of Surrey, 1989, pp. 38-9.

75 Cited in L.W. Wilson and L.R. Pfaff, *Early St Marys*, St Marys: St Marys-on-the-Thames Historical Society, 1981, nos. 34, 7, and 24; see also de Caraffe et al., *Town Halls*, p. 127; Keith Bantock, 'St Mary's Town Halls', unpublished manuscript, Environment Canada—Parks, 1978.

76 Illustrated in Saskatchewan Association of Architects, *Historic Architecture of Saskatchewan*, Regina: Focus, 1986, p. 71.

77 *Western Municipal News*, 3: 3, March 1908, p. 703; discussed and illustrated in de Caraffe et al., *Town Halls*, pp. 105-7.

78 See, for example, Colin Cunningham, *Victorian and Edwardian Town Halls*, London: Routledge and Kegan Paul, 1981; Nikolaus Pevsner, *A History of Building Types*, London: Thames and Hudson, 1976, pp. 53-62.

79 All are illustrated in de Caraffe et al., *Town Halls*.

80 Ibid. pp. 60-1, 75, 211-12; CUM (Répertoire d'architecture traditionnelle sur le territoire de la Communauté urbaine de Montréal), *Les Édifices publics*, Architecture civile I, Montreal: Communauté urbaine de Montréal, 1981, pp. 110-14; Luc d'Iberville-Moreau, *Lost Montreal*, Toronto: Oxford University Press, 1975, p. 107; Jean-Claude Marsan, *Montreal in Evolution*, Montreal: McGill-Queen's University Press, 1981, pp. 214-15; François Rémillard and Brian Merrett, *Montreal Architecture: A Guide to Styles and Buildings*, Montreal: Meridian Press, 1990, pp. 38, 80.

81 Cited in Arthur/Otto, *No Mean City*, pp. 169, 175; see also Dendy and Kilbourn, *Toronto Observed*, pp. 148-51; de Caraffe et al., *Town Halls*, pp. 61-4; Patricia McHugh, *Toronto Architecture: A City Guide*, Toronto: Mercury Books, 1985, p. 106; Marilyn M. Litvak, *Edward James Lennox: Builder of Toronto'*, Toronto: Dundurn, 1994.

82 de Caraffe et al., *Town Halls*, pp. 159-60; Irene L. Rogers, *Charlottetown: The Life in Its Buildings*, Charlottetown: Prince Edward Island Museum and Heritage Foundation, 1983, pp. 149-51.

83 Kalman and Roaf, *Exploring Ottawa*, p. 111.

84 See T. Ritchie, 'The Architecture of William Thomas', *Architecture Canada*, 44: 5, May 1967, pp. 41-5.

85 Most of the buildings, including the Coombs block, are illustrated and listed in Badger's catalogue, *Illustrations of Iron Architecture, made by The Architectural Iron Works of the City of New York*, New York, 1865; reprinted in W. Knight Sturges, ed., *The Origins of Cast Iron Architecture in America*, New York: Da Capo Press, 1970, plates 68, 74-6, 78-9, and pp. 24-5. See also Margot Gayle, *Cast-Iron Architecture in New York*, New York: Dover, 1974, p. xiii.

86 *A Sense of Place: Granville Street, Halifax, Nova Scotia*, Halifax: Heritage Trust of Nova Scotia, 1970; Harold Kalman, '"It's a Fantastic Space"', *Atlantic Advocate*, 68: 3, November 1977, pp.12-14; Harold Kalman, 'NSCAD Moves to the Waterfront', in *Rehoused in History: Nova Scotia College of Art and Design*, Halifax: Nova Scotia College of Art and Design, 1979, not paginated. Information has also been kindly provided by Garry Shutlak, Neil Einarson, and Susan Buggey.

87 Rogers, *Charlottetown*, pp. 245-51; Robert C. Tuck, *Gothic Dreams: The Life and Times of a Canadian Architect, William Critchlow Harris, 1854-1913*, Toronto: Dundurn Press, 1978, pp. 64-8. For Queen Square Gardens, see Mary K. Cullen, *A History of the Structure and Use of Province House, Prince Edward Island, 1837-1977*, Manuscript Report No. 211, Ottawa: Parks Canada, 1977, pp. 76-86; Mary Cullen, 'The Late Nineteenth Century Development of the Queen Square Gardens, Charlottetown, P.E.I.', *APT Bulletin*, 9:3 (1977), pp. 1-20. Mary Burnett, of the Prince Edward Island Museum and Heritage Foundation, kindly provided information on the buildings and gardens.

88 Arthur/Otto, *No Mean City*, p. 149.

89 Dendy and Kilbourn, *Toronto Observed*, pp. 104-8.

90 For a summary of Darling's career, see Arthur/Otto, *No Mean City*, p. 244.

91 For early American skyscrapers, see Carl W. Condit, *The Chicago School of Architecture*, Chicago: University of Chicago Press, 1964; Winston Weisman, 'Commercial Palaces of New York: 1845-1875', *Art Bulletin*, 36, December 1954, pp. 285-302; Winston Weisman, 'A New View of Skyscraper History', in Edgar Kaufmann, Jr., *The Rise of an American Architecture*, New York: Praeger, 1970, pp. 115-60; Sarah Bradford Landau, 'The Tall Office Building Artistically Reconsidered: Arcaded Buildings of the New York School, *c*. 1870-1890', in Helen Searing, ed., *In Search of Modern Architecture: A Tribute to Henry-Russell Hitchcock*, New York: Architectural History Foundation, 1982, pp. 136-64.

92 CUM, *Les Hôtels, les immeubles de bureaux*, 1983, pp. 110-12; Phillip Turner, 'The Development of Architecture in the Province of Quebec', *Construction*, 20: 6, 1927, p. 193, cited in Crossman, *Architecture in Transition*, p. 74; John Bland, 'Overnight Trains to Boston and New York Made Montreal "American"', *Selected Papers from the SSAC*, 2, 1982, pp. 46-64.

93 'The New Toronto Board of Trade Buildings', *CAB*, 3: 5, 1890, pp. 54-5; Crossman, *Architecture in Transition*, pp. 21-2, 75, and fig. 13; Dendy, *Lost Toronto*, pp. 28-9.

94 Dendy and Kilbourn, *Toronto Observed*, pp. 124-5; Arthur/Otto, *No Mean City*, p. 207.

95 C.J. Taylor, *Some Early Ottawa Buildings*, Manuscript Report No. 268, Ottawa: Parks Canada, 1975, pp. 169-75; Dana Johnson, 'The Former Bell Block, the Scottish Ontario Chambers, Central Chambers and the Fraser Building, Ottawa, Ontario', Building Reports 83-11, 12, 13, 14, Federal Heritage Buildings Review Office, Ottawa, n.d.; Kalman and Roaf, *Exploring Ottawa*, p. 44; CUM, *Les Hôtels, les immeubles de bureaux*, pp. 113-15.

96 'Quarter of a Million Cage', Toronto *World*, 6 August 1895; cited in Crossman, *Architecture in Transition*, p. 64; see also pp. 75-7; Dendy and Kilbourn, *Toronto Observed*, pp. 143-5; Arthur/Otto, *No Mean City*, pp. 188, 213; McHugh, *Toronto*, pp. 65-6.

97 Condit, *Chicago School*, pp. 92-3, 162-5, figs. 56, 123-9.

98 Burke, 'The Safety of Public Buildings', Toronto *World*, 11 January 1895; cited in Crossman, *Architecture in Transition*, p. 164, n. 24. For Langley's correspondence to Burke, see ibid., pp. 73-4.

99 Gregory P. Utas, 'The Daly Building', *SSAC Bulletin*, 7: 6, June 1982, pp. 2-4; Kalman and Roaf, *Exploring Ottawa*, p. 29.

100 Kalman et al., *Exploring Vancouver*, p. 27.

101 *Edward and W.S. Maxwell*, p. 73.

102 Ibid., pp. 17, 74-5; CUM, *Les Hôtels, les immeubles de bureaux*, pp. 69-71.

103 *Edward and W.S. Maxwell*, pp. 81-3; CUM, *Les Hôtels, les immeubles de bureaux*, pp. 38-41.

104 Louis Sullivan, 'The Tall Office Building Artistically Considered', 1896; reprinted in Sullivan, *Kindergarten Chats and Other Writings*, Documents of Modern Art, IV, New York: George Wittenborn, 1947, pp. 202-13.

105 Sheila Grover, *Reports on Selected Buildings in Saskatoon, Saskatchewan*, Manuscript Report No. 385, Ottawa: Parks Canada, 1977, pp. 5-13; Edmonton Historical Board, *Evaluation of the Heritage Building List in the Downtown Area Redevelopment Plan Bylaw*, Edmonton, 1982, p. 22; Jac MacDonald, *Historic Edmonton: An Architectural and Pictorial Guide*, Edmonton: Lone Pine, 1987, pp. 51-2.

106 Mills and Sommer, *Vancouver Architecture*, 1, pp. 173-8; Harold Kalman and John Roaf, *Exploring Vancouver 2*, Vancouver: University of British Columbia Press, 1978, p. 268.

107 Kalman and Roaf, *Exploring Vancouver 2*, p. 23; Peter Collins, *Concrete: The Vision of a New Architecture*, London: Faber and Faber, 1959, p. 87.

108 T. Ritchie, *Canada Builds 1867-1967*, Toronto: University of Toronto Press, 1967, pp. 229-51; Kalman, 'NSCAD Moves to the Waterfront', n.p.

109 Mills and Sommer, *Vancouver Architecture*, 1, pp. 165-71. For Selfridges, see Service, *Edwardian Architecture*, p. 168; Susan Wagg, *Ernest Isbell Barott Architecte/Architect*, Montreal: Canadian Centre for Architecture, 1985, pp. 13-15.

110 Robert Nisbet, 'Men and Money: Reflections by a Sociologist', in *Money Matters: A Critical Look at Bank Architecture*, New York: McGraw-Hill, 1990, p. 8.

111 Susan Wagg, 'A Critical Look at Bank Architecture', in *Money Matters*, pp. 36-8, 69-71; for the two American banks, see plates 4.1 and 5.1; Rémillard and Merrett, *Montreal Architecture*, p. 42; Joshua Wolfe and Cécile Grenier, *Montreal Guide*, n.p: Libre Expression, 1983, p. 77; d'Iberville-Moreau, *Lost Montreal*, pp. 112-15; CUM, *Architecture commerciale I: Les banques*, pp. 22-7. The Commercial Bank of Scotland is illustrated in Dixon and Muthesius, *Victorian Architecture*, p. 125.

112 Wagg, 'Bank Architecture', p. 64.

113 William Dendy, *Lost Toronto*, pp. 16-17.

114 Ye Gargoyle [Percy Nobbs], 'Montreal Notes', *CAB*, 17, July 1904, p. 111; cited in Wagg, 'Bank Architecture', p. 70.

115 Percy E. Nobbs, *Present Tendencies Affecting Architecture in Canada*, McGill University Publications, Series 13, No. 29, Montreal: McGill University, 1931, p. 4; cited in Wagg, 'Bank Architecture', p. 70.

116 David Spector, *Monuments to Finance: Three Winnipeg Banks*, Report of the City of Winnipeg Historical Buildings Committee, Winnipeg: City of Winnipeg, 1980, pp. 43-8; David Spector, 'McKim, Mead & White and the Neo-Classical Bank Tradition in Winnipeg, 1898-1914', *SSAC Bulletin*, 7: 3-4, December 1981, pp. 2-4; David Spector, *Monuments to Finance, Volume II: Early Bank Architecture in Winnipeg*, Report of the City of Winnipeg Historical Buildings Committee, Winnipeg: City of Winnipeg, 1982, pp. 51-8.

117 Spector, *Early Bank Architecture*, pp. 33-45; Spector, *Three Winnipeg Banks*, pp. 19-27; Wagg 'Bank Architecture', pp. 76-7.

118 Spector, *Three Winnipeg Banks*, pp. 31-40. See also Victor Ross, *A History of the Canadian Bank of Commerce*, Toronto: Oxford University Press, 1922, esp. vol. II, appendix 2: 'The Bank Premises Department and Its Buildings'; James Nicoll, 'Buildings of the Canadian Bank of Commerce', *Canadian Banker*, 45: 2, January 1938, pp. 204-14. The building has stood empty for some years.

119 *Brandon: An Architectural Walking Tour*, Winnipeg: Department of Cultural Affairs and Historical Resources, 1982, nos. 4-6.

120 Robert C. Tuck, 'William Harris and His Island Churches', *Island Magazine*, 2, Spring-Summer 1977, p. 20; Tuck, *Gothic Dreams*.

121 Tuck, *Gothic Dreams*, pp. 80-2; Tuck, 'William Harris', pp. 23-4; H.M. Scott Smith, *The Historic Churches of Prince Edward Island*, Erin: Boston Mills Press, 1986, pp. 87-8.

122 Tuck, *Gothic Dreams*, pp. 90-4; Tuck, 'William Harris', pp. 26-7; Smith, *Historic Churches*, pp. 76-7; Rogers, *Charlottetown*, pp. 261-2.

123 Malcolm Thurlby, 'The Irish-Canadian Pugin: Joseph Connolly', *Irish Arts Review*, 3: 1, 1986, pp. 16-21; Christopher A. Thomas, 'A High Sense of Calling: Joseph Connolly, A.W. Holmes, and Their Buildings for the Roman Catholic Archdiocese of Toronto, 1885-1935', *RACAR*, 13: 2, 1986, pp. 97-120.

124 Malcolm Thurlby, 'The Church of Our Lady of The Immaculate Conception, at Guelph: Puginian Principles in the Gothic Revival Architecture of Joseph Connolly',

SSAC Bulletin, 15: 2, June 1990, pp. 32-40; Thurlby, 'Connolly', pp. 18-20; Jackie Adell, 'Connolly, Pugin, and the Gothic in Ontario', *SSAC Bulletin*, 15: 4, December 1990, p. 110; Marion MacRae and Anthony Adamson, *Hallowed Walls: Church Architecture of Upper Canada*, Toronto: Clarke, Irwin, 1975, pp. 167-9.

125 Hitchcock, *Architecture*, p. 167. St Macartan's is illustrated in Thomas, 'Connolly', p. 101.

126 Thomas G. Browne, 'The Religious Heritage Committee of ICOMOS Canada', *SSAC Bulletin*, 18:1, March 1993, p. 19 (with an illustration).

127 Thomas, 'Connolly', pp. 101-4.

128 Arthur/Otto, *No Mean City*, p. 187.

129 Christopher A. Thomas, 'A Thoroughly Traditional Architect: A.W. Holmes and the Catholic Archidiocese of Toronto, 1890-1940', *SSAC Bulletin*, 10: 1, March 1985, pp. 5-8; Thomas, 'Connolly', pp. 113-14; *Construction*, 8 (December 1915), pp. 495-8.

130 Kalman, 'École des Beaux-Arts', pp. 4-5; Marsan, 'L'Apport de l'École des Beaux-Arts', pp. 12-15; Rémillard and Merrett, *Montreal Architecture*, p. 111.

131 CUM, *Les Couvents*, Montreal, 1984, pp. 238-43; Lazlo Demeter, *Maison-mère de la Congrégation de Notre-Dame de Montréal. Histoire, relevé et analysé*, Quebec, Ministère des Affaires culturelles, n.d.; for Guadet, see Drexler, *École des Beaux-Arts*, pp. 255-7; Egbert, *Beaux-Arts Tradition*, pp. 66-7.

132 CUM, *Les Édifices publiques*, pp. 24-7.

133 Dendy and Kilbourn, *Toronto Observed*, pp. 164-7; 'More Golden Arches', *Canadian Architect*, 31:3, March 1986, pp. 27-31, describing the rehabilitation by Howard D. Chapman and Howard V. Walken.

134 Grover, *Buildings in Saskatoon*, pp. 33-42; Sally Potter Clubb and William Antony S. Sarjeant, *Saskatoon's Historic Buildings and Sites*, Saskatoon: Saskatoon Environmental Society, 1973, no. 84.

135 Mark Fram, 'Niagara's Falls, Toronto's Power', in Mark Fram and John Weiler, eds, *Continuity with Change: Planning for the Conservation of Man-made Heritage*, Toronto: Dundurn Press, 1984, pp. 257-321.

136 Crossman, *Architecture in Transition*, pp. 58-60, 101-2; François Giraldeau, 'L'École des Beaux-Arts de Montréal, 1923-1959', *ARQ: Architecture Québec*, 25, June 1985, pp. 11-15.

CHAPTER 11 Domestic Architecture

1 See Witold Rybczynski, *Home: A Short History of an Idea*, New York: Viking, 1986; Marc Denhez, *The Canadian Home*, Toronto: Dundurn, 1993.

2 Alan Gowans, *The Comfortable House: North American Suburban Architecture 1890-1930*, Cambridge: MIT Press, 1986, p. 30.

3 Eric Arthur, *Toronto: No Mean City*, 3rd ed., rev. by Stephen A. Otto, Toronto: University of Toronto Press, 1986, pp. 96, 152.

4 Leo Cox, *The Story of the Mount Stephen Club, Montreal, Canada*, Montreal: Mount Stephen Club, 1967, not paginated; François Rémillard and Brian Merrett, *Mansions of the Golden Square Mile, Montreal, 1850-1930*, Montreal:

Meridian, 1987, pp. 104-9; CUM (Répertoire d'architecture traditionnelle sur le territoire de la communauté urbaine de Montréal), *Les Résidences*, pp. 674-81.

5 T. Ritchie, 'The Architecture of William Thomas', *Architecture Canada*, 44, May 1967, p. 41-5; Arthur/Otto, *No Mean City*, pp. 117-21, 146-7.

6 Cox, *Mount Stephen Club*.

7 Irene L. Rogers, *Charlottetown: The Life in Its Buildings*, Charlottetown: Prince Edward Island Museum and Heritage Foundation, 1983, pp. 127-8; Rogers, *Reports on Selected Buildings in Charlottetown, P.E.I.*, Manuscript Report Series no. 269, Ottawa: Parks Canada, 1974-5, p. 175; H.M. Scott Smith, *The Historic Houses of Prince Edward Island*, Erin: Boston Mills Press, 1990, p. 117.

8 Christina Cameron and Janet Wright, *Second Empire Style in Canadian Architecture*, Canadian Historic Sites: Occasional Papers in Archaeology and History, 24, Ottawa: Parks Canada, 1980, pp. 46-7; William Dendy, *Lost Toronto; Images of the City's Past*, Toronto: McClelland and Stewart, 1993, pp. 56-8.

9 Cameron and Wright, *Second Empire*, pp. 216-17.

10 Ibid., pp. 202-3.

11 Ibid., pp. 156-7.

12 Terry Reksten, *Craigdarroch: The Story of Dunsmuir Castle*, Victoria: Orca, 1987; Terry Reksten, *A Guide to Craigdarroch Castle*, Victoria: Orca, 1987; Martin Segger and Douglas Franklin, *Victoria: A Primer for Regional History in Architecture*, Watkins Glen, NY: American Life Foundation, 1979, pp. 284-7.

13 William Dendy and William Kilbourn, *Toronto Observed: Its Architecture, Patrons, and History*, Toronto: Oxford University Press, 1986, pp. 129-32; Arthur/Otto, *No Mean City*, pp. 176, 196-7.

14 Rémillard and Merrett, *Mansions*, pp. 136-7, 188-91; *The Architecture of Edward and W.S. Maxwell*, Montreal: Montreal Museum of Fine Arts, 1991, pp. 129-33.

15 Michael McMordie, 'Picturesque Pattern Books and Pre-Victorian Designers', *Architectural History*, 18, 1975, pp. 43-59 (with extensive bibliography); Michael McMordie, 'The Cottage Idea,' *RACAR*, 6:1, 1979, pp. 17-27.

16 John Buonarotti Papworth, *Rural Residences, Consisting of a Series of Designs for Cottages, Decorated Cottages, Small Villas, and Other Ornamental Buildings*, London, 1818; 2nd edition, 1832; Charles Parker, *Villa Rustica: Selected from Buildings and Scenes of the Vicinity of Rome and Florence; and Arranged for Lodges and Domestic Buildings*, London, 1832; 2nd edition, 1848; John Claudius Loudon, *An Encyclopaedia of Cottage, Farm, and Villa Architecture and Furniture*, London, 1833 (many editions).

17 James Early, *Romanticism and American Architecture*, New York: Barnes, 1965, p. 67; The entry on A.J. Downing by George B. Tatum in the *Macmillan Encyclopedia of Architects*, 1, New York: The Free Press, 1982, p. 593; Clifford E. Clark, Jr, 'Domestic Architecture as an Index to Social History: The Romantic Revival and the Cult of Domesticity in America, 1840-1870', *Journal of Interdisciplinary History*, 7:1, Summer 1976, pp. 33-56. A[ndrew] J[ackson] Downing, *Cottage Residences*; or *A Series of Designs for Rural Cottages and Cottage Villas, and Their Gardens and Grounds Adapted to North America*, New York and London: Wiley and Putnam, 1842; A.J. Downing *The Architecture of Country Houses: Including Designs for Cot-*

tages, Farm Houses, and Villas..., New York: Appleton, 1850; also A.J. Downing, *A Treatise on the Theory and Practice of Landscape Gardening Adapted to North America... With Remarks on Rural Architecture*, New York and London: Wiley and Putnam, 1841. (These three Downing books went through more than twenty editions and exist in modern facsimile editions or reprints.) Samuel Sloan, *The Model Architect: A Series of Original Designs for Cottages, Villas, Suburban Residences, etc.*, Philadelphia: E.S. Jones, 1852, 4th ed., 1873; Calvert Vaux, *Villas and Cottages: A Series of Designs Prepared for Execution in the United States*, New York, Harper & Brothers, 1857; 2nd edition, 1864; reprinted New York: Dover, 1970.

18 Marianna May Richardson, *The Ontario Association of Architects: Centennial Collection*, Toronto: Ontario Association of Architects, 1990, pp. 26, 30; Christina Cameron, *Charles Baillairgé: Architect & Engineer*, Montreal: McGill-Queen's University Press, 1989, p. 169.

19 Fern Mackenzie, 'Pattern Books in Kingston', *Frontenac Historic Foundation Newsletter*, 12:3, September 1984, pp. 5-6; Fern Mackenzie, 'Architectural Books Available in Kingston, Ontario, 1842-1854', unpublished paper, *c.* 1984. For the influence of pattern books in Canada, see Janet Wright, *Architecture of the Picturesque in Canada*, Studies in Archaeology, Architecture and History, Ottawa: Parks Canada, 1984.

20 Ralph Greenhill, Ken Macpherson, and Douglas Richardson, *Ontario Towns*, Ottawa: Oberon, 1974, n.p. See also Nancy Z. Tausky and Lynne D. DiStefano, *Victorian Architecture in London and Southwestern Ontario*, Toronto: University of Toronto Press, 1986, pp. 69-77.

21 A.J. Downing, *Country Houses* (1850), reprinted New York: Dover, 1969, p. 300; Greenhill et al., *Ontario Towns*, introduction and plate 51; Mathilde Brosseau, *Gothic Revival in Canadian Architecture*, Canadian Historic Sites: Occasional Papers in Archaeology and History, No. 25, Ottawa: Parks Canada, 1980, pp. 104-5; Jim Leonard, 'Who Was T.C. Clarke, C.E.?', *SSAC Bulletin*, 17:4, December 1992, p. 90; Anne Ingram, 'My Favorite Room', Fredericton *Daily Gleaner*, 15 July 1989, p. 8.

22 Downing, *Country Houses*, p. 51.

23 Vincent J. Scully, Jr, 'Romantic Rationalism and the Expression of Structure in Wood: Downing, Wheeler, Gardner, and the "Stick Style," 1840-1876', *Art Bulletin*, 35, June 1953, pp. 121-42; Vincent J. Scully, Jr, *The Shingle Style and the Stick Style: Architectural Theory and Design from Richardson to the Origins of Wright*, New Haven: Yale University Press, 1971.

24 *Canada Farmer*, 1:2, 1 February 1864, p. 21; *Canada Farmer*, 2, 1865, p. 244; the latter is reproduced and cited in John Blumenson, *Ontario Architecture: A Guide to Styles and Building Terms, 1784 to the Present*, Toronto: Fitzhenry & Whiteside, 1990, p. 41. The attribution to Smith was kindly provided by Robert Hill. Bargeboard trim is featured in Anthony Adamson and John Willard, *The Gaiety of Gables: Ontario's Architectural Folk Art*, Toronto: McClelland and Stewart, 1974.

25 Brosseau, *Gothic Revival*, pp. 138-9.

26 For the influence of Pliny's villas in Montreal, see Ellen James et al., 'Les Villas de Pline et les éléments classiques dans l'architecture à Montréal' and subsequent articles, *ARQ/Architecture/Québec*, 15 October 1983, pp. 10-28.

27 Wright, *Architecture of the Picturesque*, p. 90; see also Margaret Angus, *The Old Stones of Kingston: Its Buildings Before 1867*, Toronto: University of Toronto Press, 1966, pp. 86-7; Architectural Review Committee, City of Kingston, *Buildings of Architectural and Historic Significance*, 1, Kingston: City of Kingston, 1971, pp. 85-7; John J. Stewart, 'The Grounds of John A.'s Bellevue House', *Conservation Canada*, 4:2, Summer 1978, pp. 7-9; Marion MacRae and Anthony Adamson, *The Ancestral Roof: Domestic Architecture of Upper Canada*, Toronto: Clarke, Irwin, 1963, pp 149-51.

28 Terence Davis, *John Nash: The Prince Regent's Architect*, London: Country Life, 1966, pp. 37, 42-3, and figs. 8-16, 25-6; Constance M. Greiff, *John Notman, Architect: 1810-1865*, Philadelphia: Athenaeum, 1979, pp. 20-2, 63-8; the entry on John Notman by Constance M. Greiff is the *Macmillan Encyclopedia of Architects*, 3, pp. 306-7. An early 'Italian Villa' was illustrated in Robert Lugar, *Architectural Sketches for Cottages, Rural Dwellings and Villas*, London, 1805, and another in Papworth, *Rural Residences*; both are illustrated in Henry-Russell Hitchcock, *Early Victorian Architecture in Britain*, New Haven: Yale University Press, 1954, figs. II-5 and II-8. See also Blumenson, *Ontario Architecture*, pp. 52-7.

29 Wright, *Architecture of the Picturesque*, pp. 78-80.

30 CUM, *Les Résidences*, pp. 18-25; Luc d'Iberville-Moreau, *Lost Montreal*, Toronto: Oxford University Press, 1975, p. 92-4; Rémillard and Merrett, *Mansions*, pp. 78-83; Christina Cameron, ed., *Mansions of the Golden Square Mile: A Descriptive Guide*, Montreal, privately published, 1976, pp. 4-7.

31 Orson Fowler, *A Home for All or the Gravel Wall and Octagon Mode of Building*, privately printed 1853 (first edition 1848?); W. Creese, 'Fowler and the Domestic Octagon', *Art Bulletin*, 28, June 1946, pp. 89-102; Whiffen, *American Architecture*, pp. 84-6; Blumenson, *Ontario Architecture*, pp. 71-6; John I. Rempel, 'A Brief History of Polygonal Buildings with Residual Evidence in Ontario', *Ontario History*, 56:4, December 1964, pp. 235-46; John I. Rempel, *Building with Wood and Other Aspects of Nineteenth-century Building in Central Canada*, rev. ed., Toronto: University of Toronto Press, 1980, pp. 289-340; Blumenson, *Ontario Architecture*, pp. 71-6.

32 *Founded Upon a Rock: Historic Buildings in Halifax and Vicinity Standing in 1967*, 2nd ed., Halifax: Heritage Trust of Nova Scotia, 1971, pp. 108-9.

33 Indexed in Patricia J. Johnston and Paul R.L. Chénier, *Index of/du Canadian Architect and Builder, 1888-1908*, Ottawa: Society for the Study of Architecture in Canada, n.d.

34 Leslie Maitland, *The Queen Anne Revival Style in Canadian Architecture*, Studies in Archaeology, Architecture and History, Ottawa: Parks Service, Environment Canada, 1990, pp. 43, 124; Leslie Maitland, 'Queen Anne Revival', *Canadian Collector*, 21:1, January-February 1986, pp. 42-8. Many houses (and other building-types) of this kind used bricks of contrasting colours: often red brick, with buff brick at the corners and around the openings; see T. Ritchie, 'Notes on Dichromatic Brickwork in Ontario', *APT Bulletin*, 11:2, 1979, pp. 60-75.

35 See Maitland, *Queen Anne Revival*; Mark Girouard, *Sweetness and Light: The 'Queen Anne' Movement 1860-1900*,

Oxford: Clarendon Press, 1977; J.J. Stevenson, *House Architecture*, 2 vols, London: Macmillan, 1880; Robert Macleod, *Style and Society: Architectural Ideology in Britain, 1835-1914*, London: RIBA Publications, 1971, pp. 27-39.

36 J.K. Ochsner and T.C. Hubka, 'H.H. Richardson: The Design of the William Watts Sherman House', *JSAH*, 51:2, June 1992, pp. 121-45.

37 Victoria *Daily Colonist*, 20 November 1890; cited in Segger and Franklin, *Victoria*, pp. 267-9. The Temple Building is described and illustrated on pp. 110-13.

38 Maitland, *Queen Anne Revival*, p. 135.

39 Fern E. Mackenzie Graham, 'The Wooden Architecture of William Newlands', M.A. thesis, Queen's University, 1987, p. 52; Samuel and Joseph C. Newsom, *Picturesque California Homes*, San Francisco, 1884, reprinted Los Angeles: Hennessey & Ingalls, 1978, plate 1.

40 CUM, *Les Résidences*, pp. 556-7; Maitland, *Queen Anne Revival*, p. 163.

41 Harold Kalman and John Roaf, *Exploring Vancouver 2*, 2nd ed., Vancouver: University of British Columbia Press, 1978, p. 74.

42 Alan Gowans calls this a 'homestead temple-house', but the term is more appropriate to the American than the Canadian experience (*Comfortable House*, p. 94); following Gowans's example, Donald Wetherell and Irene Kmet call it a 'housestead' in *Homes in Alberta: Building, Trends, and Design 1870-1967*, Edmonton: University of Alberta Press and Alberta Culture and Multiculturalism, 1991, pp. 76-9. Virginia and Lee McAlester describe it as 'spindle-work: front-gabled roof', a sub-set of Queen Anne, in *A Field Guide to American Houses*, New York: Alfred A. Knopf, 1984, pp. 274-5.

43 See Gowans, *Comfortable House*, pp. 41-63.

44 Gowans, *Comfortable House*, pp. 84-93; Wetherell and Kmet, *Homes in Alberta*, pp. 79-80; *Identifying Architectural Styles in Manitoba*, Winnipeg: Manitoba Culture, Heritage and Citizenship, [1991], p. 47. Both the gable-front and foursquare houses are described as 'Edwardian Classicism' in John Blumenson, *Ontario Architecture: A Guide to Styles and Building Terms, 1784 to the Present*, Markham: Fitzhenry & Whiteside, 1990, pp. 172-5. Other terms that have been used for them include 'Edwardian Builder' and 'Classic Box'. For the use of concrete block in houses of this kind (and in other building-types), see Ann Gillespie, 'Early Development of the *Artistic* Concrete Block: The Case of the Boyd Brothers', *APT Bulletin*, 11:2, 1979, pp. 30-52.

45 Saskatchewan Association of Architects, *Historic Architecture of Saskatchewan*, Regina: Focus, 1986, p. 157.

46 Some informed sources on technical matters are George Hill, 'The Heating of Buildings,' *Architectural Record*, 5, October-December 1895, pp. 204-11; George B. Clow, *Practical Up-to-date Plumbing*, Chicago: F.J. Drake, 1906; Loris S. Russell, *A Heritage of Light: Lamps and Lighting in the Early Canadian Home*, Toronto: University of Toronto Press, 1968; Rybczynski, *Home*, pp. 123-71. For developments in public water supply, see Letty Anderson, 'Water-Supply', in Norman R. Ball, ed., *Building Canada: A History of Public Works*, Toronto: University of Toronto Press, 1988, pp. 195-220; Margaret W. Andrews, 'The Best Advertisement a City Can Have: Public Health Service in Van-

couver, 1886-1888', *Urban History Review*, 12:3, February 1984, pp. 19-27.

47 E. Burke, 'Some Notes on House-Planning,' *Canadian Architect and Builder*, 3:5, May 1890, p. 55.

48 John Ruskin, *The Seven Lamps of Architecture*, 1849; reprinted New York: Noonday Press, 1961, p. 39 ('The Lamp of Truth'); Alastair Service, *Edwardian Architecture: A Handbook to Building Design in Britain 1890-1914*, London: Thames and Hudson, 1977, pp. 11-12; Nikolaus Pevsner, 'William Morris and Architecture' (first published 1957), in *Studies in Art, Architecture and Design*, 2, London: Thames and Hudson, 1968, pp. 108-17.

49 W.R. Lethaby, *Philip Webb and His Work*, London, 1935, p. 1; cited in Macleod, *Style and Society*, p. 55. For the Arts and Crafts Movement in Britain, see Gillian Naylor, *The Arts and Crafts Movement*, Cambridge: MIT Press, 1971; Peter Davey, *Architecture of the Arts and Crafts Movement*, New York: Rizzoli, 1980.

50 Service, *Edwardian Architecture*, pp. 19-20; Naylor, *Arts and Crafts*, pp. 170-2.

51 Kelly Crossman, *Architecture in Transition: From Art to Practice, 1885-1906*, Kingston: McGill-Queen's University Press, 1987, pp. 86-97; Geoffrey Simmins, *Ontario Association of Architects: A Centennial History 1889-1989*, Toronto: Ontario Association of Architects, 1989, pp. 47-64.

52 Carolyn Neal and William J. Moffet, *Eden Smith Architect 1858-1949*, Toronto: Architectural Conservancy of Ontario, Toronto Region Branch, 1976. Obituary of Eden Smith by A.S. Mathers in *JRAIC*, 17:3, March 1950, pp. 112-13; cited in Simmins, *Ontario Association of Architects*, p. 50; Annmarie Adams, 'Eden Smith and the Canadian Domestic Revival', unpublished paper, annual meeting of the Society of Architectural Historians, Montreal, 14 April 1989; Crossman, *Architecture in Transition*, pp. 87-92. See also *Household of God: A Parish History of St. Thomas's Church, Toronto*, Toronto: St. Thomas's, 1993, pp. 114-21. In her chapter on Eden Smith, the architect of the church, Rebekah Smick gives his birth year as 1859 and credits Douglas Brown, who is writing a biography of Eden Smith, with providing her with this information.

53 Crossman, *Architecture in Transition*, p. 91.

54 Eden Smith, 'Architectural Education 1900', *CAB*, 13:6, 1900, p. 109; cited in Crossman, *Architecture in Transition*, p. 92.

55 Susan Wagg, *Percy Erskine Nobbs: Architecte, Artiste, Artisan/Architect, Artist, Craftsman*, Montreal: McCord Museum, McGill University and Kingston: McGill-Queen's University Press, 1982; Susan Wagg, 'The McGill Architecture of Percy Erskine Nobbs', MFA thesis, Concordia University, Montreal, 1979; Crossman, *Architecture in Transition*, pp. 122-35; the entry on Robert S. Lorimer by Peter Savage in the *Macmillan Encyclopedia of Architects*, 3, p. 33.

56 Percy E. Nobbs, 'The Late Sir Robert Lorimer', *JRAIC*, 6:10, 1929, p. 352; cited in Crossman, *Architecture in Transition*, p. 126.

57 Herrmann Muthesius, *The English House*, trans. Janet Seligman, New York: Rizzoli, 1979, p. 62; cited in Wagg, *Nobbs*, p. 20.

58 Charles Reilly, 'Some Impressions of Canadian Towns', *JRAIC*, 1, April-June 1924, p. 55; cited in Wagg, *Nobbs*, p. 24; see also Aline Gubbay & Sally Hoof, *Montréal's Little*

Mountain / La Petite Montagne: A Portrait of / Un Portrait de Westmount, Westmount: Trillium Books, 1979, pp. 100-2.

59 Martin Segger, *The Buildings of Samuel Maclure: In Search of Appropriate Form*, Victoria: Sono Nis, 1986; Janet Bingham, *Samuel Maclure Architect*, Ganges, BC: Horsdal & Schubart, 1985; Leonard K. Eaton, *The Architecture of Samuel Maclure*, Victoria: Art Gallery of Greater Victoria, 1971; Leonard K. Eaton, 'The Cross-axial houses of Samuel Maclure,' *RACAR*, 7:1-2, 1980, pp. 49-58; Ross Lort, 'Samuel Maclure, M.R.A.I.C., 1860-1929', *JRAIC*, 35, 1958, p. 114. Maclure and Rattenbury are contrasted in Segger, 'The Architecture of Samuel Maclure and Francis Mawson Rattenbury: In Search of Appropriate Form', *Canadian Collector*, 11:3, May-June 1976, pp. 51-5.

60 Segger, *Maclure*, pp. 121, 134; Eaton, *Maclure*, not paginated; Segger and Franklin, *Victoria*, pp. 300-1.

61 Lort, 'Maclure', p. 114; Eaton, 'Cross-axial Houses', pp. 50-1; Vincent J. Scully, Jr, *The Shingle Style: Architectural Theory and Design from Richardson to the Origins of Wright*, New Haven: Yale University Press, 1955; Vincent J. Scully, Jr, *The Architecture of the American Summer: The Flowering of the Shingle Style*, New York: Temple Hoyne Buell Centre for the Study of American Architecture and Rizzoli, 1989.

62 Eaton, *Maclure*; Eaton, 'Cross-axial houses', pp. 54-6; Segger, *Maclure*, pp. 108-10; Bingham, *Maclure*, p. 65.

63 For an illustration of the two-storey living-room of the Roberts house, see Vincent Scully, Jr, *Frank Lloyd Wright*, New York: George Braziller, 1960, fig. 37.

64 Segger, *Maclure*, pp. 164-5; Harold Kalman, Ron Phillips, and Robin Ward, *Exploring Vancouver*, Vancouver: University of British Columbia Press, 1993, p. 157.

65 Segger, *Maclure*, pp. 170-1, 191; Kalman et al., *Exploring Vancouver*, pp. 150, 153.

66 Emily Carr used this phrase to describe her father; author Terry Reksten has adopted it as the title of a social history of Victoria.

67 *Craftsman*, March 1908, pp. 675-81; cited in Segger, *Maclure*, p. 111-12, and in Deryck W. Holdsworth, 'House and Home in Vancouver: Images of West Coast Urbanism, 1886-1929', in Gilbert A. Stelter and Alan F.J. Artibise, eds., *The Canadian City: Essays in Urban History*, Toronto: McClelland and Stewart, 1977, p. 211, n. 48. See also Deryck W. Holdsworth, 'Cottages and Castles for Vancouver Home-Seekers', in R.A.J. McDonald and J. Barman, eds, *Vancouver's Past: Essays in Social History*, Vancouver: University of British Columbia Press, 1986, pp. 11-32; Deryck W. Holdsworth, 'Regional Distinctiveness in an Industrial Age: Some Californian Influences on British Columbia Housing', *American Review of Canadian Studies*, 12:2, 1982, pp. 64-81. For Baillie Scott, see James D. Kornwolf, *M.H. Baillie Scott and the Arts and Crafts Movement: Pioneers of Modern Design*, Baltimore: Johns Hopkins University Press, 1972.

68 William H. Jordy, *American Buildings and Their Architects: Progressive and Academic Ideals at the Turn of the Twentieth Century* (Volume 3), Garden City, NY: Doubleday, 1972, pp. 217-20, 225.

69 Craftsman bungalows are discussed in Clay Lancaster, 'The American Bungalow', *Art Bulletin*, 40:3, September 1958, pp. 239-53; Robert Winter, *The California Bungalow*, Los Angeles: Hennessey and Ingalls, 1980; Anthony D.

King, *The Bungalow: The Production of a Global Culture*, London: Routledge and Kegan Paul, 1984.

70 Segger, *Maclure*, pp. 79, 88

71 Yoho and Merritt, *Craftsman Bungalows*, Seattle: Yoho and Merritt, 1920; reproduced in Michael Kluckner, *Vanishing Vancouver*, North Vancouver: Whitecap Books, 1990, p. 25; H.R. Saylor, *Bungalows: Their Design, Construction and Furnishings*, New York: McBride, Nast, 1911; the second (Toronto) edition is cited in Blumenson, *Ontario Architecture*, p. 176. See Holdsworth, 'Regional Distinctiveness in an Industrial Age', pp. 64-81.

72 Kluckner, *Vanishing Vancouver*, pp. 28-9; Kalman and Roaf, *Exploring Vancouver*, p. 169; Holdsworth, 'House and Home', pp. 195-8. For Prairie bungalows, see Wetherell and Kmet, *Homes in Alberta*, pp. 73-6; *Architectural Styles in Manitoba*, pp. 28-9.

73 H.G. Kettle, 'The Canadian Handicraft Movement', *Canadian Forum*, 20, 1940, pp. 112-14.

74 Commonwealth Historic Resource Management Limited, contribution to Marshall Macklin Monaghan et al., *Future Use of the Guild Inn*, Toronto, 1985; Hugh Walker, *The Spencer Clark Collection of Historic Architecture*, Scarborough: The Guild, 1982.

75 Wright, *Architecture of the Picturesque*, pp. 105-110, 137-9; France Gagnon-Pratte, *L'Architecture et la nature à Québec au dix-neuvième siècle: les villas*, Quebec: Ministère des Affaires culturelles, 1980.

76 See Brendan Gill and Dudley Witney, *Summer Places*, Toronto: McClelland and Stewart, 1978; E.J. Hart, *The Selling of Canada: The CPR and the Beginnings of Canadian Tourism*, Banff: Altitude, 1983; E.J. Hart, *The Brewster Story: From Pack Train to Tour Bus*, [Banff:] Brewster Transport, 1981.

77 R.H. Hubbard, *Rideau Hall: An Illustrated History of Government House, Ottawa, from Victorian Times to the Present Day*, Montreal: McGill-Queen's University Press, 1977, pp. 69-70; John T. Saywell, ed., *The Canadian Journal of Lady Aberdeen 1893-1898*, Toronto: Champlain Society, 1960, p. 359 (entry for 12 August 1896).

78 France Gagnon-Pratte, *Country Houses for Montrealers 1892-1924: The Architecture of E. and W.S. Maxwell*, Montreal: Meridian, 1987, pp. 132-8; *Architecture of E. and W.S. Maxwell*, pp. 145-6.

79 Maitland, *Queen Anne Revival*, p. 193; information from Robert Hill.

80 Maitland, *Queen Anne Revival*, p. 192; compare buildings in Scully, *Shingle Style*.

81 Shelley Hornstein-Rabinovitch, 'The Chocolate King in Paradise: The Villa Menier on Anticosti Island', unpublished paper, annual meeting of the Society of Architectural Historians, Montreal, 13 April 1989; Maitland, *Queen Anne Revival*, p. 170; the entry on Anticosti Island by James Marsh in the *CE* I, p. 84; Donald MacKay, *Anticosti: The Untamed Island*, Toronto: McGraw-Hill Ryerson, 1979, pp. 74-7, 88-9, 110.

82 Wagg, *Nobbs*, pp. 24-8; Wagg, 'The Todd House by Nobbs: Reconciling the Distinct and the Derivative', unpublished paper, annual meeting of the Society for Architectural Historians, Montreal, 14 April 1989; CUM, *Les Résidences*, pp. 715-17.

83 Gagnon-Pratte, *Country Houses*, pp. 62-9.

84 Ibid., pp. 122-4; *Architecture of E. and W.S. Maxwell*, pp. 143-4.

85 Wright, *Architecture of the Picturesque*, illustrated on p. 68.

86 Harvey H. Kaiser, *Great Camps of the Adirondacks*, Boston: David R. Godine, 1982.

87 Alec Douglas and Larry Turner, eds., *On a Sunday Afternoon: Classic Boats of the Rideau Canal*, Erin: Boston Mills, 1989, pp. 24-5; William S. Wicks, *Log Cabins and Cottages: How to Build and Furnish Them*, 6th edition, New York: Forest and Stream, 1908; information kindly provided by Larry Turner.

88 Harold Lawson, 'The Log Chateau-Lucerne-in-Quebec', *JRAIC*, 8:1, January 1931, pp. 13-21; Allan Muir and Doris Muir, *Building the Chateau Montebello*, Gardenvale, Quebec: Muir Publishing, 1980. See also *Le Manoir Louis-Joseph Papineau*, La Collection patrimoine 1, Ottawa: Éditions de la Petite-Nation, 1978; Raymonde Gauthier, *Les Manoirs du Québec*, Quebec: Éditeur officiel du Québec/Fides, 1976, pp. 24-5.

89 Gill and Witney, *Summer Places*, p. 152.

90 Cameron and Wright, *Second Empire*, pp. 152-3; Joann Latremoille, *Pride of Home: The Working Class Housing Tradition in Nova Scotia 1749-1949*, Hantsport, NS: Lancelot Press, 1986, p. 50.

91 C.J. Taylor et al., *Some Early Ottawa Buildings*, Manuscript Report No. 268, Ottawa: Parks Canada, 1975, pp. 271-6; Harold Kalman and John Roaf, *Exploring Ottawa: An Architectural Guide to the Nation's Capital*, Toronto: University of Toronto Press, 1983. p. 56.

92 Dixon and Muthesius, *Victorian Architecture*, p. 69.

93 'Apartment Houses', *CAB*, 3:10, October 1890, pp. 111-12.

94 Kalman and Roaf, *Exploring Ottawa*, p. 51.

95 Edward Mills and Warren Sommer, *Vancouver Architecture, 1886-1914*, Manuscript Report No. 405, 2, Ottawa: Parks Canada, 1975, pp. 345-50; Kalman and Roaf, *Exploring Vancouver*, pp. 23, 123.

96 Vancouver *Province*, 26 February 1907, p. 7; cited in Mills and Sommer, *Vancouver Architecture*, 2, p. 349.

97 Vancouver *Province*, 5 March 1906, p. 7; cited in Mills and Sommer, *Vancouver Architecture*, 1, p. 37.

98 *CAB*, 18:210, June 1905, p. 85; John Bland, 'The Importance and Place of the Maxwells in the History of Canadian Architecture', unpublished paper, 1990, p. 6.

99 Information kindly provided by Robert Lemire.

100 Commonwealth Historic Resource Management Limited, *Arlington Apartments: Architectural and Historical Assessment*, prepared for the City of Edmonton, 1988; Phyllis Barham, 'History of "The Arlington"...', City of Edmonton Archives.

101 Gregory S. Kealey, *Hogtown: Working Class Toronto at the Turn of the Century*, Toronto: New Hogtown Press, 1974, p. 20; the sources of the figures are the *Annual Reports* of the Ontario Bureau of Industry.

102 Kealey, *Hogtown*, p. 21.

103 Gregory S. Kealey, ed., *Canada Investigates Industrialism: Reports of the Royal Commission, 1889*, Toronto: University of Toronto Press, 1973, pp. 10, 38-9, 56; see also

104 Hannah Shostack, 'Business and Reform: The Lost History of the Toronto Housing Company', *City Magazine*, 3:7, September 1978, pp. 24-31; Lorna F. Hurl, 'The Toronto Housing Company, 1912-1923: The Pitfalls of Painless Philanthropy', *Canadian Historical Review*, 65:1, March 1984, pp. 28-53.

105 Dendy and Kilbourn, *Toronto Observed*, pp. 183-6.

106 Jill Wade, 'Wartime Housing Limited, 1941-1947: Canadian Housing Policy at the Crossroads', *Urban History Review*, 15:1, June 1986, pp. 41-59.

Bernard Ostry, 'Conservatives, Liberals and Labour in the 1880s', *Canadian Journal of Economics and Political Science*, 27 May 1961, p. 152.

CHAPTER 12 Town Planning

1 See Gilbert A. Stelter, 'The Political Economy of Early Canadian Urban Development', in Gilbert A. Stelter and Alan F.J. Artibise, eds, *The Canadian City*, 2nd ed., Ottawa: Carleton University Press, 1984, pp. 8-38; Stelter, 'The Changing Imperial Context of Early Canadian Urban Development,' in Stelter, ed., *Cities and Urbanization*, Toronto: Copp Clark, 1990, pp. 16-40.

2 James M. Cameron, 'The Canada Company and Land Settlement as Resource Development in the Guelph Block', in J. David Wood, ed., *Perspectives on Landscape and Settlement in Nineteenth Century Ontario*, Toronto: McClelland and Stewart, 1975, pp. 141-58; Thelma Coleman and James Anderson, *The Canada Company*, Stratford: Cumming, 1978; Norah Johnson, 'Guelph and Goderich: Tadmores in Upper Canada', *JRAIC*, 35:10, Oct. 1958, pp. 386-90; Clarence Karr, *The Canada Land Company: The Early Years*, Ottawa: Ontario Historical Society, 1974.

3 For the plan of Buffalo, see Francis R. Kowsky et al., *Buffalo Architecture: A Guide*, Cambridge: MIT Press, 1981, pp. 3, 54. Galt's praise is from *The Autobiography of John Galt*, II, London: Cochrane and M'Crone, 1833, p. 85, quoted in Gilbert A. Stelter, 'Guelph and the Early Canadian Town Planning Tradition', *Ontario History*, 77:2, June 1985, p. 100. Stelter's article (pp. 83-106) is the best source for the founding of Guelph.

4 Galt to David Moir, 3 Oct. 1828, quoted in Stelter, 'Guelph', p. 102. See also Ralph Greenhill, Ken MacPherson, and Douglas Richardson, *Ontario Towns*, Ottawa: Oberon, 1974, n.p.

5 See Joseph Rykwert, *On Adam's House in Paradise: The Idea of the Primitive Hut in Architectural History*, New York: Museum of Modern Art, 1972.

6 'Guelph in Upper Canada', *Fraser's Magazine*, 2, Nov. 1830, p. 456; quoted in Stelter, 'Guelph', p. 102.

7 Orr Papers, Perth County Archives, Stratford, Ontario, Clipping 1, p. 7; cited in Coleman and Anderson, *Canada Company*, pp. 34-5.

8 Stelter, 'Guelph', p. 96; Johnson, 'Guelph', p. 387.

9 John Galt, *Bogle Corbet*, III, London: Colburn and Bentley, 1831, pp. 30-1; cited in Stelter, 'Guelph', p. 103.

10 Norman MacDonald, *Canada, 1763-1841: Immigration and Settlement*, London: Longmans, Green, 1939, pp. 303-9; Ivan J. Saunders, 'The New Brunswick and Nova Scotia Land Company and the Settlement of Stanley, New Brunswick', unpublished M.A. thesis, University of New Brunswick, 1969.

11 Report quoted in Velma Kelly, *The Village in the Valley: A History of Stanley and Vicinity*, pp. 24-5; see also 'Sketches of Stanley, New Brunswick', *History Bulletin*, Saint John: New Brunswick Museum, 14:1, Winter 1967; Janet Wright, *Architecture of the Picturesque in Canada*, Studies in Archaeology, Architecture and History, Ottawa: Parks Canada, 1984, p. 151.

12 Gerald M. Craig, *Upper Canada: The Formative Years, 1784-1841*, Toronto: McClelland and Stewart, 1963, pp. 87-8.

13 J.A. Roebuck, *Existing Difficulties in the Government of the Canadas*, London: privately printed, 1836, p. 54; cited in P.J. Smith, 'John Arthur Roebuck: A Canadian Influence on the Development of Planning Thought in the Early Nineteenth Century', *Plan Canada*, 19:3,4 (September-December 1979), p. 202.

14 Province of Canada, *Journals of Assembly*, 1856, cited in George W. Spragge, 'Colonization Roads in Canada West, 1850-1867', *Ontario History*, 49 (1957), p. 7. See also Brenda Lee-Whiting, 'The Opeongo Road—An Early Colonization Scheme', *Canadian Geographical Journal*, 74:3, March 1967, pp. 76-83; Marlyn G. Miller, *Straight Lines in Curved Space: Colonization Roads in Eastern Ontario*, Toronto: Ontario Ministry of Culture and Recreation, 1978; Helen E. Parson, 'The Colonization of the Southern Canadian Shield in Ontario: The Hastings Road', *Ontario History*, 79:3, Sept. 1987, pp. 263-73.

15 Omer Lavallée, *Narrow Gauge Railways of Canada*, Montreal: Railfair, 1972, p. 48. Jacques Lacoursière, 'Le Curé Labelle', *Cahiers d'histoire des Pays d'en-haut*, 19, September 1983, pp. 37-48; [Commonwealth Historic Resource Management Limited,] 'Pioneers of the North: The Legacy of Curé Labelle', *The Story of Canada*, folio 10, Ottawa: Excelsiors Collectors Guild, 1984; see also J.E. Caron, *Historique de la colonisation dans la province de Québec de 1825 à 1940*, Quebec, 1940; 'La Colonisation: un patrimoine du XXᵉ siècle,' *Continuité*, 48, Summer 1990, pp. 47-71.

16 Lavallée, *Narrow Gauge Railways*, p. 47.

17 Kent Gerecke, 'The History of Canadian City Planning', *City Magazine*, 2:3-4, Summer 1976, pp. 12-23; Paul Rutherford, 'Tomorrow's Metropolis: The Urban Reform Movement in Canada. 1880-1920', in Gilbert A. Stelter and Alan F.J. Artibise, eds., *The Canadian City: Essays in Urban History*, Toronto: McClelland and Stewart, 1977, pp. 368-92.

18 David Bellman, 'Frederick Law Olmsted and a Plan for Mount Royal Park', *Mont-Royal, Montréal/Mount Royal, Montreal: Une Exposition presentée au Musée McCord, Montreal/An Exhibition Held at the McCord Museum, Montreal*, in *RACAR*, Supplement No. 1, December 1977, pp. S31-S48; Jean-Claude Marsan, 'Le Parc du Mont-Royal à cent ans', *Vie des arts*, 19:75, Summer 1974, pp. 17-22; A.L. Murray, 'Frederick Law Olmsted and the Design of Mount Royal Park, Montreal', *JSAH* 26:3, October 1967, pp. 163-71; Frederick Law Olmsted, *Mount Royal, Montreal*, New York: G.P. Putnam's Sons, 1881.

19 Illustrated in Margaret Archibald, *By Federal Design: The Chief Architect's Branch of the Department of Public Works, 1881-1914*, Studies in Archaeology, Architecture and History, Ottawa: Parks Canada, 1983, p. 23.

20 Thomas S. Hines, *Burnham of Chicago: Architect and Planner*, New York: Oxford University Press, 1974, chapters 4-6.

21 Margaret Anne Meek, 'The History of the City Beautiful Movement in Canada, 1890-1930', M.A. thesis, University of British Columbia, 1979; Walter Van Nus, 'The Fate of City Beautiful Thought in Canada, 1893-1930', Canadian Historical Association, *Historical Papers*, 1975, pp. 191-210, reprinted in Stelter and Artibise, *Canadian City*, 1977, pp. 162-85. For the American version of the movement, see William H. Wilson, *The City Beautiful Movement*, Baltimore: Johns Hopkins University Press, 1989; Charles N. Glaab and A. Theodore Brown, *A History of Urban America*, New York: Macmillan, 1967, pp. 254-7.

22 Ontario Association of Architects, *Proceedings*, 1904, p. 95; Van Nus, 'Fate', p. 162.

23 *CAB*, 15:4, April 1902, p. 49; 18, June 1905, p. 82; cited in Van Nus, 'Fate', and Meek, 'City Beautiful Movement'.

24 Langton spoke to the Annual General Meeting of the OAA; cited in Geoffrey Simmins, *Ontario Association of Architects: A Centennial History*, Toronto: Ontario Association of Architects, 1989, p. 70.

25 Simmins, *OAA*, p. 71; William T. Perks and P.J. Smith, 'Urban and Regional Planning', *Canadian Encyclopedia* (*CE*), 2nd ed., Edmonton, Hurtig, 1988, IV, p. 2228. The Town Planning Institute was disbanded in 1932 and revived two decades later.

26 Edwinna von Baeyer, '"The Battle Against Disfiguring Things": An Overview of the Response by Non-professionals to the City Beautiful Movement in Ontario from 1880 to 1920', *SSAC Bulletin*, 11:4, December 1986, pp. 3-9; Edwinna von Baeyer, *Rhetoric and Roses: A History of Canadian Gardening 1900-1930*, Markham: Fitzhenry & Whiteside, 1984, pp. 66-97.

27 Wilfrid Eggleston, *The Queen's Choice*, Ottawa: Queen's Printer, 1961, pp. 154-5. See also John H. Taylor, *Ottawa: An Illustrated History*, Toronto: James Lorimer, 1986; and Harold Kalman and John Roaf, *Exploring Ottawa*, Toronto: University of Toronto Press, 1983.

28 Frederick G. Todd, 'Report by Frederick G. Todd on Parkway System of Ottawa Improvement Commission', 1903, National Archives of Canada, quoted in Eggleston, *Queen's Choice*, p. 162. For Todd, see Peter Jacobs, 'Frederick G. Todd and the Creation of Canada's Urban Landscape', *APT Bulletin*, 15:4, 1983, pp. 27-34; John Bland, 'The Landscape Architecture of Frederick Todd', *RACAR*, 7:1-2, 1980, pp. 111-13. His approach to design is expressed in Frederick G. Todd, 'Character in Park Design', *Canadian Municipal Journal*, 1:10, Oct. 1905, p. 322.

29 H.S. Holt, chairman, *Report of the Federal Plan Commission on a General Plan for the Cities of Ottawa and Hull, 1915*, Ottawa, 1916, pp. 110-11. See Janet Wright, 'Building in the Bureaucracy: Architecture of the Department of Public Works, 1927-1939', M.A. Thesis, Queen's University, Kingston, 1988, pp. 49-50; Harold Kalman, *The Railway Hotels and the Development of the Château Style in Canada*, Maltwood Museum Studies in Architectural History, No. 1, Victoria: University of Victoria, 1968, pp. 23-4. On Bennett, see Joan E. Draper, *Edward H. Bennett: Architect and City Planner, 1874-1954*, Chicago: Art Institute of Chicago, 1982.

30 See John Crosby Freeman, 'Thomas Mawson: Imperial Missionary of British Town Planning', *RACAR*, 2:2, 1975,

pp. 37-47; Geoffrey W. Beard and Joan Wardman, *Thomas H. Mawson, 1861-1933: The Life and Work of a Northern Landscape Architect*, Lancaster: University of Lancaster, 1976. Mawson—who summarized his career in his autobiography, *The Life and Work of an English Landscape Architect*, London: Richards Press, 1927—may have been related to the Mawson brothers, architects of Yorkshire (and thus also to Francis Mawson Rattenbury), but the kinship has not been established.

31 Thomas H. Mawson & Sons, *Calgary: A Preliminary Scheme for Controlling the Economic Growth of the City*, Calgary: City Planning Commission, 1914. See E. Joyce Morrow, *'Calgary, Many Years Hence': The Mawson Report in Perspective*, Calgary: University of Calgary, 1979.

32 From a speech delivered at Calgary, 1912, printed as the prologue in Mawson, *Calgary*.

33 Ronald Rees, 'Wascana Centre: A Metaphor for Prairie Settlement', *Journal of Garden History*, 3:3, July-Sept. 1983, pp. 219-32; see also Linda Martin and Kerry Segrave, *City Parks of Canada*, Oakville: Mosaic Press, 1983, pp. 72-5.

34 Paul-André Linteau, *The Promoters' City: Building the Industrial Town of Maisonneuve 1883-1918*, trans. by Robert Chodos, Toronto: James Lorimer, 1985; Paul-André Linteau, 'The Development and Beautification of an Industrial City: Maisonneuve, 1883-1918', in Gilbert A. Stelter and Alan F.J. Artibise, eds, *Shaping the Urban Landscape: Aspects of the Canadian City Building Process*, Ottawa: Carleton University Press, 1982, pp. 304-20; Paul-André Linteau, 'Town Planning in Maisonneuve', *Canadian Collector*, 13:1, Jan. 1978, pp. 82-5; CUM (Répertoire d'architecture traditionnelle sur le territoire de la Communauté urbaine de Montréal), *Les Édifices publics*, Architecture civile I, Montreal: Communauté urbaine de Montrél, 1981, pp. 18-19, 108-9, 152-5, 204-5; CUM, *Les Résidences*, pp. 214-19. The design of the public buildings is generally credited to Marius Dufresne.

35 George D. Hall, 'The Future Prince Rupert as Conceived by the Landscape Architects', *Architectural Record*, 26:2, August 1909, pp. 97-106; R.G. Large, *Prince Rupert: A Gateway to Alaska and the Pacific*, 2nd ed., Vancouver: Mitchell, 1973; Harold D. Kalman, *The Prince Rupert Heritage Inventory and Conservation Programme*, Ottawa, 1983.

36 Aline Gubbay and Sally Hooff, *Montreal's Little Mountain/La Petit Montagne: A/un Portrait of/de Westmount*, p. 102; Martin Segger, *The Buildings of Samuel Maclure: In Search of Appropriate Form*, Victoria: Sono Nis, 1986, pp. 205-18.

37 Hall, 'Prince Rupert', *passim*.

38 Raymond Unwin, *Town Planning in Practice: An Introduction to the Art of Designing Cities and Suburbs*, 2nd ed., New York: Blom, 1909. The plan was illustrated in a plate without comment, probably because it had come to Unwin's attention after the type had been set.

39 Martin Segger, 'The Architecture of Samuel Maclure and Francis Mawson Rattenbury: In Search of Appropriate Form', *Canadian Collector*, 11:3, May-June 1976, p. 53; A.A. Barrett and R.W. Liscombe, *Francis Rattenbury and British Columbia: Architecture and Challenge in the Imperial Age*, Vancouver: University of British Columbia Press, 1983, pp. 226, 245.

40 *Canadian Municipal Journal*, 7, 6 June 1911, p. 213; quoted in Van Nus, 'Fate', p. 175.

41 'Tunnel to Connect Heart of the Business District with New "Garden Suburb"', Montreal *Herald*, 20 December 1911; G.R. Stevens, *History of the Canadian National Railways*, New York: Macmillan, 1973, p. 251.

42 Jacobs, 'Todd', pp. 29-31, who attibutes the design to Frank Darling, chief engineer of the CNOR and the first mayor of the model city.

43 Jacobs, 'Todd', p. 29; H.J. Selwood, 'Lots, Plots, and Blocks: Some Winnipeg Examples of Subdivision Design', *SSAC Bulletin*, 11:2, June 1986, pp. 6-8.

44 Martin Segger and Douglas Franklin, *Victoria: A Primer for Regional History in Architecture*, Victoria: Milestone Publications, 1979, pp. 308-11.

45 Macklin L. Hancock and D.H. Lee, 'Don Mills New Town', *JRAIC*, 30:1, January 1954, 3-29; Macklin L. Hancock, 'Business Builds a City: Don Mills, Canada', *House and Home*, 6, 1954, pp. 146-51; Joan Simon, 'Don Mills—Idealism and Speculation', *Dimensions of Canadian Architecture: SSAC, Selected Papers*, VI, 1983, pp. 31-3; John Barber, 'In the Beginning There Was Don Mills', *Globe and Mail*, 29 May 1993, pp. D1, D5.

46 Sylvain Filion, 'History of the Town of Lorraine', Lorraine, n.d. Information kindly provided by M.M. Kalman.

47 'Don Mills, The Planned Industrial Community near Toronto...', *Architectural Forum*, 114:1, January 1961, pp. 63-6; John C. Parkin and Sylvia Skeldon, 'Don Mills: An Experiment in Living', in Annabel Slaight, ed., *Exploring Toronto*, Toronto: Architecture Canada, 1972, pp. 104-11.

48 Paul-André Linteau, 'Urban Mass Transit', in Norman R. Ball, ed., *Building Canada: A History of Public Works*, Toronto: University of Toronto Press, 1988, p. 63, 68.

49 Linteau, 'Development and Beautification', p. 304; Alan F.J. Artibise and Gilbert A. Stelter, 'Conservation Planning and Urban Planning: The Canadian Commission of Conservation in Historical Perspective', in Roger Kain, ed., *Planning for Conservation*, Planning and the Environment in the Modern World, III, London: Mansell, 1981, p. 19. Walter C. Hardwick, *Vancouver*, Don Mills: Collier-Macmillan, 1974, pp. 1, 82.

50 Artibise and Stelter, 'Conservation Planning', pp. 17-36.

51 Commission on Conservation, *Second Annual Report*, Montreal, 1911, p. 75; quoted in Artibise and Stelter, 'Conservation Planning', p. 23.

52 Michael Simpson, *Thomas Adams and the Modern Planning Movement: Britain, Canada and the United States, 1900-1940*, London: Mansell, 1985; Alan H. Armstrong, 'Thomas Adams and the Commission on Conservation', *Plan Canada*, 1, 1959, pp. 20-8; Artibise and Stelter, 'Conservation Planning', pp. 23-6, O.W. Saarinen, the entry on Adams in the CE I, p 14. Adams' principal Canadian publication was *Rural Planning and Development: A Study of Rural Conditions and Problems in Canada*, Ottawa: Commission of Conservation, 1917; see also Thomas Adams, 'Modern City Planning, Its Meaning and its Methods', *Town Planning Institute of Canada, Journal*, 1:11, August 1922, pp. 11-15; Smith, 'Roebuck', p. 203.

53 [Thomas Adams,] 'Civic Improvement Organization for Canada', *Conservation of Life*, 2:1, Oct. 1915, p. 4; cited in Meek, 'City Beautiful', p. 94; Perks and Smith, 'Urban and Regional Planning', CE IV, p. 2228.

54 Thomas Adams, 'The Planning of the New Halifax', *Contract Record and Engineering Review*, 32, 28 August 1918, pp.

680-1; Ernest Clarke, 'The Hydrostone Neighbourhood', in Nova Scotia Association of Architects, *Exploring Halifax*, Toronto: Greey de Pencier, 1976, pp 56-61; Joann Latremouille, *Pride of Home: The Working Class Housing Tradition in Nova Scotia 1749-1949*, Hantsport, NS: Lancelot Press, 1986, pp. 67-74; Elaine Flaherty, 'Out of the Ashes, District has Blossomed', Vancouver *Sun*, 12 January 1993, p. A6, quoting Halifax planner Ernest Clarke and citing a photographic exhibition on The Hydrostone at the Public Archives of Nova Scotia.

55 'Ottawa Architects Club: Honorary Competition for Laying Out Recreation Park, Lindenlea, Ottawa, for the Lindenlea Garden and Suburb Association', *JRAIC*, 3:4, July-August 1926, p. 172; Stanley H. Pickett, 'Lindenlea, Ottawa', *Habitat*, 4:2, March-April 1961, pp. 17-19; Eric Minton, 'Lindenlea: Growing Old With Distinction', Ottawa *Journal*, 19 October 1968; Jill Delaney, 'The Garden Suburb of Lindenlea, Ottawa: A Model Project for the First Federal Housing Policy, 1918-24', *Urban History Review*, 19:3, February 1991, pp. 151-64.

56 Linteau, 'Development and Beautification', pp. 318-19.

57 Harland Bartholomew and Associates, *A Plan for the City of Vancouver, British Columbia*, [Vancouver: City of Vancouver,] 1928, p. 300; see also Walter G. Hardwick, *Vancouver*, Don Mills: Collier-Macmillan Canada, 1974, p. 29; and Harold Kalman and John Roaf, *Exploring Vancouver 2: Ten Tours of the City and Its Buildings*, Vancouver, UBC Press, 1978, p. 194.

58 The bylaw: 13 Geo. 5, Chap. 87; see Kalman and Roaf, *Exploring Vancouver 2*, p. 147.

59 Bartholomew, *A Plan for Vancouver*; Hardwick, *Vancouver*, pp. 27-8; E.M.W. Gibson, 'The Impact of Social Belief on Landscape Change: A Geographical Study of Vancouver', Ph.D. dissertation, University of British Columbia, 1971.

60 Elizabeth Bloomfield, 'Reshaping the Urban Landscape? Town Planning Efforts in Kitchener-Waterloo, 1912-1925', in G.A. Stelter and A.F.J. Artibise, eds, *Shaping the Urban Landscape: Aspects of the Canadian City-Building Process*, Ottawa: Carleton University Press, 1982, pp. 256-303.

61 Thomas Adams and Horace L. Seymour, 'Report on the Plan of the City of Kitchener, Ontario, February 1923 to March 1924', 4 April 1925, National Archives of Canada; quoted in Bloomfield, 'Kitchener-Waterloo', p. 292. The plan was published in the *Journal of the Town Planning Institute of Canada*, January 1925.

62 Eric Arthur, *Toronto: No Mean City*, 3rd ed., rev. by Stephen A. Otto, Toronto: University of Toronto Press, 1986; J.M.S. Careless, *Toronto to 1918: An Illustrated History*, Toronto: James Lorimer and National Museum of Man, 1984; Lucy Booth Martyn, *The Face of Early Toronto: An Archival Record, 1797-1936*, Sutton West, Ont.: Paget Press, c. 1982; Eric Wilfrid Hounsom, *Toronto in 1810*, Toronto: Ryerson Press, 1970; Edith G. Firth, *The Town of York*, 2 vols, Toronto: University of Toronto Press, 1962, 1966; Edith G. Firth, 'Prologue to Toronto: The Town of York, 1793-1834', *Canadian Collector*, 19:3, May-June 1984, pp. 37-41; G.P. de T. Glazebrook, *The Story of Toronto*, Toronto: University of Toronto Press, 1971; Patricia McHugh, *Toronto Architecture: A City Guide*, Toronto: Mercury Books, 1985.

63 Firth, *Town of York: 1793-1815*, p. lxxvi; cited in Arthur/Otto, *No Mean City*, p. 20.

64 Arthur/Otto, *No Mean City*, pp. 34-9; William Dendy, *Lost Toronto: Images of the City's Past*, Toronto: McClelland and Stewart, 1993, pp. 90-1.

65 Gunter Gad and Deryck W. Holdsworth, 'Streetscape and Society: The Changing Built Environment of King Street, Toronto', in R. Hall, W. Westfall, and L.S. MacDowell, eds., *Patterns of the Past: Interpreting Ontario's History*, Toronto: Dundurn, 1988, pp. 174-205; William Dendy, *Lost Toronto*, pp. 102-3. See also Gunter Gad and Deryck W. Holdsworth, 'Building for City, Region, and Nation: Office Development in Toronto 1834-1984', in V.L. Russell, ed., *Forging a Consensus: Historical Essays on Toronto*, Toronto: University of Toronto Press, 1984, pp. 272-319.

66 William Dendy and William Kilbourn, *Toronto Observed: Its Architecture, Patrons, and History*, Toronto: Oxford University Press, 1986, pp. 51-3; Arthur/Otto, *No Mean City*, pp. 117, 122-5. See also Alan Gowans, 'The Evolution of Architectural Styles in Toronto', in Stelter and Artibise, *Canadian City*, 2nd ed., pp. 210-19; Margaret E. McKelvey and Merilyn McKelvey, *Toronto: Carved in Stone*, Toronto: Fitzhenry and Whiteside, 1984; Stephen Beszedits, *Eminent Toronto Architects of the Past: Their Lives and Works*, Toronto: B & L Information Services, 1983; Stephen Beszedits, 'Toronto's 19th Century Architects', *Canadian Geographical Journal*, 97.3, December 1978-January 1979, pp. 52-9; Stephen A. Otto and Douglas Richardson, *Meeting Places: Toronto's City Halls, 1834-Present*, Toronto: City of Toronto Archives, 1985.

67 C. Pelham Mulvaney, *Toronto Past and Present*, Toronto: Caiger, 1884, p. 41; cited in Gad and Holdsworth, 'Streetscape and Society', p. 185.

68 Careless, *Toronto to 1918*, pp. 94, 138; Paul-André Lindteau, 'Urban Mass Transit', in Norman R. Ball, ed., *Building Canada: A History of Public Works*, Toronto: University of Toronto Press, 1988, pp. 60-3.

69 Dendy and Kilbourn, *Toronto Observed*, pp. 86-8; Arthur/Otto, *No Mean City*, p. 161.

70 Dendy and Kilbourn, *Toronto Observed*, pp. 129-33.

71 Dendy, *Lost Toronto*, pp. 124-5, 129-31; Gad and Holdsworth, 'Streetscape and Society', pp. 186-8; McHugh, *Toronto Architecture*, p. 87.

72 Dendy, *Lost Toronto*, p. 186. The plan was revised and issued as *Report on a Comprehensive Plan for Systematic Civic Improvement of Toronto*, Toronto, 1909.

73 Dendy, *Lost Toronto*, pp. 186-91; Geoffrey Hunt, *John M. Lyle: Toward a Canadian Architecture*, Kingston: Agnes Etherington Art Centre, Queen's University, 1982, p. 83; Meek, 'City Beautiful', pp. 77-81. See also John M. Lyle, 'Proposed Federal and Municipal Scheme for Toronto,' *Construction*, 4, July 1911, pp. 51-3; *Report of the Civic Improvement Committee for City of Toronto*, Toronto, 1911.

74 Annabel Slaight, ed., *Exploring Toronto*, Toronto: Architecture Canada, 1972, pp. 70-95.

75 *Wychwood Park Heritage Conservation District Plan*, Toronto: Toronto Historical Board, [1986]; Dendy and Kilbourn, *Toronto Observed*, pp. 175-7.

76 Gilbert A. Stelter and Alan F.J. Artibise, 'Canadian Resource Towns in Historical Perspective', *Plan Canada*, 18:1, March 1978, pp. 7-18; L.D. McCann, 'The Changing Internal Structure of Canadian Resource Towns', *Plan Canada*, 18:1, March 1978, pp. 46-59; Norman E.P. Press-

man and Kathleen Lauder, 'Resource Towns as New Towns', *Urban History Review*, 1, Nov. 1978, pp. 78-95. See also Robert K. Maquire, *Socio-economic Factors Pertaining to Single-industry Resource Towns in Canada: A Bibliography with Selected Annotations*, Chicago: Council of Planning Librarians, Bibliographies, 1980; Norman E.P. Pressman, *A Bibliography on Canadian New Towns*, HUD International Information Sources Series, New Towns, Washington: U.S. Department of Housing and Urban Development, 1975. For a classic economic analysis of resource communities, see Harold Innis, *Settlement and the Mining Frontier*, Toronto: Macmillan, 1936.

77 G.A. Stelter, 'The Origins of a Company Town: Sudbury in the Nineteenth Century', *Laurentian University Review*, 3:3, 1971, pp. 3-37; Noel Beach, 'Nickel Capital: Sudbury and the Nickel Industry, 1915-25', *Laurentian Uniersity Review*, 6, 1974, pp. 55-74; entry on Sudbury by O.W. Saarinen in *CE* IV, pp. 2090-1.

78 T.W. Paterson, *Vancouver Island*, British Columbia Ghost Town Series, No. 1, Langley: Mr Paperback, 1983, pp. 88-105; Susan Mayse, 'Coal Town, Boomtown, Ghost Town?', *Canadian Heritage*, 11:4, 1985, pp. 17-19; David Chuenyan Lai, *Chinatowns: Towns Within Cities in Canada*, Vancouver: University of British Columbia Press, 1988.

79 Testimony of Dr M.T. Sullivan to the Duncan Commission; cited in Latremouille, *Pride of Home*, p. 62; see also entry on Glace Bay by David Frank in *CE* II, p. 901.

80 A.K. Grimmer, 'The Development and Operation of a Company-Owned Resource Town', *The Engineering Journal*, 17, 1934, p. 219; cited in McCann, 'Resource Towns', p. 48.

81 Adams, *Rural Planning and Development*, Ottawa: Commission of Conservation, 1917, p. 66; cited in McCann, 'Resource Towns', p. 48. See also Oiva Saarinen, 'The Influence of Thomas Adams and the British New Towns Movement in the Planning of Canadian Resource Communities', in G.A. Stelter and A.F.J. Artibise, eds, *The Usable Urban Past: Politics and Planning in the Modern Canadian City*, Toronto: Macmillan, 1979, pp. 268-92; Roger A. Roberge, 'Resource Towns: The Pulp and Paper Communities', *Canadian Geographical Journal*, 97, February-March 1977, pp. 28-35, 75.

82 McCann, 'Resource Towns', p. 48.

83 'Homes for Workmen', *CAB*, 20:233, May 1907, p. 83. See also Michael J. Doucet, 'Working Class Housing in a Small Nineteenth Century Canadian City: Hamilton, Ontario 1852-1881', in Gregory S. Kealy and Peter Warrian, eds, *Essays in Canadian Working Class History*, Toronto: McClelland and Stewart, 1976, pp. 83-105.

84 Pete McMartin, '"Island" Community, a Retreat Under Shadow of Noisy Jets', Vancouver *Sun*, 20 February 1990, pp. A1, A11; see also Jill Wade, '"Citizens in Action": Local Activism and National Housing Programs, Vancouver, 1919-1950', Ph.D. Dissertation, Simon Fraser University, 1991.

85 'Industry Builds Kitimat', *Architectural Forum*, part 1, 101:1, July 1954, pp. 128-47; part 2, 101:2, August 1954, pp. 120-7; part 3, 101:4, October 1954, pp. 159-61; J. Russell Baxter, 'Kitimat: The First Five Years', *Canadian Architect*, Issue 3, March 1956, pp. 19-23; B.J. McGuire and Roland Wild, 'Kitimat—Tomorrow's City Today', *Canadian Geographical Journal*, 59:5, Nov. 1959, pp. 143-61;

John Kendrick, *People of the Snow: The Story of Kitimat*, Toronto: NC Press, 1987. The technological marvels of the smelter and its power source are described in Paul Clark, 'Kitimat—A Saga of Canada', *Canadian Geographical Journal*, 49:1, July 1984, pp. 152-73; Angela Croome, 'The Kitimat Story', *Annual Report of the Board of Regents of the Smithsonian Institution, 1956*, Washington: U.S. Government Printing Office, 1957, pp. 355-62; A.K., 'The New Frontier Towns', *Urban Reader*, 6:6, 1979, pp. 25-30. Ralph Reschke, of Alcan Smelters and Chemicals Ltd, kindly provided photographs.

86 Graham Humphrys, 'Schefferville, Quebec: A New Pioneering Town', *Geographical Review*, 48:2, April 1958, pp. 151-65.

87 *Africville: A Spirit That Lives On*, exhibition organized by the Art Gallery, Mount St Vincent University, 1989; Naomi Pauls, 'Black Community's Spirit Remembered in Exhibit', *Georgia Straight*, 23-30 November 1990, p. 30; Bridglal Pachai, Don Clairmont, Charles Saunders, and Stephen Kimber, *The Spirit of Africville*, Halifax: Formac, 1991.

CHAPTER 13 The True North

1 Robert McGhee, 'Climate and People in the Prehistoric Arctic', *Northern Perspectives*, December 1987, pp. 13-15.

2 Urve Linnamae, *The Dorset Culture: A Comparative Study in Newfoundland and the Arctic*, Technical Papers of the Newfoundland Museum, No. 1, St John's, 1975, p. 12 and *passim*; Moreau S. Maxwell, 'Pre-Dorset and Dorset Prehistory of Canada', in William C. Sturtevant, ed., *Handbook of North American Indians*, 5: Arctic, Washington: Smithsonian Institution, 1984, p. 366; Peter Nabokov and Robert Easton, *Native American Architecture*, New York: Oxford University Press, 1989, p. 191.

3 McGhee, 'Climate and People', p. 14.

4 Nabokov and Easton, *Architecture*, pp. 191-3; Allen P. McCartney, ed., *Thule Eskimo Culture: An Anthropological Retrospective*, Archaeological Survey of Canada, Mercury Series, Paper No. 88, Ottawa: National Museum of Man, 1979. See also Robert McGhee, 'People of the Whalebone Houses', *Canadian Heritage*, December 1983-January 1984, pp. 28-32; Peter Schledermann *Thule Eskimo Prehistory of Cumberland Sound, Baffin Island, Canada*, Archaeological Survey of Canada, Mercury Series, Paper No. 38, Ottawa: National Museum of Man, 1975.

5 Robert McGhee, *The Thule Village at Brooman Point, High Arctic Canada*, Archaeological Survey of Canada, Paper No. 125, National Museum of Man, Mercury Series, Ottawa: National Museums of Canada, 1984.

6 Schledermann, *Thule Prehistory of Cumberland Sound*.

7 James A. Tuck, *Newfoundland and Labrador Prehistory*, Ottawa: Archaeological Survey of Canada, National Museum of Man, 1976, especially Chapter 6, 'The Thule Tradition and the Labrador Eskimos', pp. 109-18.

8 Allen P. McCartney, 'A Processual Consideration of Thule Whale Bone Houses', in McCartney, ed., *Thule Culture*, p. 305.

9 Frobisher is quoted in Nabokov and Easton, *Architecture*, p. 189.

10 Tuck, *Prehistory*, p. 118; J. Garth Taylor, 'Historical Ethnography of the Labrador Coast', in Sturtevant, ed., *Handbook*, 5, pp. 514-15.

11 Martin Weaver, 'The Polar Home', *Canadian Heritage*, 13:1, February-March 1987, pp. 28-31; Nabokov and Easton, *Architecture*, p. 194.

12 Franz Boas, *The Central Eskimo* (1888), reprinted Lincoln: University of Nebraska Press, 1964, p. 132.

13 David Damas, 'Central Eskimo: Introduction', in Sturtevant, ed., *Handbook*, 5, p. 394; Guy Marie-Rousselière, 'Iglulik', in Sturtevant, ed., *Handbook*, 5, p. 437; Bernard Saladin d'Anglure, 'Inuit of Quebec', in Sturtevant, ed., *Handbook*, 5, p. 481. For a superb photographic essay showing the construction of an igloo by Tookillkee Kiguktak at Grise Fiord, see Ulli Steltzer, *Building an Igloo*, Vancouver: Douglas & McIntyre, 1981.

14 Boas, *Central Eskimo*, pp. 135-9; David Damas, 'Copper Eskimo', in Sturtevant, ed., *Handbook*, 5, p. 405; Nabokov and Easton, *Architecture*, p. 197.

15 Marie-Rousselière, 'Iglulik', p. 433; Nabokov and Easton, *Architecture*, p. 200. The Dorset culture also had a transitional dwelling of this kind: see McCartney, 'Consideration', p. 302.

16 Taylor, 'Labrador Coast', p. 514; Boas, *Central Eskimo*, pp. 143-4.

17 Marie-Rousselière, 'Iglulik', p. 434.

18 Saladin d'Anglure, 'Quebec', p. 482.

19 Derek G. Smith, 'Mackenzie Delta Eskimo', in Sturtevant, ed., *Handbook*, 5, pp. 349-51.

20 Smith, 'Mackenzie Delta Eskimo', p. 349; Saladin d'Anglure, 'Quebec', p. 482; Nabokov and Easton, *Architecture*, pp. 203-4; Boas, *Central Eskimo*, pp. 192-3.

21 Robert McGhee and James Tuck, 'An Elizabethan Settlement in Arctic Canada', *Rotunda*, 25:4, Spring 1993, pp. 32-40; Robert McGhee kindly provided photographs and descriptions of the site in correspondence with the author, 22 January 1991. George MacDonald initially provided information on the discoveries.

22 Vilhjalmur Stefansson, ed., *The Three Voyages of Martin Frobisher*, London: Argonaut Press, 1938, p. 116; spelling modernized by the author. This text was provided by Robert McGhee.

23 McGhee and Tuck, 'Elizabethan Settlement', p. 36.

24 George Ingram, *Prince of Wales' Fort: A Structural History*, Manuscript Report Series, No. 297, Ottawa: Parks Canada, 1979; [Harold Kalman], 'Fort Prince of Wales, Near Churchill, Manitoba', in 'Radisson & des Groseilliers', *The Story of Canada*, Ottawa: Excelsior Collectors Guild, 1987.

25 Clifford Wilson, 'Forts on the Twin Rivers', *The Beaver*, Outfit 288, Winter 1957, pp. 4-11; Ralph Hedlin, 'Port of the Pioneers', *The Beaver*, Outfit 288, Winter 1957, pp. 44-9 (and other articles in this special issue on York Factory); Frank Hall, 'York Factory Saved?', *Manitoba Pageant*, 14:1, Autumn 1968, pp. 13-23; Michael Payne, *The Most Respectable Place in the Territory: Everyday Life in Hudson's Bay Company Service: York Factory 1788 to 1870*, Studies in Archaeology, Architecture and History, Ottawa: Canadian Parks Service, 1989; Bruce Donaldson, *The York Factory Depot Warehouse*, Microfiche Report Series, no. 5, Ottawa: Parks Canada, 1982; Frits Pannekoek, 'York Factory', CE IV, p. 2352. Robert Coutts, Parks Canada, Winnipeg,

kindly provided information. For recent excavation that uncovered a late-eighteenth-century fort, see S. Biron Ebell and Peter J. Priess, 'In Search of the Octagon: Investigations under the Depot at York Factory', *Research Bulletin* [Parks Canada], May 1993.

26 Cited in [Harold Kalman], 'Depot, York Factory, Manitoba', in 'The Canada Beaver & The Origins of Fur Trading', *The Story of Canada*, Ottawa: Excelsior Collectors Guild, 1983.

27 Lyle Dick, 'The Fort Conger Shelters and Vernacular Adaptation to the High Arctic', *SSAC Bulletin*, 16:1, March 1991, pp. 13-23. Peary's remarks are from Robert E. Peary, *Secrets of Polar Travel*, New York: Century, 1917, p. 154; cited in Dick, 'Fort Conger', p. 20. Dick kindly provided this material in advance of its publication. For structures and artifacts from temporary camps of another kind, see Lyle Dick, 'Defence Research Board Camps in Northern Ellesmere Island: Report on Historical Resources', *Research Bulletin*, 292, Ottawa: Environment Canada, Parks Service, June 1991.

28 Peary, *Polar Travel*, pp. 155-6; Peary Diary, entry for 20 December 1900, Peary Papers, US National Archives, Washington: both cited in Dick, 'Fort Conger', p. 21.

29 Peary, *Polar Travel*, p. 126; cited in Dick, 'Fort Conger', p. 14.

30 James de Jonge, 'Building on the Frontier: The Mounted Police in the Canadian North', *SSAC Bulletin*, 17:2, June 1992, pp. 42-54. de Jonge kindly provided a copy of the manuscript in advance of publication.

31 de Jonge, 'Building on the Frontier', p. 54.

32 Frederick A.W. Peacock, 'The Moravian Mission and The Labrador Eskimos', *Canadian Antiques Collector*, 10:2, March-April 1975, pp. 66-9; Peacock, 'The Archives of the Moravian Church Relating to Labrador', *Newfoundland Quarterly*, 78:1-2, Spring-Summer 1982, pp. 29-33.

33 Peacock, 'Moravian Mission', p. 67.

34 Allen W. Wright, *Prelude to Bonanza*, Sidney, BC: Gray's Publishing, 1976, pp. 86-7.

35 Janet Wright, *Church of Our Lady of Good Hope, Fort Good Hope Northwest Territories*, Ottawa: Parks Canada, 1986; C.J. Taylor and Janet Wright, 'Mission Church, Fort Good Hope, N.W.T.', agenda paper, Historical Sites and Monuments Board, n.d.

36 Wright, *Prelude to Bonanza*, pp. 87, 127-30; Thomas J. Sawyer, 'A History of the Church in the Yukon', unpublished B.D. thesis, University of Alberta, 1966, p. 66. For a description of competing Anglican and Roman Catholic missions at Hay River, NWT, see Joan Mattie, 'The Hay River Missions: St Peter and St Anne's', *SSAC Bulletin*, 17:4, December 1992, pp. 97-104.

37 Ken S. Coates and William R. Morrison, *Land of the Midnight Sun: A History of the Yukon*, Edmonton: Hurtig, 1988, pp. 79-82. Many histories of the Klondike have been written, the most popular being Pierre Berton, *Klondike: The Last Great Gold Rush*, Toronto: McClelland and Stewart, 1972.

38 S.B. Steele, *Forty Years in Canada*, London: Jenkins, 1915, p. 296; cited in Coates and Morrison, *Yukon*, p. 89.

39 Margaret E. Archibald, *A Structural History of the Administration Building, Dawson, Yukon Territory*, Manuscript Report Series, No. 217, Ottawa: Parks Canada, 1977.

40 Margaret Carter and Margaret Archibald, *Early Courthouses of the Yukon*, Manuscript Report Series, No. 311, Ottawa: Parks Canada, 1977; G.E. Mills et al., 'Early Court Houses of the Old Territorial North West and the Prairie Provinces', in Margaret Carter, comp., *Early Canadian Court Houses*, Studies in Archaeology, Architecture and History, Ottawa: Parks Canada, 1983, pp. 136-40; David Neufeld, *Government Roofs in Dawson City, Yukon Territory: An Assessment of Design Challenges and Building Practices*, Research Bulletin, No. 280, Ottawa: Environment Canada, Parks Service, 1990.

41 Fuller to Ewart, 13 August 1899, NAC; cited in Richard G. Stuart, *The Annex to the Commissioner's Residence, Dawson: A Structural History, 1901-1964*, Manuscript Report Series, No. 367, Ottawa: Parks Canada, 1979, p. 10.

42 Stuart, *Annex*, pp. 9-12. See also R.J.E. Brown, *Permafrost in Canada: Its Influence on Northern Development*, Toronto: University of Toronto Press, 1970, esp. pp. 56-62.

43 *Nugget*, 11 May 1901, p. 4, and 16 August 1901, pp. 1, 4; cited in Commonwealth Historic Resource Management Limited, *St Andrew's Presbyterian Church, Dawson: A Structural and Use History*, Microfiche Report Series, No. 171, Ottawa: Parks Canada, 1984, pp. 14-15.

44 Richard Stuart, *The Robert Service Cabin, Dawson, 1902-70*, Microfiche Report Series, No. 90, Ottawa: Parks Canada, 1983.

45 Edward F. Bush, *Banking in the Klondike 1898-1968*, Manuscript Report Series, No. 118, Ottawa: Parks Canada, n.d., pp. 13, 20, 29, 87-98; Commonwealth, *St Andrew's*, pp. 60, 62, 65; Victor Ross, *A History of the Canadian Bank of Commerce*, II, Toronto: Oxford University Press, 1922, pp. 137-98. Robert Moncrieff is sometimes credited with the design; however, he was likely the builder and not the architect. See also Margaret Carter, 'Talented Drifters: The Construction Industry in Dawson Y.T. 1897-1903', Society for the Study of Architecture in Canada, *Selected Papers*, 3, Ottawa, 1982, pp. 43-67; Ann H. Gillespie, 'Decorative Sheet-Metal Building Components in Canada, 1870-1930: Tin-Shop Methods of Fabrication and Erection', M.A. thesis, Carleton University, 1985.

46 Richard Stuart, *The Bank of British North America, Dawson: A Structural History*, Manuscript Report Series, No. 324, Ottawa: Parks Canada, 1979; Bush, *Banking*, pp. 77-82; Margaret Carter, *Bank of British North America, Dawson Y.T: Banking Room Interior Study, 1900-1920*, Microfiche Report Series, No. 353, Ottawa: Parks Canada, 1986.

47 C.J. Taylor, *Negotiating the Past: The Making of Canada's Historic Parks and Sites*, Montreal: McGill-Queen's University Press, 1990, pp. 170-5.

48 Robert R. Janes, 'Vernacular Architecture at a Contemporary Dene Hunting Camp', *SSAC Bulletin*, 13:2, June 1988, pp. 4-13; adapted from Janes, *Archaeological Ethnography Among Mackenzie Basin Dene, Canada*, Arctic Institute of North America, Technical Paper No. 28, Calgary, 1983.

49 Milton M.R. Freeman, 'The Grise Fiord Project', in David Damas, ed., *Handbook of North American Indians*, 5, Washington: Smithsonian Institution, 1984, pp. 676-80.

50 Bruce Stebbing, 'The Problem of Housing in the NWT', *SSAC Bulletin*, 13:2, June 1988, p. 25.

51 Northwest Territories Housing Corporation, *Northern Housing Identification Guide*, [Yellowknife:] n.d., pp. 165-6.

This, and other information, was kindly provided by Marshall Wilson.

52 G.W. Heinke, *North of 60: Report on Municipal Services in Communities of the Northwest Territories*, Ottawa: Department of Indian and Northern Affairs, 1973, p. 91; see also Gordon B. Pritchard, 'Inuvik—Canada's New Arctic Town', *Canadian Geographical Journal*, 64:6, June 1962, pp. 201-9; 'The Old and the New Aklavik', *Canadian Architect*, Issue 11, November 1956, pp. 23-8.

53 T. Ritchie, *Canada Builds 1867-1967*, Toronto: University of Toronto Press, 1967, p. 143; Letty Anderson, 'Water Supply', in Norman R. Ball, ed., *Building Canada: A History of Public Works*, Toronto: University of Toronto Press, 1988, pp. 216-17; A.F. Leitch and G.W. Heinke, *Comparison of Utilidors in Inuvik, N.W.T.*, Toronto: Department of Civil Engineering, University of Toronto, 1970.

54 John de Visser and Harold Kalman, *Pioneer Churches*, Toronto: McClelland and Stewart, 1976, pp. 183-4.

55 Erik Watt, *Yellowknife: How a City Grew*, Yellowknife: Outcrop, 1990; *Four Walking Tours of Yellowknife's Old Town*, Yellowknife: City of Yellowknife Heritage Committee, 1987; City of Yellowknife Historical Committee, *Historical Building Directory of Yellowknife*, Draft, Yellowknife, 1986.

56 Ann Peters, 'Yellowknife—A Town Without a Presence', *SSAC Bulletin*, 13:2, June 1988, pp. 33-3.

57 'Legislative Assembly of the Northwest Territories', *Award*, 7:1, April 1993. pp. 30-1.

58 Stephen Barr, 'Is There a Northern Architecture?', *SSAC Bulletin*, 12:3, June 1988, p. 40.

CHAPTER 14 Architecture Between the Wars

1 C.T. Currelly, 'Henry Sproatt 1867-1934', *JRAIC*, 11:10, October 1934, p. 151; Andrea Kristof, 'Sproatt and Rolph', *Canadian Encyclopedia (CE)* III, 2nd ed., Edmonton, 1988, p. 2064; J.M. Lyle, 'Sproatt and Rolph, an Appreciation', *JRAIC*, 2:4, July-August 1925, pp. 126-27.

2 R.H. Hubbard, 'Modern Gothic in Canada', *Bulletin, The National Gallery of Canada*, 25, 1975, pp. 8-10. The Hart A. Massey estate was reorganized in 1918 as the Massey Foundation.

3 Ian Montagnes, *An Uncommon Fellowship: The Story of Hart House*, Toronto: University of Toronto Press, 1969; Vincent Massey, *What's Past is Prologue*, Toronto: Macmillan, 1963, pp. 24-5, 52-7; William Dendy and William Kilbourn, *Toronto Observed: Its Architecture, Patrons, and History*, Toronto: Oxford University Press, 1986, pp. 194-8; Hubbard, 'Modern Gothic', pp. 10-11; Mathilde Brosseau, *Gothic Revival in Canadian Architecture*, Canadian Historic Sites: Occasional Papers in Archaeology and History, No. 25, Ottawa: Parks Canada, 1980, pp. 180-1; *Construction*, 8:5, May 1920 (issue devoted to Hart House); *Sixth Exhibition of the Toronto Society of Architects*, Toronto, 1912, no. 224; *Hart House, University of Toronto*, Toronto, 1921; J.B. Bickersteth, 'Hart House', *Architectural Forum*, 40:1, January 1924, pp. 11-17; C.H.C. Wright, 'The University of Toronto', *JRAIC*, 2:1, January-February 1925, pp. 8-9, 15-18.

4 George McCue, 'Cope and Stewardson', *Macmillan Encyclopedia of Architects*, 1, New York, 1982, p. 450; see also

Ralph Adams Cram, 'The Work of Cope & Stewardson', *Architectural Record,* 16, 1904, pp. 404-438.

5 Ralph Adams Cram, *My Life in Architecture*, Boston: Little, Brown, and Company, 1936; cited in Marcus Whiffen, *American Architecture Since 1780: A Guide to the Styles*, Cambridge: MIT Press, 1969, pp. 173-74. See also the entry by Douglas Shand Tucci on Ralph Adams Cram in the *Macmillan Encyclopedia of Architects*, 1, pp. 471-4; Robert Muccigrosso, *American Gothic: The Mind and Art of Ralph Adams Cram*, Washington: University Press of America, 1980.

6 Currelly, 'Sproatt', p. 151.

7 E.R. Arthur, 'A Review of the R.A.I.C. Exhibition', *JRAIC*, 9:12, December 1932, p. 269.

8 Hubbard, 'Modern Gothic', pp. 11-14.

9 Don Kerr, 'Building the University of Saskatchewan 1907-1930', *Prairie Forum*, 5:2, Fall 1980, pp. 157-81 (quotation on p. 162); Stan Hanson, 'The Administration Building', *Saskatoon History*, 3, Summer 1985, pp. 5-7; Michael Hayden, *Seeking a Balance: University of Saskatchewan, 1907-1982*, Vancouver, 1983, pp. 70-1.

10 Victoria *Colonist*, 11 December 1912, p. 3; cited in Douglas Franklin, 'The Competition for the Design of the University of British Columbia', *West Coast Review*, 15:4, Spring 1981, pp. 49-57. See also 'University of British Columbia, Point Grey, Vancouver, B.C.', *JRAIC*, 2:5, September-October 1925, pp. 173-9; Harold Kalman, Ron Phillips, and Robin Ward, *Exploring Vancouver*, Vancouver: University of British Columbia Press, 1993, pp. 183-6.

11 Victoria *Colonist*, 11 December 1912, p. 3; cited in Franklin, 'Competition', p. 51.

12 Sean Rossiter, 'The Firm That Built the Town', *Vancouver*, September 1983, pp. 42-52; Paul Wright, '78-Year-Old Architect Lifts Vancouver's Face', *Western Business and Industry*, 30:6, June 1956, pp. 16-18; interviews with G.L.T. Sharp by Janet Bingham (March 1972) and Harold Kalman (April and May 1972), Canadian Architectural Archives, University of Calgary.

13 'University of British Columbia', pp. 174-9; Philip J. Turner, *The University and College Libraries of Canada: Their Planning and Equipment*, Montreal, 1931, pp. 22-4 (reprinted from *Construction*, 10:11, 1931).

14 Kalman et al., *Exploring Vancouver*, pp. 186, 188.

15 Hubbard, 'Modern Gothic', p. 15; Turner, 'Librairies', pp. 22-3.

16 Saskatchewan Association of Architects, *Historic Architecture of Saskatchewan*, Regina: Focus Publishing, 1986, pp. 145-6.

17 J.N. Semmens, 'Typical Schools of Western Canada', *JRAIC*, 4:11, November 1927, pp. 403-11.

18 Allen Parker and Associates, *Vancouver Heritage Inventory: Summary Report*, Vancouver: City of Vancouver, 1986, p. 67; advertisement for Portland Cement Association, *JRAIC*, 11:11, November 1934, p. iv.

19 Chris Lund et al., *Canada's Houses of Parliament*, Ottawa: National Film Board of Canada, 1967.

20 Harold Kalman and John Roaf, *Exploring Ottawa*, Toronto: University of Toronto Press, 1983, p. 6.

21 CUM (Répertoire d'architecture traditionnelle sur le territoire de la communauté urbain de Montréal), *Les Édifices publics*, Architecture civile I, Montreal: 1981, pp. 126-7; François Rémillard and Brian Merrett, *Montreal Architecture: A Guide to Styles and Buildings*, Montreal: Meridian Press, 1990, p. 134.

22 R.L. Daniels, *Saint Mary's Church, Walkerville*, Windsor, 1954; Hubbard, 'Modern Gothic', pp. 7-8.

23 *JRAIC*, 1924; Hubbard, 'Modern Gothic', pp. 6-7 (with bibliography, n. 11); Brosseau, *Gothic Revival*, pp. 176-7; Robert C. Tuck, *Gothic Dreams: The Life and Times of a Canadian Architect, William Critchlow Harris, 1854-1913*, Toronto: Dundurn Press, 1978, pp. 175-98; 'Accepted Design for Halifax Cathedral', *Christian Art*, 1, 1907, pp. 14-15. Cram, Goodhue, and Ferguson's design for the Cathedral of St Alban the Martyr, Toronto (1911), was published but not built; see Brosseau, *Gothic Revival*, pp. 176-7.

24 Dendy and Kilbourn, *Toronto Observed*, pp. 190-1.

25 'United Church of Canada, Presbytery of Montreal, Committee on Architecture', *JRAIC*, 3:4, July-August 1926, pp. 157-64; the discussion of styles occurs on p. 162.

26 Kalman et al., *Exploring Vancouver*, p. 110.

27 'St James' Church, Vancouver, B.C.', *JRAIC*, 14:6, June 1937, pp. 106-8; Edward Mills and Warren Sommer, *Vancouver Architecture, 1886-1914*, Manuscript Report Series, No. 405, 2, Ottawa: Parks Canada, 1975, pp. 447-53; Kalman et al., *Exploring Vancouver*, pp. 49-50; Hubbard, 'Modern Gothic', pp. 4-5; Phyllis Reeve, *Every Good Gift: A History of S. James' Vancouver 1881-1981*, Vancouver: S. James' Church, 1981, pp. 99-108.

28 The two firms' designs are published in C.P. Meredith, 'Remarkable Similarity in Plans', *Construction*, 1:10 (August 1908), pp. 32-6. See Harold Kalman, *The Railway Hotels and the Development of the Château Style in Canada*, Victoria: University of Victoria, 1968, pp. 19-20; David A. Rose, 'The Hotel Architecture of Ross & MacFarlane/Ross & Macdonald', M.A. thesis, Concordia University, 1992, pp. 28-45; Kalman, *Exploring Ottawa*, p. 28. A large addition was built in 1927-9 to designs by Archibald and Schofield; see *JRAIC*, 5 (1928), p. 207, and 7 (1930), pp. 393-411. See also Joan E. Rankin, *Meet Me at the Château*, Toronto: Natural Heritage, 1990.

29 Kalman, *Railway Hotels*, pp. 20-3; Harold Kalman and Susan Wagg, eds, *The Architecture of Edward & W.S. Maxwell*, Montreal: Montreal Museum of Fine Arts, 1991, pp. 92-5; see also Rose, 'The Hotel Architecture' *passim*; David A. Rose, 'The Concordia Railway Hotels Revisited: The Château Style Hotels of Ross & MacFarlane', *SSAC Bulletin*, 18:2, June 1993, pp. 32-42; 'The Royal York Hotel, Toronto', *JRAIC*, 6:8, August 1929, pp. 246-67.

30 'Report to Council', 27 April 1927, p. 2 (the recommendations had been made in 1920); see Kalman, *Railway Hotels*, p. 24; Janet Wright, 'Building in the Bureaucracy: Architecture of the Department of Public Works 1927-1939', M.A. thesis, Queen's University, 1988, p. 50.

31 'Report to Council', p. 3.

32 Ian Doull, 'Confederation Building, Justice Building, Justice Annex, Supreme Court of Canada, Wellington Street, Ottawa', Building Reports Nos. 87-34 to 87-37, Vol. 28, Federal Heritage Buildings Review Office, Ottawa: Environment Canada, 1987; Wright, 'Building in the Bureaucracy', pp. 51-2 (Rankin's career is summarized on p. 26);

Kalman, *Railway Hotels*, pp. 24-5; Kalman and Roaf, *Exploring Ottawa*, p. 11.

33 Wright, 'Building in the Bureaucracy', pp. 81-2; Douglas Owram, *Building for Canadians: A History of the Department of Public Works (1840-1960)*, Ottawa: Public Works Canada, 1979, p. 239.

34 Doull, 'Confederation Building', p. 49; Wright, 'Building in the Bureaucracy', pp. 102-6; Kalman, *Railway Hotels*, p. 25; Kalman and Roaf, *Exploring Ottawa*, pp. 11, 22; Harold Kalman and Joan Mackie, *The Architecture of W.E. Noffke*, Ottawa: Heritage Ottawa, 1976, p. 22; Robert Hunter, 'The Central Post Office, Ottawa', *SSAC Bulletin*, 7:6, June 1982, pp. 5-7.

35 Related to the author in conversation by Ernest Cormier, 30 June 1967; this was suggested as well by E.A. Gardner, Chief Architect at the time, in a letter to the author, 29 June 1967. See also Kalman, *Railway Hotels*, p. 25; Kalman and Roaf, *Exploring Ottawa*, p. 13; Doull, 'Confederation Building', p. 28-9; Wright, 'Building in the Bureaucracy', pp. 103-5; *The Supreme Court of Canada*, Ottawa: Department of Supply and Services, 1988.

36 Related to the author in conversation by E.A. Gardner and J.A. Langford, both of whom served as Chief Architect of the Department of Public Works during King's term in office; see Kalman, *Railway Hotels*, p. 26. For the Gréber Plan, see Jacques Gréber, 'Plan for the National Capital of Canada', *JRAIC*, 26:12, December 1949, pp. 395-445.

37 Wright, 'Building in the Bureaucracy', p. 118-19, where the author suggests that it and other Quebec federal buildings reflect the *maison traditionelle* of the seventeenth and eighteenth centuries.

38 Wright, 'Building in the Bureaucracy', pp. 106-7.

39 Mathilde Brosseau, 'Canadian Pacific Railroad Stations, Past and Present - Architectural Report', collected in H.E. MacNeil, ed., *Inventory of Railway Station Buildings in Canada (Complete)*, screening paper, Historic Sites and Monuments Board of Canada, Ottawa, 1974, p. c.43; Harry Edward Prindle, 'Quebec Union Station', *Construction*, 9:1, January 1916, p. 3; Luc Noppen, Claude Paulette, and Michel Tremblay, *Québec: trois siècles d'architecture*, [Montreal:] Libre Expression, 1979, p. 311.

40 Wright, 'Building in the Bureaucracy', pp. 63-5, with an illustration of the building at Trout River.

41 Edward Mills, 'Pacific Highway Customs and Immigration Building, Surrey, British Columbia', Building Report No. 84-36, Federal Heritage Buildings Review Office, Ottawa, 1984.

42 The steel-and-concrete arch—conceived by Sam Hill, president of the Pacific Highway Association, and designed by H.W. Corbitt—was built of donated labour and materials. It is managed jointly by BC Parks and Washington State Parks. Chris Tunnoch, BC Parks, kindly provided this information. See also Cyril E. Leonoff, *An Enterprising Life: Leonard Frank Photographs, 1895-1914*, Vancouver: Talon Books, 1990, p. 31; John Pearson, *Land of the Peace Arch*, Cloverdale (BC): Surrey Centennial Committee, 1958, pp. 138-41.

43 Edward Mills, 'Federally-Owned Buildings in Riding Mountain National Park, Manitoba', Building Report 85-43/85-54, Federal Heritage Buildings Review Office, Ottawa, n.d, pp. 56-105; Dana Johnson, 'Interpretive Centre (Museum Building), Riding Mountain National Park,

Wasagaming, Manitoba', Building Report 84-32, Federal Heritage Buildings Review Office, Ottawa, n.d; Lyle Dick, 'Forgotten Roots: The Gardens of Wesagaming', *Newest Review*, November 1986, pp. 10-11. Descriptions of the gardens from National Parks Bureau, *Riding Mountain National Park*, Ottawa: National Parks Bureau, 1937, p. 18; cited in Mills, p. 60.

44 Information on the architect and date was provided by Edward Mills.

45 Edward Mills, 'Rustic Design Programs in Canada's National Parks, 1887-1950', Parks Canada, 1993.

46 Howard D. Chapman, *Alfred Chapman: The Man and his Work*. Toronto: Architectural Conservancy of Ontario, 1978.

47 Sinaiticus, 'The Royal Ontario Museum, Toronto', *Construction*, 25:11, November 1932, pp. 247-55; 'The ROM's Mosaic Ceiling: A Remarkable Work of Symbolic Art', information sheet, ROM, n.d., James E. Cruise, 'Even ROM Wasn't Built in a Day', *Rotunda*, 10:2, Summer 1977; Patricia McHugh, *Toronto Architecture: A City Guide*, Toronto: Mercury Books, 1985, p. 123.

48 A.S. Mathers, 'The Royal Ontario Museum, Toronto', *JRAIC*, 10:5, May 1933, pp. 86-91.

49 Dendy and Kilbourn, *Toronto Observed*, pp. 250-1; Sheldon Levitt, Lynn Milstone, and Sidney T. Tenenbaum, *Treasures of a People: The Synagogues of Canada*, Toronto: Lester & Orpen Dennys, 1985, pp. 76-7; *JRAIC*, 15:10, October 1938, pp. 232-3.

50 For Congregation Shaar Hashomayim, see CUM, *Les Églises*, pp. 442-5; Levitt et al., *Treasures of a People*, p. 53. For the earlier Holy Blossom, see Dendy and Kilbourn, *Toronto Observed*, pp. 146-7.

51 Claude Bergeron, *L'Architecture des églises du Québec, 1940-1985*, Quebec: Les Presses de l'université Laval, 1987, p. 40; CUM, *Les Églises*, pp. 336-9; Rémillard and Merrett, *Montreal Architecture*, p. 143.

52 Olivier Maurault, 'Un Professeur d'architecture à Québec en 1828', *JRAIC*, 3:1, January-February 1926, pp. 32-6; cited in Claude Bergeron, *Églises*, p. 36.

53 ['Ainsi dans l'ombre du cloitre est né un style nouveau. Innovée dans la tradition, cette architecture est classique dans son esprit, mais pratique et moderne dans l'execution.'] Edgar Courchesne, 'Dom Paul Bellot, O.S.B.', *JRAIC*, 11:2, February 1934, p. 30.

54 Bellot, *Propos d'un bâtisseur du bon dieu*, Montreal: Fides [1948], cited in Geoffrey Simmins, ed., *Documents in Canadian Architecture*, Peterborough: Broadview Press, 1992, pp. 171-2; Nicole Tardif-Painchaud, *Dom Bellot et l'architecture religieuse au Québec*, Quebec: Les Presses de l'université Laval, 1978; Bergeron, *Églises*, pp. 35-51; Bergeron, *Architectures du XXᵉ siècle au Québec*, Montreal: Méridien, 1989, pp. 120-6; Bergeron, 'The Influence of the Ateliers d'Art Sacré on Quebec Architecture', paper delivered at the meeting of the Society of Architectural Historians, Montreal, 13 April 1989.

55 Bergeron, *Églises*, pp. 142-3; Tardif-Painchaud, *Dom Bellot*, p. 77.

56 Tardif-Painchaud, *Dom Bellot*, pp. 58-60.

57 Tardif-Painchaud, *Dom Bellot*, pp. 56-8; CUM, *Les Églises*, pp. 286-95; Joshua Wolfe and Cécile Grenier, *Montreal Guide*, [Montreal:] Libre Expression, 1983, p. 318.

58 Robert Hunter, 'Ukrainian Canadian Folk Architecture: The Churches of Father Philip Ruh', in Gregory P. Utas, ed., *SSAC: Selected Papers*, 5, 1982, p. 24-9, Gloria Romaniuk, 'Father Philip Ruh: Missionary-priest, and Builder', *SSAC Bulletin*, 11:1, March 1986, pp. 7-8; Philip Ruh, *Missionary and Architect*, Winnipeg: Progress Printing, 1960.

59 Hunter, 'Ukrainian Canadian Folk Architecture', pp. 25-26; Kordan, 'Church Architecture in Alberta', p. 168; Radomir B. Bilash, 'Peter Lipinski, Prairie Church Artist', *SSAC Bulletin*, 13:1, March 1988, pp. 8-14.

60 Hunter, 'Ukrainian Canadian Folk Architecture', p. 26; M.C. Kotecki and R.R. Rostecki, *Ukrainian Churches of Manitoba: An Overview Study*, 2, Winnipeg: Department of Culture, Heritage and Recreation, 1984, n.p.

61 Romaniuk, 'Ruh', pp. 7-8; Kotecki, 'Ukrainian Churches'.

62 Hunter, 'Ukrainian Canadian Folk Architecture', pp. 27-8; David J. Goa, 'Three Parishes: A Study of Sacred Space', *Material History Bulletin*, 29 June 1989, pp.13-23; *Historical Driving Tour: Ukrainian Churches in East Central Alberta*, Edmonton: Canadian Institute of Ukrainian Studies and Alberta Culture and Multiculturalism, 1988, no. 1.

63 J. Edward Martin, *Railway Stations of Western Canada*, White Rock, BC: Studio E, 1979, pp. 80, 82.

64 A.H. Chapman, 'The Princes' Gates', *JRAIC*, 4:10, October 1927, pp. 351-5; Victor E. Graham, 'The Princes' Gates', *SSAC Bulletin*, 15:1, March 1990, pp. 11-19; Chapman, *Chapman*, p. 16-19; Dendy and Kilbourn, *Toronto Observed*, pp. 200, 201.

65 Kalman and Roaf, *Exploring Ottawa*, p. 122.

66 E.R. Arthur, 'A Review of the R.A.I.C. Exhibition', *JRAIC*, 9:12, December 1932, pp. 264, 269.

67 By Ronald P. Jones; cited in John Lyle, 'Canadian Architecture', *JRAIC*, 4:2, Feb. 1927, p. 65 (emphasis mine).

68 E.R. Arthur, 'Toronto Chapter O.A.A. Architectural Exhibition', *JRAIC*, 3:2, March-April 1926, p. 53.

69 W.P. Percival, *The Lure of Montreal*, Toronto: Ryerson, 1945, pp. 85-6; Jean-Claude Marsan, *Montreal in Evolution*, Montreal: McGill-Queen's University Press, 1981, p. 246; Wolfe and Grenier, *Montreal Guide*, p. 95; CUM, *Les Hôtels, les Immeubles de Bureaux*, pp. 215-20; *Construction*, 19:3, March 1926, pp. 73-88.

70 Marcus Whiffen: *American Architecture Since 1780: A Guide to the Styles*, Cambridge: MIT Press, 1969, p. 160.

71 Saskatchewan Association of Architects, *Historic Architecture of Saskatchewan*, Regina: Focus Publishing, 1986, pp. 2, 74-7.

72 Harold Kalman, *The Prince Rupert Heritage Inventory and Conservation Programme*, Ottawa, 1983, pp. 51, 69; Leslie Maitland, Jacqueline Hucker, and Shannon Ricketts, *A Guide to Canadian Architectural Styles*, Peterborough: Broadview Press, 1992, pp. 158-9.

73 Semmens, 'Typical Schools', pp. 410, 412.

74 David Naylor, *American Picture Palaces*, New York, Van Nostrand Reinhold, 1981 (citation from p. 11) and Ben M. Hall, *The Last Remaining Seats*, New York: Clarkson Potter, 1961, provide overviews of American theatres. Canadian theatres are treated in Hilary Russell, 'All That Glitters: A Memorial to Ottawa's Capitol Theatre and its Predecessors', *Canadian Historic Sites: Occasional Papers in Archaeology and History*, 13, 1975, pp. 5-125; Robert Hunter, 'Last

Performance This Season: The Architectural Legacy of Canada's 18th and 19th Century Theatres', *SSAC Bulletin*, 14:2, June 1989, pp. 32-9; Dane Lanken, 'Montreal Movie Palaces', *SSAC Bulletin*, 14:2, June 1989, pp. 40-4.

75 Russell, 'All That Glitters', pp. 21-3, with bibliography; Wolfe and Grenier, *Montreal Guide*, pp. 237-8.

76 Thomas Lamb, 'Good Old Days to These Better New Days', *Motion Picture News*, Sect. 2 (30 June 1928), p. 31; cited in Russell, 'All that Glitters', p. 47.

77 Constance Olsheski, *Pantages Theatre: Rebirth of a Landmark*, Toronto: Key Porter Books, 1989; 'New Toronto Theatres', *Construction*, November 1920, pp. 338-43; F.E. Brown, 'Constructing a Massive Proscenium Girder in Toronto's Largest Theatre', *Contract Record*, 11 Feb. 1920, pp. 122-4.

78 H. Terry Helgesen, 'The Works of B. Marcus Priteca', *Marquee*, 4:2, 1972, pp. 3-11.

79 *New Orpheum, Vancouver, B.C.*, Chicago: The Orpheum Circuit, 1927; Doug McCallum, *Vancouver's Orpheum: The Life of a Theatre*, Vancouver: City of Vancouver, 1984; 'Orpheum Theatre, Vancouver', *Canadian Architect*, 22:11, November 1977, pp. 24-9; Kalman and Roaf, *Exploring Vancouver*, p. 188.

80 'The New Empress Theatre, Montreal', *JRAIC*, 5:11, November 1928, pp. 392-6; Dane Lanken, 'Montreal Movie Theatres', paper delivered at the SSAC Conference, Montreal, April 1989; CUM, *Les Magasins, Les Cinémas*, 1985, pp. 351-2. Citation from Naylor, *Palaces*, p. 77.

81 A useful index for residences of the time is Christina Cameron, *Index of Houses Featured in 'Canadian Homes and Gardens' from 1925 to 1944*, Ottawa: Parks Canada, 1980. An illustrated survey of recent domestic architecture across Canada was published (without text) in *JRAIC*, 16:5, May 1939, pp. 98-116.

82 'Batterwood House, Canton, Ontario', *JRAIC*, 6:12, December 1929, pp. 419-24; *Canadian Homes and Gardens*, 6:4, April 1929, p. 20.

83 'Residence of G.R. Larkin, Esq., Toronto', *Construction*, 20:9, September 1927, pp. 202-6, 291-4; E.R. Arthur, 'Toronto Chapter Architectural Exhibition', *JRAIC*, 6:3, March 1929, pp. 93, 96, 101; Dendy and Kilbourn, *Toronto Observed*, pp. 236-7.

84 W.L. Somerville, 'Recent Domestic Architecture in the Province of Ontario', *JRAIC*, 5:7, July 1928, pp. 253-68. See also Somerville, 'Is Our Domestic Architecture Mediocre?', *JRAIC*, 9:4, April 1932, pp. 97-103.

85 CUM, *Les Résidences*, pp. 540-3; H.L. Fetherstonhaugh, 'Recent Domestic Architecture in the Province of Quebec', *JRAIC*, 5:5, May 1928, p. 175. The house was enlarged and the interior renovated in 1981 by architect Moshe Safdie.

86 CUM, *Les Résidences*, pp. 272-5; Rémillard and Merrett, *Montreal Architecture*, p. 143.

87 Kalman et al., *Exploring Vancouver*, p. 176; *Canadian Homes and Gardens*, 8:3, March 1931, pp. 44-5; Janet Bingham, *Samuel Maclure Architect*, Ganges, BC: Horsdal & Schubart, 1985, p. 78, 114.

88 Kalman and Mackie, *W.E. Noffke*, pp. 14-15.

89 'Address by John M. Lyle', *JRAIC*, 6, April 1929, pp. 135-6.

90 Lyle, 'Canadian Decorative Forms', *JRAIC*, 9, March 1932, p. 70.

91 H. Allen Brooks, *The Prairie School: Frank Lloyd Wright and His Midwest Contemporaries*, Toronto: University of Toronto Press, 1972, p. 274; Trevor Boddy, *Modern Architecture in Alberta*, Edmonton: Alberta Culture and Multiculturalism and Regina: Canadian Plains Research Centre, 1987, pp. 36-40. For Sullivan, see Brooks, *Prairie School*, pp. 272-9; Martin Birkhans, 'The Life and Work of Francis C. Sullivan, Architect, 1882-1929', M.Arch. thesis, University of Toronto, 1964; Birkhans, 'Francis C. Sullivan, Architect', *JRAIC*, 39, 1962, pp. 32-6.

92 Brooks, *Prairie School*, pp. 274-6; Kalman and Roaf, *Exploring Ottawa*, p. 151.

93 Brooks, *Prairie School*, pp. 277-8.

94 For Buffington's Leistikow House (1907) on Wellington Crescent, see William Paul Thompson, *Winnipeg Architecture: 100 Years*, Winnipeg: Queenston House, 1975, p. 32. Atchison's career has been studied by Philip Haese of Winnipeg.

95 Rémillard and Merrett, *Montreal Architecture*, p. 161; CUM, *Les Édifices publics*, 1981, pp. 204-5; Paul-André Linteau, *The Promoters' City: Building the Industrial Town of Maisonneuve 1883-1918*, trans. Robert Chodos, Toronto: James Lorimer, 1985, pp. 149-50, 154.

96 *Deseret Semi-Weekly News*, 2 January 1913, cited in V.A. Wood, *The Alberta Temple: Centre and Symbol of Faith*, Calgary: Detselig Enterprises, 1989, p. 36; and *Deseret Evening News*, 19 December 1914, cited in Paul L. Anderson, 'The Early Twentieth Century Temples', *Dialogue*, 14:1, Spring 1981, p. 14. See also Paul L. Anderson, 'First of Modern Temples', *Ensign*, 7:7, July 1977, pp. 6-11; Boddy, *Modern Architecture in Alberta*, pp. 33-5; 'Alberta Temple, Cardston, Alberta: Renovation/Restoration/Addition', *Canadian Architect*, 36:10, October 1991, pp. 29-33. Paul Anderson kindly provided information on the Alberta Temple.

97 Lyle, 'Decorative Forms', p. 70.

98 Geoffrey Hunt, *John M. Lyle: Toward a Canadian Architecture / Créer une architecture canadienne*, Kingston: Agnes Etherington Art Centre, 1982, pp. 10-22.

99 Hunt, *Lyle*, pp. 102-3.

100 Hunt, *Lyle*, pp. 103-104; Kalman and Roaf, *Exploring Ottawa*, p. 20. Lyle's watercolour rendering of the Bank submitted to the RCA is in the collection of the National Gallery of Canada.

101 Lyle, 'Canadian Architecture', *JRAIC*, 4:2, Feb. 1927, p. 65.

102 Hunt, *Lyle*, pp. 105-7; Lyle, 'Recent Architecture of the Bank of Nova Scotia', *Canadian Banker*, 44:2, Jan. 1937, pp. 150-7; Boddy, *Modern Architecture in Alberta*, pp. 41-8.

103 Lyle, 'Canadian Tradition Symbolized in Nova Scotia Bank Building', *Calgary Herald*, 23 Jan. 1930; cited in Hunt, *Lyle*, p. 105.

104 Trevor Boddy, 'Regionalism, Nationalism, and Modernism: The Ideology of Decoration in the Work of John M. Lyle', *Trace*, 1:1, 1986, p. 12.

105 Lyle, 'The Bank of Nova Scotia Building, Halifax', *JRAIC*, 9:1, Jan. 1932, pp. 5-13; Hunt, *Lyle*, pp. 110-114.

106 *Halifax Star*, August 1931; cited in Hunt, *Lyle*, pp. 111-12.

107 Lyle, 'Bank of Nova Scotia'.

108 Alan Gowans, *Building Canada: An Architectural History of Canadian Life*, Toronto: Oxford University Press, 1966, pl. 199.

109 'Award in Bank of Montreal Competition', *JRAIC*, 6:11, November 1929, pp. 386-8; 'The New Bank of Montreal Building, Ottawa, Ont.', *JRAIC*, 9:9, Sept. 1932, pp. 200-7; 'Sculpture on the Bank of Montreal Building, Ottawa', *JRAIC*, 9:10, October 1932, pp. 226-9; E.R. Arthur, 'A Review of the R.A.I.C. Exhibition', *JRAIC*, 9:12, December 1932, pp. 247, 264; Susan Wagg, *Ernest Isbell Barott*, Montreal: Canadian Centre for Architecture, 1985, pp. 16-19; Kalman and Roaf, *Exploring Ottawa*, p. 10; see also *Trois Architectes, Trois Quartiers*, Montreal: Canadian Centre for Architecture, 1983; D.W. Lovell, 'Historical Metaphor and the Evolution of Architectural Style', *SSAC Bulletin*, 10:3, September 1985, pp. 8-9.

110 F.H. Marani, 'Head Office Building, Bank of Canada, Ottawa', *JRAIC*, 15:7, July 1938, pp. 153-9; 'Bank of Canada', *Canadian Architect*, 23:6, June 1978, pp. 22-37; Kalman and Roaf, *Exploring Ottawa*, p. 12.

111 H.H.K., 'The Automotive Building, Canadian National Exhibition, Toronto', *JRAIC*, 6:11, November 1929, pp. 393-407.

112 Wright, 'Building in the Bureaucracy', p. 88. See also Douglas Owram, *Building for Canadians*.

113 Wright, 'Building in the Bureaucracy', pp. 88-90.

114 Ibid., pp. 96-7.

115 Commonwealth Historic Resource Management Limited, *A History of Post Office Delivery Building Depot A, Toronto*, Perth, 1989; Margaret E. McKelvey and Merilyn McKelvey, *Toronto: Carved in Stone*, Toronto: Fitzhenry & Whiteside, 1984, pp. 48-50; Maitland et al., *Guide to Styles*, pp. 142-3.

116 Wolfville *Chronicle Herald*, 28 June 1965; cited in Wayde Brown, 'Modernism and Regionalism: Influences on the Work of Leslie Fairn', *SSAC Bulletin*, 14:1, March 1989, p. 18. See also Wright, 'Building in the Bureaucracy', p. 110.

117 'Address by John Lyle', p. 136.

118 'The Aldred Building - Montreal', *JRAIC*, 8:8, August 1931, pp. 294-307; Wagg, *Barott*, pp. 14-18; CUM, *Hotels, Immeubles de Bureaux*, pp. 6-8; Rémillard and Merrett, *Montreal Architecture*, p. 177; 'The Beaver Hall Building, Montreal', *JRAIC*, 6:10, October 1929, pp. 353-72. For Lyle's Tribune Tower entry, see Hunt, *Lyle*, pp. 94-5.

119 Henry James Morgan, ed., *The Canadian Men and Women of the Time*, 2nd ed., Toronto: William Briggs, 1912, p. 11; *The Gillette Blade*, Montreal: Gillette Safety Razor Company, 1920, p. 43. Both references were kindly provided by Susan Wagg.

120 Leonard K. Eaton, *Two Chicago Architects and Their Clients*, Cambridge: MIT Press, 1969.

121 'The Marine Building, Vancouver, B.C.', *JRAIC*, 8:7, July 1931, pp. 256-63; Kalman et al., *Exploring Vancouver*, p. 88; 'Marine Building, Vancouver: Restoration and Renovation', *Canadian Architect*, 36:10, October 1991, pp. 21-5. Stimson lost the building at the onset of the Depression and it was acquired by the Guiness interests, which retained it for about a half-century. See also Gerald Formosa, *The Pleasure of Seeing*, Vancouver: Skorba, 1982, no. 1; interview with J.Y. McCarter and W.G.

Leithead, by H. Kalman, 24 Oct. 1972, Canadian Architectural Archives, University of Calgary. The late Sir John Betjeman, British Poet Laureate and a recognized authority on early twentieth-century architecture, during a visit to Vancouver in June 1975, enthusiastically declared the Marine Building (in conversation with the author) to be the best Art Deco office building in the world.

122 McHugh, *Toronto Guide*, p. 93.

123 'The Toronto Star Building', *JRAIC*, 6:4, April 1929, pp. 143-54.

124 'The New Canadian Bank of Commerce Building, Toronto', *JRAIC*, 8:4, April 1931, pp. 132-53; Dendy and Kilbourn, *Toronto Observed*, pp. 220-3.

125 Entry by Peter L. Donhauser on Jacques Carlu in the *Macmillan Encyclopedia of Architects*, 1, p. 384.

126 'The New Restaurant in the T. Eaton Company Building, Montreal', *JRAIC*, 8:5, May 1931, pp. 181-6; Jacques Carlu, 'The T. Eaton & Co. Department Stores in Toronto and Montreal', *Architectural Record*, 69 (June 1931), pp. 446-56.

127 Carlu, 'Department Stores'; Dendy, *Lost Toronto: Images of the City's Past*, Toronto: McClelland and Stewart, 1993, pp. 201-5; David Eckler, 'The Sources for and Influence of Jacques Carlu's Eaton Auditorium, Toronto, 1930', *SSAC Bulletin*, 13:3, December 1988, pp. 9-16.

128 'The Toronto Stock Exchange', *JRAIC*, 14:4, April 1937, pp. 58-66; Dendy and Kilbourn, *Toronto Observed*, pp. 226-8.

129 Kalman et al., *Exploring Vancouver*, p. 139; Eric Nicol, *Vancouver*, Toronto: Doubleday, 1970, pp. 172-7.

130 Gordon F. Pushie, 'Confederation Building', *Atlantic Advocate*, 50, June 1960, pp. 27-34; Michael Francis Harrington, 'The Eleven-Story Mountain: A New Capital for Newfoundland', *Atlantic Advocate*, January 1959, pp. 34-3. Information from Diane Duggan, Newfoundland Department of Public Works and Services, 16 May 1988.

131 Dendy and Kilbourn, *Toronto Observed*, pp. 244-5; 'A Canadian Artist's Modern Home', *Canadian Homes and Gardens*, 8:4, April 1931, p. 40; Geoffrey Simmins, *Ontario Association of Architects: A Centennial History 1889-1989*, Toronto: Ontario Association of Architects, 1989, pp. 104-12; Blanche Lemco van Ginkel, 'Slowly and Surely (and Somewhat Painfully): More or Less the History of Women in Architecture in Canada', *SSAC Bulletin*, 17:1, March 1991, pp. 9-10.

132 Dennis Reid, *Atma Buddhi Manas: The Later Works of Lawren S. Harris*, Toronto: Art Gallery of Ontario, 1985, pp. 18-19; cited in Simmins, *Ontario Association of Architects*, p. 108.

133 Simmins, *Ontario Association of Architects*, p. 112; Dendy and Kilbourn, *Toronto Observed*, p. 245.

134 Boddy, *Modern Architecture in Alberta*, pp. 68-72; Dorothy Field, 'Architecture in Alberta: The Moderne Style', *Alberta Past*, 6:1, April 1990, pp. 1, 12; Commonwealth Historic Resource Management Limited, *Garneau Theatre: Architectural and Historical Assessment*, Vancouver, 1989.

135 Kalman et al., *Exploring Vancouver*, p. 171. Information was kindly provided by Robert G. Lemon.

136 Dendy and Kilbourn, *Toronto Observed*, pp. 246-8; 'Garden Court Apartments...', *JRAIC*, 16:11, November 1939, pp. 234-9.

137 'Ernest Cormier, Architecte et Ingénieur', *Architecture, Batiment, Construction*, 2:10, Jan. 1947, pp. 12-30; entry by Phyllis Lambert on Ernest Cormier in the *Macmillan Encyclopedia of Architects*, 1, pp. 452-3; entry by Odile Hénault on Ernest Cormier in *CE* I, 517; Isabelle Gournay, ed., *Ernest Cormier and the Université de Montréal*, Montreal: Canadian Centre for Architecture, 1990, pp. 17-42, 124-31. 'The Court House Annex, Montreal', *Construction*, 20:10, October 1927, pp. 312-27; CUM, *Les Édifices publics*, pp. 180-3. See also *Trois Architectes, Trois Quartiers*.

138 Olivier Maurault, 'The University of Montreal', *JRAIC*, 3:1, Jan.-Feb. 1926, pp. 5-11; Ernest Cormier, 'New Buildings for University of Montreal', *JRAIC*, 8:6, June 1931, pp. 248-9; Cormier, 'Les Plans de l'Université de Montréal', *Architecture, Bâtiment, Construction*, 2:10, Jan. 1947, pp. 16-30; Gournay, *Cormier*, pp. 43-115, 133-71; Rémillard and Merrett, *Montreal Architecture*, p. 176; CUM, *Les Édifices scolaires*, pp. 292-5; Isabelle Gournay, 'The 1920s and the Advent of Modernism in Montreal: Contribution by Ernest Cormier', unpublished paper, Society of Architectural Historians, Montreal, April 1989.

139 E.S. McCready, 'The Nebraka State Capitol: Its Design, Background, and Influence', *Nebraska History*, 55, Fall 1974; Frederick C. Luebke, ed., *A Harmony of the Arts: The Nebraska State Capitol*, Lincoln: University of Nebraska Press, 1990.

140 Cormier, 'New Buildings', p. 248.

141 'Residence of Ernest Cormier, Esq.', *JRAIC*, 9:7, July 1932, pp. 158-64; Odile Hénault and Larry Richards, 'Cormier House', *Trace*, 1:1, 1980, pp. 25-33; Rémillard and Merrett, *Montreal Architecture*, p. 179. CUM, *Les Résidences*, p. 150.

142 Susan Bronson, 'Cormier's Seaplane Hangar: A North American Prototype', unpublished paper, Society of Architectural Historians, Montreal, April 1989; Gournay, *Cormier*, p. 26.

Chapter 15 **Modern Architecture and Beyond**

1 Henry-Russell Hitchcock and Philip Johnson, *The International Style: Architecture Since 1922*, New York, W.W. Norton, 1932; reprinted with addenda as *The International Style*, New York: W.W. Norton, 1966.

2 Percy E. Nobbs, 'Present Tendencies Affecting Architecture in Canada', Part 3, *JRAIC*, 7:11, November 1930, pp. 391-2.

3 Alexander F. Gross, 'Witness to the Passing of Victorian Architecture—the RAIC *Journal*, 1924-1935', *SSAC Bulletin*, 12:1, June 1987, pp. 9-14. Gross's modernist biases are not fully corroborated by the articles he cites.

4 *Canadian Railway and Marine World*, 418, December 1932, p. 627, cited in Shannon Ricketts, 'The Former Toronto, Hamilton and Buffalo Railway Station, Hamilton, Ontario', Railway Station Report, *Report* RSR-21, Historic Sites and Monuments Board of Canada, Ottawa, n.d., p. 9.

See also 'Toronto, Hamilton & Buffalo Railway Station, Hamilton, Ontario', *American Architect and Architecture*, July 1933; 'Toronto, Hamilton and Buffalo Railway Station, Hamilton', *Construction*, 26, September-October 1933, pp. 106-8, 112-17. Fellheimer and Wagner's unexecuted Art Deco scheme of 1930 is illustrated in Norman S. Helm, *In the Shadow of the Giants: The Story of the Toronto, Hamilton and Buffalo Railway*, Cheltenham, Ontario: Boston Mills, 1978, p. 118. For Fellheimer and Wagner's Buffalo and New York stations, see Carroll L.V. Meeks, *The Railroad Station*, New Haven: Yale University Press, 1956, p. 130, n. 28; p. 157; and fig. 219. The Bauhaus and PSFS Building are widely illustrated; see, for example, William H. Jordy, *American Buildings and their Architects: The Impact of European Modernism in the Mid-Twentieth Century*, IV, rev. ed., New York: Anchor Books, 1976, pp. 89, 132.

5 W.M. Shaw, 'Steel—A Permanent Finish', *Construction*, 26, September-October 1933, n.p; cited in Ricketts, 'Toronto, Hamilton and Buffalo Railway Station', p. 8.

6 B. Evan Parry, 'Review of the Recent Exhibition of Hospital Architecture Held in Toronto', *JRAIC*, 8:12, December 1931, pp. 423-4; *JRAIC*, 13:6, June 1936, pp. 120-1.

7 A.S. Mathers, 'The William H. Wright Building', *JRAIC*, 15:8, August 1938, pp. 173-8.

8 'Canada Packers Plant at Edmonton', *JRAIC*, 14:8, August 1937, pp. 158-60.

9 Adele Freedman, *Sight Lines: Looking at Architecture and Design in Canada*, Toronto: Oxford University Press, 1990, pp. 39-41.

10 Luc Noppen, Claude Paulette, and Michel Tremblay, *Québec: trois siècles d'architecture*, Quebec: Libre Expression, 1979, pp. 98-9; Claude Bergeron, *Architectures du XXᵉ siècle au Québec*, Montreal: Méridien, 1989, pp. 141-2.

11 M.-A. Couturier, *Marcel Parizeau*, Montreal: L'Arbre, 1945; 'House of Mr. and Mrs. Paul Laroque, Outremont', *JRAIC*, 16:9, 1939, pp. 202-3; CUM (Répertoire d'architecture traditionnelle sur le territoire de la communauté urbaine de Montréal), *Résidences*, pp. 414-15; *Canadian Homes and Gardens*, 19:9, September 1942, p. 24; Claude Beaulieu, *L'Architecture contemporaine au Canada français*, Quebec: Ministère des affaires culturelles, 1969, p. 82; France Vanlaethem, 'Le Patrimoine de la modernité', *Continuité*, 53, Spring 1992, p. 21; Dennis Reid, *A Concise History of Canadian Painting*, 2nd ed., Toronto: Oxford University Press, 1988, pp. 217, 289.

12 CUM, *Résidences*, pp. 392-4; *Canadian Homes and Gardens*, 10:9, September 1933, pp. 32-5. See also Claude Bergeron, 'Developments in Architecture in Canada', in Warren Sanderson, ed., *International Handbook of Contemporary Developments in Architecture*, Westport, Conn., and London: Greenwood Press, 1981, pp. 176-7.

13 Bruce Macdonald, *Vancouver: A Visual History*, Vancouver: Talonbooks, 1992; Patricia Roy, *Vancouver: An Illustrated History*, Toronto: Lorimer, 1980.

14 Harold Kalman, Ron Phillips, and Robin Ward, *Exploring Vancouver: The Essential Architectural Guide*, Vancouver: UBC Press, 1993, p. 159. Little has been written on Van Norman; one source is an unpublished sketch of the man and his career, compiled by Sean Rossiter for a public discussion sponsored by the Urbanarium Development Society on 10 February 1993. See also Abraham Rogatnick, 'Everything Was Up-to-Date in the 1930's', in *Vancouver: Art and Artists, 1931-1983*, Vancouver: Vancouver Art Gallery, 1983, pp. 42-8.

15 Ruby Nobbs, *Revelstoke B.C. Heritage Walking & Driving Tour*, Revelstoke, n.d.

16 Adele Freedman, 'A Pioneer Spirit', *Globe and Mail*, 1 February 1992, p. C6. See also Christina Cameron and Michael McMordie's entry, 'Architecture, Development of', in the *Canadian Encyclopedia*, 2nd ed., Edmonton: Hurtig, 1988, I, p. 104; Kalman et al., *Exploring Vancouver*, p. 244; Douglas Shadbolt, 'Postwar Architecture in Vancouver', in *Vancouver: Art and Artists*, pp. 108-9.

17 Adele Freedman, *Sight Lines*, p. 43.

18 Harold Kalman and John Roaf, *Exploring Vancouver 2: Ten Tours of the City and its Buildings*, Vancouver: University of British Columbia Press, 1978, p. 249.

19 Sean Rossiter, 'The Firm That Built the Town', *Vancouver*, September 1983, pp. 42-52, 125-6; entry by Michael McMordie on Thompson, Berwick, Pratt and Partners, *CE* IV, p. 2151; Harold Kalman, interview with Robert Berwick and C.E. Pratt, 29 June 1973, Canadian Architectural Archives, University of Calgary. These Archives hold a large collection of drawings from the practice of Thompson, Berwick, Pratt and Partners.

20 C.E. Pratt, 'Contemporary Domestic Architecture in British Columbia', *JRAIC*, 24:6, June 1947, pp. 179-98; Kalman and Roaf, *Exploring Vancouver 2*, p. 249.

21 Kalman and Roaf, *Exploring Vancouver 2*, pp. 239, 244, 248-9.

22 Mann and Downs are cited in Eleanor Wachtel, 'Ron Thom', *Western Living*, November 1984, pp. 36g-36p. See also Kalman and Roaf, *Exploring Vancouver 2*, p. 202.

23 Kalman and Roaf, *Exploring Vancouver 2*, p. 95.

24 'A Tower Built like a Tree', *Architectural Forum*, 197:1, July 1957, pp. 106-13; 'B.C. Electric Head office, Vancouver, B.C.', *Canadian Architect*, 2:4, April 1957, pp. 27-36; Kalman et al., *Exploring Vancouver*, pp. 76, 62; Adele Freedman, 'Traditions Begin With Thoughts of Heritage', *Globe and Mail*, 21 August 1993, p. C2.

25 Commonwealth Historic Resource Management Limited, *History and Evaluation of Vancouver Public Library*, prepared for The Dominion Company, Vancouver, 1992; Kalman et al., *Exploring Vancouver*, p. 91. See Douglas Simpson, 'Towards Regionalism in Canadian Architecture', *Canadian Art*, Spring 1953, pp. 110-13.

26 Kalman, *Exploring Vancouver 2*, p. 107; Kalman et al., *Exploring Vancouver*, p. 91.

27 Kalman and Roaf, *Exploring Vancouver 2*, p. 110; Kalman et al., *Exploring Vancouver*, pp. 91, 159, 146. Many architectural records from the office of McCarter and Nairne are held in the Canadian Architectural Archives at the University of Calgary. See also H. Kalman's interview with J.Y. McCarter and W.G. Leithead, 24 October 1972, Canadian Architectural Archives, University of Calgary.

28 'Simon Fraser University, Burnaby, B.C.', *Canadian Architect*, 11:2, February 1966, pp. 35-71; 'Simon Fraser University, British Columbia', *Architectural Review*, 143, April 1968, pp. 262-75; Carol Moore Ede, *Canadian Architecture, 1960/70*, Toronto: Burns and MacEachern, 1971, pp. 36-45; Leon Whiteson, *Modern Canadian Architecture*, Edmonton: Hurtig, 1983, pp. 24-7; Arthur Erickson, 'The University: The New Visual Environment', *Canadian*

Architect 13:1, January 1968, pp. 24-37; Kalman et al., *Exploring Vancouver*, pp. 216-17; Donlyn Lyndon, 'Single-Guilding Campus', *Architectural Forum*, 123:5, December 1965, pp. 13-21, 72. See also Edith Iglauer, *Seven Stones: A Portrait of Arthur Erickson, Architect*, Madeira Park, BC: Harbour, 1981; Arthur Erickson, *The Architecture of Arthur Erickson*, Montreal: Tundra Books, 1975, pp. 129-55; Arthur Erickson, *The Architecture of Arthur Erickson*, Vancouver: Douglas & McIntyre, 1988; Jill Wade, compiler, *A Bibliography of Literature on Arthur C. Erickson*, Winnipeg: University of Manitoba Libraries, 1973.

29 Arthur C. Erickson, 'The Architectural Concept', *Canadian Architecture*, 11:2, February 1966, p. 41.

30 Adele Freedman, 'A Man With a Past Looks to the Future', *Globe and Mail*, Toronto, 1 August 1992, p. C3.

31 Erickson, *Architecture*, pp. 79-87; Ede, *Canadian Architecture*, pp. 228-37; Whiteson, *Modern Canadian Architecture*, pp. 28-31; Kalman et al., *Exploring Vancouver*, p. 247.

32 'Museum of Anthropology, Vancouver', *Canadian Architect*, 22:5, May 1977, pp. 54-62; Whiteson, *Modern Canadian Architecture*, pp. 32-5; Cawker and Bernstein, *Contemporary Canadian Architecture*, pp. 145-9; Kalman et al., *Exploring Vancouver*, p. 190; 'Museum of Anthropology Vancouver', *Architectural Review*, 167:999, May 1980, p. 328.

33 Macy DuBois, 'Erickson', *Canadian Architect*, 19:11, November 1974, pp. 32-8; 'Canadian Pavilion, Expo 70', *Canadian Architect*, 15:7, July 1970, pp. 48-53; Whiteson, *Modern Canadian Architecture*, pp. 36-9; Ruth Cawker and William Bernstein, *Contemporary Canadian Architecture: The Mainstream and Beyond*, rev. ed., Markham: Fitzhenry and Whiteside, 1988, pp. 103-8 (Robson Square); Kalman et al., *Exploring Vancouver*, pp. 76, 90.

34 Dendy and Kilbourn, *Toronto Observed: Its Architecture, Patrons, and History*, Toronto: Oxford University Press, 1986, pp. 308-11.

35 Trevor Boddy, 'Erickson in Washington', *Canadian Architect*, 34:7, July 1989, pp. 24-37; Erickson, *Architecture of Arthur Erickson* (1988), pp. 212-17.

36 Ede, *Canadian Architecture*, pp. 238-45; Kalman and Roaf, *Exploring Vancouver 2*, p. 247.

37 'North Vancouver Civic Centre', *Canadian Architect*, 21:10, October 1976, pp. 40-5; Cawker and Bernstein, *Contemporary Canadian Architecture*, pp. 124-9.

38 Cited in Anthony Jackson, *The Future of Canadian Architecture*, Halifax: Nova Scotia Technical College, 1979, p. 29.

39 See Michael McMordie's entries on John Burnett Parkin and John Cresswell Parkin in *CE* III, p. 1615; Adele Freedman, *Sight Lines*, pp. 92-6.

40 'Ontario Association of Architects' New Building', *JRAIC*, 31:12, December 1954, pp. 450-4; 'Clubhouse for Canadian Architects', *Architectural Forum*, April 1955, pp. 148-51; Bill Brown and Paul Rockett, 'Architects Build a Home of Their Own', *Weekend Magazine*, 5:35, 1955, pp. 10-13. Geoffrey Simmins, *Ontario Association of Architects: A Centennial History 1889-1989*, Toronto: Ontario Association of Architects, 1989, pp. 129-36.

41 Arthur's role is recognized by John Bland in Pierre Mayrand and John Bland, *Three Centuries of Architecture in Canada*, Montreal: Federal Publications Service—Georges Le Pape, 1971, p. 117.

42 'Factory & Offices for Ortho Pharmaceutical', *Canadian Architect*, 1:7, July 1956, pp. 23-36; Bureau of Architecture and Urbanism, *Toronto Modern Architecture 1945 1965*, Toronto: Coach House Press, 1987, pp. 55-9;

43 John C. Parkin, 'Modern Architecture in Ontario', in Whiteson, *Modern Canadian Architecture*, p. 122.

44 'Toronto Airport Terminal Buildings', *JRAIC*, 35:6, June 1958, pp. 236-7; 'Toronto International Airport', *Canadian Architect*, 9:2, February 1964, pp. 41-68; *Canadian Architect Yearbook*, 1964, pp. 54-5; 'Massey Medals for Architecture 1964', *JRAIC*, 1964, pp. 67-8, 71.

45 Jordy, *American Buildings*, 4, p. 232; see pp. 228-77.

46 John Jacobus, *Twentieth-Century Architecture: The Middle Years 1940-65*, New York: Praeger, 1966, p. 102.

47 Macy DuBois, 'Toronto-Dominion Centre: A Critique', *Canadian Architect*, 12, November 1967, pp. 33-4; Bureau of Architecture and Urbanism, *Toronto Modern*, pp. 24-5, 72-7; Michael McMordie, 'Modern Monuments', *Canadian Forum*, 68:681, May 1978, p. 28; William Dendy and William Kilbourn, *Toronto Observed*, pp. 276-9; McHugh, *Toronto Architecture*, p. 96.

48 Macy DuBois, 'Toronto-Dominion Centre', pp. 33-4; emphasis mine.

49 'Commerce Court, Toronto', *Canadian Architect*, 18:3, March 1973, pp. 48-60; Dendy and Kilbourn, *Toronto Observed*, pp. 280-1; Cawker and Bernstein, *Contemporary Canadian Architecture*, pp. 119-23; McHugh, *Toronto Architecture*, pp. 96-7.

50 Entry by Alix Granger on 'Banking', *CE* I, p. 174.

51 Peter Blake, *The Master Builders: Le Corbusier, Mies van der Rohe, Frank Lloyd Wright*, New York: Alfred A. Knopf, 1961, pp. 249-52.

52 'C.I.L. House, Montreal', *Canadian Architect*, 7:6, June 1962, pp. 53-63; Jean-Claude Marsan, *Montreal in Evolution*, Montreal: McGill-Queen's University Press, 1981, pp. 348-51; Norbert Schoenauer, *Architecture Montreal*, Montreal: Province of Quebec Association of Architects, 1967, no. 22; Claude Beaulieu, *L'Architecture contemporaine au Canada français*, Quebec: Ministère des Affaires culturelles, 1969, p. 16; author's conversation with Michael Dunne, July 1960. See also Denys Marchand, 'La Conquête du ciel', *Continuité*, 53, Spring 1992, pp. 7-13.

53 Ray Affleck et al., 'Place Ville Marie', *JRAIC*, 40:2, February 1963, pp. 47-68; 'Place Ville Marie', *Architectural Forum*, 118:2, February 1963, pp. 74-89; Norbert Schoenauer, 'Place Ville Marie: Critique One', *Canadian Architect*, 8:2, February 1963, p. 57; Marsan, *Montreal*, pp. 346-8; Beaulieu, *L'Architecture contemporaine*, pp. 60-1; Schoenauer, *Architecture Montreal*, no. 21; Bergeron, *Architectures du XXe siècle*, pp. 194-5; Bergeron, 'Developments in Architecture in Canada', in Sanderson, *International Handbook*, pp. 186-7; Judith S. Hull's entry on I.M. Pei in Adolf K. Placzek, ed., *Macmillan Encyclopedia of Architects*, 3, New York: Free Press, 1982, pp. 384-6. For overviews of skyscraper development in Montreal and the underground city, see Denys Marchand, 'La Conquête du ciel', Yves Deschamps, 'Megacity Montreal', and David Brown, 'La Ville intérieure'—all in *Continuité*, 53, Spring 1992, pp. 7-

13, 23-6, 27-30 respectively. See also Fred F. Angus, 'The Fiftieth Anniversary of Central Station', *Canadian Rail*, 435, July-August 1993, pp. 134-43; 'The Queen Elizabeth Hotel', *JRAIC*, 35:7, July 1958, pp. 246-54.

54 'Place Victoria, Montreal', *Canadian Architect*, 10:7, July 1965, pp. 37-54; Marsan, *Montreal*, pp. 351-3; Schoenauer, *Architecture Montreal*, no. 24.

55 Freedman, *Sight Lines*, pp. 1-31.

56 Dendy and Kilbourn, *Toronto Observed*, pp. 206-7; Freedman, *Sight Lines*, pp. 7-9, 30; Bureau of Architecture and Urbanism, *Toronto Modern*, pp. 60-1.

57 Freedman, *Sight Lines*, pp. 22-6; Schoenauer, *Architecture Montreal*, no. 29; Marsan, *Montreal in Evolution*, p. 351.

58 Freedman, *Sight Lines*, pp. 20-2.

59 'Toronto City Hall and Square Competition', *JRAIC*, 35:10, October 1958, pp. 359-85; 'Toronto City Hall and Civic Square', *Canadian Architect*, 10:10, October 1965, pp. 45-68; Bureau of Architecture and Urbanism, *Toronto Modern*, pp. 23-4, 78-83; Dendy and Kilbourn, *Toronto Observed*, pp. 266-71; 'Singular Symbol for Toronto', *Architectural Forum*, 123:4, November 1965, pp. 15-23; Simmins, *Ontario Association of Architects*, pp. 137-46.

60 James A. Murray, in *Canadian Architect*, special issue, 1980, p. 27.

61 R.J. Thom, 'Toronto City Hall: A Critique, *Canadian Architect*, 10:10, October 1965, p. 59. For an analysis of Nathan Phillips Square, the plaza of Toronto-Dominion Centre, and other open spaces in downtown Toronto, see Detlef Mertins, ed., *Metropolitan Mutations: The Architecture of Emerging Public Spaces*, RAIC Annual 1, Toronto: Little, Brown and Company, [1989,] pp. 41-56.

62 Trevor Boddy, *Modern Architecture in Alberta*, Edmonton: Alberta Culture and Multiculturalism, and Regina: Canadian Plains Research Centre, 1987, pp. 76-9.

63 Ibid., pp. 66-7, 81-2.

64 'Edmonton City Hall', *JRAIC*, 35:5, May 1958, pp. 165-7; Boddy, *Modern Architecture in Alberta*, pp. 83-4; Edmonton Historical Board, *Evaluation of the Heritage Building List...*, Edmonton: City of Edmonton, 1982, pp. 10-11. The new City Hall is reviewed in John Bentley Mays, 'High Civic Moment', *Globe and Mail*, 2 October 1993, p. C7.

65 'Ottawa City Hall', *JRAIC*, 35:9, September 1958, pp. 323-30; Harold Kalman and John Roaf, *Exploring Ottawa*, Toronto: University of Toronto Press, 1983, p. 122.

66 Humphrey Carver, *The Cultural Landscape of Rockcliffe Park Village*, Village of Rockcliffe Park, 1985, p. 62; 'Hart Massey House, Ottawa', *Canadian Architect*, 8:9, September 1963, pp. 41-6; Kalman and Roaf, *Exploring Ottawa*, p. 136. The Farnsworth and Johnson houses are discussed and illustrated in Jacobus, *Twentieth-Century Architecture*, pp. 78, 122-3.

67 Illustrated and discussed in Erna Dominey, 'Wallbridge and Imrie: The Architectural Practice of Two Edmonton Women, 1950-1979', *SSAC Bulletin*, 17:1, March 1991, pp. 12-18. Erna Dominey kindly provided material on the firm in advance of publication.

68 William Paul Thompson, *Winnipeg Architecture 100 Years*, Winnipeg: Queenston House, 1975, pp. 47, 66.

69 Charles A. Jencks, *Late-Modern Architecture and Other Essays*, New York: Rizzoli, 1980.

70 Kalman et al., *Exploring Vancouver*, p. 114. Peter Cardew kindly provided information.

71 Barton Myers, 'Wolf Residence', *Canadian Architect*, 21:10, October 1976, pp. 28-33.

72 'Citadel Theatre, Edmonton', *Canadian Architect*, 22:7, July 1977, pp. 18-27; Michael McMordie, 'The Citadel Theatre', *Canadian Forum*, 58, October-November 1978, pp. 33-5; Whiteson, *Modern Canadian Architecture*, pp. 78-81; Cawker and Bernstein, *Contemporary Canadian Architecture*, pp. 172-9; Boddy, *Modern Architecture in Alberta*, pp. 105-7.

73 Vincent Massey, memorandum, 1960; cited in Ede, *Canadian Architecture*, pp. 10-23; 'Massey College', *Canadian Architect*, 8:10, October 1963, pp. 47-62; Dendy and Kilbourn, *Toronto Observed*, pp. 272-5; Bureau of Architecture and Urbanism, *Toronto Modern*, pp. 29, 68-71.

74 Cited, without revealing the author, in *Toronto Modern*, p. 29.

75 Ede, *Canadian Architecture*, pp. 46-57; Whiteson, *Modern Canadian Architecture*, pp. 128-31; 'Champlain College, Trent University', *Canadian Architect*, 12:12, December 1967, pp. 28-38; 'Thomas J. Bata Library, Trent University, Peterborough, Ontario', *Canadian Architect*, 16:8, August 1971, pp. 50-2.

76 'Shaw Festival Theatre, Niagara-on-the-Lake', *Canadian Architect*, 19:1, January 1974, pp. 20-8; 'Progress Report: Metro Toronto Zoo', *Canadian Architect*, 19:10, October 1974, pp. 41-53.

77 Peter Hemingway, 'Prairie Architecture: An Introduction', in Whiteson, *Modern Canadian Architecture*, p. 69.

78 Trevor Boddy, 'Ethnic Identity and Contemporary Canadian Architecture', *Canadian Ethnic Studies*, 16:3, 1984, pp. 6-7.

79 Ede, *Canadian Architecture*, p. 261.

80 Ede, *Canadian Architecture*, pp. 190-7; Whiteson, *Modern Canadian Architecture*, pp. 98-101; Étienne J. Gaboury, 'Design for Worship', *Canadian Architect*, 13:13, March 1968, pp. 33-42; Brenlee Werner, 'Three Churches by Etienne Gaboury', *Canadian Interiors*, 6:10, October 1969, pp. 28-32; 'Church of the Precious Blood St Boniface', *Architectural Review*, 167:999, May 1980, p. 317; 'Canadian Architecture: Out on the Plains', *Progressive Architecture*, 53, September 1972, pp. 126-9; Étienne Gaboury, 'Towards a Prairie Architecture', *Prairie Forum*, 5:2, Fall 1980, pp. 237-8; William Bernstein and Ruth Cawker, *Building with Words: Canadian Architects on Architecture*, Toronto: Coach House Press, 1981, pp. 52-3.

81 Boddy, 'Ethnic Identity', pp. 7-8; Cawker and Bernstein, *Contemporary Canadian Architecture*, pp. 134-9.

82 Boddy, 'Ethnic Identity', p. 9.

83 Cited in Whiteson, *Modern Canadian Architecture*, pp. 90-3.

84 Whiteson, *Modern Canadian Architecture*, pp. 74-7; 'Muttart Conservatory, Edmonton', *Architectural Review*, 167:999, May 1980, p. 316.

85 'Winnipeg Art Gallery', *Canadian Architect*, 17:7, July 1972, pp. 24-35.

86 Pierre Guimond and Brian Sinclair, *Calgary Architecture: The Boom Years 1972-1982*, Calgary: Detselig Enterprises, 1984, pp. 122-3; 'Ukrainian Churches', *Domus*, 654, October 1984, pp. 26-8.

87 Freedman, *Sight Lines*, p. 49.

88 Trevor Boddy, *The Architecture of Douglas Cardinal*, Edmonton: NeWest Press, 1989, p. 17.

89 Boddy, *Cardinal*, pp. 30-43; Ede, *Canadian Architecture*, pp. 198-205; Whiteson, *Modern Canadian Architecture*, pp. 70-3—Cardinal is quoted on p. 71.

90 Cited in Freedman, *Sight Lines*, p. 50.

91 Boddy, *Cardinal*, pp. 53-71; Peter Hemingway, 'Critique: Two Buildings by Douglas Cardinal', *Canadian Architect*, 23:2, February 1978, pp. 18-23; 'Grande Prairie Regional College, Alberta', *Canadian Architect Yearbook*, 1972, not paginated; Cawker and Bernstein, *Contemporary Canadian Architecture*, pp. 130-3; 'Douglas Cardinal: Le Centre civique et culturel de St-Albert, Alberta', *ARQ: Architecture Québec*, 14, August 1983, pp. 24-5.

92 Cited in Boddy, *Cardinal*, p. 126.

93 [Douglas Cardinal,] 'Canadian Museum of Civilization: Descriptive Notes', circulated by the Canadian Museum of Civilization, 1989; see also Boddy, *Cardinal*, pp. 82-105; Pierre Beaupré, 'Le Musée de l'Homme', and Cardinal, 'National Museum of Man', *ARQ: Architecture Québec*, 17, February 1984, pp. 24-9.

94 Geoffrey Simmins, 'Home at Last', *Rotunda*, 21:1, Summer 1988, pp. 44-53; Jean Sutherland Boggs, 'The New National Gallery of Canada', *Apollo*, 127:315, May 1988, pp. 306-10; Larry Richards, 'Ottawa's Crystal Palace', *Canadian Art*, 5:2, June 1988, pp. 50-9.

95 Claude Bergeron, *L'Architecture des églises du Québec*, Quebec City: Les Presses de l'Université Laval, 1989, pp. 252-5; Claude Bergeron, 'L'Architecture religieuse et le modernisme international, 1945-1955', in *Architectures. la culture dans l'espace*, Questions de culture, 4, Ottawa: Éditions Leméac, 1983, pp. 125-7.

96 Laurent Lamy and Jean-Claude Hurni, *Architecture contemporaine au Québec, 1960-1970*, Montreal: L'Hexagone, 1983, pp. 42-5; Bergeron, *L'Architecture des églises*, pp. 92-3.

97 Marsan, *Montreal*, p. 355; Schoenauer, *Architecture Montreal*, no. 27.

98 Claude Bergeron, 'Le Modernisme venu du Nord: les églises du Saguenay—Lac-Saint-Jean', *SSAC Bulletin*, 13:3, 1988, pp. 15-17; Claude Bergeron, *L'Architecture des Églises*, pp. 286-9; Beaulieu, *L'Architecture contemporaine*, p. 63.

99 Bergeron, *Églises*, pp. 246-51; Bergeron, 'Le Modernisme', pp. 14-15.

100 Paul Gauthier and François Giraldeau, 'Profiles d'architects d'aujourd'hui: Jean-Marie Roy', *ARQ: Architecture Québec*, 36, April 1987, pp. 20-35.

101 Melvin Charney, 'Modern Movements in French-Canadian Architecture', *Process Architecture*, 5, Tokyo, 1978, pp. 15-26; reprinted in Geoffrey Simmins, ed., *Documents in Canadian Architecture*, Peterborough: Broadview Press, 1992, pp. 74-6.

102 Ede, *Canadian Architecture*, pp. 104-13; Prince Edward Island Centennial Committee, 'The Nation's Tribute: The Fathers of Confederation Memorial Building', in *Confederation Conference Centennial, Prince Edward Island 1964*, Fredericton: Unipress, 1964, pp. 79-85.

103 Robert Fulford, *This Was Expo*, Toronto: McClelland and Stewart, 1968; I. Kalin, *Expo '67: Survey of Building Materials, Systems and Techniques Used at the Universal and International Exhibition of 1967*, Ottawa: Queen's Printer, 1969; Edouard Fiset, 'Expo '67: Design Preview', *Canadian Architect Yearbook*, 1965, pp. 89-96; Marsan, *Montreal*, pp. 364-70; Cawker and Bernstein, *Contemporary Canadian Architecture*, pp. 13-18; Beaulieu, *L'Architecture contemporaine*, pp. 88-91.

104 'Habitat 67', *Canadian Architect*, 12:10, October 1967, pp. 31-49; Moshe Safdie, *Beyond Habitat*, ed. by John Kettle, Montreal: Tundra, 1970; Ede, *Canadian Architecture*, pp. 218-27; Whiteson, *Modern Canadian Architecture*, pp. 218-21.

105 Pierre Beaupré. 'D'une station à l'autre', *ARQ: Architecture Québec*, 3, September-October 1981, pp. 10-25; Émilie d'Orgeix, 'Le Métro: un rêve magnifique', *Continuité*, 53, Spring 1992, pp. 14-18; Marsan, *Montreal*, pp. 358-64.

106 'Olympic Stadiums', *Canadian Architect*, 21:9, September 1976, pp. 32-60; Luc Noppen, 'Le Stade Olympique', *Continuité*, 53, Spring 1992, pp. 31-4.

107 'Place Bonaventure', *Canadian Architect*, 12:9, September 1967, pp. 41-66; Ede, *Canadian Architecture*, pp. 124-35; Whiteson, *Modern Canadian Architecture*, pp. 214-17; Marsan, *Montreal*, pp. 353-5; Beaulieu, *L'Architecture contemporaine*, pp. 84-5. For Affleck, see John Bland et al., 'Profiles d'architectes d'aujourd'hui: Raymond T. Affleck', *ARQ: Architecture Québec*, 34, December 1986, pp. 10-23.

108 Jane Jacobs, *The Death and Life of Great American Cities*, New York: Random House, 1963; see also Adele Freedman, *Sight Lines*, pp. 51-5.

109 E.G. Faludi, 'The Trend in Shopping Centres', *JRAIC*, 26:9, September 1949, pp. 267-79; entry by Dennis Doordan on Faludi in the *Macmillan Encyclopedia of Architects*, 2, p. 39. Some early American shopping centres are described in Richard Longstreth, 'The Neighborhood Shopping Center in Washington, D.C., 1930-1941', *JSAH*, 51:1, March 1992, pp. 5-34.

110 Entry by Harold Kalman on 'Shopping Centres' in *CE* III, pp. 1995-6; Kalman and Roaf, *Exploring Vancouver*, p. 252; Meredith L. Clausen, 'Northgate Regional Shopping Center—Paradigm from the Provinces', *JSAH*, 43:2, May 1984, pp. 144-61. For Maxwell Kalman's early shopping centres, see Bergeron, *Architectures*, pp. 158-60. See also John Barber, 'Courting Commerce', *Equinox*, 54, November-December 1990, pp. 70-84; David Lasker, 'Main Street Modern', *Ontario Living*, March 1986, pp. 26ff; William Severini Kowinski, *The Malling of America: An Inside Look at the Great Consumer Paradise*, New York: William Morrow, 1985.

111 Ian Martin, 'Le Centre d'achats Rockland, à Ville Mont-Royal', *Architecture-Bâtiment-Construction*, December 1959, pp. 28-33; Bergeron, *Architectures*, pp. 159-60. Ian Martin and Maxwell Kalman shared an office during the 1950s, although they were never partners.

112 Victor Gruen, *Centers for the Urban Environment*, New York: Van Nostrand, 1973, p. 33; cited in Anthony Jackson, *Space in Canadian Architecture*, Halifax: Technical University of Nova Scotia, 1981, p. 7.

113 Michael Hugo-Brunt, 'Yorkdale Shopping Centre, a Study', *JRAIC*, 41:6, June 1964, pp. 38-47; also further articles on pp. 48-54.

114 Peter Hemingway, 'The Joy of Kitsch', *Canadian Architect*, 31:3, March 1986, pp. 32-5; Mertins, *Metropolitan Mutations*, pp. 97-100; Marylu Walters, 'Rubin Stahl and the Monster Mall', *Edmonton*, May 1984, pp. 21-4; material provided by West Edmonton Mall Promotions Ltd.

115 'Royal Bank Plaza, Toronto', *Canadian Architect*, 22:4, April 1977, pp. 38-53; Whiteson, *Modern Canadian Architecture*, pp. 184-7; Dendy and Kilbourn, *Toronto Observed*, pp. 282-5.

116 David Lasker, 'A Towering Presence', *Report on Business*, 3:2, August 1986, pp. 52-6; Freedman, *Sight Lines*, p. 29; Robert Gretton, 'WZM', *Canadian Architect*, 16:5, May 1971, pp. 50-3.

117 Guimond and Sinclair, *Calgary Architecture*, pp. 40-1.

118 'Calgary's Plus 15', *Architectural Review*, 167:999, May 1980, pp. 310-12; Cawker and Bernstein, *Contemporary Canadian Architecture*, pp. 89-95; Guimond and Sinclair, *Calgary Architecture*, pp. 6-7; Harold Hanen, 'Multi-Level Choreography', in Mertins, ed., *Metropolitan Mutations*, pp. 71-80.

119 Peter Collymore, 'New Atria of Canada', *Architectural Review*, 167:999, May 1980, pp. 273-85.

120 'The Toronto Eaton Centre', *Canadian Architect*, 22:5, May 1977, pp. 30-50; 'The Toronto Eaton Centre: Phase II', *Canadian Architect*, 24:11, November 1979, pp. 24-31; Whiteson, *Modern Canadian Architecture*, pp. 164-7; Cawker and Bernstein, *Contemporary Canadian Architecture*, pp. 109-14.

121 *Canadian Architect*, special issue, 1980. For Zeidler, see Robert Fulford, 'The Rise and Fall of Modern Architecture', *Saturday Night*, 95:10, December 1980, pp. 23-31.

122 Nikolaus Pevsner, *A History of Building Types*, London: Thames and Hudson, 1976, pp. 261-5; Johann Friedrich Geist, *Arcades: The History of a Building Type*, Cambridge, Mass.: MIT Press, 1983.

123 Mertins, *Metropolitan Mutations*, p. 42.

124 Kalman et al., *Exploring Vancouver*, p. 88; for the other buildings at Expo 86, see Andreas Schroeder, 'A Peek at Expo 86', *Canadian Geographic*, 105:6, December 1985-January 1986, pp. 8-19; Peter Prangnell, 'Expo 86: A Misconceived Midway', *Canadian Architect*, 31:7, July 1986, pp. 20-31.

125 Peter Collymore, 'New Atria of Canada', *Architectural Review*, 167:999, May 1980, p. 285.

126 Boddy, *Modern Architecture*, p. 105-6, 126; Whiteson, *Modern Canadian Architecture*, pp. 82-5; *Architectural Review*, 167: 999, May 1980, p. 285.

127 Whiteson, *Modern Canadian Architecture*, pp. 168-71; Peter Pragnell, 'Scarborough Civic Centre, Ontario', *Canadian Architect*, 18:11, November 1973, pp. 23-47.

128 'Metropolitan Toronto Library', *Canadian Architect*, 23:1, January 1978, pp. 20-9; Dendy and Kilbourn, *Toronto Observed*, pp. 288-90; McHugh, *Toronto Architecture*, p. 80.

129 Quotations from Cawker and Bernstein, *Contemporary Canadian Architecture*, pp. 115-18; see also *Architectural Review*, 167:999, May 1980, p. 277; Bergeron, *Architectures*, pp. 246-7; Wolfe and Grenier, *Montreal Guide*, p. 180.

130 In addition to the catalogue, the exhibition produced a large, scholarly text: Arthur Drexler, ed., *The Architecture of the École des Beaux-Arts*, New York: Museum of Modern Art, 1977. The National Gallery produced the same catalogue and a narrated slide show, 'The École des Beaux-Arts and Canadian Architecture', by Harold Kalman (1976).

131 Bernstein and Cawker, *Building with Words*, p. 84.

132 Robert Venturi, *Complexity and Contradiction in Architecture*, New York: Museum of Modern Art, 1966; Robert Venturi, Denise Scott Brown, and Steven Izenour, *Learning from Los Vegas*, 2nd ed., Cambridge: MIT Press, 1977; Charles Jencks and George Baird, eds, *Meaning in Architecture*, London: Barrie and Rockliff, 1969; Charles A. Jencks, *The Language of Post-Modern Architecture*, 4th ed., New York: Rizzoli, 1984; Anthony Jackson, *The Democratization of Canadian Architecture*, Halifax: Tech-Press, 1978; Anthony Jackson, *The Future of Canadian Architecture*, Halifax: Tech-Press, 1979; Anthony Jackson, *Space in Canadian Architecture*, Bedford, NS: Technical University of Nova Scotia, 1981; Tom Wolfe, *From Bauhaus to Our House*, New York: Farrar, Straus and Giroux, 1981.

133 'Maison Bradley', *ARQ: Architecture Québec*, 9, October 1982, p. 16; 'Bradley and Marosi Residences', *Charles Moore and Company*, GA Document, Tokyo: A.D.A. Edita, 1981; Whiteson, *Modern Canadian Architecture*, pp. 234-7.

134 See Jencks, *Language of Post-Modern Architecture*, esp. pp. 39-79; and Jencks, *Late-Modern Architecture*, pp. 6-8, 19-30.

135 Charles A. Jencks, 'Pavillon Soixante-Dix', *The Language of Post-Modern Architecture*, 2nd ed., New York: Rizzoli, 1978, p. 4; Arthur Drexler, 'Pavillon Soixante Dix', *Transformations in Modern Architecture*, New York: Museum of Modern Art, 1979, p. 139.

136 Larry Richards, ed., *Centre Canadien d'Architecture / Canadian Centre for Architecture: Building and Gardens*, Montreal: CCA, 1989; Peter Blake, *The Master Builders*, New York: Alfred A. Knopf, 1961, pp. 249-52; Ken Sobol and Julie Macfie Sobol, 'One Woman's Crusade for Better Buildings', *Canadian Geographic*, 110:4, August-September 1990, pp. 68-76; Freedman, *Sight Lines*, pp. 75-9.

137 Cawker and Bernstein, *Contemporary Canadian Architecture*, pp. 202-5; 'Mississauga City Hall', *Canadian Architect*, 32:6, June 1987, pp. 20-31; Jim Murphy, 'City Image', *Progressive Architecture*, 68:8, August 1987, pp. 69-79. Anne M. DeFort-Menares, 'Issues of Hierarchy and Social Ritual: Mississauga City Hall', *SSAC Bulletin*, 10:4, December 1985, pp. 26-31; Andrew Gruft et al., *A Measure of Consensus: Canadian Architecture in Transition*, exhibition catalogue, Vancouver: University of British Columbia Fine Arts Gallery, 1986, pp. 19, 45; Freedman, *Sight Lines*, pp. 155-8.

138 Sean Rossiter, 'The Makeover Artist', *Vancouver*, September 1989, pp. 33-42, 107-11; Kalman et al., *Exploring Vancouver*, p. 93; Pete McMartin, series on Cathedral Place, *Vancouver Sun*, 23-28 May 1991; Lance Berelowitz, 'Remaking History', *Canadian Architect*, 38:6, June 1993, pp. 18-19.

139 'Award of Excellence...', *Canadian Architect*, 30:12, December 1985, pp. 14-16; Kalman et al., *Exploring Vancouver*, pp. 27, 203-4; Rhys Phillips, 'Developers Building Architectural Poetry', Ottawa *Citizen*, 9 March 1991, p. J2.

140 Adele Freedman, 'Building on the Past—Get the Connection?', *Globe and Mail*, 21 September 1991, p. C2.

141 Annette Lecuyer, 'Engaging Extrovert', *Architectural Review*, 193: 1155, May 1993, pp. 16-19.

142 'Seabird Island School, Agassiz, BC', *Canadian Architect*, 34:12, December 1989, pp. 25-7; Donald Canty, 'Aerodynamic School', *Progressive Architecture*, 73:5, May 1992, pp. 142-7; 'Native Wit', *Architectural Review*, 193:1155, May 1993, pp. 47-52; *Architectural Review*, October 1992. Richard Evans kindly provided information on the schools.

143 'Elemental Gestures', *Canadian Architect*, 31:1, January 1986, pp. 12-15; Cawker and Bernstein, *Contemporary Canadian Architecture*, pp. 206-8; Freedman, *Sight Lines*, pp. 88-91.

144 Eberhard Zeidler, 'High Tech and Victoriana', *Canadian Architect*, 31:5, May 1986, pp. 35-9.

145 E.M. Farrelly, 'Seagram Museum, Waterloo, Ontario', *Architectural Review*, 178:1065, November 1985, pp. 66-7.

146 Adele Freedman, 'Trendiness? Ugh! Jury Smiles on the Modern', *Globe and Mail*, 23 March 1991, p. C11.

147 'Leisure Centre', *Canadian Architect*, 30:7, July 1985, pp. 36-9.

148 Kalman and Roaf, *Exploring Vancouver*, p. 212; related to the author in conversation by Barry Downs, c. 1973.

149 C.J. Taylor, *Negotiating the Past: The Making of Canada's National Historic Parks and Sites*, Montreal: McGill-Queen's University Press, 1990.

150 Luc Noppen, *In the National Gallery of Canada: 'One of the most beautiful chapels in the land'*, Ottawa: National Gallery of Canada, 1988; Harold Kalman, 'Restoration of the Chapel of the Rideau Street Convent', *Journal of the Association for Preservation Technology*, 8:4, 1986, pp. 18-29; Phil Jenkins, 'Magnificent Obsession' *Canadian Heritage*, 13:5, Winter 1987-8, pp. 20-5.

151 Some of these issues are discussed in Marc Denhez, *Heritage Fights Back*, Ottawa: Heritage Canada and Toronto: Fitzhenry and Whiteside, 1978; and Ann Falker, *Without Our Past? A Handbook for the Preservation of Canada's Architectural Heritage*, Toronto: University of Toronto Press, 1977 (both of which were written early in the heritage movement).

152 Mark Fram and John Weiler, eds, *Continuity with Change: Planning for the Conservation of Man-made Heritage*, 2nd ed., Toronto: Dundurn Press, 1984, p. xix.

153 Cited in Whiteson, *Modern Canadian Architecture*, p. 16. See 'Meewasin Valley Project, Saskatchewan', *Canadian Architect*, 24:12, December 1979, pp. 23-6.

154 Susan Buggey, 'Halifax Waterfront Buildings: An Historical Report', *Canadian Historic Sites, Occasional Papers in Archaeology and History*, No. 9, Ottawa: Parks Canada, 1974, pp. 117-68; Allan F. Duffus, 'Granville Street and Historic Properties', in Nova Scotia Association of Architects, *Exploring Halifax*, Toronto: Greey de Pencier, 1976,

pp. 20-9; Harold D. Kalman, 'NSCAD Moves to the Waterfront', in *Rehoused in History: Nova Scotia College of Art and Design*, Halifax: Nova Scotia College of Art and Design, 1979, not paginated; Harold Kalman, 'It's a Fantastic Space', *Atlantic Advocate*, 68:3, November 1977, pp. 12-14; 'Halifax Waterfront Restoration and Development', *Canadian Architect Yearbook*, 1972, pp. 46-9; Cawker and Bernstein, *Contemporary Canadian Architecture*, pp. 57-64.

155 Catherine Gourley, *Island in the Creek: The Granville Island Story*, Madeira Park, BC: Harbour Publishing, 1988; Michael and Julie Seelig, 'Recycling Vancouver's Granville Island', *Architectural Record*, September 1980, pp. 76-81; Cawker and Bernstein, *Contemporary Canadian Architecture*, pp. 73-6; Whiteson, *Modern Canadian Architecture*, pp. 60-3; 'Granville Island Redevelopment Plan', *Canadian Architect*, 22:12, December 1977, pp. 43-8; 'Granville Island, Vancouver', *Canadian Architect*, 25:8, August 1980, pp. 16-27; 'Granville Island Renewal, Vancouver', *Architectural Review*, 167:999, May 1980, p. 324; Joel Shack, 'The Industrial Bricolage of Granville Island', in Mertins, *Metropolitan Mutations*, pp. 115-22; Catherine Gourley, 'Tin Shed Cinderella', *Canadian Heritage*, 17:2, Summer 1989, pp. 31-4; Kalman et al., *Exploring Vancouver*, pp. 130-2.

156 Cited in Cawker and Bernstein, *Contemporary Canadian Architecture*, p. 74.

157 Jacques Dalibard, 'The Historical Context', in Deryck Holdsworth, ed., *Reviving Main Street*, Toronto: University of Toronto Press, 1985, pp. 57-61.

158 John Stewart, 'Breathing Life Back into Downtown', in Holdsworth, *Reviving Main Street*, pp. 63-86; Heritage Conservation Branch, *Nelson: A Proposal for Urban Heritage Conservation*, Victoria: Heritage Conservation Branch [1981]. See also Walter Jamieson, 'Conservation as an Approach to Urban Renewal', *Plan Canada*, 24:2, September 1984, pp. 44-54; Ted Silberberg et al., *A Guide for the Revitalization of Retail Districts*, Toronto: Project: Saving Small Business, 1976.

159 Affleck, 'Alcan World Headquarters', *ARQ: Architecture Québec*, 11, February 1983, pp. 19-20; Norbert Schoenauer, 'Maison Alcan, Montreal: An Avant-garde Spirit', *Canadian Architect*, 29:4, April 1984, pp. 24-33; 'Maison Alcan, Montréal, Québec', *ARQ: Architecture Québec*, 20, August 1984, pp. 14-15; 'Alcan aménagera un noveau complexe immobilier pour son siège social', *SSAC Bulletin*, 7:2, April 1981, pp. 8-9.

160 Edward Lindgren, 'Market Square, Saint John, New Brunswick, Mixed Use: Rebuilding a Waterfront', *Canadian Architect*, 29:6, June 1984, pp. 20-9; Judy Oberlander, 'Market Square: St John's South Street', *Progressive Architecture*, 65:3, March 1984, pp. 34-5; France van Laethem, 'Complexe Market Square, Saint-Jean, Nouveau-Brunswick 1978-1983', *ARQ: Architecture Québec*, 34, December 1986, pp. 18-19; George Schuyler, 'Market Square: Downtown Economic Revival', *Plan Canada*, 27:1, March 1987, pp. 16-22.

161 Gruft, *Measure of Consensus*, p. 22; Kalman et al., *Exploring Vancouver*, p. 125.

162 Kalman et al., *Exploring Vancouver*, p. 92; McHugh, *Toronto Architecture*, p. 213. The idea of TDR was introduced in John J. Costonis, *Space Adrift: Landmark Preser-*

vation and the Marketplace, Urbana: University of Illinois Press for the National Trust for Historic Preservation, 1974.

163 Constance Olsheski, *Pantages Theatre: Rebirth of a Landmark*, Toronto: Key Porter, 1989; 'Pantages Theatre, Toronto', *Canadian Architect*, 34:10, October 1989, pp. 57-61; Hilary Russell, *Double Take: The Story of the Elgin and Winter Garden Theatres*, Toronto: Dundurn, 1989.

164 'Sinclair Centre, Vancouver', *Canadian Architect*, 32:3, March 1987, pp. 22-32; Kalman et al., *Exploring Vancouver*, pp. 83-4.

165 Dendy and Kilbourn, *Toronto Observed*, pp. 294-6; Don Lovell, 'Royal Ontario Museum and Queen's Quay Terminal: Two Toronto Landmarks Renovating', *SSAC Bulletin*, 9:4, December 1984, pp. 7-10; *Architectural Record*, June 1985, pp. 134-41, August 1986, p. 64. For the original warehouse, see 'Canadian Rail and Harbour Terminals, Toronto', *Construction*, 20:3, March 1927, pp. 98-102.

166 'Centre Stresses Native Culture', *Canadian Architect*, 30:3, March 1985, pp. 36-8.

167 Kalman et al., *Exploring Vancouver*, p. 187.

168 John Lyle, 'Canadian Decorative Forms', *JRAIC*, 9 March 1932, p. 70.

BIBLIOGRAPHIES
ON THE HISTORY OF
CANADIAN ARCHITECTURE

ALLAN, NORMAN R., 'Some Recent Notes on Manitoba Architectural Bibliography', *SSAC Bulletin* 11:2, June 1986, pp. 9-10.

Federal Heritage Buildings Review Office/Bureau d'examen des édificies fédéraux à valeur patrimoniale. Indexes to Reports. Ottawa.

KALMAN, HAROLD, 'Recent Literature on the History of Canadian Architecture', *Journal of the Society of Architectural Historians*, 31:4, December 1972, pp. 315-23.

KERR, ALASTAIR, 'The Growth of Architectural History in British Columbia', *SSAC Bulletin*, 10:1, March 1985, pp. 21-4.

LERNER, LOREN R., and MARY F. WILLIAMSON, *Art and Architecture in Canada: A Bibliography and Guide to the Literature to 1981/Art et architecture au Canada: Bibliographie et guide de la documentation jusqu'en 1981*, 2 vols, Toronto: University of Toronto Press, 1991.

'Newfoundland Architecture: A Bibliography', *SSAC Bulletin*, 8:2, June 1983, p. 20.

1993 Bibliography/Bibliographie 1993, Manuscripts and Publications, Research Divisions, National Historic Parks and Sites Branch, Parks Canada, Ottawa, 1993.

RICHARDSON, DOUGLAS, ed., *Architecture in Ontario: A Select Bibliography on Architectural Conservation and Architecture*, compiled by Patricia Crawford, Philip Monk, and Marianna Wood [Toronto: Ministry of Culture and Recreation,] 1976.

SIMMINS, GEOFFREY, *Bibliography of Canadian Architecture/Bibliographie d'architecture canadienne*, Ottawa: Society for the Study of Architecture in Canada, 1992.

WADE, JILL, *Manitoba Architecture to 1940: A Bibliography*, Winnipeg: University of Manitoba Press, 1978.

GLOSSARY

ACROTERION An ornamental projection at the corner, or peak, of a roof; or the base that supports the ornament.

ANTA, ANTAE, ANTIS In CLASSICAL architecture, an *anta* is the exposed end of a wall, usually decorated with a PILASTER; *antae* are two adjacent and aligned wall ends; and COLUMNS between the *antae* are described as being *in antis*.

ANTHEMION In CLASSICAL architecture, an ornamental form based on the honeysuckle or palmette.

APSE In a church, a semicircular or polygonal projection at the altar (usually east) end, beyond the SANCTUARY.

ARCADE A row of ARCHES.

ARCH A form of curved construction, usually made from MASONRY, that spans an opening in a wall and distributes the weight above it on the walls or PIERS at either side.

ARCH-AND-SPANDREL MOTIF A wall treatment similar to a PIER-AND-SPANDREL MOTIF, but in which the piers are joined at the top by ARCHES.

ARCHITRAVE A horizontal BEAM or LINTEL, that rests on COLUMNS or PIERS; or the lowest portion of an ENTABLATURE; or a decorative moulding around a door, a window, or an ARCH.

ARCHIVOLT One of several parallel curved, and often decorated, MOULDINGS on the inside of an ARCHED opening; a curved ARCHITRAVE.

ASHLAR Stone that has been cut square and DRESSED.

ATRIUM In CLASSICAL architecture, an interior courtyard that is open to the weather. In contemporary architecture, a significant interior space, often skylighted, used for circulation.

ATTIC The top floor of a building, often reduced in height and unfinished; in CLASSICAL architecture, a storey that is inserted within the ENTABLATURE.

BALDACHIN A canopy above a church altar, often supported on COLUMNS.

BALUSTRADE A railing composed of POSTS (balusters) and a handrail.

BARGEBOARD Boards or other decorative woodwork fixed to the edges or projecting rafters of a GABLED roof. Sometimes called gingerbread.

BARREL VAULT A MASONRY VAULT in the form of a semicircular ARCH.

BASTION In military architecture, an angular and pointed projection, often diamond-shaped and usually located at a corner, that enabled gunners to defend the ramparts and CURTAINS of a fortification.

BATTEN A narrow vertical strip of wood, placed over joints of wider boards to protect the joints from the weather; the combination is called board-and-batten construction. *See also* SIDING.

BATTLEMENT A notched PARAPET, originally intended for defence; the notches are called battlements or crenellations. Hence a battlemented parapet is also known as a crenellated parapet.

BAY A window, door, or other opening, comprising one visual division of an elevation or a façade.

BEAM A principal horizontal structural member.

BELLCAST An EAVE that curves, or flares, outward like the flanges of a bell.

BELT COURSE In a MASONRY wall, a distinctive COURSE that usually projects slightly and may be decorated, forming a distinct horizontal band; also called a string course.

BOARD AND BATTEN See SIDING.

BOSS In MASONRY construction, a projecting ornament, often located at the intersection of two components.

BROACH SPIRE A polygonal spire set on top of a square tower; the transitional elements are called broaches.

BRACKET A member, often triangular in form, that projects from a wall or other vertical surface and supports another component, such as an EAVE.

BUTTRESS A vertical strip of heavy masonry applied to the wall of a building to provide structural reinforcement against lateral forces (as from a VAULT or an ARCH). When the buttress is a free-standing PIER attached to the wall by one or more arches, it is called a flying buttress.

CAMPANIFORM In the shape of a bell.

CANOPY A horizontal, sloped, or arched surface that projects from a wall—usually over a door or a window—to provide shelter from the weather.

904

CANTILEVER A BEAM or other horizontal member that projects beyond a vertical support and is unsupported at one end.

CAPITAL The decorative head of a COLUMN, PILASTER, PIER, or other vertical support.

CAPONIER In military architecture, a relatively small projection that provides a firing position, similar to a DEMI-BASTION but covered.

CARTOUCHE A decorated panel, often curvilinear in form.

CASEMENT A window that opens by being hinged along one side.

CHAMFER A sloping or bevelled edge.

CHANCEL In a church, the SANCTUARY at the altar (usually east) end, used by the clergy.

CHANNEL A groove, often decorative.

CHOIR In a church, the portion between the NAVE and the CHANCEL, used by the choir for singing.

CHEVRON V-shaped decoration.

CLADDING The external, non-structural material that protects the structural wall or FRAME from the weather.

CLAPBOARD See SIDING.

CLASSICAL Derived from the architecture of ancient Greece or Rome.

CLERESTORY A row of windows located near the top of the wall of a NAVE or room or other space.

CLOCHER A belltower on a church (from the French *cloche*, or bell).

COFFER A recessed decorative panel in a ceiling, VAULT, or dome.

COLONETTE See POST.

COLUMN See POST.

CONCRETE A mixture of cement, aggregate (usually sand and gravel), and water that hardens and attains great compressive strength. When used structurally it is usually reinforced by being poured around steel rods or mesh to give it tensile strength as well. Concrete may be poured into forms (usually wood) directly in place in a structure, or it may be precast away from the site and then placed into position. Concrete blocks are precast and used as building blocks.

CORBEL A kind of BRACKET composed of a single projecting block, or of several graduated projecting courses of MASONRY, providing a ledge.

CORNICE The uppermost portion of an ENTABLATURE; often used to indicate the projecting horizontal element (to shed rainwater and for decoration) at the top of a building, or a similar feature (often in plaster) at the top of the wall of a room.

COUNTERSCARP In military architecture, the outer wall of a ditch.

COURSE A single horizontal row of brick, stone, or other walling material.

COVE A concave MOULDING or recess, usually where a ceiling adjoins a wall.

CRENELLATED See BATTLEMENT.

CRÉPI A lime plaster used as a coating on stone buildings, particularly in New France, to protect the wall and the mortar joints from the weather.

CRESTING A decorative rail, a row of FINIALS, or another feature at the top of a building, often along the RIDGE of the roof.

CROCKET An upwardly projecting repeated decorative element, often along spires and GABLES in Gothic Revival architecture.

CUPOLA A feature at the top of a roof, usually dome-shaped and opened up by windows or COLUMNS.

CURTAIN In military architecture, a wall.

CURTAIN WALL An exterior wall that is fastened to a FRAME and protects the building from the weather; it has no structural function, and supports only its own weight.

DADO Panelling, usually wood, that is applied to the lower portion of a wall, above a baseboard.

DEMI-BASTION In military architecture, a BASTION composed of only two angled faces.

DENTIL A small, tooth-like square block, used in a row as a decorative feature in a CORNICE.

DORMER A window that projects from a sloping roof, with a small roof of its own.

DOVETAIL A joint of two interlocking blocks that flare outwards in the shape of the tail of a dove.

DRESSED Of stone: cut square on all sides and smoothed on the face.

DRIP MOULDING A projecting MOULDING that is shaped to allow rainwater to drip off its edge, away from the wall below it.

DRUM A cylindrical MASONRY component that forms one unit of a COLUMN; also a cylindrical STAGE below a dome.

EARTHWORKS In military architecture, a defensive structure constructed of earth.

EAVE The projecting edge of a roof.

ECHINUS A convex projecting moulding near the top of a CAPITAL.

ENGAGED Of a COLUMN or PILASTER: attached to a wall.

ENTABLATURE The horizontal component, usually decorated, that lies directly above a COLUMN or other support; in CLASSICAL architecture, the entablature is composed of an ARCHITRAVE, a FRIEZE, and a CORNICE.

FASCIA A plain horizontal band (i.e. a vertical surface), as in a board below an EAVE.

FINIAL An ornamental projection at the top of a GABLE, roof, or other high component.

FLÈCHE A slender spire atop a tower; French for 'arrow'.

FLUTES Vertical grooves on the shaft of a COLUMN or other support.

FRAME The structural skeleton of a building; as an adjective, referring to timber structure.

FRIEZE The middle portion of an ENTABLATURE, or any decorated horizontal band.

FRONTISPIECE The central portion of the main façade.

GABLE The triangular portion of wall beneath the end of a GABLED ROOF.

GABLED ROOF A roof that slopes on two sides.

GAMBREL ROOF A roof that has a double slope, with the lower slope steeper and longer than the upper one; a MANSARD ROOF.

HALF-TIMBERED In early building, a wall constructed of timber with the spaces between the members filled with MASONRY (in French, *colombage pierroté*); since the late nineteenth century, a wall that imitates half-timbering, even if the timber members are not structural.

HAMMER-DRESSED Stone that is DRESSED with a lightly textured surface.

HIPPED ROOF A roof that slopes on four sides.

HOOD MOULDING A MOULDING located at the top of a window to deflect rainwater.

IMPOST A MOULDING, BRACKET, or MASONRY course in a wall that supports the end of an ARCH.

IN ANTIS See ANTA.

JOIST A secondary horizontal structural member, usually supported by a BEAM at each end, and itself supporting a floor, ceiling, or roof.

KEYSTONE The wedge-shaped central block, or VOUSSOIR, at the apex of an ARCH.

KING POST In a roof TRUSS, the vertical member that extends from the centre of the principal beam (called the TIE BEAM) to the underside of the RIDGE.

LANTERN A windowed superstructure at the top of a roof or dome; a small CUPOLA.

LINHAY In Newfoundland, a row of utility rooms across the rear of a house.

LINTEL The horizontal supporting member at the top of a door or window.

LOGGIA A gallery that is open on one or more sides, often with an ARCADE.

LOOPHOLE In military architecture, a narrow hole in a wall through which ordnance or arms can be fired.

LOZENGE Diamond-shaped ornament.

MANSARD ROOF A roof that has a double slope, with the lower slope steeper and longer than the upper one; a GAMBREL ROOF. Named after the seventeenth-century French architect François Mansart.

MASONRY Stone, brick, concrete, tile, or any other non-organic and non-metallic building material.

METOPE In CLASSICAL architecture, the panel between TRIGLYPHS in a Doric FRIEZE.

MORTISE In a timber connection, a slot into which a TENON is inserted.

MOULDING A shaped decorative element, usually a horizontal band, that projects slightly from the surface of a wall.

MULLION A thin upright member within a window or between adjacent windows.

MUTULE In CLASSICAL architecture, a block-like decorative element on the SOFFIT of a Doric CORNICE.

NAVE The principal room or space in a church, which accommodates the congregation.

OGEE A double curve, usually used to describe an ARCH or a MOULDING.

PALISADE A row of logs or poles inserted upright into the ground and used as a wall or fence.

PALLADIAN Related to the buildings of the sixteenth-century Italian architect Andrea Palladio, or to the eighteenth-century English revival of his style.

PARAPET A portion of wall that projects above a roof.

PARTERRE In landscape gardening, a formal area of planting, usually square or rectangular.

PAVILION An articulated portion of the façade of a building, often higher than, or projecting forward from, the rest. If it is in the centre, it is called a FRONTISPIECE.

PEDIMENT The triangular end of a GABLE, or a triangular ornamental element resembling it, defined by a MOULDING (or series of mouldings) along its three edges.

PENDENTIVE The curved and sloping surfaces beneath a dome that mark the transition from the circle of the dome (or its DRUM) to the square of the supports.

PIANO NOBILE In Italian, the principal storey, usually above the ground floor.

PIER See POST.

PIER-AND-SPANDREL MOTIF A wall treatment that emphasizes the play between vertical PIERS and horizontal SPANDRELS.

PILASTER See POST.

PILLAR See POST.

PLATE In wood FRAME construction, a horizontal component that connects the tops or bottoms of POSTS or BEAMS.

PLINTH A block used as the base of a COLUMN or other upright support.

PORTE-COCHÈRE A covered entrance porch for vehicles.

PORTICO A covered porch, often consisting of COLUMNS supporting a PEDIMENT.

POST A generic word for any upright support that has several variants. It is used either in a general sense (e.g. POST-AND-BEAM construction) or in specific reference to a timber support. Pillar is a somewhat archaic word synonymous with post. A pier is a post of square or rectangular section, usually of MASONRY. A column is a post of circular section; a steel or iron member used vertically is also called a column. A colonette is a small column. A pilaster is a shallow rectangular upright support set into a wall and used mainly as decoration.

POST-AND-BEAM A building system that emphasizes the regular use of vertical and horizontal (or slightly sloping) structural members.

PROSTYLE Characterized by free-standing columns that stand forward from a wall (contrasted with columns *in antis*).

PURLIN In timber roof construction, a secondary horizontal component parallel to the RIDGE and supported at each end by a RAFTER.

QUATREFOIL A decorative form characterized by four lobes.

QUOIN One of a series of blocks or block-like components at the corner of a wall; in a MASONRY wall, its function is to reinforce the corner.

RAFTER In timber roof construction, a principal sloping component that runs from the wall PLATE to the RIDGE.

RAVELIN In military architecture, a freestanding triangular outwork.

RETABLE In a church, a decorative wall treatment or screen behind the altar; also called a reredos.

RETICULATED Patterned, often in a net-like design.

REVEAL The surface of a window or door opening; its width is usually the thickness of the wall.

RIDGE The apex of a roof, usually horizontal; or the structural component at the top of a roof.

ROUNDEL A circular panel or decorative component.

RUBBLE Rough, uncoursed stonework.

RUSTICATION Rough-surfaced or heavily textured stonework.

SACRISTY In a church, a room for the storage of sacred objects and for the carrying-out of certain church activities.

SANCTUARY In a church, the area around the principal altar. In a synagogue, the NAVE.

SASH In a window, the wood or metal frame that holds the glass.

SCOOP A hollowed-out half-log, used on a roof as a channel to carry away rainwater.

SEGMENTAL ARCH An ARCH whose profile comprises an arc smaller than a semicircle.

SHED ROOF A roof with only one slope; also used to describe the roof of a DORMER window if it has only one slope.

SHIPLAP See SIDING.

SIDELIGHT A window beside a door, forming part of the door unit.

SIDING A facing material, or CLADDING, applied to the outside of a wood-framed building to make it weatherproof. Sometimes called weatherboarding. Several kinds of wood siding are common in Canada. Shiplap (or drop siding) consists of horizontally laid boards with notched edges that make an overlapping joint; the face of each board is parallel to the plane of the wall. Clapboard (or bevelled siding) consists of bevelled boards laid horizontally and overlapping at the top and bottom; the face of each board is oblique to the wall. Board-and-batten siding is composed of vertically applied boards whose joints are covered by narrow strips (BATTENS). Shingles may also be used as siding, and materials other than wood are often employed. Composition siding is made of asphalt, asbestos, or synthetic materials, often imitating brick or shingle. Metal siding (usually composed of aluminum or galvanized steel) and vinyl siding are also used, often imitating wood.

SILL A horizontal member at the bottom of a wall (sometimes called a sill PLATE) or a window.

SOFFIT The underside of an EAVE, BEAM, or other component.

SPANDREL The portion of wall between the top of one window and the window SILL above it; or the roughly triangular surface between two adjacent arches.

STAGE One tier in a tower or other vertically composed structure.

STRING COURSE A BELT COURSE.

STRINGER A BEAM; also a sloping structural member that supports a staircase.

STUD In timber construction, one of a series of vertical supports, or POSTS.

TENON In a timber connection, a projecting tongue that is inserted into a MORTISE.

TERRA COTTA Fired clay (literally 'baked earth') commonly shaped in a mould and frequently glazed after firing.

TERREPLEIN In military architecture, the flat roof of a fortification, on which ordnance was mounted.

TIE BEAM In a roof TRUSS, a principal beam that spans from one wall to the other.

TRANSEPT In a church, a projecting space that is perpendicular to the NAVE; the nave and transepts intersect at the crossing to produce a cruciform plan.

TREFOIL A decorative form characterized by three lobes.

TRIFORIUM In a church, a passage or gallery above the NAVE arcade and below the CLERESTORY.

TRIGLYPH In CLASSICAL architecture, one of a series of raised ornamental panels in a Doric FRIEZE that consist of three vertical bands; triglyphs alternate with METOPES.

TRUSS A structural framework, made of either timber or metal, that is composed of individual members fastened together in a triangular arrangement.

TYMPANUM The panel, usually semicircular, located between the underside of an ARCH and the top of a doorway within the arch; also the triangular space enclosed by a PEDIMENT.

VAULT An arched ceiling constructed of MASONRY materials; the undersurface, or SOFFIT, is usually curved. If the vault is generated from a series of pointed, rather than round, arches, it is called a groin vault.

VOLUTE In CLASSICAL architecture, the spiral ornament on a CAPITAL.

VOUSSOIR One of the wedge-shaped masonry blocks out of which an ARCH or VAULT is composed. The central voussoir is the KEYSTONE.

INDEX OF CANADIAN BUILDINGS

GENERAL INDEX

British Columbia, 479, 480; Barkerville, 669; Castlegar, 517; Courtenay, 670; Cumberland, 670; early architecture, 803; English influence, 868; First Nations schools, 852, 867-8; Grand Forks, 517; Illecillewaet Glacier, 493; Kaseo, 670; Kitimat, 672-5, 869; modernism, 817 (*see also* West Coast style); native architecture, 595, 852, 867-8; Nelson, 670, 860; New Westminster, 643; Point Grey, 785; Prince Rupert, 521, 655-7, 660, 672; Shaughnessy Heights, 661; Surrey, 560, 852; Town Planning Act (1925), 661; Vancouver Island Arts and Crafts Society, 623; Victoria, 553-4, 623, 624, 655, 658; West Vancouver, 787; Yahk, 482

British Columbia Electric Rail Co., 627

British Columbia Mills, Timber and Trading Co., 504, 506, 523, 634

British Museum (London), 536

Bronfman, Samuel, 803, 847

Brotman, Edel, 519

Brotman, Fanny Pelenovsky, 519

Brown, David, 709. *See also* Brown and Vallance

Brown, Denise Scott, 845

Brown, D.L., 640

Brown, Ernest, 511

Brown, E., 728

Brown, F. Bruce, 711

Brown, George, 539

Brown, John James, 573

Brown, J. Francis, 572, 711

Brown, W.M., 675

Brown and Painter, 498

Brown and Vallance, 530, 709

Browne, George, 573, 607, 627

Browne, George C., 600

Browne, Peter Charles, 587

Brussels City Hall, 538

Brutalism, 813, 833

Bryant and Gilman, 543

Bryn Mawr College, 708, 709

Bucmaniuk, J., 735

Buffalo, New York, 644

Buffington, Leroy, 752

Builder, The, 612

Building codes, 643

Bukovynians, 509, 510, 511, 512

Bungalows: colonial, 625; Craftsman (California), 625-7, 785, 797

Burgee, John, 846

Burke, Edmund, 574, 618. *See also* Burke and Horwood; Burke, Horwood and White

Burke and Horwood, 574, 725

Burke, Horwood and White, 579, 716

Burnett, Frank, 575

Burnham, Daniel H., 579, 651, 652, 667

Burton, Harold, 753

Busch, Henry F., 560

Butler, Charles, 728

Butlin, Joseph, 529

By, John, 534

Byzantine style, 718, 725, 728, 733, 734, 735

Cadbury, George, 671

Cadbury, Richard, 671

Calgary, 488, 499, 527-32, 838; Chinatown, 531-2; and CPR, 527, 532; Mawson plan, 652-3; 'oil patch', 808-9; Oliver quarries, 530; Plus 15 system, 838, 863-4; suburbs, 532

California, 615, 631, 740, 749; bungalow, 625-7; wood building, 797

Cambridge Seven Associates Ltd, 830

Cambridge University, 706

Campbell, Wilfred, 541

Campbell, Sir William, 662, 663

Canada First movement, 541

Canada Farmer, The, 604

Canada Land Co. (Canada Co.), 643-7

Canada Mortgage and Housing Corporation (CMHC), 596, 642, 858, 865. *See also* Central Mortgage and Housing

Canada, Province of, 534

Canada West: 'colonization' roads, 649; land development, 648-9; Public Lands Act (1853), 648

Canadian Architect, The, 808

Canadian Architect and Builder, 545-6, 612, 618, 625, 637, 651

Canadian Chancelry (Washington, DC), 796

Canadian Copper Co., 670

Canadian Embassy (Mexico City), 820

Canadian General Electric, 592

Canadian Group of Painters, 772

Canadian Handicraft Guild, 627

Canadian Municipal Journal, The, 657

Canadian Pacific Ltd, 490

Canadian Pacific Railway, 479-83, 531, 576, 598, 609-10, 661, 706; 'assisted settlement' programs, 499, 504; 'crop payment plan', 499; dams and canals, 499; demonstration farms, 499; Development Branch, 499; Esquimalt and Nanaimo Railway, 486, 602; forestry department, 483; hotels, 480, 485, 492-8, 718, 827; 'loan farms', 499; Ogden Shops, 499; 'ready-made farms', 499, 504, 505; service buildings, 484-6; Standard No. 4 Section House, 484; Standard No. 10 Station, 482; station gardens, 483, 651; stations, 481-3, 487-92, 532, 651, 827; and tourism, 492, 628; and Western settlement, 492-500, 521, 527, 532

Canadian Railway and Marine World, 781

Canadian style, 593, 705, 721, 754, 755, 756, 778, 869; Anglo-, 556; and natural landscape, 811; and 'northern' architecture, 541; *See also* Château style; Prairie regionalism; West Coast style

Canals, 499, 541

Candela, Felix, 824-5

Cantelon, Adam, 508

Capper, S. Henbest, 593-4

Cardew, Peter, 813, 852

Cardinal, Douglas, 818, 823-5

Carlu, Jacques, 767-8, 769, 781

Carlu, Natacha, 768, 770

Carmack, George Washington, 692

Carnegie, Andrew, 530; Carnegie Foundation, 592

Carr, Emily, 772

Carrère and Hastings, 581-2, 754

Carson Pirie Scott Department Store (Chicago), 574

Cartier, Sir George-Étienne, 539

Cartier, Jacques, 550

Carver, Humphrey, 811

Cathay, Company of, 683

Cauchon, J.-E. Noulan, 660

Cawker, Ruth, 799

Cawston, John A., 808

Cawston and Stevenson, 808

CEMP Investments Ltd, 803

James, Wesley, 632
James and James, 572
Janes, Robert, 696
Janes, S.H., 805
Janishewski, Jarema, 515
Jardine, Alexander, 667
Jarvis, Edgar Beaumont, 573, 725
Jeffers, Allan Merrick, 556
Jekyll, Gertrude, 669
Jencks, Charles, 813; *The Language of Post-Modern Architecture*, 845; co-ed., *Meaning in Architecture*, 845
Jenney, William Le Baron, 571. *See also* Jenney and Mundie
Jenney and Mundie, 574
Jews, 509; agricultural settlements, 518-19
Johnson, Ed, 526
Johnson, Philip, 779-81, 800, 845-6, 847; house (New Canaan, Connecticut), 811
Johnson, R.A., 578
Johnson and Crooks, 674
Jones, Chilion, 534, 535, 536, 538. *See also* Fuller and Jones
Jones, Edward, 848
Jones, Hugh G., 492
Jones, Jacobine, 759
Jones and Kirkland, 848
Jordy, William, 800

Kahn, Louis, 813
Kalman, Maxwell M., 635, 658, 834
Kearney, Joseph Patrick, 690
Keefer, Samuel, 534, 539, 545
Keith, B.F., 741
Keith-King, John, 703
Kelly, Douglas, and Co., 575
Kelly, Robert, 575
Kemp and Sons, 585
Kempt, William, 686
Kendall, E.N., 647-8
Kent, Edwin S., 633
Kent, Herbert Harold, 760
Kerr, P., 508
Kertland, Douglas E., 759, 772
Kimberley-Clark Corp., 672
King, William Lyon Mackenzie, 721, 722
Kingston (England) School of Art, 813
Kipawa Fibre Co., 671
Kipling, Rudyard, 527
Kipp, Theodore, Co. Ltd, 526
Kirkby, William W., 691
Kirkland, Michael, 848
Kiss, Zoltan S., 793
Klein, Maurice D., 726
Knight, James, 684
Knox, Wilm, 573
Kohn, Robert D., 728
Kutchin, 691

Labelle, Antoine, 649
Labelle, Henri S., 785
Labrador: Happy Valley, Goose Bay, 689; Hebron, 680; Hopedale (Nunaingok), 689; Moravian missions, 689-90
Ladies Home Journal, 625, 750
Laferrière, J. André, 658
Lafrenière, J.-L.-D., 563
La Haye-Ouellet, Société, 844

Lake, Ira, 756
Lake Shore Apartments (Chicago), 800-2
Laloux, Victor, 589
Lamb, Thomas W., 742, 744
Lambert, Phyllis, 803, 847-8
'Lambeth palaces', 525
Land: cost of, 596, 633, 634, 637; Crown, 643, 648, 649; development, 643-9; subdivision, 615; speculators, 643; survey (West), 479; use, separated, 566, 651, 657, 661 (*see also* Zoning)
Landau, Hermann, 519
Landscape architecture, 539-40, 653-4, 669, 703-4, 725, 774, 789, 811, 833, 848, 860; English tradition, 655; urban, 649
Langelier, J. Donat, 785
Langevin, Sir Hector-Louis, 545
Langley, Henry, 542, 574. *See also* Gundry and Langley; Langley and Burke
Langley and Burke, 613
Langley, Langley and Burke, 569
Langton, John, 541, 721
Langton, William A., 651
Lanken, Peter, 847
Lapérouse, Comte de, 684, 686
Larkin, Gerald R., 747
Larkin, Peter C., 747
Laroque, Paul, 784
Lasserre, Frederic, 787, 823, 833
Latrobe, Benjamin Henry, 579
Laurier, Sir Wilfrid, 718; government, 498, 659
Laval de Montigny, François-Xavier de Montmorency-, 550
Laver, Augustus, 534, 535. *See also* Stent and Laver
Lawrence, W.D., 728
Lawson, Harold, 633. *See also* Lawson, Bettes and Cash; Lawson and Little
Lawson, Bettes and Cash, 550, 770
Lawson and Little, 611
Leavitt Jr, Charles W., 661
Le Corbusier, 781, 783, 787, 810, 813, 818, 820, 823, 824-5
Lecourt, J.-P.-M., 551
Ledoux, Claude-Nicolas, 757
Lefuel, H.-M., 541
Legislative buildings, provincial, 550-9
Lehr, John, 511
Leman, J.-B., 785
Lemercier, 627
Lemieux, Louis, 828
Lemon, Robert G., 864
L'Enfant, Pierre, 644
Lennox, Edward James, 553, 565, 593, 709, 726
Lescaze, William, 781
Letchworth (Hertfordshire), 657, 659
Lethaby, William Richard, 619, 620
Lever House (New York), 803-4
Lipinski, Peter, 515, 733
Little, Harold, 633. *See also* Lawson and Little
Liverpool Cathedral, 717
Liverpool University School of Architecture, 621
Lloyd, George Exton, 524
Lockwood and Mawson, 554, 671
Loew, Marcus, 741, 742
Log construction, 501, 502, 503, 519, 529, 724; church, 512; country house, 631-2; horizontal, 509-11, 512; Mackenzie Basin, 698; vertical, 502, 511
Loire, Gabriele, 716